Robert Brough Smyth

The Aborigines of Victoria

with notes relating to the habits of the natives of other parts of Australia and

Tasmania - Vol. 2

Robert Brough Smyth

The Aborigines of Victoria
with notes relating to the habits of the natives of other parts of Australia and Tasmania - Vol. 2

ISBN/EAN: 9783337273057

Printed in Europe, USA, Canada, Australia, Japan

Cover: Foto ©Andreas Hilbeck / pixelio.de

More available books at **www.hansebooks.com**

THE

ABORIGINES OF VICTORIA:

WITH

NOTES RELATING TO THE HABITS

OF THE

Natives of other Parts of Australia and Tasmania.

COMPILED FROM VARIOUS SOURCES FOR

THE GOVERNMENT OF VICTORIA

BY

R. BROUGH SMYTH,

F.L.S., F.G.S., ASSOC. INST. C.E., MEM. GEO. SOC. OF FRANCE; HON. CORR. MEM. SOC. OF ARTS AND
SCIENCES OF UTRECHT, BOSTON SOC. OF NAT. HIST., ISIS SOC. OF DRESDEN,
ETC., ETC., ETC.

VOL. II.

By Authority:
JOHN FERRES, GOVERNMENT PRINTER.
PUBLISHED ALSO BY GEORGE ROBERTSON, LITTLE COLLINS STREET, MELBOURNE.
LONDON:
TRÜBNER AND CO., 57 AND 59 LUDGATE HILL; AND GEORGE ROBERTSON,
17 WARWICK SQUARE.

1878.

CONTENTS.—VOL. II.

	PAGE
LIST OF ILLUSTRATIONS - - - - - - - -	v

LANGUAGE. — Onomatopœia. — Words formed after the advent of the whites. — Sign-language.—Sanscrit roots.—Words resembling English.—Languages named after the negative.—Tables illustrative of the languages spoken by the natives of Victoria.—Pronouns.—Numeral adjectives.—Comparison of the language spoken in Victoria with the dialects of Moreton Bay, Dippil, Kamilaroi, Bulloo Creek, Lake Macquarie, Cornu tribe, Adelaide, Port Lincoln, Croker Island, Adelaide River, King George's Sound, Swan River, &c.—Sameness of personal pronouns.—Numerals.—Interjections, cries, terms of abuse, &c.—Language of the natives of Lake Tyers in Gippsland—Lake Wellington, Gippsland—Brabrolong, Gippsland—Lake Hindmarsh—Western district. — Lists of words compiled by the Local Guardians of Aborigines. — Inflections.—Vocabularies. — Yarra Yarra and other tribes.—Native names of trees, shrubs, plants, &c.—Native names of localities and natural features in Victoria - 1

APPENDICES.—A. Notes and Anecdotes of the Aborigines of Australia, by Philip Chauncy, J.P., District Surveyor at Ballarat - - - - - - 221

 B. Traditions of the Australian Aborigines on the Namoi, Barwan, and other Tributaries of the Darling, communicated by the Rev. William Ridley, M.A., &c. 285

 C. Notes on the Natives of Australia, by Albert A. C. Le Souëf - - - 289

 D. Notes on the Aborigines of Cooper's Creek, by Alfred W. Howitt, F.G.S., P.M. and Warden, Bairnsdale - - - - - - - 300

 E. Notes relating to the Aborigines of Australia, by the late John Moore Davis - 310

 F. Notes on the System of Consanguinity and Kinship of the Brabrolong Tribe, North Gippsland, by A. W. Howitt, F.G.S., P.M. and Warden, Bairnsdale - 323

 G. Notes on the Language and Customs of the Tribe inhabiting the country known as Kotoopna, by William Locke - - - - - - 333

 H. Hunting the Blacks, by the late A. F. A. Greeves - - - - 336

 I. The Crania of the Natives, by Professor Halford, of the Melbourne University - 340

THE ABORIGINES OF TASMANIA.—Physical character.—Mental characteristics.—Numbers.—Birth, &c.—Marriage.—Death and burial.—Encampments, &c.—Food.—Diseases.—Dress and ornaments.—Weapons. — Implements.—Canoes.—Stone implements.—Fire.—Language - - - - - - - - 379

INDEX - - - - - - - - - - 435

LIST OF ILLUSTRATIONS.—VOL. II.

PULPIT ROCK, CAPE SCHANCK (Frontispiece).

	PAGE
King George's Sound, 1846	to face page 221
Mirnyongs, outlet of Lake Connewarren	233
Native of King George's Sound (male)	236
Natives of King George's Sound (woman and child)	237
Kertamaroo (King John)	246
Mocata (King John's wife)	247
Natives of King George's Sound	248
War dance and a corrobhoree (No. 1)	257
Mimic war dance, hunting scenes, &c. (No. 2)	257
Groups of squatters	258
Letter	to face page 261
Head of a native with ornaments (Cooper's Creek)	302
Adze or gouge	304
Hand (sign)	308
Hand (sign)	308
Hand (sign)	308
Hands clasped (sign)	308
Hand (copy of) marked on rock	309
Diagram, showing method of figuring skulls	to face page 341

Skull of Australian (A)—
    Front view   343
    Side view   343
    Posterior view   345
    From above   345
    Inferior view   347

Skull of Morgan, the bushranger (European), (M)—
    Front view   349
    Side view   349
    Posterior view   351
    From above   351
    Inferior aspect   353

Skull of a Chinese   355

Skull of Australian (probably female), (B)—
    Front view   357
    Side view   357
    From above   359
    Inferior aspect   359

Skull of Australian (C)—
    Front view   361
    Side view   361
    From above   363
    Inferior aspect   363

ILLUSTRATIONS.

Skull of Australian (D)— | PAGE
    Front view - - - - - - 365
    Side view - - - 365
    From above - - - - - - 367
    Inferior aspect - - - - 367

Skull of King Jimmy, of the Mordialloc Tribe (E)—
    Front view - - - - - - 369
    Side view - - - - 369
    Upper view - - - - - - 371
    Posterior aspect - - - 371
    Section - - - - - 373
    Section, with base lines, chords, angles, &c. - - - 373

Necklace of shells - - - - - 399
Stone implement - - - - - 405
Stone implements - - - - - 406
Stone implements - - - - - 407
Map of Australia, including Tasmania - - - - - End of vol.

Language.

It is not possible for any one who has not lived for a long period with the natives to undertake any such task as that of writing a grammar of the native tongue. The number of dialects in Victoria alone would require careful investigation for many years before it would be practicable to give any trustworthy account of them; and it appeared to me that I would best serve the interests of philology by collecting information from gentlemen who have had the most favorable opportunities of making themselves acquainted with some of the dialects.

In addition to the native words and phrases which occur in other parts of this work, there are now given here the following papers, namely:—

1. Language of the natives, by the Rev. John Bulmer, of Lake Tyers, Gippsland.
2. Language of the natives, by the Rev. F. A. Hagenauer, of Lake Wellington, Gippsland.
3. The dialect of the Brabrolong and neighbouring tribes, by A. W. Howitt, F.G.S., &c., &c.
4. Language of the natives of Lake Hindmarsh, by the Rev. A. Hartmann.
5. Language of the natives of Lake Hindmarsh, by the Rev. F. W. Spieseke.
6. Words and sentences in the native language, by Charles Gray, Esq., Wickliffe.
7. Some words of the native language of the Western tribes of Victoria, by N. Thornly, Esq.
8. Sentences in the native language, written down by Mr. Joseph Shaw, Lake Condah.
9. Vocabulary of the language spoken by the tribes inhabiting the country about the Rivers Crawford, Stokes, lower parts of the Wannon and Glenelg, compiled by the late C. J. Tyers, Esq., in 1842.
10. Lists of words, English-Native, compiled by the Guardians of Aborigines in the Colony of Victoria.
11. Declension of noun, use of possessive pronouns, &c., by the Rev. Mr. Hartmann, the Rev. Mr. Bulmer, the Rev. Mr. Hagenauer, and Mr. John Green.
12. Vocabulary, remarks on the structure of the language, &c., by Mr. John Green, Coranderrk, Upper Yarra.

13. Succinct sketch of the Aboriginal language, by the late Wm. Thomas, Esq., Guardian of Aborigines.
14. Language of the Aborigines of the Colony of Victoria (arranged anew), by the late Daniel Bunce, Esq.
15. Dialect of the Ja-jow-er-ong race, by Joseph Parker, Esq.
16. Words in the dialects of the natives of Geelong, Colac, Goulburn, Murray, and Campaspe, and in those of the Witouro, Jajowrong, Knenkoren-wurro, Burapper, and Ta-oungurong tribes.
17. Native names of trees, shrubs, plants, &c.
18. Native names of localities in Victoria, by the Local Guardians of Aborigines.
19. Native names of localities in Victoria, from papers furnished by the Surveyor-General of the colony.
20. Native names of several hills, rivers, &c., by the late C. J. Tyers, Esq., 1840.
21. Native names of places in Victoria, by Gideon S. Lang, Esq.
22. Native words and names, Kerang, Lower Loddon, by H. Taverner, Esq.
23. A list of words compiled by Henry J. Withers, Esq., Berrembeel, Wagga Wagga, New South Wales.

The papers contributed by the Rev. John Bulmer, of Lake Tyers in Gippsland, the Rev. A. Hartmann and the Rev. F. W. Spieseke, of Lake Hindmarsh, Mr. Joseph Parker, of the Loddon, and the Rev. F. A. Hagenauer, of Lake Wellington in Gippsland, are of great value. I obtained from some of these gentlemen short stories and phrases in the native tongue, written down exactly as the natives speak, with the corresponding English words below; and I believe these will assist the philologist more than if I had given merely statements and opinions relative to the grammar and structure of the language.

The sounds of the letters that are used in writing English do not convey the sounds of the words of the native tongue. It is often impossible to write down correctly any word beginning with B. It is frequently sounded like P. *Boorp* (Loddon) is written *Poorp* (Lower Murray), and *Baramul* is in like manner written *Paramul*. D is so sounded as to perplex the enquirer. One word will suffice to show this:—

Ground	*Dyah* - - - -	Upper Richardson.
	Tyar - - - -	Lake Hindmarsh.
	Tha - - - -	Birregurra.
	Tcha - - - -	Glenelg.
	Jah - - - -	Hamilton.
	Djak - - - -	Glenorchy.
	D'tchar - - -	Murray.
	Char - - - -	Lower Loddon.
	Yar - - - -	Horsham.

D has its proper sound in such words as *Bidderup* (dead), *Turdenden* (new), *Urdin* (straight), &c.

An examination of the words in the vocabularies shows that there are numerous equally remarkable dialectical transitions of consonants.

H is sounded clearly and sharply at the end of a word, often like R, as in *Lah* and *Lar* (a stone), and *Wah* and *War* (a crow).

In such words as *Korak, Drae,* and *Merang,* the sound of R is rough, rolling, and strong.

Ng has a nasal sound, which it is not easy for Europeans to imitate.

There are no sibilants in the native tongue; no articles; and, it is supposed, no distinctions in gender (with certain exceptions noticed by Mr. Threlkeld).*

There are dual forms of speech.

There are interrogative pronouns.

The plural is usually formed by placing a numeral before the substantive, the substantive not changing its form except for euphony. This, however, is not the rule in all dialects.

The numerals are "one" and "two," other numbers being expressed by combinations of the words expressing "one" and "two;" but this rule again is not of universal application. In some dialects it is said that there are distinct and separate words for "three," "five," and "seven."

Suffixes are used.

There are no terms to express abstract ideas.

A great many words are onomatopœic in their origin.

Sign-language is used.

Words originating in sounds which the words themselves are intended to imitate are probably very numerous in all the languages and dialects, but the changes which the several tongues have undergone during a long lapse of time may prevent the discovery of the origin of many of these roots.

A few words which are undoubtedly onomatopœic will suffice to show that a thorough examination of the Australian languages would result in valuable acquisitions to philology:—

Crow	*Wa-ak* or *Waugh.*
Magpie	*Koorabaukoola.*
Mopoke	*Wook-ook.*
Dove	*Koorookookoo.*
Plover	*Petereet* or *Perret-perret.* (English, *Pewet.*)
Cat	*Uru,* or *Yurn,* or *Yoorn.*
Thunder	*Woon-duble,* or *Drumbullabul,* or *Mun-der,* or *Mooroobri.*
Laugh	*Kinka.* (English, *Kink.*)
Coughing (of one having a cold)	*Koondrakondroo.*
Teeth	*Leah* or *Teera.*
Tongue	*Tallang.*

---

* Mr. Bulmer, who is a keen observer and well acquainted with the languages spoken on the Murray and in Gippsland, informs me that in one of the dialects of the Murray the blacks will say to a man *Purragia* ("you lie"), and to a woman *Purragaga* ("you lie"). Will the peculiarities of the dialects ever be known?

Rattle	- Moorrá-moorrá.
To whistle	- Whee-ree-leu.
To blow	- Boo-roo-knin.
To sneeze	- Chee-koorn-der.
Stone plover	- Wooloo-look.
Frogs	- Kong-kang. (So called from the noise they make.)
The emu	- Kong-ko-rong. (So named from the noise it makes.)

When the white settlers brought their horses, cattle, and sheep, and many appliances of civilization to Australia, the natives were compelled to coin several new words, in order to make themselves understood. Some of these are expressive, and in their formation highly instructive. I will quote a few examples :—

Barn-door fowl	- Chuck-chuck.
Swine	- Pig-pig.
Sheep	- Yeep or Eu-ep.
Horse	- Kirt-kirt-tar-nuk or Kut-kut-tarnook (many vessels).
Cattle	- Koo-roo-m'n. (Kor-ror is the word for kangaroo.)
Dog (introduced)	- Karl (from the noise he makes when he snarls).
Spoon	- Woo-roo-knee-chal-loop (the mouth of the mussel).
Pot or kettle	- Tar-nook (the native name for the wooden vessel used by them).
Bottle	- Doom-doom-e-bur-a-mul. (Having reference to its shape, like an emu.)
Roof	- Boorp-e-lar (the head of the house).
Candle	- Marm-bull (that is to say "fat").
Gun	- Drum-bullabul (thunder).
Ship	- Bul-li-to Kooron (large canoe).
Boat	- Wye-bo Kooron (small canoe).

Sign-language is used more or less throughout Australia. Men ignorant of each other's language manage to communicate their ideas by making signs with the hand.

Mr. Alfred Howitt, in his paper on the Natives of Cooper's Creek, gives a description of the gesture-language of the people of that country, and the subject is mentioned also by Mr. Samuel Gason.

The hands and fingers are often used by the natives when they find they have no words to express their meaning—as, for instance, when they desire to convey the idea of numbers exceeding those in their vocabulary. A native will hold up his hands, spread out his fingers, and open and shut them rapidly, when he wishes to give a notion of the great numbers of kangaroos he has seen, or great numbers of blacks.

It is believed that they have several signs, known only to themselves, or to those amongst the whites who have had intercourse with them for lengthened periods, which convey information readily and accurately. Indeed, because of their use of signs, it is the firm belief of many (some uneducated and some educated) that the natives of Australia are acquainted with the secrets of Freemasonry.

Mr. Samuel Bennett, in his valuable work on *Australian Discovery and Colonization*, gives some words of the Australian tongue which in sound and meaning are allied to words used by the Aryan race. They are as follows:—

Gin or *Gun*, a woman; Greek, γυνη (*guné*); and derivative words in English, such as generate, generation, and the like.

Joen, a man; Persian, *juen;* Latin, *juven-is.*

Gibber, *Kibba*, or *Kepa*, a rock; Arab, *kaba;* Moorish, *giber*, as in Gibraltar; Hebrew, *kefas.*

Cobbera or *Cobra*, the head; English, *cob;* Spanish, *cobra;* German, *kopf.*

Tiora, land or country; Latin, *terra;* French, *terre;* English, *territory.*

Hieleman, a shield; Saxon, *heilan;* English, *helm* or *helmet* (a little shield for the head).

Moray or *Murry*, great, large, or much; Celtic, *mor* or *more;* English, *more*, the comparative of much.

Gnara, a knot or tangle; English, *gnarled* (full of knots).

Kiradjee, a doctor; Greek, χειρουργος; Persian, *khoajih;* English, *surgeon;* Old English (obsolete), *chirurgeon.*

Cabohn, good, true, great. Words of the same or similar meaning, of which "bon" is the root, are found in most of the European (Latin) languages.

Yarra, flowing; *Wallo-yarra*, the beard (hair flowing from the chin). The names of several British rivers, such as the Yare, the Yarrow, and others, as well as many Australian streams, as the Yarra-yarra (flowing-flowing), seem to have had a common origin. The word "hair" is perhaps another form of the same word; as well as "arrow," the bolt shot from a bow.

Mar-rey, wet; *Mer* or *Mar*, water. This root occurs in the names of numbers of waters, streams, and rivers in Australia, as well as in Europe; in the latter generally applied to the sea or a large body of water, as in Boulogne-sur-mer; Weston-super-mare; Windermere, &c.; Hebrew or Phœnician, *mara;* Latin, *mare*, the sea or a great river.

Bo'ye or *Bogy*, a ghost or an object of terror; English, *bogy, bugaboo.*

Kalama, a reed, the rod or staff of a spear; Greek, καλαμος; Latin, *calamus;* Hindostanee, *callum.*

Gunya, a place for shelter; Persian or Arabic, *gunn.*

Mah, to strike; Hindostanee, *mah.*

Pilar, a spear; Latin, *pilum* (plural, *pila*).

Pidna, the foot; Latin, *ped;* and English derivative words, as pedestrian.

Mr. Bennett says that "many other words might be added which afford traces of resemblance between the languages of the Australian Aboriginal tribes and the tongues spoken by the various Aryan nations. But whether they indicate a common origin, or merely suggest the probability of a small infusion of words of Sanscrit derivation through the occasional visits of Arabs or Malays, it is difficult to say. The latter supposition appears not improbable."

Mr. Threlkeld, quoting from a paper furnished him by W. A. Miles, Esq., gives the following comparisons:—

Australian.	Sanscrit.
Nau-wai, a canoe	- *Nai*, a ship; Persian, *naó*.
Murri nauwai, a ship	- *Neoya*, naval.
Makoro	- *Matsyah*, a fish.
Wonnai	- *Yuvana*, a young person.
Maiya	- —— Persian, *mar*, snakes.
Marai, spirit	- *Mara*, death.
Yuring	- *Iri*, a radical, to go.
Nukung	- *Adguna*, a woman.
Murrakeen	- *Kanya*, a girl.
Wakun, from the cry	- *Ka, ka*, a crow.
Wak-wak-wak	- *Waka*, a crane.
Punnul	- *Bhanu*, the sun.
Kui	- *Ooo*, to sound.
Bo, to be one's self	- *Bhu*, to be.
Yamma, to stop from harm, to guide, to lead	- *Yama*, to stop.
Yinal, son; *Yinalkun*, daughter	- *Yauvana*, youth.

Mr. Taplin says he made a collection, some time since, of those words of the native language which most resemble English words, or words of languages from which English is derived. The words he has given are, he adds, pure native, that is, *Yarildewallin*.

I here quote a few of these words from Mr. Taplin's work, with additions showing the derivations:—

Mr. Taplin—			
Native words.	Meanings.	English or other word which they resemble.	Derivations.
Yun	soon	soon	Moeso-Gothic, *suns*; Anglo-Saxon, *sona*.
Kurrin	enquiring	enquiring; Latin, *quærens*	
Multuwarrin	becoming many or much	*multus*, multiplying	
Poke	a small hole	pock	Anglo-Saxon, *poc*; Dutch, *pok*.
Wirrangi	bad	wrong	Anglo-Saxon, *wringan*, *wrungen*, twisted from the right.
Trippin	drenching	dripping	Anglo-Saxon, *dripan*; Danish, *dryppe*.
Throkkun	putting	throwing	Anglo-Saxon, *thrawan*.
El	will	will	Gothic, *wilja*; Anglo-Saxon, *willa*; Dutch, *wil*; Slavonic, *wolia*, *wola*; Greek, βουλή.

LANGUAGE.

Mr. Taplin—		Derivations.
Native words.	Meanings.	English or other word which they resemble.	
Merippin Lippin	- cutting	- ripping	- Anglo-Saxon, *ripan*.
Nowaiy, Tarno	- negative	- no	- Gothic, *ne, ni*; Danish, *nei*; Greek, *νή*.
Itye	- 3rd personal pronoun, he, she, it	- it	- Mœso-Gothic, *ita*.
Ngo	- go	- go	- Anglo-Saxon, *ga, gan*.
Ngia	- here! (imperative)	- nigher	- { Gothic, *nehwa*; Swedish,
Ngai	- here	- nigh	- { *nāra*; Icelandic, *na*.
Luk	- so, thus	- like	- Gothic, *leiks*; Icelandic, *likr*; Greek, ἴικελος.
Trentin	- tearing	- rending	- Anglo-Saxon, *rendan*; German, *trennen*.
Tampin	- walking	- stamping	- Danish, *stampe*.
Grauwun	- burying in the earth	- ground	- Gothic, *grundus*.
Wurti	- wet	- wet	- Anglo-Saxon, *wæt, hwet*.

The late Mr. William Hull, at one time Member of the Legislative Council of Victoria, was, I believe, one of the first to direct attention to certain apparent resemblances between some few words in the Australian tongues and the Sanscrit. Such resemblances are curious, and invite enquiry; but it is, to say the least, doubtful whether they have a philological or ethnological value.*

* In a communication to the *Athenæum* (No. 2545, 5th August 1876), entitled "*Pre-Historic Names for Man and Monkey*," Mr. Hyde Clarke states "that in Eastern Australia, as in Europe, the names for extinct races are applied to ghosts and fairies; but further in Australia, such a name is exhumed and applied to a new race. Thus *wunda*, a name of thousands of years, is applied to the newly-come Europeans. *Makoron* is only another word of the same kind, being *koro*, a man. *Wunda* is, however, a root having wider relations, and so are *murri* and *koro*. These words, and others used for man, serve not only to name man, but monkey, lizard, and frog—all four-footed or four-handed. In making some comparisons of animal names of Bribri, Tiribi, &c., of Costa Rica, Central America, which correspond with the African, as do such American names generally, it appeared that lizard, frog, and monkey interchanged. I had long suspected that monkey names were related to those for man, but the evidence was not strong until the group now pointed out was got together."—[Here follow the examples.] Mr. Clarke goes on to say that one "thing is certain, that the Aryan languages are the languages of blacks, as are most of the languages of the world; and the words supposed to represent an Aryan civilization are those of the civilization of the pre-historic blacks and savages. Looking to the facts, the differences between the languages of the Aryan stock are not all due to phonetic degradation. One chief point on this head is that roots were independently selected; and as the variations of pronunciation are found in the prehistoric languages, the probability is that some of these have been transmitted. Thus the Aryan languages are not to be regarded as the descendants of one Aryan stock, but as the languages of an amalgamation of various tribes, which having been brought together, have been subjected to what we understand as Aryan influences. Whether this was effected by the influence of white men in various black or mixed tribes assembled is a matter to be investigated. At all events, white men learned their languages from black men, and from them acquired their primitive mythology. With regard to the words *wunda*, &c., the question will naturally be put by some, what bearing they have on the Lemurian doctrine, so strongly advocated for ethnology by Prof. Huxley, philological arguments in favor of which were brought forward by the late distinguished scholar, Dr. W. H. Bleek. The facts here brought together, which form only a small part of the mass, showing how the names of animals, weapons, tools, and tribes are common to the old world and the new, well illustrate the early stages of language. . . . . The community of name of man with those animals here mentioned extends very much further among four-footed beasts; and birds were named from beasts. We have thus the probable origin of totems and totem-worship, as likewise in pre-historic philology we have the verbal origin of tree, serpent, and other kinds of worship, as I have shown in my late paper on Sibu and Siva worship." Mr. Clarke's paper is very curious and interesting.

A great many of the languages of Australia are named after the word "no." The late Mr. Bunce states that the Melbourne people used, to designate their language, the words *N'uther galla*—*N'uther* meaning "no."

The late Mr. E. S. Parker corroborates Mr. Bunce's statement. He says— "The natives distinguish the different *talle* or languages by their negations. Thus there is the *Burapper* dialect, spoken by the *Mallegoondeet;* the *Utar* dialect, on the Murray and Lower Goulburn. These words *Burapper* and *Utar* being respectively the negations of each language; and so of others."

This system of nomenclature appears to prevail in the eastern and southern parts of the continent.

The Rev. W. Ridley, M.A., eminent amongst the philologists of Australia, says—"The following are the names of some languages spoken in the interior:—1. *Kamilaroi;* 2. *Wolaroi;* 3. *Wiraiaroi;* 4. *Wailwun;* 5. *Kogai;* 6. *Pikumbul;* 7. *Paiamba;* 8. *Kingi.* The first five of these are named after their negatives. In the first, *Kamil* signifies 'no ;' in the second, *Wol* is 'no ;' in the third, *Wira* is 'no ;' in the fourth, *Wail* is 'no ;' in the fifth, *Ko* is 'no.' In *Pikumbul,* on the other hand, *Piku* means 'yes ;' so that the Australian Aborigines, in this instance, named their language on the same principle on which the French acted in distinguishing the dialects of France, as *Langue d'Oc* and *Langue d'Oyl.*"

Some thirteen years ago I obtained from a number of gentlemen resident in Victoria short vocabularies of the language spoken in their several localities (now printed in this volume). An examination of the lists, when arranged geographically, is very interesting. Thirty words, as spoken in each district, have been selected for comparison, with the following results:—

RIVER MURRAY.

English.	Tangambalanga, (Kiewa River), Upper Murray.	Barnawartha, (Indigo Creek), Upper Murray.	Echuca, Junction of Campaspe and Murray.	Gunbower, Near Mount Hope, River Murray.
Man	Gerree	Mung	Moanit	Coolie
Woman	Giree	Belagera	Layarut	Lubra
Father	Mamgah	Mamah	Kaiya	Mamook
Mother	Bigah	Gunee	Kana	Pabook
Head	Booaw	Cumbugong	Mwongery	Mooruncook
Hair	Booaw	Huran	Beko	Nurranncook
Eye	Mee	Mill	Man	Mirinook
Ear	Mirimbah	Mutha	Marrmo	Wirrinboolook
Mouth	Deirah	Erang	Kotta	Chirbook
Tongue	Tierah	Tulling	Tallye	Chalinook
Teeth	Teera	Terah	Derra	Leanook
Hand	Murrah	Murrah	Peeyin	Mununcook
Finger	Youllon	Yellon	Teechera	Mununcook
Foot	Teyrah	Jeunong	Tchinna	Chinunook
Blood	Koroo	Gornyah	Mowa	Koorkook
Bone	Kieela	Thubal	Lillima	Mirdirook
Sun	Koonda	Neera	Yongya	Mooree
Moon	Yow-warra	Cobadong	Yongwida	Wiewill
Star	Jiemba	Jemba	Truttra	Toort

LANGUAGE.

RIVER MURRAY.

English.	Tangambalanga (Kiewa River), Upper Murray.	Barnawartha, (Indigo Creek), Upper Murray.	Echuca, Junction of Campaspe and Murray.	Gunbower, Near Mount Hope, River Murray.
Night	Tooma	Burandong	Bona	Boorin
Day	Koonda	Erah	Wongda	Karook
Fire	Kurraw	Wanga	Dickya	Wannup
Earth	Merre	Towarah	Wokka	Churr
Stone	Poongah	Willong	Ecoga	Larr
Tree	Wondah	Wonder	Tainya	Becal
Wood	Tau-wa	Kegel	Mootta	Becal
Snake	Tucyon	Thoro	Kona	Goornwill
Eagle	Warrimoo	Weramu	Hwammery	Wirhill
Crow	Berontha	Wargon	Warkil	Waa
Kangaroo	Boodgoo	Murray	Kyemery	Cooray

English.	Kulkyne, Lower Murray.	Tyntyndyer, Lower Murray.	Mildura, Lower Murray.	Yelta, Junction of the Darling and Murray.
Man	Wotungi	Wortongie	Wir	Maa-lee
Woman	Lio	Liour	Coormup	Nongo
Father	Maami	Mamie	Bait	Kambia
Mother	Paapie	Baboo	Acka	Naamagh
Head	Durut-hoopi	Poorp	Turt	Therto, Kokoro
Hair	Kiut-carangie	Gneningin	Moor-il	Boorlkee
Eye	Mai	Mirnoo	Me	Maykee
Ear	Mural-wimpoli	Wirumpoolen	Mural	Uree
Mouth	Dhuck-chapie	Woorinen	Turk	Yetka
Tongue	Maat	Tchilinon	Malta	Therlinya
Teeth	Ruruc-leang	Leangin	Rurck	Nandee
Hand	Wuin	Murnungin	Wina	Mambanna, Mera
Finger	Munangi	- - -	Ak-a-quim	Merra
Foot	Jahn	Chinangin	Thina	Thinna
Blood	Kuroc	Jinka-jinka	Coorook	Kandara
Bone	Beagim	Calwe	By-imp	Pina
Sun	Nung	Nowie	Nunk	Yhuk-ko
Moon	Bait	Meatian	Pyte	Pytoa
Star	Narro-bil	Toort	Boul	Boorlee
Night	Biangri	Tolkine-nowie	Wangry	Ton-kon-ko
Day	Beianung	Keely-nowie	Bay-a-nauk	Minki
Fire	Neie-wunapi	Wanup	Mick	{ Nan-day-lee / Koon-ega
Earth	Teangi	Tungie	Nat-ya	Merndi
Stone	Kotabi	Muckie	Thauk	Yernda|
Tree	Bullot-hullandi	Boorongie	Burnell	Yarra
Wood	Leitpar	- - -	Boup	Yarra
Snake	Karnie	Cannie	Thoke	Tooroo
Eagle	Maundil	Perrit-perrit	Maw-an-dil	Bilyarra
Crow	Waak	Wangie	Walk	Waukoo
Kangaroo	Bulukone-quangi-	Koorangie	Bu-lu-cool	Bool-oolye

The words in the foregoing tables illustrate the language spoken by the tribes inhabiting the banks of the River Murray. The first place named—

Tangambalanga—is distant only twenty-two miles from Barnawartha; Barnawartha is about one hundred and three miles from Echuca; Echuca is twenty-seven miles from Gunbower; Gunbower is about fifty-seven miles from Kulkyne; Kulkyne is eleven miles from Tyntyndyer; Tyndyndyer is about one hundred miles from Mildura; and Mildura is sixteen miles from Yelta. The distance, in a straight line, between Tangambalanga and Yelta is not less than three hundred and thirty miles.

Comparing the first two in the list—Tangambalanga and Barnawartha—it is apparent that eight words in the list may be regarded as identical, and eight more, at least, as having the same roots; that is to say, sixteen words at least out of the thirty coincide. Comparing Tangambalanga with Yelta, it is seen that there are no two words in the list exactly alike, but fourteen at least have the same roots.

It will be observed that pronouns are in some cases tacked to the words in the tables, but the reader will find no difficulty in recognising these in the places where they occur.

WIMMERA DISTRICT.

English.	Lake Hindmarsh.	Horsham.	Glenorchy.	Upper Richardson.
Man	Wutyo	Wootcha	Conllee	Watcha
Woman	Leirock	Lyurock	Bibagou	Biang-Biango
Father	Mahm	Marmie	Maarm	Mamie
Mother	Bap	Barpee	Bauppee	Papie
Head	Burp	Boorpeek	Bourp	Boorp
Hair	Narraburp	Ngrah-boorup	Gnarra	Niabook
Eye	Mir	Mirrh	Mirkk	Meer
Ear	Wirmbull	Worimbull	Wearboull	Wrimbool
Mouth	Tyarp	Jarp	Wourrough	Woora
Tongue	Tyalle	Chally	Tchallee	Jallie
Teeth	Lia	Lear	Leah	Leah
Hand	Manja	Munya	Munyah	Manyah
Finger	Yullup-yullup-manja	Watchip-watchip	Wingerapp	Bap Wanyah
Foot	Kinna	Jinna	Jinna	Ginah
Blood	Gurk	Korruek	Goork	Gooak
Bone	Kalk	Kaalk	Culke	Callac
Sun	Nyau-we	Nyowee	Ghnarwee	Nyawie
Moon	Mityän	Mitchen	Yen	Yeen
Star	Turt	Durht or Turht	Dourt	Doort
Night	Burroin	Boreun	Bouroin	Booring
Day	Nyau-we	Nyowee	Ghnarweeyun	Berrip
Fire	Wan-yap	Wanyup	Wee	Wee
Earth	Tyar	Yar	Djak	Dyah
Stone	Kut-yap	Koehop	Laugh	Lach
Tree	Kalk		Gulpougarra	Galk
Wood	Kalk	Kaalk	Culke	Galk
Snake	Tyu-rang-kuk-nalluck	Kurnwill	Cournemille	Goorinmill
Eagle	Wirp-pill	Werarepil	Gnarraille	Warpil
Crow	Woa	Wah	Waagh	Wiaa
Kangaroo	Min-yo	Koray	Coorab	Goora

WIMMERA DISTRICT.

English.	Avoca.	Upper Loddon, Daylesford.	Lower Loddon, Boort.
Man	Koo-lie	Koolee	Wootho
Woman	Too-ra	Touroi	Larook
Father	Mar-mook	Marm	Marmoke
Mother	Bar-poop	Barp	Barbook
Head	Boor-kook	Boorp	Boourbook or Youyourook
Hair	Nar-boor-kook	Gnerra	Narranyuke
Eye	Myn-ook	Ma	Min-nook
Ear	Wym-bool-look	Weimbul	Weembulloke
Mouth	Woor-uk	Wooroo	Cherbook
Tongue	Tar-lee	Chalie	Charlinyook
Teeth	Lee-are	Leear	Leeanyook
Hand	Mun-nar	Mirna	Manarnyuke
Finger	Won-in-mun-nar	-	Wathep-wathep manarnyuke
Foot	Tee-nar	Jinna	Chinarnyook
Blood	Koor-kook	Gourk	Coorkgook
Bone	Karl-kook	Kolk	Carlgook
Sun	Nar-wee	Gnowee	Gnarwee
Moon	Yean	Yern	Waingwill
Star	Tourt	Toort	Doort
Night	Boo-run	Boorinen	Pooroon
Day	Kar-pul	Gnowecu	Parrep
Fire	Wee	Wee	Wannop
Earth	Kap-pen	Jaa	Char
Stone	Lar	La	Lar
Tree	Kulk	Kulk	Carlk
Wood	Moo-tuk	Kulk	Carlk
Snake	Kul-mil	Kunmil	Coonwill
Eagle	Wear-pil	Waa-pil	Warepill
Crow	War	War	Warr
Kangaroo	Kor-ror	Goura	Cooree

The River Wimmera, the River Richardson, the River Avoca, and the River Loddon, are all within the southern basin of the River Murray, and drain a generally very level country, not thickly wooded, except in the parts occupied by Mallee scrub. It is about twenty-five thousand square miles in extent; and communication between all parts of it is comparatively easy. It is not necessary to comment on the obvious inferences to be derived from a mere glance at the words in the tables. The dialects throughout this area present no such striking differences as those of the River Murray. The explanations given by my correspondents show how alterations in the dialects have occurred, without preventing the people of the several tribes from being intelligible to each other.

It may be said indeed that throughout this area there was but one language, —or, perhaps, to state the case more accurately, one dialect: the differences being no greater than are found to occur when we compare the vocabularies of the people inhabiting different counties in England.

THE ABORIGINES OF VICTORIA:

WESTERN DISTRICT.

English.	Balmoral.	Sandford.	Hamilton.	Portland.	Warrnambool.
Man -	Cooly -	Koomongmorang	Colae -	Mhara -	Maar
Woman -	Bang-bang-go -	Nooranygoulk -	Bangbaugo -	Tunumbu -	Tonambool
Father -	Marmuke -	Papic -	Mammy -	Pepint -	Tebach
Mother -	Papuke -	Noorong -	Pappy -	Nerung -	Nerra
Head -	Boorpuke -	Coolan -	Boorup -	Pini -	Pim
Hair -	Gnerraboorp -	Nullong -	Nahra -	Narat -	Aran
Eye -	Meurnok -	Moorung -	March -	Ming -	Meir
Ear -	Wroom-bolok -	Hooaung -	Brimbol -	Wing -	Wurn
Mouth -	Worro -	Mullong -	Coue -	Olung -	Knoolong
Tongue -	Chal-inuke -	Talline -	Charle -	Talian -	Tuline
Teeth -	Leanuke -	Tungung -	Layha -	Tungun -	Tongun
Hand -	Manya -	Murrong -	Monyah -	Murrung -	Merra
Finger -	Babmanya or Griting	Gridding -	Kyup -	Kiapork -	Merra
Foot -	Ginna -	Dinnung -	Chena -	Youk -	Jinnung
Blood -	Gork -	Carmarrow -	Roark -	Ghereek -	Kemi
Bone -	Calk -	Burgine -	Calk -	Buckin -	Puckine
Sun -	Nyawi -	Turrung -	Nowe -	Nuriung -	Uuna
Moon -	Yern -	Dangitt -	Yaen -	Turro -	Yer-yer
Star -	Dort -	Barite-barrite -	Toort -	Minkil -	Punjell
Night -	Boroinu -	Booron -	Borrine -	Boron -	Borone
Day -	Nyawi -	Woorum Durrong	Belpa -	Nunung -	Teern
Fire -	Wee -	Ween or Goonda	We -	Wein -	Ween
Earth -	Teha -	Maring -	Jah -	Mering -	Merring
Stone -	La -	Moorie -	Lah -	Murrai -	Merri
Tree -	Calk -	Parliep -	Galk -	Waurut -	Wooroot
Wood -	Calk -	-	We -	Wein -	Ween
Snake -	Coornwel -	Coorong -	Coornweel -	Corang -	Coorang
Eagle -	Wrappel -	Necyangarra -	Rappil -	Neunghur -	Eanger
Crow -	Wa -	Warng -	Woa -	Warl -	Wah
Kangaroo -	Cur-re -	Koorang -	Goora -	Corang -	Koroit

English.	Wickliffe.	Carngham.	Camperdown.	Colac.
Man -	Cooley -	Kolmoit -	Unimodthe -	Mondel
Woman -	Lubra -	Kolmoit-bapanet -	Unnodthe -	Noodnuwett
Father -	Marmae -	Pittong -	Pepic -	Maahma
Mother -	Parpae -	Yuttong -	Nerong -	Paahpa
Head -	Caubra or Poorpeek	Moork -	Pienatnin -	Moranyenue
Hair -	Marah -	Nuir-moork -	Harat -	Kaenmorackenue
Eye -	Macinyarack -	Mere -	Merang -	Mrinyedue
Ear -	Rinbool -	Worn -	Weiringnatnin -	Weinyedue
Mouth -	Learangcrack -	Wora -	Wooroonaugtin -	Woronyedue
Tongue -	Taleangerack -	Glannen -	Talgarnangtin -	Talanyedue
Teeth -	-	Lea -	Tonganantin -	Moerinyedue
Hand -	Munyangarack	Marna -	Moraangtin -	Macnyinue
Finger -	Munyangarack	Wonmarna -	Kittiemoraangtin -	Lerinyinue
Foot -	Kinneyangcrack	Jenir -	Dinangtin -	Kenaeyenue

LANGUAGE.

WESTERN DISTRICT.

English.	Wickliffe.	Carngham.	Camperdown.	Colac.
Blood	Cookyangcrack	Corrick - - -	Qurocantnin - -	Korockycnuc
Bone	Calleyangcrack	Nal - - -	Pnghine - - -	Yecbringycouc
Sun -	Nowic - - -	Maira - - -	Fherne - - -	Naah
Moon	Yea - - -	Yaan - - -	Borangnatin - -	Paartput
Star -	Tatinowic - -	Torporrum - -	Whythurb - -	Karrankaran
Night	Pooroin - - -	Morkalla - -	Booroon - - -	Pooroonna
Day -	Perpoamin - -	Morrayail - -	Hulogetin - -	Wooremolleen
Fire -	Ween or Wee -	Weeing - - -	Wheen - - -	Weeing
Earth	Ya - - - -	Yoruockjaa - -	Merrin - - -	Tha or Moora
Stone	Lah - - -	Law - - -	Merri - - -	Drae
Tree -	Pecal - - -	Car - - -	Woorot - - -	Coorlong
Wood	Poort - - -	Wing - - -	Doarb - - -	Kalerack
Snake	Kurowill - -	Conmoit - - -	Koorang - -	Kaanlaog
Eagle	Yannul - - -	Mairompial - -	Keroolct - -	Orlimerick
Crow	War - - -	Waa - - -	Waang - - -	Kaiwaicrook
Kangaroo -	Curah - - -	Kaima - - -	Quooric - - -	Korak

The places named in the above table lie to the south of the great spur of the Main Dividing Range, and all the waters run directly to the sea, or to inland lakes. The area is about fifteen thousand square miles, of which nearly eight thousand consist of wide, open, level plains. There are no natural barriers separating the tribes.

The distance from Balmoral to Colac in a straight line is about one hundred and thirty miles.

THE YARRA AND WESTERN PORT.

English.	Yarra Yarra.	Western Port.	English.	Yarra Yarra.	Western Port.
Man -	Koolcin - -	Koo-lin	Bone -	Neelong - -	Neyln
Woman	Baggarkruk -	Bag-rook	Sun -	Nawin - -	Ner-wein
Father	Mamaneek -	Marman	Moon	Meneam - -	Myn-e-am
Mother	Babaneck -	Parpun	Star -	Durt pirram -	To-pi-ram
Head -	Kawanug -	Kow-ung	Night	Booren - -	Bo-run
Hair -	Yarric - -	Yar-ra	Day -	Yalingboo -	Yel-lin-wa
Eye -	Merring - -	My-ring	Fire -	Wein .	Wee-en
Ear -	Werring - -	Wer-ring	Earth	Yearmoobeck -	Beek-beck
Mouth	Wooroong -	Nnng-bil-bnn-uk	Stone	Lang - -	Laug
Tongue	Jellang - -	Tallang	Tree -	Treang - -	Ter-rung
Teeth	Leeung - -	Lee-ung-er	Wood	Kalk - -	Kulk
Hand -	Maruung - -	My-rong	Snake	Kaan - -	Karn
Finger	Woonmooumillrt	Mun-ung	Eagle	Buudjell - -	Pun-gil
Foot -	Jeenoong - -	Tee-nan	Crow	Waang - -	Warng
Blood -	Kurruk - -	Kul-mul	Kangaroo -	Koocm - -	Ko-em-ko-em

The dialects of the Wooeewooroug or Wawooroug tribe (River Yarra) and the Boonoorong tribe (Coast) are the same. Twenty-three words out of thirty are, making allowances for differences of spelling and pronunciation, identical; five have evidently the same roots, and only two are widely different. It will be observed that only a very few words coincide with words of the same meaning in the dialects of the Gippsland tribes.

The people of the Yarra and the coast were separated from the Gippsland tribes by the waters of Western Port, and by dense scrubs extending from the inlets northwards to the southern rim of the Yarra basin. East of Western Port there is a tract of wild country—debatable ground—which was the scene of many battles in former times. It is said that it was held sometimes by the Western Port blacks and sometimes by the tribes inhabiting Western Gippsland.

GIPPSLAND.

English.	Bushy Park, Gippsland.	Lake Wellington, Gippsland.	Lake Tyers, Gippsland.
Man	Gun-na	Kanny	Brah
Woman	Woo-gut	Wookatt	Woorcat
Father	Mun-gunn	Moonkan	Mung-gan
Mother	Year-kunn	Yackan	Yackan
Head	Poo-ruk	Brook	Purk
Hair	Leet	Litt	Lit
Eye	Myree	Mooeh	Mre
Ear	Woor-ring	Wring	Wring
Mouth	Kart	Gad or Gaad	Kaat
Tongue	Tallan	Tyelling	Jelline
Teeth	Unduk	Ngirrndock	Nerndack
Hand	Breet	Pritt	Bret
Finger	Laa-ra-breet	Pritt	Tagnra Bret
Foot	Tey-yan	Tyain	Ja-an
Blood	Krook	Krook	Karndobara
Bone	Byrng	Pring	Bring
Sun	Woo-run	Warring	Wurrin
Moon	Nger-run	Ngirrang	Nerran
Star	Pree-cel	Breell	Brayel
Night	Pook-kan	Padd-kallack	Bookang
Day	Woo-run	Warring	Wurrin
Fire	Tow-war-rar	Towr	Towera
Earth	Turrn	Wrack	Wark
Stone	Wool-lun	Walloong	Wallung
Tree	Kulluk	Talk	Nappur
Wood	Kulluk	Mritt	Kanby
Snake	Too-roo	Toorroong	Kalang and Thurrung
Eagle	Poen-rung	Quarrnamarroo	Quornamero
Crow	Nar-ru-quon	Ngarroogall	Waygara
Kangaroo	Tir-rer	Tyirra	Jirrah

The dialects of the Gippsland tribes show closer affinities with those of the Upper Murray than with those of the Lower Murray; and it may be presumed that Gippsland was peopled from a stream coming either across the Alps or coastwards from the north-east—and not from the stream that followed the

River Darling southward to Yelta—southward to the heads of the Wimmera, southward to the heads of the Glenelg, and westward to Colac. Speculations of this kind are, however, at present of little value, and yet not altogether worthless if they set one to examine evidence more closely. There were once several separate peoples in Gippsland, differing much in appearance; and it is possible, nay probable, that some part of Gippsland was peopled from the stream that flowed southward and westward along the banks of the Goulburn, and thence across the Dividing Range, or southward from the Murray along the banks of the Ovens or the Kiewa.

Pronouns.

LAKE TYERS, GIPPSLAND.

First person.

	Singular.			Plural.	
Nom.	Ngio	I.	Werna		we.
Poss.	Ngetal	mine.	Nindethana		ours.
Objec.	Ngio	me.	Werna		us.

Second person.

Nom.	Mangee	thou.	Gnowo		ye or you.
Poss.	Koothaula	thine.	Ngingal		yours.
Objec.	Nungoo	thee.	——		you.

Third person.

Nom.	Jilly	he.	Mandha		they.
Poss.	Nungal	his.	Thanal		theirs.
Objec.	Noonga	him.	——		them.

No pronouns—Feminine gender.   No pronouns—Neuter gender.

My	Ngetal.	Who	Nan (also expresses "what").
Thy	Ngingal.		
His	Nyungal.	Which	Wunman.
Her	[no feminine.]	What	Nanma.
Our	Nindi Thanal.	That	Ketchoon.
Your	Ngwana Thanal.		

The Rev. Mr. Bulmer adds, in a recent communication, the following:—Murray—I, *Natoa;* you, *Nindoa.* Gippsland—I, *Ngio;* you, *Nindo.* Maneroo—I, *Ngiimba;* you, *Nindege.*

LAKE HINDMARSH.

	Singular.			Plural.	
Ngan		I.	Nga		we.
Ngeck		mine, my.	Ngan-dack		ours.
Ngär-rin		me.	Ngan-dank		us.
Ngar		you, thou.	Ngat		you.
Ngin		yours, thine.	Ngo-dack		yours.
Ngan-nung		you, thee.	Din		you.
Ngait		he, she, it.	Ngatts		they.
Nyuck		his, hers, its.	Ngeän-nack		theirs.
Ngun		him, her, it.	Ngin		them.

Who, *Win-yar;* which, *Win-ya-tuck;* what, *Ngan.*

NUMERAL ADJECTIVES.

	LAKE TYERS, GIPPSLAND.		LAKE HINDMARSH.
One	Koo-to-pau.	One	Ke-yap.
Two	Boolooman.	Two	Pullet.
Three	Boolooman batha Kootook.	Three	Pullet Ke-yap.
Four	Boolooman batha Boolung.	Four	Pullet-pullet.
	&c., &c.	Five	Pullet-pullet Ke-yap.

I have compared the words in these tables with numerous vocabularies from other parts of Australia, and the coincidences are striking and instructive :—

English.	Moreton Bay.	Victoria.
Eye	Millo	Mill (Barnawartha).
Blood	Kakke	Gooak (Upper Richardson).
Tongue	Tallain	Talline (Sandford).

English.	North side of Moreton Bay, thence towards Wide Bay and Burnet District. (Dippil.)	Victoria.
Stone	Kitta	Kutyap (Lake Hindmarsh).
Eye	Mi	Mai (Kulkyne).
Blood	Kuki	Gooak (Upper Richardson).
		Gurk (Lake Hindmarsh).
		Koorkook (Avoca).
Hair	Dhella	Yar-ra (Western Port).
Head	Kanr	Kowung (Western Port).

English.	Namoi, Barwan, Bundarra, Balonne Rivers; Liverpool Plains, Upper Hunter. (Kamilaroi.)	Victoria.
Fire	Wi	Wee (Glenorchy, Hamilton, &c.).
Day	Yerada	Erah (Barnawartha).
Man	Giwar	Girree (Tangambalanga, Upper Murray).
		Wir (Mildura, Lower Murray).
Hand	Murra	Murrah (Upper Murray).
Eye	Mil	Mill (Barnawartha).
Tongue	Tully	Tuline (Warrnambool).
		Tyalle (Lake Hindmarsh).

English.	Bulloo Creek, North of Darling and Warrego.	Victoria.
Sun	Tuni	Uuna (Warrnambool).
Moon	Kein	Yen (Wickliffe).
Day	Warroo	Woorun (Bushy Park, Gippsland, &c.).
Fire	Wu	Wee (Glenorchy, &c.).
Mouth	Mumnurrah	Worro (Balmoral).
Hand	Murra	Murrah (Tangambalanga).
Eye	Monaroo	Mirnoo (Tyntyndyer).
Tongue	Teeyir-tarlina	Tierah (Tangambalanga).
		Therlinya (Yelta).
Teeth	Tuyali, Durali	Lea (Glenorchy).
		Derra (Echuca).
Kangaroo	Koolar	Korror (Avoca).

LANGUAGE. 17

English.	Lake Macquarie, N.S.W.	Victoria.
Moon	Yellena	Yern (Upper Loddon). Yen (Glenorchy).
Tree	Kollai	Kulh (Avoca).
Fire	Koi-yung	Koonega (Yelta). Goonda (Sandford).
Night	Tokoi	Tolkine (Tyntyndyer).
Man	Kare	Gerree (Tangambalanga).
Tongue	Tullun	Tuline (Warrnambool).
Ear	Ngureung	Wring (Lakes, Gippsland).

English.	Cornu Tribe, North of River Darling.	Victoria.
Sun	You-ko	Yhuk-ko (Yelta). Yougya (Echuca).
Star	Poor-li	Boorlee (Yelta).
Day	Murn-ke	Minki (Yelta).
Night	Tunka	Ton-kon-ko (Yelta). Tolkine (Tyntyndyer).
Head	Thirta-walla	Therto (Yelta).
Mouth	Yelka	Yelka (Yelta).
Hand	Murrah	Mera or Mambanna (Yelta).
Eye	Maki	Maykee (Yelta).
Tongue	Tarra-langi	Therlinya (Yelta).
Teeth	Mindi	Nandee (Yelta).
Ear	Uré	Uree (Yelta).
Foot	Tiduah	Thinna (Yelta).
Hair	Tartar-burlke	Boorlkee (Yelta).
Blood	Carndarah	Kandarah (Yelta).

English.	Adelaide Tribe, South Australia.	Victoria.
Sun	Tindo	Koonda (Tangambalanga).
Moon	Kakina-Piki	Pyte (Mildura).
Star	Purle	Boorlee (Yelta).
Stone	Pure	Poongah (Tangambalanga).
Tree	Wirra	Woorot (Camperdown).
Man	Meyu	Maar (Warrnambool).
Head	Mukarta	Moork (Carugham).
Hand	Marra	Merra (Warrnambool).
Eye	Mena	Mirnoo (Tyntyndyer).
Tongue	Tadlanya	Therlinya (Yelta).
Blood	Karro	Koroo (Taugambalanga).

English.	Parnkalla, Port Lincoln, South Australia.	Victoria.
Father	Pappi	Papie (Sandford).
Mother	Ngammi	Naamagh (Yelta).
Hand	Marra	Merra (Warrnambool).
Eye	Mena	Mirnoo (Tyntyndyer).
Tongue	Yarli	Chalie, &c. (Upper Loddon, &c.).

English.	Croker Island, North Australia.	Victoria.
Sun	Muri	Mooree (Gunbower).
Hand	Yeyen	Wuin (Kulkyne).

VOL. II. C

18   THE ABORIGINES OF VICTORIA:

English.	Adelaide River, North Australia.	Victoria.
Father	Pep-pee	Pepie (Camperdown).
Hand	Man-enee	Manya (Balmoral).
Eye (or see)	Ma	Ma (Upper Loddon).
Teeth	Ya	Layha (Hamilton).

English.	King George's Sound, Western Australia.	Victoria.
Hand	Marhra	Murrah (Tangambalanga)
Eye	Kaubigur Mel	Mill (Barnawartha).
Tongue	Dtakundyl	Tulling (Barnawartha).
Teeth	N'algo	Lia (Lake Hindmarsh).
Foot	Jinna	Jinna (Horsham).
Blood	Barree	Burrabee (Barnawartha).

English.	Swan River, Western Australia.	Victoria.
Sun	Ngangga	Yongya (Echuca).
Moon	Mega, Miki	Meatian (Tyntyndyer).
Ground (or land)	Budjor	Jaa (Upper Loddon).
Father	Manman	Marman (Melbourne).
Hand	Marhra	Murrah (Tangambalanga).
Eye	Mel	Mill (Barnawartha).
Tongue	Dtallang	Tallang (Western Port).
Foot	Jinna	Jinna (Horsham).
Hair	Kattamangara	Yar-ra (Western Port).

The word for "Head" at Popham Bay, North Australia, is *Koala* (*Koolie*, Gunbower, Victoria); "Opossum" at Wellington Valley and at Regent's Lake, Lachlan, is *Willee* (*Wille*, Lake Hindmarsh); "Fire," at Karaula, in lat. 29° S., is *Wĕ* (*Wee*, Wimmera district); and "Crow," at Byrne's Creek, near the Lachlan, is *Waagan* (*Wangan*, Barnawartha).

A number of similar coincidences might be given, and it is not far wrong to say that, in the dialects of Victoria, the words for Head, Hair, Tongue, Teeth, Eye, Hand, Foot, Blood, Bone, Night, Snake, Crow, and Sun coincide; and that throughout Australia the words for Eye, Tongue, Hand, Teeth, Blood, Sun, and Moon are the same, or nearly the same. There are exceptions, it is true; but these are explained by the habits of the natives and the probability of errors having crept into the vocabularies.*

---

* Mr. John Macgillivray, in the narrative of the *Voyage of H.M.S. Rattlesnake*, refers to the "difficulty of framing so apparently simple a document as a vocabulary, and particularly to show how one must not fall into the too common mistake of putting down as certain every word he gets from a savage, however clearly he may suppose he is understood." He adds that he got at different times and from different individuals for the "shin-bone" words which, in the course of time, he found to mean respectively the "leg," the "shin-bone," and "bone" in general.

Though great care has been bestowed on the vocabularies in this work, it would be unreasonable to suppose that, in all cases, the exact equivalents of the English words have been taken down, or that the lists are free from errors.

Further evidence of the unity of the languages is afforded by the sameness of the personal pronouns, and the constant recurrence of one, at least, of the numerals—the word for "two." It is only necessary to give a few examples:—

	I.	Thou.	He.
Victoria	Ngio	Mangee -	Jilly
	Ngan	Nyar	Ngait
Moreton Bay	Atta	Inta	Ungda
Queensland (Dippil)	Ngai	Nginna	Unda
Namoi, Liverpool Plains (Kamilaroi)	Ngaia	Nginda	Ngenna
Lake Macquarie, New South Wales	Ngatoa	Ngintoa	Ninwoa
Narrinyeri, South Australia	Ngap	Nginte	Kitye
Parnkalla, South Australia	Ngai	Ninna	Panna
King George's Sound, West Australia	Adjo, Y'go	Nginni	Bal
Swan River, West Australia	Ngadjo	Nginni	Bal

TWO.
Victoria	Boolooman, Pullet.
Moreton Bay	Bullae.
Kamilaroi	Bular.
Karaula (lat. 29° S.)	Bulár.
Wellington Valley, New South Wales	Bulla.
Wollondilly River, New South Wales	Pulla.
Bulloo Creek, north of Darling and Warrego	Barkalo.
Adelaide tribe, South Australia	Purlaitye.

It would appear, from the scanty vocabularies that have been printed, that the native words for "two," "twice," "both," and "four"—common in nearly all the dialects of the eastern and a great portion of the southern parts of Australia—are different or greatly modified in the language of the districts west and north-west of the Great Bight. But they are used in the central parts of the continent. The Dieyerie tribe say for "those two," *Boolyia*.

A comparison of all the words in the tables for Victoria with words in vocabularies for other parts of the continent seems to show that the language spoken by the tribes of the River Murray and the Western districts of Victoria have closer affinities with the languages of the other parts of the continent than the dialects of the Yarra Yarra, Western Port, and Gippsland tribes have. Indeed the dialects of the Gippsland tribes appear to have been originally either greatly different, or they have been modified since the tribes settled in these parts. From their geographical position, these tribes are in a measure isolated, and any influences that might have affected the dialects of the Murray and the Western districts would not necessarily have extended to them; nor would changes in the language of the people thus situated have spread westward or north-westward.

There are many causes in operation which, in course of time, lead to alterations in the dialects; tending, however, rather to the introduction of new words and the disuse of old words than to any change in the structure of the language. From the information supplied by those best acquainted with the habits of this people, it appears it is a custom—common, if not universal—that when a person dies whose name is the same, or has the same sound, as any word of the dialect of the tribe, that word thenceforth is never used, or certainly not again resumed until the dead person is forgotten by all but near relatives. In this manner the dialects are in time slightly altered.

Again, new words and phrases would be introduced, and some peculiar modes of expression arise, in consequence of a son-in-law being prohibited from speaking to or using the name of his mother-in-law. A man with two or three wives would not seldom be placed in some difficulty; and if possessed of more than ordinary capacity, might, in extricating himself, make perhaps no trifling additions to the vocabulary.

A powerful man—a warrior, a priest, or a dreamer—would in like manner, even if he did not coin new words, greatly influence the mode of speech in his tribe. His peculiarities would be imitated by the young persons, and perhaps new substantives would be woven into verbs, and new suffixes given to parts of speech.

Indeed it is surprising that there should be a sameness in the structure of the languages throughout Australia, and no greater diversity in words. Having no signs or symbols whereby a word or a sentence could be fixed, without having direct communication with each other; and some tribes, though not far distant, being altogether separated, and being influenced by different physical aspects, different forms of vegetation, and different climates—it is astonishing that the original tongue from which the existing languages and dialects have proceeded is yet vital, and exhibits its character and method in so many almost unvarying aspects throughout such an immense tract.

INTERJECTIONS, CRIES, ETC.

The well-known call *Coo-ee*, used when the natives hail each other in the bush, is universally adopted by colonists, and this speaks strongly in its favor. It would be difficult, indeed, to utter any other sound which would be as clear and as soft, as significant, and be carried as far in the forest as this call.

The drumming or droning noise made by the men when engaged in the corrobboree, and the grunting sounds they utter, are appropriate to their action.

When a warrior is speaking, and he is interrupted, he cries *Wau-h!* *Wau-h* has a number of different meanings, varying with the tone in which it is uttered. It has as many meanings as "Hear! hear!" in our assemblies. Those words may be spoken scornfully, or encouragingly, or—and this happens with *Wau-h* —when nothing else can be said. The native of Australia is not wanting in skill when engaged in argument, and his *Wau-h*, like our "Hear! hear!" is often used to disconcert an opponent.

Waugh! is also equivalent to "Behold!" "Look out!" "Hollo!" "Stop!"

When the natives express satisfaction, or when anything strange is presented to their view, they cry *Ko-ki!* If strongly impressed by a startling statement, they say *Kanti!*—equal to "My word!" and when they wish to express their acquiescence they say *Naa!*

LANGUAGE.

"Yes," in the dialect of the Lake Hindmarsh people, is *Nyei;* in that of the Yarra Yarra tribe, *Ngie;* in that of the Coast tribe, *Um-um;* but in that of the Upper Loddon it is *Yea-yea.*

"No," is *Wur-rag* at Lake Hindmarsh; on the Yarra it is *Ta-goong;* at Western Port, *N"uther;* and on the Upper Loddon, *Low-nee-rong.*

"Hark!" in the dialect of the Yarra natives is *Ngarrngak.*

"Hush!" "Hark!" is *Ur! Ur!* amongst the Melbourne people.

"Hark!" "Listen!" is *Thooamee!* in the dialect of the Coast tribe; and "Behold!" "Be still!" is *Noo-gee!* A hoot—a shout of contempt—is, in the language of the same people, *T"thee waugh!* and when they call to each other "to come on," "to follow"—as an invitation—they say *N"ya-alinyo!* I have heard this call in the bush, and the sound is musical and clear.

"Wait!" "Stop!" at Western Port is *Burra!*

When sorrowful, they express their sorrow by a sound like *Yah!*

When highly delighted, I have heard old men utter a prolonged sound like *Ng-ng-ng.*

In the north-western part of Victoria "Listen!" is *Goorrongy!* "Stop!" "Hark!" is *Tyerrickee!* and "Ah!" "Oh!" *Nyoo!*

In the Western district "Wait!" or "Stop a bit!" is *Warma!* or *Detpa!*

Mr. A. W. Howitt, in reply to enquiries, gives the following information:— When pleased, the natives cry *Ko-ki* (Gippsland), and *Ki* (Cooper's Creek). Grief is expressed by a shrill howl like *Eaw.* It is almost impossible to convey an idea of the sound by any combination of letters. Mr. Howitt says he has heard it at Cooper's Creek and also in Gippsland.

When joyful, they say *Yackatoon* (Gippsland), a word which *Toolabar,* a native of Gippsland, could not translate. When slightly hurt, as when a finger is cut or bruised, they cry *Ko-ki!* (Gippsland).

They call to each other thus: *Yangi!* (I say! Hollo!) (Gippsland); the reply being *Bow!* (Ay! ay!); or (at Cooper's Creek) *Copperow!* which is equivalent to "Come here!" the answer being *Abbo.* The latter word is also used as a token of assent. The term *Gow,* of the Cooper's Creek blacks, is used as a salutation, and may be equivalent to the term "All right," or the "Welly good" of the Chinaman.

"Yes," is *Nya;* and "No," *Ngatbun* (Gippsland).

"Yes," at Cooper's Creek, is *Gow* or *Abbo;* and "No" is *Watta.*

An interjection of assent to a speaker is *Mut-ta-tang,* "Talk again;" and one of dissent may be *Mut-jet-bollan,* "Talk lies," or *Ngatbun,* "No."

Wukunda-da-tchuta is equal to "My word! a fine fellow!"

Wunnoo-but-kun has no precise meaning, but is used to express surprise at a great number. For instance, when a black sees a very large mob of cattle coming towards him, he cries *Wunnoo-but-kun!*

Mr. Gason says that, at Cooper's Creek, *Koopia* is used in calling a child, equivalent to "Come, child!" that *Kulie* signifies "That's enough, I have said it, that's sufficient;" and that *Choo* is an exclamation used to draw attention to an object.

The Rev. Mr. Bulmer tells us that a mother's cry of *Lathi!* when a daughter is carried off by a warrior, is peculiarly sad, and sufficient to awaken sympathy in any bosom.

The Rev. Mr. Taplin says that "the Narrinyeri often utter inarticulate sounds, in order to express their feelings and wishes. These answer to our interjections, such as 'Oh! Ah!' &c., only it is not easy to express them by letters. Their method of saying 'yes' and 'no' is very difficult to write down. A sort of grunt, which may perhaps answer to the letters *ng*, pronounced in an affirmative tone, means 'yes;' the same sort of grunt, which can only be written by the same letters, but uttered in a negative, forbidding tone, means 'no.' Their expressions of surprise are the following:—*Kai, hai!* This is a pure interjection, and only means sudden astonishment. *Porluna;* this means 'Oh! children,' and is a common expression of wonder and amazement. *Tyin embe!* is an expression too filthy to be translatable; nevertheless it is a very common interjection of astonishment amongst the old blacks. The word *Koh* is used to attract attention, or to call out to a person to come. It is uttered long, and the *o* very round. The same word *Koh*, uttered short, is a sort of note of interrogation, and is used in asking a question. The *h* is strongly aspirated. A sort of cry, used to attract attention, may be written *Nyaaaah*, the *h* strongly aspirated. It must be understood, however, that in all these cases our letters only give an approximation to the sound; it must be heard in order to be understood. Some of the old women, by way of salutation on meeting a friend, will say, *Kaw, kah-kah, kah.* It sounds very much like an old crow. All the natives, old and young, when they are hurt, cry out *Nanghai, nanghai, nanghai!* —'My father, my father, my father!' or else, *Nainkowa, nainkowa, nainkowa!* —'My mother, my mother, my mother!' Males usually say the former, females the latter, although not invariably so. It is ludicrous to hear an old man or woman with a grey head, whose parents have been dead for years, when they hurt themselves, cry like children, and say *Nanghai*, or *Nainkowa*, as the case may be. The Narrinyeri are skilful in the utterance of emotion by sound. . . . . . . After I had finished the burial service, to which they were all very attentive, they proceeded in native fashion to raise a loud lamentation over the grave. First of all, old *Kartoinyeri* and *Winkappi* uttered a keen wail in a very long, high note, gradually lowering the tone; this was joined in by all the women present. Then the rest of the men uttered a long, loud, deep-bass groan. As that rolled away, the keen wail of *Kartoinyeri* and *Winkappi*, and the women, broke in; and as that began to lower in tone, the deep groan of the men was heard. This was continually repeated for about ten minutes. . . . . As an expression of grief by sound, it was perfect." *

A correspondent of Mr. Alfred Howitt's says that a word like *Nin-ki*—the last syllable much prolonged—seems to be a usual way of arresting attention amongst all the blacks of South Australia.

These brief notes afford material which will be of assistance in future researches.

---

* *The Narrinyeri,* pp. 95-6.

LANGUAGE.

TERMS OF ABUSE.

The terms of abuse used by the natives are strong. I have made careful enquiries respecting these, and the results show that in abusing each other the Aborigines are at least the equals of Europeans. Mr. John Green collected for me several of the phrases used by the natives of the Yarra. One will say to another *Booqurring mane-mane ngabedejew nggi mila Booqurring kianto ngalim-ngalim boongarboon*—"That fellow over there is very sulky with me for nothing. It is himself that is in fault." One will tell another that he is "a liar" (*Merrinam moom*); a "great liar" (*Marangi*); a "rascal" (*Keern*); a "terrible rascal" (*Tagaraktorong*); and the reply may be possibly "You big eye" (*Taong-gala*); "You crooked eyed" (*Wantarra mrring*); "You big-headed, skin and bone fellow, you!" (*Tanggoola kaong tewrong kalk kalk bornen torong enerop warr karwan*); "You big dirty devil!" (*Torong koo-nog Ngarrong torrong*); or, "Look at that fellow, he is like a dog!" (*Werre neen mane tonda Yerrangano*).

A woman will accuse another of unchastity : she will say, "*Tagilla narra-moom;*" or, "*Karin na bibol mane boorrnoonto;*" and she could say nothing worse if she were giving evidence in a police court against an enemy.

The Rev. Mr. Bulmer, in reply to my enquiries, writes thus :—"When the natives were angry, and abused each other, they used epithets similar to those of the very lowest class of Europeans ; not so bad on the side of blasphemy, but worse on the side of filth. No doubt the reason of this is that the Aboriginal has no superior spirit to blaspheme. As you desire specimens of the epithets used, I give them, as, no doubt, it is necessary, in writing of the Aboriginals, to give both sides of their character. In their mild way of scolding, when the cause of quarrel is not very serious, they generally confine themselves to calling nick-names, or they refer to some peculiarity of person, whether deformity or otherwise. It is amusing to hear them commence at the head of the person they are scolding, and end at the toe-nails. Thus they will call a person *Poork gatti* (big head) ; *Barrat poork* (bald head) ; *Barrat mree* (squint eye) ; *Barrat birndang* (bad arm) ; *Barrat jerran* (bad leg) ; *Booloon gatty* (belly big) ; *Barrat jane* (bad foot) ; *Karlo tooloot* (crane neck) ; *Barrat nark* (crooked back) ; and so in like manner refer to all the members of the body. I may remark with regard to the word *Barrat*—which I have translated 'squint,' 'bad,' and 'crooked'—that it is used by the blacks in all these senses, and may perhaps be equivalent to 'deformed.'" *

There are other forms of abuse :—

Itemque sæpissime, ut narrat Rev. J. Bulmer, de membris pudendis loquuntur ; et rationibus vituperandi tetterrimi fœdissimique sunt.

In rem longius procedunt quum aliquid de re gravius agitur. Tunc quidem omnem colluviem ex memoria collectam in adversarios sine pudore sine

---

* The natives of the islands of the Pacific abuse each other much in the same terms. One will tell another that he is ugly, has cross eyes, has a big mouth, &c. ; and an antagonist will retaliate by calling out "big eyes," "crooked legs," and the like.—*See Wild Life amongst the Pacific Islanders,* by Lamont, p. 309.

dubitatione congerunt. Feminæque procul dubio pejores si id quidem potest quam ipsi homines. Ut in albis hominibus "damn" aut "proh! fidem" aut "Dii immortales" ita apud eos verba obscœnissima audiri potest.

Ne parentes quidem se retinebunt quominus liberos parvos sermone pudendo alloquantur; liberisque coram disserunt ea quæ nunquam impuberibus dici fas est. Matresque semper pene liberis dant nomina nostris auribus fœdissima præ illorum sententiis innoxia et pura. Puer sæpe nominant *Dango Willin* (lappa). Hoc nomen extremum difficile expressu significat ut lappa cui affigat hærebit ita homo cui nomen "lappa" sit in deliciis veneris inhærebit.

LANGUAGE OF THE NATIVES.
(By the Rev. John Bulmer, of Lake Tyers, Gippsland.)

1. In what way is the article expressed and used in the Aboriginal tongue? (*See* Remarks.)

   A house - - - - - - *Mangu ketchoon.*
   The tree - - - - - - *Gingin nyleppur.*

2. Is such a thing as gender known in the Aboriginal language? If so, how is it used?—(*See* Remarks.) Give the equivalents of—

   Stone - - - - - - - *Walloony.*
   Male kangaroo - - - - - *Brangolo jirrah.*
   Female kangaroo - - - - *Booyangan jirrah.*

   And the male and female designations of other animals if there appear to be any regularity in forming the feminine from the masculine.

3. How is the plural formed? Give examples, as—

   Kangaroo - - *Jirrah.* | Men - - -
   Kangaroos - - (No plural form.) | Tree - - - *Nyleppur.*
   Man - - - *Bra.* | Trees - - *Yail nyleppur.*

4. How are the adjectives used? Are there degrees of comparison, and, if so, how are they formed or expressed? Give examples—

   A tall man - - - - - *Wrekil kani.*
   A taller man - - - - *Gnoolo wrekil kani.*
   The tallest man - - - - *Mack gnoolo wrekil kani.*

5. Personal pronouns—

   I - - - - *Ngio.* | We - - - *Werna.*
   Thou - - - *Mangi.* | Ye or you - - *Ngoortana.*
   He - - - - *Gindi.* | They - - - *Thana.*
   She - - - |
   It - - - |

   Is gender known in respect of the personal pronouns?—(*See* Remarks.) Are there cases? If so, give equivalents—

   I - - - - | We - - - *Werna.*
   Mine - - - *Ngetal.* | Ours - - - *Ninde thana.*
   Me - - - - *Ngio.* | Us - - - - *Werna.*

LANGUAGE.

Thou	-	-	*Mangee.*	Ye or you	-	*Gnowo.*
Thine	-	-	*Koothoula.*	Yours	-	*Nyingal.*
Thee	-	-	*Nungoo.*	You	-	

He	-	-	*Jilly.*	They	-	*Mandha.*
His	-	-	*Nungal.*	Theirs	-	*Thanal.*
Him	-	-	*Noonga.*	Them	-	

She	-	-	They	-
Hers	-	-	Theirs	-
Her	-	-	Them	-

(No feminine pronouns.)

It	-	-	They	-
Its	-	-	Theirs	-
It	-	-	Them	-

(No neuter pronouns.)

6. Relative pronouns—

Who	-	*Nan* (also expresses "what").	What	- *Nanma.*
Which-		*Wunman.*	That	- *Ketchoon.*

Give one or two short sentences showing how the relative pronouns are used.—(*See* Remarks.)

7. Possessive pronouns—

My	-	*Ngetal.*	Our	- *Nindi thanal.*
Thy	-	*Ngingal.*	Your	- *Ngwana thanal.*
His	-	*Ngungal.*	Their	-
Her	-	(No feminine pronouns.)		

State how they are expressed and used, and give short sentences by way of illustration.—(*See* Remarks.)

8. Distributive pronouns—

Each	-	- *Bremba.*	Either	-
Every	-	- *Ngurtana.*	Neither	-

State how they are expressed and used, and give a few short sentences by way of illustration.—(*See* Remarks.)

9. Indefinite pronouns—

Some	-	- *Preporetha.*	One	- *Kootook.*
Other	-	-	Any	- *Nappan.*
No	-	- *Ngalko.*	All	- *Girtgan.*
None	-	- *Naatbun.*	Such	-

Are they declined, and, if so, how?—(*See* Remarks.)

10. Adverbs—

Here	-	- *Tintaka.*	Backward	- *Ngrow.*
There	-	- *Manana.*	Forward	- *Ngoolo.*
Where	-	- *Woonman.*	Homeward	- *Mellagan.*
Hither	-	- *Bootjee.*	Hence	- *Moolo.*
Thither	-	- *Thoondho.*	Thence	-
Whither	-	- *Wool.*	Whence	-

10. Adverbs—

Only		
Alone	- - -	Ngalquan.
Solely		
Again	- - -	Barrat.
How	- - -	Waykrat.
Why		
When	- - -	Nara.
Wherefore		
Whether		
Very	- - -	Mambalgran.
Together	- - -	Karobran.
Perhaps	- - -	Kanno.
Much	- - -	Waycoot.
Little	- - -	Ngoopin.
Enough	- - -	Moondhana.
Often	- - -	Mailbran.
Seldom	- - -	Plakoot.
Sometimes	- - -	Kengalapan.
Never		
Once	- - -	Kooteganman.
Twice	- - -	Boolanggan.
Thrice		

Are there equivalents in the native language for the above, and how are they used.—(*See* Remarks.)

11. Prepositions.—How are prepositions placed? Give a few short sentences showing how they are used, and give equivalents of—

Above	- - -	Booloot.	Into	- - -	Mangina.
About	- - -	Paroneta.	Near	- - -	Jenana.
After	- - -	Kendoona.	Nigh		
Against	- - -	Neerambo.	Of		
Amidst	- - -	Booth.	Off	- - -	Plakoma.
Among	- - -	Kara.	On		
Around	- - -	Mateinga.	Over	- - -	Boolootha.
At	- - -	Noondhana.	Round	- - -	Maleinga.
Before	- - -	Nulla.	Through	- - -	Moolianga.
Behind	- - -	Gandee.	Throughout		
Below	- - -	Thanga.	Till	- - -	Mana.¹
Beneath			To	- - -	Keekala.
Beside	- - -	Thinana.	Towards	- - -	Jillianga.
Between	- - -	Booth.	Under	- - -	Thanga-thanga.
Beyond	- - -	Moonda.	Underneath	- - -	Thanga.
By			Until	- - -	Keekala.
Down	- - -	Thanga.	With	- - -	Thoolo.
For			Within	- - -	Woothae.
From	- - -	Mangy.	Without	- - -	Moona-anga.
In					

12. Conjunctions.—How are they used? Give one or two sentences by way of example. Give equivalents of—

Although			Neither		
And			Notwithstanding		
As			Nor		
Because	- - -	Wakanal.	Or	- - -	Kinna guani.
Both	- - -	Boola.	So		
But			That		
Either			Than		
For			Though		
If	- - -	Woothamalkanu.	Unless		
Lest			Yet		

13. What are the common interjections?—

Kooki.
Kanti (equal to "my word").

Yay (to express sorrow).
Naa (to express agreement).

REMARKS.

1. It is a most difficult matter to get the articles; in fact I do not think they have any, for in order to express the definite article they would say "that man;" and for the indefinite article, "another man;" or in their own tongue, *Preppa kani.*

2. In expressing the masculine or feminine they say, *Brangolo jirrah* (that is, male kangaroo); or sometimes they will say, *Jirrah watty* (a big kangaroo); and a female kangaroo is *Booyanga jirrah* (a kangaroo with an ovary); but in describing other animals they say, for females, *Yackan* (mother) —thus, *Yackana koola* (a female or mother bear).

3. In expressing the plural they make no difference where they place an adjective before it. Thus—"one kangaroo" is *Kooto jirrah;* "two kangaroos," *Booloomana jirrah;* but to express a large number of kangaroos they alter the termination of the noun. Thus, they say, *Yaail manda jirrowa* (many kangaroos), or *Yaail manda koolowa* (many native bears); but this is done merely for the sake of euphony, as there seems to me no particular rule on the subject; for they say *Kootopana kani,* that is, "one man;" or *Boolooman kani,* "two men;" and to express many men they say, *Yaail manda kani*—the termination of the noun not being altered at all. So I think we may conclude that they only alter the noun when it would sound abrupt without some affix. They have no way of expressing the plural as we have. They cannot express "trees": they say *Gullepur,* or *Yaail gullepur,* or, for "one stick," *Kallack;* and *Yaail manda kallowa,* for "many sticks." Indeed the blacks have no word to express "tree." The word *Gullepur* may mean a tree, or merely a piece of stick, or even a pipe to smoke with. In just the same way, they have no word for "fish" or "bird." All are distinguished by their proper names, as, for instance, a stringybark tree is *Yangoora,* and an ironbark, *Irrick.* So, in like manner, fish are known by their proper names, as *Kine* (bream), *Tamboon* (perch), *Krinyang* (mullet), &c., &c.; but the whole is known as *Yarnda jacka* (meat which is in the water).

4. I find it difficult to express how they compare. In comparing, for instance, "big," they say *Quarrail gree* (big canoe); for one bigger, *Mack quarrail gree* (which means a very big canoe); but to express a bigger one still they say *Mack quarrail gatty gree*—that is to say, "a very big, big canoe." And in comparing the word "tall," they say, *Wreckil kani* (a tall man), *Gnolo wreckil kani* (a taller man), and *Mack gnolo wreckil kani* (the tallest man). To express "good," "better," "best," they say—*Laan manda kani* (a good man), *Mack laan manda kani* (a very good man), and *Bremmanda kani* (the best man).

5. I have found it very difficult to get the pronouns, and I may state that they have no gender.

6. To show how the relative pronouns are used, I give an example or two. For instance, "Who goes with me?" is—

Nanma gegan thulo wanga necta?
Who   goes   with   me?

And " Which is your camp? " is—

   Woonmanda baang ma gningaloong?
   Which or where camp of yours?

And " What are you carrying in your hand? " is—

   Nanma kertbato man braa guinga?
   What carry in hand yours?

 7. To express the pronoun " my," they say, " for my spear," *Waal ma gnetal* (spear of mine); " thy spear " is *Waal ma gningal* (spear of thine); and " his spear " is *Waal ma gnungal* (spear of his).

 8. The distributive pronouns I have found very difficult, as it is hard to make the blacks understand what is meant. I give you one sentence to show the way the pronoun " each " is used. " I will give each of you a spear " is—

   Bremba gegwanatha waal ma gnurtagnangno.
   To each give I spear and to all of you.

I suppose equivalent to our expression " I will give to each and all of you a spear."

 9. The indefinite pronouns are not declined.

 10. The adverbs, also, I have found difficult to obtain. The word "homeward" I have given as *Mellagan;* but this merely expresses "to return," and is mostly used to express returning to one's settled home, or to home for the time being. The words I have not given I have failed to procure. I do not think their equivalents exist in the language.

 11. Of the prepositions I have given you all I could get, and I add a few sentences to show how they are used. To express " between "—as, for instance, " I was between two kangaroos," they say—

   Moona booth jirrowa.
   I was between kangaroos.

" Put that rug over the camp " is—

   Kinowa marook munana moola booloboolotha baanga.
   Put rug that way over   camp.

" I will go with you " is—

   Kickanat thoolo uanga nindo.
   Go I there with you.

And " I was under the tree " is—

   Thangana kallacka thin ma gnat.
   Under tree   was I.

LANGUAGE.

NATIVE WORDS AND THEIR MEANINGS IN ENGLISH.

Thununa ngi pandan.
Going to I strike.

Thununa ngi wooorngan togä jacka.
Going to I seek nest bird.

Thununa ngi bàndan.
Going to I sleep.

Thununa ngi tethagengan jack.
Going to I chew meat.

Thununa ngi keppeun.
Going to I scold her.

Thununa ngi pertgana jack tyro.
Going to I catch meat line.

Thununa ngi batgejan gwian.
Going to I cut axe.

Thununa ngi màng gwan ngunga.
Going to I to watch him.

Thununa ngi jibban nat kallack.
Going to I burn I stick or wood.

Thununa ngi leckin nganatha yarn.
Going to I pour out I water.

Thununa ngi wanjani.
Going to I take it.

Thununa ngi tat tat greletha.
Going to I keep to myself.

Thununa ngi jellan boorka ge jenat.
Going to I to sharpen by myself.

Wäl ma ngetalung.
Spear of mine.

Man jilly panda ngan poorko.
He hit me head.

Tarlo jack thialan.
Small meat eats.

Wulginga bundando kàlango.
How sting (or bite) snake.

Nerndowa woona dthal.
Teeth of his.

Kinnat gan yarrowa.
I am fightable (I was angry).

[Mr. Bulmer gives a further explanation of these phrases in a letter to me. He says that he has used the word *Jack* for "bird" as well as for "meat," and this is the way the blacks always use it when they speak of birds. *Tarlo jack* is "little meat." If they were going to hunt kangaroo, they would use the term *Woorngana jacka*, meaning thereby that they were going to get "meat." He says he has failed to render one sentence, because he could not get it satisfactorily translated. It is this :—"I am going to sharpen my spear." The term *ge jenat* he thinks—he says he is almost sure—is as he has rendered it. *Nat* at the end of the word *Gejen* is a personal pronoun, first person singular ; and, he supposes, is used to render the sentence emphatic. He finds that the blacks commonly use pronouns in this manner. To translate some sentences literally is nearly impossible—the corresponding English words would appear to be without sense. For instance, the sentence "I am going to burn a stick (or wood)" would be "I am going I burn a stick"—the *ngi* being, like *nat*, a pronoun, first person singular.]

THE VERB.—TO HEAR.

INDICATIVE MOOD.

Present tense.
Wäng-gän at - - - - I hear.
Wäng-gän nungäng - - - he hears.
Wäng-gän thanä - - - they hear.

Future tense.
Wäng-günä tha oorko - - I will hear.
Wäng-gän garä - - - he will hear.
Doorowäl wangän - - - they will hear.

Compound present tense.
Wängani - - - - - - - - I am hearing.
Nung-gän garä wängän - - - - - - he is hearing.
Wängänä quoit - - - - - - - they are hearing.

IMPERATIVE.

Wängän - - - - - - - - Hear.

To Love.

INDICATIVE MOOD.

Present tense.

Woorun yän at	I love.
Woorun yän nungäng	he loves.
Woorun yän kära wåro	they love.

To Go.

INDICATIVE MOOD.

Present tense.		Future tense.	
Yan gan nat	I go.	Thun uni yän gän at	I will go.
Yan gan nungäng	he goes.	Yan gan gärä	he will go.
Yan birtan	they go.	Blanga jindan	they will go.
Yan gan wert	we go.		

Compound present tense.

Plapa nat gara	I am going.
Plapän	he is going.
Ngändä kindan	they are going.

IMPERATIVE.

Plapä	go.

Thi alanä jirah thin butha karik.	Kootopanä kani mul wangä kewita.
Eat kangaroo in the scrub.	One man will go to creek.
Kàna watha wali, bal ngat melkina.	Kootopanä kani mul wangä karika.
Give me my spear, will I kill.	One man will go to scrub.
Melkin ngat. } or, I have killed him.	Kootopanä kani mul wangä wäroin.
Killed I.	One man will go to forest.
Jibban wert bal wert thäng.	Nundeing mä wanga thungundhä.
Roast it all it eat.	Meet at the water-hole.

Wango ya il kinedä.
Where plenty fish.

Wudhä mal kanu kärnding bal wert kang keekaling mookä nungia.
If he coo-ee then we will go to him.

Wudhä mal kano wert loorapa merat wrüthun kani.
If one of us catch the strange man.

Kana watha wallung	Give me a stone.
Uä wallung ma nunga	Give him a stone.
Ucanä jinnä yarn	I give him some water.
Man yal ucanathä yarn ma ngingo	I will not give water to you.
Kana wathä lackie	Give me some bread.
Ucanä jinna ngleppur	I will give you stick.

Wackä ucan wern i-ä ngleppur ma ngingo.	Dindhä ma mung-gandan.
We give will not stick to you.	There is father of mine.
Dindhä ma breth ba ngethäl.	Thalmä mung-gan dänä.
This is hand of mine.	He is father of mine.
Watbilimba.	Wackä jinanä mung-gan douna.
Sing you a song.	This not father of mine.
Wunmanä mungan ma nginalung?	Boolooman. Kootopan.
Where is father of yours?	Two. One.

Kana watha lack bal nat thang, mack mremanat.
Give me bread for me to eat, very hungry I.

LANGUAGE. 31

"Three" would be expressed thus :—

        Boolooman batha kootook.
        Two   and   one.

"Four" thus :—

        Boolooman batha boolung.
        Two   and   two.

And so they go on repeating as far as they can. All the numerals they have are "one" and "two."

Ban yal thangha yarn.
We   drink water.

Wreckil birndang ma nat-kidha.
Long arm has my brother.

Wreckil mandhā bowan dowhan.
Long is sister of mine.

Boolithganda lathe kani mali.
Two children man that.

Kinnamā kallack bal ngin pandū baan.
Take stick and you strike dog.

Thapija kani pandando kallow baan.
The man beat (or struck) with stick dog.

Tata kandā woorin.
Rising is the sun.

Thaprā woorin.
Set is the sun.

Thaprā naran waregando.
The moon is risen.

DECLENSION OF SUBSTANTIVES AND PERSONAL PRONOUNS, WITH EXAMPLES OF THE DUAL.

	Singular.	Dual.	Plural.
Nom.	*Kani*, a man	*Boolong kani*, two men	*Womba kani*, men.
Gen.	*Wa kani*, of a man	*Wa boolonga kani*, of two men.	*Thungo wanga kani*, of the men.
Dat.	*Mo kani*, to a man	*Kinna boolonga*, to two men	*Thulona kani*, to the men.
Acc.	*Kani*, a man	*Boolong kani*, two men	*Womba kani*, men.
Voc.	*Wagrato kani*, O man	*Wagrato boolong kani*, O two men.	*Wakratgil kani*, O the men.
Abl.	*Kinanga kani*, by a man	*Kinanga boolonga*, by two men	*Thana kani*, by the men.
Exat.	*Thingo wangona kani*, from a man.	*Wanga boola*, with two men	*Wanga thana kani*, from the men.
Ergat.	*Kikana thulona kani*, with a man.	*Thula wanga boola*	*Thitana worna kani*, with the men.

First person.

	Singular.	Dual.	Plural.
Nom.	*Ngio*, I	*Ngalo*, we two	*Nango*, we.
Acc.	*Ngat*, me	*Nyalo*, us two	*Nango*, us.
Caus.	*Ngioma*, by me	*Nyango*, by us two	*Werna*, by us.

Second person.

	Singular.	Dual.	Plural.
Nom.	*Jilana*, thou	*Ngoogara*, you two	*Ngurtana*, you.
Acc.	*Jilani*, thee	*Ngoogara*, you two	*Ngurtana*, you.
Voc.	*Wakrat denana*, O thou	*Kanugara gno*, O you two	*Wakrat ngurtana*, O you.
Caus.	*Nindoma*, by thee	*Boolangara*, by you two	*Thal ngurtana*, by you.

Third person.

	Singular.	Dual.	Plural.
Nom.	*Jilli*, he ; *Malie*, she ; *Mandha*, it	*Boolagano*, they two	*Thinana*, they.
Acc.	*Ngunga*, him	*Boolagano*, they two	*Thinana*, them.
Caus.	*Kanu ngunga*, by him	*Thanouraganu*, by them two	*Thana*, by them.

The two men went away	Plapa boolung kani. Go two men.
The names of the two men	Thara boolung kani.
I gave a spear to the two men	Ukatho waal boolung kani. Gave I spear two men.
I speared the two men	Pandatho boolung kani. Speared I two men.
I slept with the two men	Baandathan wanga bulla. Slept I with two.
I ran away from the two men	Windathani thungo wanga bulla. Ran I from the two.
The two men caught me	Loorapa bulla gnan. Caught two me.
I caught the two men	Loorapa gnio bulla. Caught I two.
I saw the tracks of the two men	Tacka gnio bulla wanik. Saw I two tracks.
I go	Balnat yaning.
We two go	Yangan gnal.
We go	Plapan wert.
You go	Yan imba.
You two go	Plapimb baook.

NOUNS AND VERBS, GIPPSLAND.

NOUNS.		VERBS.	
Sleep	Bairndan.	To sleep	Bairndanweet.
A knot	Thulunba.	To net or knit	Krendang.
A cut	Bowga.	To cut	Batgejan.
A fight	Pandean.	To fight	Yarrak.
Growth (enlargement)	Berngan.	To grow	Berngan.
Love (affection)	Woorinyan.	To love	Woorinyan.
A call	Karndan.	To call	Karndogan.
A blow	Pandan.	To beat	Pandean.
A cleft	Tarregan.	To cleave	Taramban.
A smear	Maneba.	To smear	Kartaban.
A spear	Waal.	To spear	Krindha.
Speed	Minamit.	To hasten	Wutherama.
Death	Nowoot.	To die	Tirtygan.
Hunting (sport)	Warrangwan.	To hunt	Worngan.
Sweat	Blanda blanda.	To sweat or perspire	Blanda blanda.
Life	Bagwan.	To live	Warrapanana.
Rest	Gwandoban.	To rest	Gwandoban.

[I have obtained these words from the Rev. Mr. Bulmer, to show the relation that exists between nouns and verbs. They afford some hints as to the modes in which words have been formed, and the reader can easily add largely to the list by an examination of the vocabularies in this work.]

NATIVE STORY.—English—*Bundah Wark*.

Two blacks, a man and a woman, named Paddy and Kitty; the two went from Lake Tyers,
Bolung kani, bra il woorcat, thärbla Paddy batha Kitty bulla plapa mungä Wärnungatty,
to get some swans' feathers and opossum skins for sale. There was no flour at the station.
wurnalla murn mundärrä bathä märuk ualla. Nätbä lack munga bullagan.
So the two went away for one month, promising to return when the flour came.
Plapa bulla ma kootealla wanedä, bulla mellagalithä mal ngalla belligalitha lack.

The two went down the Lakes with other two blacks.   One day the two
Kicka bullä thullä   yak mullo jettah   mullo wanga preppü bullung gàna.   Mal plapa bulla

left their camp to go and hunt by themselves, and were never seen again.
thungo kooto brun thuloo woorngàllä ngäl quanä bulla, nandha kang barratha mräkandha.

One day the blacks were hunting in the scrub near some water, when one man picked up a bone.
Woorngan kani wrah thundho kàriha dundho yaru yärnda, kootoopa kani ma mutba bring.

He thought it was a kangaroo bone.   He looked again and found it was the bone of a black.
Kaang koonganu ngal yal bringa jirowa.   Kaang bürrath jungarra haany bringa kani.

Some more blacks came up and took away the mud and found the body of Kitty.
Bärrath batha kaang preperwitha kani ma kina mulla yenella tackın kani machta.

All the blacks knew the body, because she had a lame leg.   All the blacks said some
Kani thungo wango, ma kirtirra matho.   Thun garra kani mal

one had murdered her.
jelmbandho kani.

NATIVE STORY.—*Bundah Wark*—English.

Boolung kani, bra il woorcat, thärbla Paddy batha Kitty.   Bulla plapa munga Wärnungatty
Two blacks, man and woman, named Paddy and Kitty.   Two went from Lake Tyers

wurnalla murn mundarra batha märuk,   ualla.   Nütba lack munga bullagan.   Plapa bulla
to get swan feathers and opossum rug, to give away.   No flour at the station.   Went the two

ma koote ulla waneda.   Bulla mellagalithä mal ngalla belligalitha lack.   Kicka bulla thulla yak
for one moon.   To return when comes flour.   Went the two to the west

mullo jettah.   Mullo wanga preppä bullung gàna.   Mal plapa bulla thungo kooto brun.
by the sea beach.   Went with them other two men.   Went the two one day.

Thulo woorngälla ngäl quana bulla.   Nandha kaang barratha mrä kandha.   Woorngan
To hunt by themselves the two went.   Never seen were their faces again.   Hunting were

kani wrah thundo kàrika, thundo yara yärnda.   Kootopa kani ma mutba bring.
the blacks in a place where was scrub, where was also water.   One black picked up a bone.

Kaang koonganu ngal yal bringa jirowa.   Kaang barrath jungarra kaang bringa
Then thought he this is a bone of a kangaroo.   Then looking again found there the bone of

kani.   Barrath batha kaang preperwitha kani ma kina mulla yenella tackan kani
a black.   Looked another there more blacks and they got by lifting and saw a black's

machta.   Kani thungo wang-a ma kirtirra matho.   Thungarra kani mal jelmbandho
body.   Blacks knew when she was lame.   Knew blacks that she had been tomahawked

kani.
by blacks.*

NATIVE LANGUAGE, GIPPSLAND AND MURRAY.

English.	Native.
What name you?	(G. L.) *Wun-man thari gnina?*
	(M.) *Wingi a nimba?*
Where is the track?	(G. L.) *Wanick indra?*
	Track where is it?
	(M.) *Windarra yuthero?*
	Where is the track?
Where are the other blacks?	(G. L.) *Wunman preppa kani?*
	Where are other blacks?
	(M.) *Windarra karo waimbia?*
	Where are other blacks?

* In *The History of Bolgan*, in this work, Mr. Alfred Howitt gives a similar account of the finding of poor Kitty's bones.

English.		Native.
I lie	(G. L.)	*Jate bolato.* Lie I.
	(M.)	*Purragia appa.* Lie I.
You lie, &c.	(G. L.)	*Jate bolando.* Lie you.
	(M.)	*Purragia imba.* Lie you.
	(M.)	*Yaton purragia.* He lies.
	(M.)	*Purragia gnalie.* Lie we.
	(M.)	*Purragia urta.* Lie all (or, you all lie).
I am hungry, &c.	(G. L.)	*Ganuganat.* Hungry I.
	(M.)	*Wilka wilk appa.* Hungry I.
	(G. L.)	*Nindo ganuganook.* You hungry.
	(M.)	*Wilka wilkimba.* Hungry you.
Hungry	(M.)	*Yaton wilka wilk anna.* He is hungry.
	(M.)	*Wilka wilk urta.* Hungry all (or, all are hungry).
Our father, &c.	(G. L.)	*Mungan oura.* Father our.
	(M.)	*Ninnin kambia.* Our father.
	(M.)	*Kambe i. Nammarri.* Father my. Mother my.
My camp	(G. L.)	*Muck gnetal gambanja.* My camp.
	(M.)	*Yapperi.* Camp (or, my camp).
Where is the meat?	(G. L.)	*Wudha jack?* Where meat?
	(M.)	*Windarra manba?* Where meat?
No meat	(G. L.)	*Natbunda jack.* No meat.
	(M.)	*Natha manba.* No meat.
Afraid, &c.	(G. L.)	*Jer-ag anat.* Afraid I.
	(M.)	*Gno-yal nappa.* Afraid I.
	(G. L.)	*Jer-ag anda.* Afraid you.
	(M.)	*Gno-yal nimba.* Afraid you.
	(G. L.)	*Natbunda jer-ag anat.* Not afraid I.
	(M.)	*Illa gno-yal nappa.* Not afraid I.

LANGUAGE.

English.		Native.
Cut a canoe to get meat for all	(G. L.)	*Panda gnin oura gri wur iatanga.* Cut you for all canoe meat.
Go	(G. L.)	*Pangat yanning.* I go.
	(G. L.)	*Yan imba.* Go you.
	(G. L.)	*Yan ga nal.* Go we two.
	(M.)	*Paddy wappa.* Go I.
	(M.)	*Paddy waimba.* Go you.
	(M.)	*Paddy urta.* Go we.
	(M.)	*Paddy walie.* Go we two.
Where is my canoe stick?	(G. L.)	*Wunman gendook muck gnetal?* Where is canoe stick of mine?
Bathe	(M.)	*Yakake wappa.* Bathe I.
	(M.)	*Yakake waimba.* Bathe you.
	(M.)	*Yaton yakake wanna.* He bathes.
	(M.)	*Yakake walie.* Bathe we two.
I go to another country or place	(M.)	*Paddy wappa karo kara.* Go I another country (or place).
What do you think? &c.	(M.)	*Minna uring nindo?* What think you?
	(M.)	*Uring ato.* Think I.
	(M.)	*Yaton uri wanna.* He thinks.
You do not speak	(M.)	*Illa parel go rimba.* Do not speak you.
Who stole my bread?	(M.)	*Winjea karnmia mani?* Who stole bread my?
I speak not to you	(M.)	*Illa kulpera notama.* Not speak I to you.
You spoke to me	(M.)	*Nindo kulpera gnana.* You spoke to me.

Mr. Bulmer adds this note:—" I thought it best to give you specimens of both languages—Gippsland and Murray—so that you might see the construction of both. I think we may safely venture to say that the construction of all the native languages, which must have originally come from the same source, is the same. One thing I have observed with regard to the language—it is a double language. They have two words to express everything. This is very convenient to a people who have occasionally to disuse a word, on the death of a friend whose name sounded like the word they lay aside. For instance, when

I first went among the Murray blacks they used the word *Murra* for the hand. A man died who was called *Murra muto* (or bad hand), having only one finger on each hand. The blacks then changed the word *Murra* for *Mam banya*. This very practice would no doubt much assist, in the course of years, to change a language, while its construction remained the same."

Vocabulary.

English.	Murray.	Gippsland.
Wind	Yarto	Krow-a-ro.
Summer	Buckara	Jelanduok.
Winter	Koleya	Merbuck.
Star	Burley	Brael.
Sun	Yhucko	Wurrin.
Moon	Pitoa	Nar-ran.
Gum-tree	Bernarra	Ykuro.
Wood	Yarrara	Mrit.
Fire	Nandaly	Towera.
Water	Nucka	Yarn.
Stone	Yarnda	Wallung.
Rain	Mochera	Willung.
Clouds	Ninda	Note.
Sky		Warrun.
Old man	Wirta	Boredine.
Widower	Yachea	Marra walack.
Widow	Mambanya purno	Wuw-a-lack.
Blackfellow	Waimbia	Kan-ni.
Earth	Murndy	Wrack.
Egg	Purty	Bo-yang.
Camp	Yap pera	Gambanja.
To-day	Kalpo	Jilli.
Yesterday	Illour	Book-ang.
I see	Wing-e-ato	Tin tacka.
To lie	Purragia	Jate bolan.
To steal	Karnmia	Dowan-dowan jal.
Come	Kowa	Gnowan jy.
Be quick	Wal-nal weu	Wothera.
Where	Windarra	Wunman.
Good	Kandelka	Lane.
None	Natha wary	Naat-bun.
Yes	Gua	Gua.
No	Mopa	Gnalko.
Small quantity	Kate wail yo	Tarlitban.
Plenty	Ko-ua	Ya ill.
News	Berlko	Lewin.
Sun-down	Hippy yhuko	Kote bill.
Bad	Thul-logga	Din-din.
Wait	Balyarta	Targut.
Spirit or shadow	Uri-uri	Yambo.
Father	Kambea	Mungan.
Mother	Namarra	Yackan.
To die	Pucka	Tirtyga.
To perspire	Kangnarra	Blanda-blanda.
Give me	Gnokan danna	Kana watha.

LANGUAGE.

English.	Murray.	Gippsland.
Whose is this?	Arn ahie	Gnana lack a dinda.
Where is the road?	Windarra yhutero	Wanick indra.
Mine	Gnie	Gnetal.
Grass	Mutho	Bun.
Ferns		Ge uan.
Swan	Young oly	Gidi.
Pelican	Gnang kero	Burran.
Black duck	Miralie	Wrang.
Kangaroo	Bul o li a	Jirrah.
Wallaby	Marrinya	Tharogang.
Bandicoot	Doganya	Min nack.
Emu	Kalty	Mi owero.
Opossum	Pirlta	Wa-gin.
Native bear		Kullah.
Eel		No-yang.
Spear	Kalkro	Wall.
Club-shield	Marraga	Marraga.
Spear-shield	Karragame	Bamerook.
Boomerang	Wana	Wangin.
Club	Pira	Kallack.
Instrument for throwing spear	Yarramba	Mirriwan.
Eagle	Bilyarra	Quarnamerung.
Crow	Wacko or Wa-hu	Gnar-o-kal.
North		Be-ara.
South		Tha.
East		Kar-wi.
West		Yack.
Doctor	Makega	Malluy mallanq.
Tall	Barlaro	Wreckel.
Short	Pimby	Tookul a pan.
Blood	Kandarra	Karn do barra.
Hands	Murra	Bret.
Feet	Thina	Jane.
Knees	Thingee	Bun.
Elbows	Kuppoa	Jill ung.
Mouth	Yelka	Ka-at.
Chin	Wacka	Yain.
Hair	Burlhy	Lit.
Forehead	Bich ho	Nen.
Ear	Ury	W-ring.
Teeth	Nandy	Gnarn-dack.
Tongue	Tar-lin-ya	Jilline.
Throat	Bern-bu	Tull-oit.
Finger nails	Mel inya	Tagera-bret.
Liver	Thanganya	Wall-ow-alack.
Fat	Murney	Warne wan
Cheeks	Gnerly	Wa-any.
Stomach	Kurnto	Bullon.
Flesh	Wanga	Wor-ri a tang.
Eyes	Makey	Mri.
Man	Maly	Brah.
Woman	Nongo	Woor-cat.
Boy	Wilyango	Lathe.
Girl	Nongo mote pa	Tarl woor-cat.
Dog	Kad dely	Ba-an.

NATIVE NAMES OF ANIMALS, ETC., COLLECTED FROM A MEMBER OF THE KARNATHUN TRIBE, WHOSE ORIGINAL RESIDENCE WAS LAKE TYERS.

English Name.	Aboriginal Name.
Kangaroo	Jir-rah.
Black wallaby	Thărogang.
Red wallaby	Kinarra.
Paddy melon wallaby	Bowey (o as in "cow").
Kangaroo rat	Bree.
Bandicoot	Menak.
Common rat	Biak.
Wombat	Naroot.
Porcupine	Kowern.
Native bear	Koola.
Dog	Buan.
Iguana	Bathalook.
Small lizard	Keratung.
Red snake or brown	Thurung.
Black snake	Toon yarak.
Small snake	Koon gwan.
Wood or constrictor snake	Loowa birri.
Opossum	Wä jan.
Black opossum	Brak.
Water rat	Toora blung.
Platypus	Barlijan.
Native cat	Brumbin.
Tiger cat	Bindkalang.
Ring-tail opossum	Blüang.
Flying squirrel	Wäran.
Large flying squirrel	Wärnda.
Flying mouse	Toan.

Fishes, &c.

English Name.	Aboriginal Name.
Bream	Kine.
Perch	Tambun.
Flat-head	Brindat.
Large mullet	Pertpiang.
Sand mullet	Krinyang.
Sea trout	Billin.
Schnapper	Narboogang.
Silver perch	Käry.
Silver-fish	Kooey.
Fish without scales, known as "leatherjacket"	Ngat.
Golden perch	Looterak.
Shark	Yelmri.
Whale	Baawang.
Seal	Bithowi.
Crab	Krangilang.
Lobster	Derndang.
Shrimp	Wäat.
Prawn	Wertwertire.
Oyster	Koo-n warra.
Periwinkle	Wratjan.
Limpet	Yo-ngnan.

English Name.	Aboriginal Name.
Salt-water grass	Loomat.
Kelp	Koonthooi.
Water	Yarn.
Salt water	Waring.
Lake	Wrathung.

Birds.

English Name.	Aboriginal Name.
Emu	Miowera.
Native companion	Kooragan.
Crane	Karlo.
White crane	Tirtgerawan.
Eagle hawk	Quarnameroo.
Sparrow hawk	Tootooth gwan.
Fish hawk	Be win.
Magpie	K'lart.
Crow shrike	Wooryung.
Curlew	Brä walagan.
Plover	Berin-berin.
Red-bill plover	Tarlarang.
Swan	Gidi or babine.
Black duck	Wrang.
Teal duck	Natuth.
Wood duck	Yellan nandih.
Widgeon	Koortgan.
Pelican	Booran.
Seagull	Blithbrung.
Small white seagull	Tarook.
Mutton-bird	Bralak.
Cormorant	Kürney.
Large kingfisher / Laughing jackass	Quäh.
Small kingfisher	Thoormuryung.
Kingfisher with white neck	Tanyankarogan.
Black diver with white breast	Koorowera.
Mopoke	Wookook.
Crow	Ngaroogal.
Wonga-wonga pigeon	Waakquagan
Bronzewing pigeon	Tappak.
Lyre-bird	Woorail.
Swallow	Kilugan.
Martin or swift	Koornyan.
White cockatoo	Bräh.
Grey cockatoo	Käran.
Black cockatoo	Nganak.
Blue mountain parrot	Wattat.
Grass parrot	Toon.
Satin-bird	Bungil warndowan.
Musk duck	Ban.
Robin redbreast	Bulularang.
Mistletoe-bird	Chirtgang.

LANGUAGE. 39

English Name.	Aboriginal Name.
Small bird with patch of red over tail	*Bribatith.*
Small bird like tomtit	*Ya rang.*
Geese	*Nath.*
Snipe	*Klih.*
Spoon-bill duck	*Wyung.*
Darter or serpent-bird	*Tharwan.*
Mountain duck	*Karu-gnark.*
Sand-piper	*Kewet-kewet.*
White hawk	*Boon boong.*
Small grey hawk	*Troon wagga.*
Grey plover	*Bungil bowrndang.*
Quail	*Ooro bi ynanang.*
Penguin	*Tarlo birndany.*
Water-hen	*Neerloony.*

Insects, &c.

English Name.	Aboriginal Name.
Spider	*Mermandho.*
Tarantula	*Waanduna kani.*
Mason fly	*Kookoonda miowera.*
March fly	*Narrawort.*
Mosquito	*Newan.*
Cricket	*Tu jerrat.*
Small moth	*Tarlo käng-käng.*
Frog	*Tatelak.*
Bull-frog	*Blaok.*
Sting-ray	*Bäälangoork.*
Bulldog ant	*Dibban.*
Large-headed ant	*Purk gatti.*
Small black ant	*Wooyoot.*
Louse	*Niu.*
Grass tick	*Dungo.*
Grasshopper, locust	*Bapakan.*
Grub	*Krang.*
Large moth	*Bä buhan.*
Butterfly	*Ngarawert.*
Black beetle	*Ngoorin.*
Fly	*Narwon.*
Bee	*Kaangal.*
Mantis	*Bungil towera.*
Centipede	*Ngow-ook thuringa.*

English Name.	Aboriginal Name.
Scorpion	*Koongun.*
Earwig	*Ngara-ngara.*

Trees, &c.

English Name.	Aboriginal Name.
Ironbark	*Baroin.*
Box-tree	*Tä-kan.*
White-gum	*Balook.*
Mahogany of Snowy River	*Pinnak.*
Wattle	*Mart.*
Lightwood	*Yowan.*
She-oak	*Bürn.*
Cherry-tree	*Ballat.*
Stringybark	*Yangaora.*
Mountain ash	*Yowat.*
Red-gum	*Yooro.*
Tea-tree	*Birt.*
Tea scrub on hummocks	*Nowart.*
Currant-tree	*Lirra.*
Pittosporum undulatum	*Bärt-bürt.*
Honeysuckle	*Bown.*
Kangaroo apple	*Koonyang.*
Musk-tree	*Burri mebbook.*
Fern-tree	*Käruk.*
Fern, light-green one	*Geewan.*
Nettle	*Mäbun.*
Sow-thistle	*Thalak.*
Common grass	*Dan.*
Grass-tree	*Turndang.*
Cabbage-tree	*Thapalla.*
Reed	*Kowat.*
Cutting grass, used for making baskets	*Krowan.*
Rush grown on swamps, with broad flat leaf	*Toorook.*
Round rush	*Booroot.*
White-currant shrub	*Karrowert.*
Raspberry	*Yallaban.*
Tall fern-tree	*Kakawert.*
Short fern-tree	*Dagal.*

LANGUAGE OF THE NATIVES OF THE PINE PLAIN TRIBE, NORTH WIMMERA, AND GENERALLY UNDERSTOOD IN THE WESTERN DISTRICT, THE LODDON, AND SWAN HILL.

(*Carefully collected from some very intelligent blacks from that tribe living at Lake Wellington Mission Station in Gippsland.*)

(BY THE REV. F. A. HAGENAUER, OF LAKE WELLINGTON, GIPPSLAND.)

English.	Native.
I am going to strike	*Duak ginyan.*
	To strike going am I.
I am going to find a nest	*Yaak ginyan laungy-banyee.*
	To find going am I (a) nest (of a) bird.
I am going to lie down	*Goomin ginyan.*
	To lie down going am I.

English.	Native.
I am going to chew the meat	*Watye ginyan ngowee.* To chew going am I the meat.
I am going to scold her	*Tyallee ginyan.* To scold her going am I.
I am going to chop with an axe	*Taardow ginyan batye goorook.* To chop going am I with an axe.
I am going to watch him	*Maan-maan tyerry ginyan.* To watch him going am I.
I am going to burn the wood	*Werrick ginyan wanyip.* To burn going am I the wood.
I am going to pour out the water	*Gaal ginyan cattying.* To pour out going am I the water.
I am about to take it	*Gaam-maan ginyan.* To take it about am I (going).
I intend to keep it	*Woorrpamitt ynootyan.* To keep it intend I.
I am going to sharpen my spear	*Litwoony ginyan ngary balleck.* To sharpen going am I my spear.
He bit me on the head	*Tacking propanpeck.* He bit me on the head (my head).
The bird eats	*Bany tyeckelang.* The bird eats.
How does the snake bite and kill man?	*Tyanango goottilang goornmill buntinong wootye?* How does bite the snake to kill man?
With his teeth	*Lee allook.* With his teeth.
I was angry	*Goollinan.* Angry was I.

The Verb "Goongee."

TO LOVE, TO CREATE BY LOVE, TO MAKE, TO DO.

INDICATIVE MOOD.

Present tense.

Singular.		Plural.	
Goongeenon	- I love.	*Goongeenan*	- We love.
Goongeen	- Thou lovest.	*Goongeenat*	- You love.
Goongeena	- He loves.	*Goongeenatt*	- They love.

Past tense.

Goongeenong	- I loved.	*Goongeenango*	- We loved.
Goongeeno	- Thou lovedst.	*Goongeenange*	- You loved.
Goongeena	- He loved.	*Goongeenang*	- They loved.

Perfect tense.

Goongeenon mala	- I have loved.	*Goongeenango malan*	- We have loved.
Goongeeno mala	- Thou hast loved.	*Goongeenange malan*	- You have loved.
Goongeena mala	- He has loved.	*Goongeenang malan*	- They have loved.

Pluperfect tense.

Goongeenon malana	- I had loved.	*Goongenanon malanon*	- We had loved.
Goongeenone malana	- Thou hadst loved.	*Goongenange malanon*	- You had loved.
Goongeena malana	- He had loved.	*Goongeenga malanan*	- They had loved.

LANGUAGE.

Future tense.

Singular.		Plural.	
Goongeengnon maleck	- I shall love.	*Goongengnangnon maleck*	We shall love.
Goongeengon maloock	- Thou shalt love.	*Goongeengnott maloock*	- You shall love.
Goongengo maloock	- He shall love.	*Goongeengnott muloock*	- They shall love.

Future perfect tense.

Goongeengnanon mala	- I shall have loved.	*Goongeenango malano*	- We shall have loved.
Goongeengnona mala	- Thou wilt have loved.	*Goongeenang malano*	- You shall have loved.
Goongeengnonan mala	- He will have loved.	*Goongenungo malano*	- They shall have loved.

POTENTIAL MOOD.
Present tense.

Goonganeeget	-	- May I love.	*Goongareegett*	-	- May we love.
Goongareeget	-	- Mayst thou love.	*Goongateegett*	-	- May you love.
Goongangeeget	-	- May he love.	*Goongatyeegett*	-	- May they love.

Past tense.
Not to be found out; likely not to exist.

Perfect tense.

Goonganeget mala	- May I have loved.	*Goongareegett malan*	- May we have loved.
Goongareeyet mala	- Mayst thou have loved	*Goonyateegett malan*	- May you have loved.
Gvongangeeget mala	- May he have loved.	*Goongatyeegett malan*	- May they have loved.

No Pluperfect tense.

SUBJUNCTIVE MOOD.
Present tense.

Gattoongnoong goonget	- If I love.	*Gattoongunoroong goonget*	If we love.
Gattoonga goonget	- If thou love.	*Gattoonguttoong googet*	- If you love.
Gattoongoroong goongett	If he love.	*Gattoonyaroong googett*	- If they love.

IMPERATIVE MOOD.

Goongack!   *Goongack!*

SENTENCES IN ENGLISH AND ABORIGINAL.

A kangaroo is feeding in the scrub	-	-	*Miyoock goray dyickeling ganya patta yalk.* There kangaroo is feeding thick one scrub.
Get me my spear and I will kill him	-	-	*Munacke tyarrameck bovann.* Hand me here my spear him kill I will.
I have killed him	-	-	*Boyeenann.* Killed him I have.
Let us roast him	-	-	*Bovango ba towango.* Let us roast him and eat him.
One of us go down to the creek	-	-	*Kiup bangoroock yarrowa parrall.* One of us go down to the creek.
One of us will go into the scrub	-	-	*Kiup bangoroock yarrowa ganya patta galk.* One of us go into (dowu) thick one scrub.
One of us go into the forest (number of large trees)			*Kiup bangoroock yarrowa goroong goroong ngatta galk.* One of us go into large large high scrub.
We will meet at the big water-hole, where the fish are plentiful			*Weeyonbiny yungo muago goroongo yaram,* Meet we will at large water-hole, *yannoong gettyowelly werringal.* where are plenty fishes.

VOL. II.   F

English	Aboriginal
If one of us catch the stranger, let him coo-ee and we will run to him	Gatloong kiup prengoorroock garroock ginyoong goolloom-goolloom, garntallya bam tyerryngango. If one among us him catch stranger, call for (us) run all will.
Give me a stone	Woogageen kiup goottyappa. Give me a stone.
Give him a stone	Woogag kiup goottyapp. Give him a stone.
I give you some water	Woonannoong kuttyong. I give you water.
I will not give you any water	Bogee wannoong wooging kattyoong. I will not give water.
Give me some bread	Woogag geen bannyimnoo. Give me bread.
We will give you a stick	Wooging ngang tangoonoong galko. Give we will you a stick.
We will not give you a stick	Wooyeeba tangoonoong wannoong woging galko. We will you not give a stick.
Give me some bread to eat, I am hungry	Woogaggeen bannyimmo, weegann. Give me bread, I am hungry.
This is my hand	Gimpa manyaneck. Here is my hand.
Sing a song	Waarrangack yattngatteh. Sing a song.
Where is my father?	Mameck gimpa? My father where is?
He is my father	Ngooa mameck. He is my father.

Father. My father. Our father.
Mamen. Mameck. Mamengoroock.

My father comes. *Mameck woata.*	Our father comes. *Mamengoroock woata.*
Your father comes. *Mamoock woata.*	Your father comes. *Mamentack woata.*
His or her father comes. **Ginio mamoock woata.*	Their father comes. *Mamentack woata.*
(*Ginio signifies "that one's.")	That one's father comes. *Ginior mamoock woata.*

English	Aboriginal
My father is here	Gimpa mameck. Here is my father.
Our father is here	Gimpa mamengoroock. Here is our father.
He is not my father	Ngooat mameck. Not is my father.

One. Two. Three. Four. Five.
Kiup. Boollett. Boollett ba kiup. Boollett ba boollett. Boollett ba boollett ba kiup.

Six.
Boollett ba boollett ba boollett.

English	Aboriginal
A great, great many	Galloopp galloopp.
We drink water	Goopango kuttyoong. We drink water.
My brother has a long arm	Goottangeck tyowang pattyngoroock. My younger brother a very long arm has.
My sister is very tall	Tyaattyeck tyowang goroock. My sister very tall is.

LANGUAGE.

He has two children	- - - -	*Gilla boolaven boollett piampango.* He has two children.
Take a stick and beat the dog	- -	*Manacke galk tagack gall.* Take a stick beat dog.
The dog is beaten with a stick	- -	*Tackalanack* or *gall tackannack galko.* The dog he is beaten with a stick.
The sun is rising	- - - - -	*Prinna ngauoee.* Is rising sun.
The sun is set already	- - - -	*Ngoomming nyatkin ngauoee.* Already is down sun.
The moon is risen	- - - -	*Prinnon mittyaan.* Risen is moon.
What have I done to you?	- - -	*Nyannon tyam goongin tyoorr mangin?* I have what done to you?
The day after to-morrow	- - -	*Perpeck ngooa ngauoee.* To-morrow after this day.
Where is your mother?	- - -	*Winya bapooch?* Where is your mother?
My mother speaks	- - - -	*Bapeck worecka.* My mother speak.

DECLENSION OF SUBSTANTIVES AND PERSONAL PRONOUNS.

Singular. / Dual.

	Singular	Dual
Nom.	A man, *Wootye*	Two men, *Booletye wootye.*
Gen.	Of a man, *Wootyoogitg*	Of two men, *Wootyegitg booletye.*
Dat.	To a man, *Wootyoock*	To two men, *Booletye wootyook.*
Acc.	A man, *Wootye*	Two men, *Booletye wootye.*
Voc.	O man! *Wootyoh!*	O two men! *Booletye wootyoh!*
Abl.	By a man, *Wootyookal*	By two men, *Booletye wootyookal.*
Exat.	From a man, *Wootyenoong*	From two men, *Booletye wootyenoong.*
Ergat.	With a man, *Wootyell*	With two men, *Booletye wootyooll.*

Plural.

(The same as dual, only to use the word *Getyonwell* instead of *Booletye*), like—

Nom.	Men, *Getyonwell wootye.*		Voc.	O men! *Getyonwell wootyoh!*
Gen.	Of men, *Getyonwell wootyegitg.*		Abl.	By men, *Getyonwell wootyookal.*
Dat.	To men, *Getyonwell wootyook.*		Exat.	From men, *Getyonwell wootyenoong.*
Acc.	Men, *Getyonwell wootye.*		Ergat.	With men, *Getyonwell wootyooll.*

First person.

	Singular.	Dual.	Plural.
Nom.	I, *Walloreck*	We two, *Walloonganook*	We, *Walloongingorack.*
Acc.	Me, *Walloonoongeck*	Us two, *Walloongoongnock*	Us, *Walloginyorack.*
Caus.	By me, *Wallogalleck*	By us two, *Walloongnoongnallooch*	By us, *Wallogallingorack.*

Second person.

	Singular.	Dual.
Nom.	Thou, *Walloongin*	You two, *Boolet wool.*
Acc.	Thee, *Walloongin*	You two, *Boolet wool.*
Voc.	O thou! *Walloongeen!*	O you two! *Boolet woollen!*
Caus.	By thee, *Walloogallet*	By you two, *Boolet woollek.*

The Rev. Mr. Hagenauer states that he could not find out the remainder from any of the blacks belonging to the Pine Plain tribe who reside at Lake Wellington. They said that the old men knew more, but they had not learnt it from them.

A SHORT ABORIGINAL STORY, IN THEIR OWN LANGUAGE, WITH THE CORRECT ENGLISH BELOW.

Gra goongeenang   mamengorach   meg megy yowwee,   goray   perrippen   manye
(When) first made (the) great father every living beast, (the) kangaroo run off (on his) fore

ba tyinnallook ngollo gaal;   gaolloam goolloomoo   mortannin malloohoom doolloo wooyarin
and hind legs like (the) dog; (but) a strange blackfellow hunted after him until   got short

manninyook.   Nyattyementon!   Porannyatta   goolloam goolloom dorin, goray perrippen
his fore-legs. Him poor fellow! When at night (the) strange blackfellow slept, (the) kangaroo run off

tyinnalloak   nimpa yetya.   Payoongmingoo torroponen tyinnallook   gimpa mengoon.
(on) his hind-legs to this country. Since that time (it) went on   hind legs   here about till now.

COLLECTION OF WORDS IN THE ABORIGINAL LANGUAGE.

(BEING THE LANGUAGE UNDERSTOOD IN THE WESTERN DISTRICT, THE NORTH-WESTERN DISTRICT, THE LODDON, AND SWAN HILL, BUT BELONGING ESPECIALLY TO THE NORTH-WEST OR THE PINE PLAIN TRIBE.)*

Aboriginal.	English.	Aboriginal.	English.
Bunn	ashes.	Dam-dam pirney	vessel, pot.
Boorrinn	dark.	Daalka	good.
Bopoop	little boy.	Daako manye	a good hand.
Boiltack	to hate.	Derriboott	shore, bank.
Boring	smoke.	Datty oock	little river.
Bar	and.	Dennying	frost.
Bapen	mother.	Dallan	to let.
Baring	to cut.	Danta	down.
Bunn	dirt.	Danta gaamparywik	to pull down.
Boott	grass.	Daap tap kooya	to awake.
Bootety	both.	Dat-ngat	new.
Booletye	two.	Dattuck	a young tree.
Baan	hole.	Dilm-dilm	to crack.
Booywonga	to wipe.	Darn dam	to rattle.
Brann	rivulet.	Dootwillang	corner.
Bootylang	to go along with wind or water.	Darnoylong	to recover.
Brama	to press out.	Dutt yerrung	knock together.
Boottarty lang	fastening.	Goongin	to love.
Bonbonty lang	shivering.	Goongin	to make.
Biggy	to get up.	Goongin	to create.
Borungamda dera	snoring (great sleep).	Goortampy	dissatisfied.
Buring	road.	Ganylong	shaving.
Buring gy grasiny	dray track.	Garning	carrying.
Winya pirpa baring?	whither leads this road?	Gamgam	horse.
Boorrip payoong	run quick.	Goorroock	magpie.
Boorripa loga	fetch it quick.	Gaul	dog.
Doorri	star.	Gorya	kangaroo.
Dichele	to eat.	Ga	nose.
Dora	to sleep.	Girrip	leg.
Dora mameck	my father sleeps.	Goorrn	throat.
		Goorritmill	snake.

* Mr. Hagenauer states that he has found that the blacks generally have two words to express the same thing—so that words taken down by different writers, or by the same writer at different times, may vary very much even in the same tribe. He adds that, in his belief, a word having the same sound as the name of any person in the tribe was let drop, and another substituted for it, when that person died; hence the continual change in the language.

Aboriginal.	English.	Aboriginal.	English.
Gama	large wallaby.	Nganwe	sun.
Gni	little.	Nganwe	light.
Gatyiwee	come down	Ngatlye	greedy.
Galla-gallu goock	old woman.	Nga	yes.
Gotoock	younger brother.	Nyaranopan	old man.
Galick	there.	Nganiyoock	husband.
Gimpa	here.	Nya-paranginon	yes, I am tired.
Ginga leerrmdel	in the camp.	Ngyee	words.
Gilla	she.	Ngang gimpa	to dwell here.
Goolk	blood.	Ngack	hail.
Gotyoock	rock, stone.	Ngarya	she-oak tree.
Goorrack	sand.	Ngurrang	to like much.
Goottyill	dew.	Ngatoock	a piece.
Geera	leaf.	Ngacka	to immerse.
Gualk	tree.	Ngatpan	no.
Gimpa mya	about here.	Nyoorru willang	rain clouds.
Get mampa ginga	perhaps it is here.	Ngan goott	first.
Gampanyoock	deep.	Ngango	how.
Gayoowaa	stiff.	Ngango pory ?	how many ?
Gaal poongy non	I break through.	Nganwee	day.
Ginio	that.	Ngo gett	well.
Gam piplang	beautiful.	Nya ngy ring ?	what ?
Gy ga galach gimpa	his own.	Ngun win	at that time.
Gingma	this.	Ngoly	this one.
Gangeck	for me.	Ngango	beginning.
Gally tyerriwat	question.	Ngaan	place.
Gromack	answer.	Ngatta	afraid.
Gio?	where ?	Ngill pa it	thin.
Giang	they.	Ngang-ngany inong	I forget.
Gampa	shall.	Nganga gimpa ?	how is it ?
Ginia	certain.	Nyangonong	I see.
Gorack	ours.	Nyanginontong	we see.
Gam ma	to take upon.	Ngalloock-ngalloock tya	large bushes.
Gi-y-nang	vain.	Nguak	shade.
Gialpa weyoong	to understand.	Ngallenyoock	enemy
Galpa weyanong	I understand.	Ngallenyoock	evil spirit.
Gaalgoock	handle.	Nguttya	the evil spirit or devil.
Goolyee	good-natured.	Kuttyoong	water.
Goort goroock	peaceable.	Kaoppala	to drink.
Goorrongy!	listen ! hear !	Kalky pan goong	white clay.
Gattye	warm.	Kutgoorria	not willing.
Gattye wa	hot summer.	Kooya	thoroughly.
Gaalpawya	to rend or split.	Kiuh	one.
Gaanpap	thick.	Kooyoo watt	sorrowful.
Gaalkwill	rush.	Koolloollum	proud.
Gnallia	angry.	Lyeh	tooth.
Goollior ?	are you angry ?	Lanangorook	single woman.
Goollinong	I am angry.	Larundel	camp.
Goorook goorroock morang	the clouds are red.	Lit	top, point.
		Littia	sharp.
Galpuuga	to break.	Liroock	woman.
Gimpan ma	explain yourself.	Limoock timoock	heritage.
Gia-gia you wangoock	he cries.	Lou wee ying	all done, finished.
Gina ngayack	on one side.	Loud yo wa bopoop	the little boy cries.
Ngary	duck.	Loom	small wood brushes.
Ngange	whiskers.	Larpelaan	noise.

Aboriginal.	English.
Miroo-ack	fowls.
Mo-ah	eye.
Manye	finger.
Mark manye	hand (hand or mother of the finger).
Mittyan	moon.
Morang	sky.
Ming-ming ylang	give me some.
Manacka katying	give me some water.
Manacka wongip	give me some wood.
Matymoock	wife.
Mamoock	father.
Mameck	my father.
Mameck dora	my father sleeps.
Malyouwipe	useless.
Malp ma mi wa	I do not understand (never did it before).
Moom we ya	jealous.
Moom we ya on	I was jealous.
Maleck	shall.
Moom we ya on maleck	I shall be jealous.
Mittyach	rain.
Maroong	pine-tree.
Manacke	to bring.
Malack	by-and-by.
Moroon men	to save.
Moroon men on katying	I save any one from the water.
Mamengoroock	our great father.
Mamengoroock goongin	our great father loves and makes.
Mamengorook tyior monk goonging	our great father first made the world
ba goonyi boolctye wootye	and then he made both men
ba liroock ba ya uwe	and women, and beasts.
Muoh	inlet.
Mityoock	skin.
Micka	rich.
Manack ganyeck gima	fetch it for me.
Mampa	to think.
Manpanon	I think.
Mang gacka ngan	a fine place.
Mooroock	handle.
Moockin yirr	beginning.
Maring	he takes it up.
Maringanon	I take it up.
Mampy non	I am hot.
Manpy	hot.
Mi ya	winter, very cold.
Manacka	to carry.
Mode ma a long	cold, suffering from cold.
Mempy ni lang	to keep warm.
Marit-marit	a cool breeze.
Mameck woata	my father comes.
Mora	little ants.
Mootlyorong	I find it.
Maranggaock	revenge.
Mirma	selfish.
Morrang	very dark.
Moochoy	to rest.
Moock y non	I rest.
Monino	louse.
Moninoycch	I have lice.
Morriacky	very little.
Maalgoompip	nothing.
Nanye?	how? what?
Nyogoong	willing.
Nyat bonn mabra	the river upwards.
Nanyo nayoon?	how is the quality?
Nangoorna?	how is it?
Nintyerrwat	it is so-so.
Nyagack	look round.
Nyoongin	belonging.
Nyarrangynan	I know.
Nyanon?	I what?
Nyanon goongin?	what have I done?
Nyanon goongin tyoormangin?	what have I done to you?
Nya woa?	to whom does it belong?
Nyoorr tuma	to lurk.
Nyallo	spring.
Nyoo!	Ah! Oh!
Nyrren yeng non	I remember.
Nyn nin	satisfied.
Nyat woary	make room.
Nyoo nooing ngarwe!	Ah! this day.
Nap goonga wroa	to stare with the eyes.
Nyoo malook	to find again.
Nyappa wo unta	to accompany.
Noomittang	he cries loud.
Nyang non	I sit.
Nyang	to sit.
Nyantamoock	to wait.
Nyoomim	that will do.
Nyo koong	it belongs to you.
Nanyinia	to play about.
Nimpa worecka	to speak against.
Neoruenyoock ngarwe	sunbeam.
Nyongeek	belong to me.
Propoock	head.
Pattying	knee.
Poorrap	calf of the leg.
Prapa	slow walking.
Purpurria	lazy.
Prooinga	to cut himself.
Parangyary?	are you tired?
Paragio	tired.
Poorrparoock	to lie on the ground.
Poorrparnon	I lay down.
Panitya	a piece of land.
Propoock	hill, head (the same).

LANGUAGE.

Aboriginal.	English.
Pick	red clay.
Pringo ninyo	to pass by.
Prapra	to build.
Papilligatt	to go on foot.
Paan	small.
Paripa	run.
Prippalee	bring it soon.
Ponayanoe	to roast meat.
Purtpuria	slow.
Perwooa yama	to do it.
Pny-pny yama	willing.
Payucke	to flow.
Pawoya	to continue.
Purnya	swollen, to swell.
Prantoonoirang	blind.
Poornporoong	shoulder.
Pirro	sandy place.
Pangoog	a little meat.
Pah!	bark!
Pallarang	to bow down.
Parpack nyuwoa ngarwe	the day after to-morrow.
Proong gooagy	on one side.
Parpack	to-morrow.
Papoolwill	flat.
Pota	shake down.
Poollapull	little ones.
Perringgoock	tail.
Pogoock	life, spirit, soul.
Pytyick	fly.
Puring	roots.
Pirripa	to lead on.
Poorgoock	pull it off.
Pennimack	to cover.
Penpenny mill	to cover it with a blanket.
Pariya	to move on.
Tyerrap	mouth.
Tyallee	tongue.
Talyoock	arm.
Tyenna	foot.
Tyippa	to swim.
Tyiranga	a long journey.
Tantala	to walk fast.
Ton wick wonyip	to split wood.
Ton wick	to split.
Tittymee	to close.
Toonga	fear.
Tyippa mamoock	your father swims.
Turriya	to recover.
Turriyanon	I recover.
Tyagook	my land.
Tyammoonya	very dry.
Tya	earth, land.
Tya-it	island.
Tyarryman	to plant.
Tyaak	reeds.
Tyoorrmorng	he will.
Tyerroock	deserted place.
Tunnpill	cloudy.
Trinnta	bull.
Turmy-turmy	lively.
Turngatto	a swollen place or spot.
Tyo yon mack	to teach.
Tyat tying	to rest.
Tyanga-tyango	take eat.
Turrnack	on your back.
Tyerrngatt	new.
Tyootoock	the end.
Tyerrickee!	stop! listen!
Tratyegat nyalloonga	you come in spring.
Tyarryga	he stands.
Tyalla wook	not ripe, unripe.
Tyallich-tyallick	evening.
Tarrongo	stretch.
Tarra	white.
Tarrabunn	white ashes.
Tullengack	to skin.
Tyally goongack dalky tya	he makes fun about it.
Tyerry gotip	let it stand.
Taab taab!	easy! easy!
Tyerry gallang goock	stop with him.
Wy gon	to die.
Wy gonon	I am dying.
Woata	to come.
Wroagy yee	nothing more.
Willa	wind.
Woata willa	the wind comes.
Woata gorong a willa	strong wind comes.
Wary	go.
Warynon	I go.
Woarrwoock	outside.
Woatapook	inside.
Woatyema	it clears up.
Woa	crow.
Wonyip	fire.
Wogucky wonyip	give me some fire.
Woata non	I wait.
Woata non ginio	I wait for him.
Wary wya	go away.
Willyinywill	birds.
Winya bulluckneck?	how can you say so?
Woomylang	very miserable.
Wiayaty	to love, to like.
Wrawonmakatying	to take out of the water.
Wrawonmak	to take off.
Woornack	sunshine.
Woorynuck	grey fish.
Wya	to wish, to long for.
Wooggagacknon	I want it.
Willa	opossum.
Wiall	gum-tree.
Whinya?	where?

Aboriginal.	English.	Aboriginal.	English.
W*rawy*	to climb.	*Woatwoara*	black clouds.
W*ogack*	to give.	*Wallapit propooch*	on the head.
W*anyip*	wood.	*Worooa*	green.
W*agageck*	give me.	*Werona*	quiet, to soften temper.
W*agageck wanyip*	give me wood.	*Willunnen*	to change.
W*awook*	elder brother.	*Yanacka*	come on, move on.
W*aweek*	my elder brother.	*Yanacka galik*	they shall come on.
W*oreche*	to speak.	*Yanacka gio pata*	all shall come.
W*orecke mameck*	my father speaks.	*Yurang*	go away.
W*inya mamen?*	where is my father?	*Yura*	belongs.
W*oomelang*	poor.	*Yura parang*	it belongs to my ground.
W*agant*	hail.	*Yura parnag non*	I put it on my ground.
W*i woock*	to lift up.	*Yara purrack*	put it on my land.
W*i wy non*	I lift up.	*Yarram*	fine river, large river.
W*i wy non wonyip*	I lift up wood.	*Yauve*	beast.
W*orrenga*	to shake.	*Yauve*	meat.
W*orrenga propock*	to shake the head.	*Yama*	not willing.
W*oam*	to ask.	*Yally*	property.
W*oamanon*	I ask.	*Yally peck*	my property.
W*inyaroo?*	who?	*Yally pengorook*	our property.
W*ootye*	man.	*Yianya non gampa?*	why should I not?
W*illkilla*	to look round, to turn.	*Yingoorna*	to-day.
W*oak*	beyond.	*Yoompa*	to take from the fire.
W*oak tyetooch*	beyond time, endless.	*Yall yallama*	a cool evening.
W*allo*	near.	*Yirrymalla*	unfastening.
W*inyang?*	how far?	*Yampy anon*	I am better.
W*inyarangit*	to whom.	*Yowanyoock*	to shout.
W*iatt gattye*	spring time little warm.	*Yargan*	to look.
W*alpa*	burned.	*Yarganon*	I look.
W*ya-wya*	tough.	*Yarganon gamgam*	I look for the horse.
W*ityapoock*	the centre.	*Yattya*	bad.
W*oatgoorrack*	sandhill.	*Yurring*	gone away.
W*oagga*	to laugh.	*Yawirr*	animal.
W*oagganon*	I laugh.	*Yirrma*	lightly.
W*oagganinnin*	laughing at me.	*Yanginanoock*	we all together.

THE DIALECT OF THE BRABROLONG AND NEIGHBOURING TRIBES.

(By A. W. HOWITT, F.G.S., WARDEN AND POLICE MAGISTRATE, BAIRNSDALE, GIPPSLAND.)

Mr. Howitt has furnished short stories—native and English—illustrative of the dialects spoken by the Brabrolong and neighbouring tribes; and has added the following examples of the dual :—

I, *Ngin.*   You and I (dual), *Nallu.*   We (all), *Warru.*

Blabba nalla jilli moolla Nibboray.
Walk we now to Nibbor.

Nunda blabba nalla bagowrin jilli moolla Nibboray.
Not walk we sun-down now to Nibbor.

(That is to say, "We will not go to Nibbor now it is sun-down.")

Kunkerun   nalla   brundu.
Too late   we (will go) to-morrow.

Turntulla nalla jilli   moolla Nibboray.
Horseback we now (go) to Nibbor.

Turntun = Horse.

LANGUAGE.

Two blackfellows	*Bulloomanna kurni.*
Two quarrelsome blackfellows	*Bulloo yirakal kurni.*
Two women	*Bulloo wrookut.*
Two nice-looking women	*Bulloo laen wrookut.*
Two spears	*Bullum warl.*
Two sharp spears	*Bullum jullunbroo warl.*
Two meals (*e.g.*, dinners)	*Bullum darndroo luck.*
	(eat) (food)
Two great meals	*Bullum guerrule luck.*

THE OWL AND THE EAGLEHAWK.

(Brabrolong Tribe, Mitchell, Nicholson, and Tambo Rivers.)

Ebing   *tówund-jat*   *wattun*   *magwánnnumurunga.*   *Maengwarra*   *gwánnumurunga*
Owl   stole   'possum of eaglehawk.   Watched   eaglehawk
(The little brown owl)

multówundjun   *wattun*   *múlnoongal.*   *Yirrak neinda bulla, kányuboolla mangoot bittal.*
stealing   meat   of his.   Quarrel fellows two,   perhaps   fight.
                                                                                         (as fighting with a waddy or club)

Palwadinna   *daya*   *moóngabúllan*   *maggiárt-bearn*   *bulla.*   *Koonkarra*   *gwánnumurunga*
A number   see   fellows two   wrestling   two.   Perhaps   eaglehawk
                                             (or together)

maggiart-bearn   *bulla.*   *Kannyu*   *bullan*   *mabúndian.*   *Multówandjanny*   *ngrúnga*
wrestling   two.   Perhaps   two   bite.   Stealing   hole
          (together)   (tear with the beak)

wattunda ma gwánnumurunga   *nook prak a*   *ngrúnga*   *gwánnumurunga.*   *Ebing*   *turtygunny*
'possum of the eaglehawk   block up   hole   the eaglehawk.   Owl   dead

moonangrunga.
hole.

THE EAGLEHAWK AND THE OWL.

(By a Native of a Tribe near the Brabrolong.)

Bonay-chakka   *já-anju*   *gwánnumurunga*   *wóonganto*   *jirra.*   *Gwánnumurung*
Claw-flesh   foot with   eaglehawk   seeking   kangaroo.   Eaglehawk
The eaglehawk was seeking to seize a kangaroo with his talons.   The eaglehawk saw

ebing   *mum*   *mutkwut*   *wongia*   *ngia*   *ngrunga.*   *Ebing*   *woonganto*   *blang.*
owl   there   going   into   his   hole.   Owl   seeking ring-tail 'possum.
the owl going into a hole belonging to him.   The owl was seeking a ring-tail 'possum.

Mútkwuttung   *(mookun)*   *ebing*   *toondor*   *tanga*   *wanga*   *ngrunga.*   *Wully*   *ngat*   *kekán*
Went into (going into) owl   down   bottom   into   hole.   How   I   can
The owl went down into the bottom of the hole.   The eaglehawk said how shall

ma nókepalla   *gunna?*   *Tappy*   *quannal!*   *Ebing*   *tunkana*   *tang,*
shut up   him?   All   right!   Owl   spoke   words,
I contrive to shut him up?   All right, I have it!   The owl said how shall

wama   *ngat*   *jellaquan*   *tungoo?*   *Blabba*   *tungana.*   *Blabba*   *gwánnumurung*
how   I   hole make   hence?   Away   from here.   Away   eaglehawk
I make a hole to escape hence?   He made his escape.   The eaglehawk

tungoo—wangoo   *ebinga.*
hence—from him owl.
went away when the owl had escaped.

NOTE.—It seems that at that time the eaglehawk is supposed to have claimed all the 'possums as well as the kangaroos as his property. Hence he speaks of the hole in the tree in which lives the ring-tail 'possum as "belonging to him."

Told by one of the Tatoongolong tribe, which inhabited the strip of land between the Gippsland Lakes and the sea.

Tatoon = South, *e.g., Tatoon willung* = South rain, or rain from the south.

VOL. II.   G

SPECIMENS OF THE LANGUAGE OF THE NATIVES OF LAKE HINDMARSH.
(By the Rev. A. Hartmann.)

INFINITIVE.
To Come—*Woarta.*

INDICATIVE.

	Present.			*Past.*	
Singular.	I come, &c.	Plural.	Singular.	I came, &c.	Plural.
Woartin yan		*Woartun nuandang.*	*Woartin nan*		*Woartin nang-o.*
Woartin yar		*Woartin yat.*	*Woartin nar*		*Woartin nut.*
Woartun		*Woartun nitch.*	*Woartin ga*		*Woartin nitch.*

Future.

Singular.	I shall come, &c.	Plural.
Woartin yuan		*Woartin nuandang.*
Woartin yuar		*Woartin gut.*
Woarting ga		*Woartin gitch.*

POTENTIAL.

	Present.			*Past.*	
Singular.	I can come, &c.	Plural.	Singular.	I could come, &c.	Plural.
Woarti yan		*Woarti andang.*	*Woartian malla*		*Woartiyandang malla.*
Woarti yar		*Woartia gut.*	*Woartiar malla*		*Woartiyat malla.*
Woarti ya		*Woartia gitch.*	*Woartiya malla*		*Woartiyitch malla.*

IMPERATIVE.

Singular.		Plural.
Woarti		*Woarti wat.*

(To Beat—*Daka;* To Burn—*Walpa;* and many more like *Woarta.*)

ACTIVE.
INFINITIVE.
To See—*Nyä-ngă.*

INDICATIVE.

	Present.			*Past.*	
Singular.	I see, &c.	Plural.	Singular.	I saw, &c.	Plural.
Nyangan		*Nyangang-o.*	*Nyainan*		*Nyainang-o.*
Nyangar		*Nyangat.*	*Nyainar*		*Nyanut.*
Nyaing		*Nyangitch.*	*Nyain*		*Nyainitch.*

Future.

Singular.	I shall see, &c.	Plural.
Nyakinyan		*Nyakinyang-o.*
Nyakinyar		*Nyakinyut.*
Nyaking		*Nyakinngitch.*

POTENTIAL.

	Present.			*Past.*	
Singular.	I can, may see, &c.	Plural.	Singular.	I could, might see, &c.	Plural.
Nyanyan		*Nyanuang-o.*	*Nyawan malla*		*Nyawuandang malla.*
Nyanyar		*Nyanyut.*	*Nyawar malla*		*Nyawuat malla.*
Nyanya		*Nyanyitch.*	*Nyawa malla*		*Nyawitch malla.*

IMPERATIVE.

Singular.		Plural.
Ngagak		*Nyanganurnung.*

LANGUAGE.

PASSIVE.

INFINITIVE.—(None.)

INDICATIVE.

Present.

Singular.	I am seen, &c.	Plural.
Nyain naingn	- - -	Nyain niyangorin.
Nyain nyiurnung	- -	Nyain niyurding.
Nyain nyitch	- - -	Nyain nityanning.

Past.

Singular.	I was seen, &c.	Plural.
Nyain nain	- - -	Nyain niyangorin.
Nyain niurnung	- - -	Nyain niyurding.
Nyain itch	- - -	Nyain nityanning.

Future.

Singular.	I shall be seen, &c.	Plural.
Nyakin naingn	- - - - -	Nyakin niyangorin.
Nyakin niurning	- - - - -	Nyakin niyurding.
Nyakin nigtch	- - - - -	Nyakin nityanning.

POTENTIAL.

Present.

Same as future, with *Mamba* affixed.

Past.

Same as present.

IMPERATIVE.

Singular.		Plural.
Nyapa yunning	- - - - - -	Nyapa nyangorin.

PASSIVE.

Daka—To Beat.

INFINITIVE.—(None.)

INDICATIVE.

Present.

Singular.	I am beaten, &c.	Plural.
Dakun naingn	- -	Dakun niyangorin.
Dakun niyurnung	-	Dakun niyurding.
Dakun nitch	- -	Dakun nityanning.

Past.

Singular.	I was beaten, &c.	Plural.
Dakin nain	- - -	Dakin niyangorin.
Dakin niurnung	- -	Dakin niyurding.
Dakin nitch	- - -	Dakin nityanning.

Future.

Singular.	I shall be beaten, &c.	Plural.
Dakingn naingn	- - - - -	Dakingn niyangorin.
Dakingn niurning	- - - - -	Dakingn niyurding.
Dakingn nitch	- - - - -	Dakingn nityanning.

POTENTIAL.

Present.

Same as future, with *Mamba* affixed.

Past.

Same as present.

IMPERATIVE.

Singular.		Plural.
Dakabayunung	- - - - - -	Dakabuyurding.

INFINITIVE.
To Give—*Woka.*

INDICATIVE.

Present.

Singular.	I give, &c.	Plural.
Wokin yan	- - -	*Wooin yandang.*
Wokin yar	- - -	*Wooin yat.*
Wooin	- - - -	*Wooin nitch.*

Past.

Singular.	I gave, &c.	Plural.
Wooin nan	- - - -	*Wooin nuandang.*
Wooin nar	- - - -	*Wooin nut.*
Wooin ga	- - - -	*Wooin nitch.*

Future.

Singular.	I shall give, &c.	Plural.
Wokin yan	- - - - - - -	*Wokin yango.*
Wokin yar	- - - - - - -	*Wokin yat.*
Wokin	- - - - - - - -	*Wokin nitch.*

POTENTIAL.

Present.—(None.)

Past.

Singular.	I would give, &c.	Plural.
Wokian malla	- - - - - - -	*Wokiandang malla.*
Wokiar malla	- - - - - - -	*Wokiyat malla.*
Wokitch malla	- - - - - - -	*Wohiyitch malla.*

A kangaroo is feeding in the scrub.
Menjun tyakilingn ganyabegalk.

Get me my spear and I will kill him.
Managa ngek ngärimballeh bä brangum mallan.

I have killed him.
Mallan brangum (or) *brangumin nan.*

Let us roast him and eat him.
Böwang-u bä työwang-u.

One of us will go down to the creek.
Giapbengngurrak nyäkinyo gatyivinyo datyak ga.

One of us will go into the scrub.
Giapbengngurrak nyäkinyo ganyabegalk.

We will meet at the big water-hole, where the fish are plentiful.
Wöiupbenyang-o marko gurung-a yäram, gumbunung wärup tyanardi.

If one of us catch the strange blackfellow, let him coo-ee and we will run to him.
Gàdung giapburang ngurrak gärgala matmeyi wutyn gandalia bä bùrapiandang tyurmanuk.

Give me a stone.
Woka gek gutyap.

Give him a stone.
Woka guk gutyap.

I will give you some water.
Wokin yanung catyen-o.

I will not give you any water.
Bàwanung wokin catyen-o.

Give me some bread.
Woka gek banyim.

We will give you a stick.
Wokin nuandang unung galk-o.

We will not give you a stick.
Bàwuandang unung wokin galk-o.

Give me some bread to eat; I am hungry.
Wokn gek banyim jöwan; wckan.

This is (here) my hand.
Kimba manya nyek.

Sing a song.
Gigäli gikiyo.

Where is your father? My father is here.
Windya mäm? Mömek kimba.

He is my father.
Nyogung mömek.

He is not my father.
Nyo bàwa mamek.

One. Two. Three. Four.
Giap. Buletch. Buletpa giap. Buletpa buletch.

Five. Ten (hand).
Bulet buletch giap. Buletgedi manya.

Twenty.
Nyullo buletgedi manya.

We drink water.
Gopang-o catyen.

He has two children.
Galimbin buletch wörinditch.

My sister is very tall.
(younger) (elder)
Tyätych gutangdek tyuwurany batyin gurk.

My brother has a long arm.
(younger) (elder)
Wöwek gutch tyuwurany datyak.

LANGUAGE.

Take a stick and beat the dog. *Manah galk bä däka gal.*	The dog is beaten with a stick. *Gal malla däkin galk-o.*	
The sun is rising (risen already). *Nyōwi brinun brinin.*	The sun is setting (set already). *Nyōwi ngäkin ngükung.*	The moon is risen. *Mityen brinin.*
Where are you going? *Winya ngarra ngüka?*	What are you going to do? *Nyōwar gungnyin?*	What do you want? *Nyōwar guter?*
What is the matter with you? *Nyangar yuma?*	How long? *Nyutuk?*	I came yesterday. *Woartinan tyalligare.*	Come to me to-morrow. *Woartiar garek barebarp.*
Do not wait. *Nyungar mirmingn.*	Do not forget. *Nyungar mellimingn.*	Take care of yourself. *Nyar kellen nyār.*	What is that? *Nyähnyo?*
When did you come? *Nyettugar woartin?*	Make haste. *Nyet wunni.*	Tell him to come. *Geyagurt yarowaga.*	Give that to him. *Woka gaduk.*
Let me see that. *Nyow wanung.*	Come and help me. *Yanak wokar gin manya.*	Wait! (or, stop a bit!) *Warma!* (or, *Detpa!*)	

The Rev. Mr. Hartmann says that the moods and tenses given are the only ones he could get from the blacks. They have only one gender in their language. The *itch* of the third person plural scarcely expresses the sound; the *ch* should be pronounced as the German *ch* in the words *ich, mich, sich.*

AN OLD NATIVE STORY.

Duan   gupm   menjun   gumbarram   mellan   kitya   buroin.
(Name meaning squirrel) tracked (a) kangaroo (and was) sleeping out many (a) night.

Weenbulain-yo   wüpcullen Duan   ba   nyninmen   dumang.
(Name meaning spider) found out Duan and (Duan) saw him (Weenbulain)(certain way of coming).

Woartun   Weenbulain   nyum   bämbin   nyum   Duan   ba   bürpin ba wräiwin galk-a.
Come   Weenbulain   then   frighten that   Duan   and (made him) run and climb a tree.

Nyubendin   woartin   Weenbulain   bundin   nyuin galk bendinung
(When) on the tree came Weenbulain (and) bit through with one bite that tree on which was

Duan,   huikin   tyabaperumen ba   geka yuilgi galk, yingurnan yummin malluk
Duan, (the tree) falling (Duan) jumped and (got) to another tree, and so on till

brangayin Duan.   Tyamalluk bundin Weenbulain-yo galk wänmau-uiyen tyagung giap garan nyuin
tired Duan.   Then   bite   Weenbulain trees round about leaving one   that

bendinung   Duan.   Tyamalluk woartin   bundin nyum galk   bendinung   Duan, nyuin
on which was Duan.   Then   came (and)   bit   that   tree on which was Duan, then

buiken   galk.   Weenbulain-ya   bundin men Duan   nyuin.   Duan-a   nganangàuk buletchi,
fell   the tree. Weenbulain   bit (killed) Duan then.   Duan   (had) nephews two,

Bràmbambull   dädäwein bulanguh   wityuwa wanyuk   larndang, ba tyawràk bewa
Brambambull (by name) waiting both (for) his   return (to) the camp, and as he did not

woartin,   bikin   beelung   yarkin   bulang uk   nunangurn   muityen   bulang tyanang-i
come,   they went off both in search of him (and)   soon   found   track

tyarmbap bulak.   Gapin bulang   geu tyahal   bundinung   Weenbulain-yo.
of uncle (Duan). They tracked (him) to the place   where he had been bitten by Weenbulain.

Muityen bulang   huang bundinung   Weenbulain-yo, ba   ngepen bulang.   Nugung-a wauttin bulanguh
They found (him) dead bitten by   Weenbulain, and   buried (him).   Of course they went after

Weenbulain-ya,   gapin bulang   tyuiwrang gà.   Weenbulain-ya   buletyuk   mang gep.
Weenbulain,   tracking (him)   all the way.   Weenbulain (had)   two   daughters.

Nyain bulang		*tyanardi*	*wanyap*	*warhinnual*	*ngalluganukyanbal*	*nyum*
Saw they (the Brambambulls saw)		many	fires	he had made	on his way	till (they)
walluban bulang ginga ngàinung.	*Nyum*		*giyaren bulang nyan-o*		*wang-ngal gurmingn.*	
drew near where he lived.	Then (they had)		a council		how they might kill (him).	
Bràmbuk	*ngananep*	*yàrim*	*warn willang gal*		*ngüroben*	*Weenbulain-yo.*
Brambambull	the younger	went (to the)	windward		(to be) smelled	by Weenbulain.
Weenbulain-yo nyum	*ngüroben*	*bä*	*birnin lärnung*	*uk*	*tyumbin*	*leanyuk gurung-i.*
Weenbulain	then	smelled him and	came out of his	cave	showing (his)	teeth big.
Ngarambenya baingo	*nganayin*	*nguityapdakitch*	*ngarambenyi*	*Weenbulain*	*derta*	
The elder Brambambull	who was near him	to hit	old	Weenbulain	on his	
birnin	*nyain*	*drangat bulak leya*	*tyainyo*	*nuangàwuk*	*buletchi.*	*Malluk barta*
coming out	saw	the fresh teeth	belonging to	his daughters	two.	After a while
gurungnk leya tyumbulan nyertwunin		*birnin.*	*Nga rambenya*		*baingo nyum dakin*	
the big teeth themselves presently		came out.	The elder Brambambull		then hit	
men	*bropuk*	*ba leanyuk, ba*	*gutuk*	*bùrpin woiup*	*burnin bulang, ba*	
him	on the head	and teeth, and	the younger Brambambull	ran to help	to kill him, and	
yurp burninbulang	*Weenbulain,*	*ba*	*buityel wurninbulang bropuk*	*ba*	*darpin bulang.*	
thus they killed	Weenbulain,	and	knocked to pieces his head	and	burnt him.	

NOTE.—The Rev. Mr. Hartmann says in a letter to me, in reference to this story, that, according to information given by the blacks, it is known all over the country. It is only part of a long story. The two Brambambulls were rather remarkable men. The blacks' further account of them may be briefly stated thus :—The Brambambulls were invulnerable, and the elder could make himself invisible whenever he pleased. The last thing known about the elder is that he went away in a whirlwind. The younger Brambambull is said to have vanished too for a while, but to have made his appearance again in another part of the country. He was followed and found by his mother. It is said that he died from the effects of a snake-bite; that he was buried; and that he became alive again. After that he could not be found any more. The portion of the story that is sent, Mr. Hartmann says, is written in the way a black would tell it—of course considerably abridged.

NAMES OF NATIVE ANIMALS.

Kangaroos—
    fawn male - - - *Borra.*
    „ female - - - *Gooan.*
    grey male - - - *Goore.*
    „ female - - - *Meringur.*
    brown male - - - *Meendyun.*
    „ female - - *Mitch.*
Wallabies—
    large grey, two black *Kumma.*
      stripes on back
    brown - - - - *Gooyee.*
    small - - - - *Batyùk.*
    brown and grey - - *Tyallagar.*
    „ „ „ *Dya.*
    „ „ „ *Wakwee.*

Wombat - - - *Mùtye.*
Opossums—
    white-tailed - - - *Wille.*
    black-tailed - - - *Banya.*
Bandicoots—
    striped brown and white *Watyùn.*
    „ black and white *Mangen.*
    „ brown - - *Ba.*
Native cats—
    brown, with white spots *Berih.*
    black, „ „ *Beridyàl.*
Dingo, or wild dog - - *Wilkùr.*
Porcupine - - - - *Yùlowil.*
Mouse - - - - *Dgityigarap.*
Water-rat - - - - *Brepbir.*

LANGUAGE.

Reptiles, &c.

Lizards—
- large - - - - Gen.
- „ - - - - Yūrkurn.
- smaller - - - - Dūrndal.
- smallest - - - - Māni wūtchūp.

Iguana - - - - Dyoyū.
- „ with white tip of tail Watya.

Snakes—
- diamond - - - Dyallan.
- black - - - - Gūrnwil.
- death-adder - - - Lirk.
- grey snake - - - Mort mūt mrr.

Scorpion - - - - Bereguil.
Centipede - - - - Dyenga warak.
Frog - - - - Den.
Toad - - - - Dook.
Tarantula - - - - Wirnbolen.
Dragon fly - - - Gindenden.
Blue fly - - - - Būp bityik.
House fly - - - - Bityik.
Flat black beetle - - Boinka.
Grasshopper - - - Ngar-ngar.
Cricket - - - - Didibūroin.

Birds.

Emu - - - - Gūwir.
Black swan - - - Gūnowar.
Crane - - - - Goligūr.
Pelican - - - - Batyangal.
Native companion - Kūtyūn.
Wild turkey - - - Ngarūw.
„ goose - - - Ngarowar.

Mallee-hen - - - Lōwan.
Ducks—
- mountain - - - Bityangūn.
- black - - - - Ngare.
- teal - - - - Wipi.
- musk - - - - Tyūdwil.
- wood - - - - Walrang.

Eaglehawk - - - Wrepil.
Laughing jackass - Goorūnyūng.

Cockatoos—
- black, with red under wing Girin.
- „ „ yellow „ Gūrwel.
- white, with yellow top-knot Ginap.
- white, with red top-knot Kellelek.
- „ with no top-knot, but red under wing Catyagur.

Common green parrot - Tyetyūrt.
Crow - - - - Wār.
Magpie - - - - Gūrūk.
Water-hen - - - Carori.
Australian redbreast - Tyaligūritgūritch.
Blue mountain parrot - Calingat.
Swallow - - - - Gurawitchwitch.
Cuckoo - - - - Gūrimūl.
Curlew - - - - Will.

Fishes.

Cray-fish - - - Wūlūnak.
Black-fish - - - Wirrap.
Silver-fish - - - Dūrpkut.
Mussel - - - - Betyin.

SPECIMENS OF THE LANGUAGE SPOKEN BY THE ABORIGINAL TRIBES OF LAKE HINDMARSH.

(By the Rev. F. W. Spieseke.)

Nouns—Concise Vocabulary.

Mahm - - - father.
Bahp - - - mother.
Woawa - - - eldest brother.
Kut - - - youngest brother.
Tyat - - - eldest sister.
Kottuwan - - - youngest sister.
Kap-kap-tyirr - - family.
Wat-yip - - - male child.
Mang-yip - - - female child.
Ngan-nit - - - husband.
Mat-yum - - - wife.
Bo-pup - - - male infant.
Bo-pup-gurk - - female infant.
Nan-nan-gurk - - young woman.
Kol-kon - - - young man.
Jung-kum - - - virgin.

Ko-kurn - - - grandfather.
Mihm - - - grandmother (mother's mother).
Kok-wan - - - grandmother (father's mother).
Wut-yo - - - man; lirok.
Bang - - - body.
Wut-yo-pah lirok - men and women.
Burp - - - head.
Wirmbull - - - ear.
Mir - - - eye.
Kahr - - - nose.
Tyarp - - - mouth.
Li-a - - - tooth.
Burp-po-rung - - shoulder.
Tat-yack - - - arm.

Man-ya - - -	hand.	
Tyang - - -	chest.	
K'ra - - - -	leg.	
Kin-na - - -	foot.	
Bap man-yo - -	thumb.	
Yul-lup yul-lup man-ya	finger.	
Bap kin-nā - - -	big toe.	
Wat-yip wat-yip kin-nā	toe.	
Kol-kon - - -	soul.	
Bohk - - - -	spirit.	
Ngau-we - - -	sun.	
Turt - - - -	star.	
Dan-bill - - -	cloud.	
Mun-der - - -	thunder.	
Wil-lin-buck - -	lightning.	
Mit-yack - - -	rain.	
Nyak - - - -	hail.	
Nyun - - - -	storm, hurricane.	
Wil-la - - -	wind, breeze.	
Wui-yung wui-yung-ka -	whirlwind.	
Kulk - - - -	tree.	
Woar-tuck - -	branch.	
Kir-ra - - -	leaf.	
Bo-wat - - -	grass.	
Bi-al - - - -	gum-tree.	
Mah-rong - - -	pine-tree.	
Pullut - - - -	box-tree.	
Büp - - - -	white-gum.	
Wit-yin-will - -	bird.	
Kau-wirr - - -	emu.	
Ngar-re - - -	duck (black).	
Kurn-will - - -	snake.	
Lar - - - -	house.	
Kur-räck - - -	sand.	
Tyar - - - -	soil.	
Big - - - -	clay.	
Mir - - - -	hole in the ground.	
Ban - - - -	hole in a tree.	
Kut-yep - - -	stone.	
Wur-ror-lar - -	door.	
Kat-yin - - -	water.	
Kal-lei-yer-rau-will	conversation.	
Tyal-le-yer-rang -	quarrel.	
Yah-lei-e - - -	peace.	
Tat-yer-rap - -	fight.	
Tyal-le - - -	language.	
Kat-ye - - -	summer.	
Wiht - - - -	autumn.	
Mei-a - - - -	winter.	
Ngal-lo - - -	spring.	
Lei-muck - - -	inheritance, succession.	
Dat-nal-lo-kuck -	the centre.	
Ba-ruck - - -	the middle.	
Yahrm-bei-e - -	relief.	
Wuig-wa - - -	exchange.	
Meät-meät - - -	foreigner, stranger.	
Keh-le-de - - -	brightness.	
Bar-ring - - -	road, way.	
La-bul-la - - -	friend.	
Kul-lin-ye-calk -	enemy.	
Tut-ye - - -	rest.	
Worp-woa - - -	sorrow.	
Gulli - - - -	anger.	
Mo-kin-ye - - -	beginning.	
Tyir-tuck - - -	end.	
Yüp - - - -	the light.	
Bu-roing - - -	darkness.	
Bä-nau-we-rang -	obstruction, standing in the way.	
Bän-nau-wo-reang -	obstruction, lying in the way.	

There is no plural number; they express it thus only:—*Ke-yap kalk*, "one tree;" *Pul-let kalk*, "two trees;" *Pul-let ke-yap kalk*, "three trees;" *Pul-let pul-let kalk*, "four (2 times 2) trees;" *Pul-let pul-let ke-yap kalk*, "five (2 times 2 and 1) trees;" *Ke-yap ke-yap*, "some trees" (seldom used, however); *Kit-tyau-will kalk*, "many trees" (they usually make use of).

Could never detect an article as yet, neither definite nor indefinite.

Pronouns (Personal).

Singular.

Ngan - - I.	*Ngar* - - you, thou.	*Ngait* - - he, she, it.
Ngeck - - mine, my.	*Ngin* - - yours, thine.	*Nguck* - - his, hers, its.
Ngär-rin - me.	*Ngan-nung* - you, thee.	*Ngün* - - him, her, it.

Plural.

Ngo - - we.	*Ngat* - - you.	*Ngatts* - - they.
Ngän-dack - ours.	*Ngo-dack* - yours.	*Ngeän-nach* theirs.
Ngan-dank - us.	*Din* - - you.	*Ngin* - - them.

Some Relative Pronouns.

Win-yar	- - -	who.
Win-ya-rait	- - -	whose.
Win-yer	- - -	whom.
Win-ya-tuck	- - -	which.
Ngan	- - -	what.

Some Adjective Pronouns.

Yar-wo-kat	- -	each, every.
Ke-yap wullack	- -	either, one of two.
Kihng-ma	- -	this, these.
Man-yo	- -	that, those.
Yo-an-yo-dack	- -	any.
Mo-wil	- -	all.
Ying-yur-ne	- -	such.
Yo-wa	- -	other, another.
Wull	- -	both.
Ke-yap	- -	one.

Showing the Position of the Possessive Pronouns.

Mahm	- - -	father.
Mahm-eck	- -	father mine, my father.
Mahm-in	- -	your father.
Mahm-uch	- -	his, her father.
Bahp	- - -	mother.
Bahp-eck	- -	mother mine, my mother.
Bahp-in	- -	your mother.
Bahp-uck	- -	his, her mother.
Mahm-en-dack	-	our father.
Mahm-ang-ngo-dach		your father.
Mahm-en-nack	-	their father.
Bahp-en-dack	-	our mother.
Bahp-ngo-dack		your mother.
Bahp-en-nuck	-	their mother.

It will be observed that, either for convenience, or euphony's sake, the pronouns are generally slightly altered.

On the Inflection of the Verbs.

Woh-räg—To Speak.

Singular.

Woh-räg-ngan	-	I speak.
Woh-räy-ngar	-	you speak.
Woh-räg-e hinya	-	speaks that one, he speaks.

Plural.

Wo-räg-ango	-	we speak.
Wo-räy-o-ngat	-	you speak.
Wo-räy-ngatts	-	they speak.

Woh-räg-in-ngan	-	I spoke.
Woh-räy-in-ngar	-	you spoke.
Woh-räg-in kinya	-	he, she spoke.
Woh-räg-in-nang-o	-	we spoke.
Woh-räg-in-ngat	-	you spoke.
Woh-räg-in-ngatts	-	they spoke.

Mal-lan woh-räg-in	-	I have spoken.
Mal-lar woh-räg-in	-	you have spoken.
Mal-la kinya wo-räg-in		he, she has spoken.
Mal-lung-o woh-räg-in		we have spoken.
Mal-lat woh-räg-in	-	you have spoken.
Mal-latts woh-räg-in	-	they have spoken.

Singular.

Woh-räg-in-ngan mah-luck	- - - -	I shall or will speak.
Woh-räg-in-ngar mah-luck	- - - -	you shall or will speak.
Woh-räg-in kinya mah-luck	- - - -	he, she shall or will speak.

Plural.

Woh-räg-in-ngang-o mah-luck	- - - -	we shall speak.
Woh-räg-in-ngat mah-luck	- - - -	you shall speak.
Woh-räg-in-ngatts mah-luck	- - - -	they shall speak.

In the above, too, the pronouns are here and there somewhat changed.

Showing the Position of Adjectives.

Yat-yen-ke lar	-	a bad house.
Yat-yen-ke kall	-	a bad dog.
Deäl-ke lar	-	a good house.
Deäl-ke kall	-	a good dog.
Yat-yen-ke wut-yo	-	a bad man.
Deäl-ke wut-yo	-	a good man.

Kat-ye-lang-man-ya	-	a sick hand.
Kat-ye-langan	-	sick am I, I am sick.
Kat-ye-langar	-	you are sick.
Kat-ye-langait	-	he, she is sick. (See personal pronouns.)
Kat-ye-lungango	-	we are sick.

A Few Adverbs.

Ying-a	-	so.
Wur-rag	-	no.
Nyei	-	yes.
Tyurme	-	very.
Ngang-o	-	how.

Ngak	-	why.
Ngung-ya-gung	-	again.
Kit-yau-wil-lä	-	often.
Ngat-yap-gung	-	almost.

In the above, sound
- *a* as 'a' in father.
- *e* as 'a' in rake, sake.
- *i* as 'i' in sin, ship.
- *o* like 'o' no, so.
- *u* like 'uh' or 'oo' in pool.
- *ä* like 'e' in clerk.
- *ei* like the English 'ie' in die.
- *au* like the English 'ou' in thou.
- *ng* is produced by the nape bone or upper part of the mouth.

WORDS IN THE DIALECT OF THE TRIBES NEAR WICKLIFFE.

The following words and sentences in the native language are contributed by Charles Gray, Esq., of Nareeb Nareeb, near Wickliffe, in the Western district of Victoria.

Mr. Gray informs me that the names of the tribes of whose language he has given specimens are *Bak-on-date* and *Bank-neit*.

That spoken by "Sambo" and others is the *Bank-neit*.

Yanginyan tuckinyan.
I am going to strike.

Yanginyan tambullan larnook.
I am going to find a nest.

Yanginyan quombeyan.
I am going to lie down.

Yanginyan wartupin yowierie.
I am going to chew the meat.

Yanginyan pawinyan.
I am going to scold her.

Yanginyan bacottuinyan toolin coochil.
I am going to fish with a line.

Yanginyan touwenan tatarmu.
I am going to chop with my axe.

Yanginyan weerkinyan we.
I am going to burn the wood.

Yanginyan carnyunang catyin.
I am going to pour out the water.

Yanginyan moochchallan.
I am going to take it.

Mallach combœip.
I intend to keep it.

Yanginyan paitnainyan tuurach.
I am going to sharpen my spear.

Tackinang poorpanack.
He hit me on the head.

Youie chackelong.
The bird eats.

Ka-ka wattii parne.
Come to the creek.

Macongoo wearyea wee.
Let us make a fire.

LANGUAGE.

Wearie minæ cal.
  Beat that dog.

Delhi poo-poo!
  What a pretty baby!

Martok walla.
  It is raining hard.

Winnyera lar-nook?
  Whose mia-mia is that?

Nangwar kelang?
  What are you saying?

Coonara naram-naram?
  Are you a king?

Yonggalla bamba bryell coolpoosnella?
  Will you come to bark that gum-tree?

Mutchumaraten cutchukaru.
  Bring me a white parrot.

Wa wa wat peeal.
  Climb that tree.

Oka pappen.
  Give me a waddy.

Caraburanga paramæl.
  Let us hunt the emu.

Partum mechum meyattang wellango.
  I will get some opossum skins.

Mung larnoke paramæl.
  Here is an emu's nest.

Charem taratto.
  Throw the boomerang.

Bung-bung gilang.
  You are very stupid.

Tinggard newnewa wellicorn?
  Will you sew that rug?

Mung larnoke.
  Here is a nest.

Pawayat mang yowierie.
  You roast that meat.

Wireat wee.
  Make the fire.

Tawagat wee.
  Chop firewood.

Oka copongnio cutyen.
  Give me a drink of water.

Ka-ka. Yingellieyanga.
  Come on. Let us sing.

Yangewat.
  Go away.

Yanginyan nutin lannanuke nyacootinyan keetnu.
  I am going to watch him.

Ka ka wattie yat kingga cunyake Nareeb Nareeb.
  Come with me to Nareeb Nareeb.

Yangoor ootang coonmeel poondean titcooyin coolie? Mal leangerook.
  How does the snake bite to kill man? With his teeth.

NATIVE WORDS GIVEN—

	By "Willis," "Timor," "Bobby," "Jack," "Annie," and others.	By "Joe."	By "Sambo," "Caubra," and others.
The nose	Ca	Cayangerack	Caboong.
The eyes	Meyr	Meyangerack	Minantyen.
The hair	Nurrah	Nurreangerack	Nurrat.
The cheek	Moorrack	Murackyangerack	Wang.
The mouth	Woorock	Wooruyangerack	Woorocknong.
The whiskers	Nunnie	Nunnuyangerack	Merrang.
The ears	Wimbool	Wemboolyangerack	Weenyang.
The forehead	Kunnu		Middin.
The throat	Coon		Cutnong.
The chest	Chang		Murtoon.
The arms	Tatyack		Woork (arm).
The legs	Kur		Binnong (leg).
The hands	Munya		Murrang (hand).
The feet	Chinna		Tinnang (foot).

It will be observed that the words obtained by Mr. Gray from "Joe" are the same as those given by "Willis," "Timor," "Bobby," and "Annie;" but "Joe" uses the pronoun.

In speaking of the "arms," "legs," &c., "Joe," when meaning "both arms," "both legs," &c., would use the word *Boolite*.—(*See Boolicht*, "two," *post.*)

"WILLIS," "TIMOR," "BOBBY," "ANNIE," AND OTHERS.

One	Kiab.
Two	Boolicht.
Three	Cartore.
Four	Boolite be boolite.
Five	Kiamonya.
Six	Barook.
Seven	(No word.)
Eight	Boolite be boolite be boolite be boolite.
Nine	(No word.)
Ten	Boolite kiamonya.
Evil spirit	Moorope.
Good	Delcohe.
Aboriginal woman	Bang-banggo.
Aboriginal man	Coolech.
Head	{ Porpe. Porpeyangerach. Pinnoe.
Skull	{ Kalk. Barrang.
A shield	Mulca.

SOME WORDS OF THE LANGUAGE OF THE WESTERN TRIBES OF VICTORIA.
(COLLECTED BY N. THORNLY, ESQ.)

The following native words, with the meanings in English, are from the tribes of the Western district. I am indebted to N. Thornly, Esq., Land Surveyor, for this compilation. He has been so thoughtful as to place on record the native names of many localities.

Native Names.	Meaning in English.	Native Names.	Meaning in English.
Annya	beard.	Bapora	Mostyn township, old crossing place.
Ar-va-wan	black and white geese.		
Brimboal	the ear.	Braite	hail.
Booite	grass, herbs.	Bow	name of swamp, Mount Talbot station.
Beeal	gum-tree		
Bruk-bruk	the oak-tree, swamp oak.	Belar	red-ochre, paint.
Baaker	Glenelg River.	Bulart	grey hair, old.
Byambynee	woman.	Brit-brit	plover.
Baaring	road, or path.	Byjuke	kangaroo-rat.
Bramburra	name of late chief.	Bahrook	heath.
Byaduk	stone tomahawk.	Bubrooten	scrub.
Brepa	waddy.	Burumbuart	junction of the Salt Creek with Glenelg, Harrow.
Brin-brim	spring of water.		
Bunn	bank, ridge, hillock.	Byerr	meeting, hunt, Parliament.
Bacci	soft, boggy.	Booring	smoke.
Bowan	roast, to cook.	Caitian	water.
Boolite	two.	Caroopook	hill.
Boolite pre boolite	four.	Carong carack	mountains.
Beeor	sweet, honey.	Cowan or cowah	native name for Mount Arapiles.
Beerik	native cat.		
Boreang	the Victoria Range.	Corra	kangaroo.
Beeaar	stream, running water.	Cowen	emu.

LANGUAGE.

Native Names.	Meaning in English.
Cobe vidion	native turkey (bustard).
Crew	native water-hen (bald coot).
Curran geerip	adult.
Coopan	to drink.
Callcoop	bones.
Corre	mouth.
Calite	light.
Carran mell	snake.
Caite	one.
Cuite pu boolite	three.
Cooack	sand.
Coolanchurrep	anger.
Caa	the nose.
Connadoyen	Lake Wallace.
Coite urn	native companion.
Caeep	one tree.
Conawarr	swan.
Coryea	paddy melon, small kangaroo.
Conneewirrecow	head of the Tea-tree Creek, Longlands.
Connee, forehead ; wirrecow, tea-tree.	
Caper kelly	name of large salt lake.
Coleepoo	name of a lagoon, Pine hills.
Carrak	the magpie.
Corrondeeble	part of Salt Creek, near Harrow.
Culla-culla	name of lagoon, Mullagh station.
Connepra	name of lagoon, Pine hills.
Colingcclup	name of lagoon, Pine hills.
Cherrieweerup or cherrywceerup	native name of Clunie station.
Carn carmul	native name of lagoon, Pine hills.
Delk	good water.
Drajurk	reeds, bulrushes, flags.
Dank teeranite	fight, battle.
Dy jark	the arm.
Docker	bark of trees.
Dakingle	to kill.
Dewrang	high, lofty.
Drik-drik	limestone, lime.
Dyea	earth, soil.
Geayoul	forest, plenty, many.
Gurra	red.
Gurracoop	blood.
Gorra	a chief or king.
Gorran Doranan	the present chief of the tribe.
Gatum-gatum	the boomerang.
Gritjurk	mosquito.
Gatall	Maryvale old home-station lake.

Native Names.	Meaning in English.
Ill-i-ra	native hut, my-mya.
Ingturrapamba	fear, frightened.
Jerrywarrook	the White Lake of Major Mitchell.
Jell-jell	name of a lagoon, Pine hills.
Jerrigwarra	swamp near the Mallee scrub.
Kadnook	flat ; name of S. G. Henty's station near Harrow.
Kombaiy	lying down, rest.
Kiata	summer, heat
Keepa	salt.
Leanguel	a native weapon.
Lalanguite	name of a lagoon, Pine hills.
Lak	a stone, rock.
Leea	teeth.
Loomalangan	to cry, to weep.
Maen	a kind of tea-tree.
Moorang	clouds.
Murrandana	thunder ; name of one of Armitage's stations, S. Adelaide road.
Mutak	the skin.
Manya	the hands.
Merr	the eye.
Maarmun	to hear.
Mallee	thicket.
Mood	winter, cold in the abstract.
Monnott	to feel cold.
Moray	the root of a tree.
Mallee parbool	name of a tea-tree lake, Mullagh.
Mallanganee	another, Pine hills.
Mallanbool	a reedy swamp, Pine hills.
Mortart	Pleasant Banks, Affleck's station.
Manyonda	swamp on Lake Wallace station.
Moonjam	a dry lake on Mullagh station.
Merrymeric	old sheepwash on Salt Creek, seven miles from Harrow.
Morrpaga	the face or countenance.
Moonya	a house.
Marroo	pine-tree.
Moodya	St. Mary's Lake, Mount Arapiles.
Munda	Townscud's old station, Tea-tree Creek, Longlands.
Merrick	an egg.
Na a prup	hair.
Na yan can	to see, look.
Palpara	a lake on Mullagh station, twelve miles from Harrow.

Native Names.	Meaning in English.	Native Names.	Meaning in English.
Pobrick	a lake on Pine hills.	Worroh	black color.
Prop	the head.	Willa	opossum.
Pallite	cherry-tree.	Wirreccoo	a kind of tea-tree.
Pa-pidjeck	a fly.	Wanwin	black water-holes, twelve miles from Harrow, Adelaide road.
Popope	a child, infant.		
Punandeegin	salt or brackish water.		
Pirrepango	run, flight.	Wateegat	come, come here.
Rapel	eaglehawk.	Wydung	bandicoot.
Tchakel	lake.	Weetya	the blackwood-tree.
Tchakel-tchakel	lakes.	Wale	the curlew (little bustard).
Tort	stars.	Wombalano	love, pretty, lovely, beautiful.
Tord wirrup	hawk.		
Tchina	foot, footmark.	Uleart	the old Grange home-station in 1840.
Ticoyan	to eat.		
Toolang	stringybark forest.	Mulleraterong	the site of Hamilton township.
Tare	spear.		
Tooloy	wattle-tree gum.	Ulebowening	Wannon, at junction of Grange Burn.
Tar ar nite	white color.		
Toolka	the Cape Barren geese.	Tapook	Mount Napier.
Toolondo	swamp at Chas. Officer's home-station.	Bucaan	Grange Burn (running stream).
Tchila	the tongue.	Woorack	plains.
Tit-tit	strong, or strong man.	Warachoorack	honeysuckle plains.
Urangara	the sun.	Bruck-bruck-	she-oak tree.
Urancooya	snow.	Toolang	stringybark.
Wee	fire.	Murroo	pine-trees.
Wallie	rain.	Coaakwoorack	sandy plains.
Woorak or Woorack	a plain, level country.	Warwanbool	gum-trees.
Warock	honeysuckle-tree.	Wooklpooa	Glenisla swamp, near Carter's home-station.
Willkin	native dog.		
Wayang	hurricane, high wind.	Bepcha	Solitary hill, situated about four miles north-west of Carter's homestead.
Win-win tie	a boy eight or ten years old.		
Willintick	lightning.		
Walling	burnt black log.	Lootchook	swamp, east of the Glenisla home-station three miles.
Wallpar	dead tree.		
War wan bool	green color, growing tree.	Bellemenah	point of the Victoria immediately eastward of Glenisla station.
Weekeer	dead body.		
Waa	the crow.		
Winani	a hollow tree.	Lambruk	Carter's home-station.

NATIVE TERMS USED BY THE UPPER GLENELG TRIBE.

Wur het e gera	clear lake.	Car che cur	white.
Chae chagel	name of district.	Beap-beap	wood duck.
Nur coung	birds, native companion.	Choluel	musk duck.
Wooreep	grey parrot.	Jilpanger	skylark.
Moo ro curt	green leek.	Dope worra	lizards, common kind.
Raling ur	blue mountain.	Chooyoo	large tree.

NAMES OF SOME SWAMPS WITHIN THREE MILES OF CLEAR LAKE.

Jallur.
Bow (pronounced "bough").
Lurmut.
Carchap.
Weobea.
Poorpigoproe.

LANGUAGE.

Native Names obtained from Aborigines at Glenisla, with Translation, Locality, etc.

Native Names.	Pronounced.	Meaning in English.
Mekonongweerap	Mee-konong-wee-rap	The black-fish cannot get any higher up (Rosebrook).
Weerap	—	Black-fish.
Konong	—	A hill or any impediment of any kind. This is a small fall in the creek at Rosebrook.
Bujam-bujam	Boojam-boojam	A water-hole at Rosebrook home-station.
Burrai gurrai	Burr-ay gurray	A kangaroo camp. Any kangaroo camp.
Krambruk	As spelt	A sandy place.
Jahrapoohl	Ja-rap-oohl	A water-hole in the Glenelg, at the crossing of the Horsham road, by Cavendish.
Ganangenyaivie	Ja-nang-en-yaw-wee	The entrance north end of the Victoria Range.
Konangiedwara	Ko-nang-e-dura	A small creek from the mountains east of Glenisla.
Kartukil	Car-tuccle	A large swamp lying at the base of the hills east of Lambruck.
Larngebunyah	Larnge-e-bunyah	The high mountains immediately north of the Chimney-pot Gap, Victoria Range.
Ming-ming	As spelt	A large swamp in Woohlpooer, near the east boundary.
Chukilcallipurt	Chuck-il-calli-purt	A swamp at Brin Springs homestead.
Wonwondah witchoop	Won-won-dah wit-choop	Another swamp adjoining the last.
Yarragallum	Yarragallum	A swamp at Rosebrook sheepwash.
Mucatcatchin	Mu-cat-cat-chin	A spring at the base of the Black Range, east side.

Native Names.	Meaning in English.	Native Names.	Meaning in English.
Catchin	Water.	Woorak	Honeysuckle-tree.
Wallah	Rain.	Beereek	A native cat.
Wurtipook wallah	A little rain (i.e., a shower).	Rappell	Eaglehawk.
		Buor	Honeysuckle scrub.
Wallay	An opossum.	Norkwook	A native companion.
Chokivil	The musk duck.	Goroke	Magpie.
Goburt	A she-oak tree.	Boboh	Young wattle-tree.
Koray	A kangaroo.	Kolabutyin	A wild turkey.
Mooree	The black duck.	Jallakin	Kangaroo-rat.
Peeall	Gum.	Don-gan-gee	Wattle gum.
Johie	An emu.	Dakakamudah	A large crane.
Billewirrup	Rock wallaby.	Bo or Bohe	A bandicoot.

LANGUAGE.—LAKE CONDAH.

The following sentences in the native language were written down at my request, in 1870, by Mr. Joseph Shaw, of the Lake Condah Aboriginal Station:—

Purtoko	purpoyah	thinbetch	ko.		Matthala	patpattha	purpoyah	thinbetch	ko.
Strike	going	am I	to.		Meat	chew	going	am I	to.
Manoko	wortno	purpoyah	thinbetch	ko.	Keyako	thanambur	purpoyah	thinbetch	ko.
Find	nest	going	am I	to.	Scold	her	going	am I	to.
Yow	wakko	purpoyah	thinbetch	ko.	Nawhanna	pettoko	ko	purpoyah	thinbetch.
Lie	down	going	am I	to.	Watch	him	to	going	am I.

Piepie	cheka	purpoyah	thinbetch	ko.	Thokkin		purpurtin.	
Burn	wood	going	am I	to.	Eats		bird.	
Kang	oko	porich	purpoyah	thinbetch	ko.	Winthey o-o-than pundan marr kooranga purtin?
Pour	out	water	going	am I	to.	How does bite mau snake kill?
Man	eyah	purpoyah	thinbetch	ko.	Noatpey	thangan	dekoa.
Take	it	about	am I	to.	His	teeth	with.
Man	eyah	natthoat	pa	ko.	Whattka	lingan	thunkil	natthoat.
Intend	it	I	keep	to.	Angry	very	was	I.

		Purtaninna	pim	hungan	theelung.
		Hit	head	me	he.
		("on the" left out.)

| | Yeornyearn | dekoa | kutchil-kutchil | purpoyah | thinbetch | ko. |
| | Fish | with | line | going | am I | to. |

| | Natthoat | purpurkorto | dekoa | minurko | ko | purpoyah | thinbetch. |
| | My | axe | with | chop | to | going | am I. |

| | Purnukkoyah | tharana | natthoat | purpoyah | thinbetch | ko. |
| | Sharpen | spear | my | going | am I | to. |

NOTE.—Mr. Shaw, in a letter to me, states that the definite and indefinite articles are left out, as he cannot gather any letter or word corresponding to them.

VOCABULARY OF THE LANGUAGE SPOKEN BY THE TRIBES INHABITING THE COUNTRY ABOUT THE RIVERS CRAWFORD, STOKES, AND LOWER PARTS OF THE WANNON AND GLENELG.

(COMPILED BY C. J. TYERS, ESQ., IN 1842.)

English.	Aboriginal.	English.	Aboriginal.
Hair	- Nerlàng.	Stars	- Kà-kà-tìrring.
Forehead	- Kerning.	Rain	- Karpine.
Mouth	- Wullòng.	Thunder	- Mundòl.
Head	- Kolàn.	Fire	- Wenie or ween.
Eyes	- Mring.	Water	- Pàrreeh.
Nose	- Karpòng.	Moon	- Bumboòke or parrembakke.
Teeth	- Tùng-ung.	Wind	- Nùrrajùg.
Stomach	- Bollàwing or werràng.	Sky	- Mòn-bòng.
Back	- Torrùide or werrìp.	Rainbow	- Ta-ràn.
Thigh	- Karrìp.	Smoke	- Too-oùng or poyn-burtòng.
Foot	- Denòng or tenòng.	Heat or hot	- Kà-loin.
Calf of leg	- Nurròke.	Very cold	- Mote-mote.
Hand	- Murrung or murrùng.	White man	- Ammatie or kummae-mèrring.
Chin	- Nurràng.	White woman	- Narran-goòroc.
Tongue	- Terlingae.	Black man	- Kooloying.
Lips	- Werròng.	Black woman	- Port-port-nurròng.
Ears	- Werring.	Male child	- Pòpòpe.
Neck	- Norlaìm.	Female child	- Nùrrun-gooroc.
Shoulder	- Neèt.	Young man	- Kol-kòn.
Elbow	- Terling.	Young woman	- Par-roit.
Arm	- Worròc.	Old black man	- Purt-peep-port-peep.
Breast	- Naupùng.	Childbirth	- Po-ling-pà-tà.
Knee	- Perrong.	Mother	- Nerpùng.
Sun	- Tìrring.	Father	- Bebi.
Sunrise	- Wun-u-wa-tìrring.	Kangaroo	- Goràng.
Sunset	- U-wa-tirring.	Emu	- Korpring.

LANGUAGE.

English	Aboriginal
Dog	Karl.
Black-fish	Cockmun.
Bream	Kolul.
Eagle (kills opossums, kangaroos, bandicoots, &c.)	E-ung gàrra.
White cockatoo	Mruck or karrakeèt.
Black cockatoo	Wee-làng.
Bullock	Murrùndie-weèring, nurrundie-guèring.
Horse	Nharr.
Mosquito	Murro càrra.
Fly	Mannàg or monnùc.
Wild duck	Wùrren-èet.
Large wild duck	Kùrra-wàrren.
Mussel	Torlope.
Blue parrot	Turrùot.
Snake	Koorùng.
Native cat	Tùt-tàt-karreep.
Bandicoot	Currùoi.
Kangaroo-rat	Perrùok.
Lizard	Erùok.
Opossum	Karra-mùok.
Grass	Noo-tùng.
Tree	Lang.
Blackwood	Moo-tâng.
Leptospermum	Boonoùng.
Gum-tree	Tuàrt.
Banksia	Werìte.
Reedy-grass	Turràc.
Stones	Murrai.
Bone	Nerkìne.
Marrow	Tring.
Hut or tent	Bungàirie.
House	Woorn.
Large house	Màtee-worrn.
Spear	Tàiril-kripeer and yarra-yarra.
Waddy	Kunnòc.
Waddy	Màttròng [shape of leon-ile].
Boomerang	Gattom-gattom.
Basket carried on the back of women containing wood	Koo-win.
Shield	Mulcârie.
Band worn round forehead	Kinning.
Sack or bag	Koròne.
Blanket or bed	Yung.
No (negative)	Yù-a-pùh.
Little or small	Wot-a-weèt.
Large	Mà-trong.
Good	Nue-tchong.
Bring fire	Ma-na-weein.
Bring water	Ma-na-parreèt.
You walk or go	Yun-a-kùh.
You sleep	Yew-a-hà.
Go to sleep	Yew-uttiah.
I walk	Yun-nuttiah.
Talk to me	Proë-wun-nàl.
I say	La-cannùo.
I talk to you	Prayer-un-ung.
I can see	Nà-còo.
I can see a horse	Nà-còo-nharrh.
You threw	Yun-da-nin.
You threw a spear	Yun-da-nin-kripèer.
I threw	Yon-dròo.
You jumped	Pàp-coo-pà-nin.
I jump	Pàp-coo-pà.
I drink	Pà-tù.
You drink	Tà-toò.
Come here	Wat-tùi.
Dead	Gulpin or gulpin-na.
Act of pulling the hair from the chin	Kree-pin-narràng.
Child on woman's back	Wen-a-pà.

Mr. Tyers added the following, namely :—

English	Aboriginal
Watch or clock	Ka-ka-tirring.
Good sheep (mutton ?)	Noëtchong mattal.
Beef	Tarrap nooing.
Sheep	Leep.
Sheepskin	Meetong-leep-not.
Road, or dray track	Wurrowing.
Gun	Pungùite.
Boots	Wan-denòng.
Bottle	Pee-yal.*
Trousers	Kanat-kaneep.
Hat	Mopèl-kolan.

* This name probably indicated not the vessel but the contents. Beal is the name, in the Western district, of an exhilarating liquor prepared from the flowers of the Banksia.—See page 210, vol. 1.

VOL. II.　　　　I

The natives pointed out to Mr. Tyers what they said was a large hill in the sky. They indicated the place as being towards the south-west, and they informed him that it was the residence of *Ween-min-not Karing*, the Supreme Being, who, they supposed, caused rain, thunder, lightning, wind, &c. They affirmed that they did not believe in a future state, nor that this great blackfellow was the author of their existence; but they attributed to his agency all deaths from lightning.

Names of Localities.

Source of the Wando	*Pat-la-panroo*.
River Crawford, near the road	*Mirrà-noòn*.
Water-hole, four miles above the road	*Mirreep*.
Brian's Creek	*Koròite*.
John Henty's Creek	*Too-wàron*.
Frank Henty's Creek	*Woc-woc-coorn*.
Stokes'	*Boòn-a-rong*.
Winter's Creek	*Wa-coom*.
River Glenelg	*Bo-càr*.
Fitzroy	*Wungot-pàloon*.
Grampians	*Murrai-bug-gum*.
Wannon of Sir Thomas Mitchell	*Karrawàlla*.

Nick-names of Early Settlers.

Signification.

Mr. M.	*Coot-narràng*	Hair on chin (Mr. M. wears an imperial).
G. W.	*Lirrt-pidjoong*	Singing or humming.
T. W.	*Tum-terlingae*	Playing with tongue (Mr. W. has a peculiar manner of moving his tongue when speaking).
F. H.	*Terreep*	Not known.
J. H.	*Mundol-wort*	Named after a black man who was killed by thunder; probably the first musket they heard fired was by Mr. H., which they compared to thunder.
Mr. M.	*Wun-werrang*	One who pouts.

Explanation of Symbols used to Point out the Pronunciation.

à as in "cart."
à accented.

LIST OF WORDS.—ENGLISH—NATIVE.

(COMPILED BY THE GUARDIANS OF ABORIGINES IN THE COLONY OF VICTORIA.)

On the 4th July 1863, I forwarded a number of printed papers to the Local Guardians of Aborigines in the Colony of Victoria, with the request that they would write opposite to each printed (English) word the word in the Aboriginal language having exactly the same meaning. It was suggested in the circular letter accompanying the printed form that the Guardians should take care to ascertain whether more than one word was used in the same sense by the Aborigines, and, if so, to give all such words, noting the circumstances under which they were used.

The correspondents whose replies are attached performed the work with exceeding care, and the results are very valuable.

The lists are here arranged geographically.

MURRAY DISTRICT.

TANGAMBALANGA.

Pallanganmiddah Tribe.

English.	Australian.	English.	Australian.
Man	Gerree.	Star	Jiemba.
Woman	Giree.	Sky	Youivilla.
Father	Mamgah.	Night	Tooma.
Mother	Bigah.	Day	Koonda.
Son	Yuairo.	Fire	Kurraw.
Daughter	Yuariga.	Air	Kurre } only known as wind.
Brother	Waanga.	Wind	Kurre }
Sister	Tiega.	Earth	Merre }
Head	Booaw.	Ground	Merre } only known as country.
Hair	Booaw.	Soil	Merre }
Eye	Mee.	River	Kiewra } any water.
Ear	Mirimbah.	Sea	Kiewra }
Mouth	Deirah.	Stone	Poongah.
Tongue	Tierah.	Tree	Wondah.
Teeth	Teera.	Wood	Tau-wa } only name for wood.
Hand	Murrah.	Stick	Tau-wa }
Finger	Youllon.	Bird	Murregah.
Foot	Teyrah.	Egg	Narrangah.
Toe	Youllon.	Snake	Tueyon.
Belly	Moolloona.	Eagle	Warrimoo.
Blood	Koroo.	Crow	Berontha.
Bone	Kieela.	Mopoke	Bingami.
Sun	Koonda.	Kangaroo	Boodgoo.
Moon	You-warra.		

THOMAS MITCHELL, Tangambalanga.

BARNAWARTHA.

Emu Mudjug Tribe.

English.	Australian.	English.	Australian.
Man	Müng.	Star	Jemba.
Woman	Belagera.	Sky	Thuran.
Father	Mamah.	Night	Barandong.
Mother	Gunèe.	Day	Erah.
Son	Burü.	Fire	Wanga.
Daughter	Burü.	Air	Nineyara.
Brother	Carcon.	Wind	Towarah.
Sister	Mingel.	Earth	Towarah.
Head	Cumbugong.	Ground	Thagound.
Hair	Huran.	Soil	Thagound.
Eye	Mill.	River	Murrumbidyah.
Ear	Mutha.	Sea	None.*
Mouth	Erang.	Stone	Willong.
Tongue	Tulling.	Tree	Wonder.
Teeth	Terah.	Wood	Kegel.
Hand	Murrah.	Stick	Kegel.
Finger	Yellon.	Bird	Jerpeen.
Foot	Jeunong.	Egg	Cobagah.
Toe	Yellon.	Snake	Thòrò.
Belly	Burrabec.	Eagle	Weramu.
Blood	Gornyah.	Crow	Wargon.
Bone	Thubal.	Mopoke	Gogoog.
Sun	Neera.	Kangaroo	Murray.
Moon	Cobadong.		

* Natives here have never seen the sea, and consequently have no name for it.

Blacks never use a dead person's name if possible, and always feel angry when mentioned by others.

DAVID REID, Barnawartha.

ECHUCA.

English.	Australian.	English.	Australian.
Man	Moanit.	Hand	Pecyin.
A dead man	Moa.	Finger	Teechera.
Woman	Layarut.	Foot	Tchinna.
Father	Kaiya or kaiyow.	Toe	Daybon.
Mother	Kána (the a as in " ear").	Belly	Boully.
Son	Yáha (the a as in " ear").	Blood	Mowa.
Child	Koluka.	Bone	Lillima.
Daughter	Katcena.	Sun	Yongya.
Brother	Banyip.	Moon	Yongwidu.
Sister	Túigipa.	Star	Druttra or truttra.
Head	Mwóngery.	Sky	Yuráta or dátala (a as in " far ").
Hair	Bóko.		
Eye	Maa (a as in "far").	Night	Bona.
Ear	Marrmo.	Day	Wongda.
Mouth	Kotta.	Fire	Bichya.
Tongue	Tallye (the a as in "tallow").	Air	
Teeth	Derra.	Wind	Bungya.

LANGUAGE.

ECHUCA.

English.	Australian.	English.	Australian.
Whirlwind	Mommeera.	Stick	Tratyola.
Earth	Wókka.	Bird	Chonda (tchonda).
Ground	Wókka.	Egg	Patyánya.
Soil	Wyeera (to dig the soil).	Snake	Kona.
River	Tongula or tongala.	Eagle	Hwámmery.
Sea		Crow	Wárkil.
Stone	Ecoga.	Mopoke	Koko.
Tree	Tainya.	Kangaroo	Kyemery.
Wood	Moutta.	Emu	Pekerómdia.

Is the custom of giving the name of any natural object to a man or woman common, and on the death of the person so named is the word disused, and another substituted to indicate such natural object?—Such does not appear to be the case; but the blacks do not willingly mention the names of the dead.

Such a custom, it is said, leads to great alterations in the language; are there any other obvious causes in operation leading to changes in the names of things?—I have not been able to ascertain any.

The tribe in this neighbourhood is known as the Echuca tribe, and on the opposite side of the Murray as the Moama tribe, these being the native names of the localities.

C. E. STRUTT, Echuca.

GUNBOWER.

English.	Australian.	English.	Australian.
Man	Coolie.	Star	Toort.
Woman	Lubra.	Sky	Marny.
Father	Mamook.	Night	Boorin.
Mother	Púbook.	Day	Károok.
Son	Munykowook.	Fire	Waunup.
Daughter	Unyanook.	Air	Bonguchirp.
Brother	Wáuook.	Wind	Mirin.
Sister	Koortuncook or chajook.	Earth	Churr.
Head	Mooruncook.	Ground	Churr.
Hair	Nurrannevook.	Soil	Kooruck.
Eye	Mirinook.	River	Murray.
Ear	Wirrinnboolook.	Sea	Not known.
Mouth	Chirbook.	Stone	Larr.
Tongue	Chálinook.	Tree	Becal.
Teeth	Leánook.	Wood	Beeal, and goombowel (dead wood).
Hand	Múnuncook.		
Finger	Múnuncook.	Stick	Lordwill.
Foot	Chinunook.	Bird	Withebower.
Toe (big)	Bobchininook.	Egg	Mirkook.
Other toes	Wothebothechininook.	Snake (black)	Goornwill.
Ankle	Mircook.	Snake (brown)	Coobowoo.
Belly	Billincook.	Eaglehawk	Wirbill.
Blood	Koorkook.	Crow	Wáa.
Bone	Mirdirook.	Mopoke	Wówoke.
Sun	Moorce.	Kangaroo	Cooray.
Moon	Wicwill.		

Is the custom of giving the name of any natural object to a man or woman common, and on the death of the person so named is the word disused and another substituted to indicate such natural object?—It is not the custom here.

Such a custom, it is said, leads to great alterations in the language; are there any other obvious causes in operation leading to changes in the names of things?—None.

NOTE.—So far as I can learn, they use no generic terms, the application being wholly individual—unless in the case of fish, which here is generally called "*Munjey*," or "*Mungi*."

GEORGE HOUSTON, Gunbower Station, Durham Ox.

KULKYNE.

English.	Australian.	English.	Australian.
Man	Wotungi.	Morning star	Nunkumbil.
Woman	Lio.	Stars	Narre-bil.
Father	Màami.	Sky	Nerick.
Mother	Pàapie.	Night	Biangri.
Son	Piungo.	Day	Beianung.
Daughter	Muring.	Fire	Neic-wunapi.
Brother	Bullardie.	Air	Nàaung, nùandie.
Sister	Mine.	Wind	Weirreit.
Head	Durut-boopi.	Earth	Teangi.
Hair	Kiut-carangie.	Ground	Nuidt.
Eye	Mai.	River	Ludht, kolaidhe.
Ear	Mural-wimpoli.	Sea	No term for this word.
Mouth	Dhuck-chapie.	Stone	Kotabi.
Tongue	Màat.	Tree	Bullot-bullandi.
Teeth	Ruruc-leang.	Wood	Leitpar.
Hand	Wuin.	Stick	Kulyi, boop.
Finger	Munangi.	Bird	Waangi, warrandul.
Foot	Jahn.	Egg	Bait, miki.
Toe	Nagugadun.	Snake	Karnie.
Belly	Meurt.	Eagle	Maundil.
Blood	Kuroc.	Crow	Wàah.
Bone	Beagim.	Mopoke	Rorp-rorp, duni-dunit.
Sun	Nung.	Kangaroo	Bulukone-quangi.
Moon	Bait.		

Is the custom of giving the name of any natural object to a man or woman common, and on the death of the person so named is the word disused and another substituted to indicate such natural object?—The names of the deceased persons are seldom or never mentioned by them.

Such a custom, it is said, leads to great alterations in the language; are there any other obvious causes in operation leading to changes in the names of things?—I don't know.

ANGUS MACINTYRE, Kulkyne, Lower Murray.

KULKYNE, LOWER MURRAY.

[Information obtained from a native named *Wye-nye-a-nine*.]

English.	Australian.	English.	Australian.
Man	Bang.	Ground	Dtchar.
Woman	Lay-yurrk.	Soil	Dtchar.
Father	Maw-mook.	River	Lowtoohk.
Mother	Paw-book.	Sea	No name.
Son	Wedtha-book.	Stone	La.
Daughter	Meen-gawk.	Tree	Be-al.
Brother	Goodmen-yook.	Wood	Goom-bowie.
Boy	Pine-go.	Stick	Led-will.
Sister	Djaw-djook.	Bird	Wig-krook.
Head	Mooran-yook.	Egg	Mir-kook.
Hair	Gnaran-yook.	Snake	Korrn-will.
Eye	Minook.	Kangaroo	Koorr-ray.
Ear	Rimbulloh.	Opossum	Willah.
Mouth	Woorun-yook.	Eagle	Werr-bill.
Tongue	Chalin-yook.	Crow	Wah.
Teeth	Le-an-yook.	Mopoke	Wook-wook.
Hand	Man-yan-ook.	Parrot	Djee-jugk.
Finger	Ki-ab-me.	Native companion	Kood-thun.
Foot	Chin-an-yook.	Emu	Kow-ill.
Toe	Baub-chin yanook.	Wild turkey	Gnarrow.
Belly	Bill-in-yook.	Cockatoo parrot	Wir-rib.
Blood	Koor-kook.	Swan	Kon-noorr-a.
Bone	Maddarook.	Wild geese	Gnauk.
Sun	Now-ay.	Murray cod	Poin-jall.
Moon	Wine-will.	River Murray	Mill-ieu.
Star	Tordt.	Wood to make fire-stick	Marung.
Sky	Marng or marung.		
Night or dark	Poor-run.	Fire-stick	Marung wunthup.
Day	Barrb.	One	Kiab.
Fire	Wan-nap.	Two	Buled (or puled) ya.
Air	No word.	Three	Buled ya kiab.
Wind	Merrin.	Four	Buled-buled.
Earth	No name apparently.	Five	Buled-buled kiab, and so on.
Plain	Warrk.		

Guam koo-e! war warang all willah.
Come on! we will look out 'possum.

Mankatah willah.
There is a 'possum.

Willah! mankatah willah.
'Possum! there is a 'possum.

Bird-o-men willah.
I caught an opossum.

Guam! parry ang all hooray.
Come on! we will look out kangaroo.

Man-ah buledya kooyun.
You bring him two fellows' spear.

Mambangall ngar kin koorra migo mindeah.
If we see any kangaroos in the bend [of the creek] we will catch them.

Men are never named after stones, trees, &c.; but when dead their names are not again heard.

JUNCTION OF MORCOVIA CREEK AND RIVER MURRAY.

English.	Australian.	English.	Australian.
Man	Nunna.	Pine	Murr.
Woman	Burrup.	Willow	Boclgie.
Father	Bicht.	Myall	Thurla.
Mother	Gnack.	Saltbush	Naretha.
Son	Ki.	Grass	Thurlum.
Daughter	Murruin.	Gum	Thunine.
Brother	Gunn.	Spear	Mulbar.
Sister	Myie.	Camp	Rarp.
Wife	Thirtnlolo.	Stone	Mock or kibba.
Husband	Thowin.	Earth	Rue.
Step-brother	Weetincuppot.	Ground	Nithe.
Step-sister	Jackitt.	Water	Ook.
Grandfather	Perrin.	Night	Reun.
Grandmother	Mame.	Day	Nungrum.
Infant	Rinmec.	Wind	Werriel.
Small	Murlong.	Air	Yair.
Large	Yuroung.	Fire	Arronge.
Sleep	Yermun.	Murray River	Lutte.
Dream	Routhun.	Lake	Punk.
Canoe	Youngoup.	Fishing-net	Thale.
Smoke	Toum.	Fight	Thulkee.
Ashes	Bonga.	Yes	Yai.
Grave	Bumba.	No	Yetho.
Quick	Nickernurlee.	Head	Cobbra or petùwup.
Slow	Pulgark.	Forehead	Dinn.
Eagle	Mundle.	Hair	Dreut.
Bird	Bunemun.	Eyebrow	Yinmow.
Curlew	Weelne.	Eye	Langur.
Swan	Coulthou.	Nose	Cup.
Crane	Whimba.	Ear	Marl.
Cockatoo (white)	Run.	Cheek	Teek.
Cockatoo (black)	Raik.	Mouth	Moun.
Emu	Renine.	Tongue	Mutt.
Parrot	Merlingow.	Neck	Younge.
Pigeon	Cunnup.	Shoulder	Tunmul.
Crow	Tulong.	Chest	Rack.
Teal	Tuppot.	Arm	Mul.
Musk duck	Boutong.	Back	Poeum.
Black duck	Crupung.	Leg	Cuppum.
Wood duck	Wonnon.	Knee	Troot.
Opossum	Wacynag.	Skin	Look.
Wallaby	Merrince.	Flesh	Nul.
Dog	Kign.	Fat	Cutt.
Black snake	Murnin-nulma.	Hand	Woun.
Brown snake	Punpung-nulma.	Foot	Thun.
Mallee snake	Waitmarouk.	Toe	Gnde-thun.
Whip snake	Tunart.	Finger	Conwolwoun.
Carpet snake	Buccurage.	Blood	Courrouc.
Adder	Mayahwonn.	Bone	Cun.
Kangaroo	Bulyoukeurr.	Sun	Nung.
Egg	Bâte.	Moon	Bite.
Wood	Whitha.	Star	Dingée.
Stick	Burgh.	Sky	Wango.
Box-tree	Bulloot.	Rain	Mugga.

LANGUAGE. 73

English	Australian.
Frost	Lurgoo.
Fog	Mow.
Thunder	Mundara.
Lightning	Wirlilbule.
Soul	Coule.
Fish	Marm.
Cod-fish	Mentintul.
Perch-fish	Gerric.
Cray-fish	Moware.
Mussels	Muer.
Opossum rug	Mattura.

English.	Australian.
Darling River	Yane.
Edward River	Cullart.
Murrumbidgee River	Reen.
Lachlan River	Durrum.
Tomahawk	Thurin.
Club	Murrull.
Shield	Bulrill.
Summer	Welya.
Winter	Yuit.
Owl	Pupinar.
Bat	Rockeul.

TYNTYNDYER.

This paper applies to the *Watty-watty* and *Litchoo-litchoo* tribes only.

English.	Australian.
Man	Wortongie.
Woman	Liour.
Father	Mamie.
Mother	Baboo.
Son	Wortongie wertiwoo.
Daughter	Liour wertiwoo.
Brother	Wawoo, if older; and Balarin, if younger.
Sister	Minie.
Head	Poorp.
Hair	Gneningin.
Eye	Mirnoo.
Ear	Wirumpoolen.
Mouth	Woorinen (this is also applicable to the bows of a canoe).
Tongue	Tchilinen.
Teeth	Leangin.
Hand	Murnungin.
Finger	Each finger has a separate name.
Foot	Chinangin.
Toe	Each toe has a separate name.
Belly	Wootchiwoo.
Blood	Jinka-jinka.
Bone	Calwe.
Sun	Nowie.
Moon	Meatian.
Star	Toort.

English.	Australian.
Sky	Tyril.
Night	Tolkine-nowie.
Day	Keely-nowie.
Fire	Wanup.
Air	No word.
Wind	Willangie.
Earth	Tungie.
Ground	Tungie.
Soil	Tungie.
River	Milloo.
Sea	Cowie kayiny
Stone	Muckie.
Tree	Boorongie. (This applies to a number of trees; they have not any name for tree in the singular.)
Wood	
Stick	
Bird	They have not any name for bird, each bird has a distinctive name only.
Egg	Mirkoo.
Snake	Cannie.
Eagle	Perrit-perrit.
Crow	Wangie.
Mopoke	Jinny-jinny.
Kangaroo	Koorangie.

Is the custom of giving the name of any natural object to a man or woman common, and on the death of the person so named is the word disused and another substituted to indicate such natural object?—Men and women have all names with some local meaning or personal peculiarity. When a person dies, the name is forgotten from that time forward, and if a local name, it is at once changed; this causes very great difficulty in arriving at a knowledge of their history.

Such a custom, it is said, leads to great alterations in the language; are there any other obvious causes in operation leading to changes in the names of things?—There are not any other causes for changes in the language.

PETER BEVERIDGE, Tyntyndyer, Swan Hill.

MILDURA.
Yerre-yerre Tribe.

English.	Australian.	English.	Australian.
Man	*Wir.*	Star	*Boul.*
Woman	*Coormup.*	Sky	*Nurnt.*
Father	*Bait.*	Night	*Wangry.*
Mother	*Acka.*	Day	*Bay-a-nauk.*
Son	*Ri.*	Fire	*Mick.*
Daughter	*Uru.*	Air	*Nitch.*
Brother	*Coque.*	Wind	*Wirit.*
Sister	*Micka.*	Earth	*Nat-ya.*
Head	*Turt.*	Ground	*Bambill.*
Hair	*Moor-il.*	Soil	*Carool.*
Eye	*Me.*	River	*Lut.*
Ear	*Mural.*	Sea	*Wi-a-runk.*
Mouth	*Turk.*	Stone	*Thauk.*
Tongue	*Maita.*	Tree	*Burnell.*
Teeth	*Rurch.*	Wood	*Boup.*
Hand	*Wina.*	Stick	*Bull-the-bull.*
Finger	*Ak-a-quim.*	Bird	*Boyump.*
Foot	*Thina.*	Egg	*Bet.*
Toe	*Ak-a-quim.*	Snake	*Thoke.*
Belly	*Moort.*	Eagle	*Maw-an-dil.*
Blood	*Coorook.*	Crow	*Walk.*
Bone	*By-imp.*	Mopoke	*Co-cock.*
Sun	*Nunk.*	Kangaroo	*Bu-lu-cool.*
Moon	*Pyte.*		

Is the custom of giving the name of any natural object to a man or woman common, and on the death of the person so named is the word disused and another substituted to indicate such natural object?—Yes; name given always of a natural object, but not disused after death.

Such a custom, it is said, leads to great alterations in the language; are there any other obvious causes in operation leading to changes in the names of things?—Names do not alter here.

H. JAMIESON, J.P., Mildura, Lower Murray.

YELTA.

Maronra Language.—Spoken by the *Yaako-yaako* tribe, inhabiting the Murray from about ten miles above the Darling Junction to a little below the Rufus (the feeder of Lake Victoria), about fifty miles, and by all the tribes on the Darling, to about 350 miles above its junction with the Murray. About half-way between Mount Murchison and Fort Bourke a change in dialect is discernible, and at Fort Bourke the *Kamilaroi* language commences, which is understood by the tribes on nearly all the tributaries of the Darling.

English.	Australian.	English.	Australian.
Man	*Maa-lee.*	Star	*Boorlee.*
Woman	*Nongo.*	Sky	*Kara wina.*
Father	*Kambia.*	Night	*Tan-hon-ko.*
Mother	*Naamagh.*	Day	*Minki.*
Son	*Weymbra.*	Fire	*Nan-day-lee, koon-ega.*
Daughter	*Weymbra.*	Air	*Taparoo.*
Brother	*Kokquia.*	Wind	*Yerta.*
Sister	*Wertooia.*	Earth	*Merndi.*
Head	*Therto, kohoro.*	Ground	*Pom pon deroo.*
Hair	*Boorlkee.*	Soil	*Merndi.*
Eye	*Maykee.*	River	*Berlerroo.*
Ear	*Uree, munga.*	Sea	None, having no idea of it.
Mouth	*Yelka.*	Stone	*Yernda.*
Tongue	*Therlinya.*	Tree	*Yarra.*
Teeth	*Nandee.*	Wood	*Yarra.*
Hand	*Mambanna, mera.*	Stick	*Katy yarra.*
Finger	*Merra.*	Bird	*Wonga.*
Foot	*Thinna.*	Egg	*Pirty.*
Toe	*Nerlka thinna.*	Snake	*Tooroo*
Belly	*Koarntoo.*	Eagle	*Bilyarra.*
Blood	*Kandara.*	Crow	*Waukoo.*
Bone	*Pina.*	Mopoke	*Wau-poo-a.*
Sun	*Yhuk-ko.*	Kangaroo	*Bool-oolye.*
Moon	*Pytoa.*		

Is the custom of giving the name of any natural object to a man or woman common, and on the death of the person so named is the word disused and another substituted to indicate such natural object?—I believe it is; and when the person dies, all words having a similar sound are disused and others substituted. When a person of any importance dies, the change is often very great.

Such a custom, it is said, leads to great alterations in the language; are there any other obvious causes in operation leading to changes in the names of things?—I am not aware of any other cause than the above. Sometimes a word is revived after the body of the deceased is supposed to have become dust; this causes, I think, the duplicate words.

The name of a place is as frequently given as that of a bird or animal.

As an instance of the great changes which take place in the language in the course of comparatively few years, I may mention that a few months ago an elderly woman and two lads were met with on the upper part of the ana branch, who had come in from the "scrub," and had never before seen a white man. The language they speak is evidently a dialect of the *Maronra,* but it is so different that the other blacks can understand very little of what they say. I have not had an opportunity of seeing them myself, so I only speak from hearsay evidence.

The supposition is (and the older blacks have an indistinct recollection of the circumstance) that the man, having stolen his wife, escaped with her into the scrub between the ana branch and the South Australian boundary, where they have remained ever since: when the water has dried up, getting it from the roots of Mallee, or native wells, one of which has been recently discovered. Having no intercourse with any other blacks during a period of fifteen to twenty years, they would be unacquainted with the changes which have taken place in the language during that time; and speaking that which was current when they went away, and which is now, greater part of it, obsolete, they are not readily understood. The man is supposed to be dead, and the woman with her two sons have made their way to the creek. Such appear to be the facts of the case so far as I have been able to ascertain.

THOS. HILL GOODWIN.

Church Mission Station, Yelta, 15th August 1863.

WIMMERA DISTRICT.

LAKE HINDMARSH.
Kurm-me-lak Tribe.

English.	Australian.	English.	Australian.
Man	Wutyo.	Moon	Mityän.
Woman	Leirock.	Star	Turt.
Father	Mahm.	Sky	Wur-wur.
Mother	Bap.	Night	Burroin.
Son*	Watyip.	Day	Nyau-we (also used for sun).
Daughter	Many-kep.	Fire	Wan-yap.
Brother (eldest)	Woaw.	Air	Wurrän-wurrän.
Brother (youngest)	Kut.	Wind	Wellä.
Sister (eldest)	Tyat.	Earth	Tyar.
Sister (youngest)	Kurtuan.	Ground	Tyar.
Head	Burp.	Soil	Tyar.
Hair	Narraburp.	River	Bar.
Eye	Mir.	Sea	Nyam-mat.
Ear	Wirmbull.	Stone	Kut-yap.
Mouth	Tyarp.	Tree	Kalk } (also used for wood
Tongue	Tyalle.	Wood	Kalk } and bone).
Teeth	Lia.	Stick	Lead.
Hand	Manja.	Bird	Wit-yin-will.
Finger	Yullup-yullup-manja.	Egg	Mirk.
Foot	Kinna.	Snake	Tyu-rang-kuh-nalluck.
Toe	Bap-kinna.	Eagle	Wirp-pill.
Belly	Belly.	Crow	Woa.
Blood	Gurk.	Mopoke	Kar-tuk.
Bone	Kalk (also used for wood).	Kangaroo	Min-yo.
Sun	Nyau-we.		

* The father calls his son *Watyip*, but the mother calls him *Prin-yu*.

It is the custom sometimes of giving names of any natural object to men and women, and on the death of persons so named, the word is disused and another word substituted to indicate such natural objects.

F. W. SPIESEKE, Ebenezer.

HORSHAM.

English.	Australian.	English.	Australian.
Man	Wootcha.	Moon	Mit-chen.
Woman	Lyurock.	Star	Durht or Turht.
Father	Marmie.	Sky (clouds)	Mrarng.
Mother	Barpee.	Night (darkness)	Bore-un.
Son	Watchip.	Day	Nyow-ee.
Daughter	Mun-gare-wee.	Fire	Wan-yup.
Brother (elder my)	Warh-weck.	Air	Bo-ercook.
Brother (younger my)	Eoiteck.	Wind	Wil-lah.
Sister (elder my)	Jar-jeck.	Earth	Yar.
Sister (younger my)	Eoitwun-deck.	Ground	Yar.
Head (my)	Boorpeck.	Soil	
Hair	Ngrah-boorup.	River	Bu-ar.
Eye	Mirrh.	Sea (the great water)	Ngar-mutch.
Ear	Wor-imbull.		
Mouth	Jarp.	Stone	Ko-chup.
Tongue	Chally.	Tree	By its species.
Teeth	Lear.	Wood	Kaalk.
Hand	Mun-ya.	Stick	Waddy, woddy.
Three large fingers	Watchip-watchip.	Bird	Yow-wirh.
The little finger	Kerting mun-ya.	Egg	Myrh-uck.
Foot	Jin-na.	Snake	Kurn-will.
Big toe	Burp jin-na.	Eagle	Werare-pil.
Belly	Billy.	Crow	Wah.
Blood	Kor-ruck.	Mopoke	
Bone	Ka-alk	Kangaroo	Kor-ay. The male one Moit; female, Min-joon.
Sun	Nyow-ee.		

CHAS. WILSON, Walmer, Horsham.

English.	Dialect of the Lake Hindmarsh Tribe.	Dialect of the Horsham Tribe.
Man	Woot-cha	Kul-lee.
Woman	Ly-urook	Bin-gee.
Father	Mah-mee	Bah-pee.
Son	Wot-chip.	
Daughter	Mung-airwee.	
Brother (an older one)	Wah-wee.	
Brother (younger)	Kor-tee.	
Sister (an older one)	Jah-jee.	
Sister (younger)	Kortuün-dee	Kor-togeck.
Head, calf of leg	Bore-up.	
Head (my)	Bore-peck.	
Hair	Ng-rah-boreup	
Eye	Mirrh.	
Ear	Wor-imbull.	
Mouth	Jarp.	
Tongue	Chal-lee.	
Teeth	Lee-ar.	
Hand	Mun-ya.	

English.	Dialect of the Lake Hindmarsh Tribe.	Dialect of the Horsham Tribe.
Fingers (the three larger ones)	Watchip-watchip.	
Finger (the little one)	Kerting mun-ya.	
Foot	Jin-na.	
Toe (the big one)	Barp jin-na.	
Belly	Bil-ly.	
Blood, magpie	Kōi-ruck or Korruck.	
Bone, wood	Kaalk.	
Sun (day)	Nyow-ee.	
Moon	Mit-chen	Yairt.
Star	Durt or Turt.	
Sky, heavens, clouds	M-rarng.	
Thick black clouds	Tan-bill.	
Night (darkness)	Bore-un.	
Day (sun)	Nyow-ee.	
Fire	Wan-yup	Wee.
Air	Boŏr-cook.	
Spirit	Eer-arook.	
Wind	Wil-lah	Wahd-waht.
Earth	Jah.	
Ground	Jah.	
Soil.		
River	Bu-ar	Burh.
Sea (the great water)	Ng-ar-mutch.	
Stone	Ko-chup	Larh.
Stick	Wad-dy.	
Bird	Yow-wirh.	
Egg	Mirrh-uck	Mirrh-cook.
Snake	Kurn-will	Kurn-ill.
Eagle	Werare-pil.	
Crow	Wah	Wah.
Mopoke	Kah-took	Wah-pook.
Kangaroo	Kor-ay.	
Male kangaroo	Moit.	
Female kangaroo	Mun-goon.	

I have endeavoured in the foregoing list of words to write them in syllables which would give the correct sound of the word.

With regard to the question, Is it "the custom of giving the name of any natural object to a man or woman?" I would answer *it is;* but whether or not that name is changed to some other word on the death of the black I am not able at this moment to say positively. One thing is certain, *that the blacks on no account* mention the name of a deceased black (the native name), and I know of only one instance where the blacks have not taken offence at the name given to a deceased black by the whites being still retained by another black of the tribe. This black, however, brought the name from another tribe, a short time after the death of her namesake and predecessor.

Tah-chet mah-rung is *one* of the names of Tallyho, of the Lake tribe. *Mah-rung* is the name of the pine-tree. *Jaretté* is the boy Henry's name. *Jair* is the name of the tea-tree of the Mallee. I think it should be pronounced rather *Jurh.*

Wunganette is a boy's name. *Wung-ourn* is the native name of a place near Pine Plains.

Brairn-umin is a boy's name, and is the native word for "he cuts through," or "he runs," or "pierces through," as with a spear.

Nepur-nin is a girl's name; a native verb, too, which signifies "to bury, to hide."

From the foregoing remarks you will, perhaps, draw your own conclusions. I have only been about nineteen months among the blacks, and during that period have had to study their language under great disadvantages. However, I am inclined to the opinion that the Aboriginal tongue has ever been, from the causes you point out, and also with those which every language is subject to, combined, a changeable one.

Having been requested by Mr. C. Wilson, J.P., to fill up the paper forwarded to him, I have had much pleasure in doing so as far as I have been able, and would be most happy to give any other information that is in my power.

JOB FRANCIS, Walmer.

GLENORCHY.

Djappuminyou Tribe.

English.	Australian.	English.	Australian.
Man	Coullee.	Star	Dourt.
Woman	Bibagou.	Sky	Marng.
Father	Maarm.	Night	Bourain.
Mother	Bauppee.	Day	Ghnarweeyun.
Son	Watchippe.	Fire	Wee.
Daughter	Maguppe.	Air	Gnargoutch.
Brother	Waawie.	Wind	Miya.
Brother (younger)	Gouttee.	Earth	Djak.
Sister	Djaihee.	Ground	Djak.
Head	Bourp.	Mud	Bieke.
Hair	Guarra.	Soil	Bounn.
Eye	Mirkk.	River	Birke.
Ear	Wearbuull.	Sea	Waughree.
Mouth	Wuurrough.	Stone	Laugh.
Tongue	Tchallee.	Tree	Gulpaugarra.
Teeth	Leah.	Wood	Culke; same as bone.
Hand	Munyah.	Stick	Wattipeeculke.
Finger	Wingerapp.	Bird	Yarburrgurr.
Foot	Jinna.	Egg	Mirrke.
Toe	Baupjinna.	Snake	Cournemille.
Belly	Charrowine.	Eagle	Gnarraille.
Blood	Goork.	Crow	Waagh.
Bone	Culke.	Mopoke	Kartauk.
Sun	Ghnarwee.	Kangaroo	Coorah.
Moon	Yen.		

WILLIAM DENNIS, Carr's Plains.

Upper Richardson.

English.	Australian.	English.	Australian.
Man	Wutcha.	Star	Doort.
Woman	Biang-biango.	Sky	Marang.
Father	Mamie.	Night	Booring.
Mother	Papie.	Day	Berrip.
Son	Wutchepie.	Fire	Wee.
Daughter	Mongeri.	Air	Narwart.
Brother	Wu wie.	Wind	Narwart.
Sister	Gatie.	Earth	Dyah.
Head	Boorp.	Ground	Dyuh.
Hair	Niabook.	Soil	Dyuh.
Eye	Meer.	River	Boorinegatchni.
Ear	Wrimbool.	Sea	No name given.
Mouth	Woora.	Stone	Lach.
Tongue	Jallie.	Tree	Galk.
Teeth	Leah.	Wood	Galk.
Hand	Manyah.	Stick	Galk.
Finger	Bap wanyah.	Bird	Yowra-yowra.
Foot	Ginah.	Egg	Mirk.
Toe	Bap ginah.	Snake	Goorinmill.
Belly	Charawin.	Eagle	Warpil.
Blood	Gooah.	Crow	Wiaa.
Bone	Cullae.	Mopoke	Warpoke.
Sun	Nyawie.	Kangaroo	Goora.
Moon	Yeen.		

The name of the Tribe cannot be ascertained.

Is the custom of giving the name of any natural object to a man or woman common, and on the death of the person so named is the word disused and another substituted to indicate such natural object?—It is not the custom often to do so, and when done so after death it is never used.

R. McLachlan, Upper Richardson.

Avoca.

[From the two Aborigines on the late trial of *Queen v. Symes*—viz., Samson, alias *Koo-ker-mon-dur*, and Martin, alias *Ra-ker-nun*.]

English.	Australian.	English.	Australian.
Man	Koo-lie.	Ear	Wym-bool-look.
Woman	Too-ra.	Mouth	Woor-uk.
Father	Mar-mook.	Tongue	Tar-lee.
Mother	Bar-boop.	Teeth	Lee-are.
Son	Boo-poop.	Hand	Mun-nar.
Daughter	Wy-ar-poop.	Finger	Won-in-mun-nar.
Brother	Woor-wook.	Foot	Tee-nar.
Sister	Koor-took.	Toe	Won-nin-tee-nar.
Head	Boor-kook.	Belly	Kun-nar.
Hair	Nar-boor-kook.	Blood	Koor-kook.
Eye	Myn-ook.	Bone	Karl-kook.

LANGUAGE.

English.	Australian.	English.	Australian.
Sun	Nar-wee.	Sea	Woor-ree.
Moon	Yean.	Stone	Lar.
Star	Tourt.	Tree	Kulk.
Sky	Woor-woor.	Wood	Moo-tuk.
Night	Boo-run.	Stick	Kulk.
Day	Kar-pul.	Bird	Yal-war.
Fire	Wee.	Egg	Broom-boon.
Air	Narn-goot.	Snake	Kul-mil.
Wind	Mer-ring.	Eagle	Wear-pil.
Earth	Kap-pen.	Crow	War.
Ground	Tu-nyt.	Mopoke	Weel-mul.
Soil	Kun-nar.	Kangaroo	Kor-ror.
River	Wool-lar.		

WM. THOMAS, Guardian of Aborigines.

UPPER LODDON.

DAYLESFORD.

Monulgundeech Tribe.

English.	Australian.	English.	Australian.
Man	Koolee.	Moon	Yern.
Woman	Touroi.	Star	Toort.
Father	Marm.	Sky	Wrur-wrur.
Mother	Barp.	Night	Boorinen; darkness, borine.
Son	Wareep; occasionally by the mother gnanap.	Day	Gnoween; daybreak, bearp.
		Fire	Wee.
Daughter	Mangjup.	Air	No name; breath, nrngouch.
Brother	Waroe, older brother; kut, younger brother.	Wind	Merin.
		Earth	Jaa.
Sister	Jarch, older sister; kutook, younger sister.	Ground	Jaa.
		Soil	Jaa.
Head	Doorp.	River	Bur; large river, gneurae-bur; small river, wonume-bur.
Hair	Gnerra.		
Eye	Ma.		
Ear	Weimbul.	Sea	Waree; wonume warce, small sea.
Mouth	Wooroo.		
Tongue	Chalie.	Stone	Lu.
Teeth	Leear.	Tree	Kulk (every variety of tree has its distinctive name).
Hand	Mirna.	Wood	
Finger	No name; barpmirna, thumb.	Stick	Drudra.
		Bird	Yarbooka.
Foot	Jinna.	Egg	Boom-boom.
Toe	No name; barpjinna, great toe.	Snake	Kunmil.
		Eagle	Waa-pil.
Belly	Koona.	Crow	War, white-eyed crow; ma-rung-un, black-eyed crow.
Blood	Gourk.		
Bone	Kolk.	Mopoke	Kurook.
Sun	Gnowee.	Kangaroo	Goura.

Is the custom of giving the name of any natural object to a man or woman common, and on the death of the person so named is the word disused and

VOL. II. L.

another substituted to indicate such natural object?—It is the custom to give the names of natural objects to both males and females, and upon the death of a person so named for his or her relations to abstain from the use of such name for a few months or a year, the length of time depending upon the respect felt for the person; but it is not customary for the tribe to cease to use such name.

Such a custom, it is said, leads to great alterations in the language; are there any other obvious causes in operation leading to changes in the names of things?—No.

W. E. STANBRIDGE, Wombat.

LOWER LODDON.

BOORT.
Lower Loddon Tribe.

English.	Australian.	English.	Australian.
Man	*Wootho.*	Moon	*Waingwill.*
Woman	*Larook.*	Star	*Doort.*
Father	*Marmoke.*	Sky	*Talgitcha.*
Mother	*Barbook.*	Night	*Pooroon.*
Son	*Watheby paingo.*	Day	*Parrep.*
Daughter	*Popomen.*	Fire	*Wannop.*
Brother	*Warwook*, elder; *goodmanyook*, younger.	Air	*Merrin.*
		Wind	*Merrin.*
Sister	*Tarduke.*	Earth	*Char.*
Head	*Boourbook,** *youyourook.*	Ground	*Char.*
Hair	*Narranyuke.*	Soil	*Char.*
Eye	*Min-nook.*	River("Loddon")	*Gunboweroo.*
Ear	*Weembulloke.*	Sea	Inland blacks never saw it, and so have no name.
Mouth	*Cherbook.*		
Lip	*Ouroonyuke.*	Stone	*Lar.*
Tongue	*Charlinyook.*	Tree	*Carlk.*
Teeth	*Leeanyook.*	Wood	*Carlk.*
Hand	*Manarnyuke.*	Stick	*Waddy.*
Finger	*Wathep-wathep manarnyuke.*	Bird	*Watheboryhwirr.*
Foot	*Chinarnyook.*	Egg	*Merrk.*
Toe	*Parp chinarnyook.*	Snake	*Coonwill.*
Belly	*Wanarnyuke.*	Eagle	*Warepill.*
Blood	*Coorkgook.*	Crow	*Warr.*
Bone	*Carlyook.*	Mopoke	*Curdook.*
Sun	*Gnarwee.*	Kangaroo	*Cooreè* (*Coura*).

Is the custom of giving the name of any natural object to a man or woman common, and on the death of the person so named is the word disused and another substituted to indicate such natural object?— Yes; see above;* "*Bourbook*" is name of a dead blackfellow; now it is "*Youyourook.*"

Such a custom, it is said, leads to great alterations in the language; are there any other obvious causes in operation leading to changes in the names of things?—I know of no other.

HENRY GODFREY, Boort, Lower Loddon.

WESTERN DISTRICT.

BALMORAL.
Glenelg Tribe.

English.	Australian.	English.	Australian
Man	*Cooly* or *beng*, meaning either one man or a number.	Moon	*Yern.*
Woman	*Bang-bang-go.*	Star	*Dort.*
Father	*Marmuke;* my father, *marmck;* your, *marmen;* his, *marmuke* (the *u* as in "Luke").	Sky	*Dunbil.*
		Night	*Boroinu* (dark); (the *oi* as in "point").
Mother	*Papuke* (the *a* pronounced like *a* in "after").	Day	*Nyawi* (sun); (the *nya* must be pronounced as one syllable).
Son	*Wachepuke.*	Fire	*Wee* (and which also means firewood).
Daughter	*Mung-a-ok* (*a* like *a* in "mate").	Air	*Gnang-goitch.*
Brother	*Wawuke* (elder), *cotok* (younger).	Wind	*Mering.*
Sister	*Dgatyuke.*	Earth	*Tcha.*
Head	*Boorpuke.*	Ground	*Tcha.*
Hair	*Gnerraboorp* (*a* like *a* in "after").	Soil	(sand) *Coorak;* (clay) *Militur;* (mud) *Beak* (one syllable).
Eye	*Meurnok.*		
Ear	*Wroom-bolok.*	River	*Gnul-ok-ok.*
Mouth	*Worro.*	Sea	*Numaitch* (two syllables).
Tongue	*Chal-inuke.*	Stone	*La* (the *a* as in "after").
Teeth	*Leanuke.*	Tree	*Calk.*
Hand	*Manya.*	Wood	*Calk.*
Finger	(thumb) *Babmanya;* (little finger) *Griting.*	Stick	*Coo-er-ong.*
		Bird	*Your-your* (the *ou* as in "devour").
Foot	*Ginna.*		
Toe	(big toe) *Babginna.*	Egg	*Mirk.*
Belly	*Billy.*	Snake	*Coornwel.*
Blood	*Gork.*	Eagle	*Wrappel.*
Bone	*Calk.*	Crow	*Wa* (*a* as in "after").
Sun	*Nyawi* (*nya* must be pronounced as one syllable).	Mopoke	*Curtok* (*a* as in "after").
		Kangaroo	*Curre* (two syllables).

Is the custom of giving the name of any natural object to a man or woman common, and on the death of the person so named is the word disused and another substituted to indicate such natural object?—The custom of giving the name of any natural object to a man or woman is not uncommon, the following being instances in point:—*Colabatyin* (a turkey), also a man's name; *Bulltkinna* (a sheep), also a man's name; *Bonyca* (testes), also a man's name. The writer is not sufficiently familiar with the names of women to be able to give examples, but believes the same custom extends to them. Upon the death of a person named, according to the custom mentioned, the word or name of the natural object is not disused, neither is another substituted. When speaking of a deceased person, his or her name is never mentioned.

I am not aware of any causes in operation leading to changes in the names of things. None of the words or names of things *familiar to me* have been disused or altered during the last twelve or thirteen years.

C. M. OFFICER, Mount Talbot, Balmoral.

SANDFORD.

Wannon Tribe, Meerinygil.

English.	Australian.	English.	Australian.
Man	Koomongmorang.	Star	Barite barrite.
Woman	Nooranygoulk.	Sky	Murnbull.
Father	Papic.	Night	Booron.
Mother	Noorong.	Day	Woorum durrong.
Son	Cooprank.	Fire	Ween and goonda.
Daughter	Nuart.	Air	Nood maring (good day).
Brother	Wardi.	Wind	Narcejuck.
Sister	Kurkie.	Earth	Maring.
Head	Coolon.	Ground	
Hair	Nullong.	Soil	
Eye	Moorung.	River	Boogarra.
Ear	Hoooung.	Sea	Narmutt.
Mouth	Mullong.	Stone	Moorie.
Tongue	Talline.	Tree	Parliep.
Teeth	Tungung.	Wood	
Hand	Murrong.	Stick	Lurt.
Little finger	Gridding.	Bird	Mudmurdull.
Foot	Dinnung.	Egg	Coollay.
Toe	Gridding dinnung.	Snake	Coorong.
Belly	Bulline.	Eagle	Necyangarra.
Blood	Carmarrow.	Crow	Warng.
Bone	Burgine.	Mopoke	Doorreedoonit.
Sun	Turrung.	Kangaroo	Koorang.
Moon	Dangitt.		

J. H. JACKSON, Sandford.

HAMILTON.

Upper Wannon Tribe.

English.	Australian.	English.	Australian.
Man	Colae.	Belly	Belly.
Woman	Bangbango.	Blood	Roark.
Father	Mammy.	Bone	Culk.
Mother	Pappy.	Sun	Nowe.
Son	Whucheappa.	Moon	Yaen.
Daughter	Mongawwee.	Star	Toort.
Brother	Whawe.	Sky	Mauren.
Sister	Chache.	Night	Borrine.
Head	Boorup.	Day	Belpa.
Hair	Nahra.	Fire	We.
Eye	March.	Air	Wayoungwayonga.
Ear	Brimbol.	Wind	Mya.
Mouth	Cone.	Earth	Minagotya.
Tongue	Charle.	Ground	Jah.
Teeth	Layha.	Soil	Neapein.
Hand	Monyah.	River	Yurram.
Finger	Kyup.	Sea	Ammitch.
Foot	Chena.	Stone	Lah.
Toe	Patyena.	Tree	Gulk.

LANGUAGE. 85

English.	Australian.	English.	Australian.
Wood	*We* (same as fire).	Eagle	*Rappil.*
Stick	*Koyarrock.*	Crow	*Woa.*
Bird	*Weet-weet.*	Mopoke	*Cartook.*
Egg	*Mirk.*	Kangaroo	*Goora.*
Snake	*Coornweel.*		

Is the custom of giving the name of any natural object to a man or woman common, and on the death of the person so named is the word disused and another substituted to indicate such natural object?—This custom does not prevail; the father is said to dream a name for his child. The name of the dead is never mentioned, and one holding the same name in the tribe has it changed.

P. LEARMONTH, Hamilton.

PORTLAND.

Tourahonong Tribe.

(61 now living—1863.)

English.	Australian.	English.	Australian.
Man	*Mhara.*	Star	*Minkil.*
Woman	*Tunumbu.*	Sky	*Murnong.*
Father	*Pepint.*	Night	*Boron.*
Mother	*Nerung.*	Day	*Nunung.*
Son	*Copenyong.*	Fire	*Wein.*
Daughter	*Nrarton.*	Air	*Lallapcorn.*
Brother	*Wadi.*	Wind	*Urndoek.*
Sister	*Charki.*	Earth	*Mering.*
Head	*Pini.*	Ground	
Hair	*Narat.*	Soil	*Pullang.*
Eye	*Ming.*	River	*Wurran.*
Ear	*Wing.*	Sea	*Naumut.*
Mouth	*Olung.*	Stone	*Murrai.*
Tongue	*Talian.*	Tree	*Waurut.*
Teeth	*Tungun.*	Wood	*Wein.*
Hand	*Murrung.*	Stick	*Leiyt.*
Finger	*Kiapork.*	Bird	*Purpurin.*
Foot	*Youk.*	Egg	*Minyong.*
Toe	*Merriniouk.*	Snake	*Corang.*
Belly	*Torkung.*	Eagle	*Nennghur.*
Blood	*Ghereek.*	Crow	*Warl.*
Bone	*Buckin.*	Mopoke	*Mumkight.*
Sun	*Nuriung.*	Kangaroo	*Corang.*
Moon	*Turro.*		

Is the custom of giving the name of any natural object to a man or woman common, and on the death of the person so named is the word disused and another substituted to indicate such natural object?—They name the child after the spot it is born at, and *do not* change the name of the place after the death of the so-called black.

Such a custom, it is said, leads to great alterations in the language; are there any other obvious causes in operation leading to changes in the names of things?—I cannot discover that changes are made in the names of things.

J. N. McLeod.

Mr. McLeod gives the names of some of the weapons used by the natives:—

Australian.	English.	Australian.	English.
Murrawong	like the leon-ile.	*Chunuch*	a kind of club.
Mapur	a club.	*Coyong*	large spear.
Peping	a kind of club.	*Taira*	little spear.
Mulcarra	club-shield.	*Narracoort*	spear-shield.

WARRNAMBOOL.

English.	Australian.	English.	Australian.
Man	*Maar.*	Star	*Punjell.*
Woman	*Tonambool.*	Sky	*Murnong.*
Father	*Tebach.*	Night	*Borone.*
Mother	*Nerra.*	Day	*Teern.*
Son	*Tookayn.*	Fire	*Ween.*
Daughter	*Knaard.*	Air	*Urnduc.*
Brother	*Cogo.*	Wind	*Urnduc.*
Sister	*Cukia.*	Earth	*Merring.*
Head	*Pim.*	Ground	*Merring.*
Hair	*Aran.*	Soil	
Eye	*Meir.*	River	*Purcet.*
Ear	*Wurn.*	Sea	*Mertitch.*
Mouth	*Knoolong.*	Stone	*Merri.*
Tongue	*Tuline.*	Tree	*Wooroot.*
Teeth	*Tongun.*	Wood	*Ween.*
Hand	*Merra.*	Stick	*Ween.*
Finger	*Merra.*	Bird	*Purt purdce.*
Foot	*Jinnung.*	Egg	*Mernunc.*
Toe	*Jinnung.*	Snake	*Oorang.*
Belly	*Jucco.*	Eagle	*Eanger.*
Blood	*Kemi.*	Crow	*Wah.*
Bone	*Puckine.*	Mopoke	*Cooramcet.*
Sun	*Uuna.*	Kangaroo	*Koroit.*
Moon	*Yer-yer.*		

Is the custom of giving the name of any natural object to a man or woman common, and on the death of the person so named is the word disused and another substituted to indicate such natural object?—It is common, but not disused.

Such a custom, it is said, leads to great alterations in the language; are there any other obvious causes in operation leading to changes in the names of things?—None.

A. M. MUSGROVE, Warrnambool.

WICKLIFFE.
River Hopkins Tribe.

English.	Australian.	English.	Australian.
Man	Cooley.	Star	Tatinowie.
Woman	Lubra.	Sky	Tootpunue.
Father	Marmae.	Night	Pooroin.
Mother	Parpae.	Day	Perpoamin.
Son	Popoey.	Fire	Ween or wee.
Daughter	Mangowie.	Air	Waryotyangerack.
Brother	Wowie.	Wind	Miya.
Sister	Titeyae.	Earth	Ya.
Head	Caubra or poorpeck.	Ground	Ya.
Hair	Marah.	Soil	Ya.
Eye	Macinyarack.	River	Par.
Ear	Rimbool.	Sea	The blacks here have no name for "sea."
Mouth	Learangerack.		
Tongue	Taleangerack.	Stone	Lah.
Teeth (mouth)	Learangerack.	Tree	Peeal.
Hand	Munyangarack.	Wood	Poort.
Finger	Munyangarack.	Stick	Calk.
Foot	Kinneyangerack.	Bird	Pur-pur.
Toe	Poptineyangerack.	Egg	Mairt.
Belly	Billeyangerack.	Snake	Kurnwill.
Blood	Cookyangerack.	Eagle	Yannul.
Bone	Calleyangerack	Crow	War.
Sun	Nowie.	Mopoke	Yib-yib.
Moon	Yen.	Kangaroo	Curah.

Is the custom of giving the name of any natural object to a man or woman common, and on the death of the person so named is the word disused and another substituted to indicate such natural object?—Not that I can discover; but the blacks have great aversion to naming a deceased member of their tribe.

Such a custom, it is said, leads to great alterations in the language; are there any other obvious causes in operation leading to changes in the names of things?—When I have had an opportunity of conversing with some of the more intelligent of the blacks, I shall endeavour to answer this.

CHAS. GRAY, Nareeb Nareeb.

CARNGHAM.
Mount Emu Tribe.

English.	Australian.	English.	Australian.
Man	Koimoit.	Sister (elder)	Totorang.
Woman	Koimoit-bapanet.	Sister (younger)	Bambrak.
Father	Pittong.	Head	Moork.
Mother	Yuttong.	Hair	Nuir-moork.
Son	Maun.	Eye	Mere.
Daughter	Yarrangook.	Ear	Worn.
Brother (elder)	Yandang.	Mouth	Wora.
Brother (younger)	Yangat.	Tongue	Glannen.

88 THE ABORIGINES OF VICTORIA:

English.	Australian.	English.	Australian.
Teeth	Lea.	Soil	
Hand	Marna.	River	Boranborah.
Finger	Wonmarna.	Sea	Yorran.
Foot	Jenir.	Stone	Law.
Toe	Natin jenir.	Tree	Car.
Belly	Tong.	Wood	Wing.
Blood	Corrick.	Stick (a long one)	Talk.
Bone	Nal.	Stick (a short one)	Martalk.
Sun	Maira.	Bird	Yonburrah.
Moon	Yaan.	Egg	Ja.
Star	Torporrum.	Snake	Conmoit.
Sky	Lacorra, worrawark.	Eagle	Mairompial.
Night	Morkalla.	Crow	Waa.
Day	Morrayail.	Mopoke	Waanwanal.
Fire	Weeing.	Kangaroo	Kaima.
Air	Manabyupjay.	Mountain (large)	Cawa.
Wind	Mia.	Mountain (small)	Purapura.
Earth	Yoruockjaa.	Water	Yallack.
Ground	Cha.		

Is the custom of giving the name of any natural object to a man or woman common, and on the death of the person so named is the word disused and another substituted to indicate such natural object?—On a death taking place, any relations of the same name always change their names, as they never wish to hear the name of the deceased mentioned.

ANDW. PORTEOUS, Carngham.

CAMPERDOWN.

Colongulac Tribe.

English.	Australian.	English.	Australian.
Man	Ummodthe.	Little finger	Kittiemoraangtin.
Woman	Unnodthe.	Thumb	Neramoraangtin.
Father	Pepie.	Foot	Dinangtin.
Mother	Nerong.	Big toe	Qurangadinangtin.
Son	Quoburr.	Belly	Thorangtin.
Daughter	Ghnarn.	Blood	Quroeantnin.
Brother	Wardie.	Bone	Puyhine.
Young brother	Cuoghwon or kokrer.	Sun	Fherne.
Sister	Kakie.	Moon	Borangnatin.
Grandfather	Gnarpurn.	Star	Whythurb.
Uncle	Mamim.	Sky	Murnony.
Aunt	Twollier.	Night	Booroon.
Head	Piematnin.	Day	Hulogetin.
Hair	Harat.	Fire	Whean.
Eye	Merang.	Air	Undapun.
Ear	Weiringnatnin.	Wind	Urndook.
Mouth	Wooroonangtin.	Earth	Merrin.
Tongue	Talyarnangtin.	Ground	Merrin.
Teeth	Tonganantin.	Soil	Merrin.
Hand	Moraangtin.	River	Burony.

LANGUAGE.

English.	Australian.
Sea	Ummut.
Stone	Merri.
Tree	Woorot, big tree; loang, little tree.
Wood	Boarb.
Stick	Queroo; chips, pipepi.
Bird	Boetken.
Egg	Merrik.
Snake	Koorang.
Eaglehawk	Keroolet.
Crow	Waang.
Mopoke	Youitpin.
Kangaroo	Quooric.
Magpie	Qudree.

English	Australian
Minah	Poech.
Black magpie	Kilthen.
Opossum	Pieech.
Native cat	Cowbonge.
Bandicoot	Kecrooie.
Kangaroo-rat	Berrook.
Dead man	Qualbenron.
Mouse	Bunmuth or bummuth.
Duck	Doolwah.
Horse	Cupmaturah.
Eel	Quean.
Fine day	Culhine.
Wet day	Murhang.

R. D. SCOTT, Camperdown.

COLAC.

English.	Australian.
Man	Mondel.
Woman	Noodnuwett, lubra.
Father	Madhma.
Mother	Padhpa.
Son	Kraompweet.
Daughter	Woorncut.
Brother	Kraompweet.
Sister	Permborret.
Head	Moranyenuc.
Hair	Kaenmorackenuc.
Eye	Mrinyeduc.
Ear	Weinyeduc.
Mouth	Woronyeduc.
Tongue	Talanyeduc.
Teeth	Meerinyeduc.
Hand	Macnyinuc.
Finger	Lerinyinuc.
Foot	Kenaeyenuc.
Toe	Kenaeyenuc.
Belly	Woranyenuc.
Blood	Korockyenuc.
Bone	Yeerbingyenuc.
Sun	Nadh.
Moon	Padrtput.
Star (small)	Karrankaran.

English.	Australian.
Star (large)	Orlembeleet.
Sky	Poolootnoomarang.
Night	Pooroonna.
Day	Wooremolleen.
Fire	Weeing.
Air	Parkoolook.
Wind	Pearing.
Earth	Moora.
Ground	Tha.
Soil	Moora.
River	Praah.
Sea	Lamat.
Stone	Drae.
Tree	Cvorlong; lightwood tree, laan.
Wood	Kalerack.
Stick	Kooroorook.
Bird	Thitthit.
Egg	Poetchon.
Snake	Kaanlang.
Eagle	Orlimerick.
Crow	Kaiwaicrook.
Mopoke	Kaelwarra.
Kangaroo	Korak.

Pro WILLIAM DENNIS, ALEXR. DENNIS, Birregurra.

THE ABORIGINES OF VICTORIA:

THE YARRA AND WESTERN PORT.

YARRA YARRA.
Wooeewoorong or Yarra Tribe.

English.	Australian.	English.	Australian.
Man	Koolein.	Star	Durt pirram.
Woman	Baggarkruk.	Sky	Woorowoor.
Father	Mamaneek.	Night	Booren.
Mother	Babaneek.	Day	Yalingboo.
Son	Booboopeek.	Fire	Wein.
Daughter	Manggebeek.	Air	Erelark.
Brother	Worndoolong.	Wind	Moonmoot.
Sister	Leewooruk.	Earth	Yearmoobeek.
Head	Kawanug.	Ground	Beek.
Hair	Yarrie.	Soil	Nutcundra beek.
Eye	Merring.	River	Brrering (Bur-erring, R. Yarra).
Ear	Werring.		
Mouth	Wooroong.	Sea	Waring.
Tongue	Jellang.	Stone	Lang.
Teeth	Leeung.	Tree	Treang.
Hand	Marnung.	Wood	Kalk.
Finger	Woonmoonmillrt.	Stick	Y-boo kalk.
Foot	Jeenoong.	Bird	Quip-quip.
Toe	Babeen jeenoong.	Egg	Terrentra.
Belly	Booet.	Snake	Kaan.
Blood	Kurruk.	Eagle	Bundjell.
Bone	Neelong.	Crow	Waang.
Sun	Nawin.	Mopoke	Kookoom.
Moon	Meneam.	Kangaroo	Kooem.

Is the custom of giving the name of any natural object to a man or woman common, and on the death of the person so named is the word disused and another substituted to indicate such natural object?—Yes, very common; but never changed after death.

Such a custom, it is said, leads to great alterations in the language; are there any other obvious causes in operation leading to changes in the names of things?—None.

JOHN GREEN, Yarra Flats.

WESTERN PORT.
The Boon-oor-rong or Coast Tribe.

English.	Australian.	English.	Australian.
Man	Koo-lin.	Head	Kow-ung.
Woman	Bag-rook.	Hair	Yar-ra.
Father	Mar-man.	Eye	My-ring.
Mother	Par-pun.	Ear	Wer-ring.
Son	Mum.	Mouth	Nung-bil-bun-uk.
Daughter	Mou-mon-dik.	Tongue	Tal-lang.
Brother	Won-do-long.	Teeth	Lee-ung-er.
Sister	Lour-rook.	Hand	My-rong.

LANGUAGE.

English.	Australian.	English.	Australian.
Finger	Mun-ung.	Ground	Beek.
Foot	Tee-nan.	Soil	Kung-ur.
Toe	Bub-bub-bi-tee-nan.	River	War-neet.
Belly	Won-nup.	Sea	War-reen.
Blood	Kul-mul.	Stone	Lang.
Bone	Neyln.	Tree	Ter-rung.
Sun	Ner-wein.	Wood	Kulk.
Moon	Myn-e-am.	Stick	Kulk-kulk.
Star	To-pi-ram.	Bird	Koy-up-koy-up.
Sky	Woor-woor-ror.	Egg	Tir-rat-le-lirr.
Night	Bo-run.	Snake	Karn.
Day	Yel-lin-wa.	Eagle	Pun-gil.
Fire	Wee-en.	Crow	Warng.
Air	Ang.	Mopoke	
Wind	Mon-moot.	Kangaroo	Ko-em-ko-em.
Earth	Beck-beck.		

Is the custom of giving the name of any natural object to a man or woman common, and on the death of the person so named is the word disused and another substituted to indicate such natural object?—It is the custom of naming infants, male or female, on any particular incident at their birth, especially the males. *Ex.:* Gellibrand, a noted black; his Aboriginal name was *Ber-uke,* "a kangaroo-rat," from a kangaroo-rat running through the miam at his birth. Billy Lonsdale, equally noted; Aboriginal name *Polee-orong,* after "cherry-tree," where his mother brought him forth. Another particular instance: A lubra in labor, the miam caught fire; she was caught out and fire extinguished; the child was named *Weing-parn,* "fire and water." *Wonga,* the present chief of the Yarra tribe, was born at the foot of Arthur's Seat; Aboriginal name *Wonga.*

Such a custom, it is said, leads to great alterations in the language; are there any other obvious causes in operation leading to changes in the names of things?—I am aware such is the general opinion, but I have never known any material alteration, save at death they cannot and will not repeat the name for a certain time; but *Ber-uke, Poleeorong, Weing-parn,* and *Wonga,* when dead, will not alter in a single iota the original name of Arthur's Seat, &c.

WM. THOMAS, Guardian of Aborigines.
Melbourne, 17th August 1863.

GIPPSLAND.

FLOODING CREEK AND BUSHY PARK.

English.	Australian.	English.	Australian.
Man	Gun-na.	Daughter	Toot-buk.
Woman	Woo-gut.	Brother	Tunn-tunn.
Father	Mun-gunn	Sister	Bou-ung.
Mother	Year-kunn.	Head	Poo-ruk.
Son	Leech.	Hair	Leet.

THE ABORIGINES OF VICTORIA:

English.	Australian.	English.	Australian.
Eye	Myree.	Air	
Ear	Woor-ring.	Wind	Krow-woor.
Mouth	Kart.	Earth	Turrn.
Tongue	Tal-lan.	Ground	Woork.
Teeth	Un-duk.	Soil	
Hand	Breet.	River	Woon-doon.
Finger	Laa-ra-breet.	Sea	War-ren.
Foot	Tey-yan.	Stone	Wool-lun.
Toe	Tey-yan.	Tree	Kul-luk.
Belly	Bool-lan.	Wood	Kul-luk.
Blood	Krook.	Stick	Kul-luk.
Bone	Byrng.	Bird	Klurt.
Sun	Woo-run.	Egg	Poe-ung.
Moon	Nger-run.	Snake	Too-roo.
Star	Pree-eel.	Eagle	Poen-rung.
Sky	Noort.	Crow	Nar-ru-quon.
Night	Pook-kun.	Mopoke	Woor-quok.
Day	Woo-run.	Kangaroo	Tir-rer.
Fire	Tow-war-rar.		

WILLIAM THOMAS, Melbourne.

LAKE WELLINGTON.

1. *Tarrawarrackel Tribe;* 2. *Wollum, or Wolloom, or Woolloom;* 3. *Bellum-bellum;* 4. *Moomoo and Ngattban.*

English.	Australian.	English.	Australian.
Man	Kanny.	Star	Breell.
Woman	Wookatt.	Sky	Ngoorrooltt.
Father	Moonkan.	Night	Puddhallack.
Mother	Yackan.	Day	Wurring (like sun; used in the same sense as the Hebrew).
Son	Leed; also boy.		
Daughter	Toorbackan.		
Brother	Dandang, the eldest; bromang, the youngest.	Fire	Towr.
		Air	Krow-woorr.
Sister	Bawang.	Wind	Krow-woorr.
Head	Brook.	Earth	Wrack.
Hair	Litt.	Ground	Wrack.
Eye	Moöeh.	Soil	Wrack.
Ear	Wring.	River	Bongurra.
Mouth	Gad or gaad.	Sea	Warringa.
Tongue	Tyelling.	Stone	Walloong.
Teeth	Ngirrndock.	Tree	Talk, large tree; gallach, small tree.
Hand	Pritt.		
Finger	Pritt.	Wood	Mritt.
Finger nail	Dackerpritt.	Stick	Kallooch.
Foot	Tyain.	Bird	Ngalloong.
Toe	Yackanytyainda.	Egg	Booyang.
Belly	Bullum.	Snake	Toorroong.
Blood	Krook.	Eagle	Quurrnamarroo.
Bone	Pring.	Crow	Ngurroogall.
Sun	Wurring.	Mopoke	Wookooch.
Moon	Ngirrang.	Kaugaroo	Tyirra.

Is the custom of giving the name of any natural object to a man or woman common, and on the death of the person so named is the word disused and another substituted to indicate such natural object?—Each blackfellow has his Aboriginal name, which is no more mentioned after his death, except at fights; but none could give me a satisfactory answer to the question.

Such a custom, it is said, leads to great alterations in the language; are there any other obvious causes in operation leading to changes in the names of things?—It seems to me that the greatest reason of the many changes is, *that it is not a written language*, and, consequently, they cannot all be taught after the manner and in the same forms. The same changes would naturally take place in any other language. The construction of the language, however, remains the same, the personal pronouns ending in all cases at the end of the substantive or verb, which makes it short and beautiful.

F. A. HAGENAUER, Lake Wellington Mission Station.

LAKE TYERS.

Bundah Wark Kani, or the Swan Reach Tribe or Men.

English.	Australian.	English.	Australian.
Man	Brah.	Star	Brayel.
Woman	Woorcat.	Sky	Note.
Father	Mung-gan.	Night	Bookang.
Mother	Yaekan.	Day	Wurrin.
Son	Latheba.	Fire	Towera.
Daughter	Turtbakan.	Air	Watputjan.
Brother	Tandha-gnunert.	Wind	Krowaro.
Sister	Landha-gonert.	Earth	Wark.
Head	Purk.	Ground	Wark.
Hair	Lit.	Soil	Munduekan.
Eye	Mre.	River	Bourgari.
Ear	Wring.	Sea	Waring.
Mouth	Kaat.	Stone	Wallung.
Tongue	Jelline.	Tree	Nappur.
Teeth	Nerudack.	Wood	Kanby.
Hand	Bret.	Stick	Kalack.
Finger	Tagara bret.	Bird	Tuin.
Foot	Ja-an.	Egg	Bo-yang.
Toe	Tagara ja-an.	Snake	Kalang and *thurrung*.
Belly	Bullou.	Eagle	Quornamero.
Blood	Karndobara.	Crow	Waygara.
Bone	Bring.	Mopoke	Wokuk.
Sun	Wurrin.	Kangaroo	Jirrah.
Moon	Nerran.		

JOHN BULMER, Lake Tyers, Gippsland.

Church Mission Station, Lake Tyers,
18th August 1863.

SIR,—I have the honor to acknowledge the receipt of yours of the 4th July. I am sorry I could not answer it sooner, but it arrived so late in the month that I had not time to get it ready by return of post. I have given you a list of words; I think they are correct; I have used every caution in collecting them. You will observe, on examining my list, that the blacks have two or three words to express the same thing.

It is customary among these blacks to disuse a word when a person has died whose name was the same, or even of the same sound. I find great difficulty in getting blacks to repeat such words. I believe this custom is common to all the Victorian tribes, though in the course of time the word is resumed again. I have seen among the Murray blacks the dead freely spoken of when they have been dead some time. I have seen them have a little *Uram* (fun) at the expense of a dead black, though I dare say the man had been dead nearly twenty years; though I do not think they would refer to the dead, even at that distance of time, in the presence of any relatives who might be alive. I have no doubt this custom alters the language a little. I know of no other obvious causes which might alter the language, though I should think languages which are not reduced to writing must alter in the course of years, more especially where they have customs similar to the Australian Aborigine.

With regard to the giving of names, they sometimes name a person from the country where he was born. The blacks have great objections to speak of a person by name. In speaking to each other, they address the person spoken to as brother, cousin, friend, or whatever relation the person spoken to bears. Sometimes a black bears a name which we would term merely a nick-name, as the left-handed (*Yanguia*), or the bad-handed (*Murra muthi*), or the little man (*Kato wirto*). They would speak of a person by this name while living, but they would never mention the proper name. I found great difficulty in collecting the native names of the blacks here. I found afterwards that they had given me wrong names; and, on asking the reason why, was informed they had two or three names, but they never mentioned their right name for fear any one got it when they would die.

With regard to the list of words, I found sometimes, when they had more than one word to express the same thing, that the other word related to something else. For instance, the word "brother;" they gave me the words *Thandhagunert* and *Thandhay*, which means an elder brother, while *Brammun* means a younger brother; and the word "mother"—*Yackan* and *Loombaruk;* the latter word refers to a mother's sister. While the mother is alive her sister is called *Preppa yackan*—that is, another mother—but when she is dead the *Preppa yackan* is changed to *Loombaruk*. Again, the kangaroo is called *Jirrah*, and also *Pangilowertan;* the latter word refers to the animal when he is full of grass, looking corpulent. I have found no words exactly to express mercy, justice, faith, and other words which it is so necessary for

Missionaries to know. I found a word among the Murray blacks to express compassion for anything; it is *Thangan-appel*, a word equal to "bowels of mercy," but literally it is the liver, as *Thanganya* refers exclusively to the liver, and all the affections are placed there, as *Thangan patolana*, to be hungry, *Thangan thillia*, to be hard-hearted or strong in the liver, &c. The above word is the only one I have met which expresses any feeling of compassion. With regard to "justice," I have not found a word to express it, though the blacks in this district have the word *Na-a* to express satisfaction when justice is done. The word "faith" I do not think is represented at all; they merely say, if they believe a person, "You are telling the truth," or, *vice versâ*, "You are telling a lie."

I hope I have given you the information you require. Should you again need my services, I may state I shall be happy to get all the information I can.

I have the honor to be, Sir,
Faithfully yours,
JOHN BULMER.

R. Brough Smyth, Esq.,
Secretary to Central Board for Protection of Aborigines.

The Bundhul Wark Kani, the Swan Reach Tribe.

English.	Australian.	English.	Australian.
Man	Brah, bragnolo.	Moon	Nerran, waan.
Woman	Woorcat.	Star	Brael, tirnmil.
Father	Mungan, mamang.	Night	Bookang, lallat, booknat.
Mother	Yackan, wandack.	Day	Wurrin.
Son	Latheba, gnowia.	Fire	Towera, kumballan.
Daughter	Turtbackan, tharagunang.	Air	Watputjan.
Sister	Landhagunert, tatagunert.	Wind	Krowero.
Brother	Tandhagunert, gnuloi.	Earth	Wrah, mundhukan
Head	Purk, gnowang, whyera.	Ground	Mrairra.
Hair	Lit, mundha-mundha.	Soil	Same as ground.
Eye	Mri, meragut.	River	Bowgari, warndwan.*
Ear	Wring, nucko-nucko.	Sea	Waring, nerkubundha.†
Mouth	Kaat, gna-angat.	Stone	Wallung, nerowera.
Tongue	Jelline, mambarrang.	Tree	Nlappur, kunbal.
Teeth	Nerndack, yadat.	Wood	Kallack.
Hand	Bret, yowan, gnarranman.	Stick	Kallack.
Finger nails	Tagara, bret.	Bird	Tarlo jaak (small meat).
Toe	Tagara, jaan.	Egg	Bo-yang, tha, thuja.
Foot	Jaan.	Snake	Kalang, thurrung.
Belly	Bullon, wertan, tarndan.	Eagle	Quornamero, thuronack.
Blood	Karndobarra, krook, nurruk.	Crow	Wa-gara, gnuro-jal.
Bone	Bring.	Mopoke	Wokuk, abin.
Sun	Wurrin, kalyarro.	Kangaroo	Jirrah.

* The word *Warndwan* is at present not used on account of the death of a black. I was told the word in confidence; I was not to repeat it again.

† The word *Nerkubundha* refers to its being boundless. When they look upon the sea and see no trees, they say *Nerk ubundha!* The sea-water is called *Karrang-garrang*, on account of its bad taste.

DECLENSION OF NOUN, USE OF POSSESSIVE PRONOUN, ETC.

The following papers were prepared at my request by the gentlemen whose names appear at the head of each list:—

(FROM THE REV. A. HARTMANN, LAKE HINDMARSH.)

English.	Native.
I see an opossum	*Nyängan wille.* See I opossum.
An opossum is eating the leaves	*Janga willetch gera.* Eating opossum leaves.
The tail of an opossum	*Berehi wille.* Tail opossum.
I gave leaves to an opossum	*Woyinan gerang* wille.* Gave I leaves to opossum.
I took the food from an opossum	*Märinan banyim willenyung.* Took I food opossum from.
The heart in an opossum	*Woityibük mangaga willejal.* Heart inside opossum.
I found a young one with an opossum	*Moityinan watyibi wille bapanyuck.* Found I young one opossum mother with.

English.	Native.		English.	Native.
Hand	*Manya.* Hand.		Their hands	*Manyanganak.** Hands their.
My hand	*Manyangek.** Hand my.		Tree	*Kalk.* Tree.
His hand	*Manyanyuk.* Hand his, *or* of him.		A tree	*Kiapi kalk.* A (*or* one) tree.
Her hand	Same.		The tree	*Nyninma kalk.* The tree.
Your hand	*Manyangin.** Hand your.		This tree	*Ginma kalk.* This tree.
Hands	*Manya.* Hands.		That tree	Same as the tree.
My hands	Same as singular.		Trees	Same as tree.
His hands	Same as singular.		The trees	Same as the tree.
Her hands	Same as singular.		Some trees	*Kiap-kiap kalk.* Some trees.
Your hands	Same as singular.			

* *Ng* as in "sing."

(FROM THE REV. JOHN BULMER, LAKE TYERS, GIPPSLAND.)

English.	Native.
I see an opossum	*Tahana wadthan.* See I opossum.
An opossum is eating the leaves	*Dhanda wadthanda jerrang.* Eating opossum an leaves.
The tail of an opossum	*Wreka wadthanda.* Tail opossum.
I gave leaves to an opossum	*Ukatha jerrang wadthango.* Gave I leaves opossum to.

LANGUAGE.

English	Native
I took the food from an opossum	*Kinnya nath lak thunga wanga wadthana.* Took I food from an opossum.
The heart in an opossum	*Päpaka wadthanda manyina.* Heart opossum in an.
I found a young one with an opossum	*Mulbana latha wadthana uanga yakanart.* Found I young opossum with mother its.

English.	Native.
Hand	*Bret.*
My hand	*Bretitha.* Hand my.
His hand	*Bretha.* Hand his.
Her hand	*Bretha nungowa.* Hand hers.
Your hand	*Bretjinna.* Hand yours.
Hands	No plural form. Would be expressed thus: One hand, two hand, or many hand. Thus: *Kootopana bret*, one hand; *Boolomana bret*, two hand; *Yail bret*, many hand.
My hands	*Bret bathal.* Hand mine.
His hands	*Bret kinna.* Hand his.
Her hands	*Bretha.* Hand hers.

English.	Native.
Your hands	*Bret githa kara.* Hand of yours.
Their hands	*Brethana.* Hand theirs.
Tree	*Nyleppur uatti.* Wood great.
A tree	*Kallak jinanna.* Wood that is.
The tree	*Ngarra kallak.* The tree or wood.
This tree	*Dinthaka kallak.* This tree.
That tree	*Maudthaka kallak.* That tree.
Trees	*Yail kallak.* Many tree.
The trees	*Manyina nara kallak.* That is the tree.
Some trees	*Wagut kallah.* Some trees.

(FROM THE REV. F. A. HAGENAUER, LAKE WELLINGTON, GIPPSLAND.)

English.	Native.
I see an opossum	*Takana wadthan.* See I opossum.
An opossum is eating the leaves	*Daanda wadthando yerrang.* Eating opossum leaves.
I gave leaves to an opossum	*Ukatha yerrang wadthango.* Gave I leaves opossum to.
The tail of an opossum	*Wrecka wadthanda.* Tail opossum.
I took the food from an opossum	*Kinnga nattack thunga uango wadthana.* Took I food from an opossum.
The heart in an opossum	*Papaka wadthunda manyina.* Heart opossum in an.
I found a young one with an opossum	*Mulbani latha wadthunda wanga yackan.* Found I young opossum with mother.

English.	Native.
Hand	*Bret.*
My hand	*Bretitaa.* Hand my.
His hand	*Breta.* Hand his.
Her hand	*Breta nungowa.* Hand her.

English.	Native.
Your hand	*Bretyina.* Hand you.
Hands	*Yail bret.* Many hand. (No plural.)
His hands	*Bret kinna.* Hands his.

THE ABORIGINES OF VICTORIA:

English.	Native.	English.	Native.
Her hands	Breta. Hands her.	This tree	Dintacha kallack. This tree.
Your hands	Bretgitaa kara. Hand yours.	That tree	Mandacka kallack. That tree.
Their hands	Bretana. Hand theirs.	Trees	Yail kallack. Many trees.
Tree	Ngleppaa watty. Wood great.	The trees	Mangina nara kallack. That is the tree.
A tree	Kallack yennana. Tree that is a.	Some trees	Wangoot kallack. Some trees.
The tree	Ngara kallack. The tree.		

(FROM MR. JOHN GREEN, CORANDERRK, UPPER YARRA.)

English.	Native.
I see an opossum	Walert ngangonin. Opossum see an I.
An opossum is eating the leaves	Ba walert tangerboon moorrin da. Is opossum eating leaves the.
The tail of an opossum	Walert kanee moocborren. Opossum the tail of.
I gave leaves to an opossum	Yurama din benjeroo moorrin da walert. Gave I two leaves to opossum.
I took the food from an opossum	Konga din tangee ba walert on. Took I food from opossum an.
The heart in an opossum	Daronggo me walert da. Heart in opossum the.
I found a young one with an opossum	Brimbonga din walert booboop nga look. Found I opossum young one with.

English.	Native.	English.	Native.
Hand	Manang.	Their hands	Noot to manang. Their hand.
My hand	Manangeek. Hand my.	Tree	Tarang. Tree.
His hand	Manangoo. Hand his.	A tree	
Her hand	Jedo manangoo. Her hand.	The tree	Kanee tarang. The tree.
Your hand	Manango jenna. Hand your.	This tree	Mance tarang. This tree.
Hands	Benjeroo manang. Two hand.	That tree	Managa tarang. That tree.
My hands		Trees	Tarang benjeroo. Tree two.
His hands		The trees	
Her hands		Some trees	Youange tarang.
Your hands			

LANGUAGE.

YARRA TRIBE.

The following vocabulary of the language of the tribe of Aborigines inhabiting the River Yarra, and a few short sentences in the native tongue, with translations, were compiled by Mr. John Green, the Inspector of Aboriginal Stations in Victoria.

English.	Native.
Abandon	*Waltan'i.*
Abate	*Wykrook.*
Abdomen	*Boojin.*
Abed	*Karenboon.*
Abhor	*Booang.*
Ability	*Balet'tak.*
Abject	*Nulim.*
Able	*Kyinandoo.*
Ablution	*Karwarboun.*
Abolish	*Meleemak.*
Abominable	*Booang.*
Abortion	*Nitprang'i.*
About (near)	*Kyn'oo.*
Above	*Koov-ee.*
Absent (in mind)	*Abenden ngargit.*
Absent (not here)	*Yani'jak.*
Abstain	*Nin'wilt-teni.*
Abuse (v. to abuse)	*Nilimjak.*
Accelerate	*Woonudongnak.*
Accept	*Wandan-nata.*
Accidentally	*Nyabenden-ngain'gi.*
Accommodation	*Milliptah.*
Accompany	*Yané bangal.*
Accomplish	*Moongkanin.*
Accusation	*Malle tombangin.*
Adjoin	*Nalléi jerring.*
Adjourn	*Waltan'i.*
Adjudge	*Kooptoon-nga-ge.*
Admire	*Boorndup.*
Admit	*Tylbydin.*
Adoption	*Wangoong'i.*
Adorn	*Tirredoon-boorndoen.*
Adult	*Karre-nen.*
Adulterate	*Boorroam.*
Adulterer	*Barmeen.*
Away	*Yan'i.*
Babbler	*Yar'an-nul.*
Babe	*Booboop.*
Bachelor	*Yan'yean.*
Back	*Ngark.*
Backbite	*Perangoolin.*
Bad	*Nilim.*
Bag	*Bilang.*
Bait	*Toorron.*
Bake	*Nangeebuk.*
Bald	*Taweet.*
Bare	*Yearrn.*

English.	Native.
Barefoot	*Yearrnjenong.*
Bashful	*Wiling-jek.*
Bat	*Boléang.*
Battle	*Jelpchering.*
Bawl	*Marr-roong.*
Beak	*Bargimboon.*
Beard	*Ngarrin.*
Beat	*Tingkurtini.*
Bee	*Manerlony.*
Beef	*Bulgana.*
Begone	*Yane-toee.*
Belong	*Noogal.*
Bewail	*Marroen.*
Beyond	*Kaberring.*
Birds	*Queep-queep.*
Birth	*Tongberang'i.*
Bitter	*Balim-balim.*
Black	*Woogar'ring* or *Koonarrtbeen.*
Bladder	*Balk.*
Blind	*Bamooen.*
Blood	*Goorrk.*
Blue	*Woorrkarreen.*
Blunt	*Warrup.*
Boat	*Koorong.*
Body	*Toolcroom.*
Bone	*Nea'ling'o.*
Boot	*O'look* or *jenongolook.**
Bosom	*Birring.*
Bottom	*Moom.*
Boy	*E'an'in.*
Brain	*Torn'do'un.*
Brat	*Nilinjak.*
Bread	*Noorong.*
Breast	*Brim-brim.*
Breath	*Nga-angò.*
Breathing	*Wan-ang-goon.*
Bring	*Wan'da-gat.*
Brother	*Bang-gan'oo.*
Brow	*Meené-an.*
Brown	*Yalleen.*
Bucket	*Tarrnook.*
Build	*Ngi-a-yat.*
Burn	*Nang-goun.*
Bustard	*Warrn-murn.*
Butterfly	*Balam-balam.*
Buttock	*Jerrar-nu.*

* *Jenong is foot.*

THE ABORIGINES OF VICTORIA:

English.	Native.	English.	Native.
Canoe	Koorong.	Daughter	Meeng-gip.
Cap	Kamper kaóng.	Daunt	Bamboon.
Carve (wood)	Néaroo.	Dauntless	Ngabon-bamboon.
Cat	Be'de dil.	Dawn (of day)	Brarungun.
Catch	Bangagat.	Day	Karremeen.
Cave	Merring-jak-horen.	Daybreak	Brarungun.
Centre	Bagora.	Daylight	Weandahgoongen.
Change	Wookè hirè-bang-al.	Dead	Wykit.
Chant	Engeng.	Deaf	N'gawoon.
Charcoal	Kanendurr.	Dear	Yeadabilling
Chat	Toomjerring bolin.	Debase	Nilimjak-kooroo'gi.
Cheek	Wangò.	Debate	Tomehringnin.
Child	Boopoop, or Boopup, or Booboop.	Decamp	Waltani.
		Decay	Buderanangi.
Choke	Gather-moun.	Deceit	Manerang-ngoon.
Clay	Bigoorn.	Deck (to dress)	Kun-berrbay.
Clean	Barmberring.	Deep	Boon-gim.
Climb	Warrnagat.	Defeat	Kinandak-koongnoon.
Coat	Goattak.	Defend	Moorrndak-koongadán.
Cold	Mooter ween.	Defile (v. to defile)	Nilimjak-kooroo'gi.
Colic	Jerren-nen.	Defy	Kinandah-koongnoon.
Come	Wandeat.	Delicious	Yering yim.
Comfort	Boordup.	Deliver	Moorrndak-koongad'an.
Coming	Boorrnoone.	Demon	Ngurrang.
Conjoin	Jerrboongun.	Dent	Barrip.
Converse	Toomcherring.	Deny	Ngabeden-dak.
Cord	Woodol-woodol.	Depart	Yeanéato.
Corn (on foot, &c.)	Berrpeet.	Descend	Barrawee.
Corpse	Werrgabil.	Desire	Indankoongnunjunu.
Costive	Balert-tak.	Destroy	Jel'bud'ool.
Cough	Koonin-goon.	Dew	Warroong.
Cramp	Jennaboorré.	Dim	Boorreen.
Crane	Karween (the first man).	Din	Tallgarru.
Create (to make)	Boocegigat.	Dinner	Tangerboon.
Creator (maker of all things)	Bunjel.	Dirge	Toomé karra nun.
		Dirt	Mun-neep.
Creek	Gurrnoong.	Dirty	Nilimjak.
Creep	Derrindoen.	Discomfort	Jeengngaring.
Creeping	Derrinjee.	Discontent	Wakè karroong ngon.
Cripple	Ngarrboun.	Dish	Wilin-wilin.
Crooked	Wanderring.	Ditty (song)	Engeng.
Crow	Wang (the second man).	Dive	Gorron goun.
Cruel	Nilimjak-hoorring.	Divide	Loong-goonak.
Cry	Marroun.	Dizzy	Ngiren-nen.
Cudgel	Kudjerrong.	Do	Jneeng-gooak.
Cut	Bendi.	Doctor	Werrerup.
Cutting	Bendadol.	Dog	Earingin.
Damage	Nilim.	Down	Be or we.
Damp	Taban.	Drag	Koorbi-gat.
Damsel	Burnnè or moonmoondik.	Dread	Bamboon.
Dance	Ngarry'eè	Dream	Yioohgen.
Danger	Nilim.	Dress	Boodin-gin.
Daring	Ngabon-bamboon.	Drink	Obá-gat.
Dark	Booreen.	Dry	Goon-boon-noon.
Darling	Yadabiling.	Duck	Toolim.
Dastard	Bamboon.	Dull	Deem-deen-dak.

LANGUAGE.

English.	Native.
Dung	Koonoong.
Dust	Maneep.
Dwarf	Moorec.
Dwelling	Elim or wil'im.
Dying	Weargarangûon.
Eagle	Bunjel.
Ear	Wooring.
Early	Moolookoo.
Earth	Y'éamen'cenbik.
Ease	Ngawcbi.
Eat	Tangarrbéd.
Eaten	Tangarrbathan.
Edge	Lany'o.
Edging	Ngeroo.
Eel	Eok.
Efface	Woorewogat.
Effects	Nowalekno.
Egg	Dirrandirr.
Eject	Databéágat.
Eke	Permbagat.
Elope	Man'ngan.
Elude	Welipteen.
Emaciate	Nilimjak-korring.
Embrace	Moondani.
Emigrate	Yean'i.
Empty	Tendebik.
Encounter	Toomjerringan.
Encumber	Bardon'ngan.
End	Kangoo.
Ending	Tendebik.
Enjoy	Yarwinboo'dek.
Enlarge	Woorrto-kon'ga-gat.
Every	Yearmeen.
Evident	Iuinburdi.
Evil	Nilimjak-kooring.
Excellent	Qeeing boordup.
Excite	Toomb'igat.
Expend	Tendebik.
Expire	Werrurang-ngon.
Fable	Marrening.
Fact	Twarren-nga-gi.
Fade	Wergi.
Fain	Boodambunin.
Faint-hearted	Bamban.
Fair	Qeeute boordup.
Fall	Baderin boon.
False	Marrcen.
Father	Marmun.
Fame	Boordup.
Fameless	Nilimjak.
Family	Booboop narrkwarren.
Famine	Taong-gan.
Famish	Nerribrenin.
Fancy	Boodamboo'in.
Farewell	Twaginin.
Far	Booér.

English.	Native.
Fast (swift)	Berren-berren.
Fat	Marrimbool.
Father-in-law	Kondo'lang'o.
Fatherless	Moorré.
Fear	Bamboon.
Feast	Tangárbè.
Feeble	Murrineren.
Feed	Tangerboun.
Feel	Bang'adinen.
Feet	Jenongbertoorr.
Feign	Marrnen.
Felon	Nilimjak-koorren.
Female	Badjurr.
Fetch	Windága.
Feud	Wakering.
Few	Wálak-wálak.
Fib	Marrening.
Fiend (bad spirit)	Ngarrong.
Fight	Jeltehering.
Fighter	Koonòmoon.
Fill	Jaboon.
Fire	Ween.
Fish	Malloren.
Fishing	Gooluk-keni.
Flat	Woork.
Flay	Ter'embeyat.
Flea	Moon-ong.
Fleabitten	Boondo'ang moononga.
Flee	Berren-berren.
Flesh	Weeringam.
Flew	Gamagooen.
Fling	Booembegat.
Float	Yarragoon.
Flock	Boolodoon.
Flour	Noorrong.
Flown	Gamagooen.
Fly	Gamagooen.
Fog (mist)	Bowrang.
Folk	Koolinjerrh.
Fond (to love)	Yeadabilin.
Food	Qeeup.
Foot	Jenong.
Footpath	Bajejenoug.
Fop	Toolap.
Forbid	Toomatining-goongak.
Foreknowledge	Ngargoonin twarn.
Forerun	Bamborrnang'i.
Foretell	Toombadinin twarn.
Forget	Nabidin ngaringi.
Fornicator	Barmeen.
Forsake	Yeaninin.
Frail	Marrinernen.
Fret	Wa itken.
Frost	Tangbilk.
Full	Doorneen.
Fume	Booang.

English.	Native.	English.	Native.
Fun	Jellikcha.	Heart	Dorroong.
Fur	Beelyooren.	Heat	Nanger-baun.
Gale	Boolwotò moonmot.	Heavens	Lark.
Gape (to yawn)	Yarramoen.	Heavy	Barnboon goorreen.
Gather	Burgoongagat.	Hell	Nilimjak-yclim.
Gave	Wongadain.	Help	Tamboonamon.
Geese	Bikmoom.	Here (in this place)	Nag-golee or màng.
Girdle	Milargarin.	Hide (keep out of sight)	Willip-keen.
Give	Woonga gat, or umalek, or yumma-leek.	High	Yarrbat.
Glad	Barbornenin.	Hill	Banool.
Glow	Yanggemdakgoon-non.	Ice	Tangbulk.
God	Ronjel.	Idea	Ngang-yarra-moamin-in.
Going	Yan'i.	Identity	Nngalek-ki-noo-changoon-twan taka.
Gone	Yan'i'j.		
Good	Boordup.	Idiot	Nganga-dak-ki-no.
Grandmother	Maloong-goongò.	Ignorant	Intank-a.
Grass	Banneem.	Ill	Cherarmen.
Grasp	Banga-gat.	Ill-nature	Bookquaren.
Grease	Marrambool.	Imbibe	Nuboun.
Great	Boollootò.	Imbolden	Babert-ching-ka.
Greedy	Balert-kang.	Imitate	Burrong-gi.
Green	Woorrwarren or Woorwarreen.	Immediate	Wat-ching-ka.
		Immense	Wourrt-ta-boo.
Greyhead	Lamboun-kawang.	Immerse (cover with water)	Gooroong-ki.
Grim	Nilimjak-koorren.		
Groan	Tirrt-toolcen.	Immovable	Tam-marrneen.
Growl	Wa keen.	Immure (shut in)	Tarrt-koorim-bagat.
Grub	Milerrk.	Impaint	Merrebagat.
Grumble	Wa keen.	Impeach	Ngat-twonan.
Guide	Loorendé-gat.	Impede	Toort-koo-dong-a din.
Gum	Kerrang.	Impel	Urrduk ju-at.
Gun	Trang boolábil.	Impiety	Tankirra-bil.
Ha!	Ki!	Impostor	Marrin-ing-juno.
Haggard	Jeeng-ngarring.	Improve	Marrin-ing.
Hail	Kav-ing.	In	Koorrngee.
Hair	Yarré.	Inconstant	Moor-moor-ween.
Hairy	Moorram-marren.	Increase	Karri-nun.
Half	Marroo.	Incurable	Ngabin-na win.
Hamstring	Karra-gora.	Independent (free)	Yering-garrine.
Hand	Marnong.	Inquire	Bila-doin.
Handful	Jaboon-marnong.	Insane	Anga-woo-in.
Happy	Barrbon-neen.	Insects	Toombak.
Hard	Balert-tak.	Inside	Boojc.
Hark!	Ngarrngak!	Insnare (to catch)	Bang-un.
Haste	Berrn-berrn.	Instantly	Bangoon-narroa.
Hat	Komperkawang.	Insufferable	Man-doin-qua-neen.
Hatchet	Karrgeen.	Insult	Book-o-warren.
Hawk	Bulok-bulok.	Intend	Yan-kranginin.
Head	Kawang.	Intestines	Boore-boore-do.
Headache	Lulerneen-kawang.	Intoxicate	Ngirin-nen.
Headband	Birrbak-kawangin.	Introduce	Geerp.
Heal	Ngarra-jarra-noun.	Invade	Boonbree-kaling-i.
Health	Boon-marrit-tak goorcen.	Invalid	Charen-neen-mel-bo.
Hear	Ngarrn-gak-go.	Invisible	Ngabina-mang-oon.
Hearing	Ngarrngar-boodin.	Invite	Toomba-din-juno.

LANGUAGE. 103

English.	Native.
Ire	Bouk-hooring.
Irregular	Na-boon-tin marr-neen-manee.
Is	Ma-gi-gal.
Island	Ba-gerr-brip.
Jaw	Wang-at-ta.
Jealous	Bang-neen.
Jesting	Laga-ba-boo-en.
Join	Kerr-boo-on-ool.
Joint	Toor-rong.
Joy	Burd-up.
Jugular	Berr-up.
Jump	Yurrm-up.
Kangaroo	Mirrm.
Kangaroos (two)	Mirrm-bootor.
Kangaroos (many)	Mirrm-booloh.
Keep	Murrn-ak.
Kick	Karrak.
Kidney	Marr-up.
Kill	Chil-buk.
Kin	Kerr-up-mon.
Kiss	Moo-porn-dak.
Knee	Barreng.
Kneel	Barreng-ye-gorree.
Knew	Ngarrn-gi.
Knife (sharp stone)	Kal-boon-kal-boon.
Knock	Toondook.
Know	Ngarr-gi.
Lad	Wyu-luk.
Lake	Bol-lok.
Lame	Ngarrboon.
Lament	Woorrbaun.
Land	Bik.
Language	Ngnool.
Large	Woort-to.
Last	Wan-qunde.
Lazy	Wa-boorrn.
Leaf (of tree)	Jerrang.
Leak	Boee-goun.
Leap	Yurnee.
Least	Wy-krook.
Lice	Moon-ong.
Lick	Jam-bak.
Life	Mooroop.
Light	Yu-ang-gim.
Lightning	Derreng-o.
Like	Bootham-narra.
Lip	Woorroong.
Listen	Nyang-gak.
Little	Wy-krook.
Liver	Bootho.
Lizard	Toorrop.
Load	Barn-burn.
Loath	Booang.
Locust	Na lang na lang.
Log	Woorrec-kalk.

English	Native.
Lonesome	Gan-gan.
Long	Boorr.
Longing	Mel-both-a dak-barring.
Look	Nang-nak.
Lost	Yu-burn-angi.
Love	Onem-da.
Low (not high)	Morrt.
Lungs	Woorba-oollook.
Lurk (hide)	Marra-go.
Lying	Karrem-bin.
Mad	Nanga-wo-en.
Made	Ela-mong-gi.
Maggot	Moona long.
Maid	Burnnie.
Malady (sick)	Jerrin-neen.
Man	Kolin or koulin.
Man-eater	Tak-jerran-i-a.
Manful	Boo-gi il.
Manhood	Jeebouak.
Manna	Kun-am boora.
Many	Woort-tin-do.
Mark	Danda-gat.
Marriage	Yuram-magat.
Marrow	Birrm.
Marsh	Tool.
Massacre	Ull-ull.
Mate	Jerrup.
Meat	Queeup.
Melt	Bullan-doon.
Memory	Ngargerr-moon.
Men	Kolin dorr.
Men (two)	Koolin-bootor.
Men (many)	Koolin-boolok.
Met	Nakorany-an-ang.
Meteor	El-a-lang-i.
Midday	Til-ang-ge-karrá-meen.
Midnight	Til-ang-ge-nala-go.
Midway	Bag-garr-doee.
Milk	Brim-brim.
Milky-way	Tirrn-galh.
Mind (my mind)	Nga-ang-garra noominin.
Mine (belonging to me)	Nooga-leek.
Mist	Boorr-arrang.
Mistletoe	Bulee.
Mistake	To-ton-taw-dan.
Mock	Boorr-go-neen.
Moon	Meene-an.
Moonlight	Meene-an-toon.
Mosquito	Go-gook.
Moth	Tarr-ien.
Mother	Báboop.
Mountain	Ngarrak.
Moustaches	Nyarrin.
Mouth	Nga-angdak.
Move	Togip.

English.	Native.
Much	Woot-too-korreen.
Mud	Bey-gooreen.
Murder	Chil-bâ-dol.
Murderer	Moon-a-bil.
Mushroom	Beah-goorn.
Musk-tree	Tall.
Myself	Wan.
Naked	Yerran.
Name	Narreen.
Narrow	Tarri-mang-garr.
Nasty	Bilim-bilim.
Navel	Meendook.
Near	Tang-an-doea.
Neck	Koorra.
Need	Boo-dom-boun.
Neglect	To-yoom-boun.
Nephew	Karri-karri-imboo.
Nest	Elmo-garang.
Net	Garrt-kirrh.
Never	Ta-goong.
News	Kooeeon.
Next	Koon-at-tew.
Nice	Boorrd up.
Night	Boorren-de.
Nimble	Warrk-warrk.
No	Tú-goong.
Noise	Werreng-jerren.
None	Tú-yoo.
North	Win-malee.
Nose	Ká-ang.
Notch	Burrip.
Now	Mangee.
Nurse	Moonda-gat.
Oar	Kana-goo-ulom.
Offer	Toom-bal-ang-anin.
Oft	Mel-boo.
Oil	Yn-nok.
Old	Turrde-boop.
Once	Kooptoon-doe.
One	Kooptoon.
Open	Yurra-me.
Opinion	Moonung-narruhi.
Orator	Moondá toom-dae-neen.
Orphan	Moorree-yak.
Out	Berrnat-to.
Over	Koonda-lût.
Owl	Go-goom.
Pain	Brreng-gerre-neen.
Pair	Boolla-oen.
Palm (of hand)	Boothe-manang.
Pap	Brim-brim.
Papa	Marrn-moon or warree-geek.
Paroquet	Yu boop.
Parrot	Bro-gil.
Part (of anything)	Long-ye-gerre-bi.

English.	Native.
Pay	Murrmoomle-ak.
Peace	Daminon-inon.
Pebble (stone)	Moonowroong.
People	Moorre kolindirr.
Perfect	Tende beck.
Perspire	Mooroun-mooroun.
Piece	Kongi-yik-wy krook.
Pinch	Chile-buh.
Pit	Mirreeng.
Pith (in wood)	Brong-gi.
Play	Chilak-herreng.
Please	Onemdà.
Plenty	Woot-tun-oo.
Plover	Perret-perret.
Point	Chin-chin-mirrn.
Polish	Boornerr-win.
Pregnant	Koonoong-warren.
Press (to squeeze)	Moondak.
Pretty	Burrd up-orren.
Prevent	Me-am bak.
Pride	Doleen.
Promise	Toomballangin.
Protect	Dill-bâ-din.
Provide	Ge-gu-boo-dani.
Provoke	Toomboon e angin.
Pull	Koorr-bak.
Pursue	Tarra-gak.
Putrid	Booderinin.
Puzzle	Nga-boon-din-nga-goen.
Quarrel	Wá-herrá-bil.
Quartz	Barrwong-ge-moong.
Racing	Boon-gerreen.
Rage	Chipjerreng.
Rain	A-l.
Rainbow	Bren be-al.
Ramble	Yabb-lunn.
Rap	Moonee-muk.
Rattle	Moorrá-moorrá.
Raveu	Wâng.
Ready	Jim bree nin.
Receive	Gong a dirr.
Recital	None-ninde-toom-bik.
Recoil	Yurrder-boon.
Rectify	Burdup-tâgo-konga-din.
Red	Grook-warreen or krook-krook warrabil.
Reed	Jerrerr.
Reek (smoke)	Boorrt.
Refresh	Larrge-gi-ang-ing-in.
Regret	Woorr-ba din-dâ.
Reject	Boorrdadin.
Rejoice	Barrboon in in dâ.
Rejoin	Bonde-mah.
Relative (same blood)	Gerrbik.
Relieve	Nga-ongak-kan.

LANGUAGE.

English.	Native.	English.	Native.
Remain	Mang-an.	See	Naug-ak.
Remove	Warrongak.	Seek	Ye-â-yak.
Rend	Torroomuk.	Self	Kanje groong.
Renew	Wa-dam-buk.	Send	Woorree-mak.
Repent	Wilke.	Sepulchre (grave)	Mirreng.
Reply	Toombuk-tâ.	Sew	Marrgak.
Reproach	New-lün-quen-noolin.	Shade	Yunak.
Reprove	Nga-bo-darra-ngugo-konga-da.	Shame	Wol-anin.
		Shell	Tal-lang.
Resound	Karang krom-ya breen.	Shin	Kal-ge-grang.
Rest	Nga-we.	Shine	Bathel-moon.
Restless	Wilke-wilke ni-e-â.	Short	Morrt.
Retrace	Nook-kindan-twakin-a-â.	Shoulder	Ngang-gerr.
Retract	Twa-gorrak-ngooleen.	Shower	Che-brong.
Reward	Mabrim-boon-neen.	Shrub	Yerrin.
Rib	Darrneen.	Shut	Tootkorak.
Right	Boordup.	Shy	Bam-be.
Rigid	Balerrt.	Sick	Cherrin-neen.
Rip	Berre-muk.	Side	Marr.
Ripe	Toegocen.	Sigh	Nyanat-â.
Rise	Koma-gee.	Sinew	Berr boo.
Road	Parreng.	Sing	Engeng.
Roast	Nang-am-buk.	Sister	Lâtingata.
Rock	Moojerr.	Sit	Nyalimbe.
Rod	Parrim.	Skin	Morrok.
Root	Werrook.	Skull	Galk-ka-áng.
Rope	Woodel-woodel.	Sky	Woorrworrâ.
Rotten	Boderrin-in.	Slay	Gil-boak.
Rough	Newlim-grook.	Sleep	Ngi-gool.
Round	Wallan-wallan.	Sleepy	Bonde-ang-nan-ngi-golt la.
Rug	Tadool-todool.	Sleet	Kabbing.
Rumbling	Moorrn-moon.	Slender	Kalk-kalk-mirrin broong.
Run	Worre wee.	Slip	Borror goidin.
Runaway	Worrar-anginee.	Slow	Bidjit-bidjit.
Sad	Woorrboon.	Small	Wy krook.
Said	Mallee-go-ia.	Smoke	Boorrt.
Same	Noone-in-de.	Snake	Koormiel.
Sand	Breg-gerr.	Snore	Newaragolin.
Sang	Engi.	Snow	Kabbing.
Sap	Doo-â-no.	Soft	Dogil-dugil.
Sarsaparilla	Wattee-mulleen.	Some	Wonga geek.
Sassafras	Ching koong.	Something	Ngin-ing-oo-milla.
Sat	Ngorrn-i.	Son	Boo-boo-gorrt.
Satan	Ngorrang.	Sou-in-law	Koon-de-loug.
Satisfy	Twarn-de-groong.	Song	Enguk-eng-eng.
Save	Murr-mak.	Soon	Moolo-ko.
Saw	Ngany-â-din.	Soot	Woogarrâ-bil.
Say	Any-ing-uar-goen.	Sorry	Woobedin.
Scab	Ba-borrom.	Soul	Moorop.
Scabby	Ba-brom â olok.	Sour	Karrm-karrm.
Scar	Boorran.	South	Mirreen or wa-boorn.
Scare	Noorrbil-bong-ak.	Spark	Be-be dinen.
Scatter	Ki-e bo-ling-go-â grak.	Spawn (of fish)	Drre-drre-mâlun.
Sea	Bullim-be warreen.	Speak	Toom-nee.
Secure	Moong-moong-gak.	Spear	Dúrr.
Seed	Koorr.	Speed	Wondil.

VOL. II. O

THE ABORIGINES OF VICTORIA:

English.	Native.
Spend	Loott koradin.
Spew	Koorr-mi.
Spit	Jug-an-dak.
Spittle	Ká-gooll.
Split	Lal go-mak.
Spoke	Toom nangi.
Sport	Likje bi.
Spring (of water)	Bun-ding.
Spy (a)	Merrtt.
Squat	Brrim-brrim.
Squeeze	Moon-dak.
Squint	Ngut-warra-mirreng.
Stab	Dorr-gi.
Stake	Ngarrm bool.
Stand	Tarre-dee.
Star	Toorrt.
Stare	Tan-gong-i.
Start	Noorrp-tang-a-din.
Steep	Moorr.
Stench	Boo-ang.
Stick	Kalk.
Stiff	Yul-orrt-ten.
Still-born	Weah a bil-mamboodil.
Sting	Birringun.
Stomach	Ba-boogoorrn.
Stone	Moojerr.
Stoop	Mije korree.
Stream	Wane-wan.
Stride	Yulerrt-te.
Strife	Boomool-lunga dool.
String	Purrt-tean.
Strong	Ballerrt.
Struck	Chil-bi-eng-an.
Stupid	Nang-â-ween.
Subtle	Err-neen-bordon-munee.
Suck	Brim-buk.
Suffocate	Moom-goonga-nool.
Sulky	Chipjerreng.
Summer	Ngumi-e-ak-korreen.
Sun	Ngumi.
Sunburnt	Nangi-ngumeâ.
Sung	We-eng-â-din.
Sunk	Kan-dongadin.
Sunrise	Bukje-korreen-ngumi.
Sunset	Kroong kontew-ngumi.
Sunshine	Birkjen-ngumi.
Supple	Doober-doober.
Suppurate	Karre noon.
Sure	New-noon.
Surfeit	Ebeing-god-a-din.
Swallow	Bett-bett ngom bil.
Swam	Erra ga din.
Swamp	Boollok.
Swan	Goon â-warr.
Sweat	Moorreen-moorreen.
Sweet	Doo-en.

English.	Native.
Swim	Erra-ge.
Swing	Boorra-boorra ben.
Tail	Mooee boo.
Take	Kongak.
Talk	Toom-nee.
Talking	Toom-nangi.
Tall	Krang-niel.
Taste	Barra-dak.
Tattle	Erraneen-barrong-neen.
Tears	Pawnje mirreng.
Teeth	Leeang.
Tell	Toom-buk.
Tempest	Wett-mulleen.
Tendon	Beerip.
Terror	Bambadin.
Testicles	Moortt.
Thanks	Ngoon godjin.
That	Kon-nooe.
The	Gee.
Their	Mallee goblin.
Thief	Be at tangi.
Thigh	Ngarrge jerrin.
Thin	Gal-gal mirran.
Thirsty	Kon bon-non.
Thistle	Brugl-brugl.
Thorn	Warr.
Those	Waooll.
Thought	Non noo-ngarrang-kana noo-noon.
Three	Boollo-ween-bagoop.
Throw	Bo-em badin.
Throat	Korren.
Thumb	Ba-bo-ún marnang.
Thunder	Woonda bil.
Thy	Wan.
Tie	Berrbak.
To	Kondee.
Told	Toomba-dool.
Tomahawk	Karrgeing.
To-morrow	Yeram-boo-ee.
Tongue	Jällin.
Top	Koong-jerrang.
Topple	Baderrambe.
Torn	Toorrm-toorrm-mi.
Tortoise	Bundabun.
Track	Barreng.
Travail	Mam-badool.
Travel	Yanon-inon.
Traveller	Bren-nonooll.
Tree	Kalk or bajerrang.
Tribe	Marra-nee-guna-guna.
Trick	Ngon-bong-ngak.
Tripe	Brra-brra-doo.
Trouble	Wabong-ngon-boo-jeek.
True	Goon-golong-ngi.
Trust	Tarrn-doon-nonin.

English.	Native.
Try	Bramuk.
Tumour	Karre-ni.
Turn	Wilke.
Twilight	Ban-bam-errim.
Twist	Minak.
Two	Bolloween.
Ugly	Jeng-yerring.
Ulcer	Boom-borre-meang.
Unable	Mon-tooleen-narr.
Unborn	Nabadool-man-na-gi.
Unclean	Intarr-worra-baleen.
Under	Koon-doe.
Understand	Nyang-kon-narr-an ta.
Uneasy	New lim-tea-korre nin.
Uneaten	Nga-be-din-tangerr-bi.
Uneven	Nga-boun-bolin-tarrengbren or wan-wan-dirra-bil.
Unfair	Ngaboon-noon-koorreen.
Unfaithful	Marrangi.
Unfasten	Boodvom-ngak-kannooi.
Unfit	Nilimjak.
Unfold	Boo-dong-nak or boorm-mak.
Unfortunate	Mirrinta kooangdin.
Unfrequent	Ngabondu koojetanin.
Unhappy	Nga-be-din-da-wang-een.
Unite	Boonde-mak ballettak.
Unjust	Wy-hoorong koogajeh.
Unkind	Nga-boun-da, or burrd-up korre-nowee, or ngaboon-boodom-babon.
Unseen	Nga-be-din-da-nang-i.
Unsound	Boodorranin.
Untrue	Man-in-da.
Untruth	Man-in-da.
Unweary	Nga-be-din-da-wa-borreen.
Unwelcome	Nga-be-din-da-boodom-boun.
Unwell	Nillamturrong.
Up	Koobi.
Uphill	Wangerrip.
Upper	Kabbareng.
Upright	Utten.
Uprise	Kooma-ge-hoobi.
Upward	Kabbareng.
Urine	Ballge.
Us	Wy.
Uvula	Doo-mak.
Vale (a valley)	Doon-ngorrm.
Vanish	Euk-bood-eng-ngi.
Vapour	Boorrong.
Vast	Woorr-woorr.
Vein	Barring-ge krook-nat.
Venom	Bon-non-gi.
Verdant	Woon-waren.

English.	Native.
Vexed	Chip-jerrbiengin.
Vile	Newlum.
Villain	Nullim.
Virgin	Burne-burne.
Visible	Nga-ga-din.
Visit	Du-wan-koo-nongi.
Voice (sound emitted by the mouth)	Ngoloo or in-nong-ool-toom-neen.
Vomit	Krrum-mee.
Wail (lamentation)	Jale marrn-ngol.
Wailing	Mamjerring.
Wake	Tarra be
Walk (v.)	Yan.
Wand (a small stick)	Jerrer.
Wandering	Yalbilum-korrneen.
Want	Nono-no-bodom-boun.
War	Ngulang.
War (s.)	Terrok-trangi.
Warm	Toom-badin.
Wart	Perrpe.
Waste (to diminish or spend)	Toorongjering-noorong.
Water (s.)	Paen.
Water (fresh)	Paen.
Water (salt, as of the sea)	Palem warren.
Wattle (the tree so called)	Kirrang.
Wax (s.)	Bejering.
We	Wat.
Weak	Barrbontak-korreen.
Wear (to waste)	Tooroongjering-noorong.
Weather (the state of the air)	Berring tak.
Weep (to shed tears)	Eb-ngoling.
Welcome (kind reception)	Womin je ka.
Well (a spring of water)	Ban-ding.
Well (not sick)	Boordup tak kooreen.
Wet (rainy, moist)	Karrgaling.
Whale (a large fish)	Be-ti-el.
What (p.)	Ining-jak.
Wheeze (v.)	Kart tirring.
Whelp (a puppy dog)	Boobop yerranginin.
When	Narooe.
Whence	Inongo.
Whenever	Moolok rangino.
Where	Intoorring.
Whereabouts	Intoorring.
Whet (to sharpen)	Kirk-kirk-konak.
Which	Wenerop.
While	Kooingkoono-angin.

English.	Native.	English.	Native.
Whirring (noise by a bird's wing)	Kart-tirring.	Word (part of speech)	Ngol.
Whisper (a low voice)	Bran-bran-koejuraboline.	World (the earth)	Beek tak maen.
		Worm	Torro.
Whistle (the sound made by the lips)	Dort tangia.	Worse	Nulim.
		Would	Koodong-ninerr.
White	Lamboorreen.	Wound (s.)	Meangatta.
Whither	Either.	Wrangle (to dispute)	Toorerup.
Who	Ela.		
Whole	Luttrin-nangi.	Wrap (to roll together)	Mone-mone mak.
Whose	Edal.		
Why	Ain-ing-tali.	Wrath	Boogil.
Wide	Wilt-korring.	Wrench (to pull forcibly)	Koorrbak.
Widow	Moolin grook.		
Widower	Wurrbil.	Wrest (to twist)	Koorrbak.
Wife	Brimbano.	Wriggle (to move to and fro)	Borrtjerin bolan.
Will (choice, command)	Ngabedin.		
		Wring (to twist)	Mim nak.
Win (to win a game)	Toengorrt tani.	Wrinkle (as in the face)	Nanborrjerin.
Wince (to shrink with pain)	Wan-noonin.	Wrist	Ngoangnatta.
		Writhe (to distort)	No word.
Wind (n.)	Moonmoot.		
Winding (turning about)	Winder-boring.	Wrong (s.)	Nullimdak.
		Wry (crooked)	Wy-drring.
Windy	Kooreentak-korranen.	Yam (the root so called)	Barrm.
Wing (part of a bird)	Turago.		
		Yawn (to gape)	Yerram-yerram mooni.
Wink (to shut the eyes)	Milip-milip-boni.	Yell (to make a noise)	Karrim-neen.
Winter	Berrentak.	Yellow	Babedirreen.
Wish (longing, desire)	Intak-kongi.	Yelp (to yelp as a dog)	Warram boorboon.
Wish (to have a strong desire)	Intak-kongi.	Yes	Ngie.
		Yesterday	Yollinkoe.
Withhold	Twabongon.	Yet (nevertheless)	Kooing.
Within	Mangkie.	Yield (to produce)	Woort tanoo.
Wires	Boolim-korrttin.	You	Warr.
Woe	Woo.	Young (not old)	Tarrango.
Woman	Daggarrook or bajor.	Young (the offspring of any creature)	Booboopreek.
Womanhood	Woortbarrmgrookje.		
Womankind	Woortbarrmgrookje.		
Womb	Korreen-korreen-noo.	Your	In or din; your hand, manongin.
Women	Woortanobajer.		
Women (two)	Baggarrook-bootor or bajor-bootor.	Youth (a young person)	Wylak.
Women (many)	Baggarrook-boolok.	Youthful	Yean yan.
Wonder (s.)	Inta-barra kong-gani juno.	Zeal	Toolangi.
Wood (a forest)	Kalk.	Zig-zag (winding)	Toonda nulm buting ta kojen.
Wood-ashes	Bona be maneep.		

The plural of all living creatures is expressed by adding "*bootor*" if only two, and "*boolok*" when more than two, to the singular noun.

The plural of nouns—of stone, stick, star, &c., &c.—is expressed by adding *pirm*. Thus—

Stone	-	Lung.	Sticks	Kalk-pirm.
Stones	-	Lung-pirm.	Star	Turrt.
Stick	-	Kalk.	Stars	Turrt-pirm.

LANGUAGE.   109

The sexes are distinguished by adding "*ly-goon*" (male), and "*booner*" (female). Thus—

Male kangaroo   -   *Mirrm-ly-goon.* | Female kangaroo   -   *Mirrm-booner.*

Possession is indicated thus—

Stick my   -   -   *Kalk-eek.* | Stick his   -   -   -   *Kalk-o.*

English.	Native.
My hand	*Manang-eek.*
My hands	*Benjere manang-eek.*
My foot	*Jenang-eek.*
My feet	*Benjere jenong-eek.*
My leg	*Jerring-eek.*
My legs	*Benjere jerring-eek.*
My head	*Ka ang-eek.*
My body	*Miram-eek.*
My hair	*Yarr-eek.*
My eyes	*Mirring-eek.*
My ears	*Wering-eek.*
My nose	*Kang-eek.*
My teeth	*Leang-eek.*
My mouth	*Nanda-eck.*
My lips	*Worang-eek.*
Your hand	*Manang ng na.*
Your hands	*Benjere manang ingna.*
Their hands	*Manang noota me kia weet.*
My horse	*Katadarnook-eek.*
Your horse	*Kata darnook ingna.*
My house	*Willim-eek.*
Your house	*Willim mina.*
Their house	*Noota kia weet willim.*
My dog	*Maramb-eek warraing.*
My kangaroo	*Miramb-eek koue em* or *quoo-eem.*
My face	*Meni ba gan-eek.*
Man	*Kolin.*
Old man	*Weekubil.*
Young man	*Yean in.*
Grandfather	*Biring groong.*
Father	*Marman.*
Father-in-law	*Gonkilang.*
Stepfather	*Yuong-marman.*
Husband	*Naing groong.*
Widower	*Warbil.*
Son	*Mamam moo.*
Son-in-law	*Karry-karry imboo.*
Brother	*Wondowlong* or *bang gan.*
Brother-in-law	*Kooreit.*
Stepbrother	*Tuti.*
Uncle	*Garrgook.*
Nephew	*Woorning.*
Cousin	*Beeninang.*
Woman	*Baggarrook.*
Old woman	*Moondegrook.*
Young woman	*Moondik.*
Girl	*Moon-moondik.*
Children	*Booboop nark.*
Grandmother	*Maling tra.*

English.	Native.
Mother	*Pa-pa.*
Stepmother	*Wardè grook.*
Wife	*Brim bin.*
Widow	*Bundun grook.*
Daughter	*Mang keep* or *kerin.*
Sister	*Lee woork.*
Sister-in-law	*Yum murrk.*
Aunt	*Bum boora.*
Niece	*Ba pi.*
Wedding	*Karbo baggarrook yeram mial.*
Friend	*Kireep.*
Ancestors	*Lee wik.*
Tribe	*Nara nce kanie-kanie.*
I hear	*Nyarnkadin.*
They hear	*Noollang ngarngit.*
We hear	*Ngargian.*
Come	*Warry wec.*
I come	*Ye'ye'yan ue won.*
We come	*Brenen ngan.*
Go	*Berr yance.*
I go	*Malan yanéá.*
We go	*Berr yanee bit.*
They go	*Yanina moonaga.*
I am going	*Wentoom moang yaninin.*
We are going	*Wendit ka yanin.*
They are going	*Yanooyul moonaga.*
Give me a stone	*Koongageek lung.*
Give him a stone	*Koongogoona lung.*
I gave you some water	*Woongana ngalun bawn.*
I will not give you some water	*Ngidibaner nelena woongana bawn yeóta.*
Give me some bread	*Koontabageek noorong.*
We will give you a stick	*Woongana ngana kalk.*
We will not give you a stick	*Ngabeninalina woongan kalk.*
Give me some bread to eat, I am hungry	*Woongageek noorong nery bery nen.*
This is my hand	*Kabbe marnong-eek.*
Sing me a song	*E'ingook e ing e ing.*
Where is your father?	*Intoom marman?*
He is my father	*Myo marman.*
My father is here	*Marman-eek myo.*
He is not my father	*Ngaboon myo marmaneek.*
We drink water	*Nyobenin bawn.*
My brother has a long arm	*Panggangen-eek nerem tarago.*
My sister is very tall	*Leearook-cek nerem ta.*
He has two children	*Benjeroo booboop.*
The sun is rising	*Naween wary ween.*

110   THE ABORIGINES OF VICTORIA:

English.	Native.	English.	Native.
The sun is set	Naween koorgoén.	I am well	Burdup koory enin.
It is raining	Purmen bawn.	Take a stick and beat the dog.	Koongak kalk teilbok.
It is a fine day	Naweenda.		
It is a cold day	Moater boon pan'dill.	The dog is beaten with a stick.	Teibok kaka kalk.
It is frosty	Tang billk.		
It is snowing	Kuving.	Where are you going? Wether yanon?	
That is a fine tree	Burdup tirang.	I am going to the mountain.	Yanenin-nagara goit.
That is good grass	Burdup booit.		
I am sick	Tae win.		

A kangaroo is feeding in the scrub.
   Quooeem   tangarboom   yerrin oot.

Get me my spear and I will kill him.
   Konga gee   daruk   pardé-yan.

I have killed him.
   Malanong pardé-ya.

Let us roast him and eat him.
   Perr   toncebit   tangé it.

One of us will go down the creek.
   Mirram nga'at   yané bit mithe   koorong noot.

One of us will go into the scrub.
   Mila   yanina miléé   yerrin oot.

We will meet at the big water-hole, where the fish are plentiful.
   Mala-doang nangee'a   tumbaor   teenoo,   noo-noo kooding (*taobet ba by eook).

                                                               * Fish and eels.

One.	Two.	Three.	Four.	Five.
Kanbo.	Benjero.	Benjero kanbo.	Benjero-benjero.	Benjero-benjero ba kanbo.

Six.
Benjero-benjero ba benjero, &c.

Sun	Ngumi or na-ween.	Night (dark)	Marp-poreen.
Sunrise	Windar-ring.	Moon	Tra-bujeen or meane-am.
Morning	Bar-ring or yar-am-bring.	Light (day)	Karry-mean.
Sunset	Qurm-qun.	Stars	Turt pir'am
Evening	Mallok-mollok.	Star	Turt.

I am going to strike   -   -   -   Mángee* yean-noonjó'in† koondee chil-bunen.
                                         Am   going   I   to   strike.

I am going to find a nest   -   -   Mángee yean-noonjó'in kooandee yeákinin ellum'ó.
                                        Am   going   I   to   find   nest a.

I am going to lie down   -   -   Mángee yean-noonjó'in koondee kanam'boobik.
                                        Am   going   I   to   lie down.

I am going to chew the meat   -   Mángee yean-noonjó'in koondee tángárrboonin koeap'ta.
                                        Am   going   I   to   chew   meat the.

I am going to scold her   -   -   Mángee yean-noonjó'in koondee wygan'au.
                                        Am   going   I   to   scold her.

I am going to fish with a line   -   Mángee yean-noonjó'in koandee haolook-chabik ind'o wood'l-wod'l.
                                        Am   going   I   to   fish   with   a line.

I am going to chop with my axe   -   Mángee yean-noonjó'in koondee tibarrábik karrgeen tak.
                                        Am   going   I   to   chop   axe my.

I am going to watch him   -   -   Mángee yean-noonjó'in koondee náng-narra-noominin.
                                        Am   going   I   to   watch   him.

I am going to burn the wood   -   Mángee yean-noonjó'in koondee werrgá-ni-wan kalk.
                                        Am   going   I   to   burn   the wood.

I am going to pour out the water   -   Mángee yean-noonjó'in koondee je-gan'iú-wan páen.
                                        Am   going   I   to   pour out the water.

---

* *Mángee* might be rendered "Be," thus :—" I be going to strike."

† *Yean-noonjó*, "going," or *yanon*, "go," in all cases signifies that the person has to walk to do the thing : I am going to strike—*Mángee chilbunen'in.*
                Be   strike I.

LANGUAGE.

I am about to take it - - -	*Mángee koon'gin'in wan.*
	Am about take I it.
I intend to keep it - - -	*Mángee marrn-non-in wan.*
	Am intend keep I it.
I am going to sharpen my spear -	*Mángee yean-noonjó'in koondee burr-narrab'ik goeeon'tak.*
	Am going I to sharpen spear my.
He hit me on the head - - -	*Chilb'áng-an káwáng'oo malee.*
	Hit on the head my he.
The bird eats - - - - -	*Qui'ip-qui'ip tangárboun.*
	Bird eats.
How does the snake bite to kill a man?—With his teeth.	*Moorrdak kooderboún boonderboon koolon-noong werrp-poderboún koolin'tak?—Bondang'in leángoo.*
	How does bite snake kill man a?—With his teeth.
I am very angry - - - -	*Mángee chipcher'non'in.*
	Am angry very I.

Me - - -	*Wán* or *wár.*		Her pipe -	-	*Piptoo.*
He - - -	*Mainée.*		Their pipes -	-	*Pipoo'gob bilin.*
They - -	*Jánúboolin.*		I go - -	-	*Mángee yean-onin.*
We (two) -	*Wy.*		We go -	-	*Mángee yeanébi*
We (many) -	*Wy-jak.*		They go -	-	*Mángee yeanébool.*
My pipe -	*Pipeek.*		He go -	-	*Mángee yeanéboom.*
Your pipe -	*Pipin.*		She go -	-	*Mángee yeani-dool-ching-ká.*
His pipe -	*Pipjin.*				

NOTE.—You will notice that the word *Mángee* is used in the plural as well as in the singular. The same word (*Mángee*) is used thus:—*Mángee:* There in that place, *or* there it is; *Máng:* Here in this place, *or* here it is.

My dog -	-	*Yeráng-in'eek.*	Her dog -	-	*Yeráng-in'ó.*
		Dog my.			Dog her.
His dog -	-	*Yeráng-in'din.*	Their dog -	-	*Yeráng-in oogob-bilin.*
		Dog his.			Dog their.

At that time there were a great many men, women, and children, but now there are but few of us. But since we began to settle and live in our own houses, we have improved much.

We are now happier, and glad to see so many children about us.

Some are coming home; they are now tired of the bush.

Noogalloe kolin ba badjurr ba boobop boola doi. Mange walak-walah koorong-korreta boonto-y boom-brong-ngi lak-broongi ba billi ngalamboo-naje ellim-mong-atta maen borrdoptak koorreeni.

Mauge jen-de-y borrdoptak korre-galeen barndoen nangonoado warrt-toon-to boobop koorreen barr-neen yarr-wal-an-e bo-ongatta.

Twagoon-nile wa bongarrby worroro balk-tak.

Song—*Wak-wak.*

[Very old Song, made on the occasion of an Earthquake.]

Twarde kan noo toombi, jewa-to-me-me-jet Wanellima i i i iningjak barra-milla brinbolene wonto nyiar-grroen bel-bel targel-booel-beek karwen mall.

LITERAL:—That will do of that kind of things. What is that noise at the back of my camp? It makes the ground shake and the gum-trees tremble.

SHORT SENTENCES, ETC.

English	Native
There are two to each of you	*Mange bollawooen noogal bol.*
Give us one each	*Brring brrang billing wangarbe.*
Every one of us will go	*Tende wy laterr noong ngani-you mango.*
Either of us will go	*Yan'e bangatto.*
Neither of us will go	*Nga banabol yanan yourang.*
Neither of us has got it	*Ngi a boon tong ka you anga wantoen.*
I killed a female kangaroo	*Jelbadin ba boondo mirramtak;* or *Jelbadin mirram boonerrtak.*
I killed a male kangaroo	*Jelbadin twarde boop torong mirramtak;* or *Jelbadin mirram ly gorrntak.*
My head is very sore	*Kaongeek jerreneen youronge.*
Thy hand is very dirty	*Manongin werreneen woorrk-koorrie kanneentak.*
His hand is very sore	*Manongo jerrerneen.*
Her hand is very sore	*Manongo jerrerneen.*
Our house is very cold	*Werreneen ellimatta bandal-tak koorren.*
Your house is very good	*Bamena ellimin borrdoptak koorreen.*
Their house is very bad	*Werreneen jen-noo ellimtan newlimtak koorreen.*
What is that?	*Weeneroptak?*
Who is that?	*Weenerop newan?*
That is a stone	*Ka jeng ka mojertak.*
It is a stone	*Newan mojer.*
If any do not like Coranderrk, they can go away, and come back by-and-by.	*Ngia boon bodoom boon maen beek ki yanep wyadak mooloko twagie maga Coranderrktea.*
This place (Coranderrk) is very good. It is better to live here than to go about and drink.	*Bordop manbeek koorreen ngaboon nga koorreen toonta kiongia bambo ngo opka tongia balimta.*
The Government has gathered us from the drink.	*Mange moork-moork karboon ngarringe magalo balimtalo.*
Bad white men have nearly killed all our men and women.	*Magalo newlamtew hoomideet noongo weerki lattrang mangi kolin ba badjewer.*
I am going to the mountain to-morrow. I will make a hut; and I will hunt two days for the lyre-bird. I will then come back to my own house.	*Yankrang a din errimbooe kabanda bolaga ngiarrangin din ellime koorong nem-manin boli wyin nin boln-boln nemaroongin wyrongan nga gan malongngam mada twagonngi kone bolage ellimtoje mong poje.*
We are going to bed now; for we must get up to-morrow at break of day, because we are going over the mountain.	*Mange youma brrea-ang-il, boorrnea koma krriangilo boorrntoe jente, bolage wendanin nang-nal ngurraktoe.*
They are all very bad men and women the people who live in the bush.	*Quing-ke newllinjak kolin ba badjurr, mangby-en yanone balk-toe.*
Before the white people came to our country we were all very happy together; but when they came they gave us grog, and it made us mad.	*Maga bigangatta brreni hoomoje noogal booda-do borrdoptak kroong-i-a, mal brreni noogal-looe woongerby balimta ba bolage nganga boongerrboon.*
Then we became unhealthy, and began to die off.	*Noome nearroka-dak werrk boongerby.*

ARTICLE.

English	Native
A house	*Koinee ellim.* A house.
The house	*Koogik ellim.*

GENDER.

English	Native
Male kangaroo	*Mirramly goorrn.*
Female kangaroo	*Mirram booerr.*

LANGUAGE.

PLURAL.

Kangaroos	Mirram woottan noo.
Trees	Kalk-byjerrang.
Tree	Kalk.
Men	Koolinboolick.

ADJECTIVES.

A tall man	Karnangnile koolin.
A taller man	Tong-tong korrin.

PRONOUNS.

English.	Native.	English.	Native.
Personal.			*Possessive.*
I	Wan.	Yours	Noogalin.
Thou	Warr.	His	Noogalo.
He	Moonee.	Ours	Noogalangin.
She	No equivalent.	Theirs	Noogaltan.
We	Wanginin.		*Relative.*
You	Wangan.	Who	Weenerop.
It	No equivalent.	What	Ining.
They	Dool.	Which	Ining-jack.
		That	Manen.

My house	Ellim eek.
	House my.
Thy house	Ellim ngoot.
His house	Ellim o.
Her house	Ellim o.
Your house	Ellim in.
Our house	Ellim atta.
Their house	Jew do wal ellim.
Each	Bring-bring biling.
Each man is going	Bring-bring biling yanep koolin.
Either	Mandoroong.
Either of you may go	Mandoroong wangin yane.
	May you go.
Neither	Ngabedin.
Neither of you is going	Ngabedin walangin yanep.
Some	Wonga.
Give me some	Wonga koonga-geek.
	Some give me.
Other	Youong.
Give me the other	Youong koonga-geek.
	Other give me.
None	Ngaboondok.
Any	Kalla millee.
Here	Woo.
There	Mongdew.
Here (putting something into your hand)	Woo.
Here it is (showing you something)	Mang.
There (pointing to something at hand)	Mangdew.
Over (there before you)	Mange or Mango.

VOL. II.   P

English.	Native.	English.	Native.
Backward	Nyarrgeegonen.	Again	Toolo.
Above	Ngirr-ngirrwan.	About	Mang bajin.
How	Noorotqurongi.	After	Wande tew.
Why	Ining tala.	Against	Weta brangi.
When	Ngurroie.	Before	Bambo.
Little	Wyhrook.	Behind	Wane jeeh.
Enough	Twarn.	Below	My-je-de-dak.
After	Wang karring.	Beside	Nga to jeek.
Never	Ngabondak.	Between	Bageroe.
Once	Kooptoon-toe.	Beyond	Jeyou.
Twice	Balboot-toe.	Down	Mi e.

English	Native
Between the hands	Bageroe manongoe.
Under the stone	Mangadin mon ki wyjun mojer ta.
Into the water	Poje pawntoe.
Into the fire	Poje weentoe.
Into the hole	Poje nringtoe.
At the fire	Jeyou weentoe.
So was he	Toonda koorrangi mandew.
That is it	Nga i e.
Unless you go	Maller emer toolo.
Bigger than that one	Woorttu koorreen kanano.
Yet he would not do it	Wangadino nga bejak-kongi.
Go round there	Mongtew koorrnee kallé.
Here it is	Mange.
There it is	Kaleno.
Where is it?	Intaje koornento?
Only one more	Kooptoonje toolo.
How did you go?	Norrar korrnang-ngi?
Why did you come?	Inongar-krong ngi?
That is enough	Twarje newan new.
Very often	Noje-noje.
He comes sometimes	Brrnon negol jew-jew tak.
He came once	Brrenaje coopton-toe.
He did it twice	Nol kong ngi bulabil-toe.
I will go again	Yaninin toolo.
Go through the creek	Yanin niwan breen brong-inin kuladerr-toe.
Go round the road	Waluen-waluen kone killing-inin barranggat-twe.
I go over the mountain	Mange bring-krrong inin ngurrak-toe.
We are going over the mountain	Mange yan kong jerring neen ngurrak-toe.
He has gone over the mountain	Yani jeeng ka ngurrak-toe je kub-anty.
Will you go over the mountain?	Yanini warr ngurrak-toeje bin krranginni?
I would go and hunt, but I have no gun	Yanadan toongka ba mein ga ngia drung boolubil tak.
I will go if you will go	Yaninin tak kallangnarr yanan.
Go and kill the cat	Yane me ba tywagera bededool.
Come back soon	Twagar nigon nerrnoo.
Bring me some fire	Wanta geu ween kanan noo.
We will go and fish to-morrow	Golok jada korrnde mallon.
And the fish will bite, and we will eat them.	Milajele nagrot bondar ban boli nonaje tangurea errimboe.

LANGUAGE.

NAMES OF NATIVE ANIMALS.

English.	Native.	English.	Native.
Bear	Koab-burr.	Plover	Peret-peret.
Native cat	Beth-e-del.	Pelican	Bil-e-gin.
Kangaroo	Mirrim.	Lyre-bird	Bulin-bulin.
Wallaby	Wimbâ.	Jay	Balcen-bulcen.
Wombat	Warreen.	Eagle	Bunjel.
Native dog	Yearangin.	Pigeon	Moongoob-bárrá.
Opossum	Walert.	Laughing jackass	Koarring-koorring.
Squirrel (large)	Poong-goong.	Bat	Billeang.
Squirrel (small)	Warrin.	Platypus	Wad-dirrang.
Lizard (large)	Pudjeing.	Magpie	Parr-warrang.
Swan	Goon-â-warr.	Parrot	Boorrgil.
Native companion	Goorrook.	Bustard	Breu-el.
Crow	Wang.	Porcupine	Kâ-warren.
Cockatoo (white)	Ngiah.	Kangaroo-rat	Barrook.
Cockatoo (black)	Na-u-na-duk.	Snake	Ka-ân.
Duck	Tulum.	Quail	Born-gin.
Wood duck	Bik-moon.	Hawk (little)	Klu-roong.
Mountain duck	Winak-hi.	Grubs (in trees)	Milork.
Emu	Boorri-mul.		

GOULBURN TRIBE.

A kangaroo is feeding in the scrub.
Mirrim tangarboon ngarup toe.

Get me my spear and I will kill him.
Gong-naget dear burenoo.

Let us roast him and eat him.
Beer nangebethoo tang-ado.

Give me a stone.
Gong-naget moorrer.

Give him a stone.
Gong-ngago moorrer.

I gave you some water.
Kyinen wongi pawn.

I will not give you some water.
Ngabenan wanin wongin pawn.

We drink water.
Nooboonni pawn.

Give me some bread.
Gong-chabagaeck noorong.

We will give him a stick.
Gongangallu kalk.

We will give you a stick.
Wungiunio wanin kalk.

We will not give you a stick.
Nyabenan wanin kalk.

Give me some bread to eat.
Intarrik wook taboun noorong tangunoo.

This is my hand.
Maggulle manangeek.

Sing me a song.
Intarr wengin.

Where is your father?
Inta koonin warrijin?

He is my father.
Mang-nuin warrijin.

My father is here.
Warrijeek maggullee.

He is not my father.
Naboontanka warrijeek.

One.
Rooptin.

Two.
Balubil.

Three.
Bulawin ba goop.

Four.
Bulawin-bulawin.

English.	Native.	English.	Native.
Bone	Kalhyn.	Blow	Telbuk.
Blood	Koorh.	Cut	Pentuck.
Matter	Boothen.	Kick	Meranak.
Brain	Doonden.	Fall	Batherembi.
Heart	Dorong.	Swelling	Karrenin.
Liver	Booing-ata.	Heaven	Woor woon.
Kidney	Marp-ata.	Sky	Woor woon.
Bowels	Meiang-ata.	Cloud	Lark.

116 THE ABORIGINES OF VICTORIA:

English.	Native.	English.	Native.
Thick cloud	Mondirking lark.	He hears	Ngarrngoon mallee.
Mist	Boorang.	They hear	Ngarrnkarrbon mang'ee.
Rain	Ael.	I go	Mangee yanunin.
Hail	Moorcer.	I am going	Mangee yaninin.
Snow	Kabing.	We go	Intace yanoni.
Ice	Tangbelh.	They go	Yanool tongka.
Thaw	Ten'debeek tangbelk.	I am sick	Jerrinin tongka.
Flood	Woorlbilly pawn.	He is sick	Jerrinin mang'ee.
Air	Wanang-wanang.	They are sick	Jerrinin kal buncherin.
Wind	Gooreen.	We are sick	Jerrinin ingen tongka.
Storm	Wondoaebel.	I was sick	Jerrinin athin tongka twan.
Calm	Dereming.	I am well	Boorndup kooren-nun.
Sound	Woondo.	He is well	Boorndup kooren mang'ee.
Noise	Wering gering.	We are well	Boorndup kooreningen mang.
Silence	Timince.	They are well	Boorndup hoorenool mang'ee.
Lightning	Jerringoo.	I am hungry	Mangka nearebrea nun.
Thunder	Woodobil.	They are hungry	Nearebrenool mang'ee.
Fire	Ween.	We are hungry	Mangka nearebren kal buncherin.
Spark	Bevdinen.	He is hungry	Nearebren mang'ee.
Blaze	Ye up kanun.	I am hot	Mangoolwon tak koorin-nun.
Smoke	Boort.	He is hot	Wooloon tak koorin mang'ec.
Ashes	Muneep.	They are hot	Wooloon tak koore kal buncherin mangee.
Heat	Woolen.		
Cold	Mooter ween.	We are hot	Wooloon tak hooren mang.
Sun	Ngumi.	I am cold	Loork-loork kooren-nun mang.
Moon	Menan.	You are cold	Loorh-loork cher koorenar.
Star	Turt.	Look	Nyarar mang'ee.
Meteor	Goorbenee turt.	Look here	Ngunak mang.
Planet	Luan.	Look yonder	Nyanak chew.
Seven Stars	Moon-moondik.	Go	Yanee.
Spring	Kom brook.	Come	Wonde.
Autumn	Berreen.	Go up	Yaneedo.
Light	Yearam.	Go over	Yuneedo ban.
Darkness	Booreen.	Go down	Barang-barang yanee.
Day	Karry mean.	Come up	Wende.
Night	Booreen.	Come over	Koondelee kado.
Sunrise	Wondang ngumi.	Come down	Barrawee miee.
Twilight	Moolok-mooloh.	Come in	Koong ke hado.
I hear	Nyain koninda.	Go out	Bene'do miethering.
We hear	Koby ngarrugoon.		

LAKE CONDAH TRIBE.

English.	Native.	English.	Native.
My hand	Murungan.	There	Wonda.
My foot	Tinungan.	Over there before you	Moong'o or moong'e.
Your hand	Murung ngo.	Up there	Kan noo.
His hand	Murung newang.	Down there	Wan new.
I will go	Boor peer.	Look there	Na ka go e ot.
I am going	Boor poea.	Look here	Na ka.
He is going	Boor pa.	Look, look!	Na ka! na ka!
They are going	Boor ee.		

LANGUAGE.

English.	Native.
Go and look	Na ka booree.
I say	Nga took.
To die	Kal prena.
Dead	Noo kati yab wonda.
He is dead	Nga ga.
All done	Bang ngat lia ook kin'o.
Give me bread	Yung mita yung mita.
Food (general)	Ngool balin gootin.
Meeting (general)	Quorun.
Track	Tarn.
This track	Moombe tarn.
Stone tomahawk	Mod'e cher.
Grass	Pootong.
Father	Bepi.
Mother	Ngrrong.
Brother	Warti.
Sister	Kuki.
Son	Koping ung.
Daughter	Ngart un.
Husband	Ngun up.
Wife	Malbung.
Hand	Murung.
Foot	Tin ung.
Head	Pim.
Body	Koong.
Eyes	Meeng.
Nose	Kapung.
Ears	Wing.
Mouth	Nyulling.
Teeth	Tangang.
Hair	Ngarat.
Tongue	Tal lang.
Sun	Nya ung.
Moon	Taroo.
Wind	Ngondok.
Stars	Ming-gal.
Rain	Mic-ung.
Snow	Yurngarang.

English.	Native.
Thunder	Marndal.
Lightning	Wilim nung.
Light (morning)	Kal at.
Dark (night)	Boorong.
Whirlwind	Weeung-weeung gor.
Water	Parech.
Opossum	Koora mok.
Kangaroo	Korang.
Cockatoo	Na nuk.
Crow	Wang.
Kill the kangaroo	Kal prena na koorin.
Are you going?	Watoongen?
Throw the spear	Mia tara.
Going away	Boorenen.
Come here	Wata.
Coming here	Wat tok mar tin ba.
Going to stay five days	Kart murung goot a koat.
One	Ki upa.
Two	Bolita.
Three	Bala mea.
Four	Bolita-bolita.
Ten	Bolita murung (two hands).
Stone	Mari.
Fish (general)	Yarar.
Eel	Queang.
Black-fish	Qulil.
Duck	Mooee.
Swan	Koona wara.
Emu	Koping.
Blood	Kerch.
Breath	Nganga.
Spirit (soul)	Moorop.
Bad	Ammengar.
Good	Otung.
God (or big man)	Prenheal.
Devil	Ngot hoot.
Seven Stars	Me patoom.

SUCCINCT SKETCH OF THE ABORIGINAL LANGUAGE.

(By WILLIAM THOMAS, ESQ., GUARDIAN OF ABORIGINES.)*

GRAMMAR.

From observations I have been led to make, and attentively noticing their expressions, I am led to conclude that, like many of the civilized languages, much is abridged by the use of prepositions and terminations, which give a musical tone to savage languages not to be found in civilized tongues. Such has been observed in the South Sea Islanders, and generally among other barbarous nations; in fact, every Aboriginal is a true child of nature, and nothing more than what is actually required will be found in their language. Reduplication is a feature in the Aboriginal language of the two Melbourne tribes, which renders it at one and the same time simple and harmonious. The degrees of comparison in the adjectives are generally formed thus—*Worbrinun*, tired; *Worbrinunun*, very tired; *Worbrinununun*, excessively tired—regularly done. *Nerrebrunin*, hungry; *Nerrebruninun*, very hungry; *Nerrebruninunun*, regularly famished; and so on, though they sometimes say *Kungee nerrebrunin*, excessively hungry.

Articles are seldom used, the numeral adjectives answering fully their purpose. The article is always used (though at the termination) when describing any part of the human frame, and that in an elegant manner. *Arter*, the: thus—*Myng*, eye; *Myngarter*, the eye; *Tallan*, tongue; *Tallanarter*, the tongue. They, however, often use the participle *o* for "the," as—*Tenung*, foot; *Tenungo*, the foot; *Myngo*, the eye, &c.

Plurals are generally formed with the numerals, though sometimes (quite an original method) by *ge* to the end of the first singular, making both the the substantives plural, thus—*Koolin*, man; *Bagrook*, woman; *Koolingeebagrook*, men and women; and often dispensing with the conjunction altogether; thus—*Wein*, fire; *Parn*, water; *Wein-parn*, fire and water.

Verbs are more regular; in fact, they appear one and all upon one general footing, like the French, but destitute of the irregular and reflective. Their verbs invariably terminate in *eit*. The *eit* cut off, and the verb may be conjugated; though I could never go through or find out, as in the French and English grammar, the whole of the tenses. I select a few of the principal verbs.

Bauganeit - - - to have.	Komargeit - - - to get up.
Burgoneit - - - to spear.	Koonaneit - - - to hold.
Bouldoneit - - - to fall.	Mardoneit - - - to cry.
Boundoneit - - - to bite.	Monkeit - - - to make or do.
Gnolbuneit - - - to carry.	Marngoneit - - - to mend.
Gormurgeit - - - to cover.	Narngoneit - - - to hear.

* An extract from a *Report of a Select Committee of the Legislative Council of Victoria on the Aborigines*, 1858-9.

LANGUAGE. 119

Ngarneit - - -	to see.	Umoneit - - - to throw.
Nobeaneit - - -	to drink.	Koomoneit - - - to bury.
Pundarroneit - -	to dig up.	Wolwooneit - - - to run.
Purrumboneit - -	to rub out.	Weagolaneit - - - to die.
Paarthrabuneit - -	to steal.	Wongoruneit - - - to be stupid.
Tunganeit - - -	to eat.	Yenioneit - - - to dwell.
Toewangeit - - -	to go.	Yaarkoneit - - - to look for.
Tomboneit - - -	to enquire.	Yarwoneit - - - to swim.
Toomdereneit - -	to talk.	Yannoneit - - - to walk.
Tiowoneit - - -	to be sick.	Yangowlaneit - - to go away.

Thus—*Bangan,* have; *Banganerdon,* I did have; *Yarwon,* swim; *Yarwonerdon,* I did swim; *Tanganaraka,* did I eat? *Bouldonerdon,* I did fall; and so on. Since they have been with the white people they, however, use the pronouns I, you, &c., thus—*Murrumbeek yarwon,* I swim; *Murrumbinner tanganan,* you eat; &c., &c., &c.

Pronouns are also subject to reduplication by abridging or annexing to the terminations, thus—

Murrumbeek - - -	I or me.	Murrumbinner - - Thou or you.
Murrumbick - - -	Mine.	Murrumbianner - - Yours.

Adverbs in like manner, as—

Ganbo - - - -	One.	Bengero - - - Two.
Ganboden - - -	Once.	Bengeroden - - - Twice.
Ganbony - - -	First.	Bengerodenum - - Second.

Particles are seldom used separately, and are so strangely interwoven with verbs, adverbs, and the other parts of speech, that, in a brief sketch like this, it would be useless to enter upon.

Conjunctions they have but few; but all that are necessary.

I will now give a list of the principal adverbs, particles, prepositions, conjunctions, &c. The verbs have been briefly given, and the adjectives will come in the regular vocabulary.

Adverbs of Number.—*Ganboden,* once; *Tindee,* only; *Tindee bengero,* only two; *Tindee bengeroganmel,* only three.

Adverbs of Order.—*Ganbony,* first; *Ganbronun,* first time; *'Bengeroudin,* second; *Telutkin,* before; *Kurrengerin,* after; *Wunadak,* behind; *Werneit,* last; *Mingo,* beginning; *Toloma,* middle; *Moibo,* end.

Adverbs of Place.—*Korbe,* here; *Temon,* there; *Mihu,* these; *Notto,* here; *Winda,* where; *Windowring,* whither; *Monkir,* thither; *Karboit,* above; *Kubberdon,* below.

Adverbs of Quantity.—*Bullito,* much; *Kertherba,* together; *Wyebo,* little; *Nogee,* enough; *Uunga,* more; *Bullitodebar,* too much; *Wyebo-debar,* too little; *Wootunno,* abounding; *Nungulbudin,* how many; *Nunggudbuddin,* how much.

Adverbs of Time.—*Netbo,* now; *Wombo,* sometimes; *Moloco,* presently; *Yellewa,* to-day; *Baboreen,* to-morrow; *Mola molok,* yesterday; *Molo guan,* by-and-by; *Yerramboot,* day after to-morrow; *Yellingout,* another day; *Banban cram,* morning; *Kurren munnebo,* noon; *Krungine ngervein,* evening; *Borun,* night; *Gnanbo,* long time; *Tutanbo,* short time; *Nierbuddlun,* never; *Nunnelliner,* then; *Borundut,* midnight.

Adverbs, Negatives.—*Nier,* nay; *Utur borak,* no.

Adverbs, Interrogatives.—*Wener,* which; *Winnerdon,* which one; *Windower,* to which; *Wener,* what; *Winnerer,* what is; *Winda,* where; *Windart,* where did they; *Kunne,* this.

Interjections.—*Ki! ki!* surprise; *Ur! ur!* hush, hark; *Yarka!* grief, pain; *Wa! wa!* look out.

Particles affixed, &c.—*Ut,* in; *Oot,* on; *Dap,* in; *Wea,* in the; *Wa,* to, at; *Arter,* the; *O,* the; *Burnin,* at; *Ter,* add; *Teno,* at the.

Conjunctions.—*Bar,* and; *Ge,* occasionally, and; *Tey,* also.

Pronouns.—

Singular.		Plural.	
I or me	Murrumbeek.	We	Murramaner.
Thou or you	Murrumbinuer.	You	Murrumbinner.
He or him	Munniger, kargee.	They	Murrumnuller.

Possessive.

Mine	Murrumbieek.	Us	Nurnin.
Yours	Murrumbianner.	Them	Murthiger.
Ours	Murrumbunarter.	Myself	Ganicek.
His	Kargeeicek.	Yourself	Ganninner.

N.B.—It will be necessary here, in order to give an idea of the use Aborigines make of these small particles, to give examples, thus:—*Ut*, in; *Beek*, ground or earth; *Beekut*, in the ground. *Willum*, house or miam; *Willumut*, in the house. *Dap*, in; *Koorong*, boat; *Koorongdap*, in the boat. *Wa*, in the; *Weing*, fire; *Weingwa*, in the fire. *Wa*, to or from; *Sydneywa*, to Sydney. *Oit*, to or at; *Melbournoit*, to Melbourne. *Arter*, the; *Tallanarter*, the tongue; *Myngarter*, the eye. *O*, in the; *Weingo*, in the fire; &c., &c.

The aforesaid will, I trust, be to the committee and philologists some clue to the language of the two Melbourne tribes, comprehending no small extent of country along the coast and inland to the Goulburn, Ovens, Broken, and Devil's Rivers, which may serve as a key (as far as my experience goes) to a chain of communication throughout Victoria, and, upon the same rule, throughout the whole of New Holland. I leave this sketch and my remarks for what they are worth, and now proceed to the vocabulary.

Succinct Language.—Mort Noular.

ADJECTIVES.

English.	Native.	English.	Native.
Bitter	Ballin.	Free	Poo-tun-uk.
Broad	Yerringooden.	First	Gan-bro-nun.
Big	Bullitto.	Good	Mar-na-meek.
Blind	Toutmyng.	Good (very)	Boon-dup.
Bad	Nillam.	Greedy	Bul-let-garn.
Black	Woorkoordin.	Giddy	Lar-lun-en-et.
Blue	Wookurrerble.	Hot	Num-mun-in.
Clean	Kurrebully, or worrework, or woorrebully.	Hot (as fire)	Tou-nar-bon.
		Heavy	Bern-bern.
Dry	Kuubebel.	Hungry	Ner-re-brun-in.
Dry (dead)	Bidderup.	Hoarse	Kiel-bul-un-in.
Deaf	Toutweing.	Industrious	Tar-tuk-ur-nup.
Dirty	Woorgurrin or woorgulbunna.	Idle	Tour-nur-nin.
		Lazy	Tour-lin-tab-lun.
Dark	Boorundara.	Lazy (very)	Tour-nur-ne-nun.
Deep	Mer-rim.	Lazy (sluggish)	Tal-lun-der-ner.
Deeper	Mer-rim-er.	Long	Ner-rim.
Flat	Koy-eon.	Light (weight)	Bul-ler-bul-ler.
Fat	Marm-bull.	Little	Wyc-bo.

English.	Native.	English.	Native.
Lame	Nar-boon.	Sick (very)	Gee-gee-ry.
Last	Yan-neite.	Straight	Ur-din.
Mighty	Bool-ut-pall-eet.	Smooth	Barm-burdin.
Nasty	Nil-lam.	Slow	Port-be-uk.
Narrow	Win-nin-koo-dip.	Stinking	Buun-koon.†
New	Moo-lo-good.	Sweet	Lal-lee-woon.
New (fresh)	Tur-den-den.	Tall	Kur-nile.
Old	Wag-ga-bell.	Thick	Bun-neet.
Poor	Wa-wat-tun-ner.	Thin	Lal-lum.
Proud	Tou-lup.	Thirsty	Kurn-brun-in.
Pretty	Bourn-dup.	Tired	Wor-brun-in.
Round	Pi-o-bu-bur-din.	Ugly	Nil-lam.
Round (as tree)	Piou-bur-rin.	Upright	Murm-bull.
Rough	Te-rip-te-rip.	Upright (as a stick)	Ter-ree-dee.
Rotten	Brun-guit.	Wet	Toln-go-don.
Rich*	Narn-get.	Wet (as damp)	Tul-gru-min.
Red	Be-bet-ur-nin.	Weak	Bo-rup.
Short	Mort-ku-ding.	Wicked	Me-ung-o-wor-gile.
Sweet	Bab-ber.	Wicked (bad)	Nil-lam.
Strong	Pal-leet.	Well (not ill)	Ko-rum-din-in.
Sloping	Kur-nurm-bil-ber-ding.	White	Tarn-der-din.
Square	Purk-bun.	Wise	Narn-ger-bon.
Stupid	Naw-lun-niu.	Wide	Wyl-gul-ter.
Sound	Pal-let-ku-ding.	Young (male)	Yan-yean.
Sick	Tarn-der-bun-in.	Young (female)	Mon-mon-deek.
Sick (not well)	Toy-yon.	Yellow	Ki-er-lin.

SUBSTANTIVES.

Parts of the Body.

English	Native	English	Native
Body	Mur-rum.	Jaw	Eurt.
Hair	Yarra.	Beard	Yar-ra-nun-duk.
Hair (of the head)	Yar-ra-kow-an.	Moustache	Yar-ra-mou-tu-be-run.
Head	Kow-an.	Neck	Koarn.
Head (crown of)	Troot-toop.	Shoulder	Buck-ur-er.
Skull	Turp-turp.	Arm	Ter-ruk.
Brain	Tourn-tourn.	Elbow	Ko-rum.
Forehead	Myng-nin.	Armpit	Wou-gu-ruk.
Bone over eyes	Tourn-a-myng.	Wrist	Un-ung.
Ear	Wer-ring.	Hand	Mun-ung.
Eye	Myng.	Hand (palm of)	Ber-ring-ber-ring.
Eyebrows	Yar-ra-myng.	Fingers	Mun-nong.
Eyelashes	Yar-ra-de-myng.	Finger (first)	Won mun-mill-uk.
Eyeball	Woor-wor-ri-mer.	Finger (little)	Won-mun-mill-uk-wye-bo.
Nose	Gaarn.	Thumb	Bar-bin-bar-bin.
Nostrils	Myng-gaarn.	Nails	Tir-re-bee-mun-ung.
Mouth	Kun-der-ner.	Breast	Bar-nu-boom.
Mouth (open)	Um-ble-bun-ark.	Breast (nipple of)	Brem-brim.
Lips	Woor-roon.	Bosom	Ber-ring.
Teeth	Lee-ang.	Belly	Boart.
Tongue	Tal-lon.	Navel	Tour-luk.
Cheeks	Woung.	Back	Bnn-nin-bun-nin.
Cheek-bone	Tourt-woung.	Backbone	Nilgn-er-ur-ruk.
Chin	Un-duk *or* nun-duk.	Ribs	Nilgn-o-tur-min.
		Posteriors	Bill-ake.

* Not in our sense—wealth; but estimation—eloquence, advice, or war.
† A nasal long drone.

English.	Native.	English.	Native.
Hip	Kow-an-bour-no.	Evening star	Mar-be-ang-rook.
Thigh	Ngar-ke-ter-rang.	Dew	Boo-re-arn.
Knee	Bur-din.	Fog	Ng-err.
Leg	Lour-ko.	New moon	Burm-bo.
Leg (calf of)	Lourk.	Half moon	Bul-go.
Ankle	Tour-rum-ke-kun-uk.	Full moon	Tu-an-de-boop.
Foot	Te-nan.	Thunder	Woon-du-ble.
Instep	Ngar-te-nan.	Lightning	Moor-rin-no.
Heel	Pern.	Ice	Tarn-bulk.
Toe	Kow-an-te-nan.	Snow	Kab bin.
Toe (big)	Bar-bun-te-nan.	Hail	Tu-dee-war-ree.
Toe (little)	Wye-bo-te-nan.	Rainbow	Brin-beal.
Skin	Tar-bo.	Storm	Ko-reen.
Bone	Nilgne-ka-rook.	Wind	Morn-moot.
Flesh	Ngar-huk.	Whirlwind	Burt-ko-reen.
Windpipe	Tur-tur kur-rum.	Hot wind	Weet-mul-lin.
Lungs	Nin-nin-e-bourt.	Rain	Parn-min.
Heart	Toor-oor.	Spring	Moo-dee-e-ram.
Breathing	Ang.	Summer	Mer-rim-nger-wein.
Throat	Tum.	Autumn	Moo-dee-nger-wein.
Gullet	Tal-ler-be-goûrn.	Winter	Per-ring-nger-wein.
Stomach	Tur-rum-ber-lin.	*Cardinal Points.*	
Guts	Moon-mur.		
Liver	Boûr-doo.	East	Kul-lin-bi-rem.
Kidney	Woor-ror-marp.	West	Nut-bro-ki.
Kidney (fat of)	Marm-bul-lâ.	North	Bur-gee.
Bladder	Mour-rut.	South	Koor-reen.
Urine	Bul-gi.		
Vein	Gour-uk.	Sea	War-reen.
Sinews	Pee-reep.	River	Woor-neet.
Blood	Kul-mul.	Spring (rise water)	Gan-noon.
Marrow	Dee-dit.	Creek	Kun-nung.
Sweat	Moor-run-moor-run.	Water-hole	Tăm-boore.
Of the Heavens, &c.		Water-hole (temporary)	Pun-pun.
God (or first cause)	Pundgyl-Marman.		
Devil [some tribes have]	Bull-gen-kar-nee.*	*Four Elements.*	
Heaven	Woor-woor-rer.	Earth	Beck.
Hell†	Moo-eep-nall-ook.	Air	Ngrn tou-râ.
Soul	Moor-roop.	Fire	Weing.
Spirit	Nar-roon.	Water	Parn.
Ghost	Moor-roo-bull.	*Five Senses.*	
Apparition (of one dead)	Lam-bar-moor.‡	Taste	Bar-ro-muk.
		Smell	Ngar-o-buk.
Sun	Nger-wein.	Feel	Purn-boo-nuk.
Moon	Myn-cam.	See	Ngar-noon.
Star	To-py-rum.	Hear	Ngar-goon.
Cloud	Lark.	*Face of Countries.*	
Sky	Woor-woor.	Mountain	Bun-null.
Morning star	Woo-to-ko-rook.	Ranges §	Noo-ur-ro-ur-rook.

* My blacks state this only means ugly.

† They have several terms for the abode of bad souls. This is the most impressive, continued descending through a narrow opening, and never stopping.

‡ A long solemn drone.

§ Every range has its name; likewise every mountain has its particular name; so that blacks can state the precise mountain or hill in an extensive range where they will meet. I have upwards of 200 names of mountains in the Australian Alps. Aborigines require neither latitude nor longitude; plain nature by day and the stars by night.

LANGUAGE.

English.	Native.
Hill	Wye-bo-bun-null.
Rise	Mill.
Flat	Taul.
Swamp	Bull-ook.

Stone, Clay, &c.

English.	Native.
Stone	Larng mong.
Flint (white)	Oo-work.
Red (ochre)*	Wee-rup.
White (ochre)	Nar-rum-ble.
Brown (ochre)	Ter-reel.
Brick	Der-re-kul-mul.
Clay	Nut-kun-tare.
Gravel	Ter-ree-beck.
Coal	Lourn.
Charcoal	Kun-nun-dare.
Sand	Kar-ga-ruk.
Ashes (dust)	Mun-nip.

Kindred.

English.	Native.
Man	Koo-lin.
Woman	Bag-rook.
White man	Hom-mer-geek.
Black man	Woor-gur-din-koo-lin.
Old man	Wag-a-bil-koo-lin.
Old woman	Moon-deg-rook.
Infant (male)	Wye-bo-bo-pup.
Infant (female)	Wye-krook.
Child	Bo-pup.
Girl	Mon-mon-dik.
Young man	Yan-yean.
Young woman	Mon-mon-dik.
Husband	Nan-go-ron.
Wife	Bren-bun.
Son	Mum-mum.
Daughter	Man-gip.
Father	Mar-man.
Mother	Par-pun.
Grandfather	Ner-bun-ger-ron.
Grandmother	Ko-kung-e-up.
Sister	Leur-rookong.
Brother	Woon-do-l.
Elder brother	Barn-gun.
Elder sister	Lun-dun.
Uncle	Kurn-kurn.
Aunt	Bum-boon.
Niece	Pa-ren-ger-roon.
Nephew	Nar-bung-ur-roon.
Half-caste	Tree-be-mur-rum.
Friend	Kor-ki.

Clothes, &c.

English.	Native.
Coat	Woor-kud-der-bil.
Trousers	Ta-rang-ar-look.
Shirt	Ta-run-a-look.
Shoes	Te-nan-a-look.
Hat	Kum-bra-kow-an.
Mur-ri-guil	Worn over secret parts of males till married.
Nour-rite or kiar-yeun	Worn over secret parts of females till married.
Leek	Band round forehead, worn by male and female.
Mur-rur-kul-lim	Band neatly made of thread.
Til-bur-nine	Fine apron made of emus' feathers, goes all round the waist, worn by females in a single dance.
Mur-ri-kle	Strips of opossum skin worn to hide the fundament in males when in a dance.
Kourn-but	Necklace made of reeds.
Kourn-ur-run	Fine necklace, made of the sinews from emus' legs.
Wal-ler-wal-lert	Opossum rug.
Yel-ler-ne-bre	A blanket.
Yell-un-cet-tur-ruk	Band round the arm to strengthen arm.
Ber-buk	Belt round the belly to keep off hunger.
Mi-am or wil-lum	A house or place to lie down in or live.
Yel-low-dung	Sapling from one end to the other of the miam.
Lee-an	Forked sticks to support the sapling of miam.
Tourn-der-ry	Thick bark with which the blacks make miam.
Bol-loom	Thin bark which blows off trees, kindles in an instant.
Tar-nuk	Native bucket, made from the elbow or wart of trees.
Kul-bul-ling-ur-rook	Native tomahawk, made from a blue flat pebble stone, found in certain ranges. The blacks had great labor to get them to cut ; the handle was bent wood.
Min-der-min	Native nails or pegs made by hardening wood in fire.
Pee-reep	Native thread.
Moo-gra-moo-gra	Kangaroo bag, in which the black holds all his wealth but his spears.
Be-lang-be-lang	Native bag, made of grass.
Bin-nuk	Native basket, made of native flags of grass.
String (Europ.)	Woo-gle-woo-gle.

* These ochres are used promiscuously in painting their bodies for corrobborees, &c.; but two of them for sacred purposes : viz., the white for mourning ; red, for joy when a victim has been offered up for their dead.

English.	Native.	English.	Native.
Looking-glass*	Woor-un-dul-min.	Native companion	Kur-ur-rook.
Gun	Trang-bul-la-bill.	Turkey	Woon-mar-bel.
Powder and shot	Mor-ra-doo.	Pelican	War-gill.
Flint (of gun)	Pel-lin or oour-uk.	Swan	Koon-war-ror.
Knife	Kul-pen-kul-pen-gee-up.	Mulligan	A large bird of prey, lives only on birds and fish by the coast.
Fork	Kal-lup.		
Spoon	Tourn-der-ry (made of bark).	Eagle (very large)	Pun-dyl.
Basin	Ko-ron-er.	Eagle (smaller)	Ber-pip.
Box	Lil-le-ry.	Sparrow hawk	Par-rite.
Brush	Wor-oor-wort.	White hawk	Kab-bin.
Dish	Wel-len-wel-len.	White hawk (very small)	Tur-rer.
Pannikin	Pan-ni-kin.		
Candle	Marm-bull.	Lyre-bird	Bulln-bulln.
Hammer	Num-bert.	Nankeen-bird	Kar-warn.
Chisel	Beum-bean.	Pigeon	Moon-go-bra.
Saw	Pinder-bul-lup.	Cockatoo	Gnur-uile.
Axe	Num-be-mon.	Black cockatoo	Gnur-nan.
Gimlet	Man-mure-bul-lup.	Cockatoo parrot	Kar-mile.
Spade	Bel-ler-rer.	Parrot (general name)	Tan-dun.
Hoe	Wye-bo-bal-ler.		
Ship	Bul-li-to-koo-ron.	Parrot (Magella)	Bro-gil.
Boat	Wye-bo-koo-ron.	Parrot (blue mountain)	Lar-guk.
Paddle (as canoe)	Kun-ne-ko-lon.		
		Parrot (king)	Uu-gup.
Animals.		Parrot (very small kind)	Nel-la-woon.
Kangaroo	Koo-im.		
Wallaby	Wym-bir.	Satin-bird	Ngar-ran.
Wombat	War-reen.	Whip-bird	Yan-yan-gak. [So named from its noise, like the cracking of a whip.]
Bear	Kur-bur-rer.		
Bandicoot	Boe-ung.		
Opossum	Wal-ler-wal-lert.	Wattle-bird	Yan-guk.
Flying squirrel (three kinds)	Eur-run.	Leather-bird	Be-rat-be-rat.
		Mopoke	Goor-koom (night-bird).
Smaller kind	Ku-an-boo.	Cuckoo (noise like)	Woork-woork.
Very diminutive	Tu-an-tu-an.	Magpie	Per-er-warn.
Kangaroo-rat	Ber-uke.	Gean-gean	A bird between a crow and magpie. [The natives have strange superstitious notions of it.]
Rat (common)	Ty-ung.		
Ringtailed opossum	Be-min.		
Mouse	Bar-rut.		
Dog	Wer-run-un.		
Dog (wild or native)	Wer-ren-wil-lum.		
Cat	Urn or yurn.	Crow	Warn. [Superstitious of this.]
Water mole	Tu-la-or-ong or pal-la-rale.		
		Laughing jackass	Tour-ur-rong. [Called the bushman's timepiece.]
Platypus	Mur-rin-moor-roo.		
Hedgehog	Kow-an.	Bell-bird	Trin-war-reen.
Horse	Kul-ken-tur-nuk.	Redbreast	Tee-ung.
Bullock	Bul-gan-ner.	Fowl	Bowl.
Sheep	Eu-ep.	Duck	Tou-loom.
		Kor-rung-un-un	Very large water fowl.
Birds.		Goose	Nup-nup.
Bird (general term)	Koy-up.	Quail	Tre-bin.
Emu	Bur-ri-mil.	Snipe	Kruk-wor-rum.

* When white people had regularly made a footing at Port Phillip, one, Budgerry Tom, was noted for giving names to European things and animals. These names are mostly of his giving.

English.	Native.
Soldier-bird	Bill-bill-man-nere. [So named by the whites from its always being on the *qui vive*, and alarming the forest, to the great mortification of the sportsman.]
Tug-gan-kow-an	A small bird, makes a howling, distressing noise.
Bat	Pol-ly-ong.

Fishes, &c.

English.	Native.
Tu-at	General name of fish.
Whale	Pet-ti-heel.
Shark	Tal-lan-nur-run.
Porpoise	Bar-bar-kă.
Salmon (a kind of)*	Kur-nur-guil.
Cod (in Goulburn and Murray)	Mal-lun.
Lobster	Kur-rite.
Cray-fish (fresh-water)	Tar-luk-purn.
Cray-fish (salt-water)	Toy-yon.
Oyster	Tou-at.
Mutton-fish	Woor-din.
Cockle	Mur-yoke.
Mussel	Mur-bone.
Periwinkle	Pid-de-ron.
Sprat (a kind of)	Tal-li-bal-li.
Herring	Tar-uk-war-ra-bil.
Leech	Ter-rum-be-leet.
Frog	Nar-rut.

Miscellaneous.

English.	Native.
Insects (general term)	Kam-kam-koor.
Locusts (green wings)	Tee-een.
Locust (a large kind)	Karl-kal. [The duog of this insect is sweet; it is generally termed manna, though not generally known to be the soil of this insect; but such is the case. I have gathered as much as a quart from the tar-gau (or box-tree) at its base of a morning.]
Moth	Bar-lum-ber-lun.
Butterfly	Bol-lom-bol-lom.
Grasshopper	Nar-rite.
Fly (common)	Kow-urk.
March fly	Kurm-bur-ra.
Mosquito	Koor-gook.
Flea	Man-nun.
Louse	Noo-noon.
Lizard	Eu-roke or tun-per-rim.
Lizard (small kind)	Nur-rung.
Lizard (very large)	Per-ren-un. [At the Ovens and Broken River, and to the north, they run to four, five, and six feet long. I have measured one five feet.]
Lizard (another kind, very fat, but small)	Pudg-gen. [Eaten by the blacks generally.]
Snake	Karn.
Snake (black)	Tar-run-del.
Snake (diamond)	Koon-mill.
Worm	Tur-ror.
Grub	Ver-ring. [Very large and fat; blacks eat them raw. Said by Europeans to be fine eating, when roasted or fried.]
Grub (smaller)	Bear-uk.
Grub (very small)	Yeour-ong. [Not bigger than a small maggot. I have seen quarts and pecks of them got from near the roots of the trees. The blacks mix them with charcoal, and thus separate them from the rotten tree and eat them.]
Centipede	Ter-run-mur-ruk.
Ant (common)	Murrub.
Bull ant	Oeur-rong. [Awfully sharp bite.]

Trees, Shrubs, &c.

English.	Native.
Tree (general name)	Tur-rung or kulk.
Tree (blossom of)	Kurn-brook.
Tree (seed of)	De-ran-dell.
Tree (root of)	Wen-eu-ruk.
Tree (trunk of)	Wee-reep.
Branch	Ter-ru-galk.
Leaves	Mur-run.
Veins	Mur-rer-mur-uk.
Sap	Tu-un-no.
Bark	Tourn-der-ry.
Gum-tree (red)	Be-al.
Gum (white)	Yar-ra-bin.

* Shoals of these in muddy rivers at Western Port.

English.	Native.
Be-nup (a gum)	[Grows stately, but very irregular in its branches; pure snowy white bark. From the elbows of this tree the blacks formerly made their tar-nuks or water buckets, which appear by a kind Providence to be designed for that purpose.]
Box-tree	Tar-gan.
Box (bastardy)	Beet.
Stringybark	Bun-ger-look.
Stringybark (inferior kind)	Way-out.
Light or black wood	Burn-nar-look.
Light or black wood (spurious)	Marn-gan-noy-an.
Peppermint	Eur-look.
Honeysuckle	War-rak.*
She-oak	Tur-run.
Turpentine (tree)	Vi-al. [The oozing from this tree the natives use as a plaster for wounds.]
Wattle-tree (common)	Kur-run.
Wattle-tree (silver)	Moy-yan.
Wattle-tree (mimosa)	War-our-e-rup.
Wattle-tree (dwarf)	Eurt.
Cedar (bastardy)	Wy-gout.
Cherry-tree	Poo-lyte. [The stone grows outside, and not inside, as in Europe.]
Fern-tree	Kum-ba-da.
Fern-tree (short fern-tree)	Ku-der-ron.
Cabbage or grass tree	Kum-be-deek.
Privet (shrub)	Kar-ran.
Myrtle (native)	Tid-e-am.
Strawberry (native)	Koo-gor-ruk.
Rush	Bourt-bourt. [Good substitute for candles in the early history of the colony; grows a fine size at Western Port, and used by the primitive settlers there for candles.]
Flag (many kinds, principal)	Kur-ra-wan. [Black lubras make fine baskets and mats of them split.]
Fig (native)	Bung-bur-rulk or kum-me-ree.
Buttercup	Kurm-bur-root.
Convolvulus (three kinds)	Nur-rur.
Grass	Bo-curt.

Vegetables (indigenous), &c., eaten by Blacks.†

English.	Native.
Tal-le-rup	Grows 3 feet 6 inches high on the rich land and swamps; they eat it raw; tastes like cabbage.
Yep-pere	Small sweet bulb.
Mur-nong	A nourishing bulb, grows on poor loamy soil; blacks very fond of it.
Kurn-ger-rer	Tapering root, like a carrot; eaten raw, or thrown into the fire.
Boo-yeat	Grows high, like kum-be-duk. They bruise the outside, with which they make a kind of dough; eat the inside raw.
Kur-run	Gum; a valuable portion of Aboriginal diet. In dysentery they use it as a medicine made up into pills—a good medicine too.
Kurrn	A small maggot; eaten in thousands.
You-urn	Larger kind; eaten also.
Knu-nal	Eggs of ants.
Nurm-nurp	Large vegetable, grows in rich land and swamps, as high as celery and not inferior.

---

* Tree generally stunted, not more than six or eight inches in diameter; but on the Ten-mile Beach, between Mordialloc and Mount Eliza, between the two first inlets of the sea, on mere sand, they grow as high and in diameter as a huge gum-tree.

† It would be well here to state that these roots are all indigenous, and were in abundance before the whites came among them. Civilized or tamed animals and enclosures have much diminished their dependence. All were eaten by the blacks. To avoid touching upon the like subject again, I may state that all animals, except the snake and a few other animals, were eaten by the two Melbourne tribes; and tribes to the westward—even the Geelong blacks—used to eat snakes and bodies of large moths.

English.	Native.	English.	Native.
Bourt-deet	A superior fibrous vegetable; blacks eat it raw or cooked.	Biscuit	Pal-let-ner-rong.
		Soup	Lil-le-bro.
		Tea	Mor-an-doo.
European Food, &c.		Butter	Brim-brim-o.
Bread or flour	Ner-rong.	Milk	Brem-brem.
Rice	Kur-ran.	Herbs	Par-rum.
Sugar	Gaem-gaem.	Carrots	Kam-bo-duk.
Meat (general)	Win-gar-um.	Tobacco	Kun-ang-ner-ro-men.
Beef	Bul-gan-ner.	Spirits	Bal-lam.
Mutton	Ee-up.	To drink spirits	No-bi-an-bal-lam.
Pork *	Tal-lum.	To get drunk†	Bul-li-to no-bi-an.

A Few Leading Sentences.

English.	Native.	English.	Native.
Come here	War-ra-wee.	Take it	Koon-uk.
Go away	Tan-na-to-a.	Go and fetch	Yan-na-no.
Give me	U-mar-leek.	Cut it	Ti-buk.
Lend me	We-am-be-kan.	Put it down	Mar-buk.
Bring me	Won-da-nun.	Sit down there	Nor-lum-bee-not-to.
Send me	U-ro-ma-kun.		

English	Native
Come here to-morrow, and cut me some wood, and me give you white money.	Ba-bo-ring mur-rum bin-ner wo-man, bar til-ben-er kulk, bar murrumbeek umarleek white money.
What for you stupid, and get em big one drunk; by-and-by you die like it another one black fellow.	Kundee vener wong ruunin murrumbinner, bar bul-lito nobean ballam molocho weakon tan-dowring uungo koolin.
Will you go with me?	Tan-na-noul?‡
Where are you going?	Winda lingo murrumbinner?
This way, that way	Temon-o, temon mihu.
What going for?	Kundee vener?
To look out kangaroo	Kundee koim.
Where are your spears?	Winda tarren-o?
Here, in my miam	Mihu willumut.
No good spear. Very good gun	Nillam tare. Marnameek tranbulla-bel.
Now, let us go	Yan-na-wat.
Me see kangaroo; no you make noise, me shoot him.	Narnardun koim nier bunner tomnboonner murrumbeek vioner.
Go on, fire. Ah! tumble down dead	Mangkouuk vioner. Wa trantublulneit.
No dead, only gammon; you see run away that one.	Borak weakoner, tindee moyup; murrumbinner ngarren woolwoor.
Big one stupid. Now, go look out opossum	Nowlununartun, warrentenul, kundee waller wallert.
Me see tracks up the tree §	Nangerdon munnung kalligi myngnoit.
Blackfellows' corrobboree to-night	Koolin ngargunner borundut.
No; too much tumble down rain	Utur; bullito parn-min boldoneit.

---

* I must remark that, when I first came among the Aborigines, they would not eat any part of the pig. I soon found, however hungry a black might be, that he would not partake of a rasher of bacon. They could not explain why, only "no good pig." They, however, have long got over this prejudice, and now enjoy it much.

† The first black I ever saw drunk was of the Goulburn tribe—a man in years. Poor fellow! He was brought up to my tent by his wife and others, to know if he would die—had he been poisoned. He cried, staggered, and lay down in my tent. This was early in 1850. I believe, such was their innocence at that time, that the blacks thought he had been poisoned. Alas! now they crave this poison.

‡ This "noul," at the termination of the verb "go," answers to "will you with me?"

§ Blacks can tell by the bark if an opossum is up, by claw marks.

You tell 'em blackfellows to corrobboree, and me give them white money.
Tombannerrennun ngargun, bar murrumbeek umallen white money.

Blackfellows big one stupid, no corrobboree — Kooliner, wongrunin bullito, borak ngargun.

What for blackfellows no corrobboree? — Kundee vener borak ngargee kooliner?

Blackfellows die last moon — — — Koolin weakun ninncam werneit.

Blackfellows' corrobburee to-morrow night — Baborin burundut kooliner ngargee.

Yes, big one corrobboree; all blackfellows dance. Don't you know another one moon come?
Yea, ngargoon waga-bil, umarko koolin yeilve nier. Mangeit mincam uungo womon?

Dialogues.

ON RISING IN THE MORNING.

Awake! get up, get up, get up! — — — Ngiemuk! kommergee, kommergee, kommergee!

I will get up directly; stop, stop! my trousers are wet.
Murrumbeek kommergee tudan; burra, burra! murrumbiek tarrunarlook tulgunner.

Get up and make the fire; the sun is high — Kommargee werigut vein; ngervein karboit.

You are lazy; get up; chop some wood; the sun is up; dry your trousers.
Tandnni murrumbinner; kommagee; tilberner kulk; ngervein karboit; biderup tarrunarlook.

What for you tell 'em lie? sun only little up. Where tailwork?
Wenerrer wa moyutpin murrumbinner? ngervein tindee wyebo. Winda tailwork?*

Tailwork not dry; name who leave it on the ground last night.
Tailwork nier bidderup; nerreno welain narlumboon nge bukerborin molomolae.

Now it is dry; go on, turn away. Ah! I see smoke; fire soon come.
Netbo bidderup; ure, purrumbon. Ah! ngeren port; molocho vein woman.

Very good now, big one fire; now sit down and smoke your pipe.
Marnameek netbo, bullito vein; narlumby prombean pipe.

All good white men when they get up say their prayers, and thank God for taking care of them all night.
Bondup kommergee-ker nerdoit kommergee pardogurrabun, bar thank Pundgy'l Marman tuduk kununurner nerrembee borundut.

Big one stupid me and all blackfellows; no like it white man.
Wongrunin murrumbeek bar koolinner; nier tandowring bommageek.

ON GOING A JOURNEY.

Now, my blackfellows, make haste and get your breakfast; we will be going.
Eur barbullin kunarkut yanner bullen kunnee wat; kunnee wat.

Where are the bullocks? — Winda wottering bulganna?

Over there, behind that hill — — — Karbering miring bunnul wā.

Did you see their tracks? — — — Narnadarta parren teno?

Yes; I saw them this morning — — Yer; narnnerdonerun banban eram.

Where did they bed last night? — — Windart kudunger borundut?

By the big tree; don't you see their dung? — Narnnarlonniart karlto; kuddalling tarrung kunar?

Go and fetch them, that's a good fellow; I will lend you my horse.
Kungargewat wallarboyun nullinner; kulkelturnegieck.

Very well; where? — — — — — Kungargewat?

Bridle and saddle, I will go and fetch them; put my bag in the cart.
Worong kukedo nunnieck pelan minebuk; ngargee karber voit.

Now get the things together. Where are the pannikins? Don't leave anything behind.
Perkart yarrite ketherbā. Windowring tarnuk? Tumart now volumbernner yarrite.

Here are the bullocks. You are a good fellow, Bugup; here is a stick of tobacco for you.
Mihu pinnuk tudeyoul. Kungewā boundup, Bugup; moode yanner kunnunne murromanner.

Now, blackfellows, hold up the pole of the dray, and two of you hold on the back of the cart.
Netbo tarmbar karteckulgo, bengeronewat mummedo karter.

There, now, that will do; stop, let us see if anything is left behind; look about.
Nogeeballing, nageeballing; tudan, yartkun nut terredee yarrite; ngarreen.

---

* When I first came among the blacks, not an adult male or female were without their tailwork—a wood from which they procure fire; not by friction, as the Sydney blacks, but perpendicular, as working a drilling-bow.

LANGUAGE.   129

OF EATING AND DRINKING.

Put the pannikin on the fire. Where are the tea and sugar?
Korourk pannikin velnoit. Winda morrador bar gaem-gaem?

There is no water. Tell the lubras to get some water; pannikin in miam.
Nier parn. Toom bergee bagrook wantagu parn; pannikin willumut.

I cannot see the pannikin; it is not in the miam; I have looked all about.
Nier ngerren paonikin murrumbeek; miring willun; nier yarkunner.

Oh! big one, stupid me; it is behind the miam by that gum-tree.
Oh! wongurrunin, murrumbeek; monkir willumut karbe nge beal turrung.

Wash the pannikin. Very good clean, no good dirty.
Kurworbun pannikin. Marnameek kerwoneit, nillam kunnit pin.

Me big one hungry. Where is the kangaroo, the opossum, and the bandicoot?
Nerrebrunin bullito murrumbeek. Windowring koem, waller wallert, bar boong?

There they are, also the bear, wallaby, and wombat; put them all to the fire. Plenty of food in the bag. Sit down to-day; no look-out, only eat, sleep, and sing.
Notto nangeit, bar wimbi, warren, turnanook umarko, bar kurborä; bullito tanganan narlumby woollaminin, quombä yellnewä; utur, koondee, tinde tanganan, yemen bar yengerk.

Here, pickaninny, give that to the lubras, and tell them when they have eaten to go and look out gum for blackfellows to eat.
Wä! bopup, kunuk kunnee bagrook, tombanna bagrook tinderbuk tanganan dado koondee kurruntuduk koolinner bullito tanganan.

This kangaroo is very good, it is a joe; here is another, young lubra, ah!
Kunne koem marnameek, joe kargee; bar unngo marnameek, monmondeek, ki!

The water boils; put in the tea, and give some to the children, and they fetch us more water.
Parn touloppun; quambä morador, bar umarleek bopup, tudun bopup wantagee parn uungo.

You too much greedy, pickaninny; you give some of that kangaroo to that pickaninny out there.
Bullito garn murrumbinner, bopup; umerleek bopup monkyne nge tanganun koem tudau.

Now let us sleep, big one stupid; white man work every day, no like 'em this. No you make a noise, pickaninny; play out there. Big one bellyful me.
Netbo mallyemena, bullito wongorunin hommageek mongan yellenwä yellenwä. Nier tandowring nge-nier, bopup; tillutkerin monkyne nge. Bullito marp murrumbeek.

PLAYS AND DIVERSIONS.

What shall we play at first? - - - -
Wener ganbony tillutkerrin?

We will play at ball; you make it up, very high, don't you see one? Very good that one, go on kick.
Mangut marnameek, mongun ganbony murrumbinner, marnamuk kunnup; ure kurruk ngerin karboit.

Come, come; me get it; make haste! - -
Kolly-warree, wolley kungardon!

Take care of the child; no me throw it down; no me stupid.
Tartbuk bopup; niup badan umite nier; wongrunin murrumbeek.

Throw it out again, out further. Call the boys outside.
Umark worreder, wentbuk, marnameck. Tombargee bopup millurree.

Take care of the stumps, take care now, you go on too fast.
Warregerry kulk, warregerry kullerbrook, kulberlin woovoneit murrumbinner.

No more; that will do; the ball broke; sit down
Nogee; nogee; mangut tinderbeek; narlumby.

Play at soldiers. Come here. Stand up. Hold up your head. That will do, that will do.
Tillutkerrin policemen. Warrä wee. Terridee, kommergally, berunggally. Nogee, nogeemee.

Right about face - - - - -
Pierup koodelly.

Stand at ease - - - - - -
Tilbert munuuinner.

Attention - - - - - - -
Tilbert terreninna.

Quick march - - - - - -
Yanna uree.

Another one day get 'em guns - - -
Uung yellenwä kundu trangbullabil.

No more play now, it is too hot. When go down sun, then play at wavoit.
Nogeemee woodu ngervein tournaboon. Nerdoit narlumby, ngervein wavoit.

Now koolin, where wavoit? Come all blackfellows.
Netbo koolin, winda wavoit? Womenderrewat.

Now let us see who throw out the farthest. Throw it out.
Malnangyer, wida umeit warreete, umuk perperduuk.

VOL. II.   R

You can't catch me. No you'take it, my wavoit. This is mine. No, no; me give it you.

All done play. Dark now. Come on, come on. You walk and I will run.

Sit down. Where pipe? Outside, inside miam; make haste and get it.
Sit all around. Stop, just stop - - - -

Nier benerak bunner, nier paarthrabun, wavoit murrumbick. Kunne murrumbiek. Utur, nier urbinan umanner.

Tinderbeck tillutkerrin. Borun netbo. Warrawee murrumbinner yannou, murrumbeek woovon.

Narlumby. Winda pipe? Kiering, mihu willum; ure urebuk.
Wan-wan broodewat. Pingoody, pingoody.

Translations.

THE CXXI. PSALM.

1. I will lift up mine eyes unto God; from Him cometh my help.

2. My help cometh from the Lord, who made the heaven and the earth.

3. He will not suffer thy foot to be moved; He that keepeth thee will not slumber.

4. Behold! He that keepeth Israel shall neither slumber nor sleep.

5. The Lord is thy keeper; the Lord is thy shade, upon thy right hand.

6. The sun shall not smite thee by day, nor the moon by night.

7. The Lord shall preserve thee from all evil; He shall preserve thy soul.

8. The Lord shall preserve thy going out and thy coming in, from this time forth, and even for evermore.

1. Murrumbeek woorunderoneit mynginiek kuding Pundgyl Marman; weda womonner nunlbeunnul.

2. Murrumbick nunlbeunnul womoner Pundgyl Marman, wellainer monkeit woor-woor bar becker.

3. Kargee nier malbodoneit murrumbiek tinan; mungither wellainer koonark murrumbinner nier yemoner.

4. Wa! Mungither wellainer Koonark murrumbinner nier yemee nier yemoner.

5. Pundgyl Marman kunark murrumbinner; Pundgyl Molarick ulbinner munung.

6. Nier ngervein tilbunner murrumbinner yellanwā nier mineam boorundut.

7. Pundgyl Marman nulworthun murrumbinner; nier nillam woman mungither moorupiek nulworthununner.

8. Pundgyl Marman nerdoit murrumbinne yannon nulworthun, bar nerdoit womoneit nulworthun murrumbinner, netbo bar wootunno yearamboot tille mille nanbo.

THE FIRST CHAPTER OF GENESIS.*

1. In the beginning God created the heaven and the earth.

2. And the earth was without form, and void, and darkness was upon the face of the deep. And the Spirit of God moved upon the face of the waters.

3. And God said, let there be light: and there was light.

4. And God saw the light that it was good; and God divided the light from the darkness.

5. And God called the light day, and the darkness he called night. And the evening and the morning were the first day.

1. Ganbronin Pundgyl Marman monguit woorworer bar beek.

2. Nier beck nowdin netbo, beek tandowring tarkate; nier boit, nier mill, nier taul, nier turrong, nier uungo; bar boorundara kormuk bumile. Bar Moorup Pundgyl warrebonnk narlumbanan parn.

3. Bar Pundgyl Marman tombuk, womear yangamut : bar yangamut woman.

4. Bar Pundgyl Marman nangeit yangamut bar tombak boundup nge ; bar Pundgyl Marman borungnergurk yangamut boorrundara.

5. Bar Pundgyl Marman nerreno yangamut yellenwo, bar borundara borundut. Bar krunguine bar banbaneram nerreno ganbronin yellenwā.

---

* Abridged in some of the verses, in order to simplify the chapter to suit Aboriginal capacity, but the full purport is retained.

6, 7. And God said, let there be a firmament. And God made the firmament; and divided the waters which were under the firmament from the waters which were above the firmament: and it was so.

8. And God named the firmament heaven. And the evening and the morning were the second day.

9. And God said, let the waters under the heavens be gathered together unto one place, and let the dry land appear: and it was so.

10. And God called the dry land earth; and the gathering together of the waters called he seas: and God saw that it was good.

11, 12, 13. And God said, let the earth bring forth grass, herb, and trees, whose seed is in itself: and it was so: and God saw that it was good. And the evening and the morning were the third day.

14, 15, 16, 17, 18, 19. And God said, let there be light above, to divide the day from the night, and let them be for lights to give light upon the earth: and it was so: and God made two great lights; the greater light to rule (or make) the day; and lesser light to rule (or make) the night. He made the stars also. And God saw that it was good. And the evening and the morning were the fourth day.

20, 21, 22, 23. And God said, let the waters bring forth abundantly of fish, great and small, and fowl that may fly above the earth. And God saw that it was good. And the evening and the morning were the fifth day.

24, 25. And God said, let the earth bring forth all living creatures after its kind: and it was so. And God made beasts of the earth, and all cattle after its kind. And God saw that all was good.

26, 27. And God said, let us make man in our image. And God made in his own image man; in the image of God created he him; male and female created he them.

28, 29. And God blessed them, and said, increase and replenish the earth; and have power over the fish of the sea, and fowl of the air, and all living things. And God gave man every tree and herb bearing fruit and seed for man's food.

6, 7. Bar Pundgyl Marman tombak, malwomear firmament. Bar Pundgyl Marman mongeit narng; bar borungnergurk parn kubberdon beck, bar nungonuk parn kuding karboit tandowring nowdin netbo.

8. Bar Pundgyl Marman nerreno firmament woorwoorrer. Bar krunguine bar banbaneram nerreno bengerrowlin yellenwă.

9. Bar Pundgyl Marman tombit, malwomear parn kubberdon woorwoorrer kundee ganbony tombor, bar malwomear palletdebuk: bar nowdin netbo.

10. Bar Pundgyl Marman nerreno hidderup beck (earth); bar wotonno parn nerreno warreenwarreen: bar Pundgyl nangeit kooding ngə marnameek.

11, 12, 13. Bar Pundgyl Marman tombit, warra wee boit, bar kunnulderbil kurrenum, bar terrung willainer kooding nge: bar Pundgyl Marman ngerren bar tombak marnameek. Bar krunguine bar banban eram yellingwă bengero ganmel.

14, 15, 16, 17, 18, 19. Bar Pundgyl Marman tombak, malwomear yangamut karboit, bar nungonuk yellenwă bar borundut, tuduk yangamut becker: tandowring netbo: bar Pundgyl Marman monkeit bengero bullito yangamut; koonge bullito narngate yellenwă, bar wyebo yangamut narngate borundut. Mungither monkeit wotunno topiram nowdin netbo. Bar Pundgyl Marman nangeit koodin marnameek. Bar krunguine bar banbaneram bengero bar bengerowlin yellenwă.

20, 21, 22, 23. Bar Pundgyl Marman tombak, malwomear tuat wootunno, wyebo bar bullito narlumbunner parn, bar koyup woolwoin karboit becker. Bar Pundgyl Marman ngerreen boundup nge. Bar krunguine bar banban eram bengero bar bengero ganmelrowling yellenwă.

24, 25. Bar Pundgyl Marman tombak, mallongener beck wantagee umarko kunup togan nge: bar tandowring nge. Bar Pundgyl Marman monkeit tukin ungut tandowring nge. Bar Pundgyl Marman nangeit marnameek kuding.

26, 27. Bar Pundgyl Marman tombak, mallun monkeit kooling tandowring murrumbunick. Bar Pundgyl Marman monkeit tandawring kargeeiek koolinner; nowdin kargeeiek monkeit munniger; kooling bar bagrook monkeit murrumnuller.

28, 29. Bar Pungyl Marman tombit boundup murrumnuller; geanboon koolingee bagrook bar wootunno bepup kuding beckar; bar umanaro umarko tuat kuding warreen, koyup worworrow bar umarko yeareit togan. Bar Pundgyl Marman uninară koolin umarko turrung, bar umarko uungo tunganan koolinge bagrook.

30, 31. And God gave every living thing to man for food; and it was so. And God saw everything that he had made, and behold it was very good. And the evening and the morning were the sixth day.

30, 31. Bar Pundgyl Marman umanarer kunnulwarrable tuduk tanganan; kuding nge. Bar Pundgyl Marman ngarren umarko kargee mongon, bar wă tombak koongee boundup. Bar krunguine bar banban eram, nerreno bengero, bengero, bar bengerowling yellenwă.

THE CREED.

I believe in God the Father Almighty, Maker of Heaven and Earth ; and in Jesus Christ His only Son our Lord; who came down from heaven to save man, and die for his people ; who was by wicked men killed and hanged on a tree ; who was dead and buried ; who rose again the third day from the dead, and ascended into heaven, and sat down at the right hand of God the Father ; from whence He shall come again and make all mankind stand before Him ; and separate the good from the wicked.

I believe in the Holy Ghost, the resurrection of the body, and the life everlasting.—Amen.

Murrumbeek nunurrunkella kuding Pundgyl Marman, koongee palleek mongeit woorwoorrer bar beeker ; bar kuding Jesus Christ Tindee mummum murrumbununner Lord ; wellainer burrawee woorwoorrer mongonner koolinge bagrook marnameek ; wellainer nillam koolinglil buk weakeit bar berbuk, narlumboon burrung ; wellainer wengoulaneit bar numbuk ; wellainer tinderbeek bengero ganmel yellenwă, kuding commargee nunnume, bar kubboweer woorwooroit bar narlumby ulbinner munung Pundgyl Marmanicck ; uungo yellenwă Jesus Christ nerlingo mongoin umarko koolinge bagrook terridee kargeeiek ; bar pindoner boundup bar meungo.

Murrumbeek nunurrunkellă Boundup Moorrup, commargee murrum, bar moorrup, tillee millee nangbo.—Amen.

THE LORD'S PRAYER.

Our Father who art in Heaven ; hallowed be Thy name ; Thy kingdom come ; Thy will be done on earth like it in heaven. Give us this day our daily food ; and forgive us our bad deeds as we forgive them that do us bad ; and keep us from sin this day, and from all evil.

Only Thou, O Great Father, can keep us now and ever.—Amen.

Marmanellă Marman wellainer narlumhoon karboit ; nerrino murrumbinner koongee boundup ; woman trangbulk murrumbinner mongon tandowring becker. Umarleek nurnin yellenwă tauganan ; bar narlarnarny nurnin nowdin murrumarter narlarnarny ungo ; bar kunark nurnin watticar koolin yellenwă nier nillam womeit.

Tindu Murrumbinner, Boundup Marman, nulworthen nurnin netbo bar nanbo.—Amen.

FROM CHURCH SERVICE.

My dear blackfellows,—God's book tells us in many places to acknowledge and confess our many sins, and that we should not hide them before the face of Almighty God, but confess them with sorrow, that we may have forgiveness of them through His great goodness; and though every day we ought to tell God our sins, yet more so on Sunday, when we all meet together ; to thank him for all his goodness ; to hear His good book; and to ask all good for our bodies and souls. So let us all, as many as are now here, fall upon our knees, and pray to our Great Father in heaven, saying—&c., &c.

Murrumbick koolin,—Kunne paper wă Pundgyl Marman tombak wongonon dado pardogurrabun tomboon nillam nurnin koongee meungo, bar nier eulethee nillam nurnin tuduk nier wongrunin pallat Pundgyl Marman, tindee mardon mallun tombak mongderrewat mardoneit kunnup Pundgyl Marman yangally narrite umarko boundup rige ; bar nelnwă pardogurrabun banban eram bar krunguite Pundgyl Marman, nerdoit bullito Sunday womon wotunno pardogurrabun narlumby umarko ; thank Mungither tuduk umarko boundup narngon kargeiek berkerk ; tombarlarnon yarrite boundup murrum bar moorup ; netbo, malpardogurrabun umarko, marlumbunun mibu bullito Pundgyl boundup Marman narlumboon karboti tom-der-run en-er—&c., &c

LANGUAGE.

HYMN TO OLD HUNDRED.*

1 Pund-gyl Mar-man, bar mar-na-meek
   Nun-guk kub-ber-don mur-rum-beek
   Mong-der-re-wat koo-lin netbo
   Tan-dow-ring koon-gee mur-rum-bo.

2 Mal-yeng-erk par-do-gur-ra-bun
   Tu-duk yar-rite ko-dun-un-un
   Ner-rem-bee bo-run yel-len-wa.
   Nul-wor-then bo-pup Koo-linner.

3 Ner-doit ye-men-ner mur-rum-beek
   Lack-boo-ding myng-ner kar-gee-ick
   Bar ner-doit yan-na-ner war-reet
   Kar-gee nger-ren-er mur-rum-beck.
   &c., &c.

* The black children at Merri Creek school used to sing this admirably.

CATECHISM.

Q.—Tell me, my child, who made you? - -
A.—The Great God who made the heaven and the earth.

Q.—Tombannerek murrumbiek bopup, wellainer mongeit murrumbinner?
A.—Pundgyl Marman weda mongut woor-woorrer bar beeker.
&c., &c.

LANGUAGE OF THE ABORIGINES OF THE COLONY OF VICTORIA.

This vocabulary, compiled by the late Daniel Bunce, Esq.—"English—Native"—is now arranged for greater convenience in a new form—"Native—English." Mr. Bunce was a careful and conscientious observer, and, on the whole, his vocabulary is very accurate. It appears to relate almost exclusively to the dialects of the Yarra Yarra and Coast tribes.

Directions in Pronunciation.—In all cases the vowels must be sounded, and the vowel *a* sounded broad as *ah*. Where a word terminates with *tha*, its sound is sharp, as in *thank*. If *tho* is the concluding syllable, it should be pronounced soft, as in *though*.

By speaking this language with a soft Italian accent, the reader will have little trouble in making himself understood by the natives.

Aboriginal.	English.
Ah-ah *or* weenthunga - - -	Peradventure, perhaps.
Allambee - - - - -	To recline, seated, sitting, to sit on a seat, to sojourn, to remain a while.
Allambee ba'anth - - -	To float, ducking under water.
Allambee beek - - - -	To fall, to tumble down.
Allambee myaring mulloko jeetho -	A lodging, a temporary abode.
Allambee weenth - - -	Inflame, to set on fire.
Allambee willam - - -	Occupy, reside.
Ba'anji myrring - - -	Tear, water from the eye.
Ba'anji ba'anth - - - -	Water.
Ba'anth mellaba - - -	Rain, a shower.

Aboriginal.	English.
Baggarook	Female, woman.
Baggarook bulgana	Cow.
Baggarook n'u'd'lam	Beldam, a scolding woman.
Bambra	Mushroom.
Bang'ath	Overcome, to subdue.
Banyock brearback	Abjugate.
Barawag	Breast-high.
Barding	Knee.
Barem-burbywa	Lactation, giving suck.
Bargan	Cool.
Bargarro	Shoulder.
Barmburrim	Clean, unsoiled, pure, to cleanse, to rinse.
Barnboon	A load, a burden.
Barraback	Bandage, knot, to tie.
Barroworn	Magpie.
Beally goonong	Loins of the body.
Beebeethu'ung	Red, color of blood.
Beek	Clay, country, dirt, mud, earth, ground, land, soil, mould.
Beelmeek	Pus, corrupt matter from a sore.
Beelong	Bag.
Beenack	Basket, flasket, band-basket.
Beenthuck gooroomulla	Bleed, to let blood.
Belling-atha	Abdomen, paunch, the belly.
Beertherriboon	Bilk, to cheat.
Benjeroo	Both, a couple, a brace, double, a pair, two, second, next to the first, two wives.
Benjeroo allambee	To brace, to bind together.
Benjeroo baggarook	Women (two).
Benjeroo cooleenth jumbuck	Dialogue.
Benjeroo vor carnboo	Three, third.
Benjeroo vor benjeroo geenong	Quadruped, four legs.
Benjeroo vor benjeroo geenong'atha	Four-footed.
Benjeroo vor benjeroo vor benjeroo	Six.
Benjeroo vor benjeroo vor carnboo	Five.
Benjeroo vor benjeroo vor benjeroo vor carnboo	Seven.
Benjeroo vor benjeroo vor benjeroo vor benjeroo vor carnboo	Nine.
Benjeroo vor benjeroo vor benjeroo vor carnboo noweenth	A week or seven days.
Berring	Midwinter.
Bibberoom	Abscess, sore, blotch, scabby.
Bilim	Alcohol, spirits, brandy.
Bilim-bilim	Ale or beer.
Bilim ponraneen	Stagger, to reel.
Bilim umaraleek	Intoxicate, to make drunk.
Billarng	A line, a string.
Bindack	To cut, to carve, to hew.
Bindurk	Bowels.
Birmabuck	A fly, an insect.
Bolk	Urine.
Bollam-bollam	Butterfly.
Bollardy week	Shallow, not deep.
Booboop	Baby, child, infant, offspring, children, urchin, young.
Boobooroom	Scurvy or scabby.
Booboop mongoobera	Cygnet, young swan.

LANGUAGE.

Aboriginal.	English.
Booboop n'uther parbine n'uther marmoonth	A foundling.
Boodankin	Deep, far from the bottom.
Boodurk co'ondo'ong	To choke, stifle, strangle, suffocate.
Booith	Liver, one of the entrails.
Boonboop powreenth	Born.
Boonduck	To gnash, to grind the teeth in rage.
Boonthung thung allen	To bite.
Boorong	Firmament.
Booran	An ant.
Boorooee	Black, dark.
Booroointh *or* lark	Murky, dark, cloudy.
Booroonth	Dark, gloom, want of light, obscure, to darken.
Booronthooith	Midnight, night.
Booronthooith yannathan	Nightfaring, travelling in the night.
Boorurn	Sky, the heavens.
Bootboon	Cancer, pustule, a pimple or sore, scabby, sores, a tender place.
Boothonakoon	Cough.
Bouthoon geenong a'ta	Chilblain.
Booyboorooing	To-morrow.
Borap	Debility, weakness.
Boroug	Lip of the mouth.
Borong'ooth	Brittle.
Bowyceth	Bald.
Brimbinuree	Bride.
Brim-brim	Milk.
Brim-brimgatha	Bosom, breast, nipple, a teat.
Brimbynthon	To find, to discover.
Brimerriburn	To burrow, to make holes, a hole, a hollow place.
Bucknalook	Conjuror.
Bulgana	Beef, bull, meat, ox, bullock.
Bullar-bullar	Light, not heavy.
Bullarto	Abundance, big, broad, bulky, capacious, colossal, large, copious, extensive, exuberant, abundant, fertile, fruitful, great, large, huge, immense, most, the greatest in quantity, much, a great deal, plenty, profusion, quantity, bulk, redundance, total, universal, all, vast, very great, exceeding, satiate, full.
Bullarto ba'anth	Deluge, inundation, a lake, overflow of water.
Bullarto ba'anth mellaba	Storm, rain.
Bullarto bilim	Bacchanalian, debauch, drunkenness, inebriated, drunken, sot, drunkard, tipsy, drunk.
Bullarto carndooth	Concupiscence, sensuality, whorish, unchaste, wanton, lascivious.
Bullarto conong	Diarrhœa.
Bullarto corong	A ship or large vessel
Bullarto cooleenth	Chief, command, commander.
Bullarto cooleenth allambee	A gang, a number of men together.
Bullarto cowongatha	Chub-head, stupid.
Bullarto dullally	Incivility.
Bullarto dullallally	To plume, to make proud.
Bullarto dumbalk	Winter.
Bullarto ecip	A flock of sheep.
Bullarto cumaraleek	Hospitality, munificent, open-hearted, generous.
Bullarto garng	Greedy, inhospitable, parsimony.

Aboriginal.	English.
Bullarto jaalbunna	Cut throat.
Bullarto ja'alburt	Slaughter, to slay.
Bullarto jindivick	Demolish, to lay waste.
Bullarto jumbuck	Brawling, loquacity, too much talk, vociferous, noisy.
Bullarto jumbunna	Babbler, to talk idly, chat, chatter, to cluck, to talk fast, clamorous, noisy, to expostulate, hubbub, great talking, jabber, verbose.
Bullarto jumbunna eumaraleek	Importunate.
Bullarto lark	Cloudy, fog, mistiness, overcast, clouded.
Bullarto marden	Deplore, to lament, dirge, funeral ditty, heartache, sorrow, inconsolable, misery, to pine, to grieve, sad, sorrowful.
Bullarto marmingatha	Almighty God, clergyman, God, devotion, the Supreme.
Bullarto monomeeth	Delight, enrapture.
Bullarto mooyoopgo'onong	Delusion, a cheat, sham.
Bullarto mornmoot	Hurricane, a violent storm, storm, tempest.
Bullarto nandubber	Glut, overmuch.
Bullarto nang'ana	Stare, to look with wonder.
Bullarto nerreburdin	Ravenous, hungry, unfed.
Bullarto noweenth	Meridian, mid-day, noon-day.
Bullarto n'u'd'lam	Dislike, to hate, to detest, scandalous, shameful.
Bullarto n'ulam	Despicable, worthless, worse, worst.
Bullarto nurong	Feast.
Bullarto n'ya'alingo conong	Lax, diarrhœa.
Bullarto n'ya'arunning	Driveller, a fool.
Bullarto n'yeelam	Diabolical, abominable, damnable, most wicked.
Bullarto n'yellam	Enormity, villany, intolerable, very hard.
Bullarto n'yoweenth	Summer.
Bullarto pa'amboonth	Coward, cowardice, daunted, dread, great fear, chicken-hearted, cowardly, to quake, to shake with fear.
Bullarto porkwadding	Crabbed, peevish, impatient, passionate, impetuosity, fury, infuriate, enraged, rage, violent anger, unpeaceable, quarrelsome.
Bullarto poromboon	Mar, to spoil.
Bullarto queeop-queeop	Flock of birds.
Bullarto torong	Brig, a ship.
Bullarto tutbyrum	Comet.
Bullarto umaleek	Liberal.
Bullarto umaraleek	Munificent, open-handed, generous, open hearted.
Bullarto umina	Oversleep, outsleep.
Bullarto weenth	Blaze, flame, bright, conflagration, general fire, hot.
Bullarto weeakabull	Longevity, length of life.
Bullarto wonthaggi	Gather, to collect.
Bullarto yannathan	Unfixed, vagrant.
Bullarto yarragondock	Unshaved.
Bumbuck	Hack, to cut in pieces.
Bundarraboon	Inhuman.
Buudike	Chip, to cut in pieces.
Bungal	Division, equal, each.
Burnburn	Burden, a load.
Burra	Forbear, to pause, a pause, a stop, tush, wait, stop, rapid.
Burra-burra	Abrupt, apt, quick, bestir, busy, directly, outright, immediately.
Burraguck morobeek	Likeness.
Burribarridth	Plover, a bird.
Byawark lark	Incantation, a charm.
Ca'anboo myruongatha	Digital, a finger.

LANGUAGE. 137

Aboriginal.	English.
Ca'anboo meniyan	Month.
Ca'andect	Amorous.
Ca'andooith	Immodest, shameless, impure, unchaste, indecently, indecorous, indelicate.
Caarndooith	Foul-mouthed, bad language.
Ca'arneek	Lonely.
Ca'arnduce	Abuse.
Ca'arnthooith	Lewd, wicked, hurtful.
Ca'arrdooce	Lust, carnal desire.
Cabbe melemung'il	Greeting, a salutation.
Cabbin	Chill, cold.
Cabbing	Snow, sleet.
Carbeenthon or carbethon	Gay, cheerful, hilarity, humorous, play, to sport, to chuckle, to laugh, glad, gleeful, merry.
Carmboonith	To amuse, merry.
Carmuggy or carmuggie	To rouse up, ascend, to arise, awake, convalescent, to raise, to raise up, to rise, get up, up, waken, to rise from sleep.
Carmuggy carmuggy	To rouse, to wake up.
Carmuggy noweenth	East.
Carmuggy n'yoweenth	Sunrise.
Carnboo	A, one, once, unit.
Carnboo coolcenth	Individual, one person.
Carnboo dandridibhle	Shilling.
Carnboo myrring'atha	Monocular, one-eyed, one eye.
Carnboon	Jesting, laughing, joke, jolly.
Carnboo meniyan	Lunation, the revolution of the moon, month.
Carnboo n'uther benjeroo	Entire.
Carndeeth	Lascivious, lustful.
Carndooith	Carnal, sensual, unbecoming, indecent, unchaste, unseemly, vice, wicked, vicious, vile.
Carnic n'ya'llamboonon	Alone, singly, by one's self.
Carrangall	Athletic.
Caryoong	A belt, a girdle of opossum wool.
Chuck-chuck	Chanticleer, a cock.
Cobhera cowong	A cap, a hat.
Cobbeya nerregootha	Summit, top.
Cobboboonee	To part, to separate.
Cobborin	Local, in that place, there, at that place, thither, yonder.
Concenoram	To corrode.
Cong'ack	Hold, to keep.
Cong'atha	Nasal, belonging to the nose, nose.
Conong	Compost, dung, excrement of animals, human dung, excrement, manure, muck, soil, stool, evacuation.
Coogurra	Clothe, to cover with a rug, covering, dress.
Coolcenth	Black man, creature, man, male, the he of any species, adult of the human species, a mortal, a human being, a person (man or woman)."
Coolcenth bullarto bilim	A drinker, a drunkard, drunk.
Coolcenth bullarto jumbunna	Gabbler, a prater.
Coolcenth dullallally	Uncivil.
Coolcenthebaggarook	A person (man or woman).
Coolcenth jeetho	Delegate, to send away.
Coolcenth mooyoop goonong	Impostor, a cheat.
Coolcenth nang'eeth	Eye-witness.
Coolcenth n'ya'alingo uong'a beek	A foreigner.

VOL. II. S

Aboriginal.	English.
Cooleenth n'ya'arunning	Milksop, derision, a laughing-stock, dolt, stupid fellow, mad, a fop, humdrum, a stupid person, lunatic, madman, maniac.
Cooleenth pimberlally	Dishonesty, a thief.
Cooleenth uther mooyoop	Faithful.
Coolonyeebaggarook	Wife.
Coomuckawabilly	Infold, wrap up.
Coong'ack	To feel, sense of touch.
Coongamea brimbine	Adultery.
Coong-uck	Infection.
Coongurt	To accept.
Coonoojee	Nab, to catch.
Coopbarninthyoowung	Incurable.
Cooragook	Stop, to pause.
Coornburt	Chain, a necklace, ornaments worn round the neck.
Coorng-uck	Impede, to hinder.
Coornmill	Serpent, a snake.
Coornong	Brook, a creek.
Cooroonoing	Athirst, thirsty.
Coorowork	Interchange.
Corowock	To wash.
Corrobboree	Dance.
Cowong	Costard, cranium, skull, head.
Cowongatha	Pate, the head, skull, scalp.
Cowong n'ya'arunning	Deranged in mind, light-headed.
Cowurndy	Crawl, to creep.
Croobuck	Clinch, to hold fast.
Cubboot	Mute, silent, dumb.
Cubbout nangooith	Beware, mum, hush.
Currumburra	Flesh-fly, a blow-fly.
Dandredibble	Small change, money.
Darnum	A parrot.
Dirundirri	Eggs of birds.
Doonburrim	Lizard.
Dorong	Core, heart.
Drumbullabull	Blunderbuss, gun, carbine, detonation, thunder, a firelock, fowling-piece, a musket.
Drumdlemera	Bottle, a flask.
Dullallally	Brag, to boast, bounce, conceited, ambition, wish for power, arrogantly, proudly, audacious, bluster, to bully, boaster, swagger, coxcomb, a fop, despotic, egotist, effrontery, elated, pride, proud, gasconade, officious, ostentation, pert, saucy, pompous, presumptuous, arrogance, rudeness, shameless, impudent, to strut, to walk affectedly, upstart, vain, vanity, to vaunt, grumbling, growling, opinionative, barefaced, flippancy, pertness, high-minded, imperious, impertinent, impudence, insolence, lofty, haughty.
Dullallally cooleenth	Bouncer, a bully.
Dumbalk or dumbulk	Bleak, chilly, frosty, ice, freeze, frost, hail, frozen rain, hoar-frost.
Durong'y burn	Heel, the hind part of the foot.
Durooke lark	Rainbow.
Eeburra or yucca-yucca	Anguish, pain, plaint, lamentation, plaintive, shriek, a cry of anguish.
Eeburra woorarra rummeethan	Alas! denoting pity.
Ecip	Mutton, sheep.

LANGUAGE.

Aboriginal.	English.
Ellinging	Brow, forehead.
Eoke	Eel.
E'u'd'lam cooleenth	Scoundrel.
Eumaleek	Recompense, to gain.
Eumaleek bulgana	Meat offering.
Eumana	Dormant, sleeping.
Eumaraleek	Ask, beseech, bestow, give, cede, to give up, consign, to give over to another, contribute, crave, demand, deign to give, to claim, entreat, furnish, supply, to hand, implore, beg, petition, supplicate, to present, to restore.
Eumaraleek dandridribble	Imburse, to give money.
Eumaraleek mirambeek	To claim.
Eumaraleek nurong	Feed, to supply food.
Eumina	Asleep, repose, sleep.
Eyearoothin	Dream.
Galbarmuck	Gash, a deep cut or wound.
Galbiling n'garrook	Tomahawk.
Galboorack	Apiece, to divide.
Galburnin	Broken, lame, cripple, to maim.
Gallopin-gallopin gweeop	Knife, penknife.
Geenong	Mark, footmark.
Geenongalook	Boot, shoe.
Geenonga'tha	Ankle of the foot, foot, step, footstep, toes.
Geerar	Reed.
Geerar oordiyalya	Reedy, many reeds.
Geetho	Proceed.
Geetho youarrabuck	Run, to go quick.
Gooroomul	Blood.
Goorang	Demon, evil spirit.
Gullagothoon	Inside.
Gweeon	Lance, a long spear.
Iroontha wothoingun	Pulse, motion of the blood.
Ja'aburt	Injure.
Ja'albuck	Scream.
Ja'albunna	Butchered, killed, massacre, murder, murderer.
Ja'albunna booboop	Infanticide.
Ja'alburt	Assault, to beat, to strike, destroy, kill, deprive of life, murder, scourge, punish, slay.
Ja'alburt marmoonth	Parricide, who kills his father.
Ja'alburt parbine	Matricide, killing a mother.
Jajidtch	Marrow in bones.
Jeed-tho	Abscond.
Jeeluckgeerework	Dandle, to play.
Jeerar	Lance, a long spear (made of reeds).
Jeeraboon	Ashamed, shy, bashful, coy, modest, coyish.
Jeetho	Depart, detach, send away, dismiss, exit, fly, to go away, go, to walk off, hence, liberate, to set free, loose, on, go forward, onward, repulse, to drive away, retire, send, to despatch, went, gone, withdraw.
Jeetho booroonthooith	Nocturnal, by night.
Jeetho corong	Ferry in a boat or canoe.
Jeetho mornmoot	Blow, driven by wind.
Jeetho uonga beek	Remove, to go away.
Jeetho uonga willam	Decamp, to shift, migration, removing, to move.
Jeetho youarrabuck	Hie, to go quickly.
Jeetho uther jumbuck	Elope.

140   THE ABORIGINES OF VICTORIA:

Aboriginal.	English.
Jeetho willam	Homeward.
Jen-jen moon	Point, sharpened.
Jim jerrum	Cod-fish.
Jindarning thung'oith	Food, nourish, to support, nutriment, provisions, victuals, refreshment.
Jindy neelingo	Gaunt, thin, slender.
Jindivic	Burst, asunder, consume, destroy, decay, falling off, devoid, empty, disappear, to vanish, eaten, all gone, emptiness, escaped, exhaust, extinct, fade, wither, irrecoverable, lost for good, lose, to suffer loss, none, out, not here, past, rid, clear away, vacant, gone, vanish, to disappear, went, fade away.
Jindivic ba'anth	Leak, to run out, parched, dried up.
Jindivic boothoone	Cure, heal up, heal, to cure, recover, get well again.
Jindivic booyaroong	Eunuch.
Jindivic kidnong	Earless.
Jindivic n'yowcenth	Sunset.
Jindivic weeinth	Quench, to extinguish fire.
Jindivic yarragondock	Shave.
Jindi woraback	Annex, to join together.
Jingeelbark	Knock.
Jiruduck	Contempt, scorn.
Jirnkee	Cascade.
Jooruduck !	Ah ! denoting contempt.
Jonediah myrrinbiangoo	Alike.
Jumbuck	Announce, confer, converse, declaim, to harangue, divulge, to reveal, impart, communicate, enquire, to ask, interpret, to explain, narrate, to tell, oration, a speech, to speak.
Jumbunna	Colloquy, a conference, discourse, inform, to tell, language, mention, to repeat, pronounce, to speak, reply, to say, speech, talk, to utter.
Jumbunna allen	Attention.
Jumbunna porkwadding	Altercation, dispute.
Kaarmbee	Blithe, merry.
Kalburning n'g narragoo	Misshapen, deformed.
Kalk	Chump of wood, log, a piece of wood.
Kalk-kalk	Bludgeon, thick stick, cane, walking-stick, stick, piece of wood.
Kang'an	Feather, plumage.
Karbeethong	Mirth.
Karkarook	Sand.
Karung	Shin.
Keelonith	Suppose.
Kidnong'atha	Ear.
Kie ! monomeeth	Amaze, confusion, cheer, gaity, hurra ! shout of triumph.
Kirrack	Kick, with the foot.
Kirring	Hooked.
Kirtkirtarnook	Hackney, a horse, mare, steed.
Kirtkirtarnook geenong'alook	Horseshoe.
Kirtkirtarnook yarragong-atha	Horsehair.
Kong'arra muggy	Regain.
Kongwak	Catch, to stop.
Koogurra	Apparel.
Koonangonan	Childbearing.
Koon-warra	Swan.
Koorknatha	Calf of the leg.

LANGUAGE.

Aboriginal.	English.
Koorn	Neck, part of the body, throat.
Koortworko	Reserve, keep some back, retain.
Korong	Canoe, boat.
Korramoonith	Retch, to vomit.
Korrong	Gum, viscous juice of wattle and other trees.
Korroorook	A stork.
Korumburra	Maggot.
Kulburnin	Break, crash.
Kullap	Needle of bone.
Kurrambeo	Laugh.
Kye!	Acclamation; Ha! an expression of wonder; O! interjection; soho! wonder.
Kye! quantbee!	Hey! exclamation.
Kye mirambeena nang'ooith	Look! lo! behold!
Lark	Haze, cloud.
Leongatha	Check-tooth, dental, relating to the teeth, teeth, tooth.
Liketeu	Burlesque, to mimic.
Lillereboo	Juice.
Ling'an-ling'au	Hook, fish-hook.
Long	Cliff.
Lo turneen	Deaf.
Mailburningnul	Associate.
Maimborogul	Beetle, an insect.
Mardan	Bewail, calamity, cry, to weep, doleful, dolour, pain, gloomy, melancholy, glum, sullen, grief, groan, fetching deep sighs, lament, low-spirited, dejected, miserable, unhappy, moan, to grieve, pule, regret, sob, wail.
Mardan bullarto	Bemoan, sorry, weep, to cry, wept.
Marguck	Sew, to join together, unite.
Marmingatha	Divine, minister, Lord, Supreme Being, orison, a prayer, religion.
Marming'utha n'g'amoojidtch	Preacher.
Marmoonth	Father of a family, papa or father, parent, father or mother, sire.
Marp	Bloat, puffy, fleshy, inflation, obese, plump, fat, pot-bellied, stout.
Marron	Leaf of trees or plants.
Marrooing	Howl like a dog.
Maynthook	Navel, part of the body.
Meilburdeen	Permanent, perpetual.
Meniyan	Moon, lunar, relating to the moon.
Miarum-miarum	Camp.
Minejeerimering	Deformed, ugly.
Mirambena vor mirambiak	We, you and me.
Miram	Bough of a tree, branch.
Mirambeek	Due, one's own, mine, belonging to me, myself, own, belonging to one's self, prerogative.
Mirambeek alambee	Inhabit, to dwell.
Mirambeek beek	District, belonging to a tribe, indigenous, native.
Mirambeek buggarook marmoonth	Father-in-law.
Mirambeek eumaraleek	Grant, a thing granted.
Mirambeek jeetho	Disunite from a friend, leave, to go away, vacate.
Mirambeek jeetho mirambeena	Escort, to go with.
Mirambeek junubuck	Intimate, to tell, to relate.
Mirambeek nangana	Apparent, conspicuous, easily seen, saw, to see.
Mirambeek nangith	Detect, to find out.

Aboriginal.	English.
Mirambeek nangooith	Recognise.
Mirambeek n'ya'alingo	Ingress, entrance.
Mirambeek willam	Home.
Mirambeek wonthulong	Intimate, familiar friend.
Mirambeena	Thee, thou, thine; ye, nominative, plural of thou; you, yourself, your, belonging to you.
Mirambeena jetho	Expel, to drive out.
Mirambeena jeetho burra-burra	Despatch, to send away quick.
Mirambeena jumbuck	Answer, explain.
Mirambeena mirambeek	Ours, ourselves.
Mirambeena monomeeth	Esteem, to think well of.
Mirambeena nangana	Denote, to point out, enlighten, exhibit, offer to view, show, to show to another.
Mirambeena n'ya'alingo	Remand, to call back, revocate, calling back.
Mirambiak	Appertain, belonging to, belong, self, one's self.
Mirambiak booboop	Son.
Mirambiak nangooth	See, to perceive with the eye.
Mirboo	Kidneys, reins,
Mirmbull	Corpulence, fat.
Mirring	Hear.
Mirring-ian	Pensive.
Mogormeenth	Saliva, spittle.
Mollokin	Sister.
Molong molook	Afternoon, evening, sun-down.
Monomeeth	Agree, amity, appreciate, approve, beauty, benevolence, bravo, generosity, gentle, mild, well done, charming, comely, commendation, darling, a favorite, desert, worthy, elegant, endearment, enjoyment, fair, beautiful, famous, fidelity, honesty, good, indulgent, kindness, kind, benevolent, laud, to praise, merit, odoriferous, sweet, pleasant, precious, costly, pretty, handsome, prime, first-rate, properly, pure, in a fit sense, not sullied, rapture, delight, rejoice, relish, right, proper, satisfied, seemly, decent, serene, splendid, spotless, deserving, zest, to relish.
Monomeeth'baanth	Stream, running water.
Monomeeth cong'atha	Fragrance.
Monomeeth cooleenth	Ally, a friend, charitable, estimable, incorrupt, honest, just, plain-dealing, true-hearted.
Monomeeth jumbunna	Conversable.
Monomeeth mirambeek cooleenth	Chum, messmate.
Monomeeth mirambeena	Thanks.
Monomeeth mirambeena n'ya'alingo	Welcome.
Monomeeth myrring-atha	Perspicuous, quick-sighted.
Monomeeth nang'ooith	Smile, to speak kindly.
Monomeeth nojee	Coincide, to agree with.
Monomeeth n'uther pa'amboonth	Magnanimous, brave, manful, bold.
Monomeeth u'uther pimberlally	Honest.
Monomeeth poath	A grassy plain, a lawn.
Monomeeth worong'atha	Luscious, sweet.
Mooboop wooringwillam	Cub, young of native dog.
Moola	Shadow, a shade.
Moomgatha	Back, the hinder part, bottom, fundament.
Mooumoondick	Damsel, young maid, deity, God, the Pleiades, divinity, supreme, girl, a young female, a virgin, miss, young unmarried person, vestal, pure; youth, past childhood, if a girl.

LANGUAGE. 143

Aboriginal.	English.
Moongoobera	Wood-pigeon.
Moonip	Embers.
Moonong	Louse.
Moorburnduck	Caress.
Moordiyal jumbunna	Carnage.
Moort	Abridge.
Moortring-an	Quake, to shake with cold.
Mooyoop	Artful, cunning, dally, to trifle, delude, to cheat, duplicity, deceit, evasion, flam, a pretext, flatter, hoax, imposition, hypocrite, a dissembler, insincerity, misinform, to give a false account, overreach, deceive, outreach, trick.
Mooyoop goonong *or* myopego-onong	Banter, crafty, deceitful, dissemble, fawn, to flatter, feign, to dissemble, fib, a lie, frivolous, gammon, to deceive, gull, to cajole, to cheat, incredible, not to be believed, a juggler, a cheat, a liar, ludicrous, burlesque, misguide, lead wrong, mockery, mummery, buffoonery, nonsense, palaver, talk idly, plot, to scheme, pretence, a pretext, pseudo, false, quibble, quirk, a taunt, ridicule, scoff, slyness, cunning, stratagem, unreal, not real, raillery, satire, to joke, to exaggerate.
Mooyope	Cheat.
Morack	Hill.
Mornmoot	Blast of wind, gale of wind, wind.
Mornmoot bullarto	Windy, very stormy.
Mulloko	Defer, to put off, delay, ere long, immediate, postpone, presently, soon, refrain, by-and-by, shortly, quickly, soon.
Mulloko booboop	Breeding, to hatch, conceive, pregnant, pregnancy.
Mulloko bullarto	Enlarge, increasing.
Mulloko carmuggy nowinth	Dawn, break of day.
Mulloko cuminna	Drowsy.
Mulloko jeetho	Going.
Mulloko jindivle	Wane, diminish.
Mulloko monomeeth	Hope.
Mulloko murmbull	Dying.
Mulloko nojee	Embryo, unfinished.
Mulloko n'ya'alingo	Coming, expectancy, something expected.
Mulloko porkwadding	Enrage, exasperation, offend, to make angry, provoke.
Mulloko umarrong'ook	Fate, destined to die.
Mulloko unnina	Lethargic, sleepy.
Mulloko weeakabull	Elderly.
Mulloko wyeeboo	Reduce.
Mung-mung	Note, observe, remark, to mark, perceive, recollect, remember.
Munnip	Ashes, cinder, dust.
Murmbull	Dead, death, die, lifeless, perish, deceased, inter, to bury.
Murra-murra bargoagan	Shiver with cold.
Murrack	Grasshopper.
Murringian	Ponder, to think.
Myaring	Before, here, in this place, local, present, not absent.
Myarring'inna	Lag behind.
Myarum-myarum	Bower of boughs.
Myeering	Exterior.
Myogo'onong	Relic.
Myooith coruee uonga n'gerroodjeeth	After, behind.
Myoop	Counterfeit.

Aboriginal.	English.
Myarring'inna	Behind.
Myrnong	Finger, thumb.
Myrnong kalk	Walking-stick.
Myrnongatha	Claw, foot of a bird, fist of the hand, paw, the forefoot of a beast.
Myrongatha	Hand.
Myrringano	Countenance, form of the face, face.
Myrringata porkwadding	Frown.
Myrringatha	Eye.
Myrring leong'atha	Eye-tooth.
Myrwarradredoing noon	Benumbed.
Na'aboonthang'arraboonth	Fast, to abstain from.
Na'ang'naroonum	Bethink, to remember.
Na'anwoodthina	Breathless, fagged, harassed, tired, jaded, pant.
Na'arangabbeernee	Gently, slowly.
Na'arung'uith	Inaudible.
N'allambee bungal	Between, centre.
Namburk	Burial, bung.
Nangana	Compare, to examine, distinguish, eyesight, to see, sight.
Nangana geenong	Vestige, footmark.
Nangana geenong'atha	Track, to follow, trail.
Nang'ana mirambeek	Evident.
Nangana wirrate	Espy, see at a distance.
Nang'ark	Peep, a sly look.
Nangathan	Combine, to unite.
Nangooith	Behold! lo! seen.
Nangurk thurtbuck	Caution.
Napp	Bridge.
Narheethong	Lively.
Narbethong	Cheerful, fun, levity.
Narring-oboornee	Late, slow.
Narringyan	Moody.
Narrobuck	Smell.
Nayook	Cockatoo.
Needly-ooing	Paroquet.
N'eelam	Collusive, bad, corrupt, graceless, abandoned, to annoy.
N'eelam baggarook	Hussy, bad woman.
N'eelam warrabuck	Fetid, stink.
Neelum	Prejudice, dislike.
Neerim	High, elevated, long, not short, spear, long pointed weapon, tall.
Nelwork	Heed, caution.
Nenborongooith boganna	Apologize.
Nerdunning	Faint, not strong.
Nerreburdeen	Voracious, indigent, in want, starving, hungry.
Nerrena	Name.
Nerrurt	Frog.
N'ga'an	Breath, air drawn by the lungs, breathe.
N'gaang	Hiccup.
N'gammojiggerook	Lady, white woman.
N'gammoodjidtch	Englishman or white man.
N'gammoodjitdch marmingatha	Parson, priest.
N'garrabooen	Limp, to halt.
N'garrambul	Chalk, paint.
N'giaboopoop	Infertile, barren.
N'gondook	Chin.

LANGUAGE.

Aboriginal.	English.
N'gorack	Mountain, peak, a hill.
N'gorack bullarto	Mountainous.
N'groorook	Flint, a pebble.
N'gubborner	Grog.
N'gull	News.
N'neeruroon	Cement, gum.
Noobuck	Drink, to swallow.
Noogee	Complete, correct, content, desist, to leave off, end, finish, ho! enough, hold, be still, mature, perfect, needless, that will do, cease, done, exactly, full, satisfied, clear, manifest, successfully, overmuch, quantum, sufficient, quash, to crush, quell, quietus, a full discharge, quite, completely, replete, ripe, settled, confirmed, suffice, suitable, agreeable, unnecessary, satisfactory, valid, well, properly, satiate.
Noogee-noogee (spoken sharply)	Wearied, harassed by another.
Noogee monomeeth	Concur, to agree.
Noolenthethan	Miss, not to hit.
Noongoong jeeraing nuit	Asunder.
Noorturninum	Pain.
Notti run joomboilong'oith	Promise.
Noweenth	Disc, face of the sun, light, rays of the sun, sun.
N'u'd'lam	Antipathy, dislike, depravity, disreputable, evil, false, faulty, infamous, bad, insipid, want of taste, knave, a rascal, mean, contemptible, misbecoming, unseemly, naughty, wicked, nuisance, obscene, disgusting, odious, opprobrium, disgrace, perfidious, prevaricate, to lie, refuse, worthless, shameful, unfaithful, treacherous, unpalatable, unsound, corrupt.
N'u'd'lam cong'atha	Fusty.
N'u'd'lam cooleenth	Fibber, one who lies, ignoble, worthless, ingrate, an ungrateful person.
N'u'd'lam cowong	Loggerhead, thick skull, a dolt.
N'u'd'lam jumbuck	Evil speaking.
N'u'dlee	Bound, to spring.
N'ulam	Horrible, shocking, paltry, pollution, shabby, mean, sinful, wicked, unmeet, improper, venal, bad.
N'ulam cooleenth	Desperado, faithless, miscreant, a wretch, reprobate, abandoned, rogue, vagabond, villain, a wicked wretch, a worthless person.
N'ulam cong'atha	Rancour, striking.
N'ulam jumbuck	Falter in speech.
N'ulam jumbunna	Swear.
Nulling'arung	Shark, sea fish.
Numbuck	Charnel, place of sepulchre, grave for the dead.
Nungooring	Cockle.
Nuringian	Sedate, quiet.
Nurong	Bread, flour, loaf of bread.
Nurring'ian	Meditate, think, study, melancholy, quiet, not to speak, quietude, muse, to study, consider, contemplate.
N'uther	Denial, to deny, nay, no, negation, not, refuse.
N'uther allambee willam	Away, absent.
N'uther ba'anth	Drought, dry weather.
N'uther baggarook	Unmarried, single man.
N'uther barmburrim	Nasty, dirty.
N'uther booboop	Childless.
N'uther boolong	Nothing.
N'uther booboop carmuggy	Barren.

VOL. II.   T

Aboriginal.	English.
N'uther bullarto	Dearth, want, indigence, scarce.
N'uther bullarto nurong	Famine.
N'uther burra-burra	Tardy, slow.
N'uther ca'anthooith	Decent, becoming.
N'uther carmuggie	Cureless, incurable, restive, unwilling to stir.
N'uther cooleenth	Unmarried, single woman.
N'uther cooleenth allambee willam	Uninhabited, untenanted, unoccupied.
N'uther dandridibble	Penniless, no money, moneyless, poor.
N'uther dullallally	Humble, lowly.
N'uther eumaleek	Disallow, to deny.
N'uther geenong'alook	Unshod, no shoes, barefoot.
N'uther jeetho	Continue, to remain, stay, don't go.
N'uther jindivic	Durable, exhaustless.
N'uther jumbuck	Inconversable, unsocial, silent, sulky, sullen, surly, unsaid, not yet uttered.
N'uther jumbunna	Dumb, incapable of speech.
N'uther kurrambull	Cogitation, thought.
N'uther kurrick-kurrick	Blunt-pointed, not sharp.
N'uther lark	Unclouded, no clouds.
N'uther ma'amoonth n'uther parbine	Orphan.
N'uther mardan	Callous, light-hearted, unmourned, not wept for.
N'uther marming'atha	Blasphemous, immoral, irreligious, profanely, wickedly.
N'uther marmoonth	Fatherless.
N'uther marp	Lank, long and thin, lean, without fat, meagre, thin, skinny, wanting flesh, slender.
N'uther marron	Leafless.
N'uther mirambeek	Disown, renounce.
N'uther mirambiak nang'ana	Unforeseen.
N'uther monomeeth	Abject, dirty, clumsy, nasty, inferior, inharmonious, not sweet, loathe, to hate, repugnant, unjust, unkind, unneighbourly, unfriendly, wrong, injury, scurvily.
N'uther monomeeth cooleenth	Brutal.
N'uther monomeeth jumbuck	Inarticulately, to speak indistinctly.
N'uther mooyoop	Credit, belief, determination, discreet, earnest, fact, frankly, without reserve, genuine, real, heartiness, sincerity, innocence, matchless, natural, unaffected, powerful, profess openly, punctual, renowned, verify, to prove true, eminent, truth, true, undeceive, unfeigned, sincere.
N'uther mooyoopgoonong	Serious.
N'uther mooyoop myrring'ata	Sheeps' eyes, loving look.
N'uther myarum-myarum	Houseless.
N'uther nangana	Blindfold, invisible, miss, not to be seen, unperceivable, not to see, unseen.
N'uther nang'ooith	Imperceptible, not seen, indiscernible, not to be seen, seal, to close the eyes.
N'uther noogee	Imperfect, unfinished, incapable, unfit, incomplete, incorrect, inept, unfit, insufficient, nugatory, no good, no use, unserviceable.
N'uther n'ya'alingo	Absence.
N'uther n'ya'alingo conong	Costive.
N'uther n'ya'arunning	Dignify, experienced, handily, with skill, ingenious, learned, clever, manœuvre, skilful, sagacity, sane, sound of mind, science, knowledge, sensible, understand, wise, wot, to know.
N'uther n'ya'arunning mirambeek	Comprehend, faculty, ability.
N'uther oodiyalyal umaraleek	Frugal, miserly.

LANGUAGE. 147

Aboriginal.	English.
N'uther oodthenong	Few, a small number.
N'uther parmboonth	Dare, to defy, daring, gallant, brave, heroic, intrepid, fearless, champion, prowess, bravery, bold, confident, resolute, firm, undaunted, unterrified, valiant, valour, courage, courageous.
N'uther pardin	Pathless, trackless.
N'uther permberlally	Equity, justice, fairly, honestly, commit, to entrust.
N'uther porkwadding	Composed, calm, convivial, gay, diverting, merry, lenity, kindness, merciful, compassionate, passive, easy, patient, peaceable, quiet.
N'uther tartbanerra	Listless, heedless, negligent, careless, unguarded, unmindful.
N'uther tuthyrum	Starless, no stars.
N'uther umalcek	Illiberal, mean, niggard, covetous, ungenerous.
N'uther umaralcek	Grudgiugly, unwillingly, rapacious, greedy.
N'uther umina	Awake, not asleep, restive, without sleep, wakeful.
N'uther u myoa	Preserve, to keep, provident.
N'uther uonga	Nobody, not any one, not another, unparalleled, none other like it.
N'uther uonga cooleenth nangana	Secret, private.
N'uther weeakabull	Juvenile, young, youthful.
N'uther wirrate	Environs, not distant, near, close at hand, nigh, vicinity.
N'uther yan yean	Bridegroom.
N'uther yarragondock	Smock-faced.
N'uther youarrabuck	Easily, gently.
N'ya'alingo	Aback, backwards, appear, approach, come, to draw near, to countermarch, emerge, enter, hither, recede, fall back, return, to come back.
N'ya'alingo ba'anth	Fountain, a spring.
N'ya'alingo willam	Invite.
N'ya'arunning	Absurdity, to make a blunder, weak, brainless, silly, clodpole, stupid, confound, perplex, crack-brained, crazy, delirium, loss of mind, dull, fantastical, finical, foppish, folly, fool, half-witted, ignorant, lapse, to forget, impolitic, imprudent, inadvertence, carelessness, incongruity, indiscreet, to act foolishly, insane, mad, madly, misapprehend, mistake, not to understand, omit, forgot, preposterous, absurd, puerile, childish, remiss, careless, silliness, simpleton, unintelligent, unknowing, unmeaning, unskilful.
N'ya'arunning cooleenth	Natural, fool, ninny, noddy, a simpleton, numskull.
N'ya'arunning cowong	Distraction, madness, forgetfulness, loss of memory, idiot, a fool.
N'yallambee ba'anth	Drench, to soak in water.
N'yallambee moamgatha	Couchant, squatting on the hams, couch, to lie down.
N'yeelam	Crime, wicked.
N'yeelam baggarook	Coquette.
N'yeelaug	Bone, bony.
N'yeelingo turnin	Rib.
N'yeemoonth or yallambee	Bask, couch, to lie down, lay, lie, prostrate, laid flat, recumbent, lying.
N'yeerurkooleen	Snore.
N'yelam beek	Desert, a wilduerness.
N'yelambooreen	Abhor.
N'yellam	Bad, base, mean, execrable, hateful, incorrigible, iniquitous, sinful, mischief.
N'yellam cooleenth	Rascal, profligate, wicked.
N'yellam myrring'ata	Blear-eyed, dimness, dullness of sight.

Aboriginal.	English.
N'yellam warrobuck	Stink.
N'yellan therrongatha	Bow-legged.
N'yuther wirrate	Close, not distant.
Odthenong	Countless, innumerable.
Odthenong queeop-queeop	Covey, a number of birds.
Ongue hook	Indebted, to owe.
Oodiyalyal cooleenth	Crowd, a multitude.
Oodthenong	Congregation, many.
Oodthenong cooleenth	Confluence, a multitude, party, a number of individuals.
Oodthenong jindivic	Desolate, laid waste.
Oodthenong umaraleek	Devote, give up.
Oodyyallyal tootbyrum	Constellation.
Oordiyalyal allambee	Altogether.
Oordiyalyal	Hundred, divers, several, drove, a crowd, inexhaustible, infinite, immense, manifold, many in numbers, many, numerous, most, the greatest in number, multiplicity, myriads, great numbers, number, plural, quantity, numbers, sundry, swarm.
Oordiyalyal baggarook	Throng, multitude.
Oordiyalyal cooleenth	Throng, multitude.
Oordiyalyal cooleenth geetho	Procession, a train marching.
Oordiyalyal cowong'atha	Many-headed.
Oordiyalyal jumbuck	Communicative.
Oordiyalyal nang'ana	Frequent, often seen.
Oordiyalyal nang'ooith	Gaze, to look earnestly.
Oordiyalyal n'ya'alingo	Collect together, muster, to assemble.
Oordiyalyal jindivic	Destitution.
Oothanong booboop	Children.
Pa'amboonth	Dastard, coward, dismay, faint-hearted, cowardly, flinch, to shrink from pain, heartless, wanting courage, poltroon, pusillanimous, terror, fear.
Palrurt	Able, able-bodied, active, brawny, dexterity, indefatigable, industrious, lustily, with vigor, mighty, powerful, muscular, strong, robust.
Pany'ath	Capture.
Parbine	Dam, mother, mamma.
Parbine n'uther booboop	Motherless.
Pardin	Path, footpath, track, road, a way.
Parmboonth	Afraid, consternation, fear, dread, fright, recreant, cowardly, scare, frighten, shudder, quake with fear, timid, fearful.
Parmboonth n'uther	Fearless.
Parooth	Mouse.
Parramouth	Blind.
Path'eron	Caterpillar, a grub, a destructive worm.
Pellong	Net.
Permberlally or pimbullally	Defraud, to rob, depredate, filch, to steal, fraud, to cheat, despoil, imposition, light-fingered, thievish, peculate, pilfer, pillage, plunder, purloin, ransack, rifle, theft, stealing.
Permberlally baggarook	Seduction.
Permberlally booboop	Kidnap.
Pidjering	Scar, mark of a wound.
Po'ath	Blade of grass, grass, turf, covered with grass.
Poggoomuck	Gut, to draw out the guts.
Poojeering myrringa	Blink, to wink.
Poorneet	Tadpole.
Poowong	Carrion, putrefaction, rottenness.

LANGUAGE.

Aboriginal.	English.
Porkwadding or porquarrin	Chafe, to fret, anger, crossgrained, discord, displeasure, feud, quarrel, fretful, fury, passion, gruff, surly, harsh, austere, hotheaded, passionate, incensed, provoked, indignation, ire, malice, spite, morose, peevish, wrath, rancorous, malicious, umbrage, choler, contentious, quarrelsome.
Powerding	Accident, fell down, tumble.
Pundruyong cowong'onock	Nod, to bend the head.
Pung'ock	Nip, to pinch.
Purring	Highway, road.
Quanthee	How, query, question, to enquire, what.
Quanthee n'y'aling	Whence, from what place.
Quanthueeneera	Sudden, surprise, what for, why.
Quanthueeneera n'ya'alingo	Intrusion.
Queeop-queeop	Bird.
Queeop-queeop willam	Nest, bird's nest.
Quiukee monomeeth	Love, affection, limpid, clear, pure.
Roaturninang	Incision, a wound.
Tany a goon	Taste.
Tarkeeth	Marsh, a bog, swamp.
Tarmbuck	Lift up.
Tarnook	Basin, to hold water, bowl, a vessel, bucket, cup, a drinking vessel, jug, mug, a vessel to drink from, pot, pannikin.
Tartbanerra	Care, careful.
Tatbee	Hide, a skin.
Tatekorhee	Blab, to tell tales.
Teed'thung	Bat-mouse.
Tha'ambuck	Heave, to lift.
Tha'arabuck	Itch, scratch, tear with the nails.
Thallarabegoon	Gorge, the throat.
Thang'arth	Eat.
Thang'arreeoath	Breakfast.
Tharrack gully'buyth	Chase, to hunt, to course, pursue.
Tharrajidtch	Cessation, stop.
Tharrin	Buttock.
Theema koing'ack	Procrastination, delay.
Therrangalook	Apparel.
Therray	Aloud.
Therreoermyrnong	Nails on the fingers or toes.
Thirrock	Arm, limb of the body.
Thirrong	Thigh.
Thirrong'alook	Breeches, trousers, cloak, to cover, coat, frock, gown, shirt.
Thirrong'atha	Elbow, haunch, thigh, leg.
Thirumaleek	Horseleech, leech.
Thittle	Glutton, gormandizer.
Thocamee	Hark! listen! to hearken, listen.
Thoomee	Peace, silence.
Thooraweenth	Noise, outcry, report, a loud noise, riot, an uproar, squall, to scream.
Thoronee	Abdomen, belly.
Thort borra hoon	Precaution.
Thoumeenmella	Mouth, to grumble, mumbler, a mutterer, murmur, pout, to look sullen.
Thoumeenmeenmella	Peevish, pettish, quarrelsome, scold, to chide, scowl, to frown, snappish, cross-tempered, snarl, spleen.
Thullarabeegoon	Weasand, windpipe.
Thung'ook	Mastication, chewing.

Aboriginal.	English.
Thurrijee	Halt, to stop.
Thyowon	Ill, sick, illness, sickness, indisposition, invalid, sick person, languid.
Tonimbuck	Burn, to char, scorch.
Tooiyung	Cray-fish.
Toolome	Duck, a bird.
Toonn'gin	Blight, a sore.
Toombyling goonock	Conqueror.
Toorong'a	New, not old, modern.
Torndoin	Brain.
Torra'aweenth	Loud, much noise.
Totekarrawa	Incarcerate, tie, to fasten.
Tote kooda waugh	Shut, close the door.
Tote korrawaugh	Bind, confine, detain, keep in custody, to join together.
Touit	Fish.
Towrambuck	Lick, to touch with the tongue.
T'see waugh or jirnduck	Contempt, scorn, despise, to scorn, detest, disdain, hoot, shout of contempt, insult, jeer, to treat with scorn, nausea, feeling of disgust, pish ! pshaw ! interjection.
Turkeeth	Moorland, marshy ground, morass.
Turnoma'ay	Eyebrow.
Tutbyrum	Star.
Uarrabuck	Begin, quick.
Uguck	Grease, to smear with fat.
Ulertbee	Avoid, to shun.
Umaleek	Deliver, distribute, relief, render, to give, request, to ask, reward, solicit, vouchsafe.
Umaleek booboop brimbrim'gatha	Suckle, a child at the breast.
Umaraleek	Beg, dun, to ask, offer, to give.
Umaraleek nurong	Diet, supplying with food.
Umarongack	Corpse, a dead body.
Umarraleek	Accommodate.
Umina	Doze, to slumber, rest, sleep.
Umina n'uther	Sleepless.
Umina uther carmuggy	Drowsily, idly.
Umuck	Cast, to throw, hurl, fling.
Umuck yang'ana	Gasp for breath.
Um-um	Aye, yes, sign of compliance, yea.
Um-um monemeeth	Like, pleased with.
Um-um noogee	Conclude, to determine, penetrate, to understand.
Uonga	Alteration, change, to alter, lieu, taking another thing instead, other, not the same, reverse.
Uonga beek	Abroad, outlandish, foreign.
Uonga carnboo	Encore.
Uonga cooleenth booboop	Bastard.
Uonga cooleenth n'ya'alingo mirambeek willam	Visitor.
Uonga umaraleek	More, in greater number.
Uonga willam	Elsewhere.
Urimembergat	Couple, to marry.
Urongee jaalburt	Belabor, to beat soundly.
Uther jumbuck	Grave, serious.
Uther mooyoop	Candid, downright, open-minded.
Uther mooyoop myrring'ata	Eagle-eyed.
Uther myoop	Clever.
Uther n'ya'alin	Exclude, to shut out.

LANGUAGE. 151

Aboriginal.	English.
Uther n'yeelam	Chaste, pure.
Uther umaleek	Ill-nature.
Uther umina	Disquiet.
Uthur weeakabull	Energy, power.
Wa'ajuck	Chide.
Wa'ang	Crow, a bird.
Warragul	Ferocious, savage, wild, opponent, an enemy.
Warragul cooleenth	Enemy, foe, hostile, savage, wild, antagonist.
Warrain	Beach, marine, belonging to the sea, ocean, sea, coast.
Warrain ba'anth	Brackish.
Warring-aboornee	Linger, to remain, to loiter.
Waugh kye!	Holla! stop! shout.
Weengoon	Life, animal being, live, to be in a state of life.
Weeakabull	Aged, ancient, senior, oldest, antique, old, decrepitude, old age, dotage, dotard, inferior.
Weeakowleen	Carcass.
Ween'gamool currungmeen	Alarm.
Weenth	Fiery, fire.
Weenth kalk	Fire-brand.
Weenthunga	Doubt, to question, dubious, mistrustful, doubtful, perplexed, misunderstand, precarious, seemingly, doubtfully, suspicion, uncertain, unsettled, vague.
Weenthuga-weenthunga	Indecision, hesitation.
Wilgul	Hawk, a bird.
Willam	Building, a habitation, cottage, hut, dwelling, house, place of abode, rind, bark of trees, residence.
Winjeel	Eagle.
Winter	Where.
Wintharra n'gurrung'uith	Harbinger, a messenger.
Winthathith koordee	Crack, noise.
Winthoonth	Birth, coming into life.
Winthunga	Somewhere.
Wintowrding	Whereabouts, whither, where.
Wintowring ba'anth	Dry, thirsty.
Wirrack	Clamber, to climb.
Wirram	Left, opposite to the right.
Wirrate	Afar, beneath, beyond, bottomless, distance, far, distant, furthest off, remote, wide, remotely, at a distance.
Wirrate bullarto	Farther, more distant.
Wirraway	Challenge, incite, to stir up, menace, to threaten, dare, to defy, daring.
Wirock weenth	Kindle, to set on fire, enkindle, ignite, light, kindle a fire, a fire.
Wollard-wollard	Fur, opossum rug.
Wollawordock	Unimportant, never mind.
Wong	Cheek.
Wonthaggarook	Mealy-mouthed, meek, gentle, mild, kind, reserved, modest.
Wonthaggi	Borne, drag, to pull along, get, to bring, haul, to drag, lug, procure, to fetch, obtain, convey.
Wontbulong	Acquaintance, confederacy, friend, favorite, neighbour, partner, a sharer, companion, brother.
Woodheno	Abound, plenty.
Wookooardjilly	Labor, to work.
Woolen boorin	Warm, not cold.
Woolerreby	Whistle.
Woolwee	Flee, to run away, fleet.

Aboriginal.	English.
Woonmabill	Bustard, native turkey.
Woonthalongooth	Brethren.
Woorap	Ochre.
Wootheel-wootheel	Cord.
Woowookarung	Bounteous.
Wordiyalyal geenong'ata	Centipede.
Worong'atha	Mouth.
Worrowing	River, a stream.
Worrowing wyceboo	Rivulet, a small river.
Worthaggarook	Shame-faced, modest.
Wurrook	Flat, level.
Wurroor	Perspiration.
Wyandoorin	Bow, to stoop.
Wyeeboo yeeram	Betimes, early, daylight.
Wyeeboo	Brief, concise, short, jot, a tittle, least, superlative of little, less, little, small in quantity, minikin, small, minute, mite, modicum, morsel, a small piece, petty, puny, scrap, a bit, shred, tiny, wee.
Wyeeboo ba'anth	Damp, dew, ford, shallow water, humid, moist.
Wyeeboo ba'anth mellaba	Mizzle, rain in small drops, drizzly.
Wyeeboo bilim	Dram of spirits, a nobbler.
Wyeeboo bulgana	Calf.
Wyeeboo chuck-chuck	Chicken.
Wyeeboo cooleenth	Dwarf, small man, mannikin, a little man, pigmy, runt.
Wyeeboo drumbullabull	Pistol.
Wyeeboo eeip	Lamb, a young sheep.
Wyeeboo jumbuck	Calm, laconic, whisper.
Wyeeboo kirtkirtarnock	Colt, young horse, foal, nag, young of horse, pony.
Wyeebob lark	Mist, a low thin cloud, misty.
Wyeeboo mornmoot	Puff of wind.
Wyeeboo nang'ana	Glance, quick view, half-sighted.
Wyeeboo noweenth	Early, soon.
Wyeeboo nurong	Crumble of bread.
Wyeeboo n'uther wirrate	Short, not long.
Wyeeboo weenth	Spark of fire.
Wyeeboo pa'amboonth	Apprehension.
Wyeeboo roomera	Half.
Wyeeboo toolome	Duckling, young duck.
Wyeeboo unina	Nap, a short sleep, slumber, light sleep.
Wyeeboo warrin	Channel, narrow sea.
Wyeeringana n'gell	Abettor, aid, help, assist, to help, conduce.
Ya'arumowgarangamite	Combat, to fight, conflict, contention, strife, contest, fight, quarrel.
Yainyaing	Sing, music, carol, chant.
Yallambee	Bide, to remain, dwell, ease, quiet, put, to place, lay, tarry, stay.
Yallambee ba'anth	Bathe, dabble in water.
Yallambee beek	To lie on the ground, motionless, lying down.
Yallambee brimbrimgatha	Imbosom, to hold in the bosom.
Yallambee lark	Aloft.
Yallambee uonga beek	Exile.
Yallanibberon	Blanket, bedding.
Yallund'aruck	Chaplet, wreath round the head.
Yan-boorneen	Naked, uncovered, nudity, nakedness.
Yannaboothoointh	Pass, to go beyond.
Yannanayowoit	Always.

LANGUAGE. 153

Aboriginal.	English.
Yannathan	Jaunt, to walk about, motion, the act of moving, perambulation, promenade, walking, ramble, to wander, roam, rove, travel, walk.
Yannathan ba'anth	Wade, to walk through water.
Yannatherra aha	Adieu.
Yannathooec	Move, to change place.
Yannay wirrate	Journey, to travel.
Yannethoce	Messenger, scout, one sent to look for an enemy, courier.
Yan yeau	Bachelor, unmarried, boy, boyish, lad, minor, not of age, stripling, youth, a youth, past childhood if a boy.
Yarragondock	Beard, moustache.
Yarragondockatha	Whiskers.
Yarragongatha	Curl, a ringlet of hair, forelock, hair on the forehead, hair.
Yarragongatha bullarto	Hairy, covered with hair.
Yarrarthinmingan	Bustle.
Yarwee	Swine.
Yea nurk	Chine, back-bone.
Yecleelinthung	Bruise.
Yecrang	Brake, a thicket.
Yellana durruk	Decorate.
Yellingbo	To-day.
Yellingbo marming'atha	Sabbath, a day of worship, Sunday.
Yellingboith	Daily, diurnal.
Yellingoith	Overnight, yesterday.
Yerrallerning	Idleness, lazy, inactive, indolent, inert, sluggish.
Yetyeteemyrring	Eyelash.
Yillertbee	Cover, to hide, deposit, screen.
Yimmerboordy	Jacent, lying at length.
Yonduck	Jostle, to push.
You myoo	Prodigality, wasteful.
Youanga	Another.
Youarrabuck	Accelerate, eagerly, keenly, haste, expedite, fast, quick, hasten, hurry, be quick, instant, the present moment, precipitate, to hurry, prepare, prompt, to make ready, readily, with speed, smartly, briskly, speed, swift, velocity, brisk.
Youarrabuck geetho	Scamper, to run with speed.
Youdlee	Jump, leap.
Youdleenth	Agility, nimble, quick.
Youcyook	Oily, greasy.
Young'yee	Hum, to sing low.
Youonga	Anew, over again.
Youonga cooleeuth	Follower, attendant.
Yucca-yucca	Lackaday! alas! oh! smart pain, denoting sorrow.

DIALECT OF THE JA-JOW-ER-ONG RACE,

With a short account of their Traditional History and Superstitions, &c., &c.

(BY JOSEPH PARKER, FRANKLINFORD.)

[The following paper and vocabulary have been prepared by Joseph Parker, Esq., son of the late Edward Stone Parker, Esq., some time Member of the Legislative Council of Victoria, and for many years Assistant Protector of Aborigines. Mr. Joseph Parker has had unusually favorable opportunities of learning the native language and of becoming acquainted with the manners and customs of the Aboriginal natives of Victoria.]

The *Ja-jow-er-ong* race at a remote period numbered about one thousand beings, and were divided into seven distinct tribes—the *Leark-a-bulluk*,* the *Pil-a-uhin-goon-deetch*,* the *Kalk-kalk-goon-deetch*, the *Wong-hurra-ghee-rar-goon-deetch*, the *Gal-gal-bulluk*, the *Ton-nim-burr-lar-goon-deetch*, and the *Way-re-rong-goon-deetch*. They claimed as their territory the country extending from Ballan on the south to the junction of the Serpentine and the Loddon on the north, and from the eastern slopes of Mount Macedon on the east to the Pyrenees on the west.

With but a few trifling exceptions, the dialect of these tribes was the same. They were considered by all other Aborigines a formidable and important race of people, not merely because they possessed a large extent of fine country especially adapted for hunting and other purposes, but because within their territory was found the only rock known from which their *Bur-reeks* (tomahawks) were made; and the locality in which this rock was found bears the name of Bur-reek to this very day, the literal English of which is "axe."

It was their custom at certain seasons of the year, usually spring or summer, to meet on friendly terms the natives of other tribes who came from all quarters to procure portions of this stone. Though the sanguinary propensities of the *Ja-jow-er-ongs* made them a terror to all other Aborigines, the messengers from the distant tribes were treated as sacred visitors.

These messengers travelled by means of friendly signals, and when passing through hilly and timbered country they would fill a hollow tree (generally on some elevated spot) with green boughs and set fire to it at the base, thus causing a column of smoke to ascend to such a height that it could be seen many miles off. If it were found necessary for these messengers to send up a signal in country void of timber, they would carefully cut the bark off a stout sapling, from fifteen to twenty feet in length, thus forming a tube or funnel, which was filled with boughs and carried by them until required. They would generally select a calm and clear day for these signals, and if no return signal was given, they would retrace their steps with all possible speed, believing that those natives to whom they had been sent were at enmity with them. But when approaching those they intended visiting, they would carry a green bough in their right hands, which was an emblem of peace.

---

* The terms "*bulluk*" and "*goon-deetch*" signify "people" and "men."

No distinct and settled form of religion or worship existed among them. They, however, believed in the existence of an evil spirit, and the occasional existence of a good one whose powers were limited to certain periods.

The "Eagle," "Crow," and "Bat" were regarded as sacred animals, each having distinct powers. The Eagle and Crow possessed, at a remote period, the same influence and power, and worked their "miracles" in harmony together; but having quarrelled and fought, they separated for ever, and worked "miracles" and "wonders" distinct and at variance with each other. The Eagle was "lord of the forests and mountains," and the Crow "lord of the hills and plains." The Bat, it was affirmed, had certain protective and enchanting powers: it would watch over the lonely and weary traveller, and could warn him of impending danger, and guide him into the path of safety.

They did not believe in death from natural causes, except in the two extremes of life—old age and infancy; but assert that there were two forms of death—the *Moo-char-moo-roop* (literally, "take the spirit") and the *Boor-kur-moo-rar* (or, "break the kidney-fat"). The first of these terms, *Moo-char-moo-roop*, applied only to those who had been removed by a very sudden death without any apparently previous illness. The spirits of those who died in this way were said to have gone to the West (*Whar-ree-whin-knam-mytch-oo*), and would re-appear at some future time brighter and more perfect beings. Under this belief, mothers, whose infants had died in the way here described, have been known to carry the dead body on their backs for months after death, affirming that the longer they carried the corpse in this way the more future happiness would their child and themselves enjoy, and believed that its departed spirit had the power of granting to its parents the influence of "witchcraftism."

The other form of death—*Boor-kur-moo-rar*—a horrid superstition, was the cause of perpetual murder and blood-shedding. If one of their number died from natural causes, or was killed, no matter how, the moment life was extinct the body was tied up and prepared for interment, and carried to a piece of clear soil; two of the companions of deceased would then dig a small trench round the body, generally of an elliptical form, which would be carefully swept and minutely examined in order to find a hole. Should they succeed in finding one, they would place a straw in it, and carefully mark the bearing it pointed to. They would then proceed in the direction indicated by the straw, and take a similar life to the one they had lost; that is to say, should a man die, the life of another man would be taken, and if that of a woman or child, a similar life would also be taken.

In the year 1846 an incident occurred which painfully illustrated this superstition. The Melbourne or Coast natives lost a man of their tribe, generally supposed from natural causes. A number of the deceased's friends resorted to the usual mode of trench-digging, and, strictly in accordance with the straw-pointing, proceeded to Knee-rarp—now known as Joyce's Creek—and there at mid-day attacked a party of the *Ja-jow-cr-ong* natives, who were at the time hunting, and killed a fine young man who was at the time unable to defend himself. The friends of this young man, although eye-witnesses to his murder, and in the full knowledge of who the guilty parties were, proceeded in the usual way to tie up the body and dig the trench. The straw pointing in the direction of the Goulburn, a strong party, consisting of eighteen men, were then equipped with spears, &c., and in about a week from the Knee-rarp tragedy a similar life was taken by this party in the locality named. Thus it was that this horrible superstition kept these people in constant fear of molestation, and caused them to be continually moving from place to place.

Their burial ceremonies were characteristic of their life. In preparing the corpse for interment, they would double it up in the smallest possible compass, and wrap the body in all the articles of clothing the deceased possessed, and generally bury the body in a grave from four to five feet deep, and all the deceased's property would be placed in the grave at the time of interment. The grave would be finished off in an oblong form, and the ground carefully scraped and swept for some distance around it. A small tuft of emu feathers tied on a stick would be placed at the head of the grave, and a fire kindled and kept constantly burning for eighteen or twenty days at the foot of it.

Their lamentations were of the most savage description; they would resort to various methods of torturing themselves, in order that they might suffer pain for those they had lost. The men would cut their heads with any sharp-edged instrument that was available, and the women scratch the flesh from their cheeks, and sear their legs and arms with fire, and break their heads with sticks.

The family and social relationship of these people was one of the darkest features of their history. No marriage bond or law of any kind existed among them, and in the matter of choice or selection the woman had no voice, for she was virtually the property of her nearest male relative, and in a matrimonial sense could be disposed of by him at any time. Plurality of wives was very common among them, and any of the women could be put away at the will of the husband, and the strongest mark of friendship that could be displayed by one man to another was to present him with one of his superfluous wives.

A stupid custom existed among them, which they called "*Knal-oyne.*" Whenever a female child was promised in marriage to any man, from that very hour neither he nor the child's mother were permitted to look upon or hear each other speak nor hear their names mentioned by others; for, if they did, they would immediately grow prematurely old and die.

If the term "intelligent" could be applied to a people who were so naturally low and ignorant, and as devoid of moral restraint as the Aborigines of Australia were reputed to be, certainly that term could be applied to the *Ja-jow-er-ongs*, for they displayed marked aptness and ability and were highly imitative. Their skill and aptitude have been clearly shown in the preparation and manufacture of their native weapons and other articles of war, and their imitative powers on their opossum-skin rugs, on the furless side of which, with the assistance of sharpened mussel-shells, they have scratched all kinds of figures and characters, some of which were copied from nature; and their accuracy and correctness have often been a matter of astonishment to the more skilful and cultivated eye of the European.

LANGUAGE.

This short and frail narrative alludes only to a few of the many peculiar habits and traditions of a race once numerous and strong, and whose voice yet calls for the solving of that question which asks—Why is it that, in a country where colonization and Christianity have made such marked progress, this race, who but a quarter of a century since could be counted by the thousand, are now virtually a people of the past?

Vocabulary.

The correct pronunciation of the words in this vocabulary can only be arrived at by adopting the simple rule of giving to every letter used its full sound, and the long sound in the case of ee, oo, and rr. It will be observed that the *Ja-jow-er-ong* alphabet contains neither F, Q, S, V, X, nor Z.

English.	Aboriginal (with literal English).
Man (white)	Knam-i-gheetch.
Men (white)	Knam-i-gheetch-bul-luk.
Woman (white)	Knam-i-gheetch-goork.
Women (white)	Knam-i-gheetch-bul-luk-goork.
Man (half-caste)	Moo-coo-lom-beetch.
Men (half-caste)	Moo-coo-lom-beetch-bul-luk.
Women (half-caste)	Moo-coo-lom-beetch-bul-luk-goork.
Man (black)	Goo-lee.
Men (black)	Goo-lee-bul-luk.
Woman (black)	Too-ree.
Women (black)	Too-ree-bul-luk.
Grandfather	Knam-jam.
Father	Marm.
Son	War-reip.
Sons	War-reip-kal-ick.
Stepfather	Kar-re-kar-rim-book.
Father-in-law	Kar-re-kar-rim-book.
Old man	Knar-em-been.
Young man	Kool-koon.
Youth	Kool-koon.
Boy	Boorp-boorp.
Child	Boorp-boorp.
Infant	Kneel-lar-moom.
Children	Boorp-boorp-kal-ick.
Brother (elder)	Wharr.
Bachelor	Kneel-la mur-ram.
Brother (younger)	Koot.
My brother (elder)	Wharr-eck.
My brother (younger)	Koot-eek.
Your brother	Wharr-inn *or* koot-in.
His brother	Wharr-wook *or* koot-ook.
Our brother	Wharr-ell *or* koot-ell (brother ours).
Their brother	Wharr-jhan-uck.
Husband	Knan-eiteh.
Widower	Doo-ring-yetch.
Son-in-law	Knál-oyne.
Stepson	Kuan-nap.
Brother-in-law	Coo-reetch.
Uncle	Chár-chi.
Nephew	Coor-whan-dook.
Cousin	Coó-ki.
Old woman	Moyn-nim-goork.
Young woman	Biang-biang-gó.
Girl	Boó-ní-hoó-ní.
Grandmother	Mé-mán-dook.
Mother	Bárp.
Mother-in-law	Knal-oyne-goork.
Stepmother	Ber-mén-án-goork.
Wife	Mur-ram.
Widow	Doo-ring-yetch-goork.
Daughter (elder)	Máng-gáp.
Daughter (younger)	Jhin-narp-ang-goork.
Stepdaughter	Kuan-nap-guork.
Sister (elder)	Chár-choók.
Sister (younger)	Koo-took-goork.
Aunt	Bár-rip-jar-bine.
Niece	Yee-rat-goork.
Marriage	Marn-ga-long.
Widowhood	Doo-ring-yetch-goork.
Family	Woi-noit-yere-hil.
Male	Goo-lee.
Race	Goon-deetch.
Tribe	Bul-luk.
Female	Too-ree *or* goork.
Man and woman	Goo-lee-bar too-ree.
Men and women	Goo-lee-bar too-ree-bul-luk.
God	Wo-reip-ar-pel (prayerful).
God	Marm-ing knoo-rack (Father of us).
God	Knoo-rar-rook-knair-kneetch (Great Master).
Body	Bang.
Spirit	Moó-roóp.

158   THE ABORIGINES OF VICTORIA:

English.	Aboriginal (with literal English).
Ghost	Koo-chél.
Head	Boorp.
Forehead	Ghin-nee.
Back of head	Knan-ning-e-boorp.
Temples	Tor-toitch.
Face	Myrr-bar-karr (eyes and nose).
Cheek	Moo-rark.
Eyeball	Woórr-woorer-myrr.
Eyebrow	Tar-nó-myrr.
Eyelash	Wir-ren-e-myrr (feather of the eyes).
Eyelid	Knar-ree-myrr.
Tear	Whync-yer-am-e-myrr (water of the eye).
Cross-eyed	Dur-rick-myrr.
Nostril	Boitche-karr.
Nose	Karr.
Smell	Knar-rùp.
Mouth	Woo-roo.
Lip (upper)	Mee-chee-woo-roo (skin of the mouth).
Lip (lower)	Yarn-ba-yée-woo-roo.
Gum	Bang-geé-leár (flesh of the teeth).
Tooth or teeth	Lear.
Front teeth	Warng-gúm-lear.
Back or double teeth	Terr-kee-lear.
Tongue	Chal-leé.
Jaw	Moo-rark.
Chin	Boorp-c-knar-nee (head of the beard).
Spittle	Chow-irre.
Ear	Wirr-m-bool.
Lobe of the ear	Boiche-wirr-m-bool.
Hearing	Knare-nar.
Hair	Knar-arr.
Whisker	Kneen-nce or knar-ree.
Moustache	Koy-on-e-woo-roo (spear of the mouth).
Beard	Knun-nee or knar-nee.
Neck	Coorn.
Throat	Coora-de-chow-irre.
Back	Wharr-yin.
Chest	Jhung.
Belly	Boitch.
Ribs	Lun-ing.
Side	Chool-loom.*
Private parts (male)	Whirr-er.
Testicles	Boo-nar.
Private parts (female)	Boi-yúrre.
Navel	Warr-oó.

English.	Aboriginal (with literal English).
Shoulder	Buk-er-roó.
Arm	Tar-ruck.
Upper-arm	Bun-dar-rúp.
Elbow	Bol-loitch.
Fore-arm	Cun-darp.
Wrist	Toor-nen.
Hand	Mun-nar.
Palm of hand	Boitche-mun-nar.
Hand (back of)	Wharr-ym-e-mun-nar
Thumb	Barp-e-mun-nar (mother of hand).
Finger (first)	Win-dár-ráp.
Finger (second)	Mar-ron dyarp.
Finger (third)	Kiam-bul-lar.
Finger (fourth)	Kir-ring-mun-nar.
Right hand	Yoolp.
Left hand	Whar-rum.
Finger nails	Lietch-e-mun-nar (scales of the hand).
Knuckle	Tar-ro-gee-mun-nar.
Fist	Moo-ree-mar-mun-nar (a crooked hand).
Leg	Kar-rip.
Hip	Kalk-é-móo-lóo.
Thigh	Móo-lóo.
Knee	Bar-ring.
Knee-cap	Boorp-e-bar-ring (head of the knee).
Calf of the leg	Boor-rárp.
Ankle	Mark.
Instep	Jhung-gee-jhin-nar (the breast of the foot).
Foot	Jhin-nar.
Foot (sole of)	Boitch-e-jhin-nar (the stomach of the foot).
Heel	Kun-nárk.
Toe (large)	Barp-e-jhin-nar (the mother of the foot).
Toe (second)	Why-knam-e-jhin-nar.
Toe (third)	Boorp-boorp-e-jhin-nar.
Toe (fourth)	Boorp-boorp-ook.
Toe (fifth)	Kiam-goork (a lonely girl).
Skin	Meetch.
Flesh	Bang.
Muscle	Knar-rám.
Bone	Kalk (stick).
Joint	Tur-ring.
Blood	Goó-roók.
Matter	Boi-chún.
Brain	Toorr-toín.
Heart	Toor-wg.
Lungs	Jhar-jha-róok.
Liver	Boitch.
Stomach	Boo-ring-goòp.

* The "C" in this word should be sounded like "c" in cheese.

LANGUAGE.

English.	Aboriginal (with literal English).
Bowels	Boo-reétch-loo-reetch.
Vein or artery	Koár-rám.
Dung	Koo-nár.
Urine	Ghy-rre.
Sweat	Woo-rér.
Rump	Moom.
Breast or paps	Coormb or coormb-oók.
Hair of the head	Knar-rar-knee-boorp.
Skull	Kalk-e-boorp.
Temples	Toor-toítch.
Jaw (upper)	Kalk-e-lear.
Gullet	Jhee-coórn.
Windpipe	Jhal-larp-e-coórn.
Armpit	Kar-rarp.
Collar-bone	Wee-ring.
Spleen	Baa-reetch.
Breath	Bee-ra-wer-coórn.
Kidney-fat	Pap-ool-e-márrk.
Gall	Ming.
Bladder	Larr-nee-ghyrre.
Kidney	Marrk or marrp.
Blister	Bil-nil-long.
Blow	Máirrm-e-long.
Cut	Tél-lén.
Kick	Kúr-rùck.
Wound	Wée-reép.
Horse	Kút-kút-tar-noók (many vessels).
Horses	Kut-kut-poo-piárré.
Cattle	Koo-roó-m'n.
Sheep	Yeep.
Swine	Pig-pig.
Kangaroo	Goó-rá.
Wombat	Knoorre-knoorre.
Australian bear	Knurrm-bul-moom (forked rump)
Dog (native)	Whill-kúr.
Dog (common)	Karl.
Native cat	Yoorn.
Kangaroo rat	Bar-roók.
Rabbit rat	Chu-roytch.
Burrowing rat	Bar-row-eitch.
Water rat	Yerr-ék.
Common mouse	Túr-nine.
Opossum	Wee-lár.
Ring-tailed opossum	Bun-nár.
Squirrel (grey)	Poo-roól.
Small blue squirrel	Knoorre kyé.
Black flying cat	Yun-dool.
Bandicoot	Boó.
Ant-eater or hedge-hog	Yool-á-nil.
Platypus	Wy-chár-arng.
Wallaby	Jhin-bong-goore.
Bat	Knun-ar-knun-mytch.
Emu	Bar-ra-múl.

English.	Aboriginal (with literal English).
Swan (black)	Koon-oó-worra.
Eagle	Wairrp-il.
Eagle hawk	Kneár-aytch.
Large ground hawk	Bee-yérng.
Falcon hawk	Yán-yérng.
Sparrow hawk	Wher-rain wher-rain.
Wood duck	Knun-núck.
Black duck	Knarr-ee.
Mountain duck	Mein-yœ-luck.
Musk duck	Knún-neé-níl.
Teal	Bán-nairre.
Little grebe	Koo-ra-noo-rá.
Blue crane	Karr-náine.
Nankeen heron	Yàp-peél.
Ibis	Pyte-pyte-char-roók.
Native companion	Koo-roón.
Turkey bustard	Knár-rów.
Curlew	Koo-hy-eirrp.
Pelican	Bar-rang-gul.
Spur-winged plover	Baa-ritch-baa-ritch.
Snipe	Ming-eŭ-waller.
Landrail	Lerrp.
Partridge quail	Choo-irrp.
Common quail	Boo-rong-gi.
Three-toed quail	Koo-nám-moól.
Small yellow quail	Knán-náp.
Small plover	Moon-yar-reetch.
Pigeon (bronze-wing)	Dupp.
Cockatoo (black)	Ware-aine.
Cockatoo (white)	Jhin-núp.
Parrot (white)	Kar-rar-kur.
Rosella parrot	Tur-nim-burt.
Crimson parrot	Poo-roo-kil.
Green leek parrot	Moo-ra-kane.
Blue mountain parrot	Kul-ling-er.
Cockatoo parrot	Woo-reép.
Small paroquet (green)	Ukip.
Small paroquet	Knil-leé-noyne.
Ground paroquet	Derre-nál.
Large grey parrot	Yaa-rár.
Laughing jackass	Koo-nork.
Swallow	Wool-ér-ing-boiteh.
Martin	Lel-lerrp-koon.
Magpie	Koo-roork.
Small magpie	Jheerm-jheerm.
Black magpie	Mooyn-un-kil.
Crow	Warr.
Owl	Wheer-múl.
Cuckoo	Kar-roók.
Small ant-eater	Beeyng.
Large ant-eater	Bul-lén bul-lén.
Minah (grey)	Burrp-púr.
Small ground lark	Wheet-goork.

THE ABORIGINES OF VICTORIA:

English.	Aboriginal (with literal English).	English.	Aboriginal (with literal English).
Large ground lark	Toort-ee-chár-oók.	Eucalyptus—	
Rook	Mar-rang-un.	White-gum	Ban-napp.
Blue jay	Yar-ra-yar-ak.	Blue-gum	Bapp.
Brush turkey	Low-an.	Red-gum	Bu-al.
Kingfisher	Dy-ring dy-ring-uong.	Ironbark	Yee-ripp.
Swift	My-erre.	Grey-box	Boo-loitch.
Murray cod	Wee-ráp.	Yellow-box	Tarrk.
Black-fish	Woo-lk.	Red-box	Tee-ring.
Perch	Ghee-rar-núl.	Brown-box	Wy-all.
Eel	Boyn-knúrt.	Acacia—	
Cray-fish	Yap-peetch.	Golden-wattle	Wy-kalk.
Mussel (fresh-water)	Chal-loop.	Lightwood	Mootch-ong.
		Silver-wattle	Whar-rar-rark.
Mussel (salt-water)	Byte-bytch.	Brown-wattle	Too-lain.
Turtle (fresh-water)	Woo-room-oók.	Callitris (Murray pine)	Murr-nroong.
Minnow	Birnm.	Exocarpus or Australian cherry	Pul-loitch.*
Whitebait (Australian)	Wool-coot.		
Water frog	Dein.	Banksia, commonly called Australian Honeysuckle	Woo-rack.
Large brown frog	Doom.		
Leech	Pil-leetch.	Myrtle (native)	Tch-oóp.
Carpet snake	Koorn-núl.	Tea-tree (native)	Poo-noó.
Black snake	Koo-loo-nòng.	Native peach	Bee-ree-kúl.
Whip snake	Káir-roòk.	Casuarina—	
Large Murray snake	Min-dye.	She-oak	Koo-loitch.
		Forest-oak	Chu-rarng.
Sand snake	Bein-gárl.	Grass-tree	Buck-kup.
Small brown lizard	Kuark-e-knoo-áck.	Reed or Victorian bamboo	Charr-ak.
Spotted lizard	Dong-dong.		
Jew lizard	Kann.	Edible rush, commonly called Loddon down	Boo-reetch.
Grey lizard	Bein-beirrk.		
Iguana	Your-koon.		
Scorpion	Be-ree-kil.	Basket rush	Wit-chee.
Centipede	Jhe-reen-nu-rark.	Grass (generally)	Booyn.
Tarantula spider	Mun-nar-kar-reek.	Fern	Moo-laa.
Ant	Ma-rah.	Tubular rush	Boong-knóort.
March fly	Moo-roon.	Underbush or bramble	Jheerp-jheerp.
Mosquito	Lee-ree.		
Sand fly	Moon-keen.	Yam	Moo-nar.
Bee	Moom-oom-bar-ar.	Orchis (yellow)	Boo-ni-loo-ni (a young woman).
Flea	Lain.		
Louse	Moon-yir.	Orchis (brown)	Kool-koón (a young man).
Flesh fly	Bee-reek.	Brown-wattle gum	Too-lain.
House fly	Toor-toytch.	Gum or resin	Choo-tch.
Butterfly	Ballam-ballam.	Honey	Chee-noyne.
Large moth	Boo-room-beetch.	Manna	Lerrp.
Earth-worm	Jhoom-pilleetch.		
Pupæ of ants	Kal-keetch.	*Native Weapons.*	
Eucalyptus—		Large spear	Yal-litch.
Stringybark	Wong-burra.	Jagged spear	Koy-oon.
Messmate	Boorr-knúl-oók.	Reed spear	Charr-ák.

* This tree was highly prized by the *Ja-jou-er-ongs*, from the fact that it was said the juice of its bark was a powerful and sure antidote for snake-bite, and they affirmed that in numberless cases the victims of snake-bite had been cured by an application of this juice.

LANGUAGE.

English.	Aboriginal (with literal English).
Small spear	Taire.
Throwing-stick	Yer-rick.
Boomerang	Tat-tem tat-tem.
Battle-axe	Leer-uil.
Round-headed club	Moo-uoop.
Stone tomahawk	Moon-oo-bun-goit or barr-eek.
Pointed club	Woy-woytch.
Iron tomahawk	Barr-eek.
Small bent stick	Bee-rip-ayne.
Shield (large)	Mul-kur.
Small light shield	Gearra-mul.
Yam-stick	Karr-née.
Weapons collectively	Bulk-bulk.

Miscellaneous.

English.	Aboriginal (with literal English).
Bag	Mook-oor mook-oor.
Reed-necklace	Char-ak-koon.
Head-band	Mul-lar-kar-wyne.
Wooden shovel	Lan-kat.
Opossum rug	Jhar-roon.
Apron of feathers	Tirree-burnee.
Fishing-net	Kar-lyne bar-mirree.
Canoe	Yoong-goip.
Dagger and cord	Knar-rarm.
Net	Koo-rare.
Apron (men's)	Bar-rine-jhim.
Apron (women's)	Knoo-roytch.
Mat	Yal-lán.
Basket	Balk.
Wooden bucket	Tarr-noók.
Good	Tól-koók.
Bad	Yur-ring.
Great	Knoo-rar-ook.
Little	Why-nee-mook.
Alive	Moo-roón.
Dead	Dee-ri-ung.
Hungry	Mahr-re-ung.
Thirsty	Goorn-már.
Frightened	Parm-ber.
Long	Kar-poól.
Short	Moort.
Lazy	Terrm-mil-ong.
Stupid	Bung-lung-gil.
Active	Knen-knen.
Dark	Boo-royne.
Light	Bairrp.
Fast	We-ra-poo-nong.
Slow	Wom-boo-nong.
Full	Knoop-po-rong.
Empty	Dak-coo-rong.
Sick	Jon-er-ong.
Lame	Knurrp-per.
Blind	Knee-már.
Deaf	Knock-in-wirr-m-bool (shut ear).

English.	Aboriginal (with literal English).
Cold	Bine-jhul.
Warm	Woym-ber.
Hot	Woo-koo-kool.
Dirty	Woo-koo-rong.
Clean	Peetch-un-doo-rong.
Strong	Pal-lert.
Weak	Yil-lert.
Raw	Koo-mar.
Cooked	Joy-coy-knin.
Withered	Koi-yu-wharr.
Blunt	Too-roop.
Sharp	Knar-rytch.
Sharp-pointed	Knar-rytch mirrb.
Pregnant	Boorp-boorp-or-rong.
Dazzling	Mil-lip-pár.
Bald	Bil-lick boorp (bare head).
Tall	Kar-pool.
Fond	Wart-yee-long.
Ripe	Lein-yer.
Lofty	Tur-rer-an-gu-long.
Best	Boo-noong-loo-uooug.
Shining	Bee-la-rong.
Hanging	Ban-doo-rong.
New	Derrng-knet-took.
Old	Jhew-an-dook.
Dark	Boo-royne.
Bashful	Koo-lool.
Smashed	Jhal-jhal-ly-en.
Careless	Lang-lang moo-roop.
Worry	Whir-ring-mil long.
Rotten	Boytch-boytch.
Double	Boo-lan-yer-boorp (double head).
Enough	Kar-chow-min.
Grey-headed	Lar-chick-boorp.
Gorged (with food)	Too-hire-ung.
Angry	Koo room-by-ung.
White	Tarrh-noo-rong.
Black	Woor-koo-rong.
Red	Bit-too roug.
Green	Mal-lak.
Blue	Woorer-woorer (sky).
Yellow	Ghee-rar-mil-ong.
Brown	Koorm-koorm mur-meetch.
Sleepy	Knoo-rar-kool.
Drowsy	Bool-ar-ong.
Tired	Bar-rap goo-rong.
Heavy	Poon-woort.
Light	Wool-loong.
Straight	Yoolp.
Crooked	Wy-an-du-rong.
One	Kiarrp.
Two	Boo-laytch.
Three	Boo-laytch kiarrp (two and one).

VOL. II.

English.	Aboriginal (with literal English).	English.	Aboriginal (with literal English).
Four	Boo-laytch boo-laytch (two, two).	Snow	Kap-páng.
Five	Kiarrp-mun-nar (one hand).	Hail	Larr-nee-wol-ler (house of the rain).
Six	Boo-laytch boo-laytch boo-laytch (three twos).	A spring	Yer-rarm.
		Lake or pond	Bo-lok.
Eight	Pan-yer-an-geetch.	Sea	Wharr-ree.
Ten	Boo-laytch mun-nar (two hands).	River	Burr or gun-bung-goorre.
		Wave	Booing-boolng.
Twenty	Boo-lar-ra.	Creek	Burr.
Many or plenty	Kut-knt.	Drop	Doorm-mar.
All	Knul-doo-rong.	Stream	Ya-loók.
Pretty or handsome	Yar-rang-ghin.	Flood	Wol-ler-wol-ler.
Greedy	Lair-lait.	Marsh or bog	Bamm.
Strange	Main-maytch.	Earth or ground	Jharr.
Cruel	Boo-gil.	Dry ground	Boi-boi-e-jharr.
Fierce	Koo-loo-mun-dar.	Mud	Bup-ál.
Like	Knoo-lar-go-roug.	Loam	Bup-jharr.
Soft	Boolk.	Sand	Koo-rúk.
Hard	Pal-lert.	Dust	Moo-nál.
Mistake	Knut-tow-er-roug.	Stone	Larr.
Mad	Bung-lung-gee-long.	Pipeclay	Bup-al.
First	Karl-lee-goon-deetch.	Mountain	By-nooell.
Last	Bark-goon-deetch.	Hill	Yon-arng.
Quiet	Tam-mia-long.	Plain	Wherrk.
Sweet	Gheerm-gheerm.	Country	Tar-bilk.
Bitter	Ghurr-ghurr.	Valley or gully	Tar-rar-rark.
Sour	Girre-girre.	Road	Bar-ring.
Diseased	Wee-rip nee-rip.	Track	Bark.
Wide	Mel-lapp.	Wind	Myrr-ine.
Narrow	Whin-née.	Thunder	Mun-dar.
Deep	Tee-yál.	Lightning	Mil-lark-ook.
Shallow	Eu-róng.	Sky	Woor-er-woor-er.
Near	Doo-mee.	Cloud	Marng.
Far	Boo-rre.	Rainbow	Tar-ruck-e-woorer-woorer (arm of the sky).
Round	Men-goo-rong.		
Square	Bil-bil-ung.	Fog	Woo-room e woller.
Hollow	Knár-noŏn.	Fine weather	Woo-roo-kool.
Bent	Mil-pa-long.	Cold	Byne-jhúl.
Smooth	Main-main.	Heat	Woym-ber.
Distant	Whar-reetch-oo.	Sun	Now-éy.
Dry	Boi-boi.	Moon	Yearn.
Wet	Nim-meetch.	Star—Jupiter	Boond-jhil (bold).
Poor	Oyn-nim-óok.	Star—Venus	Charch-e-now-ey (sister of the sun).
Fire	Wee.		
Flame	Yal-lan-yer.	Stars (generally)	Toort.
Smoke	Boort.	A meteor	Yal-lee-nil-long (tumbling over).
Spark	Knen-knen (quick).		
Ashes	Jule-jule.	Comet	Boi-woo-rarng.
Ashes (hot)	Bar-ree.	To-day	Now-ey-u-mong.
Charcoal	Wir-ring.	Day	Now-ey-u.
Water	Wy-knurr-ám.	Morning	Bairp-er-now-ey (morning sun).
Rain	Wol-ler.		
Mist	Boo-rong.	To-morrow morning	Bairp-bair-bairp.
Dew	Toor-meetch.		
Frost	Tarn.	Sunrise	Bang-ar-now-ey (the sun climbs).

LANGUAGE.

English.	Aboriginal (with literal English).
Noon	Kar-pool-e-now-ey (long sun).
This evening	Chal-lik chal-lik.
Last evening	Chal-lik-gee.
Sunset	Knock-er-now-ey (gone in sun).
To-night	Boo-royne-nu.
Midnight	Kar-pool-e-loo royne-nu (long night).
Light	Yap.
To-morrow	Bair-re-bec.
Darkness	Boo-royne.
A month	Yearn.
A year	Kar-rie bur mir-reen (summer and winter).
Spring	Knal-low.
Summer	Kar-rie.
Autumn	Woo-reetch.
Winter	Mir-reen.
New moon	Why-nee-me-yerrn (small moon).
Full moon	Knoo-rar-ook-yerrn (great moon).
North	Knar-ram-e-now-ey (rays of the sun).
South	Coo-marr (cool).
East	Bairp (morning).
West	Knam mytch (white or bright).
North-west	Wee-rin-mal-lee.
North-east	Kail-lee-bairp (mark of the morning).
South-east	Mar-recu mar-reet.
South-west	Larr-nee-kap-pang (house of the snow).
House	Larr.
Native hut	My-am-bert.
Chimney	Ghee-ree-kil-moom.
Window	Whar-lun-dool-myrre.
Door	Kal-lee-larr.
Roof	Boorp-e-larr (head of the house).
Forked stick	Knam-bool-kalk.
Fence	Knal-lap-coon.
Food	Yarre-boo-gar.
Bread	Nurong.
Meat	Bang.
Milk	Coorm.
Sugar	Gheerm-gheerm.
Rice	Kar-rine.
A drink	Knoo-per.
A knife	Kal-poon kal-poon (cut, cut).
A plate	Wel-lain wel-lain.
Spoon	Woo-roo-knee-chal-loop (mouth of the mussel).
Pot or kettle	Tar-nook.
Bottle	Doom-doom-e-bur-ra-mul.
Bucket	Tar-nook.
Doctor	Barng-bar-knul.
Boil or abscess	Boitchun.
Scab	Bar-bar-room.
Cold	Boit-chun-e-coorn (matter in the throat).
Dysentery	Jhu-row-er.
Syphilis or excrescence	Wombi.
Small-pox	Moo-nool-e-min-dye (the dust of the serpent).
Pox-marked	Lil-lipp-e-min-dye (the scales of the serpent).
Headache	Lar-ly-ang-boorp (split head).
Rheumatism	Tur-ree-nil-long.
Blight (eye)	Kar-ring-e-myrre.
A vomit	Kerre-már.
Invalid	Jow-er-ar-pil.
I or me	Wan or un.
Thou or you	Warr.
He, she, or it	Marl.
We	Knell.
Ye	Warr.
Mine	Wang-eck.
Thine	Warng-knen.
His or hers	Warr-nook.
Ours	Warr-knen-déck.
Yours	Warr-knen.
Theirs	Warr-jhan-nook.
Us	Warn-doóng.
Myself	Kian-eck.
Yourself	Kian-in.
Himself or herself	Kian-ook.
They	Hytch.
This	Mong.
That	Nuyne-ar.
That's it	Nuyne-ar-min.
Where	Whin-jar.
To sleep	Knoo-ra-kool.
To find	Tum-bar.
To tear	Choo-roo-nar.
To speak	Woo-ra-kur.
To tell	Ghee-yin.
To give	Woo-kin.
To go	Yan-kuar or knun-nee.
To walk	Yar-rin or kar-rim-bin.
To run	Wheerr-win.
To make	Moong-garr.
To form	Birn-nin.
To build	Barrp-per.
To swim	Whe-rar-kur.
To eat	Jhak-er.
To drink	Knoo-per.

English.	Aboriginal (with literal English).	English.	Aboriginal (with literal English).
To hear	Knair-nur.	To put	Yoorrp-per.
To see	Knar-kur.	To pray	Woi-woi-poe.
To feel	Carrk-er.	To put (down)	Jhar-ree-muck.
To smell	Knar-roop-per.	To boast	Boorn-dar.
To sneeze	Chee-koorn-der.	To lift	Wy-mar.
To laugh	Wairk-er	To lie (in ambush)	Ghee-ram-bein (in the boughs or leaves).
To cry	Mar-ree.		
To beat	Chil-pin.	To whistle	Whee-ree-len.
To split	Larl-groo-war.	To shiver	Moorr-moorr-ne-long.
To bake	Mar-roo-knar.	To change	Wook-jha-rong.
To rise	Py-keen.	To peep	Euy-pa-lung.
To kneel	Bar-ring-coo-nee.	To mix	Kur-ree-pee-ring.
To shoot	Dok-ker.	To rub	Knar-ree-muck.
To turn	Wil-keen.	To scratch	Wol-lin-go-mar.
To fetch	Moo-cheen.	To extinguish	Boot-koo-mar.
To scratch	Kul-lar mil-leen.	To dry	Boitch-koo-nar.
To jump	Birrp-jhan-nin.	To form	Knar-roo-kur.
To creep	Kow-in-deen.	To tread	Kar-reen.
To grow	Kar-ring-in.	To fly	Py-keen.
To suck	Barp-pa-lin.	To sweep	Knar-row-neen.
To lick	Chow-am-bin.	To watch	Koom-be-rar.
To vomit	Kurr-min.	To straighten	Buck-am-en-darr or yoolp-uck.
To blow	Boo-roo-knin.		
To pick up	Tum-bin.	To feed	Jock-kaa-leen.
To chop	Tel-leen.	To stink	Boo-ang-ghin.
To send	Jhar-ra-min.	To descend	Chew-lak-kee.
To wrestle	Bar-room-jhar-reen.	To go (up)	Bang-kneen.
To hate	Me-tow-e-yur.	To climb	Bang-knee.
To breathe	Knarng goytch-oo-nar.	To open	Bart-koo-nar.
To make haste	Yon-harrp-er.	To shut	Mum-goorr-ween.
To hold	Kark-keen.	Yes	Yea-yea.
To tie	Bairp-peen.	No	Low-nee-rong.
To shake	Yil-ling-ghin.	Presently	Ying-oo-nee.
To spill	Karng-knil-lin.	By-and-by	Nee mytch.
To take	Mootch-al-le.	Long since	Jhoo-an-dook.
To bark	Loorrp per.	Here	Mong-mere.
To hide	Non-rar.	Where	Whin-jhar.
To return	Choo-wen-u-war.	There	Ghin-ym.
To twirl	Moo-ree-moo-ree-mar.	When	Nar-roo-gee.
To whisper	Woo-yam-lar.	Not	Knul-lar.
To swell	Kar-ring-er.	More	Jhool-loo.
To play	Wee-ra-mar.	Always	Mell-loo-ra-pyang.
To fling	Yoong-gee-lee.	Across	Wharr-am-jee-rong or kar-roong-ee.
To scatter	Mee-ta-ra-mar.		
To pinch	Win-nee-puck.	Gently	Wom-boo-nee.
To lend	Woo-ra-mar.	Enough	Kar-chew.
To teach	Jim-haa-yer.	Over there	Yer-hytch-jhee-ree.
To show	Chew-y-mar.	What for	Koon-dee-nar (for what).
To rest	Koo-man-goo-nong.	And	Bar.
To mark	Choorn gar.	For	Knoon-dee.
To cut	Tel-luck.	In	Ee.
To paint	Bee-kar-mil-leen.	Of	Yu.
To light	Yapp-uck.	Under	Wai-char or my-er-ghar.
To forget	Knar-knootch-who-ar.	Over	Wharr-ym-ee.
To remember	Jhal-poon-dar.	Down	My-er-ghar or koomb up.
To thrash	Berr-marr.	Beneath	Koorn-ee.

English.	Aboriginal (with literal English).	English.	Aboriginal (with literal English).
Beyond	Ging-gow-er-ong.	Upon	Jha-ra-mim.
Inside	Boitch-ee.	Within	Boitch-ee-nook.
Before	Knun-go.	Without	Knulla - boitch - ee nook (not within).
Behind	Karr-oong or mi-you-ghar.		
If	Knet-toong.		
Below	Lim-ning-gee.	*Parts of Birds, &c.*	
After	Knar-rook-gee.	Wing	Tar-rark.
From	Ghee-ym.	Tail	Beer-ak.
Past	Lut-ty-in.	Claws	Leetch-e-jhin-nar.
Since	Ying-oo-nee.	Feathers	Whee-rain.
Through	Bree nane.	Nest	Larr.
Until	Marl-hytch-oong.	Egg	Boom-boom.
Up	Py-kee.	Fin	Ballin-ook.

A FEW PROMISCUOUS SENTENCES, WITH THEIR LITERAL TRANSLATIONS.

Aboriginal.	English.
Knun neen-in-hairp hair bairp yerrk keen un koon dee goo-ra.	Going me to-morrow morning look me for kangaroo.
Marl-un-mooch-ar-why knurr-am	Let me fetch water.
Whin knar knat knun neen?	Where are you going?
Wharr-tin main maytch goo-lee yerrk kee long lytch kondee jhuck keetch.	Come strange men looking for food.
Knul-lar burt koo unk	Don't wake (him or her).
Burt-tuk loorp pa long karl	How bark the dogs.
Ghee yuck-en dayne knar wharr knar kin jhal-la gee.	Tell us what you saw yesterday.
Knar-kin-un kulng ga long kuam nu geetch goork.	Saw me dancing white women.

The following tables illustrative of the dialects spoken by the natives of Geelong, Colac, Goulburn, Murray, and Campaspe, and those of the *Witouro*, *Jajowrong*, *Knenkoren-wurro*, *Burapper*, and *Ta-oungurong* tribes are extracted from Mr. Eyre's work. He states that they were published for the House of Commons, with other papers on the Aborigines, in August 1844.*

CORIO AND COLAC.

English.	Woddowrong, or Corio Natives.	Koligon, or Colac Natives.	Dautgart, or Natives to the west of Colac.
Head	Mor-rok-gnet-ok	Mor-rok-grun-ok	Be-nia-nen
Eyes	Mer-gnet-ok	Merg-nen-ok	Mer-gun-nen
Forehead	Ment-gnet-ok	Gner-on-gnen-ok	Mer-then-quan-nen
Nose	Kanug-gnet-ok	Kong-gnen-ok	
Lips	Wor-ung-gnet-ok	Wor-ung-gnen-ok	
Arm	Far-ong-guet-ok	Ken-e-gnen-ok	
Leg	Kar-gnet-ok	Kar-e-gnen-ok	
Foot	Gen-ong-gnet-ok	Ken-ong-gnen-ok	

* *Journals of Expeditions of Discovery,* vol. II, pp. 399 to 402.

CORIO AND COLAC.

English.	Woddowrong, or Corio Natives.	Kolìgon, or Colac Natives.	Dautgart, or Natives to the west of Colac.
Sun	Mer-c	Na	Derug
Moon	Yern	Bard-bard	Bar-i-nan-nen
Star	Fot-ba-rum	Kar-art-kar-art	Bom-mar-a-morug
Earth	Du	Ta	Mering
Stone	Lu	Tre	Mor-i
Fire	Weang	Wean	
Water	Gno-bet	Kan	Baret
Kangaroo	Ko-im	Ko-ra	Ko-rin
Emu	Kar-wer	Por-i-mul	Por-i-mul
Opossum	Wol-ard	Pong-o	Pi-c
One	Ko-i-moil		
Two and two	Bul-ad-barp-bul-ad	Bul-ad-duk-bul-ad-duk	Bul-ad-da-bul-da-da

GOULBURN, MURRAY, AND CAMPASPE.

English.	Jhongworong, or Goulburn Natives.	Pine-gorine, or Natives of Junction of Goulburn with the Murray.	Gnurellean, or Natives west of Campaspe.
Head	Mor-rom-gna-ta	Po-ko	Tong-go-gnen-a
Eyes	Mer-ing-gna-ta	Ma	Mer-e-gnen-a
Forehead	Me-guen-gna-ta		Mean-de-gnen-a
Nose	Kaw-ing-gna-ta	Kow-o	Tan-de-gnen-a
Lips	Wor-ro-gna-ta	Wor-o	Wor-om-de-gnen-a
Arm	Far-ok-gna-ta	Po-re-ne	Tar-ok-e-gnen-a
Leg	Ho-ra-gna-ta	Tut-eu-ga	Ko-rom-bo-gnen-a
Foot	Gnen-ong-gna-ta	Gen-a	Gen-ong-be-gnen-a
Sun	Now-an	Yourug-ga	Now-wer
Moon	Yambuk	Yourug-kud-a	To-rong-i
Star	Fort	Tut-ta	Tort-tok
Earth	Beak	Wok-a	Mil-a
Stone	Lang	Bo-ren-a	Kor-dob-e
Fire		Pe-da	Wem be
Water			Kor-den-ok
Kangaroo	Mar-ons	Ki-e-me	Kori-e
Emu			Kow-wer
Opossum			Wo-i-e
One	Kap	You-a	Lu-a
Two and two	Bul-mo-gur-nen-bul-mo-gur-nen	Bul-tu-bul-bol-tu-bol	Bo-ri-de-bo-ri-de

Mr. Eyre says that the letters "*gn*" at the commencement of words and syllables represent a peculiar nasal sound common in the dialects of Port Phillip: to form this sound, the organs of speech must be placed in the same position as they are to sound *g* hard, and then the sound is emitted through the nose like the letter *u*.

LANGUAGE.

WITOURO, JAJOWRONG, KNENKOREN-WURRO, BURAPPER, AND TA-OUNGURONG TRIBES.

English.	Witouro.	Jajowrong.	Knenkoren-wurro.	Burapper.	Ta-oungurong.
Father	Pedouring ettuk	Marmook	Marmak	Marmook	Warredoo
Mother	Knardon knettuk	Barbook	Barpanorook	Barbook	Barbanook
Son	Boron	Boboop	Wat ye pook	- - -	Boboop
Daughter	Bagorook	Tor roi	Mangapook	Layurook	Baguroo
Brother	Warnoong	Warwook	Warwook	Warwook	Parngannoo
Sister	Wairn ga knettuk	Kotook	Kotoogan garook	Kotook mennook	Bainbainoo
Husband	War ringoor tannooh	Nannetook	Nannetook	Nannetook	Nangorouoo
Wife	Nannapoon gooranook	Marrarbook	Nettargorook	Mater mennook	Beembannoo
Man	Gole	Gole	Gole	Woitu-bullar (pl.)	Goleen
Woman	Bagorook	Ture	Bien biengu bullar	Layurook	Badyuroo
Old man	Wooring-wooring	Knarmbeet	Lalli bullar	Onyim	Ti yin gular
Old woman	Mondegorook	Ony im gorook	Ony im gorook	Ony im gorook	Week-week
Black man	Bangondedook	Bango-dedook	Bangodedook	Bangondeyook	Mararmgondeg
Body	Bangik	Bangook	Bangook	Baugook	Marramboo
Soul	Murrum knook	Mooroopook	Mooroopook	Knanbileknook	Mooroohoo
White man	Amygeet	Amygeet	Amygeet	Moandeet	Amygee
Skin	Tallanook	Meetook	Meetook	Meetook	Darboo
Fat	Koreetook	Bairpulluk	Bairpulluk	Bairpulluk	Mambooloo
Bone	Goorook	Kalkook	Kalkook	Mairderook	Kalgoo
Blood	Goortan yook	Gorook	Goorkook	Goorookook	Gurugoo
Head	Moorayook	Bourpook	Bourpook	Bourpook	Kowanoo
Eyes	Mirrook	Minnook	Minnook	Minnook	Mingoo
Ears	Wingook	Wimbulook	Wimbulook	Wimbulook	Wirringoo
Mouth	Woorutanyook	Wooruknook	Wooranyook	Wooranook	Woorungoo
Nose	Karn yook	Garnook	Garnook	Garnook	Garknoo
Beard	Nareen gan dau yook	Knarneknook	Knarni knook	Nannin yook	Kner nin yoo
Teeth	Lean yook	Learnook	Learnook	Learnook	Leangoo
Tongue	Tallan yook	Talkknook	Talkknook	Talleknook	Tallanoo
Fore-arm	Yoondap	Yoondap	Yoondap	Nanne wannoo	Yoondaboo
Hand	Munangin	Munnar	Mun ne knook	Munnanook	Munangoo
Thigh	Karreem nook	Karrepook	Karrepook	Karreboo	Tarrangknoo
Leg	Loortam nook	Burapook	Burapook	Burapook	Gooramboo
Foot	Tinnanook	Tinnanyook	Tinnan jowook	Tinnanook	Tinnanoo
Fire	Wing	Wee	Wee	Wannap	Wein
Water	Moabeet	Wonyeram	Kat yin	Karteen	Parn
Rain	Mundur	Woller	Woller	Metark	Yayal
Thunder	Mundur	Mundur	Mundur	Mundarra	Moondabil
Earth	Dar	Dar	Dar	Dar	Be-cek
Stone	Lar	Lar	Lar	Lar	Moid yerre
Wind	Moonmoot	Mirreen	Mya	My-ya	Gooree
Sky	Woorer-woorer	Woorer-woorer	Woorer-woorer	Woorer-kalkook	Woorer-woorer
Sun	Mirri	Nowe	Nowe	Nowee	Nummi

WITOURO, JAJOWRONG, KNENKOREN-WURRO, BURAPPER, AND TA-OUNGURONG TRIBES.

English.	Witouro.	Jajowrong.	Knenkoren-wurro.	Burapper.	Ta-oungurong.
Moon	Minyan	Yern	Yern	Wiying wil	Minnun
Stars	Toort baram	Toort	Toort	Toort	Toort
Cloud	Lark-	Murrong	Murrong	Murrong	Lark
Yesterday	Taleyu	Talego	Talego	Tallegallegor	Yullongoi
To-morrow	Yeramun	Bairpobarrah	Bairpobarrah	Bairpoorm	Yeramboin
Day	Mirriyu	Noweyu	Noweyu	Nowegal	Karremeen
Night	Moorkalyn	Boorroinyn	Boorroinyu	Booroinyetta	Booroindyee
Kangaroo	Goim	Goora	Goora	Gooreyeer	Marram
Opossum	Wollert	Weila	Weila	Weela	Wollert
Dog	Garl	Garl	Garl	Werengun	Yerangun
Emu	Kowe	Barramul	Yowerre	Kowe	Barramul
Tree	Koor par gerong	Kalk pu gherra-	Kalk pu gherra-	Tark tawooh	Kalk-par-ge-rong
Grass	Bohiet	Boin	Bohiet	Bohiet	Barnoom
Bark	Mooriet	Myabert	Marrartak	Moorartap	Moorartap
Leaf	Mooran	Gerrar	Gerrar	Gerrar	Gerong
Flower	Goora	Duwin	Goen-goen	Goorr	Gooroo
Large spear	Karp	Kouiyun	Koiyun	Koiyun	Koiyun
Reed spear	Tark	Tark	Dark	Tarr	Derar
Boomerang	Wangim	Tatim-tatim	Tatoom-tatoom-	Warn	Wangim
Battle-axe	Leangil	Learwil	Learwil	Learwil	Leungail
House	Karrong	Lar	Lar	Larr	Yillum
Great	Detarbul	Knooreetabook	Murtyowook	Koorconandook-	Woortabook
Little	Nauy a korooh	Wanemook	Wardebook	Murtook	Wikorook
Alive	Mooron	Mooron	Mooron	Moorun	Mooron
Dead	Detarwa	Deryung	Detyung	Weekin	Werregi
Bad	Noolam	Yurrong	Yartin yar	Yettowarndook-	Noolam
Good	Koenebanyook	Talkook	Talkook	Talkook	Wan-wan goo
Long	Nerrim	Karpool	Tuwurnge	Tuwarnandook	Yurobot
Short	Moert	Moet	Moet	Tuluwandook	Moert
Cold	Molongetting	Motangiu	Motangorin	Lokan yurain	Motangan
Warm	Narwoorarning-	Wootyeep	Wootyeep	Boorook	Narworing
One	Koen moet	Kiarp	Kiarp	Kiarp	Koopt you
Two	Bullait	Bullait	Bullait	Bullait	Bullarbil
Three	Bullait par koen-moet	Bullait par kiarp	Bullait par kiarp	Bullait kiarp	Bullarbil bar-boop
Four	Bullait-bullait	Bullait-bullait	Bullait yown bullait	Bullait-bullait	Bullarbil-bull-arbil
Plenty	Wurreyoolyool	Kurt-kurt	Kurt-kurt yar	Parrook	Woortyannoo
I	Bangeek	Bangak	Bangak	Bangak	Murrumbik
You	Bangen	Bang-in	Baug-in	Bang-in	Murrumbyeu
Where	Wear	Windya	Windyaya	Windya	Inda
Here	Kimbarne	Kinkio	Kinkio	Kingooda	Kalarwe
Another	Yarknook	Yuwannook	Yuwannook	Yuwannook	Yuwangoo
What for	Wekartook	Wenarra	Wenarra	Wenarra	Nannin gartook
To tell	Keyak	Keyak	Keyak	Koongak	Toombak
To give	Wowak	Wokah	Wokak	Wohak	Wooknak

WITOURO, JAJOWRONG, KNENKOREN-WURRO, BURAPPER, AND TA-OUNGURONG TRIBES.

English.	Witouro.	Jajowrong.	Knenkoren-wurro.	Burapper.	Ta-oungurong.
To speak	Nartun whoorakeeh	Woorakeyak	Woorakeyaku	Woorakeyar	Mallam doon yer
To eat	-	Mullun tak-kah-	Mullon tank-beka	Tak kwan nek-nin	Tangeyer
To drink	Knurtul-nopeet-	— oppellar	— opellanyook-	Kopallanyoo	Opear
To hear	Gnarwah	Kneerknak	Kneerknak	Knaryin	Knarngak
To see	-	Nark ar	Narkinnewa-noong	Naryin	Knar nar
To sleep	Komkarneetyan	Kombeyan ak	Kombeyanak	Kombeyan win-	Karnambeyan
To steal	Pilmirringoora-	Kunnundillar	Kannand yinnar	Moug kargurar-	Peart yin
To fight	Peet yalleet yan	Dorkt yerar	Dorkelyeer	Dork alley an	Wialley an
To kill	Bannargak	Berkagak -	Berkin agak	Talkowak	Berkagat
To dance	Kneerekeyan	Yepenyun	Yepenneknen	Warrepin knan-	Knarger nan
To make	Mongak	Mongak	Moyoopah	Tal gonak	-
Yes	Ye-ye	Ye-ye	Ye-ye	Knaar	Knary ea
No	Borack	Lowurrong	Nullun yer	Burapper	Targoon
By-and-by	Numiet	Numiet	Mallin yook	Kimbarm	Malle mal
A long time since	Tuwurngee-yomeer	Tuwurn keey oomeer	Mallarmeer	Kim howa	Parmboet

NATIVE NAMES OF TREES, SHRUBS, PLANTS, ETC.

Some years ago I sent paper covers, properly arranged for preserving botanical specimens, to three of the Managers of Aboriginal Stations in Victoria, with the request that they would collect specimens of the foliage of trees, shrubs, and plants, and obtain from the natives their names for the trees, &c.

The Managers very kindly undertook the task. From Mr. John Green, of Coranderrk (greatly assisted by Mrs. Green, to whom I am much indebted), I obtained sixty-nine specimens; from the Rev. Mr. Hartmann, of Lake Hindmarsh, fifty-nine; and from Mr. Joseph Shaw, of Lake Condah, twenty-four; all admirably arranged and neatly labelled.

These fasciculi were placed in the hands of the Government Botanist, and he was asked to write opposite to each native name the correct botanical name; and, owing to his zeal, I am now able to give these lists to the public in such a form as to be of permanent value. If I had contented myself with setting against the native names the corresponding English names, the work would have been valueless; as the latter are applied often carelessly and without knowledge. Baron von Mueller's determinations make—what was a mere collection of strange words—a list which will be of great interest hereafter;

because nearly all the trees and plants here named by the natives can now be easily identified.

It will be observed that in some cases the natives have given different names to the same plant. Great care was taken by my correspondents, and I cannot believe that any error has crept in. It is not improbable that there are, in the same tribe, more names than one for a plant, and that a plant in one stage of development may have a different name when it is in another stage.

In Mr. Green's list, *Wetomellen* (No. 2), collected by Mrs. Green, is not to be distinguished from *Minamberang* (No. 63), collected by Mr. Green; and No. 30 (*Merwan*) is exactly like No. 31 (*Nyaring*).

I point out these apparent discrepancies, not to lessen the value of the work, but to increase it. Probably Mr. and Mrs. Green had not with them on every occasion the same native; and a native might on one occasion give the name of the foliage, on another that of the fruit, and on another perhaps that of the root. It is exceedingly difficult to procure information from the natives with respect to these matters; but I am satisfied that the work has been done with every regard to accuracy.

The collection of plants and the list of native names received from the Rev. Mr. Hartmann are of more than ordinary value. He has taken the greatest care in performing the work; and his abilities and his education are sufficient guarantees that it is accurate, and as complete as one man, with other heavy duties to attend to, could make it.

The contributions of the Managers of the Stations are not alone of importance as showing what names the natives give to plants; but the plants having been gathered in the several localities specified at the head of each list, something is added to our knowledge of the geographical distribution of some species; and even from a strictly botanical point of view are worthy of preservation.

Plants, with native names, received from Mr. John Green, of Coranderrk:—
(*Examined and named by Baron von Mueller, C.M.G., F.R.S., Government Botanist, &c.*)

No.	Native Name.	Identified by Baron von Mueller as—
1	Kurwan	Bursaria spinosa. Cavanilles.
2	Wetomellen	Clematis aristata. R. Brown.
3	Panaryle	Mentha Australis. R. Brown.
4	Coranderrk	Prostanthera lasianthos. Labillardière.
5	Eepaeep	Rubus parvifolius. Linné.
6	Mooiung	Apparently the young state of Acacia melanoxylon. R. Brown.
7	Wyett	Young state of some species of eucalyptus.
8	Kalertiwan	Pomaderris apetala. Labillardière.
9	Waar	Leaf only.
10	Pooibooy	Helichrysum ferrugineum. Lessing.

LANGUAGE.

No.	Native Name.	Identified by Baron von Mueller as—
11	Dalurp - - - - -	Sonchus oleraceus. Linné.
12	Merndorrt - - - - -	No flower nor fruit.
13	Neringnerit - - - -	Helichrysum scorpioides. Labillardière.
14	Ballangin - - - - -	Cymbonotus Lawsonianus. Gaudichaud.
15	Murreyuke - - - -	Acæna sanguisorbæ. Vahl.
16	Burunbeet - - - -	Platylobium obtusangulum. Hooker.
17	Burumkulwill - - -	Leaf only.
18	Koolin (the native word for "man")	Caladenia pulcherrima. F. von Mueller.
19	Pimpat - - - - -	Craspedia Richea. Cassini.
20	Ballangin - - - - -	Erechtites arguta. Candolle.
21	Burgilburgil - - - -	Aroetriche serrulata. R. Brown.
22	Kadsekadsek* (one can scarcely observe the sound of "s")	Rumex Brownii. Campdira.
23	Kurranungun - - - -	Pimelia humilis. R. Brown.
24	Errienellam - - - -	Drosera auriculata. Backhouse.
25	Pimpat - - - - -	Brachycome cardiocarpa. F. von Mueller.
26	Terrat - - - - -	Geranium dissectum. Linné.
27	Nerringnganin (the root is eaten by the natives)	No name given.
28	Mulling-mulling (the root is eaten by the natives)	No name given.
29	Tabungin (the root is eaten by the natives)	No name given.
30	Merwan - - - - -	Diuris pedunculata. R. Brown.
31	Ngaring (the root is eaten by the natives)	Diuris pedunculata. R. Brown.
32	Pike (the root is eaten by the natives)	Bulbine bulbosa. Haworth.
33	Kaanung (the root is eaten by the natives)	No name.
34	Taberup - - - - -	Villarsia reniformis. R. Brown.
35	Tallak-tallak - - - -	Eryngium vesiculosum. Labillardière.
36	Moriyoke - - - -	Acæna sanguisorbæ. Vahl.
37	Genineemoongoon - - -	Epacris impressa. Labillardière.
38	Naringarnik - - - -	Diuris corymbosa. Lindley.
39	Moambill - - - -	No name.
40	Toolimerin - - - -	Xanthorrhœa minor. R. Brown.
41	Toolim - - - - -	Juncus vaginatus. R. Brown.
42	Tangnau - - - - -	Gratiola Peruviana. Linné.
43	Mudrurt - - - - -	Cæsia corymbosa. R. Brown.
44	Woorun - - - - -	Eucalyptus amygdalina. Labillardière.
45	Nareenguan (eaten by the natives)†	Hypochœris glabra. Linné.
46	Daal - - - - -	Aster argophyllus. Labillardière.
47	Toolemerin - - - -	Xanthorrhœa minor. R. Brown.
47a	Woolerp - - - -	Leptospermum lanigerum. Smith.
48	Berry yung - - - -	Acacia stricta. Willdenow.

* More like *Kadthekadthek*.

† Mr. Green states that the natives eat this plant, and probably the roots afford them food in certain seasons. "*Hypochœris, Seriola, Robertia,* &c., form Lessing's sub-tribe Hypochœridæ. Swine are said to be fond of the roots of *Hypochœris radicata,* the long rooted cat's-ear, whence indeed its generic name."—*Burnett,* p. 636.

It is not referred to in Hooker's *Flora Ciberia* as given in his great work on the *Flora of Tasmania.*

No.	Native Name.	Identified by Baron von Mueller as—
49	Burny-burny	Diuris maculata. Smith.
50	Tirba twebin	Eucalyptus fissilis. F. von Mueller.
51	Karrawang	Billardiera scandens. Smith.
52	Kiukinquouggerin (a shrub of which opossums are very fond)	Daviesia corymbosa. Smith.
53	Moéang	Acacia melanoxylon. R. Brown.
54	Tre tal	Goodia lotifolia. Salisbury.
55	Koonadiang (bearing fruit like white currants)	Panax sambucifolius. Sieber. (Varietas dendroides.)
56	Warraworup	Acacia decurrens. Willdenow. (Varietas mollissima.)
57	Morr	Coprosma microphylla. Allan Cunningham.
58	Gaggawar	Lomaria Capensis. Willdenow.
59	Kabin	Kennedya prostrata. R. Brown.
60	Boe-boe	Aster ramulosus. All. Cunningham.
61	Kanberr	Pultenæa juniperina. Labillardière.
62	Nanggert	Glycine clandestina. Willdenow.
63	Minamberang	Clematis aristata. R. Brown.
64	Poocet (the heart of this fern is eaten by the natives)	Alsophila Australis. R. Brown.
65	Kombadik	Dicksonia antarctica. Labillardière.
66	Wyeeboo gaggawar	Lomaria discolor. Willdenow.
67	Koordrung	Davallia dubia. R. Brown.
68	Woorike (a cone of the honey-suckle; the natives soaked the cones in water, and obtained therefrom a pleasant drink)	Banksia Australis. R. Brown.

Plants, with native names, received from the Rev. Mr. Hartmann, of the Aboriginal Station at Lake Hindmarsh:—

(*Examined and named by Baron Von Mueller, C.M.G., F.R.S., Government Botanist, &c.*)

No.	English Name.	Native Name.	Identified by Baron von Mueller as—
1	Shrub	Gingimrick	Dodonæa cuneata. Rudge.
2		Watchûpga	Dodonæa viscosa. Linné.
3	Shrub	Liriginaangijooyû	Hakea flexilis. Ferd. von Mueller.
4	Shrub	Ngûral	Myoporum platycarpum. R. Brown.
5	Shrub	Küllüdct	Cassia artemisioides. Gaudichaud.
6	Box-tree	Bulloitch	Eucalyptus.
7	Tea-tree	Bûnû	Melaleuca.
8	Mallee, No. 3	Gûnamalary	Eucalyptus uncinata. Turganinow.
9	Mallee, No. 2	Bûnûrdùk	Eucalyptus dumosa. A. Cunningham.
10	Mallee, No. 1	Tyalla	Eucalyptus.
11	Bitter quandong-tree	Gûtchû	Santalum acuminatum. Candolle.
12	Pine-tree	Märung	Callitris verrucosa. R. Brown.
13	White gum-tree	Bëyal	Eucalyptus.
14	He-oak tree	Ngäröe	Casuarina glauca. Sieber.

LANGUAGE.

No.	English Name.	Native Name.	Identified by Baron von Mueller as—
15	Shrub - - - -	Gĭo - - - -	Hakea leucoptera. R. Brown.
16	Shrub - - - -	Gŭkwonbĕyurgalk	Grevillea ilicifolia. R. Brown.
17	Shrub - - - -	Brémgŭ - - -	Acacia salicina. Lindley.
18	Honeysuckle-tree	Woreck - - -	Banksia marginata. Cavanilles. (B. Australis. Br.)
19	Shrub - - - -	Gŭtchamŭl - -	Melaleuca pustulata. J. Hooker.
20	Quandong-tree -	Bĭtchĭgal - -	Santalum Preissianum. Miquel.
21	Shrub - - - -	Bŭrŭpga - -	Acacia argyrophylla. Hooker.
22	Shrub - - - -	Dĕrŭck - - -	Beyera ledifolia. Klotzsch.
23	Native currants - {	1. Gŭinyŭgŭr -	1. Steuanthira conostephoides. } Sonder.
		2. Goring - -	2. Brachyloma ericoides. }
24	Shrub - - - -	Gŭkĕrbŭk - -	Casuarina stricta. Aiton.
25	Shrub - - - -	Wĭtchwĭl - -	Leptospermum myroinoides. Schlechtendahl.
26	Shrub - - - -	Nyărpĭrn - -	Neither flower nor fruit.
27	Shrub - - - -	Wallowa - -	Acacia calamifolia. Sweet.
28	Native yams -	Bam—Mŭnyà -	Microseris Forsteri. J. Hooker.
29	Wild rhubarb -	Lanangárangal -	Rumex (neither flower nor fruit).
30	(Used as medicine)	Gŭkwonderŭk -	Myriogyne minuta. Lessing.
31	- - - -	Gŭtyamul - -	Melaleuca parviflora. Lindley.
32	- - - -	Bŭrorong - -	Neither flowers nor fruits.
33	Kind of yam -	Dyarrŭk - -	Geranium dissectum. Linné.
34	Mallee - - -	Gŭnamalang -	Eucalyptus (wants flowers and fruits).
35	Mallee - - -	Danyo - - -	Eucalyptus (no developed flowers or fruit).
36	Kind of yam -	Yŏwàndŭk - -	Convolvulus erubescens. Sims.
37	She-oak - -	Bräkbrŭk - -	Casuarina quadrivalvis. Pentenat.
38	- - - -	Beal - - -	Loranthus pendulus. Sieber.
39	- - - -	Bŭrpangoreetch	No flower or fruit.
40	- - - -	Geapga - -	Bursaria spinosa. Cavanilles.
41	Currant - -	Wining - - -	Exocarpus aphylla. R. Brown.
42	- - - -	Gartiya - -	Acacia (no flowers, no fruit).
43	White-gum -	Bap - - -	Young shoot of an eucalyptus (without flowers and fruit).
44	- - - -	Kŭrong bŭwitch -	Juncus pallidus. R. Brown.
45	- - - -	Mŭrmbal - -	Dianella revoluta. R. Brown.
46	- - - -	Bărep - - -	No flower or fruit.
47	- - - -	Manginbŭwitch -	No flower or fruit.
48	- - - -	Gŭraybŭwitch -	No flower or fruit.
49	- - - -	Wĭrpmrr - -	Xerotes (no fruit).
50	- - - -	Gŭllĭbărkityallan -	Festuca distichophylla. J. Hooker.
51	- - - -	Dŭro - - -	No flower or fruit.
52	Oats - - -	Marmoitch - -	No flower or fruit.
53	- - - -	Yullam - -	Erodium cicutarium. C. Heritier.
54	One-leaved wild potato	Mărŭngĭn - -	No flower or fruit.
55	Broom, No. 2 -	Bŏwŭrr - -	Bæckia Behrii. F. von Mueller.
56	Broom, No. 1 -	Dyŭrr - - -	Melaleuca uncinata. R. Brown.
57	Golden-wattle -	Wĭtch - - -	Acacia pycnantha.
58	Native cherry -	Nyŏra - - -	Exocarpus spartea. R. Brown.
59	- - - -	Ngenyenyegowandullang	Aster pimeloides. Ferd. von Mueller.

174 THE ABORIGINES OF VICTORIA:

Plants, with native names, received from Mr. Joseph Shaw, of the Aboriginal Station at Lake Condah:—
(*Examined and named by Baron von Mueller, C.M.G., F.R.S., Government Botanist, &c.*)

No.	Native Name.	Identified by Baron von Mueller as—
1	Karingan	Pultenæa stricta. Sims.
2	Wikerich	Pimelea humilis. R. Brown.
3	Popoto	Burchardia umbellata. R. Brown.
4	Nallako	Leptospermum juniperinum. Smith.
5	Wauworan	Caledenia pulcherrima. Ferd. von Mueller.
6	Pokancheong	Eryngium rostratum. Cavanilles.
7	Pinnoug	Stylidium graminifolium. Swartz.
8	Mawkun	Cheilanthes tenuifolia. Swartz.
9	Nall	Kennedya prostrata. R. Brown.
10	Punnun	Leptospermum lanigerum. Smith.
11	Thingan-pattherat	Potentilla anserina. Linné.
12	Mookich	Solanum aviculare. Forster.
13	Tharook	Convolvulus sepium. Linné.
14	Currong	Acacia decurrens. Willdenow. (An older name for Acacia mollissima.)
15	Burnburne	Sambucus Gaudichaudiana. Candolle.
16	Billhook	Cassinia longifolia. R. Brown.
17	Parrapurpun	Pteris rotundifolia. Forster. (Var. falcata.)
18	Ballot	Exocarpus cupressiformis. Labillardière.
19	Murinmuch	Cynoglossum Australe. R. Brown.
20	Poopunong	Helichrysum bracteatum. Willdenow.
21	Mawkum	Pteris aquilina. Linné.
22	Wankutch	Veronica Derwentia. Littlejohn.
23	Mayakich	Solanum aviculare. Forster.
24	Wingoyan	Correa speciosa. Aiton.

NATIVE NAMES OF PLACES IN VICTORIA.
(Compiled by the Local Guardians of Aborigines.)

On the 31st July 1869, I forwarded a circular letter, with a portion of the map of Victoria, to each of the Local Guardians of Aborigines, with the request that they would ascertain the native names of the rivers, creeks, hills, ranges, and other natural features in their several districts, and the results are contained in the following papers:—

NATIVE NAMES OF PLACES IN THE UPPER MURRAY DISTRICT.
(Compiled by T. Mitchell, Esq.)

Name as given on Map.	Native Name.	Meaning in English.
Mitta Mitta River	Mida-modunga	From reeds called *modunga*.
Beethan	Beeth-an-da	From weed called *monanda*.
House Creek	Tarrōo-uringa-minga	Mussel Creek.
Huon's Creek	Koan-dudda	From hill so called (Lady Franklin).
Toolangatta	Toolan'gutta	Currejong trees abound.

LANGUAGE. 175

Name as given on Map.	Native Name.	Meaning in English.
Tan-gam-ba-langa	Tan-gam-boo-lam	Cray-fish.
Little River	Kiewa	Derived from *cy-a-nun-a*, sweet, and *wher-ra*, water.
Murra-ma-rang-bun	Muri-ga-rung-doon	Derived from *mung-ya-rung-a*, tall, and *doon*, a hill.
Yackandandah	Yag-gun-dóo-na	From *yag-gun*, native name for the country, and *doon*, a hill.
Barranduda	Bar-ran-di-da	Swamp.
Kerguina	Kur-ra-gui-na	From *hur-ra-in-ede*, silent camp.
Sandy Creek	Kurrain-ga-ah	Windy Mountains, where it rises.
Middle Creek	Kerree-bana	Green Creek, from numerous weeds growing in it.
Wagra	Wagra.	
Cooy-ya-long	Coo-ye-dong.	
Granya	Cranya.	
Talgarna	Talgarna.	
Thurandolong	Thur-an-doó-long	From hill near of same name.
Cudgewong	Cud-ya-wa	From *cud-ya-wa-da*, skin of kangaroo.
Womaatong	Wair-me-da	Big water-hole at Junction.
Bongella	Bongella	Small island.
Belvoir	Woodanga	From an edible nut or plant found in lagoons.

NATIVE NAMES OF PLACES ON THE LOWER MURRAY.
(Compiled by B. W. Gummow, Esq.)

Name as given on Map.	Native Name.	Meaning in English.
Lake Yanga	Ya'hngro	First view narrow, then spreading out into an expanse of water.
Funbaw	Purn-purn	Dwarf Mallee pine.
Weimey	Wáilie	Name of the curlew.
Cuttanb	Cútiúp	Pine resin.
No. 1	Wen'domel	Where are you going?
Naroween	Norówong	I want to go along a blackfellow.
No. 2	Buck-buck	Bubbling of water.
Yolkie	Yí'lkie	Not known.
Bung	Bo'inghóo.	
Mount Templar	Nanúwie	A corner.
No. 3 (creek)	Wirrállie	Black cockatoo.
Calandom	Not known.	
Burra-burra	Búrra-búrra	The cord that bears a satchel.
No. 4	Gúnbówer	Tortuous.
No. 5	Máipie	I made a spear.
Toliobook	To'oliboóck	The yolk of an egg.
Coomaroop	Co'omarúo	A species of acacia.
Palk	Pálkie	Enlarged abdomen.
Piancill	Pi'anghill	Not known.
No. 6	Jerówe	Large smoke.
Woortwort	Wo'ort-po'or	Bulrush.
No. 7	Pa'ni-millie	Little river.
Byndir	Pu'nbi	A small oven.
Guyer	Ngíghyer	A waist-belt.
Koronelorehleur	Kúróng'olotehieur	Large sheet of water.
Tyntynder	Tyntyndye'rr	An acrid lichen.
Babel	Babel	A dull heavy thud.
Gunboa	Gunbour	Tortuous.

Name as given on Map.	Native Name.	Meaning in English.
Swan Hill	Martyrócquert	Platypus.
Marraboor River	Pani-millie	Little river.
Lake Baker	Bormbendil	Honey-dew.
Towan	Towan	Being speared.
Lake Boga	Kooem	Milk.
Garnouk	Garnouk	A leg.
Manunor	Manangwoore	A louse.
Bingeroup	Binjarnp	A shoulder.
Bael-bael	Bael-bael	Gum-trees.
Kerang	Kerang	A parasite.
Mering	Merinkie	It will stick.
Leagur	Leargur	Teeth.
Quambartook	Quambartook	A rat.
Lalbert	Lalbert	A creeper.
Titybong	Titybonga	Root of a tree.
Towaniny	Towaninie	A blow on the back of the head.

NATIVE NAMES OF PLACES IN THE DISTRICT OF LAKE HINDMARSH.

(COMPILED BY THE REV. A. HARTMANN.)

Name as given on Map.	Native Name.	Meaning in English.
The River Wimmera, and the adjoining country as far as Lake Hindmarsh	Burr.	
Lake Hindmarsh	Guru.	
Rocky Point	Gürndägauer	*Gauer* means emu.
The outlet creek between Lakes Hindmarsh and Albacutya	Krumclak.	
Lake Albacutya	Ngelbakutya	*Kutya*, sour quandong.
Outlet creek and country below Lake Albacutya	Tyăkil bä tyăkil.	
Jerrewirrup	Jerriwirrup	Wart on a tree.
Mount Jenkins	Gärnditg.	
Wirringres Plains	Wirringer.	
Sandhills at Pine Plains	Gärdennung wändyel.	
Yallamjib	Yallamjap	Crab-hole.
Yarriambiak Creek	Yarriambink.	
Lake Coorong, and country round about	Yarak.	
Avon River, and country	Wityellibar.	
Mount Jeffcott	Bràbrauer.	
Buloke	Bŭlŭk.	
Morton Plains country	Wàndyin marungŭ.	
Tyrrell	Tàril.	

To most of these names, as you will observe, the blacks could give no meaning.—A. H.

NATIVE NAMES OF PLACES IN THE GLENELG DISTRICT.

(COMPILED BY H. L. McLEOD, ESQ.)

Name as given on Map.	Native Name.	Meaning in English.
Crimugal	Crimugal	Riding up.
Mongrel	Moangull	Well, come up.
Cadnite	Canite	Not known.
Koom	Koomboornambarambum	Lying down.
Wooratanbulli	Wooratanbulli	Stomach.

LANGUAGE.

Name as given on Map.	Native Name.	Meaning in English.
Cuapinyo	Bunnia	Ring-tailed opossum.
Binum	Binnum-binnum	She-oak.
Benayeo	Benyeo	The act of throwing.
Sandy Creek	Brum-brum momo	A kind of rush.
Warkur	Not known.	
Mosquito Creek	Brah	To stab.
Boraccrooer	Not known.	
Tor	Tor	Water-hole.
Penola	Boyng burk	Sandy back.
Apsley	Kiòtacha	Native cat.
Camm	Ghar	Nose.
Elderslie	Langap	A hollow in the ground.
Carrante	Carrante	Cherry-tree.
Lemon Springs	Gnalp	Spring.
Bring Albert	Bring albit	Sandy spring.
Edenhope	Guniah	Green bank.
Power's Creek	Guagaguck	Emu.
Glenelg	Barker.	
Mooree	Morce	Middle of a tree.
Chetwynd	Gunarry	Swamp-oak.
Mullach	Mullengera	Ferns.
Kout Mann	Not known.	
Longlands	Not known.	
Koolomert	Koolermert	Little bird.
Pigeon Ponds	Not known.	

NATIVE NAMES OF PLACES IN THE WANNON DISTRICT.

(Compiled by Peter Learmonth, Esq.)

Name as given on Map.	Native Name.	Name as given on Map.	Native Name.
Mountains.		*Lakes.*	
Mount Napier	Tapook.	Lake Linlithgow	Tunneyare.
Mount Rouse	Kollor-kollor.	Kennedy	Mumyawoune.
Mount Bainbridge	Kreekore.	*Plains.*	
Dundas Ranges	Punyole.	Linlithgow Plains	Warrock Plains.
Victorian Ranges	Pillewcane.	*Creeks.*	
Rivers.		Muddy Creek	Not known.
Wannon	Boar-ang.	Muston's Creek	Bunyong.

NATIVE NAMES OF PLACES IN THE VICINITY OF GLENORCHY.

(Compiled by S. Wilson, Esq.)

Name as given on Map.	Native Name.	Meaning in English.
Lake Lonsdale	Dyael *or* jackle	Swamp.
Glenwylln	Aring	She-oak or casuarina.
Hill near Glenwylln	Woorac-woorac	Honeysuckle or Banksia.
Horsham	Wopet-bungundilar	House of feathers.
Longerenong	Longerenong	The dividing of the waters.
Sandhill at Longerenong	Wyn-wyn-ballyma	The direction of the mouse's dwelling.
Ashens	Lauganong-joruk	The reedy branch or fork.
Glenorchy	Djarrah	A job, a piece of work.

VOL. II.   Z

178   THE ABORIGINES OF VICTORIA:

Name as given on Map.	Native Name.	Meaning in English.
Pleasant Creek	Yerip	Ironbark gum-tree.
Grampians	Cowa	Mountain.
Mount Zero	Mullup-cowa	Little mountain.
Boga Lakes—Pine Lake (No. 2 in map)	Boninjeb	Salt water.
Boga Lakes—Duck Lake (No. 3 in map)	Buckanyany-jowk	Reedy-neck (descriptive of the shape of this lake).
Boga Lakes—Drung-drung (No 1 in map)	Drung-drung.	
Walmer	Tulgamurny catyin	Water of the visitors.
Vectis	Yawmbul	A swim.
Polkemmet	Witchi	Sedges or bulrushes.
Norton Creek	Malibar	A blind creek.
McKenzie River	Bun-nah	Tea-tree scrub.
Burnt Creek	Purtit	Bulrush or sedges.
North Brighton (in map Darlot and McLachlan)	Becatyin	Chalk (or lime) water.
Swamp at North Brighton	Dooen.	
Wimmera River	Barrh	Proper name, no meaning ascertainable.
Half-way Inn	Greech*	Fat.
Irrewarra	Nawallah	What's that?
Rosebrook	Boyop-butyum-butyum	Mesembryanthemum or pig's-face.
Rose's Gap	Barregowa	The middle of the mountains.
Ledcourt	Ledcourt	A spear-point.
Richardson River	Wirchilleba	A dry watercourse.
Marnoo	Marnoo	Finger.
Carr's Plains	Cattiong nyam-nyam†	Flowering climber.
Warranooke (Nicol and Ayrey's station)	Warranooke	The upper lip.

* The blacks assure me it is the native name, although the meaning suggests an English origin.—S.W.
† Pronounced one syllable.

NATIVE NAMES OF PLACES IN THE DISTRICT OF CARNGHAM.
(Compiled by A. Porteous, Esq.)

Name as given on Map.	Native Name.	Meaning in English.
Mount Cole	Bereep-by-bereep	Wild mount.
Fiery Creek	Baringa yallar	Rapid floods.
Middle Creek	Calpin bartic	Resort of many birds.
Raglan	Gereep-gereep	A rough country.
Shirley	Wonagarack	Sandy ground.
Beaufort	Yarram-yarram	Cannot interpret.
Trawalla	Trawalla	Much rain.
Mount Beckworth	Nananook	Behind.
Mount Mitchell	Ornop bonark.	
Mount Bolton	Boriga	Loose ground.
Mount Misery (No. 1)	Langayan	Moon.
The Cardinal	Largagorockfort.	
Peak of Almond	Kam-kam.	
Lady Mount	Lepokworan.	
White-stone Lagoon	Pore.	
Cockpit Lagoon	Morekana	Wild.
Burrumbeet	Bormbeet	Muddy, dirty water.

LANGUAGE.

Name as given on Map.	Native Name.
Mount Ross	Jame.
Spring Hill (No. 1)	Warra.
St. Mary's Hill	Waranganack.
Ravenscroft Hill	Bungel.
Lake Learmonth	Tombine.
Mount Blowhard	Mortello.
Hepburn	Morakile.
Birch Hill	Michacola.
Coghill's Hill	Coratcoork.
Forest Hill	Lightyarang.
Spring Hill (No. 2)	Barangoan.
Creswick	Calembeen.
Hollow-back	Langerguping.
Miners' Rest	Drawill.
Ballarat	Ballarat.
Mount Pleasant	Portello.
Yuille's Swamp	Wendource.
Mount Warrenheip	Warrancip.
Sebastopol	Uran-uran.
Mount Buninyong	Bonanyong.
Yarrowee Creek	Yaramlock.
Hardie's Hill	Barengleowell.
Smythesdale	Naringook.
Black Hill	Nawrightwidwid.
Carngham	Kurnum.
Gold workings, Snake Valley	Nimbuck.
Baillie's Creek	Neperiok.
Chepstowe	Ganing-gering.
Mount Emu	Tokorambeet.
Bainjamie	Langi willi.
Skipton	Woran.
Borriyallack	Borriyallack.
Anderson's Hill	Widderin.
Caramballack	Welergate.
Mount Vite-vite	Molo-molo.
Mount Bute	Coromellock.
Happy Valley	Melong-gap.
Lucky Woman's	Workgogerk.
Mount Erip	Nollo.
Pitfield	Mindi.
Mount Misery (No. 2)	Wadgap pyangra.
Mount Mercer	Garaug gollock.
Rokewood	Convreyalk.
Gnarkeet	Noran ket.
Woady Yaloak	Woady Yaloak.
Mount Elephant	Gerinyclam.
Lismore	Bongcrem-mucn.
Mount Clark	Larra.
Tooliorook	Lar.
Little Corangamite	Napart.
Foxhow	Miter.
Cressy	Bitup.
Weering	Wopillingcalebgecing.

Name as given on Map.	Native Name.
Shelford	Lauy-y-pigan.
Green Hill	Beringworwor.
Mount Hesse	Mokatook.
Lake Murdeduke	Mundeduke.
Mount Gellibrand	Walar-walar.
Birregurra	Birregurra.
Kerangemoorah	Worayao.
Lake Colac	Koram.
Lake Korangamite	Korangamite.
Purrumbete	Purrumbete.
Mount Porndon	Bondon.
Mount Woridgil	Yaretgall.
Mount Myrtoon	Meton.
Pirron Yalloak	Pirron Yalloak.
Morass	Kupurp.
Great Warrion Hill	Koirurk.
Elephant Bridge	Cocorn.
Colac	Bobonorok.
Mount Poolongoork	Mecornam.
Lake Gnarpart	Gnarpart.
Mount Cavern	Bangeratcoret.
Mount Pisgah	Morambuelbullet.
Lake Goldsmith*	Yangrawill.
Stockyard Hill*	Bapcl.
Bald Hill, west of Burrumbeet Lake*	Gunnpan.
Small hill near Skipton*	Monmot.
Forest around Beaufort	Eurambeen.
Lexton	Mahmab.
Head of Wimmera Creek	Culcotok.
Hill east of Skipton	Chilerep.
Small hills south of Mount Emu	Nanami.
Amphitheatre	Yapal.
A forest hill north of Raglan	Bork-bork.
Glenlogie station	Berumgower.
Mr. George Thomson's hill	Gaymorran.
Mr. Ware's hill	Coron.
Mr. Ritchie's hill	Allaynep.
Sago Hill	Collargateyaller.
Black Hill	Collargateyaller.
Burrumbeet Creek	Drawill.
Mr. F. Ormond's hill	Wetaran.
A large cave in ditto	Larnook.
Leigh Creek	Wahwilcurtan.
Emu Creek, after junction with Baillie's Creek	Tariwoodcot.
Moorabool Creek	Moorabool.

* Not mentioned on the map.

NATIVE NAMES OF PLACES IN THE TALBOT DISTRICT.
(Compiled by P. C. Crespigny, Esq.)

Name as given on Map.	Native Name.	Meaning in English.
Mount Glasgow	Tout Bour Nay	Unknown. A volcanic mount known as Mount Glasgow.
Wonge Kurrup	Wonge Kurrup	Unknown. A volcanic mount on the west side of Tullaroop Creek, eight miles north of Clunes.
Wall Walp	Wall Walp	Unknown. At Major Mitchell's crossing over Tullaroop Creek, nine miles north of Clunes.
Big Swamp	Merrin-merrin	Unknown. A large swamp north of Clunes.
Big Water-hole	Moorangapil	Unknown. A lagoon near Talbot.
Tullaroop	Tullaroop	Unknown. A large creek running through Clunes.
Timor	Timor	Unknown. A creek running through Adelaide Lead into the Bet Bet Creek.
Naragil	Naragil	Unknown. A small creek running through the parishes of Amherst and Craigie.
Bet Bet	Bet Bet	Unknown. A large creek on the western side of the division.
Caralulup	Caralulap	Unknown. A parish in the south-western part of the division.
Lilicur	Lilicur	Unknown. A parish in the western part of division.
Bung Bong	Bung Bong	Unknown. A parish in the north-western part of the division.

NOTE.—There are no means of ascertaining the meanings of the native names in English. I have questioned some gins, but they are ignorant of them.—P. C. CRESPIGNY.

NATIVE NAMES OF PLACES IN THE COUNTIES OF HAMPDEN AND HEYTESBURY.
(Compiled by Robert Scott, Esq.)

Native Name.	Meaning in English.	Parish or Run.
Allamiditnu	Part of the bank of Lake Terang	Terang.
Allawookur	Creek	Terang.
Allonggowyong	Marsh	Colantet run.
Alloom	Knoll on bank of Lake Colongulac	Colongulac.
Aloome	Part of the bank of Lake Terang	Terang.
Allumbaa	Spring	Terang.
Alumbah	Spring	Keilambete.
Aluretnitt	Part of the bank of Lake Terang	Terang.
Amelkilbint	Marsh	Purrumbete.
Anaki boornok	Spring	Larra.
Arryaringuhar	Creek (Blind Creek)	Struan.
Arryyarrup	Blind Creek; runs in winter; water brackish	Connewarren.
Bangal	A. Anderson's homestead and name of Mount Emu Creek opposite Bangal.	
Barrandar	Creek	Maridayallock.
Bayrong	Creek	Terang.
Bimalloom	Knoll on bank of Lake Colongulac	Colongulac.
Binebaccallooke	Knoll on bank of Lake Colongulac	Colongulac.

LANGUAGE. 181

Native Name.	Meaning in English.	Parish or Run.
Birdebush	Brackish lake	Koort-koort-nong.
Bugadanectch	Spring	Larra.
Bolajup	Spring	Borriyalloak.
Boigdeet	Marsh	Larra.
Bookaar	Brackish lake	Koort-koort-nong.
Boonuap	Muston's Creek	Connewarren.
Boorite youong	Dam	Corangamite.
Booronuit	Marsh	Larra.
Borriyalloak	F. Ormond's homestead	Borriyalloak.
Bonelwithitnick	Spring on the bank of Lake Gnotuk	Colongulac.
Boniyarook	Part of the bank of Lake Terang	Terang.
Bourg	Mount Shadwell	Mortlake.
Buckerang	Rise	Corangamite.
Buiclaccaluke	Site on which W. Adeney's homestead is built	Colongulac.
Bulkilnarra	Salt lake	Corangamite.
Bunbunyer	Spring	Borriyalloak.
Bundar	Marsh	Struan.
Buranggurtwooroot	Tributary of Curdie's Creek (gum-tree, wooroot)	Tandarook.
Burrah	Hopkins River (the name of the lake it runs from).	
Bullenmerri	Brackish lake	Colongulac.
Carawa	Creek	Terang.
Carnoorong	Timbered land between Lake Keilambete and Noorat	Glenormiston.
Carpundergil	Marsh	Terang.
Chocolyn	W. Adeney's homestead	Colongulac.
Chocolyne	Knoll on bank of Lake Colongulac	Colongulac.
Colan	Marsh	Purrumbete.
Colantet	W. Allen's homestead and a marsh.	
Colladal	Spring	Maridayallock.
Colongulac	Brackish lake	Colongulac.
Colpoombooruak	Part of Bostock's Creek	Tandarook.
Coorcknerite	Part of Curdie's Creek (nerite meaning small fish or spawn)	Tandarook.
Coradgill	Salt lake	Corangamite.
Corambliting	Marsh	Poligolit.
Corangamarajah	Mack's homestead (good water).	
Corangamite	Salt lake.	
Connewarre	Dam	West Cloven Hill.
Connowarren	Fresh lake	Ellerslie.
Corn-corn natong	Point running into Lake Corangamite	Corangamite.
Corookorookerdiec	Salt lake	Terinallum.
Corum	Marsh	Terang.
Culer-culer	Sugarloaf Hill	Jancourt.
Culliawor	High bank overlooking Lakes Bullen, Merri, and Gnotuk	Colongulac.
Cunduro	Spring	Terang.
Cunongeeyeuk	Tea-tree springs (cunong means dung)	North Keilambete.
Currungurrun	Small rise	Corangamite.
Currycong	Hugh Scott's homestead, Jancourt	Jancourt.
Curtbiel	Salt lake (dry in summer)	Terinallum.
Dunnawalla	Brackish lake	Larra.
Eyang	Brackish lake (drying up fast)	Bolac Plains.
Geelengla	Spring	Larra.
Geritger	Spring and small creek	Purrumbete.

THE ABORIGINES OF VICTORIA:

Native Name.	Meaning in English.	Parish or Run.
Gheringal	Brackish lake	Terinallum.
Giringcall	Spring (signifies that wild dog was killed there)	Colongulac.
Gnarkeet	F. Begg's homestead and chain of ponds	Gnarkeet.
Gnarkeet dungurk	Salt lake	Borriyalloak.
Gnotuk	Salt lake and slightly brackish spring on the east side of lake	Colongulac.
Gnarpurt	Lake (very bitter or salt).	
Goodwitch	Salt lake	Corangamite.
Jeeler	Marsh east side of Mount Widdern	Borriyalloak.
Jehura	Marsh	Purrumbete.
Karaiar	Brackish lake	Kariah.
Karawah	Outlet from Pejark	Terang.
Kart Dirk	N. Cole's homestead (carry water)	Kilnoorat.
Keilambete	J. Thomson's homestead and salt lake.	
Kerbyleet	Marsh	North Purrumbete and Colongulac.
Kirwecton	Mount	Koort-koort-nong.
Kohlear	Marsh	Tandarook.
Koleaur	Small hill on which Hugh Scott's homestead is built	Tandarook.
Kolora	Fresh lagoon	Kolora.
Kong	West Cloven Hill (like a bandicoot)	Koort-koort-nong.
Konnenonar	Fresh lagoon	Keilambete.
Koopup	Marsh (dry)	Bangal.
Koonanguric	Fresh lake	Tooliorook.
Koort-koort mouthang	Sloping bank at the south-west corner of Lake Guotuk	Colongulac.
Koort-koort-nong	J. G. Ware's homestead (land crabs)	Koort-koort-nong.
Koreetnong	Brackish lake	Kariah.
Konawallo Karra	Mrs. Robertson's homestead (the place of the old wattle-tree)	Connewarren.
Koroot-koroot	Black swamp (fine land and water)	Connewarren.
Kurthaulen	Stony Rises (islands of stone)	Struan.
Lakulang	Salt lake	Terinallum.
Langi Willi	W. Mitchell's homestead	Skipton.
Larra	J. L. Currie's homestead and small spring	Ettrick.
Leura	Mount (volcanic)	Colongulac.
Maingar	Swamp (Port Fairy)	Connewarren.
Malleen	Hill	Tandarook.
Mambally	Small creek	Connewarren.
Maridayallock	J. McKinnon's homestead	Maridayallock.
Martingmiring	Marsh	Purrumbete.
Mawwick	Marsh	Maridayallock.
Meeton	Mount	Kariah.
Mejirinuke	Creek	Colongulac.
Meningorott	P. McArthur's homestead and mount	Kilnoorat.
Merrit	Marsh	North Purrumbete and Colongulac.
Merriwidgill	Marsh	Corangamite.
Mertonimburich	Gully north end of Lake Gnotuk	Colongulac.
Mingham	Marsh	Purrumbete.
Moigoniutch	Marsh	Larra.
Mont-mont mithin	Part of the bank of Lake Terang	Terang.
Morragilynon	Small Bald Hill	Bangal.
Mullah	Spring (profuse growth of the nettle)	Keilambete.

LANGUAGE.   183

Native Name.	Meaning in English.	Parish or Run.
Mulleen	Tea-tree spring (Dairy station)	Jancourt.
Mumbythaca	Mount	Connewarren.
Murramong	Marsh (dry)	Bangal.
Myrnong	H. H. Gibson's homestead (*mirnong* or *murnon*, a root used by the natives, like a carrot, and very abundant here)	Mortlake.
Naikoneburrimon	Little muddy water-hole in the south-west of	Colongulac.
Narribool	Creek	Terang.
Narrokeeing	Ewan's Hill	Maridayallock.
Noorat	Mount (volcanic)	Glenormiston.
Olangone	Salt lake (high bank)	Connewarren.
Ornaweewit	A. S. Robertson's homestead (first swallow of the season)	Struan.
Oorate	The Sisters (stony, and many kangaroo)	Kolora.
Palayratuoe	Open ground between Lake Keilambete and Noorat	Glenormiston.
Parp	Spring	Purrumbete.
Pejark	Marsh	Terang.
Penourong	Marsh (dry in summer)	Terinallum.
Perikywarn	Spring	Purrumbete.
Piel	Salt lake	Terinallum.
Poligolit	J. Dodd's homestead.	
Pollong gowyong	Marsh	Colantet.
Poolongoork	Small hill (pickaninny elephant).	
Porndon	Mount (volcanic)	Purrumbete.
Port bullong	Spring	Purrumbete.
Pourpeatberry	Spring (water gushing out)	Keilambete.
Poyetete	Tea-tree	North Keilambete run.
Puckerwuro	Bank at outlet from Pejark	Terang.
Puckarwooro	Bank at the north-east corner of Lake Ballenmerri	Colongulac.
Puladyabook	Issue of marsh to Lake Corangamite	Corangamite.
Pullnar	Marsh	Tandarook.
Punpundhal	Salt lake	Corangamite.
Puntiyerraman	Creek running past Mr. Robertson's	Struan.
Purdieurong	Salt lake	Terinallum.
Purrumbete	Messrs. Manifold's homestead, and fresh lake 156 feet deep	Purrumbete.
Purtmundal	J. Hasler's homestead	Corangamite.
Put-put	Marsh	Purrumbete.
Sangoyie	Tea-tree spring	Bangal.
Tandarook	Dr. Curdie's homestead and limestone hill (derived from a vegetable root found there called *darook*)	Tandarook.
Taragill	Spring (place where rushes grow)	Keilambete.
Tarangmuckar	Tributary of Curdie's Creek (*tarang*, the leaf of the lightwood; *muckar*, a vegetable root)	Tandarook.
Tarncuboo	A prominent part of the eastern bank of Curdie's Creek (from *tarin*, a road; *cuboo*, the nose)	Tandarook.
Tataitong	Spring	Larra.
Tatutong	Salt lake	Corangamite.
Tayrangweyuk	Stony ridge at the foot of Mount Noorat to the east	Glenormiston.
Terang	Fresh lake	Terang.
Terang-pom	Brackish lake	Corangamite.

Native Name.	Meaning in English.	Parish or Run.
Terrara merri	Salt lake (dry in summer)	Terinallum.
Terrinallum	Mr. Cumming's homestead and Mount Elephant.	
Terrie-terrie murrie	Tributary of Curdie's Creek (means a stony creek)	Tandarook.
Timboon	Creek	Maridayallock.
Tirangal koort-koort	Marsh	Larra.
Tircarra	Marsh	Larra.
Tirtoo	The Blind Creek	Between Kilnoorat and Maridayallock.
Tocoureeit	Marsh	Maridayallock.
Tooliorook	Brackish lake.	
Tooloomolong	Large marsh	Jancourt.
Toorak	Tea-tree springs, township of Mortlake	Mortlake.
Trelwyte	Marsh north-east of Mount Widdern	Borriyalloak.
Tyrrer	Marsh	North Purrumbete and Colongulac.
T'wroghadeen	Marsh	Colantet.
Vita-vita	Mount	North Elephant.
Wanan	Small rise on which A. S. Robertson's house is built	Struan.
Wanandor	Creek (young emu)	Struan.
Warawwill	Brackish lake (lake of reeds)	Struan.
Warntwintch	Spring, western boundary of parish of Colongulac.	
Warron	Name of Mount Emu Creek at Skipton.	
Wawallock	D. Craig's homestead.	Kilnoorat.
Weerang	Point of land in cultivation paddock	Connewarren.
Weerpurich	Spring on the west side of Lake Gnotuk	Colongulac.
Weranganuc	Brackish lake	North Purrumbete.
Weright	Marsh	Purrumbete.
Werong	Marsh	Purrumbete.
Weriwerikoort	Tea-tree springs, brackish	Mortlake.
Widdern	Mount (volcanic), (two caves)	Borriyalloak.
Willackbirk	Spring (bad water) and creek	West Cloven Hill.
Wiritgill	Mount (volcanic)	Purrumbete.
Wirraan	Brackish lake	Koort-koort-nong.
Wirrburo	Marsh	Terang.
Woamgooduate	Rises	Tandarook.
Wookur	Creek	Terang.
Wookurmta	Part of the bush	Terang.
Woolonguwong	Fresh lagoon	Koort-koort-nong.
Woombiher	Marsh	Terang.
Wooramouil	Creek	Struan.
Wooriobolook	Elephant Marsh	Tooliorook.
Wooriwyrite	G. Shaw's homestead	Wooriwyrite.
Woorodirb	Part of Bostock's Creek	Tandarook.
Warrnporon	Part of the bank of Pejark	Terang.
Warrnonorn	Part of the bank of Pejark	Terang.
Warteroe	Spring, resembling the shoulder	Keilambete.
Yunbect	Marsh	Purrumbete.
Yarmon	Marsh	Purrumbete.
Yelletger	Marsh	Purrumbete.
Dharugill	A spring, &c. (a plant)	Kilnoorat—Mr. McArthur's
Baakaarabooitch	Dam on Blind Creek (brackish water)	,,
Goloigh	The Blind Creek	,,
Gonogovitch	Swamp (kangaroo)	,,

LANGUAGE.

Native Name.	Meaning in English.	Parish or Run.
Keenitch	Swamp	Kilnoorat— Mr. McArthur's
Koamnu	Swamp, and continuation of same (kidney)	,,
Meningord	Hill (a maggot)	,,
Moomakeekur	Sheepwash (dogwood)	,,
Nareedbudgill	Dam near Basin Banks (a frog)	,,
Warnarick	Dam, home-station (waddie)	,,
Boolitewooran	East Cloven Hill (two bandicoots)	Mr. Ware's run.
Won	East Cloven Hill	,,
Booliteherioon	Cloven Hills	,,
Boolirtkilock	West Cloven Hill	,,
Cornite	Swamp	,,
Kerrnite	Swamp	,,
Burntah	Currie's Swamp (long thatch grass)	,,
Burntah	Large swamp at stone hut	,,
Giranghabum	Mr. Robertson's swamp (native root like onions)	,,
Giranghabum	Large swamp, Mr. Currie's	,,
Kirongiwiwit	(First swallow of the season)	,,
Kurtpurlicu	Stony Rises	,,
Koort-koort-nong	(Land crabs)	,,
Medouranook	Timboon Creek (small fish)	,,
Murton	The Green Hill	,,
Pankaar	Lake	,,
Poonoong	Tea-tree	,,
Tarouck	Swamp (large reeds)	,,
Toorak	Small swamp north of Lake Poonah (reeds)	,,
Teringyellum	Mount Elephant	,,
Woorabbeeal	Lake at limekiln (gum-tree, *bual*)	,,
Wooriworah	Tea-tree at Sweet Creek	,,
Wooriwyrite	Honeysuckle bank near the church, Kiluoorat	,,

Native Name.	Meaning in English.
Natural Names, &c.	
Tirren	Sun.
Purrang nut ning-	Moon.
White churt	Stars.
Koouk cutrine too	Comet (*too*, to smoke).
Taarin-taarin paa-root	Rainbow (*paaroot*, like mouth).
Myiang	Rain.
Wallart	Hail.
Naark	Frost.
Wirndook	Wind.
Moorndou	Thunder.
Yerkone	Lightning.
Marnong	Sky.
Merring	Clouds, also earth.
Burect	Water.
Cut-cut	Grass.
Merri	Stone.
Animals.	
Turro	Bunyip.
Koora	Old man kangaroo.

Native Name.	Meaning in English.
Murrin	Forester kangaroo.
Narkwoor	Forester "Joe."
Cullurn	Wallaby.
Curn-duig	Wallaby "Joe."
Parre	Small kangaroo, rabbit size.
Pee jack	Species of kangaroo with a beard like a goat.
Werringal	Native bear.
Mooragil caboo	Wombat (*caboo*, the nose).
Booruong	Native dog.
Wirron	Kangaroo rat.
Carrooie	Bandicoot.
Cabong	Tiger cat.
Woomenite	Native cat.
Mooroug	Native water rat (means black).
Woolonguloe	Porcupine (from *woolung*, sharp).
Y-eetick	Flying squirrel (signifies a wing and long bushy tail).
Burroot	Squirrel mouse (signifies little).

Native Name.	Meaning in English.	Native Name.	Meaning in English.
Purt mur	Small mouse (very small).	Tolorim	Robin redbreast.
By-iete	Opossum.	Waigh week	Swallow.
Pooyook	Ring-tailed opossum.	Arrin	Quail.
Mullin	Bat.	Terang pundete	Snipe.
		Paturaal	Plover.
	Birds.	Tuaroo	Small white bird seen about lakes.
Burrinmool	Emu (signifies a long leg and long neck).	Mirnin-mirnin	Small wren.
Cooro	Native companion (light color).	Thereri	Wattle-bird.
Burrum-burrum	Wild turkey (signifies big).	Bullan	Drab-colored bird.
Koorno-woour	Swan.	Yoongar	Cormorant.
Purndurgul	Grey goose.	Tindeu	Kingfisher.
Naunch nack	Black goose.		
Curt perap	Pelican.		*Snakes, &c.*
Cooie	Water-hen or coot.	Corang	Diamond snake.
Weerungooi	Dark heron.	Murrh	Black snake.
Cooroy cory	Mountain duck.	Cartook	Big yellow snake.
Too-too boro	Black duck.	Wrock	Iguana.
Law wook	Wood duck.	Toorootgil	Lizard.
Currie boodnook	Teal duck.	Torauk	Big lizard.
Nallitgill	Platypus.	Moowny	Small lizard.
Braich bird	Musk duck.	Woorakcoole	Small iguana.
Coolonal	Small gull.		
Neangar	Large eaglehawk.		*Timber.*
Mullen-mullen	Small eaglehawk.	Moothang	Lightwood.
Willan	Black cockatoo.	Wooroot	Large gum.
Niooke	White cockatoo.	Mirright	Honeysuckle.
Coorookite	Small white cockatoo.	Coorung	Stringybark.
Coornate	Laughing jackass.	Pullate	Cherry-tree.
Waa	Crow.	Purnong	Tea-tree.
Coora	Magpie.	Currang	Wattle.
Mooan noogul	Black magpie.	Wareet terra	Wattle.
Co cock	Mopoke.	Narang	She-oak.
Wirrimul	Grey owl.	Pea all	Red-gum.
Toord	Red parrot.	Yull-yull	Tea-tree.
Cull callingi	Green parrot.	Taroon	Scrub.
Wirt tooro	Blue mountain parrot.	Purn-purn dum	White-gum.

NATIVE NAMES OF PLACES IN THE VICINITY OF WARRNAMBOOL.

(Furnished by H. B. Lane, Esq.)

Name on Map.	Native Name.	Name on Map.	Native Name.
Allansford	Wurrurmuayer.	Warrnambool Bay	Cowarndichnu.
Camperdown	Murrunkinarong.	Warrnambool	Wheringkornitch.
Curdie's River	Narrarwhurrut.	Lake Pertobe	Pehrtupe keellink.
Dunmore	Coonogeull.	Tower Hill	Koroitch (a small fish).
Drysdale	Murhtmihrtinyah.	Greenhill H. S.	Gnegne (no good).
Belfast	Puyeepkill.	Minjah H. S.	Pechamihronk.
Ballangeich H. S.	Woornwaking (a crow's nest).	Quamby H. S.	Wooromuckcalin.
		Tarrone H. S.	Yabng (a long swamp).
St. Helens H. S.	Gnerrang (she-oak tree).	Yambuk	Yambuk.
Moyne River	Yalloak (a shallow swampy stream).	Lake Yambuk	Yambuk keelink.
		Orford	Pehrrit.

LANGUAGE. 187

Name on Map.	Native Name.	Name on Map.	Native Name.
River Shaw	Pehrrit puhreitch.	Keilambete H. S.	Keilambete keeling.
Kirkstall	Woombeyer.	Glenormiston H. S.	Mukrrit.
Eumeralla River	Woorromkeelum (a long river).	Emu Creek	Gnurrarpookrnpookn.
		Keyang H. S.	Karngeeyang.
Branxholme	Kurtuk-kurhrtuk.	West Cloven Hills	Warroue.
Mount Eccles	Puint pino.	Terang	Turroug.
Castlemaddie H. S.	Kill kuhrr.	Merri River at Dennington	Wheringkerneitch.
Ettrick H. S.	Kurtoneieth.		
Mount Napier	Tappoke.	Woodford	Kurtmulluk.
Mount Rouse	Kolor.	Woorwoorite H. S.	Woorwoorite.
Lake Condah	Condam keelink.	Menineoort H. S.	Menineoort.
Woolsthorpe	Lleeroot.	Eddington H. S.	Warranillook.
Woodlands	Karngkuhrtong.	Lake Booker	Corangamitch keeling.
Hawkesdale	Tuhrarmukri.	Mount Leura	Lee-hurah caark.
Kilmorey	Kuhrngkringkore.	Glenelg River	Wurri-wurri.
Mangoon Lake	Mang-oom keeling.	Mount Clay	Pinambul caark.
Hexham	Perrelleit.	Whittlebury H. S.	Whurtkirrnyangork.
Hopkins H. S.	Murri-mukrri bukrrikill.	Darlot's Creek	Killkurk whurrionnew.
Muston Creek	Woorongkeuppirn.	Black fellows' Creek H. S.	Kahrnkeenu.
Connewarren H. S.	Werrang.		
Merrang	Wirrangelleen.	Scrubby Creek	Punooppine.
Salt Lake	Mullangohne keeling.	Spring Creek H. S.	Krickkora.
Hopkins River	Pukrruhng.	Spring Creek	Mopohr.
Connewarren	Coonnewanne keeling.	Kennedy's Creek	Puhrtinikook.
Liberton H. S.	Tinnertoong.	Union H. S.	Puhrtinihook.
Framlingham	Teerak.	Portland	Pulambete.
Bryne O'Lynn H. S.	Pillook-pillook.	Stony Rises H. S.	Poorkarr.
		Birdebush	Wiraan.
Nelson H. S.	Coorong.	Lake Colongulac	Cohnggulac keeling.
Grassmere H. S.	Meekri.	Lake Gnotuk	Gnutook keeling.
Mount Garvoe	Wukrnnumbol caark.	Lake Bullen Merri	Bullen Merri keeling.
Fresh Lake	Mumdereen keeling.	Cobrico	Cobrico yallock.
Panmure	Hurrimk.	Mount Emu	Narrowhane.
Mount Shadwell	Poohrk caark.	Ecklin Swamp	Ecklin yalloack.
Mount Shadwell H. S.	Turnapohk.	Lake Elingamite	Elingamitch keeling.
		Childers Cove	Narring gnuyun.
The Sisters H. S.	Cooningdar.	Port Campbell	Purroitchihoorrong.

The list is the most correct I can give. I have made enquiries from the different blacks I have met. I have written them so as to give an idea of pronunciation.—W. GOODALL.

NATIVE NAMES OF PLACES IN THE VICINITY OF BELFAST.

Name on Map.	Native, with English meaning.	Name on Map.	Native, with English meaning.
Dunmore	Koonongal (station hill).	Condah	Carrap (lake).
Eumeralla	Warrongittong (waterhole).	Mount Eccles	Boot-beam (mountain and lake).
Korong	Korong (big swamp).	Camperdown	Lawarra.
Orford	Par-ed.	Mount Napier	Tapook.
Belfast	Nourmath.	Yambuk	Yambuk (water).
Allansford	Terong (Hopkins River).	Yalloak	Yallonk (water).
Squattlesea	Poo-ambete.		Winnie-waw (fire).
Hexham	Bulla-bulla (good).		Monegol (little round swamp).
Mortlake	Boorook (mountain).		

NATIVE NAMES OF PLACES OBTAINED FROM THE ABORIGINES OF THE RIVER YARRA YARRA.

Mount Riddell, *Koranderrk* or *Turnim-be-waang*.
Badger Creek (whose sources are in Koranderrk), *Kurr-nung*, a little watercourse.
Mount Juliet, *Tink-a-koo-lara-ghin*.
Yer-rang (erroneously named *Yering*), scrubby. The flats of the Yarra were once covered with scrub.
Keruk-yerang, wattle scrub.
Olinda Creek, near Lilydale, *Gnurt-bille-worrun*.
Yarra Yarra River, *Birr-arrung*. [The word for mist is *Boorr-arrang*.]
Place on which the City of Melbourne is built, *Narr-'m*.
Moor-ool-burk or *Moor-ool-beek*, on the River Yarra. (The earth is basaltic, and of a rich chocolate color.)
Kangaroo Ground, *Moor-rull* (also basaltic, but generally of a deeper color than the soil of *Moor-ool-burk*.)
[A volcanic hill, near Creswick, where the soil is like that found at *Moor-ool-burk* and the Kangaroo Ground, is named *Moorokyle*.]
Ban-null, a high hill or mountain.
Nut-kundrah, very stiff soil.
Mirring-gnay-bir-nong, the Saltwater River.

NATIVE NAMES OF PLACES IN GIPPSLAND.

(COMPILED BY A. W. HOWITT, ESQ.)

Name as given on Map.	Native Name.	Meaning in English and Remarks.
Reed bed at the end of the Mitchell River (shown upon the map as a kind of delta)	Wan-gan.	
Eagle Point (shown on some maps)	Nur-rung	Moon.
Bairnsdale	Wy-yung	A kind of duck.
Bairnsdale Backwater	Cow-oung.	
Clifton Morass	Nen-duck.	
Mount Taylor and Mount Lookout	Bullung-warl	Two spears. (These are two very prominent hills overlooking the low country.)
Boggy Creek	Ngurke-yow-wut.	
Lindenow	Moor-murn.	
Sarsfield (Nicholson)	Turt-toong.	
Nicholson River Backwater	Yowen-burrun.	
Mouth of the Nicholson River, east bank	Ngarka-wallung	Back-stone (literal translation).
Deep Creek at Bruthen	Nyelluog.	
Bruthen*	Murloo.	
Kilmorie	Boo-yow.	
Sec. 16 Parish of Tambo	Bruthen.*	
Inlet from the Tambo River into Kilmorie Morass	Toole-ne-yarn	Water come in.
Mossyface, Tambo River	Marlung-dun	Mussel-shell.
Ramrod Creek	Boung-warl	Camp-spear.

* It will be seen from the above that the name of Bruthen does not belong to the locality now known by it.

LANGUAGE.

Name as given on Map.	Native Name.	Meaning in English and Remarks.
Dead-horse Creek; enters the Tambo River near Ramrod Creek, from the eastward, and is crossed in the Maneroo road about ten miles from Bruthen	Gurrun-gurrun-yarn	Very little water.
Stony Creek; crossed by the Maneroo road about twelve miles from Bruthen, and runs into Lake Tyers	Crocken	Quartz.
Mouth of the Tambo River	Gwannung-bourn	Pelican.
Swan Reach	Wook-gook	Morepork.
Tambo River near Bindi	Bindi memial.	
Tambo River near Tongio	Tongio memial.	
Tongeo East	Carrara wira.	
Swift's Creek	Bunjuragingee mungee.	
Mount Tambo	Tambo.	
Mount Bindi Range	Nonniyong.	
Tongio Gap	Mungobabba.	
Lake Tyers	Wannan-gatty	Kangaroo apple. Is sometimes pronounced Koor-nung-gatty.
Ewing's Marsh	Boom-boy.	
East bank of Snowy River at mouth	Murloo.	
West side of Snowy River	Mardgee-long.	
Mount Raymond	Dubbil.	
Cabbage-tree Creek	Can-tchin.	
Cape Conran	Murrow-gunnie.	
Pearl Point	Py-yoot.	
Mount Cann	Berrn.	
Sydenham Inlet	Binn.	
Mount Willie (is shown upon some maps at the head of Lake Tyers, and just south of Maneroo road; a most prominent landmark)	Nowr-nowr.	
Red Bluff (entrance to Gippsland Lakes)	Ninnie.	
Grant	Poork-poork-gill-yarn	Head of the water.
Good-luck Creek	Groggin	Quartz.
Cobbannah Creek	Boolloot	Kind of gum scrub.
Pretty Boy's Pinch	Tulloo-bowie	Kind of wallaby.
Davy's Noo	Darn-gwennet	Bell-bird.
Bulgurback Creek	Crung-grurk	This creek is shown on the maps between Castleburn and Cobbannah. The word *Bulgurback* is corrupt, being part native and part English. *Bulgur*, mountain back—behind—that is, behind the mountains.
Castleburn Creek	War-dur.	
Waterford (Mitchell crossing on Crooked River road)	Dalu-mlarng	Yam.
Orr's Creek	Dal-gowut	Reeds.
Dargo station (Mackintosh)	Boulāng-deera	Kangaroo.
Creek at Connolly's Dargo Inn	Lown gurrut	Mountain ash. This tree has a rough bark at the butt, and a gum top; grows about 4,000 feet above sea; a white wood.
First creek up stream west side	Martgutty	Wattle-tree.
Quackmungee Hill	Kou-ark-mungee	Laughing jackass.
Quackmungee Creek	Bannur-ghur	White-gum.

Name as given on Map.	Native Name.	Meaning in English and Remarks.
Mount Birregun	Gner-ing	Gang-gang cockatoo.
Mount Steve	Koor-nung-gatty	Kangaroo apple.
Mount Baldhead	Tarl-darn	A little snow.
Notch Hill	Der-rung	Skin or hide.
Wannangatta River	Wontwun	
Wentworth River	Tally-yalmy	Shark. It is said that, a long time ago, "old man blackfellow" caught a little shark at the mouth of the Wentworth River.
Wongungarra River	Gwannam-o-rook	Eaglehawk.
Crooked River	Dow-wirra	Dry tree. The trees at the head on the Dividing Range are all dead.
Castle Hill	Browlt-dar-darnda	Always snow there.
Mount Kent	Nigga-the-rook	A yellow snake.
Snowy Bluff	Gellung-brook-wollung	A sharp-pointed stone. The words *brook* and *poork* (see above) are the same; *gellung-warl*, the name of Rottemah Island in the lakes, means "spear point."
Mount Howitt	Toot-buck-nulluck	Like a rope, or "tie him up side."
Mount Alfred (Boggy Creek), near Bairnsdale	Nuggur-yowatie	Mountain ash. This tree has a bark like ironbark, and the ends of branches are smooth-barked; it grows at a lower elevation than the true mountain ash.
Upper Boggy Creek	Taloo-lumbruck	Tadpole.
Merrijig Creek	Nunga-bruggu-lar	Wind-hole. There is said to be a rock through which the wind blows.
Iguana Creek	Callad-euru	Red-gum.

NOTE.—Boggy Creek is shown upon the maps as Prospect Creek.

NATIVE NAMES OF PLACES IN THE VICINITY OF LAKE WELLINGTON, GIPPSLAND.

(COMPILED BY THE REV. F. A. HAGENAUER.)

Name as given on Map.	Native Name.	Meaning in English.
Thomson River	Carrang-carrang	Brackish water.
La Trobe River	Durt'yowan	Finger.
Aberfeldy River	Nambruc	Plenty of black opossums.
McAlister River	Wirnwirndook'yeerung	Song of some bird.
Avon River	Dooyeedang	
Perry River	Goomballa	Climbing.
Wentworth River	Daberda'bara	Rocky bank.
Mitchell River	Wahyang	Spoon-billed duck.
Nicholson River	Dart'yung	Root of water plant.
Tambo River	Ber'rawan	
Tarra River	Blindit'yin	
Albert River	Lurt'bit	
Flooding Creek	Way-put	
Merriman's Creek	Dur'lin	
Cowar Creek	Bandow'ara	
Freestone Creek	Wurrundyan'garla	

LANGUAGE.

Name as given on Map.	Native Name.	Meaning in English.
Tom's Creek	Warrigallac.	
Stony Creek	Darlinurla.	
Sandy Creek	Warriballat	Water-holes.
Donnelly's Creek	Darliblan.	
Lake Wellington	Murla	A kind of clay found in it.
Lake Victoria	Toonal'look	Long narrow water.
Lake King	Narran	Moon.
Lake Bunga	Wurndoang	Salt lake.
Lake Reeves	Walmuuyee'ra	Shallow lake.
Raymond Island	Grag-in	Stony island.
Snake Island	Ngirna.	
Crooked River	Nailung	Plenty of water-hens.
Jones' Bay	Dahduck	Tail of the lake.
Swanreach	Wang	Breadbasket.
Seacombe or Straits	Boollum-boollum	Plenty of tea-trees.
Hills south of Merriman's Creek	Dambo-byo.	

NATIVE NAMES OF PLACES IN THE VICINITY OF LAKE TYERS, GIPPSLAND.

(COMPILED BY THE REV. JOHN BULMER.)

Name as given on Map.	Native Name.	Meaning in English.
Lake Bunga	Lāne Beuk	Good water.
Lake Tyers	War nang gatty	Big lake.
Ewen's Morass	Yä yung	Morass.
Snowy River	Kärang gil	From great quantities of water-weed about.
Cape Conran	Kerlip	A corner.
Broadribb	Wrak thun bälluk	Place of gum-trees.
Pearl Point	Tarlo wyak	A small seagull.
Point Ricardo	Marout ganny	A rocky point.
Sydenham Inlet	Birn	A fish-hawk.
Stony Creek	Lāne glan	An edible root.
Boggy Creek	Närkä kowera	A flint, being got there.
Yellow Water-holes	Wäth	A shrimp.
Buchan station	Tirtäläck	A frog.
Murrandale	Tooruk	A bulrush.
Mount Dawson	Bärrät purk	Bald head.
Murrandale Hill	Koorag angy	A deep stony gully.
Black Mountain	Woorarra	A mountainous place.
Rourke's River	Inja gut barapa	Flowing from a rock.

The Snowy River is also called *Doorack*; but I could not get the meaning from the blacks. The name (*Kärang gil*) I have given refers to its lower part, near the sea.—JOHN BULMER.

NATIVE NAMES OF HILLS, RIVERS, LAKES, AND OTHER NATURAL FEATURES IN VICTORIA.

(FURNISHED BY THE SURVEYOR-GENERAL OF THE COLONY.)

Name on Map.	Native Name.	Meaning in English.
Mount Cole	Bereep-bercep	Wild.
Fiery Creek	Boringa yallar	Flood, to carry away trees.
Middle Creek	Calpan bartick	Habitation of a bird.
Raglan	Gerup-gerup	Rough place.
Shirley	Wonagreek	Sandy ground.
Beaufort	Yarram-yarram.	
Trawalla	Trawalla	Wild water.
Mount Beckwith	Nananook	Behind.
Mount Mitchell	Ornopbonork.	
Mount Bolton	Boriga.	
Mount Misery, No. 1	Langi yan	The resting-place of the moon; as from a favorite camping-ground of the natives the moon appeared to rise over that hill.
The Cardinal	Langi gorockfort.	
Peak of Almond	Cam-cam.	
Lady Mount	Lefrokwaran.	
White-stone Lagoon	Poar	Many waters.
Cockpit Lagoon	Moracana	Wild.
Burrumbeet	Borombeet	Muddy water.
Mount Ross	Tam	Wild.
Spring Hill, No. 1	Woora	Wild (by natives near Trawalla).
St. Mary's Hill	Woronganack.	
Lake Learmonth	Tomblin.	
Mount Blowhard	Mortillo	Wild.
Hepburn	Moorokyle.	
Birch Hill	Mishacola.	
Coghill's Creek	Corotcork.	
Forest Hill	Light yarang.	
Spring Hill, No. 2	Barangoan.	
Creswick	Colembene.	
Hollow-back Hill	Languguhinggoork.	
Miner's Rest	Drawall.	
Ballarat	Ballaarat	Resting place, or reclining on the elbow. *Balla* means elbow; vide *History of Ballarat.*
Mount Pleasant	Portilla.	
Wendouree	Wendouree.	
Mount Warrenheip	Warrenheip.	
Sebastopol	Wran-wran.	
Mount Buninyong	Buninyong.	
Yarrowee	Yaramlock.	
Hardie's Hill	Boring leawell.	
Smythesdale	Naringook.	
Black Hill, Scarsdale	Nawnight-widwid.	
Carngham	Kurnum	Home of the blackfellow.
Snake Valley, Carlisle	Nimlock.	
Bailie's Creek	Neporiak.	
Chepstowe	Gening-gering.	
Mount Emu	Tokarambeet *or* Dahcorambeet.	

LANGUAGE.

Name on Map.	Native Name.	Meaning in English.
Banjamie	Langi-willi	Banjamie also a native word, the name of the little creek falling into Mount Emu Creek near the homestead of Langi-willi.
Skipton	Woran.	
Borriyallock	Borriyallock	Salt water, the Emu Creek at this point being very brackish.
Anderson's Hill	Widderin	Warm place, place of heat.
Carumballac	Walargate.	
Mount Vite-vite	Molo-molo.	
Mount Bute	Coromollock.	
Happy Valley	Molong ghip.	
Pitfield	Mindai	The native name of a large snake said by the natives to frequent the large water-hole at junction of creek immediately north of the township.
Mount Misery, No. 2	Wadgap-p-waugra	This place is east of Smythesdale.
Mount Mercer	Gorong-golack.	
Rokewood	Conoreyalk.	
Gnarkeet	Noranket.	
Wardy Yalloak	Wardy Yallock	Standing water. *See History of Ballarat.* *Yallock*, water; *wurdi*, large; *pirron*, small. Wurdi Yallock falls into Lake Corangamite at north extremity; Pirron Yalloak at south end.
Mount Elephant	Gerinyelam.	
Lismore	Bongerimennin.	
Mount Clark	Larra	*Terinallum* is the name of Mount Elephant or Mount Clark, as I have always heard from the natives. *Larra* the name of the spring at Mr. Currie's homestead.
Toolirook	Lear.	
Little Corangamite	Gnarpurt.	
Foxhow	Miter.	
Cressy	Bitup.	
Glenlogie	Berrumgower.	
Shelford	Langi ligan.	
Green Hill	Borong woor-woor.	
Mount Hesse	Mookatook.	
Modewarre	Moodewarr	The musk-duck. *Cuonewarr*, black swan.
Mount Gellibrand	Walar-walar.	
Birregurra	Birrigurrah.	
Kerangemoorah	Werayan.	
Lake Colac	Coram.	
Lake Corangamite	Kronimite.	
Purrumbete	Purrumbete.	
Mount Porndon	Bondon.	
Mount Wiridgil	Yaratgill	
Mount Myrtoon	Metoon.	
Pirron Yalloak	Pirron Yallook	The little creek or water.
Corangi	Kutmik.	
Warrion Hills	Coirwrook	
Elephant Bridge	Cocorn.	
Creek at Colac	Babenorek.	

THE ABORIGINES OF VICTORIA:

Name on Map, &c.	Native Name.	Meaning in English.
Mount Pollock	Micornom.	
Lake Gnarpurt	Gnarpurt.	
Mount Cavern	Bangareet cort.	
Mount Pisgah	Morambulbullet.	
Hill south of Langi-willi	Chelorip.	
Hill north of Skipton	Monmot	The place of cold.
Stockyard Hill	Bapal.	
Lake Goldsmith	Yengerahwill.	
Lillerie	Liller.	
Langi-kal-kal	Langi-kal-kal	*Langi*, the resort or resting-place; *kal-kal*, the cicada.
Beaufort Forest	Eurambeen.	
Amphitheatre	Yapal.	
Waterloo Swamp	Tounear.	
Range at head of Waterloo	Bork-bork.	
Lexton	Mahmah.	
Wimmera	Culcatok.	
Langi-geran	Lang-muchan	*Langi*, as above; *Gheran*, the black cockatoo.
Yalla-y-poora	Yalla-y-poora.	
Bald Hills, near Yalla-y-poora	Coron.	
Ritchie's station	Allayuck.	
Small hill east of Ritchie's station	Weshort.	
Ormond Hill and Cave	Weturanbornok	Ormond's Hill, *Widderin*; cave at the Hill, *Weturanbornok*.
Highest range at Carngham	Bora.	
Black Hill, No. 2	Colonyokgallan	This is west of Burrumbeet.
Bald Hill, Burrumbeet	Gunapan.	
Horseshoe Lake	Gara.	
Junction of Bailie's and Emu Creek	Toriwoodcot.	
Leigh River	Waywateurtan.	
Moorabool	Moorabool	The curlew, according to Geelong natives.
Creek falling into Burrumbeet	Drawall.	
Piggoreet	Piggoreet.	
Lake or large swamp	Chakil, Toombal, Booloc	These are all names of particular swamps. It is almost impossible to obtain from an Aboriginal a *generic* name, such as for a *swamp*. If asked for name, he will give that of the particular swamp referred to.
Hut	Larb.	
Water	Katyil	Parish name north of Kewell.
Creek	Pah burrh.	
Peppermint-tree	Darrk	Species of eucalyptus.
Flooded gum-tree	Moolerrh.	
Old male kangaroo	Koorch.	
Sand	Koorac.	
Charcoal	Tchirree	Parish name north of Eversley.
Ground	Charrh *or* Tarrh.	
Opossum	Wehla.	
Curlew	Wail	Parish name west of Kewell West.
Very good	Boorndup	Parish name west of Kewell West.
Very good	Talgooc.	
Crestless white cockatoo	Kuracca	County west of Kewell West.
Cockatoo	Kellalac.	
Sleeping lizard	Wallup	Name of country at Kewell.

LANGUAGE. 195

Name on Map, &c.	Native Name.	Meaning in English.
Broad-leaved Mallee	Borung.	
Narrow-leaved Mallee, water-yielding	Weah.	
Emu	Barrimal.	
Mount Franklin	Langi barrimal	The resting-place or resort of the emu.
Home or dwelling-place	Langi.	
Bone	Kalke.	
Stringybark	Warngar	Name of parish north of Moremore, Avoca district.
Ironbark	Yelirip.	
Gold	Kara-kara.	
Native oven	Kordkutchup.	
Black magpie or shrike	Moonyegel	Name of shrike.
Paddy melon	Kooyea or Gooye.	
Shell paroquet	Tchuterr.	
Flooded red-gum	Bealiba	Beal, red-gum; ba, flooded.
Murray River	Millie or Millewa.	
Towaninnie (station)	Towan'nganignie	Head cut off.
Swan Hill (town)	Martiragnir.	
Reedy Creek station	Pingarumpit.	
Bael-bael station	Bael-bael	Gum-trees.
Wycheproff station	Wyechipoorp	Poorp, head or hill.
Glenloth station	Buckerabanyule	Banyule, hill.
Long Lake	Towan.	
Lake Baker	Bombendil.	
Pentland Island	Gnetnembir	Near Swan Hill.
Panamilly	Panamilly	Little Murray River.
Lake Tyrill	Tyrill	Tyrill means sky.
Avoca River	Yangeba.	
Richardson River	Wirtilleba.	
Wimmera River	Barbarton.	
Hindmarsh Lake	Koor.	
Narowen	Narowen	Station on Lower Murray.
Youngera	Youngera	Station on Lower Murray.
Tyntynder	Tyntynder	Station on Lower Murray.
Bumbang	Bumbang	Station on Lower Murray.
Quambatook	Koornbatook	Station on Avoca.
Lake Koorong	Koorong	Station.
Beveridge Island	Tiper.	
End of gums below Swan Hill	Chitobiel.	
Gunbower	Gunbower	Ana branch.
Eureka	Gnoletkor	Station.
Swamp on Tyntynder	Babool.	
Lake Cope-cope	Gope-gope.*	
Murray River	Millewa.	
Goulburn River	Koriella.	
Broken River	Marangan	Deep pond or lagoon.
King	Boumea.	
Delatite	Delatite.	
Fifteen-mile	Tharanbegga.	
Back	Bungeet	A swamp.
Freshtown	Youanmite.	

* While in the neighbourhood recently, I met an Aboriginal native who informed me that the correct name of the lake was Gope-gope, the meaning of which he gave me as follows:—"You take one big bottle, and two, three little ones. You pour water out of little fellows into big fellow, then big fellow same as Gope-gope, cause he takes all the water away from little fellows." I thought this a very clear explanation, as this large lake undoubtedly drains the several smaller lakes in the neighbourhood.—F. FEARN.

THE ABORIGINES OF VICTORIA:

Name on Map, &c.	Native Name.	Meaning in English.
Wagandery	Wagandery.	
Boweya	Boweya	Corruption of Boughyards.
Mokoan Creek	Mokoan.	
Bungeet Creek	Bungeet	A swamp.
Faithfull's Creek	Balmattum.	
Moonie-moonie	Moonie-moonie	Spur of range at McKellar's.
Back	Branch of Moonie.	
Glen		Black swamp.
Brankeet	Brankeet	Swamp on Borodomanin.

Name on Map, &c.	Native Name.	Name on Map, &c.	Native Name.
Mount Terrible	Warrambat.	Small circular plain at racecourse	Odipna.
Paps	Maindample (Conical hill).	On the Murray above Echuca	Towrick.
Mount Battery	Beolite.		
Mount Barrenhit	Barrenhit.	Eight-mile Forest, six miles west of Echuca	Witherup.
Balmattum	Balmattum.		
River	Tonnla.	Goulburn River	Koriella.
Kangaroo	Keimeer.	Campaspe River	Yalooka (generic name).
Emu	Bigaumcha.		
Opossum	Pipca.	Tall tree	Pangorang.
Fish	Manica.	Another name for Murray	Tiregola (a particular bend in the river. Every marked feature in the river has a distinctive name).
Native companion	Cobuna.		
Wild turkey	Mincha.		
Wild pigeon	Taponga.		
Wild goose	Macorna.		
Lagoon	Patho.		
Fire	Pitha.		
Sandhill in Echuca	Maloga.	Black swan	Mia.
Dead-house Point, on Murray, near Echuca	Congabba or Torngabba.	River Murray	Millewa.
		Blue paroquet	Yarrowalla.
Three-mile Forest at Echuca	Momboana.	Name of a chief	Ballendalla. Coolynaga.

Name on Map, &c.	Native Name.	Name on Map, &c.	Native Name.
Mount Buller	Marrang.		Talangalook or Talangalute Creek.
Mount Timber-top	Warrambat.		
Mimamiluke	Mimi-mimi maluke.		Warrambat.
Devil's River	Callathera.	A swamp	Durok.
Beolite	Badlwite.	Plenty water	Carrap.
Maindample	Maindample.	Place of fish	Weesk.
Big Rushes Lagoon	Mungo.	Creek	Palamarra (name of particular hole or bend in the creek).
Water-hole at Bargard (Dueran, P.R.)	Dueran.		
Yams	Murrnong.		
Native bear	Carboor.	Name of a weed	Mullangear.
Native chiefs	Beolite.	Nettles	Mulak.
Son of Beolite	Barwite. Delatite.	The crossing-place	Nullam.
		The war-camp	Mamburn-burn.

LANGUAGE.

The following names are attached to creeks and other features without fixing their locality:—

Pygnrkoo.
Wallaroo.
Buruna.
Arenutha.
Ingarouka.
Wadeenea.
Beriaroo.
Ildornka.
Malangora.

Ilitanka.
Illimpna.
Warrabeal.*
Nannella.*
Tarragal.
Timmering.*
Kalemura.
Balladero.

* Name of parish in Echuca district.

Name on Map, &c.	Native Name.	Meaning in English.
Kangaroo run	Tarben	Plenty meat.
Butcher's Flat run	Kitara	Rushes or flags.
Castle Maddie	Kurt	High land.
Dartmoor	Pokar	Big place.
Portland	Laywhollot	The place of the long grass.
Scott's Water-holes and Drumborg	Wombiknik	The small lake.
Oak Bank	Wangot	Concealed hill.
Crawford River, Hotspur	Yallok	Deep holes. *Yalloak* general term for water.
Mount Clay	Benamball	Big hill.
Mount Mistake	Pyrtpartee	The fighting-place.
Mount Vandyke	Ban-bangill	Pretty place.
Mount Richmond	Benwerrin	The long hill.
Eumeralla	Wallonkillin	Long creek.
Mount Eccles	Poythim	The mount.
Mount Rouse	Coloro	A weed which grows only there.
Hicks' run, Condah	Poud	Small mound.
Messer's run	Popit	Bald hill.
Price's Sawmills	Potpotcallick	Thick rushes.
Darlot Creek	Killara	Always there, permanent.
Knebsworth	Waratta	Plains.
Muntham	Gallam	Tree wide apart.
Sandford	Watchropat	The place of bream.
Turnbull's run	Waak	Hummocks.
Tahara	Thar	The spring.
Second River	Bottran	Good fish.
Bridgewater	Panith	The bonik.
Narrawong	Yarnk	The long river.
Echuca	Echuca	Meeting of waters.
Murray River	Millewa	Big one water.
Campaspe	Yallkaw.	
Gotterra	Gottera	A water-hole.
Koyuga	Koyuga	A plain in the midst of a forest.
Bundarra	Bundarra	Head of a plain.
Cornelia Creek	Bourneea.	
Nanneella	Nanella.	
Rochester	Wattneel.	
Restdown Plain	Piavella	A large plain.
Timmering	Timmering	Derived from *Tymna*, the kangaroo.
Corop	Corop.	

Name on Map, &c.	Native Name.	Meaning in English.
Carag-carag	Carag-carag.	
Burnewang	Burnewang.	
Burramboot	Burramboot	A high hill.
Cooper's Lake	Pawbeenbolock	A shallow lake.
Girgarce	Gigarra.	
Kyabram	Kyabram.	
Mount Scobie	Porpanda	A large sandhill.
Merrigum	Merrigum	A small plain.
Gulgila	Gulgila	A large plain.
Wyuna	Wyuna	Clear water.
St. Germain	Yandarra.	
Kotupna	Kotupna	A kind of grass used by the natives to make nets.
Ardpatrick	Camboona.	
Goulburn River	Goyla, by Goulburn tribe ; Guugupnas, by Murray tribe.	These names refer to particular points on the river.
Mooroopna	Mooroopna	Deep water.
Shepparton	Kanny goopna.	
Parish of Ballark	Ballark	Told by natives that *Ballark* meant all about streams.
Lal-lal	Lal-lal	Dashing of waters.
Mount Wallace	Menngorn.	
Station Peak	Youang	Large hill; every peak had a name; one is called Villa Manata; this is the name recorded by Hovell and Hume when in this locality in 1825.
Yarra Yarra		Ever running.
Blackwood	Myrniong	Blackwood.
Ingliston station	Three hills (Nimbuk, Darriwell, Gorong)	*Darriwell*, the bustard.
A decoy for ducks	Duduck.	
A little bird with long tail	Deegd'gun.	
The moon	Naa'run.	
The mange in dogs	Toon'doon.	
Apple-tree	Bin'nue	Name given to parish near Aberfeldy.
Red gum-tree	Nro.	
Lightwood	Yowan.	
Box-tree	Dagon.	
Wattle or mimosa	Mort.	
Good grass	Toom bon	Name given to village at the Springs, Edwards' Reef, D. 158°.
Recamermeta	Recamermeta	Tea-tree.
Gnamingbinnet	Gnamingbinnet	Ant-hill.
Wy-yung	Wy-yung	Spoon-bill duck.
Krookayan	Krookayan	Beard.
Gooroom	Gooroom	Name of a hunting-ground.
Gow	Gow	A bird that calls out this note at night.
Doodwuk	Doodwuk	A round lump of earth in swamps.
Wonnenerbree	Wonnenerbree	Kangaroo-rat.
Geremoot	Geremoot	Name of a point on lakes.
Cowagil	Cowagil	A reed.

LANGUAGE.

Name on Map, &c.	Native Name.	Meaning in English.
Nurkin wallinga	Nurkin wallinga	Rocks or large stones.
Delbit	Delbit	Tree with a cleft.
Dead iguana	Dirdi-de-bodulook.	
Clumps of wattle	Doom morl.	
Name	Bolodhun.	
Name of salt-water creek	Grang.	
	Anakie Youang	Twin hills; they are, however, Irish twins, the number being three.
	Wurdi Youang	Station Peak, the big hill; *Wurdi Yalloak*, the big river.

English.	Native.	English.	Native.
Bulrush	Dolodrook.	Name of swamp, Mount Talbot station	Bow.
Blindness	Baragwonduc.		
A small bird	Nang'gnannet.	Red-ochre paint	Belar.
Pelican	Guanemburn.	Grey hair, old	Bulart.
Blackwood or lightwood	Toolayowan.	Plover	Brit-brit.
Sore lips	Lancart.	Kangaroo-rat	Byjuke.
Name	Coongerdick.	Heath	Babrook.
Little plain	Berper gulty.	Scrub	Babrooten.
Black gin	Wermberooket.	Junction of Salt Creek and Glenelg	Burumbuart.
Sore eyes	Naaragin.		
Sponge	Ballegon.	Meeting of bunt and Parliament	Byerr.
Name	Dooyaman.		
Beard	Anoya (name given to parish west of Myamya).	Smoke	Booring.
		Water	Caitian.
		Hill	Caroopook.
		Mountains	Carong carack.
Black and white geese	Ar-va-wan.	Native name for Mount Arapiles	Cowan or Cowah.
The ear	Brimboal.		
Grass herbs	Booite.	Kangaroo	Corra.
Gum-tree	Becal.	Emu	Cowen.
Oak-tree, Swamp-oak	Bruk-bruk.	Native turkey (bustard)	Cobe vidion (Darriwill, Geelong natives).
Glenelg River	Baaker.		
Woman	Byambynoe.		
Road or path	Baaring.	Native water-hen (bald coot)	Crew.
Name of (late) chief	Bramburra.	Adult	Curran geerip.
Stone tomahawk	Dynduck.	To drink	Coopan.
Waddy	Brepa.	Bones	Callcoop.
Spring of water	Brim-brim.	Mouth	Corre.
Bank, ridge, hillock	Bunn.	Light	Calite.
Soft, boggy	Bacci.	Snake	Carran mell.
Roast, to cook	Dowan.	One	Caite.
Two	Boolite.	Three	Caite pu boolite.
Four	Boolite pu boolite.	Sand	Coonck.
		Anger	Coolanchurrep.
Sweet honey	Becor.	The nose	Caa.
Native cat	Beerik.	Lake Wallace	Connadoyen.
Victoria Range	Doreang.	Native companion	Coite urn.
Moyston township	Bapora (old crossing-place).	One tree	Cacep.
		Swan	Coonawarr.
Hail	Braite.	Paddy melon	Coryca.

THE ABORIGINES OF VICTORIA:

English.	Native.
Head of Tea-tree Creek (Longlands)	Conneewirreco.
Forehead	Connee.
Tea-tree	Wirrecow.
Name of large salt lake	Caper kelly.
Name of a lagoon, Pine Hills	Coleepoo.
The magpie	Carrak.
Part of Salt Creek, near Harrow	Corrondeeble.
Name of lagoon, Mullagh station	Culla-culla.
Name of lagoon, Mullagh station	Colingeelup.
Name of lagoon, Pine Hills	Connepra.
Good water	Delk.
Reeds, bulrushes, flags	Drajurk.
Fight a battle	Dank teeranite.
The arm	Dy jark.
Bark of trees	Docker.
To kill	Dakingle.
High, lofty	Dewrang.
Limestones, lime	Drik-drik.
Earth, soil	Dyea.
Forest, plenty, many	Geayoul.
Red	Gurra.
Blood	Gurracoop.
A chief or king	Gorra.
The present chief of his tribe	Gorran Doranan.
Boomerang	Gatum-gatum.
Mosquito	Gritjurk.
Maryvale old home-station lake	Gatall.
Native hut, Mia-mia	Ill-i-ra.
Fear, frightened	Ingturrapamba.
The White Lake of Major Mitchell	Jerrywarrook.
Name of a lagoon, Pine Hills	Jell-jell.
Swamp near the Mallee scrub	Jerrigwarra.
Flat; name of S. G. Henty's station near Harrow	Kadnook.
Lying down, rest	Kombaiy.
Summer heat	Kiata.
Salt	Keepa.
A native weapon	Leanguel.
Name of a lagoon, Pine Hills	Lalanguite.
A stone, rock	Lak.
Teeth	Leea.
To cry, weep	Loomalangan.
A kind of tea-tree	Maen.
Clouds	Moorang.
The skin	Mutak.

English.	Native.
The hands	Manya.
The eye	Merr.
To hear	Maarmun.
Thunder (name of one of the Armytages' stations, South Adelaide road)	Murrandana.
Thicket	Mallee.
Winter, cold in the abstract	Mood.
To feel cold	Monmott (name of bare hill west of Skipton).
The root of a tree	Moray.
Name of a tea-tree lake (Mullagh)	Mallee parbool.
Another lake (Pine Hills)	Mallanganee.
A reedy swamp (Pine Hills)	Mallanbool.
Pleasant Banks (Affleck's station)	Mortart.
Swamp on Lake Wallace station	Manyonda.
A dry lake on Mullagh station	Moonjam.
Old sheepwash on Salt Creek, seven miles from Harrow	Merrymeric.
The face or countenance	Morrpaga.
The forehead	Murroon.
A house	Moonya.
Pine-tree	Marroo.
St. Mary's Lake, Mount Arapiles	Moodya.
Townsend's old station, Tea-tree Creek (Longlands)	Munda.
An egg	Merrick.
Hair	Na a prup.
To see, look	Na yan can.
A lake on Mullah station, twelve miles from Harrow	Palpara.
A lake on Pine Hills	Pobrick.
The head	Prop.
Cherry-tree	Pallite.
A fly	Pa-pidjeek.
A child, infant	Popope.
Salt or brackish water	Punandeegin.
Run, flight	Pirrepango.
Eaglehawk	Rapel.
Lake	Tchakel.
Lakes	Tchakel-tchakel.
Stars	Tort.
Hawk	Tord wirrup.
Foot, foot-mark	Tchina.
To eat	Ticoyan.

LANGUAGE.

English.	Native.
Stringybark forest	Toolang.
Spear	Tare.
Wattle-tree gum	Tooloy.
White color	Tar ar nite.
The Cape Barren geese	Toolka.
Swamp at C. Officer's home-station	Toolondo.
The tongue	Tchila.
Strong or strong man	Tit-tit.
The sun	Urangara.
Snow	Urancooya.
Fire	Wee.
Rain	Wallie.
A plain level country	Woorak or Woorack.
Honeysuckle-tree	Warock.
Native dog	Willkin.
Hurricane, high wind	Wayang.
A box-tree ten years old	Win-win-tie.
Lightning	Willintick.
Burnt black log	Walling.
Dead tree	Wallpar.
Green color, growing tree	Warwanbool.
Dead body	Weckeer.
The crow	Waa.
Magpie	Parwan or Barwon.
A hollow tree	Winani.
Black color	Warrock.
Opossum	Willa.
Black water-holes, twelve miles from Harrow, Adelaide road	Wanwin.
Come, come here	Wateegat.
Bandicoot	Wydung.
The blackwood-tree	Weetya.
The curlew (little bustard)	Wail.
Love, pretty, lovely, beautiful	Womhelano.
The old Grange home-station in 1840	Yulecart.
The site of Hamilton township	Mulleraterong.
Wannon at junction of Grange Burn	Uebowening.
Mount Napier	Tapook.
Grange Burn	Bucaan (running stream).
Plains	Woorack.
Honeysuckle plains	Warackoorack.
The she-oak tree	Bruk-bruk.
Stringybark	Toolang.
Pine-trees	Marroo.
Sandy plains	Coonkwoorack.
Glenisla swamp, near Carter's home-station	Woohlpooa.
Solitary hill, about four miles north-west of Carter's station	Bepcha.
Swamp east of Glenisla home station	Lootchook.
Lizards, common kind	Dopeworra.
Large tree	Cuiyin chooyoo.

Names of some swamps within three miles of Clear Lake:—

English Name.	Native Name.	Meaning in English.
Jalur	Jallar.	
By		pronounced "Bow."
Lurmut	Lurmut.	
Carghap	Carchap.	
Wewlea	Weolea.	
Tirpigoproc	Poorpigoproc.	

Black-fish	Weerap.	
Fall on creek at Rosebrook	Konong	A hill or impediment of any kind.
A water-hole at Rosebrook home-station	Bajam-bajam.	
A kangaroo camp	Burrai gurray.	
A landing place	Kram bruk.	
A water-hole in the Glenelg, at the crossing of the Horsham road by Cavendish	Jarapoobl.	
Ganangenyawie	Ja-nang-en yawi-wee	The entrance north end of Victoria Range
A creek from the mountains east of Glenisla	Kouangedura.	
Swamp east of Lambruck	Cartuccle.	

English Name.	Native Name.	Meaning in English.
Swamp in Woohlpooer	Ming-ming.	
Chuckilcallipurt	Chuck-il-calle purt	A swamp at Brin Springs homestead.
Wonwondah witchoop	Wonwon-dah witchoop	Another swamp adjoining the last.
Yarragallum	Yarrogallum	A swamp at Rosebrook sheepwash.
Micatcatchin	Mit-cat-cat-chin	A spring at the base of the Black Range, east side.

English Name.	Native Name.	Meaning in English.
Water	Catchin.	
Rain	Wallah.	
A little rain (a shower)	Wurtspook wallah.	
An opossum	Wallay.	
The musk duck	Chokuil.	
A she-oak tree	Golurt.	
A kangaroo	Koray.	
The black duck	Mooree.	
Gum	Pecall.	
An emu	Jobir.	
Rock wallaby	Billewirrup.	
Honeysuckle-tree	Woorak.	
A native cat	Beerak.	
Eaglehawk	Rappell.	
Scrub	Bnor.	
A native companion	Norknok.	
Magpie	Goroke.	
Young wattle-tree	Boboh.	
A wild turkey	Kolabatyin (*Darriwil* by Geelong natives).	
Kangaroo-rat	Tallakin.	
Wattle gum	Don gan gee.	
A large crane	Dakakamundah.	
A bandicoot	Bo *or* Bobe.	
Clear Lake	Wurcekgera.	
Mount Napier	Tapook.	
Victoria Range	Boreany *or* Bullawin.	
St. Mary's Lake, Mount Arapiles	Moodya.	
Mount Sturgeon	Murranaswn.	
Mount Talbot	Tolando.	
Black Range	Burrong.	
Grange Creek	Buccan.	
Hamilton township	Mutleraterang.	
Mount Rouse	Kalor.	
Junction of Wannon and Grange Creek	Ulebowening.	
Schofield's Creek	Goren.	
Harrow township	Karook.	
Black swamp	Wamlook.	
Balmoral township	Daarangurt.	
Murray River	Tangula	Some particular point of river.
Tongala	Tarnumra.	
Moira	Moira	Reedy swamp.
Echuca	Echuca	Junction of rivers.
Campaspe	Yelka.	
Wyuna	Wyuna	Clear water.

LANGUAGE.

English Name.	Native Name.	Meaning in English.
Koyuga	Koyuga.	
Gottrea	Gottrea	Water-hole.
Kotupna	Kotupna	A grass used for nets.
E. Vineyard	Chamberna	A creek.
Taripta	Taripta	Small box-trees.
Embra	Embra.	
Sandhill	Mologa	Large sandhill.
Mount Scobie	Porpanda	High mountains.
Cooper's Lake	Tangalum.	
Gilgila	Gilgila.	
Kiabram	Kiambram	Thick forest.
Lock Garry	Bimberta	Lots of fish.
St. Germains	Undera.	
Nine-mile	Tatchera	Large plain.
Merrigum	Merrigum	Little plain.
Tallygaroopna	Tallygaroopna	Large tree.
Goulburn River	Gila.	
Ardpatrick	Coomboona.	
Mooroopna	Mooroopna	Deep hole.
Shepparton	Kongoopna.	
Toolamba	Patura	Small lagoons.
Me'ran	Windella	No water.
Meering	Windella.	
Pyramid Creek	Yaramie.	
Murray River	Millewa.	
Dry Lake	Barrto.	
Sandhill Lake	Luchur Lake.	
Nine-mile Creek	Yarramie	Little creek.
Gumiawarren Sandhills	Moicuyurrt.	
Tragowel Swamp	Pouey-pouey.	
Five-mile Creek	Tintinbarren.	
Two-mile Creek	Tiengule.	
Reedy Creek	Booraire.	
Reedy Lake	Bingarumbirrt.	
Marung Lake	Marung.	
Lake Leaghur	Leaghurr.	
Murdering Lake	Lcharin.	
Kangaroo Lake	Kurmburr.	
Boga Lake	Coorm.	
The North Terrick hill, which is the largest of the two	Bullyang or Bulliyang	A cherry-tree.
South Terrick	Wangat	A kind of wooden spade for digging up grubs.
Diamond Hill, a part of Terrick Range two miles north of Main Terrick	Gydwill or Gigwill (doubtful which).	
Mount Pyramid	Byrmbowil.	
Paddy's Clump, a small clump on Pyramid Plain, an old out-station	Myrtgun	A single egg of any kind.
Cooper's old home-station, near Paddy's Clump.	Djulun	Salt-bush.
Bullock Creek, lower course station	Bullop Byoway	No meaning except for the locality.
Bullock Creek, at old Sheepwash	Goom Goorudwon-yeran	Means water escaping under ground.
The Pickaninny Creek, about three miles north of boundary	Narronynarnaby	Plant with edible root.

Name on Map.	Native Name.	Meaning in English.
The swamp commonly called Kow	Ghow.	
Pickaninny Creek, at a dam three miles north of house	Yayat	A small frog which climbs trees.
A swamp two miles S.S.E. of creek, through which a branch of the Pickaninny coming out on Kelly's run joins again at Pickaninny Creek	Waagworil.	

The following is a list of the names of places and words obtained by Philip Chauncy, J.P., District Surveyor, during the years 1862 and 1866, from Aborigines belonging to the tribes inhabiting the districts watered by the Rivers Loddon, Avoca, Richardson, Wimmera, and the Upper Hopkins; to which is added the Swan River (Western Australia) word when there is an analogy in the sound. The list, as regards the names of creeks, rivers, and mountains within the Dunolly survey district, is respectfully submitted to the Honorable the Minister of Lands and Agriculture, in compliance with his request. The names of many places in the north-western part of the colony are added. The corresponding Swan River words are noted for the purpose of suggesting the common origin of the languages. The sound of the letters accords with that recommended by the Royal Geographical Society; thus u is to be pronounced like *oo*. A supplementary list is attached, which should be used in connection with the first list. In the first column the letter S. denotes that the word was obtained from natives at Swanwater near St. Arnaud, D. from natives at Dunolly, L. at the Lower Loddon, A. at Ararat, W. at the Wimmera, C. at Camperdown, and S.R. at Swan River.

The words marked thus (*) were not obtained directly by me, but by Mr. Spieseke and two or three other reliable persons.—P. CHAUNCY.

Native Word.	Colonial Name or Description of Locality.	Signification.
Berring-a (D.)	A village south from Smythes- dale.	The rainbow-bird or bee-eater, *Merops*, with two long feathers extending from the tail.
Berrin-berrin (S.R.)		
Bukrabanyul (S.)	A certain hill, also a squatting station, near East Charlton station	*Bukra*, the middle, and *banyul* or *panial*, a hill—*i.e.*, the middle of three, as viewed from Swanwater.
Burrumbuchee (S.)	-	The white crane.
Boorpuk	-	A little hill or rising ground.
Boytch *or* Bo-ytch (S.)	-	Grass.
Bŏlap (S.)	-	A "native oven," an ash mound, camping-place.
Bo-nn (S.)	-	Ashes.
Bomgurt (S.)	-	*Bom*, a tuberous edible root, probably a kind of orchis.
Berrimal (D.)	A parish in the Dunolly district.	The emu.
Parimal (C.)		
Boorp *or* Purp (S. & A.)	-	The head.
Bulee manya (A.)	-	Fingers to count with.

LANGUAGE.

Native Word.	Colonial Name or Description of Locality.	Signification.
Bula (S.R.)	-	Many fingers, i.e., more than three, many.
Bulytch (A.)	-	Four or more fingers, many.
Bulytchee (Adelaide)	-	Four or more fingers, many.
Bullarook †	A township and forest north-east from Ballarat.	
Bomenya (A)	-	The thumb.
Burt (L.)	A station on the west side of the Lower Loddon	Smoke.
Buln-buln	A county of Victoria	The lyre-bird.
Brapbrim	Mount Jeffcott.	
Bolac or Boloke ‡ (A. & L.)	-	A lake.
Banyenong § (W.)	A parish at Lake Boloke	*Banye*, a burning, but only applicable to roots and stumps; *nong* denotes the past.
*Banyobudnut (W.)	The Mission Station on the Lower Wimmera	*Banyo*, the back.
*Bellenbirra or Bellellen (W.)	A parish	A certain kind of smooth grass.
*Boneekauwer (W.)	Bonneeyawer, a part of Edols' run on the Lower Wimmera.	The dust raised by a running emu.
Burrumbeet	A lake, 12 miles from Ballarat	*Burrum*, muddy, dirty; ‖ *beet* is a word for water.
*Burrum-burrum (W.)	A parish	Very muddy.‖
*Brim (W.)	A station on the Yarambiak Creek.	A spring or well with water.
*Back (S.)	-	Muddy water-holes.
*Billinn (S.)	-	The bull-frog.
Bick (S.)	-	Pipeclay.
Kow (in the north-west of Victoria).		
*Boor-boor-up	-	A spring, or where water may be found by digging.
*Bolang-um (S.)	A parish and station	Two cousins.
*Bardi-dart (S.)	-	Seeing a dog jump up and bite a falling star.
*Balpa or Bilpa (S.)	Banyena station, Shannahan's station	A natives' old camp.
*Bindowrim	Great Western township.	
*Bútchúk	Mount Drummond.	
*Bomjinna	Mount William	*Jenna*, a foot.
*Búrn	The Black Range.	
*Burnacre	Allanvale station.	
*Butingitch	Town site of Ararat.	
*Bvarree	Deep Lead, Pleasant Creek.	
*Dang-dang	-	Bad shells used for marking an opossum rug, and which spoil it.

† Bullarok, at Swan River, is the name of one of the four great divisions or families of the Aborigines of that part of Australia. They may not intermarry, but must seek a partner from some other division.

‡ Lake Bolac is situated 60 miles W.S.W. from Ballarat, and receives the waters of Fiery Creek. "Lake Boloke" is the name given on the maps to the basin which receives the waters of the Richardson River. The natives' name of this basin is "Banyenong."

§ When full, this lake covers an area of 25 square miles, all of which is grown over with reeds and bulrushes. In very dry seasons the water disappears, and then the natives used to set fire to the reeds and bulrushes, the stumps of which, after the burning, presented an extraordinary appearance—hence the name.

‖ These meanings are doubtful. A Camperdown native told me that *burrum* means "round" or "roundabout," which is the more probable signification.

Native Word.	Colonial Name or Description of Locality.	Signification.
*Daubinger Berakŭp	- - - - - -	Two natives who fought in the moon and broke it.
*Derril (S.)	- - - - - - -	The boundary or limit of a native's territory.
Darrkbonee (S.)	- - A parish near St. Arnaud -	Darrk is the peppermint gum-tree.
*Drung-drung or Jung-jung (S.)	A parish and lake; a parish -	Spoiling, making a mess of it.
*Dooen (S.)	- - A parish - - - -	The limits of a circular piece of country.
Enta (S). -	- - - - - - - -	No.
Gré-gré (S.)	- - A parish north-west of St. Arnaud	The lagoon called Swanwater.
Gowar (S.)	- - A hill on Yowan Spring station	A high hill.
Genna (see Jenna)	- - - - - - -	The foot.
*Gerrigurup	- - - - - - -	A stony place.
*Gorambeep bārak	- - Mount Ararat.	
*Gurkederkŭt -	- - Opossum Gully, Ararat.	
Jenna (A.)	- - - - - - -	The foot.
Jenna (S.R.)	- - - - - - -	The foot.
Jinna (Queensland)	- - - - - -	The foot.
Jeenong (Condamine River)	- - - - -	The foot.
Jenang (Goulburn River)	- - - - -	The foot.
Jeenong † (Darling River)	- - - - -	The foot.
*Jak-wurro-wil -	- - - - - -	Reeds in a creek.
*Jurn-gher-toul -	- - - - - -	A large bat like a man (a fabulous creature).
*Jalúka	- - - - A parish - - -	The valley between the Grampians, Serra, and Victorian Ranges.
*Jaraugbi-jakil -	- - The township of Moyston.	
*Jakyl	- - - - Lake Lonsdale.	
*Janŭkin -	- - - Glenorchy.	
*Kobram -	- - - Stawell town site.	
*Konkongella -	- - Concongella station.	
Koorac (D.) -	- - A parish on Avoca River -	Sand.
Kooreh (S. & D.) -	- - A parish in the Dunolly district	A large male kangaroo.
Koolee (S.)	- - - - - - -	An Aboriginal man.
Karrap (D.) -	- - A parish between Lexton and Amphitheatre	Quartz.
Karr (A.)	- - - - - - -	The nose.
*Kuyura -	- - A parish and hill near Kingower	The mountain of light.
Kinyapanial (L.)	- - A parish, a station, and a creek	Kinya, the head; banyul, of the hill.
Katyil (S.)	- - - - - - -	Water.
Kal-kal (plural) (W.)	- - A parish and station - -	Large edible grub in decayed wattle-trees; the larvæ of a species of cerambyx.
*Karangajarŭk -	- - - - - -	The valley near Ararat called Cathcart.
*Kru-kruk (Geelong)	- - - - - -	The bull-frog.
Lang-i kal-kal (A.) -	- - - - - -	The locality in which the edible larvæ of a large kind of cerambyx are found.

† The same at Fitzroy Downs, Darling Downs, and Wide Bay; Dinnong at Macquarie River; at Omeo it is Jeenongyana; at King George's Sound, Jeena, &c., &c.

LANGUAGE.

Native Word.	Colonial Name or Description of Locality.	Signification.
Lang-i gherin (A.)	The mountain on the Great Dividing Range called Mount Mistake by Mr. La Trobe, situated 7 miles east by south from Ararat. It is incorrectly spelled Laruegerin on the new map of Victoria	*Langi*, the home; *gherin*, the yellow-tailed black cockatoo (*calyptorhyncus*); i.e., the home or habitat of the black cockatoo, also its nest.
Lang-i Logan (A.)	-	The home or run of Mr. Logan.
Leer or Lea (D.)	-	The teeth.
Larr (S.)	-	A hut.
Leaghur (L.)	A station on the Lower Loddon	*Lea*, the teeth; *gorh*, the blossom of the box-tree, which is sucked by the natives for its honey.
Laal bit (S.)	Lalbert on the maps is the basin which receives one branch of the Avoca River	*Laal*, the parasite which grows on the Mallee, *bit* is the knot at the end of it.
Lal-lal, *also* Lal-lat (A.)	Two parishes	*Lal* is supposed to signify a crack or crevice.
*Ledcourt (W.)	A parish, also station	*Led* means sharp.
Longérrinong (W.)	Longerinong is a station on the Wimmera	A creek branching off the Wimmera, bifurcates at this place or splits.
Long-ernong-narri (W.)	-	A she-oak split by lightning.
Lang-i-dorn	Doctor's Creek	The nest of the bell-bird.
Lagallik	Barton's station near Moyston.	
Moliagulk (D.)	Moliagul, a town and parish nine miles north-north-west from Dunolly	A wooded hill.
Morak (D.)	-	The cheek.
Mouytye (D.)	-	The moustache.
Munya (D.)	-	The hand.
Marrong (A.)	-	The middle finger.
Maara (S. R.)	-	The hand.
Maarh (King George's Sound)	-	The hand.
Moolerr (S.)	A parish near St. Arnaud	The flooded or red gum.
Mehrin (L.)	Spelt Merin, also Meerin, on the maps; a station on Lower Loddon	The lake, an outlet of the Loddon River.
Marong (L.)	Town and parish ten miles west from Sandhurst	The Murray River pine (callitris).
Murdook (L.)	-	Small.
Morre-morre (S.)	A parish north from Malakoff, county of Kara-kara	Little hills.
*Mullak or Mullah	A place west from the White Lake, and north from the Glenelg River	A kind of shrub growing on Mount Talbot, in the Glenelg district, the roots of which are edible.
*Metinjonye	-	A Mallee rise near Mount William.
*Martang	The Black Swamp.	
*Mitye	Barton Morass or Nekeeya Swamp.	
*Mulpal	Lexington station.	
*Merpatyal	Fyan's Creek.	
Ngarree (S.) (*see* Long-ernong-narri)	-	A she-oak tree.

Native Word.	Colonial Name or Description of Locality.	Signification.
Nganyc (D.)	-	The beard.
Nganya (S. R.)	-	The beard.
Ngarra (D.)	-	The hair.
Narrepurt (S.)	A lake near Merin, on the Lower Loddon; also a station in the north-east of the county of Borung.	
Na-lnan	A parish; Nallan Nullan, another parish in the county of Borung.	A spring in the Mallee.
*Nallijup	-	I find a water-hole.
*Nimmel-mer	A water-hole near Bolangum	A native with bad eyes (*mel*) washed them and died here.
*Naram-naram	The Grampian Range.	
Panyul or Banule (D.)	-	A hill.
Pitye (S.)	-	A fly.
Tchallee	-	The tongue.
To-roee or To-roi (D.)	-	A woman.
Tu rung irriple (D.)	-	Certain she-oak water-holes.
Tyo worrk (D.)	Old Dunolly station	Manna on a gum-tree.
Tartyak (A.)	-	The arm.
Toombal (L.)	-	A lake.
Tardt (S.)	-	Crab-holes.
Tittibong (S.)	Station on Lower Avoca	*Tittit*, hard; hard ground.
Towaninnie (S.)	A certain little creek on the Lower Avoca; also a station	A blow on the back of the neck, where the soul or spirit is.
Tyin-wull (W.)	Kewell, a station and parish north of the Wimmera	The seed or fruit of the mesembryanthemum.
Woorak (D.)	-	A species of Banksia tree common near Dunolly.
Woore (D.)	-	The lips.
Whroo (Lower Goulburn)	A town and parish	The lips.
Witchi poorp (D.)	A station on the Lower Avoca (incorrectly spelled Witcheproof and Witchepraaf, and Witchipool); also the name of the hill fifteen miles north-north-west from East Charlton	*Witchi*, rushes, and *poorp*, the head or top of the hill—*i.e.*, the plant called *witche* grows on the top of this hill.
Weinbool (D.)	-	The ear.
Woongarup (A.)	-	The forefinger.
Wirting (A.)	-	The collar-bone.
Warrin (A.)	-	The back.
Wehla (S.)	A parish between Dunolly and St. Arnaud, the town called Jericho	The common grey opossum.
Wail (S.), Wailo (S. R)	-	The bird called a curlew by the colonists.
Wabbee (L.)	-	The small fresh-water lobster.
Wabbee (S. R.)	-	A kind of small fresh-water fish.
Wanwanda (W.)	A place near Horsham	A kind of shrub.
Wurranjibeel (W.)	Warraknabeal station, on the Yarrambeak Creek	*Wurra*, lip; *ngi*, its; *beal*, flooded gum-tree—*i.e.*, lip of a flooded gum-tree.
Wurra nyuk (W.)	Warranook parish	*Wurra*, lip; *nyuk*, its—*i.e.*, its lip.
Wurra-wurra (W.)	Warra-warra parish	Lips.

LANGUAGE.

Native Word.	Colonial Name or Description of Locality.	Signification.
Werrikgbor (W.)	Werrigar, a village near Warraknabeal	*Werrik*, cleaning; *ghor*, the blossom of the box-tree—*i.e.*, cleaning the ground from the fallen blossoms before encamping.
Witchelliba (W.)	A parish	*Witchelli*, a dry stick; *bah*, a creek. The Avoca River.
Wyn-wyn (W.)	A place north from Mount Arapiles	A little stick or thin switch used for feeling for an opossum in a hollow gum-tree.
Wammera	-	Probably a New South Wales word for the throwing-board.
*Warrogarbin	Near Bolang-um	A place where a native came with lips so swollen that he could not drink.
*Warrowitur	-	A camping-ground.
*Wein-wein-gurk	-	Wild, wild wind. *Wein* signifies fire in the Western district of Victoria.
Yoorndup (S.)	-	The wrist.
Youanduc (S.)	A granite rise near West Charlton	A basin in a rock.
Yuerngrun (S.)	A run near East Charlton	*Grun* or *gurn* is a certain kind of low bush.
Yarram-yuk (W.)	Yarrambeack Creek, an effluent from the Wimmera River	*Yarram*, a dry hole or blind creek; *yuk*, their, pronoun third person plural.
Yalla-y-poora	Ware's station on Fiery Creek	A pollard-tree or a gum-tree which has been cut and has sprouted.
Yawong (W.)	Springs on the east of the Avoca River between Wedderburn and St. Arnaud.	
*Warwino	Pleasant Creek.	
*Wurro-garra	Glenwillan station.	
*Wurro-nook	A place in Irrewarra parish.	
*Wurra-will	Schoular's water-hole.	
*Williwit	Newington station.	
*Wal-wal	Little Wimmera River	Reeds, full of reeds.

Additional names and words of the natives of the Lower Loddon, Avoca, and Richardson Rivers, and Pine Plains.

NOTE.—In this second list some words occurring in the first have been repeated, having been obtained from independent and different sources.—PHILIP CHAUNCY.

Native Word.	Colonial Name or Description of Locality.	Signification.
Amical	-	A white man.
Banule *or* Panyal	-	A hill.
Barp	A parish near Dunolly	The white or hill gum-tree.
Bayup	The village at Barrie's Reef, near Blackwood	A kind of gum-tree.
Beal-ba (*or* pah)	Bealiba is the name of a town and parish	*Beal*, the red or flooded gum-tree; *ba*, a creek; *i.e.*, the red gum-tree creek.
Boloke	Lake Bauyenong	A lake, *i.e.*, any lake of this kind.
Bulert	-	Grey beard.

VOL. II.   2 D

210 THE ABORIGINES OF VICTORIA:

Native Word.	Colonial Name or Description of Locality.	Signification.
Bunyeelgal	Seven-mile hut on Antwerp station.	
Boorndeep		Very good.
Bolertch	A parish on the west side of Avoca River	The box-tree (eucalyptus).
Birr-imal	A parish	An emu.
Chulwil		A musk duck.
Coolce		A native man.
Darrk		The peppermint gum-tree.
Djarree	Plains of Thalia station.	
Dyarr (Budjar at Swan River)		The ground.
Eng-eng malyan or Enta; (Yuorta on the Lower Goulburn; Yuarda at Swan River)		No.
Jenna (Jenna at Swan River, Jennang at the Goulburn River, &c.)		The foot.
Gillay or Jilleh		Perhaps.
Gnarree		The black duck, also the she-oak tree.
Gnerre	Mount Egbert Range, near Wedderburn.	
Gooro or Ghur	Lake Hindmarsh.	
Ghynup		The large yellow-crested white cockatoo.
Kara-kara	A county	Gold.
Karrap	A parish between Lexton and Amphitheatre.	
Kalkebanya	Lake Tyrrell	Foliated hydrous sulphate of lime, which is abundant in Lake Tyrrell.
Kallallac		Mitchell's cockatoo.
Katcheen garragalk	Antwerp station, near Lake Hindmarsh	Water and wood.
Koodeheal	Bealiba station	Underneath a red gum-tree.
Koolce		A native man.
Koonawarrh		The black swan.
Kooreh (Koroit)	A parish	A male kangaroo.
Kooyea		A kind of small kangaroo.
Kow		Pipeclay found on some plains 35 miles west-north-west from Pine Plains.
Kumma		A wallaby (at Lake Tyrrell).
Kurraca		Small white cockatoo, without crest, commonly called a corrella.
Mal		No.
Marong	A parish	The Murray River pine-tree (callitris).
Marmangorak		God (at Lake Tyrrell). It is doubtful whether any Australian Aborigine has any idea of a Supreme Being.
Marrambook		A wife.
Matynleework	Bealiba diggings.	
*Meyrr heu		Wind.
Murdook		Small.
Moolerr	A parish	A kind of gum-tree.
Ngannibeen-yam		Myself.
Nannee-chuk		A husband.
Ngatyar		The chief evil spirit.

LANGUAGE.

Native Word.	Colonial Name or Description of Locality.	Signification.
Ngaanga	-	The soul. *Nganga*, at Swan River, signifies the sun, also a man's beard, also the roots of trees and plants. *Nganga batta*, sunbeams.
Ngarranan, at Richardson River; or Nullaan yeerna, or Kannung enna, or Ngin jarriga, at Boort station	-	Do you understand?
Ngarropon	The lake at the back of Miller's Inn, at Cope-cope.	
Ngarre	-	The black duck; also she-oak.
Nganyak (Ngannup at Swan River)	-	To sit down.
Ngyne	-	To see.
*Ngadg (Ngadgo at Swan River)	-	Me (personal pronoun).
*Nyarritch	Eddington township.	
Ngarrewarrawil	Burnt Creek.	
Ngan-wee (Nganga at Swan River)	-	The beard.
*Pinmi	-	An evil spirit in the ground causing a whirlwind or swirl of wind.
Pittigul	-	The quandong fruit at Lake Tyrrell.
Lea kuribur	Dunolly.	
Tallja	A water-hole north-north-east from Pine Plains.	
Tchuterr	A parish	The small shell paroquet.
Toombal	-	A lake.
*Toor hi or To ro ee	-	A woman.
Turrung irripil	She-oak water-holes.	
Tyowork	Dunolly pre-emptive section	Manna which occurs on some kinds of eucalypti.
Wallup	-	The sleeping lizard.
Warrk	-	You.
Wattee or Warre wee	-	Come here, or come along. *Watto*, at Swan River, means "go," or "walk away."
Wanyebra	Ten-mile hut on Antwerp station.	
Warngarr	-	Stringybark-tree.
Warranyukbeal	Warranackbeal, Scott's station on the Yarramheac Creek	Large flooded gum-tree.
Warre jo	-	Far away.
Weerbak, or Toolgook, or *Boorndup	In three languages	Very good.
Wehla	A parish (Jericho) near Kingower	The large grey opossum.
Winjallok	Name given to parish north of Navarre	Where is it?
Woorrek (Oorar at Swan River)	-	Far away, very far.
Wonga	A small lake below Albacutya, at Bremer's station, on the outlet.	

Native Word.	Colonial Name or Description of Locality.	Signification.
Wookak	-	Give it to me.
Woonck	-	The common Banksia tree.
Wooro	Whroo is the name of a town near Rushworth	The lips. There is surface water only at Whroo, hence it is called "the dry diggings." The lips are put to the ground to drink.
Yannak	-	Go away.
Yea-a *or* Yea-yea	-	Yes.
Yellanjip	The salt lakes about 50 or 60 miles north-west from Pine Plains station.	
Yehrip	A parish on the west of the Avoca River	The ironbark tree.

Supplementary list of words obtained from Aborigines by P. Chauncy, at (C.) Camperdown, (A.) Ararat, (D.) Daylesford, (H.R.) Hopkins River.

Native Word.	Colonial Name or Description of Locality.	Signification.
Barng (H.R.)	The Hopkins River	No.
Barwong (H.R.)	The Barwon River.	
Boreitch (C.)	-	Water (?). Probably the same as *Pareitch*, salt water.
Berrimbool (H.R.)	A lake on the east of the Hopkins, six miles below Chatsworth.	
Bornong (H.R.)	The tea-tree swamp at Mortlake.	
Boonjarup (D.)	-	To bite, to slay.
Boongarup (D.)	-	To throw spears.
Buckup (D.)	-	A species of grass-tree.
Barrk (D.)	-	Tracks or to track.
Burrupa (D.)	-	To run away.
Barkna (D.)	-	To dig, scrape, bury.
Berrh (D.)	-	A river or creek.
Berrp (D.)	-	Daylight, the day.
Berpabup (D.)	-	To-morrow.
Bowitch (D.)	-	Grass, vegetation.
Boorgangoo (D.)	-	To blow with the mouth.
Barjangal (D.)	-	A pelican.
Boort (D.)	A lagoon, &c., on the west of the Loddon River	} Smoke.
Booya (at Swan River)	-	
Bayt (D.)	-	Quartz.
Barnbuyal (D.)		
Boyle *and* Boyl-ya (Western Australia)	-	A sorcerer, a power of witchcraft.
Boyne (D.)	-	Fat, handsome, grease.
Bopup (D.)	-	A baby boy.
Bihago (D.)	-	A woman.
Burrupa (D.)	} -	} Running water.
Katyeen		
Berripa (D.)	-	To run.

LANGUAGE. 213

Native Word.	Colonial Name or Description of Locality.	Signification.
Challecpepin (A.)	The hill with the steep escarpment on the south side of Mount Lang-i-gherin.	
Chalee (D)		The tongue.
T-Characar (D.)		To stand.
Dtarkjarrup (D.)		Fighting, contest.
Dtarka (D.)		To beat, to strike, to kill.
Danbil (D.)		A big cloud.
Eilyer (H.)	A small mount or rise near Austin's station on the Salt Creek between Lake Bolac and the Hopkins River.	
Gherănjemăraja (H.)	Synott's Creek at Berrybank.	
Goonang-a (D.)		Joking, jesting, telling untruths.
Garakeen (D)		A species of paroquet.
Gonowarah (D.)		A black swan.
Ghera (D.)		A gum leaf.
Jenang (C.)		The foot.
Jillup-jillup (D.)		To pinch, to squeeze.
Jence (D.)		The forehead.
Jarrb (D.) / Budjar (at Swan River)		The ground.
Karkart (D.)		A friend.
Karkoi (C.)		A pretty kind of bandicoot.
Kanarpanook (H.)		To cough, a cough.
Karamook (C.)		The common opossum.
Kallern (C.)		The brush kangaroo.
Karlk (C.)	The site of Camperdown.	
Kŏlong-ŭlak (C.)	Lake Colongulac	To cooee or call.
Kooloor (H.)	Mount Rouse.	
Kowang (C.)		A native cat.
Kielambeet, also Parc-itch (H.)	Lake Kielambete	A brackish lake.
Korite (C.)	The parish of Koroit	The large male kangaroo.
Kerurot (H.)	The Leura Swamp near Camperdown.	
Kooree (C.)		The large magpie, break-o'-day bird, *gymnorhina tibicen*.
Koroon (C.)		The "native companion," large crane.
Kooneewŭrong (H.)	Connewarren Lagoon in the county of Hampden.	
Kokeher (H.)		An orphan.
Kooneet (H.)	Austin's station on the Salt Creek.	
Katyeen (D.)		Water.
Kayanook (D.)		He himself.
Kar (D.)		A leg.
Koork (D.)		Blood.
Koolabeetyin (D.)		A native turkey or bustard.
Kalkburghera (D.)		The bush, the wooded parts of the country.
Kart-tebi (D.)		The summer season.
Kart-kart (D.)		Several, plenty, more than two.
Kalk (D.)		A tree, wood.
Kahl (D.)		A male dog.

Native Word.	Colonial Name or Description of Locality.	Signification.
Kalpooma (D.)	-	To cut.
Koong-a (D.)	-	
Eoong-a or Yoong-ee (at Swan River)	-	To give.
Kiup (D.)	-	One.
Kyn (Swan River)	-	
Koneja (D.)	-	Waterless, dry.
Laang (C.)	-	A species of gum-tree.
Lchura (C.)	Mount Leura	Lava (of which the hill is composed).
Lajeranyen (H.)	A spring S.W. from Waranet (which see *infra*) near Lake Colongulac.	
Lah (D.)	-	A stone.
Lah-wowerring (D.)	-	Rocky, covered with stones.
Larh (D.)	-	A hut or house.
Moorup (D.)	-	A spirit. It is difficult to understand their conception of a spirit or the soul of the departed.
Melion (D.)	-	Hungry, empty.
Marit (C.)	-	A female kangaroo.
Milpa-milpa boornum (H.)	-	A round swamp.
Marh (H.)	-	A man. (*Marh* is a band at King George's Sound.)
Moolung-er (H.)	-	A woman or wife.
Merreen mia (D.)	-	The south.
Melya (D.)	-	To be angry.
Marmee (D.)	-	The sky.
Ngoora (C.)	Mount Noorat	The name of an ancient "King" of the country.
Ngyuk (C.)	-	A species of white cockatoo.
Narrin (C.)	-	The large brown quail.
Ngarkarup (D.)	-	He, she, or it.
Ngarliyuhoor (D.)	-	Near, not far.
Natowalong (D.)	-	Deceit.
Ngowee (D.)	-	The sun.
Ngatta (D.)	-	To think, to believe.
Ngarree-checritch (D.)	-	A wattle-tree.
Ngooning (D.)	-	Crooked.
Porr-hue or Poork (H.)	Mount Shadwell	A cold in the head.
Purnung (C.)	-	A native dog.
Pycet (C.)	-	The large opossum.
Pooyooh (C.)	-	Ring-tailed opossum.
Purrim-purrim (C.)	-	Native turkey or bustard.
Parook (C.)	-	Kangaroo rat.
Parcitch (H.)	-	Brackish water.
Purrumbeet (C.)	Lake Purrumbete	A round lake.
Peepee (H.)	-	A father.
Tirrenehillum or Tarrinallum (C.)	Mount Elephant	A hill of fire.
Timboon (C.)	A spring and little creek on S.W. of Lake Bullen-meri, and not the place so called north of Camperdown.	
Terang (C.)	The township of Terang	A bough of a tree.
Talang (C.)	-	A strip of dry bark for lighting a pipe.
Torng (C.)	-	Smoke.

LANGUAGE. 215

Native Word.	Colonial Name or Description of Locality.	Signification.
Tulip or Toolip (C.)	-	The little magpie or magpie lark.
Tipperippet (C.)	-	The snipe.
Warrnat or Waranat (C.)	The little creek north of Camperdown, improperly named *Timboon* on the map.	
Worrn (C.)	-	A hut or camping-place on a "native oven."
Wein (C.)	-	Fire.
Warrou (C.)	The volcanic hill near Mr. Nicholas Cole's station north from Camperdown. It is in shape like an animal coiled up asleep	The common bandicoot.
Wäang (C.)	-	A crow.
Wirringbil (C.)	-	The native bear.
Wulungoon (H.R.)	The salt lagoon near Connewarren Lagoon, a few miles north from Hexham.	
Wenöön (H.R.)	The family name of the Hopkins tribe.	
Wendee (H.R.)	-	A brother.
War-war (D.)	-	To climb.
Wewar (D.)	-	To lift up.
Wurr-ip (D.)	-	Sore.
Watching (D.)	-	The knee.
Whroo or Wurroo (D.)	A township in the county of Rodney. "The dry diggings," no water but on the surface after rain. The natives had to put their lips to the ground to suck up the water.	The lips, the mouth.
Warhoe (D.)	-	The sea.
Wayet or Wayt (D.)	-	The season of April and May.
Walla-walla (D.)	A parish so called	Much rain, a great flood.
Yatching (D.)	-	Bad, foolish, childish, weak.
Yaranmillalwit (D.)	-	A species of bat.
Yeebkööng-a (D.)	-	Lost.
Yangung-o (D.)	-	To go, to move off.
Yeernoonce (D.)	-	By-and-by, presently.
Yu-ngoonee or Eu-ngünee	-	Just now.

I must here remark that the natives from whom I obtained the above words were all intelligent men, but it was not always easy to make them understand precisely what I wanted to know, as whether a word was a verb or a noun; e.g.,—Is *Kanarpanook to cough* or *a cough?* or is it used in either sense? Several natives told me that *Kielambeet* and *Pareitch* both signify brackish water, but I could get no explanation of the distinction, if any; though of course it would easily be obtained by any one who understood their dialect or was long with them.—P. C.

NATIVE NAMES OF SEVERAL HILLS, RIVERS, ETC.

(Derived from the Information of the Native Blacks "Tommy" and "Billy.")*

Station Peak	Youángh *or* Villamanata.
Mount Gellibrand	Loolúrruug-oo-lah.
Mount Elephant or Clarke	Tirrinállum.
Mount S.E. of Caráugamite	La Báam.
Mount Shadwell	Dooroobdoórabul.
Mount Abrupt	Wirribeot.
Mount William	Tó-ol.
Mount Cole	Corrong-ah-jéering.
Range east of Mount Cole	Béerbarbáirey.
Eastern Range of Pyrenees	Bemgower.
Pyrenees	Péerick.
Hill S.E. of Pyrenees	Corróonyang.
Mount Observation	Tuckerimbid.
Volcanic Hill, seven miles S.W. of Observation	Nanimé.
Hill five miles S.S.E. of Nanimé	Widderim.
Wooded hill three miles E.N.E. of Nanimé	Moonmot.
Hill seven miles S.S.E. of Observation	Mnánibadár.
High Range whence the Lea takes its rise	Bóninyon.
Hill six miles north by east of Boninyon	Wárraneep.
Hill seven miles east of Warraneep	Kirrit-barréet.
River Lea	Nurriwillún.
River N.E. of Carángamite	Wá-dy-állac.
River S.W. of Carángamite	Párranyállac.
River Taylor	Póoringh-y-jálla.
Eastern branch of River Taylor	Caranbaláe.
Large Salt Lake	Car'angamite.
Large Fresh Lake	Cólac.
Another Fresh Lake	Bolóke.
Small Salt Lake	Wirring-witring-due.
Fresh-water Lake N.E. of Observation	Bárrambeet.
Plain between Station Peak and Wa-dy-allac	Wárrac-búrran-ah.
Plain between Wa-dy-allac and Poorring-y-júlla	Pollóc.

* Extract from a Report of an Expedition to ascertain the position of the 141st degree of east longitude, being the boundary line between New South Wales and South Australia, by order of His Excellency Sir George Gipps, Knight, &c., &c., by C. J. Tyers, Surveyor, 1840.

NATIVE NAMES OF PLACES IN VICTORIA.

(By GIDEON S. LANG, ESQ.)*

Mr. Lang says :—The following names were obtained by Mr. John Currie, from a very intelligent black at Queenscliff, a few years ago, and are very expressive :—*Ballarat, Balladurk, Ballarine* (corrupted Bellarine), were favorite and extensive camping places; *Balla,* signifying elbow, or the attitude of reclining on the elbow.†

Boona-tall-ung, Point Nepean, signifies "kangaroo hide," descriptive of the angular shape of the point, like a stretched hide.‡

Woorang-a'look, Swan Island, describes the rushing sounds of the surf through the narrow opening between the island and mainland.

Euro-Yoroke, St. Kilda, the name is given from the sandstone found there, which they used to fashion and sharpen their stone tomahawks.

Koort-boork-boork, Williamstown, signifies "clumps of she-oak," the country being formerly dotted with them.§

Yowang, Station Peak, signifies "big hill."—(*See* page 199.)

Bunning-yowang, corrupted Buninyong, "big hill, like a knee;" *bunning* signifying "knee." The hill, seen from certain directions, resembles a man lying on his back with his knee drawn up.‖

Warrenyeep, corrupted Warrenheip, "emu feathers," from the peculiar appearance given to the hill by the ferns and foliage upon it.¶

Burrumbeet (Lake), "muddy water."**

---

* *The Aborigines of Australia,* by Gideon S. Lang, Esq., 1865.

† "Elbow," in the Melbourne dialect, is *Ko-rum;* in that of the Coast tribe, *Thirrong'atha;* and in that of the Upper Loddon, *Bol-loitch.*

‡ *Tallang* is the word for "tongue." The tongue of land terminating at Point Nepean is fitly described by the word. "Hide" or "skin," amongst the Coast blacks, is *Tatbee.*

§ The word for "she-oak," as given by Thomas, is *Tur-run;* amongst the Upper Loddon people it is *Koo-loitch;* and in the Western district, *Bruk-bruk.* The name quoted by Mr. Lang is therefore probably formed from the latter.

‖ The word for "knee," amongst the Yarra blacks, is *Burreng;* amongst the Western Port people it is *Burding* or *Burdin;* and in the Western district it is *Parring. Bun-nin-bun-nin* is the word for "back" in the dialect of the Melbourne tribe.

¶ *Wir-ren* is the word for "feathers," in the dialect of the Upper Loddon tribe.

** *Booreen-beek* is "dark soil;" and lakes are sometimes named by the natives from the character of the soil or clay that is found in or near the lake. The country is volcanic, and the color of the soil is a dark-chocolate. Purrumbete, another lake in the Western district, is also within the volcanic area. *Buranbeet* is the name of a shrub, *Platylobium obtusangulum* (H.).—(*See* also page 205.)

NATIVE WORDS AND NAMES.

(Obtained by Nathaniel Munro, Esq., from Henry Taverner, Esq., of Kerano, Lower Loddon.)

English.	Native.	English.	Native.
Woman	La-arook.	Give	Napouda.
Girl	Curigul.	Where	Winjalook.
Boy	Coolgoork.	Who or which	Winyatook.
Duck	Gnurre.	By-and-by	Keelamin.
Turkey	Gnurro.	The Murray River	Milloo.
Emu	Cowry.	Pyramid Creek	Yaran.
Country	Tanuck.	Nine-mile Creek	Pickaninnie yaran.
Swamp	Pocy-poey.	Two-mile Creek	Tyengule.
Lightning	Toolibue.	Five-mile Creek	Tintinbarrin.
Fire	Wamp.	Sandhills	Moingurt.
Lend	Nuella.	Tragowel Swamp	Tragowel poey-poey.
Sleep	Coombin.		
You	Gulin.	Kerang Swamp	Kerangup.
Me	Ic-ic.	Reedy Creek	Booraire.
Him	Kenya.	Kangaroo Lake	Kurmbur.
Quick	Burra warrein.	Lake Boga	Crorm.
Yes	Gno.	Dry Lake	Burto.
No	Wamba.	Sandhill Lake	Lueher.
Good	Talcook.		

LIST OF NATIVE WORDS AND NAMES.

(Compiled by Henry J. Withers, Esq., of Berrembeel, near Wagga Wagga, in New South Wales.)

English.	Native.	English.	Native.
A tribe	Eunonyhareenyah.	Nose	Mornda.
Man	Gooen.	Mouth	Nunth.
Boy	Burl.	Teeth	Erong.
Woman	Mookeen.	Hair	Ourang.
Girl	Miki.	Beard	Yarreen or Yarrun.
Head	Bultong.	Skin	Eulung.
Hand	Murra.	Blood	Goohun.
Foot	Geenong.	Bone	Thubbul.
Back	Birri.	Dead man	Bulloo.
Breast	Noonong.	Blind	Mookeen.
Neck	Wooroo.	Dead	Yalgoon.
Leg or thigh	Thurong.	Day	Yeari.
Knee	Nulgnng.	Night	Booroonthun.
Side	Thulburr.	Sun	Eri.
Shoulder	Gunuar.	Moon	Keerong.
Arm	Bulgal.	Stars	Gerrilong.
Elbow	Noouongan.	Light	Mullun.
Eye	Mill.	Moonlight	Nulgerong.
Ear	Woother.	Thunder	Mooroobri.

LANGUAGE.

English.	Native.	English.	Native.
Lightning	Marroo.	Scrub	Burgoo.
Rainbow	Euloo burgeen.	A reedy place	Jerilderie.
Clouds	Eurong.	Bark (of a tree)	Thurong.
Rain	Eurong.	Tree	Keegul.
Snow	Coonamah.	River	Murrumbidjah.
Hail	Thunthulla.	Lake	Gurwell.
Wind	Thouwarra.	Brook or creek	Thurong.
Water	Culleen.	Wet	Geether.
Ice, frost	Juggur.	Dry	Boorong.
Flood	Goonbaim.	Bird	Jibbeen.
Fire	Wing.	Wood-duck	Goonaroo.
Hot	Hoogil.	Parrot	Jibbeen.
Cold	Bulloothi.	Cockatoo	Moori.
Smoke	Cudthul.	Eagle	Mullen.
Sweet	Gilkurrijong.	Crow	Waggra.
Very pleasant, agreeable, very good	Murrumbung.	Kangaroo	Woombeen.
		Wallaby	Murrowong.
Bad	Mirri.	Water-rat	Biggoon.
Dislike	Widi murrumhung.	Opossum	Willie.
Large	Moonoon.	Native cat	Marbee.
Small	Boolee.	Native dog	Guegee.
One	Noonbee.	Horse	Yarraman.
Two	Bulla.	Snake	Cuddee.
Three	Bulla noonbee.	Fur	Keejung.
Four	Bulla-bulla.	Feathers	Boobil.
Five	Bulla-bulla noonbee.	Bee	Gubbee.
		Fish	Cooyah.
Six	Boolonbee-boolonbee.	Flowers	Bautherong.
		Drink	Weejelly.
Seven*	Bulla-bulla - bulla-courabah.	Charcoal	Gooreen.
		Road, a track	Murroo.
Yes	Nah.	A row	Berrembed.
No	Wirri.	Run	Moonbutha.
Red	Keerie-keerie.	Walk	Yannah.
Black	Boothong.	Stand up	Warother.
White	Burra-burra.	Lie down	Weerejah.
Yellow	Goonong-goonong.	After the crows	Wagga-wagga.
Blue	Burringun.	Give	Noongah.
Ground	Thug-oon.	Give it here	Noongah thine.
Dust	Boonoon.	Give me a boomerang	Noongah bulgong.
Mud	Moorong.	Come here, man	Mang thanyahuah.
Sand	Gurri.	I want to speak to you	Yalleelee.
Plains	Goonegul.	To throw a boomerang	Berrembah bulgong.
Hills	Jerrimah.		
Swamp	Bulgari.	To throw a spear	Juri jurelow.
Grass	Boogoon or Bulgoon.	To throw a barbed spear	Thoorah thooloogoo.
Wood	Geegul.		
A shrub (name of)	Euri.	To throw a hone	Doobuloo berroomali.
Leaves	Curreel.		
Red-gum	Yarra.	Will you?	Yanima?
Seed (barley grass)	Gooloo.	I have got nothing for you	Mungee minyambul yinno.
Seeds	Woonyoul.		
Dogwood	Honey-jerry.	Did you dream?	Yahmondoo yahdurnee?
River-oak	Billaway.		

* Any number beyond seven is, the blacks say, like the leaves—not to be counted.

English.	Native.	English.	Native.
You and I will	Nulleebil.	I will	Nartboo.
When shall I see you again?	Thanguar millee nangallah yalagerry?	You will	Mudoobel.
		I am going to leave you now	Neenyah thoowyah oneah bunyah.
Have you had anything to eat?	Yalwondoo thay?	Swim	Barbidgee.
		Dive	Woobunijah.
No	Wirri.	Sleep	Euri.
Sit down	Weejah.	Canoe	Murring.
Have you slept well?	Yahwondoo monyroom curi werring?	Paddle	Bunderhan.
		Honey	Naroo.
		Wild	Gelgel.
To throw a nulla-nulla	Berrembah boondeegue.	Tame	Mooroogbeeong.
		Heavy	Butherri.
Will you?	Yammah?		

King George's Sound, 1816.

APPENDICES.

APPENDIX A.

NOTES AND ANECDOTES OF THE ABORIGINES OF AUSTRALIA.

(By Philip Chauncy, J.P., District Surveyor at Ballaarat.)

INTRODUCTORY REMARKS.

As the reader will naturally desire to know what my claims are as an authority on the subject of the Aboriginal inhabitants of Australia, I may say that I arrived at Adelaide from England in 1839, and have resided in the Colonies of South Australia, New South Wales, Western Australia, and Victoria ever since. I held the appointment under the Imperial Government of Assistant Surveyor in Western Australia for about twelve years—from 1841 to 1853.

My observations of the Aborigines were made chiefly in that colony, where they were, during the period mentioned, very numerous. In 1841 they numbered about three thousand in the located portions of the territory, according to the statistical returns, whereas the white population was much smaller, and, as a consequence, we had to learn to speak to the natives to a great extent in their own language, and thus had frequent opportunities for observing their social position and habits.

The following statements are written down partly from memory and partly from a miscellaneous collection of notes which I have from time to time made. I have also occasionally availed myself of such authorities as I have at hand, for the purpose of elucidating facts with which I was previously acquainted. These are principally the valuable little publications of the late Mr. G. F. Moore, Advocate-General of the Colony of Western Australia, and of the late Mr. E. S. Parker, formerly Assistant Protector of Aborigines in Victoria, with both of whom I was personally acquainted.

As will be seen, I do not even touch on many subjects connected with this singular race of mankind. My observations are intended rather as a record of such incidents as I happen to remember, and of such facts as I have thought noteworthy, with the view of assisting in the compilation of a general history, than to afford complete information on any point.

Painted Caves.

It has been stated by Professor Huxley that the natives of Southern and Western Australia are probably as pure and homogeneous as any race of savages in existence. And yet there are some slight indications of another and possibly a more ancient people having at one time dwelt in Australia. These consist of certain red marks on the walls and roofs of caves, chiefly the imprints of human hands, as though a hand had been immersed in some red dye and then pressed against the side of the cave. These "signs-manual" are generally accompanied by some other marks or drawings.

They have been noticed in Eastern, Western, and Northern Australia; on indurated sandstone in a cliff on Dunmore's station, near the Goulburn River, in New South Wales, where they consist of hand-prints and drawings of animals; in a granite cave, about ten miles south from York, in Western Australia; and in other places.

I visited this cave in 1849, and saw the marks on the roof; they are quite indelible, and begin low down, near where the roof and floor meet. At first there is the imprint of the full-spread hand and fore-arm, in such a position that the person making it must have been squeezed as far as possible into the wedge-shaped space; then there is the mark of the hand with the fingers spread, mark after mark, and finally of the fingers only, where the roof arches up almost out of reach; but higher and just over the mouth of the cave is a circular figure, drawn with the same red substance, about fifteen inches in diameter, and filled up with lines and cross-bars. It must have been made by a person who was raised from the floor of the cave. This cavern is not easy of access, being in the face of a granite cliff overhanging the valley of the Avon River.

On my questioning the natives about these marks, they could give no rational account of them. They have very little curiosity about the cave, and pay no respect whatever to it; it does not seem to concern them or to belong to their people. On enquiring what they thought of the marks, one of them amused me with the following absurd story. He stated that his people believed that the Moon once dwelt in that cave, but becoming tired of the confinement, he[*] ran up the roof of the cave, leaving his imprint at the top as he jumped up into the sky, where he has been wandering about ever since. Nor were they acquainted with the substance used to stain the rock,—it might be cinnabar but that none is known to exist in that part of the country.

Mr. Robert D. Hardey, when making an excursion some years ago into the sandy desert which extends east from York, found the prints of five or six hands in caves nearly seventy miles east from the valley of the Avon River, but he could not ascertain what they were made with.

Capt. Flinders found paintings in caves in Chusan Island, in the Gulf of Carpentaria, made with charcoal and a sort of red paint. There were porpoises, kangaroos, turtles, and *a human hand;* also a kangaroo with thirty-two persons following it.

---

[*] The moon is masculine, the sun feminine.

Mr. Cunningham, in *King's Voyages*, saw paintings in Clack's Island, off the north-east coast.

Messrs. Grey and Lushington, in 1838, found caves with well-executed figures done in different colors, on the north-west coast; but Capt. (now Sir George) Grey thought they had no connection with the red hands in the cavern near York.

It is stated by a recent writer in the *Colonies** that ancient carvings exist in considerable numbers upon the flat rocks and headlands surrounding the harbour of Port Jackson, and at other places along the coast, primitive enough in design, yet highly interesting to the archæologist and ethnologist. At the North Head the carvings exist in great numbers, as well as impressions of human hands on the sides of perpendicular rocks; the whole of the subjects represent indigenous objects—kangaroos, opossums, sharks, shields, boomerangs, and human figures in the attitudes of the corobboree dance.†

How far these relics, or any of them, found in different and remote parts of Australia, may lead to the inference of a race having existed in the country prior to the advent of the people whom we now call Aborigines, is, I think, a question worthy of consideration.

Stephens, in his work on Central America, refers to vermilion impressions of human hands on the old Toltic buildings of Yucatan.

The stamp of the hand on a document is the sign-manual in Borneo of a native prince.‡ The red color is esteemed sacred, in many instances, by the inhabitants of a great portion of Asia.

BARBAROUS CONDITION OF THE NATIVES.

Some of the earliest discoverers of Australia saw natives of the present race when they landed. These barbarians were in a state of mere savage nature, never having heard of any other people than their own, nor having the least idea that other tribes existed beyond a very limited range of country around their own hunting-grounds. They knew nothing whatever of the conventional forms of gesture and expression which are generally understood and received as indications of amity among strange races. Whenever, therefore, they could be brought to parley, the situation was both critical and embarrassing.

The Australian Aborigines in their wild state are not only suspicious of treachery in their neighbours, but often have a superstitious terror of distant tribes, with whose existence they are only acquainted by report. It was not, therefore, suprising that they viewed with alarm the arrival of persons differing in color and appearance from any they had before seen or heard of, and of whose nature, power, and intentions they were wholly ignorant.

---

* The signature is G. F. A.—probably George Fife Angus; date 21st April 1877.

† Some of the figures of sharks and other fishes measure twenty-five feet in length, while those of men in dancing attitudes are life size. The natives say that the tribes did not reside in the places where the carvings occur, as they are sacred to the *koradjee* or sorcerers or priests.

‡ *See* Rajah Brook's work.

Some tribes had a vague idea of the white men being spirits or re-appearances of dead persons, and were restrained by awe alone from attacking them. This dread of strangers seems to be the natural result of ignorance, and reminds us of the restrictive policy, until lately, of the Japanese, and of the religious prejudices of the Hindoos and strict Mahommedans.

In the south-eastern portion of Australia, the old men used to say that the forms or spirits of the dead went to the westward, towards the setting sun; and the natives of Western Australia had the same belief. When, therefore, they saw white men coming over the sea from that quarter, they at once took them to be their deceased relatives re-incarnated, and called them *Djenga*, or ghosts, as distinguished from *Yung-ar*, or persons.

In almost all cases where there has been an opportunity of coming to an understanding, and a desire on the part of the Europeans to conciliate the Aborigines, they have evinced a friendly disposition. It has, however, often happened that the earliest interviews left anything but favorable impressions on their minds.

In the year 1699, William Dampier, an Englishman, landed on the north-west coast, and soon fell in with some natives, who ran away from him and his men. Soon after, nine of them were seen approaching with angry gestures and making a great noise, but taking a sudden panic, they fled away as fast as they could. Dampier then formed an ambuscade, and tried to seize some of them; but failing, one of his men was wounded by a spear; he then fired on the blacks with ball, and one, at least, of them fell, and was carried off by his comrades.

This occurrence may be taken as a fair example of the misunderstandings and collisions which from time to time have disgraced the history of Australia.

The dominant and arrogant race, despising the ignorant barbarian, has paid but little respect either to his rights or person, and has too often treated him as though he were a wild beast; while the savage, in accordance with the instincts of his nature, has resented the aggression; and thus some fearful outrages have occasionally, even to the present time, been perpetrated by both parties;—the white man, with his boasted civilization, being the more accountable of the two.

The landing of Capt. Cook at Botany Bay was disputed by the natives, but he found those at Moreton Bay better disposed.

The murder by the blacks of Mr. Kennedy, the explorer, with whom I was personally acquainted, near Cape York, in 1848, was in all probability committed for the purpose of retaliating aggressive action on the part of a ship's crew.

Capt. Pasco, R.N., formerly of H.M.S. *Beagle*, when she was engaged in the survey of Torres Straits, has informed me that, on the 24th June 1841, they called in at what was termed "the post office" on the uninhabited "Booby Island," and examined a book which was kept there in order that masters of ships might record any circumstance of interest during the run through Torres Straits, and found an entry by one *Greyburne*, master of *The Brothers*, in which he recorded the fact that "he had killed *only one* native." It is therefore not improbable that the master of *The Brothers* is indirectly accountable for the death of Mr. Kennedy.

This view is supported by Mr. Macgillivray, the Naturalist on board H.M.S. *Rattlesnake*, who states* that the *Yagulles* are the tribe who were concerned in the murder of the unfortunate Kennedy. The circumstances were related by an old woman named *Baki*, at Cape York, who, when questioned, corroborated the statement of that noble native lad *Jacky*, Mr. Kennedy's attendant after he had left all his other men, and in whose arms he died. She further stated that some years before—that is about the time that *Greyburne* landed from *The Brothers*—a *Yagulle* woman and child had been shot by some white men who landed from a small vessel near Albany Island, and that the tribe had been anxious to revenge their death, until they had the opportunity of doing so by killing Mr. Kennedy.

The more recent murder of Mr. Wills in Queensland was probably owing to the conduct of some white men who had shortly before captured and forcibly carried off to Sydney two lads belonging to the tribe which subsequently perpetrated the deed. Such examples, taken very much at random, are illustrative of the mutual misunderstandings and occasional harsh treatment of the natives, followed sometimes by savage murders perhaps of innocent persons, which again were succeeded by prompt and equally indiscriminate punishment of "the blacks."

In the early days of the Swan River settlement a wholesale massacre of some assembled tribes was ostentatiously designated the battle of Pinjarrah.

The Government having been informed that several tribes were to meet at a place called Pinjarrah, about forty miles south from Perth, proceeded against them with a detachment of troops led by Capt. Ellis, and headed by the Governor in person accompanied by a number of civilians.

As the natives are in the habit of occasionally meeting for the adjustment of differences among themselves, for arranging hunting expeditions, and for other purposes of a like kind, I know of no reason for supposing that on this occasion they intended to organize any force for attacking the settlers. Indeed I believe the natives would never think of assembling in large numbers with any such object in view.

The soldiers shot down a great number of them, and then dragged their bodies into heaps and covered them with sand. These mounds are, I believe, visible at the present time. In this unequal, if not treacherous affair, only one white man was killed, and this was Capt. Ellis, who fell by the spear of a native.

The published accounts of such occurrences are often partial and unfair. The natives have no newspapers and few advocates, and are therefore placed in a worse position than a criminal at the bar of English justice.

About the year 1835, some tribes had arranged to meet on the south side of the Swan River opposite Perth, and while two of them were proceeding thither, and walking along a path leading to the hut of an Indian fisherman near the

---

* See foot-note on first page of vol. II. *Voyage of the Rattlesnake.*

mouth of the Canning River, one of them was caught by the heel in a dog-trap which had been set in the narrow path by the fisherman. The native and his companion were, of course, much terrified, but succeeded in reaching the place of rendezvous, a distance of five or six miles, with the iron trap firmly grasping his heel. Here they found their assembled countrymen in a state of great excitement at intelligence which had reached them from the opposite direction that a Swan River native had been killed at Guildford by a white man. The result was that a party went the next morning to the Indiaman's hut—killed him, and so mangled the body that it could scarcely be recognized. They also threw a spear at an English gentleman who happened to be there, and who just escaped being killed by swimming the Canning River; he received a barbed spear in the back of the arm, and ran with it up to Capt. Hester's, where it was taken out.

At about the same place, though two or three years earlier, a powerful leader and two of his companions were ensnared by stratagem and made prisoners. They had been inveigled into a boat which for this purpose had put off from Perth, the embryo capital, to the opposite side of the water, where a number of natives were fishing. So soon as the men in the boat got their victims into their power, they seized, bound, and carried them off, in view of their tribe, who stood amazed and mad with indignation at the perfidy thus practised on them.

The names of these men were *Yagan*, *Doumera*, and *Nyinyinnee*. *Yagan* was a chief of the Upper Swan tribe; he was tall, athletic, and muscular, with a strong dash of the savage in his countenance. When animated in conversation, or even a little excited, scarcely a peer of the realm could excel him in dignity of demeanour or urbanity of manners. The passions of the savage, however, occasionally flitting across his brow, kept confidence in check; and yet, when conciliating, he exhibited a disposition so candid, cordial, and generous that the most timid would feel at ease in his presence. His was a fine character, but withal he had been the terror of the infant colony.

Doumera was a well-disposed, mild-looking youth, and a great favorite with many of the colonists.

Nyinyinnee, on the other hand, was dark, reserved, and cunning—"a thorough savage," as an old settler remarked.

These prisoners were conveyed to Perth and banished to a barren rock called Karnac Island. A Mr. Milne voluntarily took charge of them, accompanied by a soldier, with a view to their civilization; but after a short period they effected their escape in a boat, and landed at Woodman's Point, whence they made their way across the bush to the Swan; but in crossing the Canning road they unfortunately fell in with two young men, John and Thomas Velvich, both of whom they killed. I shall have to recur to *Yagan*, and will now only add that the Government offered thirty pounds for his head, for the purpose of obtaining which a boy named Richard Keats treacherously killed him.

This boy with his brother John were tending Capt. Bull's sheep at the Upper Swan, *Yagan's* country, and were well acquainted with him and all his tribe, numbering some seventy or eighty, when one day he asked *Yagan* to look for wild-ducks in the river for him to shoot. *Yagan* was in the act of stepping softly and looking over the bank down into the river, when Richard Keats deliberately shot him in the back of the neck, killing him on the spot, in view of the tribe, who were encamped not a quarter of a mile off. Keats then threw down his gun and ran for his life down the side of the river, but the natives soon gained upon him, and when he jumped in to swim across, they riddled his body with spears. These lads had been in the habit of daily frequenting the natives' camps for years; their treachery was therefore the greater. Capt. Bull, I believe, sent *Yagan's* head to the Directors of the British Museum after it had been smoke-dried.

The following anecdote will further illustrate the general character and disposition of the Australian natives when they first saw the white men come among them:—

Towards the end of 1848, Capt. Fitzgerald, the Governor of Western Australia, visited the newly-discovered country to the northward near Champion Bay.

While returning from the Bowes River to that Bay, accompanied by Mr. Rivett H. Bland, his Private Secretary (now of Clunes), Mr. Augustus Gregory, three soldiers and a servant lad, they saw several natives following them, who increased in number as they got into the thickets at the foot of King's table-land, and came closer to the party every step they advanced. Notwithstanding an order to keep off, one laid hold of Mr. Bland by the arm, with the intention of striking him on the head with his dowak; but on a soldier running towards him, he let go.

Mr. Bland had a pistol in his hand, but, with praiseworthy forbearance, was reluctant to commence the affray by using it. Shortly afterwards the natives, armed with spears, kileys,* and dowaks,† having closed upon the party, a spear was thrown at Mr. Gregory, but without effect, and the Governor, having dismounted, shot the man nearest to him, who appeared to have some influence in directing the movements of the others. He was a splendid fellow, more than six feet high. He suddenly sprang in among the party, his eyes flashing and his spear quivering in the *miro*,‡ ready to throw, when he received a ball through the heart, for he fell forward on the knees with his head to the ground, and did not even roll over or stir again.

The soldiers then fired, and the natives threw a shower of spears, kileys, and stones. The party had now nearly cleared the thickets, and were between two small rocky hills, from the summits of which and from the thickets behind the natives were throwing their spears, when one struck His Excellency the Governor just above the knee, passing through the thigh and protruding about a foot. Fortunately, he was warned the spear was coming, and made a sudden step forward, or it would have struck him in the back.

During the remainder of the journey, for twelve or fourteen miles, to the beach, the savages used every effort to cut them off. After a fatiguing walk of ten

---

* Boomerangs.   † Small clubs.   ‡ Throwing-board.

hours, the party reached Champion Bay, and got away in the boats, from which they saw the beach lined with natives.

The attacking party numbered about fifty or sixty. They were described as being a much finer race of men than those in the located districts, and fought with great determination and bravery.

The number of Aborigines killed and wounded could not be ascertained, but the former were believed to be three. On the part of the expedition, the Governor was the only one wounded. I do not know whether this attack, which was quite unprovoked at the time, was made from motives of revenge for some old injury, or from fear and a desire to prevent the intruders from taking possession of their country.

It has been remarked that children have a keen sense of justice, and so have the natives, if *Yagan* may be taken as an exponent of their sentiments.

Mr. G. F. Moore, when Advocate-General of the colony, had won the confidence of the natives by uniform kindness. He endeavoured to ingratiate himself with them for the purpose of learning their language and customs.

One day, in June 1843, as I was sitting with Mr. Moore at his station at the Upper Swan, he gave me the following account of a wild native's idea of justice. The incident had occurred at the door of the room in which we were sitting. It was thus:—A number of armed native men had surrounded the house, when Mr Moore went to the door to speak to them, having his fire-arms close at hand. He soon recognised *Yagan*, but the natives near the door denied that he was present. However, when the outlaw perceived that he was known, he stepped boldly and confidently up, and resting his arm on Mr. Moore's shoulder, looked him earnestly in the face, and addressed him, as the first Law Officer of the Crown, to the following effect—" Why do you white people* come in ships to our country and shoot down poor blackfellows† who do not understand you? You listen to me! The wild blackfellows do not understand your laws; every living animal that roams the country and every edible root that grows in the ground are common property! A black man claims nothing as his own but his cloak, his weapons, and his name! Children are under no restraint from infancy upwards; a little baby boy, as soon as he is old enough, beats his mother, and she always lets him! When he can carry a spear, he throws it at any living thing that crosses his path, and when he becomes a man, his chief employment is hunting. He does not understand that animals or plants can belong to one person more than another. Sometimes a party of natives come down from the hills, tired and hungry, and fall in with strange animals you call sheep; of course, away flies the spear, and presently they have a feast! Then you white men come and shoot the poor blackfellows!" Then, with his eagle eye flashing, and holding up one of his fingers before Mr. Moore's face, he shouted out—" For every black man you white fellows shoot, I will kill a white man!" And so with "the poor hungry women; they have always been accustomed to dig up every edible root, and when they come across a potato

---

* *Djenga*, or ghosts.   † *Yung-ar*, or people.

garden, of course, down goes the wanna (yam-stick), and up comes the potato, which is at once put into the bag. Then you white men shoot at poor black-fellows. I will take life for life!" *

Retribution.

A law prevails, among some tribes at least, which renders it compulsory on the nearest male relative to take the life of some one of the tribe to which the slayer belongs. And even if a man dies a natural death, they believe he has been killed by some unseen hand, in which case they resort to divination, to ascertain the tribe from which the slayer came. The avenger is generally not actuated so much by personal ill-feeling as by the desire to perform a supposed duty, and thereby maintain his good name among his own people. He therefore sometimes kills the first of the tribe he meets, without for a moment considering whether or not his victim was even an accessory. Justice is then supposed to be vindicated. Blood for blood is their universal law; revenge becomes a sacred duty; and if a man withhold his hand from taking a life as a satisfaction for his brother's, he is ever after looked upon as a coward.

As the wild blacks supposed that all white men knew and approved of each other's deeds, they held it a sacred duty for the avenger to slay the first white person in his power, of whatever age or sex, as a satisfaction for his murdered relative.

In some of the Australian settlements the colonists for the most part evinced a very friendly feeling towards the sable occupants of the country. This was especially the case at Swan River after the first few years of the settlement, and in South Australia from its commencement. The natives on their part reciprocated the expression of good-will, and became most useful and faithful assistants to the colonists.

Instances are not wanting of kindness by wild Aborigines to white men when in their power. The surveying operations of the *Beagle* during the years 1837 to 1843 were confined chiefly to those parts of the northern coast which had not been visited by other navigators. At one time, when some of the crew lived ashore, one of the men always exhibited a great antipathy to the natives; but getting lost in the bush for three days, he lay down, as he supposed, to die. His great dread was that he should be found by the natives. To his horror, on awaking from a slumber, he saw a number of them armed and standing around him. They, however, led him to their camp, fed him and kept him until the following morning, when they took him in safety to his companions,† thus exhibiting a kindly disposition in one of those tribes which are deemed the most fierce of the Australians, when not actuated to deeds of violence by motives of fear or revenge.

---

* I published this anecdote some years ago in the *Church News*, signing myself "An Old Australian."—P. C.

† I am indebted to Capt. Pasco for this anecdote.

Loss of the Austrian Bark "Stefano" north of Shark's Bay, on the North-West Coast, in October 1875.

The following particulars were furnished to the *Fremantle Herald* by Mr. John Vincent, who acted as interpreter to the survivors:—"The *Stefano*, 1,300 tons, of Fiume in Austria, with a crew of seventeen persons, was wrecked on the coast, and only ten of the men got ashore. They lived on raw shell-fish and such provisions as were washed on the beach. They had little hope of ever being rescued, and were in great dread of the natives, whom they believed to be cannibals. As everything had been lost, they had no means of ascertaining on what part of the coast they were, or in which direction lay the nearest settlement. After several days of great suffering, the natives came down to the beach, and, much to the surprise of the castaway sailors, made overtures of friendliness, which, after some hesitation on the part of the shipwrecked seamen, were accepted. The natives showed them where water could be obtained, caught fish and cooked them for them, and completely relieved the party of all fear on their account. Among the *débris* of the wreck washed ashore the natives picked up a chart of the West Coast of Australia, by which the party were enabled to make out pretty well where they were; and, after consultation, it was determined to make an attempt to get to Shark's Bay. The party started southwards, and after six days' travelling reached Cape Cuvier. Finding no water, and being afraid to proceed, they returned to the scene of the wreck, which they reached in safety. For some six weeks after their return the party lived on rock oysters, and suffered intensely from want and exposure. On Christmas Day two of the men died; and a few days after six more, including the first-mate, succumbed to their sufferings. The two remaining survivors, Baccich and Jurich, who now despaired of ever being rescued, determined to join the natives, and travelled inland for this purpose. They joined the tribe with which they were already acquainted, and found them extremely hospitable while they remained with them. They had long despaired of ever being rescued from their pitiable condition, when relief came in a most unexpected manner. Capt. C. Tuckey, of the cutter *Jessie*, engaged in the pearl-fishing, on his voyage from Roebourne to Fremantle, put in near the north-west coast to land some native divers belonging to that locality, who had been engaged in the pearling. After landing them, the *Jessie* proceeded on her voyage; but the weather getting rough, the captain thought it as well to run in towards the land and anchor in smooth water till the weather abated. Having anchored in a protected spot, Tuckey determined to send some flour and sugar ashore to the natives, with a view to establishing friendly relations with the tribes thereabout, in the event of his wanting to engage them, at any future time, for the pearling. While pulling on shore in the ship's boat, one of the hands remarked that there were two Malays on the beach with the natives. On landing, they proved to be the two survivors of the crew of the *Stefano*, and from them Capt. Tuckey learnt the sad tale of the loss of the ship and the sufferings of the crew. He brought them to Fremantle, and informed the proper authorities of what had occurred. The natives made no reference to their having had any previous acquaintance with white men during the time these young men remained with them."

The *Herald* of the 27th May 1876 adds—"The hospitality of the natives at the north-west towards the crew of the *Stefano* has been recognised by the Government, and is to be rewarded. The *Rosette*, Capt. Vincent, takes two bags of flour, one bag of sugar, twelve looking-glasses, one dozen sheath knives, and ten pounds of tobacco, for distribution among the natives at Point Cloates."

Many of the early settlers of Western Australia were much attached to the natives who had so often helped them in their greatest need, with a patience of fatigue, and with intelligence superior to that of the white men, especially in times of flood, when, but for them, many of them would have been ruined. Some of the settlers on the Canning River and in the York district were, at times, almost dependent on the natives for food, and this during a course of years. They would bring them in game, tend their little flocks, help to clear and cultivate the land, and be their messengers and letter-carriers with a cheerful unselfishness and fidelity which were quite exemplary. It was only necessary to understand them and treat them judiciously to make them very valuable allies and helps.

If Messrs. Burke and Wills, on their return to Cooper's Creek, after their daring dash across the continent, had understood the natives whom they found there, and exhibited a friendly bearing towards them, they would, in all probability, have learned from them that the party who had been left in charge of the depôt camp was only a day's journey ahead. A communication would have been opened up, and in the meantime the natives would have sustained them with fish; instead of which, these brave men were driven by hunger to eat some fish-bones which had been left by the blacks, and finally perished from starvation.

Aversion to strangers appears to be the natural result of ignorance. Until recently, when the diffusion of knowledge has become more general, we find that absurdly disparaging notions regarding their neighbours prevailed even among the most civilized nations—as, for instance, it used to be believed, within the last half-century, in England, that one Englishman could beat three Frenchmen. The savage, who has no knowledge of any people beyond a very limited area around his own territory, naturally views strangers with alarm and dislike.

When, therefore, we find that weary travellers, such as Burke, Wills, and King, were unmolested by a large and comparatively powerful tribe, it does not seem too much to assume that these people are not always so treacherous and bloodthirsty as some writers would have us believe. Indeed, as soon as Burke and Wills died, King fraternized with them, and was supported by them until succour arrived.

Information regarding the Aborigines and their Relics.

It is very desirable that authentic information should be obtained before it is too late from persons who have long resided among the Aborigines and have become conversant with their languages and peculiarities. These Europeans, as well as the natives themselves, are fast passing away, and unless the information be soon recorded, it will be lost for ever.

To the student of languages the native dialects are most valuable, and, if now preserved, might hereafter fill the most critical gaps in the history of mankind.

Some gentlemen now reside in Western Australia who have been more than forty years among the natives, and have made them their especial study. They could, doubtless, supply most valuable intelligence not otherwise obtainable.

The time is near at hand when not only the race itself will have disappeared, but no record will remain of many of their peculiarities, of the traditions of the tribes, of their characters and characteristics, and of the acts of those individuals whose biographies would be useful and interesting as being typical of this family of mankind.

Even now, as we travel through the country, we find but few indications of a previous race having occupied it. Two of these are, the marks cut on trees, which will soon disappear; and the "native ovens," or mirnyongs.

1. The marks on the trees are merely where pieces of bark have been cut out for various purposes, or where notches have been made to assist in climbing; of course, these will soon be obliterated, but, fortunately, the other monuments of a more durable description will remain.

2. These are the mirnyongs, called by the colonists "native ovens." They occur, so far as I am aware, only in the eastern and south-eastern portions of Australia, where the soil is less absorbent and the climate wetter, and in some parts colder, than the sandy territory of Western Australia.

They are what Sir Charles Lyell terms "kitchen refuse heaps," when writing of similar mounds under the peat mosses of Denmark, and are composed of ashes, fine charcoal, fragments of bones, and other remains after cooking and eating.

They are found in the valleys of rivers and creeks, on the margins of lakes and lagoons, just inside the "points of timber" or portions of forest which project into the plains, on rising grounds in the plains, near the sea-shore, and in every locality where fish, game, or food of any description is to be found.

The positions of the mirnyongs have been carefully selected, so that, as far as possible, the occupants may obtain an extensive view of the surrounding country, while they themselves are screened from any passer by.

When a company of natives returns after a day's hunting and foraging, the women take a fresh supply of firewood and stones. These last are sometimes found on the "ovens" in localities remote from where any stones are known to exist. Thus, in the course of centuries, they become large mounds, affording comfortable camping-places as compared with the often wet and scrubby ground around. There they bake their opossums, kangaroos, lizards, fish, frogs, roots, and whatever else they may have taken during the day.

These ash-heaps vary in size from ten to one hundred feet in diameter, and from a few inches to eight or ten feet in height, depending on their age, the frequency of their use, and the number of persons resorting to them. They doubtless conceal many lost stone hatchets and other implements and ornaments.

I subjoin a sketch (Fig. 247) of some large *mirnyongs* which occur at the outlet of Lake Connewarren, about five miles south-west from Mortlake, in the County of Hampden, Victoria.

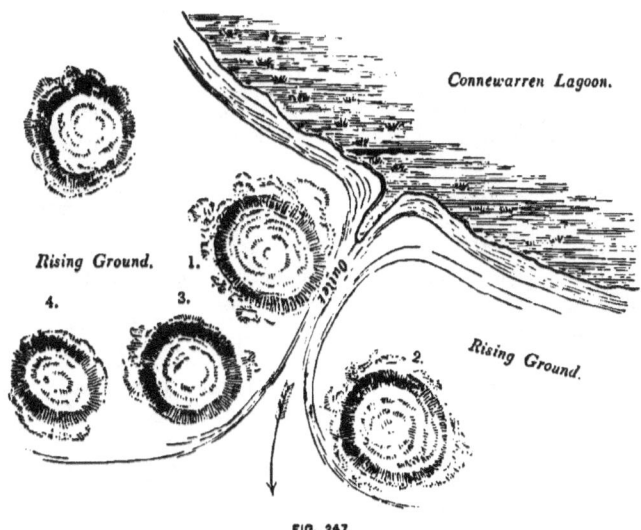

FIG. 247.

"Native ovens" are called by the natives of the Werribee, *Goorung;** of Fiery Creek, *Tallum;* of the Lower Avoca, *Bolap;* of Mount Emu, *Moornung;* and by others *Mirnyong;* in which they bake eels, roots, &c.

No. 1 is 102 by 90 feet in diameter, 310 feet in circumference, 8 feet high from the east side, and 6 feet from the west side.

No. 2 is 104 by 99 feet in diameter, 318 feet in circumference, and 5 feet high.

No. 3 is 96 by 84 feet in diameter, and 3 feet high.

No. 4 is 87 by 75 feet in diameter, 3½ feet high on east, and 2 feet high on the west side.

There are no trees within about 200 yards.

They must be of great antiquity, for there is but little firewood in the vicinity, and only small fires would suffice to cook the eels taken from the adjacent lagoon. It abounds with large eels, and a few years ago, when the flood-waters overflowed, the eels escaped from their overcrowded breeding basin

---

* A parish near Ballan is named *Gorong*.

in scores of tons. It was on that occasion that a few natives, the remnant of their tribe, stood beside the outlet bewailing the sad fact that there were no more blackfellows to eat the eels.

There are also some large shell-mounds on the coast, especially near Cape Otway, where the largest is about three hundred feet long, forty or fifty feet wide, and sixteen feet high. It must have taken ages for the fish-eating natives of the coast to build up such heaps.

In many parts of the country the mirnyongs have been destroyed by the agricultural settlers, who use them for manure. In future years the ethnologist will doubtless search many of them for relics of a lost race whose condition and habits they will indicate.

As they are the oldest, so they will be the most durable records of perhaps the most primitive people on the face of the earth. They resemble, as I have said, the *Kjökenmoddings*, or kitchen refuse heaps, of Denmark, in which pieces of stone have been found, and fragments of the bones of animals on which the savages of that country and remote period fed. From the texture of the bones, Professor Owen has been able to determine the kinds of animals to which they belonged.

I would suggest that some of the largest of these mounds be scientifically examined, with a view of ascertaining whether they contain any relics or implements differing from those in use at the present time.

At a meeting of the Ethnological Society in London, in 1864, Sir Charles Nicholson alluded to the discovery of great numbers of flint implements by Mr. Gregory, in immense tumuli near the sea, during his explorations in Australia.

Major Mitchell mentions circular mounds with trenches round them, being the tombs of a tribe on the Darling Downs. I am not, however, aware of any tumuli in Western, Southern, or South-Eastern Australia, although the natives have sometimes buried their dead in the mirnyongs which I have just described. I have taken out portions of the skeleton of an Aboriginal man from one of these mounds near Lake Purrumbete, not far from Camperdown; and as many as five or six skeletons have been found in one mound. But I think they have only latterly been used as places of interment, when the natives had so diminished in numbers as no longer to require them for camping purposes. It is very likely, too, that they were induced to use the forsaken mounds as burial-places by the consideration that the deceased would like to repose in so comfortable a place, which he had so often tenanted during life, and also because of the greater facility with which they could burrow the grave in the ash-mound than in the hard ground.

There are, however, still other memorials of the late numerous but now almost extinct inhabitants of the extensive basaltic plains of the Western district of Victoria. Some stone *mia-mys*, or shelters, may still occasionally be found; there are a few on the western margin of the Stony Rises, south of Lake Purrumbete.

In one of Chambers's Tracts on *The Monuments of Unrecorded Ages* it is stated that "stone-circles" are numerous in Victoria—that they are from ten to one hundred feet in diameter, and that sometimes there is an inner circle;

also, that the Aborigines have no traditions regarding them; that when asked about them they invariably deny knowledge of their origin.

I can safely affirm that these statements are quite incorrect—there are no such circles, and never were. I am convinced that no structures of a monumental character were ever erected by any of the Aborigines of Australia. Nor can the megalithic circles alluded to be referred to any natural appearance in any of the more recent overflows of basalt.

The authority for the statement regarding the stone-circles in Victoria is a paper by the late Sir Jas. Y. Simpson, in the Proceedings of the Society of Antiquaries (Scotland), quoted in Sir J. Lubbock's *Pre-Historic Times*. Mr. Ormond, in a letter to Sir. J. Y. Simpson (page 122), says that he has seen many, especially near the Mount Elephant Plains in Victoria, and he then gives the above description of them.

Mr. Ormond may possibly have alluded to the *mia-mys* or camping-places which have been found in open and exposed places, where the natives formed rude stone-circles merely for the purpose of shelter from the keen winds which sometimes sweep over the plains. Flat stones of basalt often occur only a few inches thick, and having two or three square feet of surface; these have been collected by the natives and set on edge, but have generally been removed by the settlers for the purpose of building the stone walls with which the country is now intersected in every direction.

Mr. Peter Manifold, who has resided on his estate in the district in question for more than thirty years, has kindly given me the following valuable information on the subject:—

"The stone-circles are made by the natives, and are always found in exposed situations where timber is difficult to obtain. The natives there formed these break-winds of stones, placed on edge in a circular form, some of them very perfect, leaving the opening generally towards the east, the prevailing winds coming from the north-west and south-west. These circles are common on the plains or eastern part of this property, where branches of trees could not be procured for giving shelter. When we first occupied this country, it was quite common for the natives to use these circles as camping-places, always having the fires in the centre. The fires were very small, as they had frequently to carry the wood long distances. The circles are generally formed of large stones set on their edges, and bedded in the ground close together, without any other stones on the top, thus forming good protection from the wind as they lay around the fire. The stones are of the common basalt, there being no other in the district. The situation selected was generally where water was convenient, or in some favorable place for game. The circles were about the size of the ordinary *mia-mys*, that is from ten to twenty feet in diameter."

I may add that the European shepherds have been in the habit of constructing rubble-walls in circles for the same purpose of protection from the winds.

On a little basalt islet in Lake Wongan, about seven miles north-east from Streatham, I observed an ancient Aboriginal work consisting of extensive rows of large stones, forming passages up and down, like a maze, at the foot of a little hill. A semicircular walk, ten feet wide, has been made by clearing and smoothing the rough rocky surface up the hill and down again leading into the maze. This work was possibly executed for the purpose of carrying on some mystic rites, or probably only for the amusement of running between the rows of stones and up the hill and down again.

Also, Mr. A. C. Allan, Inspector-General of Surveys, has informed me that during a recent journey in the Tattiara country, near the South Australian

FIG. 248.

border, he noticed a number of stone walls, two or three feet high, which had been constructed by the natives, radiating from a little cave in the ground, and forming irregular passages.

I can only conjecture that these and other similar works have been used by the Aborigines, in times past, for purposes of incantation.

ILLUSTRATIONS OF PHYSICAL CHARACTERISTICS.

The men are rather active and sinewy than strong and muscular. They are well-formed and broad in the chest, though generally rather slender in the limbs.

Mr. Knight, of Western Australia, in his little book on that colony, says—
"The limbs of a well-formed Australian man exhibit a nice symmetry and a fine muscular development. His agility and flexibility of body when running or otherwise actively engaged are advantageously displayed; his posture when throwing a spear is extremely graceful; and his gait and bearing when walking are even dignified."

The annexed engravings (Figs. 248 and 249) of a King George's Sound native, with his old wife and child, are from drawings by the late Deputy Assistant Commissary-General Neill.

FIG. 249.

They are very characteristic and true to the life.

The natives appear to have just risen from the camp-fire, being equipped for a day's foraging excursion within their own territory, for the man has but one spear. They wear the usual cloak (*boka*) made with three or four skins of the female kangaroo, the furry side being next to the body, while the outside of the boka, as well as the faces and bodies of the wearers, are anointed with *wilghee*. The man is ornamented with a bunch of emu feathers on each arm, and feathers of the black cockatoo on his head, which is bound round with string (*nulban*) made of opossum (*koomal*) fur. The barbed spear (*kidyi*) is fixed in the throwing-board (*miro*) ready for use.

The woman (*yago*) is evidently the old wife or fag, the relict of some deceased relative. The younger wife is probably more lazy, and will follow by-and-bye.

This old woman carries the indispensable *wanna*, or yam-stick, the pointed end being rounded on one side and flat on the other, and charred to make it hard. With this she hopes to supply the (*koto*) bag at her back with the roots of orchids and other tubers. She will also put into it frogs (*guyé*), opossums (*gumal*), killed by her husband, and anything else she may desire to carry. Her frightfully attenuated limbs remind one of the hardships she has endured, but it is not to be supposed that they illustrate the limbs of the women generally, some of whom have very good arms and legs. The little boy will of course make his mother carry him all day.

Stature is doubtless much influenced by local circumstances. The average height in Western Australia is, I think, equal to, but in Victoria rather below the European standard. In the former colony, some tall men and women used to be seen about Fremantle, the Murray estuary, and King George's Sound. Indeed the tribes frequenting those places included some very fine specimens of the human figure; a sculptor might select some of either sex as models of human beauty. I remember when on an expedition, in 1851, to the north-east of the Toolbrunup (or Stirling) Range, my party was one day joined by a huge native and his little wife. This brawny savage man was about six feet two or three inches in height, and broad in proportion, with enormous limbs, and was covered all over with hair. His wife, who was carrying a child at her back, did not appear to be more than thirteen or fourteen years old. Then, among the tall women, the old residents of Fremantle will remember one remarkably tall fine old woman, who used occasionally to visit the town from Pinjarra. The limbs of some of these women were as well developed as in the European type, the calves of the legs being as large. This is not, however, generally the case in most parts of Australia. The lower extremities are often very attenuated in those tribes where food is scarce and not easily obtained; yet, with this apparent defect, there is much greater pliability of muscle than in other races.

Dwarfs or cripples are never seen among the natives.

The skin is as soft as the finest velvet. This is probably caused to some extent by the use of *wilyhee*—an unguent composed of red-ochre and grease—with which they anoint themselves. A supply of *wilyhee* is generally carried by the women in their bags for the use of the party when they encamp in the evening. They then rub it over their faces and often over the whole body as they sit round their fires. Once, when travelling with a native guide, he saw that I was much inconvenienced by the great heat and the clouds of mosquitos and flies, and said—"What for white fellow all same fool? use um soap too much, instead of *wilyhee*."

In the warmer parts of Asia travellers carry oil with them, not only for food, but also to anoint their limbs in the evening, which have been scorched during the day by the sun and blistered by the winds. The ancient Hebrews sometimes anointed the whole body, though generally only the head and feet; and Niebuhr states that in Yemen the anointing of the body is believed to strengthen and protect it from the heat of the sun, by which the inhabitants of that province are so liable to suffer.

The skull of a native is thick and strong; the frontal process consists of compact bone of great thickness overhanging and protecting the eyes. The cranium often exhibits deficiencies in those organs which are regarded as indicative of the moral qualities.

My friend the late Dr. Henry Landor, in one of a series of letters to the Perth *Inquirer*, dated June 1842, writes as follows:—

"Whilst describing the form of the Australian skull, I shall point out the difference between it and those of some other races without giving a description of skulls in general, which would unnecessarily lengthen my letter.

"Of all the peculiarities in the form of the bony fabric, those of the skull are the most striking and distinguishing. It is in the head that we find the varieties most strongly characteristic of the different races. The characters of the countenance, and the shape of the features, depend chiefly on the conformation of the bones of the head. The Australian skull belongs to that variety called the prognathous, or narrow, elongated variety; yet it is not so striking an example of this variety as the negro skull. If the skull be held in the hand so that the observer looks upon the vertex, the first point he remarks is the extreme narrowness of the frontal bone, and a slight bulging where the parietal and occipital bones unite. He also sees distinctly through the zygomatic arches on both sides, which in the European skull is impossible, as the lateral portions of the frontal bone are more developed. The summit of the head rises in a longitudinal ridge in the direction of the sagittal suture, so that from the sagittal suture to that portion of the cranium where the diameter is greatest the head slopes like the roof of a house. The forehead is generally flat; the upper jaw rather prominent; the frontal sinuses large; the occipital bone is flat, and there is a remarkable receding of the bone from the posterior insertion of the occipito-frontalis muscle to the foramen-magnum.

"It is a peculiar character of the Australian skull to have a very singular depression at the junction of the nasal bones with the nasal processes of the frontal bone. This may be seen in an engraving in Dr. Pritchard's work. I have before described the teeth. I also mentioned in my last letter the remarkable junction of the temporal and parietal bones at the coronal suture, and consequently the complete separation of the sphenoid from the parietal, which in European skulls meet for the space of nearly half an inch. Professor Owen has observed this conformation in six out of seven skulls of young chimpanzees, and Professor Mayo has also noticed it in the skulls he has examined. But although this is a peculiarity found in this race alone, it is not constant. I have a skull in which the sphenoid touches the parietal on one side, whilst on the other they are separated a sixth of an inch; and in the engraving before referred to the two bones are slightly separated, but by no means to the extent that they are in European skulls. The supra and infra orbital foramina are very large, and the orbits are broad, with the orbital ridge sharp and prominent. All the foramina for the transmission of the sensiferous nerves are large—the auditory particularly so; while the foramen, through which the carotid artery enters the skull, is small. The mastoid processes are large, which might be expected, as their hearing is acute. The styloid process is small; in monkeys it is wanting. The position of the foramen-magnum, as in all savage tribes, is more behind the middle transverse diameter than in Europeans, but this arises in a great measure, though not entirely, from the prominence of the alveolar processes of the upper-jaw. Owing to constant exposure to all seasons, the skulls of savages are of greater density and weigh heavier than those of Europeans:—

		Avoirdupois.	
		lbs.	oz.
Skull of a	Greek	1	11½
„	Negro	2	0
„	Mulatto	2	10
„	Chinese	1	7½
„	Gipsy	2	0
„	Australian	1	12½

" Upon an examination of the foregoing points of diversity, it is unquestionable that the Australian skull is inferior in development to the European, and the capacity of the cranium much less."

The doctor proceeds to say:—" Their morality cannot be at a lower ebb than it is at present. The females are, many, if not most of them, prostitutes from childhood, and the men not only connive at, but openly offer their wives for the worst of purposes. It is lamentable that the iniquitous example set to the Aboriginal inhabitants has, in all countries occupied by the English, been attended with the like evil results—the retardation of Christianity, and the introduction of European vices and fatal diseases (some of the latter have not yet arrived in this colony, but they assuredly will come whenever immigration is extensive). It needs only to refer to our own experience, and to the Report of the Select Committee on Aborigines published in 1837, to prove all this. There, three able Missionaries are asked, 'Is it your opinion that Europeans coming into contact with native inhabitants of our settlements tends to deteriorate the morals of the natives, to introduce European vices, to spread amongst them new and dangerous diseases, to the seduction of native females, to prevent the spread of Christianity, and that the effect of European intercourse has been upon the whole a calamity on the heathen nations?' Mr. Ellis, Mr. Beacham, Mr. Coates: 'Yes, yes, yes.' 'As far as you know, in instances of contention between Europeans and natives, has it generally been found that Europeans were in fault?' Mr. Coates, Mr. Beacham: 'Yes, yes.' Mr. Ellis: 'I have not met with an instance in which, when investigated, it has not been found that the aggression was on the part of Europeans.'"

I have now before me the skulls of five Australian Aborigines, one New Zealander, an Englishman, a Chinaman, a Negro, and a North American Indian. They are all fully-developed specimens. No. 1, from South Australia, is a very large and heavy skull, of the lowest Australian type of any that I ever examined. It nearly accords with Dr. Landor's description. No. 2 is in every respect a better head. Nos. 3 and 4 were taken out of a mirnyoug near Fiery Creek in Victoria; they are very like each other in all the parts referred to by Dr. Landor, but are not long or narrow, nor is there the bulging where the parietal and occipital bones meet, as there is in the American skull. If held in the manner described, the observer cannot see through the zygomatic arches, although he can plainly do so in No. 1. The summit of the head does not rise as stated; the forehead and occipital bone are not flat. The supra and infra orbital and the auditory foramina are very large in both specimens. The point of the mastoid process from the edge of the auditory foramen is under half an inch in these skulls, while in No. 1 and the Negro skull it exceeds an inch. The styloid processes are well developed. I submit, therefore, that Dr. Landor's conclusion that the Australian skull is unquestionably inferior in development to the European has been arrived at on insufficient data. His residence in Western Australia was brief. Bad heads in the European type are not uncommon, but cannot be accepted as fair examples of the race.

"The present state of degradation and immorality of the natives is beyond a question; that it is also owing in a great measure to evil example is not to be denied. It is also undeniable that no effort of Government could have prevented this result. More has undoubtedly been done, and is doing, in this colony than in any other, to improve and protect them, but there is also much remaining to be done. Strenuous are the efforts now making to teach them the blessings of the Gospel; and it would be well to provide them with the means of honestly maintaining themselves by teaching them some handicraft, or by planting the castor-oil tree, which will flourish in any situation; they might pick the seeds preparatory to pressing, and the oil might eventually become an article of export to any extent. Silk might also find them employment.

"Although their conformation precludes them from arriving at great attainments, individuals are to be met with possessing well-made heads, and perhaps with talents superior to many white men—and cultivation will undoubtedly in a few generations effectually improve them. Experience and research have shown that inferior mental powers accompany inferior development, and that gradual cultivation of the mind improves the development. In the examination of the skulls found in the barrows and burial-places of the Ancient British there is a striking departure from the Grecian model; the amplitude of the anterior parts of the cranium is very much less, giving a comparatively small space for the anterior lobes of the brain. In this particular the ancient inhabitants of Britain appear to have differed very considerably from the present. The latter, either as the result of many ages of greater intellectual cultivation, or from some other cause, have much more capacious brain-cases than their forefathers.

"It may be urged that I have drawn conclusions from too few facts, and too limited observation. I admit that the observations are more limited than I could have wished; but if facts as well authenticated be opposed to these, and observations more extensive be made, I shall not hesitate to alter my opinions."

Mr. Buckle, in his *History of Civilization* (London, 1867), says:—" It may be that, owing to some physical causes still unknown, the average capacity of the brain is, if we compare long periods of time, becoming gradually greater; and that therefore the mind, which acts through the brain, is, even independently of education, increasing in aptitude and in the general competence of its views. Such, however, is still our ignorance of physical laws, and so completely are we in the dark as to the circumstances which regulate the hereditary transmission of character, temperament, and other personal peculiarities, that we must consider this alleged progress as a very doubtful point; and in the present state of our knowledge we cannot safely assume that there has been any permanent improvement in the moral or intellectual faculties of man; nor have we any decisive ground for saying that these faculties are likely to be greater in an infant born in the most civilized part of Europe than in one born in the wildest region of a barbarous country. Whatever, therefore, the moral and intellectual progress of men may be, it resolves itself, not into a progress of natural capacity, but into a progress of opportunity; that is, an improvement in the circumstances under which that capacity, after birth, comes into play. The progress is one not of internal power, but of external advantage. The child born in a civilized land is not likely, as such, to be superior to one born among barbarians."

The facial angle approaches closely to the Caucasian type, and is sometimes identical with it. The phreno-metrical angle in skull No. 1 measures 40 degrees from a horizontal line, taking the opening of the ear as the centre. In No. 3 it is 29 degrees; in No. 4, 30 degrees; in my own head it is 25 degrees. It may, however, be remarked that the physical endowments of a tribe cannot be fairly estimated by these angles, which do not measure the quantity of the brain.

I have examined many skulls of the Aborigines, and have observed much diversity of shape. A few years ago I excavated portions of a number of skulls of a tribe from the cliff overhanging the sea on the east of the Gellibrand River in Victoria. I have also seen sections of skulls sawn asunder, and my humble opinion is that a correct idea cannot be formed by the inspection of only a few skulls, such, for instance, as were examined by Mr. H. Landor, or probably were seen by Sir Charles Lyell in the Hunterian Museum.*

The hair is usually black and straight, wavy or curly; but, as in the case of *Wengal*, a native boy whom I educated, it is sometimes brown. It is thick and rather coarse, and being matted together with *wilghee*, serves the purpose of an artificial covering,

At Swan River, and on the east of the Darling Range, the men let their hair grow long, while the women cut theirs. A woman lays her head on the lap of another, who saws the hair off with small splinters of quartz. The practice of wearing the hair long is not peculiar to these men. The men of the better sort of people among the Chinese let theirs grow long, and it seems

---

* *See* the profiles opposite page 248.

to grow much longer than that of the Australian Aboriginal men, who sometimes tie their hair into a tuft on the top of the head, instead of letting it hang down in a long queue, for which indeed I have never seen it long enough. The Hebrews in the time of David considered it a glory to have their hair long and abundant, though in later times it was "a shame" for men to wear it long.

The usual color of the skin is a chocolate-brown. *Wengal*, who lived with me for six and a half years, was of this color; his skin was beautifully soft, and so transparent that a blush could be plainly seen on his face.

I measured an active fellow named *Kibra*, for the purpose of comparing the length of his leg from the sole of his foot to the top of his knee-cap with my own. My proportions are a fair average for an Englishman. I found my total height to be sixty-seven and a half inches, and to the top of the knee-cap twenty and a quarter inches, and that of *Kibra* sixty-nine and a half inches and twenty-four and a half inches, showing a greater length of the tibia in proportion to his height, as compared with my own, of about four inches.

The flexibility and strength of the toes of a native are remarkable. He can seize anything with his toes almost as well as with his fingers. When he ascends a tree, it is his great toe placed in the notch he has cut that supports his weight. I have often been amused at seeing native lads riding wild young horses with only the great toe in the stirrup.

They have an active grasping power in the feet and toes, which gives them so firm a tread, or so determined a stand, that they seem to lay hold of or grasp the ground in a manner inconceivable to those the power of whose feet is cramped by the habitual use of shoes or sandals.

As an instance of the wonderful adaptation of the natives to their mode of life, I may mention that during parturition the women stand against a tree or stump, while another woman assists in the delivery. When this takes place during a journey, the mother travels on as soon as the event is over, having first rubbed the infant over with sand.

The children are not generally weaned until they are three or four years old, but the girls always sooner than the boys—just as in Persia and other Asiatic countries, where the male children are often kept to the breast till three years old, but the girls not so long. The children are not carried in the arms, but when very young in a bag at the back, and afterwards sitting astride on the mother's shoulder.

Although no children are now born to the few poor wretches who remain to wander about the goldfields of Victoria, yet they are on the increase at some of the Aboriginal stations. Several pure Aborigines have recently been born at the Moravian Station near Lake Hindmarsh.

The natives may be said to be hardy in some respects, but delicate in others; as, for instance, the irregularity and uncertainty of their diet would be fatal to a white man. They often remain at their huts in a listless state for days and nights together, when suddenly some of them will undertake a long and fatiguing journey, travelling night and day, or other violent exercise, as the corobboree.

hunting, &c. Again, after enduring the scorching heat of the sun during the day, they will often lie on wet ground, exposed to the bitter cold of the night, quite uncovered. They will also recover from injuries, such as spear wounds through the body, which would certainly be fatal to any person who had been in the habit of living in a house. Yet, with all this apparent hardiness, we see them fade away before the white man; change their mode of life, put them to live in houses, and they inevitably perish.

Agility and Skill.

Some of the men are great runners. The apparent ease with which they get over the ground is astonishing. At one time, when I was encamped in the Darling Range, a man used to run five miles to a station and the same distance back every morning before breakfast for a bottle of milk, and was well satisfied with a pannikin of flour and a cup of tea by way of payment. So great is the tendency to resist aggression, that the skin of the soles of the feet of these men becomes a quarter of an inch thick.

The muscles of the body and limbs follow the eye with a wonderful rapidity, and the men will execute any attempted feat with almost unerring precision.

I may refer to the eleven Victorian Aboriginal cricketers, who, a few years ago, with great credit, met not only some of the best colonial clubs, but when in England proved that some of them, at least, were almost unrivalled in some parts of the game. *Mullagh*, if I remember rightly, was acknowledged to be one of the best of batsmen.

When we consider from what a very small number of men these indigenous sons of the soil were chosen, what little and desultory practice they had, and what a favorable opinion they evoked both here and in England, I think some of the prejudice which so generally prevails against the Australian Aborigines will in some measure be removed; and I may here remark that this prejudice is seldom if ever found to exist among those old colonists who had the opportunity of observing the natives when the white people first came to their country.

Wherever whaling stations have been established, the natives have proved themselves to be very valuable assistants. They make the best of "look-out" men. I have known a native sit day after day on a promontory in the keen wind or burning sun looking out to sea for a whale. They enter heartily into the sport, and make excellent "pull-away hands" in the whale-boats.

I knew at least one boat at King George's Sound in which the headsman and all the crew were Aborigines. In this dangerous employment they evinced great enthusiasm and considerable physical power and endurance. Of course their energies were stimulated by the prospect of the feast they would have if successful; but it must be confessed that the manner in which they gorged themselves when a whale was captured was very disgusting.

I have sometimes been astonished at the strength of the women in carrying burdens and lifting weights. I remember on one of my excursions we stopped to encamp late one evening at a place where firewood was scarce. Two of the soldiers of my party, who went in search of some, came to a large log, which I saw them try to lift—one at each end—but, considering it too heavy, they left it to go further. Shortly afterwards, a party of natives coming up, the soldiers sent some of them for wood, and I saw a woman go and take up the same log and carry it on her shoulders to our camp.

When travelling, the women often carry all the possessions of the tribe, sometimes including the spare weapons of the men, together with those children who are too young or too lazy to walk.

I have seen, on the Melbourne Cricket Ground, a native stand for probably half an hour dodging cricket-balls, which were thrown at him with great force by skilled bowlers, from a distance of only about ten or fifteen yards. Had some of the balls struck him in certain parts of the body, they might have killed him. Yet he depended, with the utmost self-possession, on the quickness of his eye and his agility, aided only by a narrow wooden shield.

We have seen the daring and clever acrobats in Chiarini's circus turn summersaults over seven or eight horses; but, a few years ago, I saw a New South Wales Aborigine spring from a low board, heels-over-head, over eleven horses, and it was stated that he sometimes jumped in a similar manner over fourteen. I saw the same man leap from the ground, and in going over he dipped his head, unaided by his hands, into a hat placed in an inverted position on the top of the head of another man sitting upright on horseback—both man and horse being of the average size. The native landed on the other side of the horse with the hat fairly on his head. The prodigious height of the leap, and the precision with which it was taken so as to enable him to dip his head into the hat, exceeded any feat of the kind I have ever beheld.*

All the men in Western Australia appear to be, in their wild state, good climbers. They climb the tallest and largest trees, even when straight, by cutting small notches, in which they insert the great toe, helping themselves up by leaning with the hand on the pointed handle of the hammer or *kadjo*, which they strike into the soft bark like a spike.

Sir George Grey notices the skill displayed by the Aborigines in well-sinking in Western Australia. Mr. Eyre also met with similar constructions in his journey, in 1841, from Port Lincoln to King George's Sound. He says— "These singular wells, although sunk through loose sand to a depth of fourteen or fifteen feet, were only about two feet in diameter at the bore, quite circular, carried straight down, and the work beautifully executed."

Similar wells may be seen in the sandy desert in the north-western portion of Victoria and in South Australia. I have also seen both men and women sinking in loose sandy soil for an edible root called *warran*, one of the dioscoreæ,

---

* Some years ago, on the Upper Murray, on a public holiday, when the population was assembled to witness the athletic games, a number of white men were engaged throwing a cricket-ball for a prize; the greatest distance that any one of them could deliver it was ninety-six yards; when a little native man standing by was called upon to compete—to the astonishment of all, he threw the ball one hundred and nineteen yards.

which generally grows about the thickness of a man's thumb, and to the depth of four to six or eight feet. It has a delicate sweetish flavour when roasted in hot ashes, something like that of a chestnut, and is much sought after. It is dangerous to travel on horseback through the country where it grows, on account of the frequency and depth of the holes, which are not more than about eighteen or twenty inches in diameter. I have sometimes been made aware of their proximity by seeing small quantities of sand jumping up before me, and, on going to see the cause, have suddenly come on a small hole among the scrub, so small that I could scarcely believe a human being could be at the bottom of it in a stooping position, with the knees on each side of the head. In this position the native dexterously throws the sand by a sudden jerk of the hand

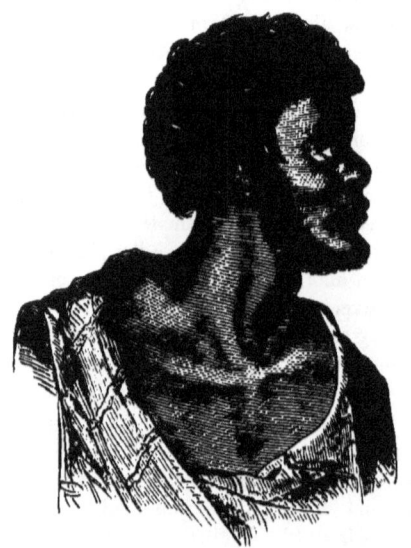

KERTAMAROO (King John).
FIG. 250.

backwards, under the arm and up behind the shoulder. The only bald natives I ever saw are the *warran* diggers, who are said to wear the hair off the head by pressing it so frequently against the sides of these holes.

Besides sinking wells, they have other means of obtaining water in the deserts, where none is to be found on the surface of the ground. In the Mallee scrubs they find water in the roots of the narrow-leafed Mallee, but only in some of the larger trees, and it requires an expert to know which trees contain it. They trace a root that runs near the surface of the ground as far as possible, and then tear it up and let the water trickle out of it. I have never seen this species of eucalyptus in Western Australia; but there they obtain water—sometimes as much as a gallon at a time—from fissures in the wood of the paper-bark tree, a large species of *melaleuca;* they make a hole through the thick bark, and the water gushes out; they then plug the hole up, and find a fresh supply next time they pass that way.

The powers and endurance as divers and swimmers of those Aborigines who inhabit the borders of rivers and the sea-coast are worthy of note. I have timed a man diving in the Goulburn River, and found he could remain under water from one minute fifty seconds to two minutes; but some of them could probably continue longer than this. The greater number of vessels engaged in pearl-fishing off the coast of Western Australia prefer employing the natives as divers to undertaking a voyage for Malays.

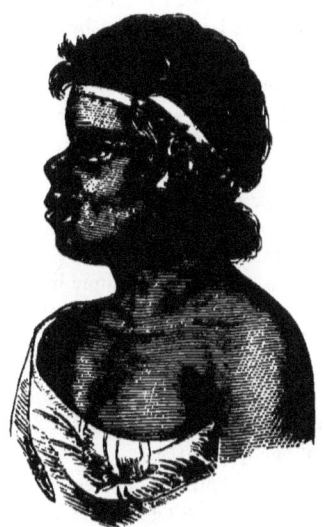

MOCATA (King John's wife).

FIG. 251.

I have often been surprised at the flexibility of the muscles even of the old people. They are in the habit of sitting round their fires with their feet and legs doubled under them for hours together, in a manner that would be most painful to a European, even if he could do it at all. They sometimes sit on their feet.

Annexed are a few profiles of some King George's Sound Aborigines, which I took in 1846. They are good likenesses. No. 7 is *Wylie,* the lad who so faithfully accompanied Mr. Eyre in his perilous journey round the coast, in 1841, from Port Lincoln to King George's Sound, and to whom Mr. Eyre afterwards sent, from England, as an acknowledgment of his fidelity and services, a handsome double-barrelled gun. No. 8 is his wife, whose hair stood erect from her forehead. No. 1 was nearly six feet high. His nose did not project beyond the upper lip. The poor fellow soon after died in a consumption. Nos. 2 to 6, 9 and 10, were prisoners who were sent to Perth to be tried for spearing cattle and sheep and stealing rice and sugar.

ACTIVITY, INGENUITY, PERSEVERANCE, CUSTOMS, WEAPONS, ETC.

When we consider that indolence is the natural consequence of the condition of these people, we shall not be surprised at finding them listless and unwilling to perform any act which involves the least more exertion than is necessary for their immediate purpose. Thus, a native never thinks of stooping to pick up anything from the ground when he can with less trouble raise it to his hand with his toes. But when roused to exertion by the chase, the corobboree, or war, he is not like the same being, but displays great activity, considerable powers of endurance, and much skill in effecting his purpose.

His patience and skill in emu stalking,* in spearing ducks, kangaroos, and native turkeys are sometimes quite extraordinary. As he walks through the bush, his step is light, elastic, and noiseless; every track on the earth catches his keen eye; a leaf or fragment of a stick turned, or a blade of grass recently bent by the tread of one of the lower animals, instantly arrests his attention; in fact, nothing escapes his quick and powerful sight on the ground, in the trees, or in the distance, which may supply him with a meal or warn him of danger. If a decayed grass-tree be near his path (and Western Australia abounds with them), he knocks it down with his foot and to pieces with his *kadjo*, and is sure to find a supply of the larvæ of a species of cerambyx called *bardi*. It has a delicate aromatic flavour, and affords him a delicious treat. They are about an inch long, and sometimes fifty or a hundred are found boring their way through one grass-tree.

A little examination of the trunk of a tree which may be nearly covered with the scratches of opossums ascending and descending is sufficient to inform him whether one went up the night before without coming down again or not. If it is up the tree, he ascends, and seldom fails in obtaining it, even though he may have to cut off a limb a foot thick with no better instrument than his stone hammer.

They have a variety of methods of catching fish. At King George's Sound I have seen them take a quantity of whiting in the following manner:—Two or three women watch the shoal from the beach, keeping opposite to it, while twenty or thirty men and women take boughs and form a semicircle out in the shallow bay as far as they can go without swimming, and then, closing gradually in, they hedge the fish up in a small space close to the shore, while a few others go in and throw them out with their hands. By this primitive method, skilfully executed, I have seen a large quantity of fish caught. At Swan River, I have watched them drive a shoal of large schnappers into water

---

* *See* Fig. 253, from a native drawing.

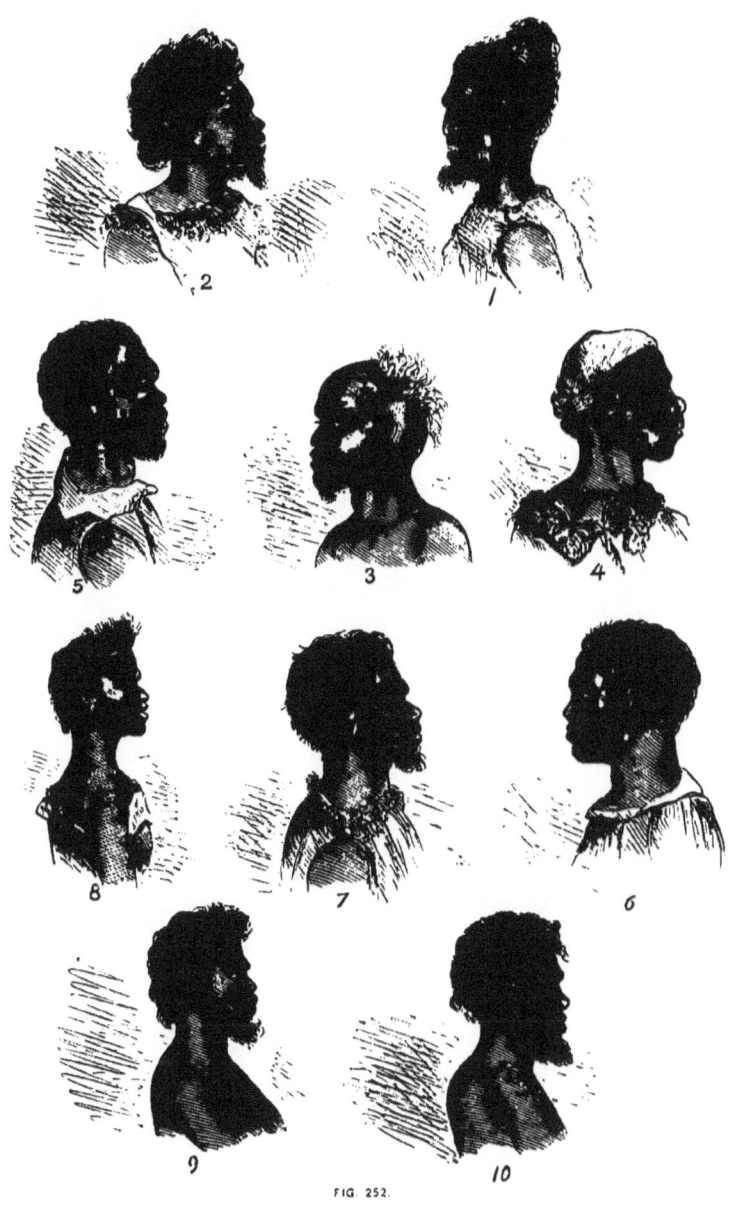

FIG. 252.

NATIVES OF KING GEORGE'S SOUND.

too shallow for them to swim in, and spear and catch a great number of fish weighing from ten to fifteen pounds each.

On the Murray River they use boats made of a single sheet of bark, and on the north-west coast of Western Australia they make rough log canoes for fishing. In South Australia I have seen them take out to sea a beautifully-made net, five or six feet wide and fifty or sixty feet long, weighted at one edge so that, while treading the water and holding it out at full length, parallel with the shore, it is in a vertical position six feet deep. Others—men and women—would then swim out for a quarter of a mile or more, and, closing in, drive the fish against the net and then spear them.

The Murray River natives use spears for fishing made of the reed which grows in vast beds from Swan Hill downwards for thirty miles, and also at Lake Moira above the confluence of the Goulburn River. These spears are pointed with bones of the emu, or such substitute as they may be able to procure. They also use heavy jagged spears made of miall or other very hard wood for fishing.

Much ingenuity is displayed in the manufacture of nets by the Coast tribes and the natives of the Murray River, from string which, where bulrushes grow, is made from the fibrous root of that plant, called on the Murray *Balyan*. They peel off the outer rind of the root, and lay it for a short time in the ashes; they then twist and loosen the fibre, and by chewing obtain a quantity of gluten, somewhat resembling wheaten flour, which affords a ready and wholesome food at all times to the tribes which inhabit the vast morasses in which the reeds and bulrushes abound. They chew the root until nothing is left but a small ball of fibre, which somewhat resembles hemp. These balls are then drawn out, and rubbed with the palm of the hand on the bare thigh of the operator, while a small wooden spindle twirled with the fingers of the other hand twists and receives the string. Among the few specimens of art manufactured by these primitive people none are more like our own than the nets of South Australia and Victoria.

Fishing with nets seems to have been a very ancient practice in different nations. Suetonius states that Nero was accustomed to fish with a net of gold and purple. Plutarch mentions corks and leaden weights as an addition which nets had received. Homer supposes that nets were not used by the ancient Egyptians. The Egyptians did, however, use weirs and toils in their fisheries. The use of fish-spears appears very clearly in the paintings of ancient Egypt.

The modes of preparing skins, and the manufacture of cloaks, bags, mats, and the various weapons and implements of the Australian natives, have been so often described that I need say but little more about them, my observations being merely of a desultory and fragmentary character.

The *kadjo* or stone hammer of Western Australia differs from any other on this continent. That of Victoria consists of *one* stone *rubbed* to an edge at one end, and resembles those of North Australia, as described by Sir Charles Lyell,*

---

* *Antiquity of Man*, p. 113.

while the *kadjo* is formed of *two chipped* stones stuck on the end of a stick of the common wattle-tree about twelve inches long and three-quarters of an inch thick. The stones are chipped, the one to an edge for cutting, the other is left blunt for hammering. They are fragments of whinstone, which occurs in veins running north-east and south-west through the granite of the Darling Range, and are *stuck* on each side of the stick with the resinous gum of the tough-topped grass-tree, or *xanthorrhœa*. The strength of this gum is extraordinary, for I have seen a native use his *kadjo* to cut large limbs off gum-trees without at all loosening the stones.

Flints and other hard stones formed the tools and cutting instruments of almost all nations before the art of working iron was discovered. They are still in use among savages, and are found buried in various parts of Europe and Asia, showing the universality of their use where the people were ignorant of the use of metals.

The Western Australians use small splinters of quartz for making the long deep cuts which may be seen on almost every native—both men and women—across the breast and arms.* With a similar fragment stuck to the end of a stick they dress and cut their kangaroo skins in preparing them for use as cloaks. They also stick thin splinters of quartz, broken with their teeth, in a row like teeth to the side of a short stick, to serve as a saw.

The natives use the stem of the grass-tree to produce fire by friction. This is done by rapidly twirling between the hands one piece of the stick in a little hole bitten out of another piece placed on the ground, and retained in its position by the feet, the operation being assisted by a little dry grass or the dry fuzzy material of the withered seed-head of the grass-tree laid in the hole, and which soon smokes and ignites. In cold weather, native men and women may be seen carrying† pieces of lighted *Banksia* bark, which burns like touch-wood, under their cloaks, and with which, and a few withered leaves and dry sticks, a fire may soon be kindled.

It is a remarkable ethnological fact that a people should be found now to exist who have no means of heating water or of cooking liquid food, or without any culinary utensil or device of any sort; yet such was the condition of the Aborigines of Western Australia when we came among them. Their only mode of cooking was to put their food into the hot ashes, sometimes wrapping small fish and frogs in paper-tree bark. In some other parts of Australia they plaster large birds, such as the black swan, with a thick coating of mud, and then, having made a suitable hollow in the middle of the ashes of a large fire, they place the mud pie into it, and cover it well over with hot embers and ashes, keeping up a good fire until the bird is cooked; when they take it out, the feathers come away with the hard crust, leaving it clean and juicy. This practice does not very much differ from that of the Arabs and some other Asiatic people, who not unfrequently at their entertainments serve up a lamb or kid that has been baked whole in a hole

---

* *See* Exodus iv., 25.
† Abraham carried fire when he was going to offer up Isaac.

in the ground, which, after being heated and having received the carcass, is covered over with stones.

The natives use several kinds of spears for different purposes. In Western Australia the men never moved about without their spears, which consisted, when fully equipped, of eight, of which five were barbed and three serrated near the point with splinters of quartz stuck on with grass-tree gum. They do not throw with precision more than twenty or thirty yards; but when not flurried, their aim is very accurate, and the spears are delivered with surprising rapidity.

Spears are among the most ancient and universal of offensive weapons, as shields are for defence. A stick sharpened at one end and hardened in the fire was probably the first spear, and it continues to be the principal offensive weapon with the Australian natives.

Shields are unquestionably the oldest and most general defensive armour in the world. They are mentioned in the Bible long before helmets, and are the only defensive armour mentioned in the books of Moses.

Some of the ancients took much delight in ornamenting their shields with all sorts of figures—birds, beasts, and the inanimate works of Nature. In like manner, the natives of Western Australia—at least some tribes north from Perth—adorn their narrow shields which are made of the soft wood of the *Nuytsia florabunda*. They are only about two and a half feet long by four inches wide in the middle, and taper to a point at each end. They are convex, with a handle inside, cut out of the one piece of wood, and are almost as light as cork, and generally elaborately carved. Many of the tribes, however, use no shield at all.

The boomerang or *kylie* of Western Australia may possibly indicate an early communication with some more civilized people, or the enjoyment of a much higher degree of knowledge among themselves before they relapsed into their present state of utter barbarism. There is much variety in the shape of these weapons in different parts of Australia.

The natives use a number of different kinds of ornaments, especially the men,* who paint their bodies all over with various devices in red and white ochre on such important occasions as a corobboree. They wear bunches of emu feathers on the arms, a wild dog's tail round the head just over the brow, and bunches of the beautiful long feathers of the large black cockatoo or of the white cockatoo on the top of the head. The young men wear the small bone of the leg of the kangaroo through the cartilage of the nose as a sign of their having attained the age of puberty.

On some parts of the coast the women make very pretty necklaces, two or three yards long, of small shells, which they string together and wind round their necks, letting them fall in graceful curves over the breast. I have a very handsome necklace of this kind which was made by a Tasmanian native.

The Murray River women make pretty but delicate necklaces with the small bones of the fresh-water lobster. They have several other ornaments, which I need not here refer to.

---

* *See* the cut at page 236.

The huts of the Western Australian natives are quickly and ingeniously constructed, and are admirably adapted to the requirements of a nomadic people in such a climate. In the warmer weather of the more northern parts of the territory they seldom make any huts, and generally go without any clothing whatever.

I have seen two native women construct and complete a well-built and symmetrical hut in half an hour from the time they arrived on the ground and began to collect the materials. The huts on that side of the continent are always made with the grass-tree (*Xanthorrhœa arborea*), except where the paper-bark (a species of *melaleuca*) is occasionally used.

These women, immediately on arriving on the ground with their tribe, set about collecting bundles of dead, and therefore hard, flowering stems, six or seven feet long, of the grass-trees which were growing around; they then skilfully made holes in the ground with their "yam-sticks," to receive these stems. They made the holes about eight inches deep in the sand, enlarging them at the bottom without increasing the size at the surface of the ground, about ten inches apart in a row, in the form of a horseshoe, the heel representing the door-way. They then proceeded to fix the grass-tree sticks in the holes, adjusting them carefully, so as to converge to a common centre at the top. The framework being now ready, they covered it with withered curled grass-tree rushes, which were kept from slipping down by the hard-pointed seed-vessels of the sticks. The next operation was the thatching. Each woman having gathered a bundle of green straight grass-tree rushes, which she held under the left arm, proceeded expertly to throw them with her right hand, handful after handful, at an angle of forty-five degrees, so that when the sharp points stuck among the covering of dead rushes the heels or thick ends of the green rushes bent down by their own weight, thereby causing them to remain in their places. The thatching was begun at the ground, and continued up to the top, and when a second coating had been given, the hut was rain-proof and complete. The next day the heat of the sun caused the thatch to settle down and look smooth; it then received a third coating. This thatch would remain compact and good, if not disturbed, for many months, requiring only the top to be renovated. The natives of Western Australia never, however, return to a hut once vacated.

The Swan River colonists often use grass-tree rushes to thatch cottages and barns; but I am sure no white man could thatch with them as well as an old native woman. The Europeans *tie* them; but as the rushes dry, they slip down; whereas in the native method there is a bend or key which prevents them from slipping.

The large stone house erected in 1848 by the Spanish Missionaries, at the Moore River, took them many weeks to thatch with grass-tree rushes, which *would* fall off nearly as fast as they tied them on.

The natives inhabiting the lacustrine district to the north of the Glenelg River in Victoria, and some of the tribes in North Australia, used to construct substantial huts, and plaster them on the outside; but they only used them periodically.

The following instance of ingenuity in a native guide occurs to me. We had been travelling on the Darling Range for many hours on a very hot day, without water, when he suddenly stopped, and squeezing his head between two stems growing out of the hollow stump of a jarrah tree, saw water about four feet down at the bottom. The question arose how it was to be got at, the hole at top, between the stems, being very small. I confess I could not have obtained any of that water; but the blackfellow, without a moment's hesitation, made a sort of besom with some heath which he tied to the end of a long stick, and having scooped a basin in the ground, adroitly filled it by repeatedly and rapidly drawing up the water with the besom. He covered the basin with grass-tree rushes, which prevented the water from becoming muddy as it trickled out of the besom. All this he did without uttering a word until it was finished, when he invited me to drink first.

As has been shown in the case of the cricketers, a native's hand and eye work together with marvellous rapidity and effect, and his powers of imitation are very great. I once saw a stockman put his whip into the hands of a native who had never before handled one. The handle of the whip was fourteen inches long, and the lash fourteen feet, of cow-hide, about one and a half inches through in the thickest part of the plait. The stockman had been showing his dexterity in cracking this formidable weapon, and handed it to the blackfellow, who, after two or three attempts, performed the difficult feat nearly as well as the Englishman.

Endurance under Suffering.

One day the clothes of the boy *Wengal*, whom I have before mentioned, caught fire when he was alone in a room. Instead of calling for assistance, he shut the door and silently tried to extinguish the flames. His back, hands, and arms were so burnt that the hospital surgeon asserted that he believed a European so injured could not have survived; he, however, recovered rapidly.

In 1852, I saw a tribe at the Moore River who were nearly all blind. The warm climate and their uncleanly habits caused flies to swarm about these poor wretches all day long. They seemed to be eating their eyes out of the sockets almost uncared for. I was much surprised at beholding so many blind men, women, and children, apparently so contented, and the younger ones even cheerful. The old women always whine when they are suffering; but in this instance they seemed to be unusually happy, probably because when I passed their camp they had several kangaroos which had recently been speared by the few men who could see. There was one very large, stout, blind old woman among them; she had a snowy-white beard about half an inch long.

Frequent privations and brutal treatment are too often the lot of the women, who, as a rule, prematurely decay, though I have seen many who appeared to be sixty or seventy years of age.

When on an excursion in the Darling Range on 30th May 1846, I ascertained the age of a native in the following manner. He showed me a grass-tree against which his mother stood when he was born. His father had cut the top off to commemorate the event, after which a shoot grew out of the side of the stem which showed distinct annular rings; these were forty-five in number, which represented no doubt the age of the man.

I have never observed insanity, or hereditary or chronic * complaints among the natives. But when Swan River was first settled, in 1829, several of the old people were marked with small-pox, which had been among them many years before.

The courage and endurance of the natives under privations and physical suffering has often attracted attention. They will endure painful surgical operations with scarcely a murmur. They are too plucky to complain. *Wyenwyen* signifies a coward, and is a term of great reproach. *Bugor* means a brave man.

The following interesting narratives in illustration of the wonderful powers of endurance of bodily pain were related to me by the Rev. Henry N. Wollaston, of Trinity Church, Melbourne, who was formerly an Assistant Colonial Surgeon in Western Australia. I copy from his own writing:—

No. 1. "In the summer of 1852–3, I started on horseback from Albany, King George's Sound, to pay a visit to Mr. George Cheyne at Cape Riche, about seventy miles south-east from the former place, accompanied by a native on foot. We travelled about forty miles the first day, and camped for the night in a clump of tea-tree scrub, called spear-wood, near a water-hole. After cooking and eating our supper, I observed the native, who had said nothing to me on the subject, collect the hot embers of the fire together, and deliberately place his right foot in the glowing mass for a moment, and then suddenly withdraw it, stamping on the ground, and uttering a long-drawn guttural sound of mingled pain and satisfaction. This he repeated several times. On my enquiring the meaning of his strange conduct, he only said—'Me carpenter make-em,'† and then showed me his charred great toe, the nail of which had been torn off by a tea-tree stump in which it had been caught during the journey, and the pain of which he had borne with stoical composure until the evening, when he had an opportunity of cauterizing the wound in the primitive manner above described. He proceeded on his journey the next morning as if nothing had happened, his toe bound up in a piece of the native tea-tree bark."

2. "When residing at Picton, near Bunbury, a native about twenty-five years of age applied to me, as a doctor, to extract the wooden barb of a spear, which, during a fight in the bush some four months previously, had entered his chest, just missing the heart, and penetrated the viscera to a considerable depth. The spear had been cut off, leaving the barb behind, which continued to force its way by muscular action gradually towards the back; and when I examined him

---

* Except in those vitiated by the white people.
† That is "I am mending my foot."

I could feel a hard substance between the ribs below the left blade-bone. I made a deep incision, and with a pair of forceps extracted the barb, which was made, as usual, of hard wood about four inches long and from half an inch to an inch thick. It was very smooth, and partly digested, so to speak, by the maceration to which it had been exposed during its four months' journey through the body. The wound made by the spear had long since healed, leaving only a small cicatrix; and after the operation, which the patient bore without flinching, he appeared to suffer no pain. Indeed, judging from his good state of health, the presence of the foreign matter did not materially annoy him. He was perfectly well in a few days."

3. "When residing at King George's Sound, as Assistant Colonial Surgeon, a native presented himself to me with one leg only, and requested me to supply him with a wooden leg, which some settler had told him he could procure in Albany. He had travelled in this maimed state from Kojenup, about ninety-six miles in the interior, for this purpose. I examined the limb, which had been severed just below the knee, and found that it had been charred by fire, while about two inches of the partially calcined bone protruded through the flesh. I at once removed this with the saw; and, having made as presentable a stump of it as I could, I covered the amputated end of the bone with the surrounding muscle, and kept the patient a few days under my care, to allow the wound to heal, which it did very rapidly, as I have observed is usually the case with the Aborigines of this country. On enquiring, the native told me that in a fight with other blackfellows a spear had struck his leg, and penetrated the bone below the knee. Finding it was serious—and I suppose taught by experience that he could not hope to save his leg, and fearing mortification—he had recourse to the following crude and barbarous operation, which it appears is not uncommon amongst these people in their native state. He, or his companions, made a fire, and dug a hole in the earth only sufficiently large to admit his leg, and deep enough to allow the wounded part to be on a level with the surface of the ground. He, or they, then surrounded the limb with the live coals or charcoal, which was replenished until the leg was literally burnt off. The cauterization thus applied completely checked the hæmorrhage, and he was able in a day or two to hobble down to the Sound with the aid of a long stout stick, although he was more than a week on the road. I got a wooden leg made for him by a clever carpenter in the town, with a suitable cup and straps and padding, and fitted it carefully to the stump; and the patient seemed highly delighted with his new acquisition, and took his departure for his home with apparent ease and comfort. A few days afterwards, however, to my surprise and amusement, another native brought the wooden leg back to me, with a message to the effect that my patient had travelled as far as Kendenup, about fifty miles from Albany, with his new leg, but then got tired of it, as an encumbrance, and sent it back to me, preferring to spend the remainder of his days with but one leg, rather than having two legs, one of which was only a 'make believe,' which had no sense, or motion, or feeling of its own. I saw and heard no more of my friend."

On some of their Mental Characteristics.

Mr. Wake* says that "to speak of intellectual phenomena in the Australian Aborigines is somewhat a misnomer. This race presents, in fact, hardly any of what are usually understood as the phenomena of intellect. Nor could it be otherwise with savages, who—almost without clothing or ornament, with few implements or manufactures, and with very inferior habitations, or means of water locomotion—have no aim in life but the continuance of their existence and the gratification of their passions, with the least possible trouble to themselves. When, therefore, I speak of intellectuality, I refer to that simple activity of mind which is necessary to the performance of the actions required for the maintenance of life, and for the display of those simple phenomena, almost instinctive nevertheless, in their nature, which may be supposed to result from the reflective exercise of the human mind on external objects, as distinguished from the merely instinctive thought of the animal."

It is probable that when Mr. Wake wrote this he had no personal experience of the Australian Aborigines. On the other hand, Mr. Parker, who was for many years Assistant Protector of Aborigines at the Loddon Aboriginal Station, expresses his opinion as follows:—"Let it not for one moment be supposed that there are any intellectual obstacles to the Christianization and civilization of these people. I have always maintained that the obstacles are purely *moral*. It is the utter sensuality of their habits and dispositions that is the main hindrance to be overcome. They are just as capable of receiving instruction, just as capable of mental exercises, as any more favored races. And it is just because their association with the European has, in so many instances, tended to foster and encourage this sensualism, that so little success has been attained in the efforts that have been made to reclaim them."

My own humble opinion is, that the adults, whose habits are confirmed, are beyond the hope of reclamation; but that the children, if taken young enough, are quite as capable of receiving and of profiting by instruction as the children of untaught parents among the white race.

Their perceptive faculties and memory are of a superior order, but they find it difficult to grasp abstract ideas, or to follow out a train of abstruse reasoning.

Mr. Wake's remarks refer to these people *as they are*, in their wild state, rather than to their capacity if taken young enough for mental exertion. The absence of all moral restraint, combined with habitual indolence—which, I suppose, is a characteristic of all savages—seems to be the immediate cause of their mental degradation.

---

* Paper read before the Anthropological Institute "*On the Mental Characteristics of Primitive Man as exemplified by the Australian Aborigines*" on 17th April 1871.

One of the greatest thinkers of our time, who has recently passed from this life, remarks on the supposed differences of race:—"Of all vulgar modes of escaping from the consideration of the effect of social and moral influences on the human mind, the most vulgar is that of attributing the diversities of conduct and character to inherent natural differences."—*Mill's Principles of Political Economy*, vol i., p. 390.

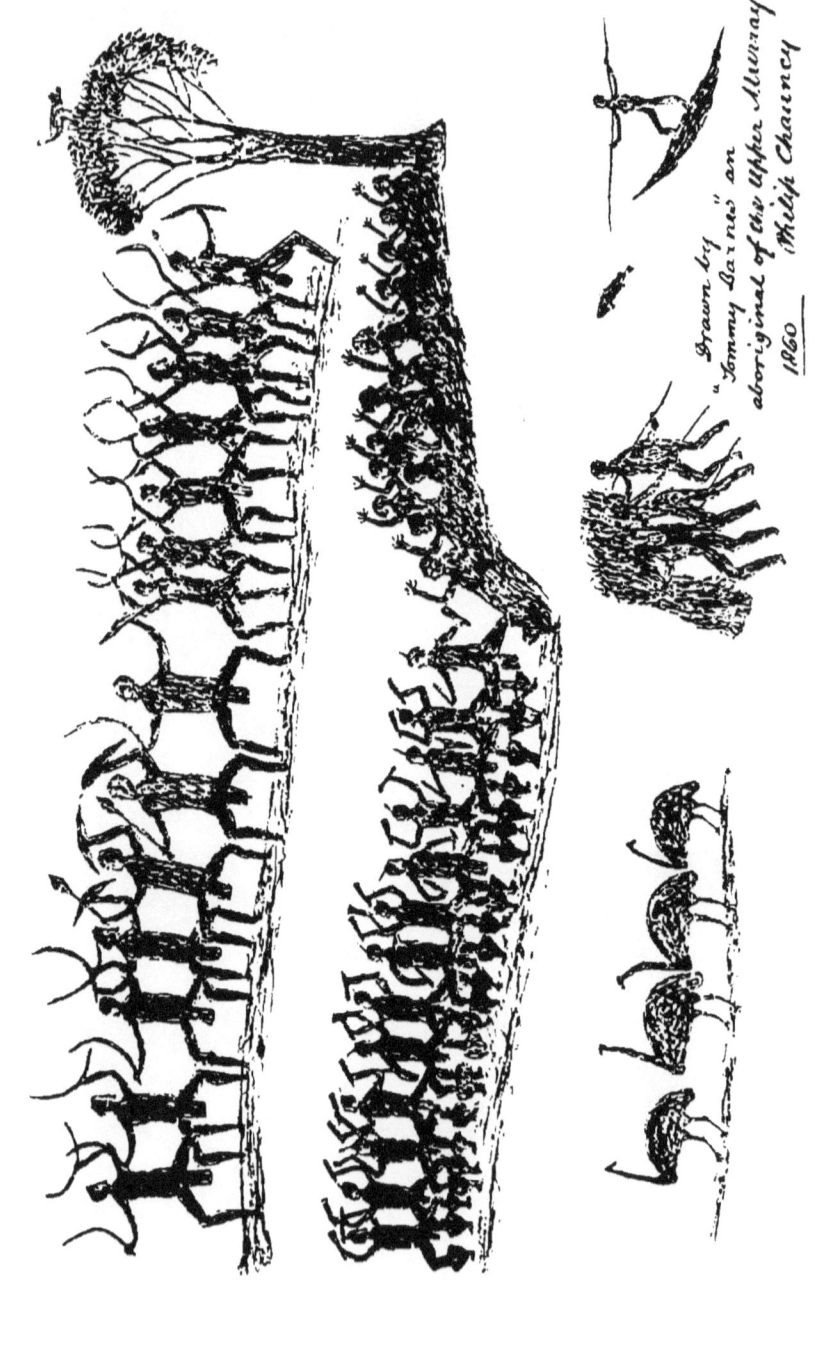

Drawn by "Tommy Barnes" an aboriginal of the Upper Murray
Philip Chauncy
1860

Mr. Oldfield, as quoted by Mr. Wake,* declares that the Aborigines of Australia "cannot distinguish the picture of a man from that of any other object, unless all the lesser parts, such as the head, &c., are much exaggerated." This, as the following anecdote indicates, cannot with truth be said of the generality of the young men and women, although it is quite likely that a stupid old woman, who had never seen a picture before, would not be able, at first sight to recognise the resemblance. And are there not many uneducated people of our own country who would be equally at a loss to know what a picture meant if they had never before seen one?

Soon after the settlement of the York district, the natives came to believe that we divined with paper on which there was any writing or drawing. It originated in this way:—Some natives had speared some of Mr. Bland's pigs, and a man was arrested on suspicion at York, but no proof could be obtained against him, when the officer in charge of the police, Mr. Norcott, son of the late Sir Amos Norcott, drew a sketch on the fly-leaf of a book of this man running after a pig with a spear sticking out of its back, and showed it to the prisoner, who instantly recognised his own likeness, and was so struck with terror that he trembled all over, and admitted the offence at once, at the same time begging Mr. Norcott to put away the *Djenga*, or devil's book.

I have sometimes shown pictures to natives who had never before seen any, and they generally, at once, recognised the objects represented.

Mr. Wake remarks, regarding their own drawings—"They may sometimes exhibit a certain amount of rude vigor, but, as a rule, they may be classed with the productions of children." Yet, placed under similar circumstances, I believe at least as much, and often considerably more, artistic skill is exhibited by them than by the untaught of our own people.

The annexed plates (Figs. 253 and 254) are from drawings with pen and ink by an untaught Aboriginal lad of the Upper Murray, known as "Tommy Barnes."

No. 1 gives a good idea of a war-dance at the top and a corobboree beneath, in which the dancers wear girdles round their bodies, and fillets of emu feathers or of small boughs round their legs, and hold waddies in their hands, which they energetically strike together, keeping time with the dance. The women, fourteen in number, sit together, with their hands uplifted, in the act of beating time on stretched skins, while behind them is a tree with a bird on the top of it. In the same picture the artist indicates the method of emu-stalking and of fish-spearing.

No. 2 also illustrates a variety of subjects: a native man in a canoe catching a turtle; a pair of emus standing by their nest, and a man throwing a spear at one of them; another man throwing his dowak at a large lizard; another in a canoe spearing a fish, which is very well drawn; nine men are engaged in a mimic war-dance for the amusement of a squatter and his wife, who are looking on; they are brandishing boomerangs, clubs, and shields, and one has a pipe in his mouth. A tame emu is standing by, doubtless belonging

---

* Paper read before Anthropological Institute, 17th April 1871.

to the station, which stands in the background. There is much spirit in these drawings; the attitudes of some of the figures, and the faces of some of the women, are very good. If carefully examined, I think we cannot avoid the conclusion that Tommy Barnes is a close observer, and is possessed of some artistic skill, which, if cultivated, would have enabled him to draw well. These sketches were hastily drawn, with no particular object in view, and probably only for his own amusement.

The following (Fig. 255) is a copy of a very spirited sketch of two groups of squatters drawn by a native lad. The attitudes are admirable, and clearly indicate the humourous train of thought passing through the mind of the lad, who must have been a close observer and a good mimic.

FIG. 255.

Many of the young people are capable of delineating objects and of practising the art of design. In an old treatise, dated 1803, the writer, referring to the natives, says:—"They have some taste for sculpture, most of their instruments being carved with rude work effected with pieces of broken shell. On the rocks are frequently to be seen figures of fish, clubs, animals, &c., not contemptibly represented."

On the Murray River, where they used to cover their huts with bark, the young men often amused themselves with carving, or drawing with charcoal, on the inside of the bark, various objects and scenes in illustration of any events which they desired to record, in the same way as I have known a gentleman ornament the walls of his *boudoir* with scene paintings.

Many of the young men have a taste for drawing, and sketch with rapidity; but we must not suppose that a wild blackfellow, when in the humour for drawing, would leave off and rise from his camp-fire to procure more bark or paper merely because he wished to commence a fresh subject. They often record events deemed worthy of note on their throwing-sticks.* I feel convinced that the powers of observation and of delineation in the Australian Aborigines will compare favorably with those of any other people who had no better opportunities for mental culture, or better materials for practising the art. The ancient Romans sometimes used the fine inner bark of such trees as the lime, ash, maple, or elm, as a substance for writing or drawing. It was called *liber*, and this word came permanently to be used for all kinds of books.

The results of the various native schools which have been established in different parts of Australia from time to time will doubtless afford ample illustrations of the general intelligence of the Aboriginal children. It is said "that the native school at Coranderrk, on the Yarra, has gained the highest percentage of passes of any school in the colony of Victoria."

I will now proceed to give some account of a native school which is perhaps not so well known as most of the other establishments for the Aborigines. I refer to that which formerly existed at King George's Sound. It was originated by the excellent and benevolent wife of the late Mr. Henry Camfield, Resident Magistrate at that place, and continued for many years under her care. The following trivial incident was the immediate cause of its origin. In June 1852, when I was residing at the Sound, the natives one day went off on a bush excursion, leaving *Kojonotpat*—a solitary, naked little girl, about three and a half years old—to wander about the settlement at Albany. She came to our gate for breakfast every morning, saying, "Me very hungry," and at length we mentioned the circumstance to Mrs. Camfield, our near neighbour, who took her in, and soon afterwards obtained the consent of her mother to keep her. Her father had been killed a short time before this. In 1858, Mrs. Camfield published a report of her school, from which I extract the following particulars.

There were then eighteen children—thirteen girls and five boys—in the establishment; the six older girls being from ten to sixteen years of age. Every attention was paid to their comfort and cleanliness. The bigger girls were taught all useful domestic works—they washed, ironed, and mangled all the clothes of the institution; baked, cooked and scrubbed, and made butter. The school routine did not extend beyond reading and writing and a little arithmetic. They read well, marking the stops, and could spell very correctly. In writing from dictation they seldom misspelt a word.

Among the younger girls there was one bright-eyed intelligent Bessie, who aimed at excelling all the big girls, and repeated the collect and gospel on each Sunday as well as the best of them. She worked with her needle, too, almost as well as they did. She was a gentle, loving little girl, and was never happier than when she could get to sit by *Missie* (the pet word for Mistress), and insinuate her little hand in Missie's.

Her younger sister was also a pleasing, promising child. One little boy, who was subject to fits, did not care to play with the other children, but would

---

* The Hebrews wrote on sticks (*see* Ezekiel xxxvii., 20), and so did the early Greeks; the laws of Solon were inscribed on billets of wood, and the Ancient Britons used to cut their alphabet on sticks. The use of sticks in keeping accounts has even remained in some country places in England to our own day.

sit apart from them, and putting his hands on each side of his face, would sit rocking himself backwards and forwards, singing softly and sweetly some hymn he had learned; sometimes it would be the line, "When they die, to heaven will go," but he would always put it, "When *I* die, to heaven *I'll* go." He died fourteen months after he entered the school.

Little *Kojonotpat*, who had increased in favor with all who knew her, died suddenly three years after Mrs. Camfield took her.

It is contended in the report that their faults are not greater than those of children of European descent, and that they are quite as capable of comprehending the truths of the gospel as any white child is. Some of them take particular pleasure in reading the Scriptures, and all the elder girls will answer questions on them with as much intelligence as the generality of children in Sunday-schools, and they quickly find any passage referred to.

The eldest girl was engaged to be married to a well-conducted, sober, industrious "conditional-pardon" man on 1st August 1858. She was by her usefulness and other good qualities in every way calculated to make a happy home for her future husband. Another girl was married to a young man, a European. She will bear comparison with any white woman among the most respectable of the laboring population, as a sensible and companionable girl. Two other girls—one black and the other half-caste—make good wives to their respective husbands, one of whom is an old settler.

The children in the asylum are a merry-hearted set, and are now engaged in working on the marriage outfit of Rhoda, who is greatly beloved by all of them. They are intelligent beings, capable of great improvement, if not as great as Europeans are.

I will here relate a little anecdote of Rachel, one of the school girls mentioned by Mrs. Camfield.

In 1863, I visited the Moravian Mission near Lake Hindmarsh, and again in 1872, on which last occasion there were sixty-four Aborigines permanent residents, of whom a considerable number were children. Mr. Spieseke, the Missionary in charge, informed me that since these people became married and led regular lives, dwelling in their own cottages, their children had greatly increased in number.

On my first visit, in 1863, I was chiefly concerned to see Rachel, or Mrs. Pepper as she then was. Her husband was an Aborigine, I believe of the Lake Hindmarsh tribe, who had been educated and had visited England. On his return voyage, the ship called in at King George's Sound, where he was introduced to Mrs. Camfield's school; and being fascinated with the charms of Rachel, proposed marriage, and was accepted, with the understanding that she should follow him to Victoria, which in due time she did, and they were married and residing at the Mission Station when I was there.

I called at the station on a Sunday, and found the village nearly deserted, many of the people being at church. Mr. Spieseke, the Moravian Missionary in charge, was preaching to them. There were about thirty-five present—men, women, and a few children. They appeared to be very attentive; and I was much pleased with their singing, good behaviour, and cleanly appearance.

Annesfield House
March 5th 1866.

My dear Miss Mitchell

I thank you very much for the beautiful cake you sent me. When it arrived on Wednesday afternoon Mrs Camfield did not know who it was for, until she read Annie Courthope's letter and then we found that it was for me. Mr Camfield said that he was jealous that it was not for him. I must thank you too for the pretty needle-book that came with Miss Trimmer she arrived on Saturday the 3rd we were looking for the cart all day on Friday and on Saturday morning it came about ten o'clock we are all glad to see Miss Trimmer back again and we are glad to see Mrs Mitchell too. In the afternoon he went with Mr Camfield to see the Church and he said that it was the prettiest little Church he had ever seen.

Last month a ship came from Adelaide with two thousand eight hundred and fifty sheep in it they looked so pretty

Three days after they went to the eleven miles, they kicked up such a dust going along. The road runs past our paddock.

Mr Camfield was delighted with the pretty watch bags and the garters he said they were the very things he wanted

The doll that was sent for Louisa Mrs Camfield gave it to Lela because she has not had one and Louisa has had three or four Lela has had her feet scalded she is such a dear thing

Mr Camfield said to her one day "Lela I will cut your hair" she has beautiful curly hair nearly white & she said "you'd better not Miss Mattie" you'd better not"

Louisa is so fond of Mr Mitchell she helped him yesterday afternoon to pick up the apples and when she can she will always be with him.

I have nothing more to say my dear Miss Mitchell so I must conclude with best love to yourself

I am your grateful

Bessy Flower

[The foregoing is a *fac-simile* of a letter written by an Australian pure Aboriginal girl, a pupil at Mrs. Camfield's school, King George's Sound.]

After church, Mr. Spieseke took me to Pepper's cottage, where we found his wife still in bed after a recent confinement. From the comfortable little parlor we were introduced to her bedroom by her husband. She was lying with her face towards the wall, but turned her large, lustrous black eyes on us with a look of surprise at seeing strangers enter her room. I spoke to her in her own language of Mr. and Mrs. Camfield, of King George's Sound, and of the native establishment there; as I did so, large tears stood in her eyes. She then asked her husband to hand down from a bookshelf a daguerreotype case, which she opened, and I at once exclaimed, "Ki! Neeja, Mr. Camfield," at which she seemed much delighted, as I was doubtless the first person she had seen since she left the Sound who had been acquainted with her native place and early friends. Several of the men and women afterwards read portions of the Bible to me, and sang some hymns, in which the children joined.

Among the passengers taken by the *Charles Edward* from Melbourne to Port Albert, in Gippsland, in June 1867, were five "Aboriginal ladies," from Western Australia, in charge of the Rev. Mr. Hagenauer, named respectively Ada, Norah, Rhoda, Emily (half-caste), and Elizabeth. Two of them proceeded to the Mission Station "Ramahyuck" to be married to Christian Aborigines of the Tarra tribe. One of these—James Matthews—was found by Mr. Hagenauer, about six years before, nearly naked, and almost wild. He was better known at Port Albert as James Fitcher, where he used to wander, for the purpose of begging. He subsequently joined the station, and became a respectable, industrious man, working readily and perseveringly at agricultural pursuits, and was baptized at the opening of the Aboriginal church at Lake Wellington. He induced all the males of the Tarra tribe to go up to the Mission Station. Mr. Hagenauer experienced great difficulty in finding suitable helpmates for the men, as it was the native custom to fight for a wife; so he hit on the happy expedient of exchanging portraits with the Christian natives of King George's Sound, which, I believe, resulted in the marriage of two of them with two of the Tarra tribe. One of the party, Betsey or Elizabeth Flower, is accomplished and highly educated. She was adopted by Mrs. Camfield at Albany, and not only passed a creditable examination in the Government school, but acted as organist in the Church of England there.

I have just received a letter, dated 16th October 1877, from the Rev. F. A. Hagenauer of Gippsland, from which I extract the following regarding the five native girls from Western Australia:—"Bessy Flower is now twenty-six years of age. She married Donald Cameron, who came with me years ago from the Wimmera district. He is a half-caste man of very superior character, fair education, pleasant manners, and considerable talents. He is here at Ramahyuck my right-hand man, and acts as overseer. He works very well in all the branches of our business at this station. Formerly the Camerons had charge of our orphans' house for Aboriginal children, but Bessy got tired of it, and they left, and live now in a neat cottage on the station. They are doing well, and live happily and faithfully together, but could do much better if Mrs. Cameron had more tact for her household duties. The great hopes we entertained of her future usefulness among the natives have not been fulfilled, though of course her superior education helps her on wonderfully well. She is still playing the harmonium in our church, and I still entertain the hope that she may be of great use some day to the black people, especially to the children here. I enclose you a photograph of herself and her husband, also one of her two little girls. Of the other four girls who came here, one died a happy death—Ada, Bessy's sister. One, Rhoda, is suffering from consumption; she is a good wife and mother, and keeps her house in good order. Norah and Emily have both large families, but they are careless, and will not attend to their household work, and neglect their children very much. Bessy's younger brother Harry is here also; he is very clever, but careless, and always ready for some mischief."

I must not omit to say something about the Roman Catholic Mission to the Aborigines of Western Australia, which was established in 1848, at a large pool or reach of the Moore River, some eighty miles north from Perth. The natives' name for this pool is *Mourin*, and the establishment was first known by the euphonious name of "The Mourin Mission;" but I find that the place is now called by the awkward and inappropriate appellation of "New Norcia."

In 1848, a ship arrived at Fremantle from Lisbon, bringing about forty Spanish and Italian priests and students, headed by Don Serra, Bishop and Administrator of Temporalities. They came out under the auspices of the Queen of Spain, for the purpose of propagating their faith among the sable tribes of Western Australia. Among them were some well educated and gentlemanly men, who, although they could speak several European languages, seemed to have no aptitude for acquiring a knowledge of either the language or turn of mind of the natives. They purchased 2,500 acres of land at the Mourin, carted up a supply of stores, and erected a large rubble-stone house, which they thatched with grass-tree rushes. Their nearest neighbour was a young English gentleman, who had sailed with them from Portugal, and who took a pleasure in teasing them. He took up some land, and built a house at a place called Bindoon, thirty miles nearer the settled districts. There was a large tribe of natives at Mourin, and another at Bindoon. A number of the former were baptized by Bishop Serra; and on such occasions the newly-made "Christians" received a small supply of rice or potatoes. The natives, on their part, brought in kangaroos to the Missionaries.

Thus all went well for a time, but mistakes began to be made on each side. The Missionaries imagined that the blacks presented them with the produce of the chase in recognition of the spiritual advantages received; whereas the natives supposed that these friendly white men gave them the rice as a payment for submitting to the ordeal of baptism. When, therefore, some of these novel Christians presented themselves to the Bishop, asking to be baptized over again, he became irate; and the more so when he found that some of them had surreptitiously obtained the rite a second time by disguising themselves. He exclaimed—"Don't you know, you ungrateful fellows, that we have come all the way from Europe for your benefit?" "*Kiar!*" they shouted, "*Nganya eulup boola*," "Yes, I am very hungry" (mistaking the word Europe for *eulup*, hungry). "*Nyinnee maryne yunge*"—"You give me some food."

All this time the master of Bindoon had been making friends with his tribe, and got plenty of work done by them, for he was a good-natured merry fellow, and readily picked up their language. He used to amuse himself and them by telling them stories about the priests, whom he represented as having "plenty of rice and potatoes," the proper way to obtain which was to use an expression in one of Lever's novels—" Bloody end to the Pope!"

They used, therefore, to learn these words, and practise saying them when sitting by their camp-fires at night, without, of course, having the least idea of their import. The futile attempts of some new learner to repeat the sentence would evoke the most boisterous merriment, in which Mr. H. heartily joined when present.

In course of time an arrangement was made by the two tribes for a friendly meeting at a certain intervening rendezvous ; and one fine morning the Missionaries were astonished and disconcerted at finding that the natives, Christians and all, had decamped. They little thought that no offer of reward or fear of punishment would deter a native from leaving, once he had determined to do so.

For three weary days Bishop Serra was chafing at the unaccountable absence of his new converts, when he determined on making a journey, accompanied by one or two coadjutors, to the settled districts. On their way they fell in with a large encampment of natives, which proved to be the assembled tribes from Mourin and Bindoon. He thought it a fitting opportunity for expostulation, and accordingly the three venerable clergymen rode slowly up with all possible dignity of demeanour. The natives had evidently had a corobborce the night before, for some seventy or eighty of the men were so painted and ornamented as not to be easily distinguished by those who knew them.

No one who has never seen a camp of friendly tribes can have an idea of what a lively, noisy scene it is. There are groups of huts scattered about, each hut with its fire and family sitting round. Conversation is kept up between distant parties as though they were near each other—some are quiet and moody, but the greater number are shouting, laughing, and talking. On this occasion they had much news to tell each other—the Mourin tribe of what queer fellows the priests were, of the big house, the baptizing, and, better than all, of the rice and potatoes, and of their attempts to get more by offering to be baptized again. But the Bindoon tribe knew of a far better method of getting the good things ; they had been teaching their friends to repeat the pass-words which were to have so desirable an effect.

As the clerical party advanced, they were met by a number of boisterous, laughing, painted, naked savages ; but they rode into the middle of the camp before alighting. The young men then swarmed round them, clapped the Bishop on the shoulders, pulled his long beard in admiration, and by way of the greatest compliment they could pay him, told him he was *goombar*—that is, "very big," "as big as a gum-tree!"* But he motioned them to stand back, and then began—" Don't you *savez* you have been made Christians, you ungrateful fellows ? We have come all the way from Europe for your benefit, and now you

---

* Like the Asiatics, they practise the most preposterous flattery.

leave the station." "*Kiar! nganya culup boola!*—Bloody end to the Pope!" shouted a number of voices at once. "Why? what for? what harm has the holy Father done you, you ungrateful fellows?" "*Nganya culup, nyinnee maryne yunge*"—"I am hungry; you give me some food." "No! I did not say *culup*—I said Europe," exclaimed the haughty Spaniard, beginning to lose his temper, as he found that his venerable and dignified appearance had no effect on these barbarians, who now closed round him, shouting at the top of their voices, "Bloody end to the Pope!" "You give me rice!" until the good Missionaries had to mount their horses and ride off as fast as they could, with a troop of savages running after them, laughing and yelling, and shouting with all their might.*

This occurred a short time after the Mission Station had been established, and a little before I visited it. It has since then prospered, and I believe has for years past exported wine and wool, the produce of the labors of the domesticated natives.

Don Rosendo Salvado, with whom I was acquainted, is the present Bishop. He is a gentleman possessing much learning and ability, and is an accomplished musician. A fine-toned bell, one of the largest in Australia, dating from the period of Charles V., and consecrated to St. Anna (if I remember rightly) calls the people to church.

As guides in travelling, or assistants in the bush, the intelligence and skill of the natives is generally superior to that of the white men, who by comparison appear rather stupid. If there are difficulties to be overcome, food or water to be obtained, or the best travelling ground to be selected, their advice and assistance are invaluable. The late Sir Thomas Mitchell † says—"I have found those who accompanied me on my expeditions into the country superior in penetration and judgment to the white men comprising my party."

These people never evince surprise at any novel or extraordinary sight. Once, when travelling alone in the Darling Range, I fell in with a native lad, who had recently come down with some of his tribe from the far interior, and had seen very little of the white people;—he had certainly never beheld a mask. I alighted from my horse, and walked with him for the purpose of conversation. After a while, I let him get a little in advance of me, when I took a mask out of my pocket, which I had brought with me on purpose to show it to the natives, and putting it on, stepped up to him, and looked him in the face. On beholding the hideous sight instead of the white man who he supposed was talking to him, he evinced no sign of emotion, but just looked for an instant, and then went on talking just as though no change had taken place. Another Aboriginal lad, on seeing the sea for the first time, just took one comprehensive gaze, and then turning away, quaintly remarked—"Big fellow water-hole that." He had evidently never before seen a waterhole the opposite side of which his keen eyes could not descry.

---

* I published this anecdote some years ago in the *Church News*, signing myself "An Old Australian."—P. C.

† *Tropical Australia*, p. 412.

The Aboriginal men have often been employed in considerable numbers, and with much success, as frontier police in the several Australian Colonies. Indeed, without their aid, it would generally have been impossible to capture offenders among their own people; and they have not unfrequently been employed to take white men against whom warrants had issued but who had successfully eluded the English police.

That the Aborigines sometimes display much readiness of invention under difficulties, and uncommon skill and courage in the execution of the plan formed, is amply illustrated by the two following anecdotes, for which I am indebted to Mr. Bland, of Clunes, who in the early days of Western Australia was for many years Resident Magistrate and Protector of Aborigines in the York district.

An Aborigine, one of the crew of the Twofold Bay whalers, apprehended an escaped European convict whom the police were unable to capture. He took one of his mates with him, and on the next day brought the man in. When asked how he succeeded in taking the convict, whom he had never before seen, he gave the following story :—He met the man on a road, and thinking he might be the right person, went up to him, and said—" Who are you?" The man gave some name; the native then, pistol in hand, said— " You are a ticket-of-leave man, arn't you?" " Yes, I am." " Then show me your pass." The man gave him a piece of paper, which turned out to be an old public-house bill. The native could not read, but stood in front of the man, holding the paper up before his eyes as though reading it, but he was really looking over it into the convict's face; his quickness of perception and intuitive knowledge of human nature enabled him to see that the man looked frightened, and he shouted to his companion—" Oh! this is the right man." They caught him, put the handcuffs on him, and took him in to the police station. A London detective could not have done better.

The other example is as follows :—A desperate native offender had for some time eluded capture, when a constable, accompanied by a blackfellow from another tribe, went to a native camp, where they saw the man they were looking for, but did not know how to catch him. The constable's native assistant said to him—" Oh, I will pretend to be in a great passion, as if I were going to spear some one; the other, being a strong man, will then come and hold me, to prevent me from doing mischief, and then you can put the handcuffs on him." This ingenious and bold plan was carried into execution, and was quite successful, as they brought the culprit away as their prisoner. I should, however, here remark, by way of explanation, that when a native works himself up into a passion for some grievance in which the others do not sympathize, some one always holds his arms, to prevent him from injuring any one. I have frequently seen this done. Men hold the angry man, and women the angry woman; the person so held being often rather glad than otherwise to find that he has produced an effect great enough to induce some champion thus to interfere to prevent him from doing a mischief which he would rather be credited with than really accomplish.

The perceptive faculties of the Aborigines are very clear, and their powers of observation and imitation sometimes quite extraordinary. They are therefore excellent mimics, and display much original humour.

Monotonous and harsh as their chants are, the natives are by no means unsusceptible of the power of music. The young people readily learn to sing, and some of them to play on instruments. Often, when approaching a native encampment on one of those lovely mornings which, at Swan River, shed an indescribably balmy influence on all around, I have heard the plaintive morning song—the men as they sat sharpening their spears, the women as they lazily put together the smouldering embers, while the others slept around. The following is a line of one of their chants :—

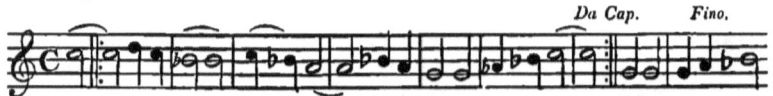

They have names for all the conspicuous stars, for every natural feature of the ground, every hill, swamp, bend of a river, &c.; but not, in Western Australia, for the river itself—the water, a native laconically remarked, runs away into the sea; it is no use naming that.

LANGUAGE.

As so much has doubtless already been written about the numerous languages or dialects of Australia, I will only remark that I have observed many words in Victoria, especially on the Goulburn River and Upper Murray, which are identical with or similar to those denoting the same thing in Western Australia. This may be noticed particularly with regard to parts of the body, indicating, I think, notwithstanding the opinion of Count Strezelecki, the common origin of the several languages. In the Darling Range the language is not always sex-denoting. I have known the masculine *he* used to women as well as to men.

The dialects change with almost every tribe. *Some* tribes name their children after natural objects; and when the person so named dies, the word is never again mentioned; another word has therefore to be invented for the object after which the child was called. I knew a man whose name was *Karla* (not *Calor*), which signifies "fire" or "heat;" when he died, another word had to be used for "fire;" hence the language is always changing.

I am not aware of any word in Western Australia to denote a Supreme Being or even a good spirit.

INTERMARRIAGES.

My friend the late Mr. W. H. Knight, of Swan River, kindly sent me, last year, a copy of Bishop Salvado's Genealogical Tree of the natives of Western Australia, from which it appears that they are divided into six families, and intermarriages within a family are prohibited. There are the—1, *Tirarop;* 2, *Nyocoynok;* 3, *Palarop;* 4, *Tondorop;* 5, *Mondorop;* 6, *Jiragiok.* Every native, male and female, belongs to one or other of these six families. The names are inherited by the children not from the father, but from their mother. No native can marry any of his family name, nor any one of some of the other families, but of those only which their law allows.

The Perth and Murray natives are *Ballarok;* then there are the *Dtondarup* and the *Ngotak*, probably identical with some of the above. As the children take the mother's name, and the hunting ground or landed property descends in the male line, it follows that the land is never for two generations in the hands of men of the same family name; and in the event of a man having several wives of different family names, his lands are at his death divided between so many new families. His male children owe certain duties to men of their own family at the same time as to their half-brothers, which often clash with each other, and give rise to endless dissensions.

The natives being divided into six families, and intermarriages being prohibited, it follows that a *Tirarop* cannot marry a *Tirarop*, a *Mondorop*, or a *Tondorop;* but he may marry either a *Jiragiok*, *Palarop*, or *Ngocognok;* and the children of a *Tirarop* man and a *Palarop* woman would belong to the *Palarop* family or branch, whose choice of marriage is also limited. I believe this theory is correct, and obtains throughout the whole western coast with some slight variations; the same law prevails amongst the natives of the northwest coast, the only difference being in the names of the families.

Customs and Superstitions.

The natives of Western Australia, when the white men arrived, had no religion, no trace of idolatry, and no idea of a God; no government, no chief, properly so called; and, as regards their social condition, much may be imagined when it is stated that they had no cooking utensil whatever, nor did they know the use of any metal; they went almost naked, and in the northern and warmer parts, quite so; their dwellings, as has been already stated, were of the most fragile and temporary description, and their means of water locomotion of the rudest kind, even in those parts where they used any sort of canoe.

Although they seem to know nothing of a Supreme Being, they believe in the existence of various local demons. The Swan River Aborigines say that an evil being, called *Nyoralong*, wanders about in the night-time, in the *Banksia* forests, collecting the gum of the *Nuytsia floribunda*,* which he puts into bags hanging all round his body. They assert that he is like an old man walking about in a half-sitting attitude, and carrying a *wanna*, or yam-stick, and that he utters a short, sharp screech at every step. I enquired why they never speared him; but they were indignant at the idea, and replied— "One might as well try to spear a grass-tree, he is so surrounded with gum bags." Although they eat the gum which exudes from the acacias, hakeas, and other trees, they never touch the *Nuytsia* gum; for, were they to do so, they say

---

* Native name *Mutyar*. A loranthus that grows by itself, I believe only from suckers, and cannot, so far as I know, be propagated. It bears splendid orange-colored blossoms.

Nyowalong would certainly do them some secret injury; but the fact is, it is not an edible gum—they make a virtue of necessity. Then there is a demon, named *Winniung*, who resides in the winter-time on a hill on the south of the Helena River, near Mount Dale, in the Darling Range; but in the summer he dwells on the other side of the river, *because he cannot cross it when flooded.*

These imaginary beings are all material, and subject to the same physical conditions as themselves. Yet they have some undefined notion of a spirit, or soul, or perhaps of a personal identity which is independent of their present corporiety. They think that if they are buried they will rise again with some different body; hence their desire to take down and bury the two men who were gibbeted for the murder of Mrs. Cook.* In like manner, the low-caste natives of the Orissa district in India, who migrate to the sugar plantations of Mauritius, often become home-sick, and commit suicide in the firm belief that they will enter through the portals of death into their own country again—but only if their bodies are not mutilated. They, therefore, often hang themselves, but would have a serious objection to be decapitated. Mons. de Chazal, of Port Louis, effectually put a stop to any more suicides on his plantation by telling the coolies that he would cut off the feet of any one who killed himself.

An old Swan River native explained to me that the soul (*Noytch*) dwells in the back of the neck, and that it is by striking a man there that he is surreptitiously killed, when asleep, by some evil being, or by a *Wailo*, that is, a northern man. "*Wailo*" is a name given to all people living to the north of them by every tribe in Western Australia, be the latter situated where they may. The *Wailo* men are much dreaded, and are believed to possess supernatural powers.

The chief demon of the hill natives is *Waugal*,† dwelling in the large brown snake, which they carefully avoid, and never kill, though they are in the habit of eating other snakes equally venomous. I was one day travelling on horseback near the River Dale, with a native guide, when I suddenly came upon a large brown snake coiled up and fast asleep. I immediately alighted to kill it, at which my sable friend was much alarmed, and tried to pull me back, declaring that, if I killed the snake, *Waugal* would *quibble Gidgee*, or spear me by stealth when I was asleep, and he urged me to have one of the soldiers of my escort to sleep in my tent for protection.

On the south-west of Victoria, near Port Campbell, several caverns have been washed out under the cliffs by the force of the Southern Ocean. One of these extends under ground nearly a quarter of a mile, and in one place the rain-water has washed a small hole from the surface of the ground down into the cavern. There is a continual draught of air blowing up through this hole, so that if a leaf or any light substance be thrown over it, it is immediately carried up into the air. For ages past the natives were in the habit, whenever they approached this air-hole, to throw a piece of wood into it to propitiate the demon

---

* *See* page 280.

† *Waug* signifies a spirit. *Waugal* is a being analogous to *Mindi* of South-Eastern Australia— a mighty serpent.

supposed to reside within its profound and mysterious depths. When the late Mr. Superintendent La Trobe examined this part of the coast, in 1842, some of his men made a rope ladder, and went down over the cliff and explored this cavern. When they came to the part nearly under the hole communicating with the surface, they found an enormous pile of wood, which must have been the accumulation of ages, as the natives had to carry the pieces of wood from the distant forest. The men set fire to the pile, which lit up and displayed a magnificent vaulted chamber, bedecked with long glistening stalactites, and tenanted by vast numbers of bats, whose whirring, whizzing noise was probably that which the natives attributed to some supernatural being.

At Mount Gambier also there are some very large caverns in the limestone rock, believed by the natives to be haunted.

To return to Western Australia. *Waugal*, with some tribes, is an aquatic monster, endowed with supernatural powers; and as the natives do not believe in natural disease or death, they attribute all ailments for which they cannot otherwise account to *Waugal*, or to some other demon, or to the *Wailo* men.

I am of opinion that the natives generally do not believe that their women have a future state or are endowed with souls. Yet they certainly believed that the white people, when they first arrived, were their deceased ancestors re-incarnated.

Before the arrival of a ship from Europe, the Swan River natives supposed that the spirits of the deceased passed into the cormorants which frequent the Mewstone, a granite rock some miles out in the sea opposite the mouth of the Swan River, called by them *Gudu mitch*, a compound of *Gu-urt*, the "heart," and *mit* or *mitch*, the "medium" or "agent"—signifying that this island is the medium or agent by which the spirit of the departed one enters the body of a cormorant. Large flights of these birds used to pass up the estuary of the Swan every morning on fishing excursions, and return to the Mewstone in the evening, and the natives refrained from killing them lest thereby they should be slaying their ancestors. When, however, they saw ships coming from the same direction, and bringing white people, they called them *Djenga*, or ghosts, supposing them to be the re-embodiments of their progenitors who had come back to the land of their birth.

At first I doubted whether this was really their spontaneous belief, and thought it probable that the colonists had originated the idea. Afterwards, however, I had good reason to believe that they thought some at least of the white men were re-incarnations of their deceased relatives. I was supposed to be *Bogan*, a native of the Middle Swan tribe, who had been killed in single combat with another man some time before my arrival. An account of the fight, and of the person of *Bogan*, was given to me by some of the settlers when I went to reside at Guildford, on the Swan; and on the 19th October 1841, about two years after his death, the grave having been shown to me, I took up the skeleton, and sent it to the late Dr. Jacob, of Dublin, who had it set up in Trinity College Museum, as I was afterwards informed by his son in Melbourne. On questioning some members of his tribe about *Bogan*, I found they thought I was he.

I knew a gentleman who had a scar on his leg similar to one which had been on the leg of a deceased native man. This gentleman was the first to settle in a new district, at Chittering, near Bindoon, where the natives had then seen very little of white people. On perceiving the scar, they immediately asserted that he was their deceased friend, and the widow claimed him as her husband.

Europeans were frequently claimed as relations by the old people, who seemed sure of their identity, and treated them with the love they bore to the individual supposed to be recognised. This belief, however, began to die out as they saw that children were born to the white people.*

In Victoria, where hot winds and other electrical disturbances of the atmosphere are common, the natives used to think that the ground was haunted, and that the swirls of dust, so often seen in the summer-time, were caused by demons passing along in the ground. It was sometimes amusing to see a whole encampment of lazy natives hurrying out of the way of an approaching whirlwind charged with dust. The crashing of trees during a hurricane was also attributed to the same occult influence.

Some of the old people appear to be stupid; but this may be the result rather of mental indolence and want of culture than of the absence of intellectual faculty when young.

In Western Australia, a *Bulya-gadak* †—that is, a magician or sorcerer—is considered a very wise man, and advises the young men, who greatly respect him.

The old women, too, have much influence over the younger members of the tribe. They are often great termigants, and the instigators of many of the quarrels. When there is a disturbance in the camp, one of them will be sure to fan the kindling flame. When there is a death to be revenged, or an enemy to be punished, or a quarrel to be adjusted, some nude old virago will be seen pacing backwards and forwards with great rapidity, pouring forth in a declamatory tone—a sort of chant—a volley of abuse against the adverse party ; and calling on her own people to take signal vengeance by tearing out his liver, or otherwise tormenting him; and it is surprising what an effect this often has on the men.

Thus it will be seen that the old people, if not greatly respected, were at least looked up to as the guides of the young, They always were, so far as I have observed, treated with kindness, fed and attended to when sick or decrepid, and never left to starve or die, as is too often the practice among the Boschmen of Southern Africa.

The *Bulya-gadak*, like the magicians of ancient Egypt, is applied to for explanation and aid in all things that lie beyond the circle of common knowledge and action. Thus, in cases of sickness, he is the only physician called in, as in Egypt, where the profession of medicine was in the hands of the lowest of the three orders into which the priestly caste was divided.

---

* The ancient Egyptians believed that when the body perished the banished soul began its career anew in connection with physical existence.

† Called *Koradgee* by the Port Jackson tribe.

The *Bulya-gadak* professes to cure diseases by enchantment; that is to eject the evil spirit, called *Bulya*—the supposed cause of all sickness and disease. The operation was as follows:—The magician would squeeze the affected part with both hands, and then, drawing them down, would attract *Bulya* to the extremities, and finally bring it out, shaking and blowing upon his hands each time, in order to get rid of *Bulya*, who was supposed to make his escape without being seen by the uninitiated, but who sometimes appeared as a piece of quartz, which was kept as a great curiosity.

A Port Jackson native stated that the *Koradgee* men became possessed of their supernatural powers in the following manner:—A man sleeping at night on the grave of a deceased person would be freed from the dread of future apparitions; for during that fearful sleep the spirit of the dead would visit him, seize him by the throat, and, opening him, take out his bowels, which the spirit would afterwards replace and then close up the wound.

I have seen their incantations in South Australia during the ceremony of changing a boy into a man.

Mr. G. G. McCrae, in his pretty but fanciful poem, "*Mamba, the Bright-eyed*,"* when alluding to this rite, says:—

> "Not ours the wisdom or the light
> To shadow forth that solemn rite;
> Nor what the word, nor what the way,
> That moulds a man from boyish clay."

I did, however, witness the whole ceremony near Adelaide, in the year 1839. I was the only white person present, and was conducted to the place by a friendly native. There were probably a hundred or more Aborigines on the ground. The spot selected was a small open space partly surrounded by a forest of large trees, facing the thickest part of which, and about twenty yards from the edge of it, sat a youth with his head hanging down, and his legs stretched out before him. My sable friend took me close up to him; and from him, as the apex of the angle, diverged two lines of men, in the form of the letter **V**, with the open part towards the forest; and about twenty yards behind was a semicircle of fires, each surrounded by a group of women, sitting on the ground, who made a great blaze with branches of dead leaves during the most important parts of the ceremony. The night was very dark, and the effect quite imposing. The glare of the fires only tended to make the darkness of the forest more visible. When all seemed to be ready, there was a dead silence. I whispered to my friend, but he motioned to me to be still. Every one was waiting in breathless anxiety, when suddenly, out of the dark forest, three naked, weird-looking old men came shrieking, yelling, and jumping in a zig-zag course, and gesticulating in the most frantic manner. The fires were all instantly lighted up, and displayed a scene far more remarkable than any I have ever seen in a theatre. The old sorcerers were streaked with white, and otherwise ornamented. They gradually approached the lad in a devious course, until their frenzy reached its climax, when one of them suddenly stooped down before him at my feet, and a perfect silence ensued while he tickled him with a

---

* Canto 1., stanza 23.

small bunch of emu feathers, which he twirled between his fingers, from the lad's shoulders, down his arms, to the ends of his fingers, making a chirping noise between his closed lips the while; this he did several times, and then all three of the old men darted back into the darkness of the forest. The blaze of the fires had now died out, all was enshrouded in darkness, and a dead silence was maintained for about ten minutes, when the whole ceremony was repeated, except that this time the *Bulya-gadak* twirled the feathers down the boy's body and legs to his feet; then there was the running and jumping back into the wood; and the scene was enacted over and over again, with some addition each time to the process of mesmerism, if such it really was. The subject of this solemn rite appeared to be in an unconscious slumber during the whole performance. The same magician performed the operation each time; and when he seemed to have thoroughly mesmerized his subject, he took a small splinter of quartz between his fingers, and, having wetted it on his tongue, cut a great gash across the lad's breast, but the latter did not appear to feel it in the slightest degree. He then tickled him over with the feathers, and gave another and another cut, passing the quartz between his lips each time, and keeping up the chirping noise. The three then rushed back into the wood, the moon began to rise, and all was over. My kind friend must, I presume, have been a man of influence, or he could never have prevailed on the tribe to allow me to witness this rite. He confidently assured me that when the three *Bulya-gadaks* ran back into the wood they plunged into the moon, which soon after rose in that direction.

The next morning I rode out to the encampment, and found one of the old men standing before the novice, giving him some solemn advice, just as illustrated by Major Mitchell, at page 322, vol. I., of his first expedition.

Circumcision is practised by one or more tribes on the north-west coast. I have not myself witnessed this, but have reason to credit the reports I have heard respecting it. A most extraordinary practice was resorted to by some of the natives inhabiting the country near Port Lincoln. They used to cut open as great a length of the urethra as possible from underneath.

There seems to be no doubt of some tribes occasionally, and under particular circumstances, practising infanticide, and they sometimes—though, I believe, very rarely—eat their offspring.* Can it be that these revolting practices are unnatural methods—unintentional it may be—of keeping in check the too rapid increase of a barbarous people in a region where the indigenous productions afford a very scanty supply of food? In some countries, pestilential diseases or failure of the crops thin overcrowded populations; in others, war accomplishes the same end; and, as civilization progresses, the only natural and reasonable method is adopted—that of transplanting the people to unpopulated and suitable areas of the earth's surface.

Twins are occasionally born. *Wengal*, the boy whom I educated, was a twin—the other being a girl, whom its mother killed in infancy. Her name

---

* Mr. Stephens, in his *Incidents of Travel*, says of the Bedouins—"I never knew them refuse anything that could be eaten. Their stomach was literally their god."

was *Bukanyeen*, and she was considered a very decent old woman by the settlers on the Swan. I asked her, eight years afterwards, how she could bring herself to kill her child. She replied, pointing to the bag at her back, that there was only room for one, and she could not possibly carry another. On pressing her for further information, she informed me that soon after it was born she scratched a hole in the sand behind her hut, and, having given it a " little " knock on the head, laid it in the hole, and kept on crying, the child crying too, till she could bear it no longer; and then went out and gave it another " little " knock, which, however, killed it; and then she cried for several days.

I have already stated the very general belief that the spirit of a deceased person assumes a fresh corporeal form; but I think some tribes must have thought that the re-embodiment took place some time after death, for they displayed great care in the interment of a dead man by firmly tying the thumb of the right hand to the great toe of the left foot, the body being doubled up, with the knees touching the chin. There were various modes of interment by different tribes. Some placed the body in a sitting posture, with the face towards the north, and others lying on the left side, with the face towards the rising sun. The grave was scratched out with the hands about three or four feet deep, and the body, being placed in it, was covered with thick logs of wood, to prevent native dogs from molesting it. The surface of the grave was flat or hollow, and a semicircular mound was made on one side of it, opening to the east. The weapons which had been used by the deceased, and whatever else the affection of the relatives prompted them to bestow, were laid on the grave. A fire was kept burning before it for several days, and a hut was sometimes built over it. They seemed to think that, notwithstanding their efforts to keep their friend down, he got up and warmed himself.

While the interment was being made, the *Balya-gadak* sat at the head of the grave, bending from time to time his head to the ground to listen for the flight of the spirit, and the information it might have to give him as to the evil being who had caused his death.

From the time of death until after the burial, which took place within twenty-four hours, the wives and female connections of the deceased kept up their lamentations by shrieking, howling, and declaiming. They scratched their noses and cheeks until the blood flowed down, and deep cicatrices were left which always helped to disfigure them.* They also smeared their heads with pipeclay.†

The following account of an Aboriginal funeral is given in the *Central Australasian* of the 30th January 1875:—" Towney, four years attached to the Bourke police as tracker, died on Wednesday, from injuries received by a kick from a horse, and was buried on the following day with all the ceremonies of

---

* See Matthew vi. ch., 16 v. A similar custom still maintains its ground in Moslem countries, though Mahomed endeavoured to put a stop to it. The men sometimes wound themselves in excess of grief with knives, but the women are content to lacerate themselves with their nails. Examples of this custom might be obtained from many parts of the world in different stages of civilization.

† The putting dust upon the head was and is still a sign of great affliction in many countries of Asia, as it also was among the ancient Egyptians.

his tribe. Soon after death, the body was covered with gum leaves, and rolled in an opossum rug and a blanket. His gin lay with her head resting on the corpse, and one of the oldest men lay in a similar manner. All were silent, and remained so for twenty-four hours. When preparations were made for the burial, two widowed gins, with hair cut short and heads covered or plastered with pipeclay, took prominent parts in the arrangements. The oldest men carried the body to the grave (some half a mile from the camp) on a pole, one end resting on each shoulder, and passed through the cords which secured the blanket and opossum rug on the corpse. A grave was dug in the shape of a well, about four feet six inches deep. When it was ready, the bier was raised by two old warriors, and at this moment a pitiful cry was raised by all the blacks. After silence was partly proclaimed, an old warrior named *Kangaroo*, with a small branch of a gum-tree in his hand, commenced addressing the corpse, with his head close to the body. He continued doing this incessantly for twenty minutes, and was answered by an old man in a stooping posture on the opposite side of the bier. Two men in the grave laid an opossum rug round it to receive the remains, which were lowered down amidst the cries of every black present. Gum leaves were then thrown over the body. And now comes the revolting part. Two men adjusting the body in the grave, stand up. One takes a boomerang, the other stoops and receives a blow which draws blood freely. The boomerang is handed to the other; he then strikes, and both bleed copiously over the corpse. They are then removed, and three men go into the grave and strike each other till they bleed, bowing down their heads the while. One throws himself down, and is with difficulty removed. Three others repeat the same thing. These men all bled freely, and in submission, till the grave was covered with blood. The bleeding men now retired in sadness under trees; the gins applied gum leaves till the blood was stopped, meanwhile keeping up an incessant cry. They submit, it seems, to their heads being cut in order to strengthen the deceased in the grave, and assist him to rise in another country—not, as is generally supposed, a white man, but a black. They carefully covered in the grave, and built a sort of *gunyah* over it, with a bush fence round it. They swept round all the old graves, and returned to camp, leaving the wife of deceased and the widowed gins to mourn."

On one occasion, Mr. Bland, in endeavouring to refute their belief that the white men were re-embodied blackfellows, said—"Nonsense! I was never here before;" and was answered by an intelligent lad, named *Kowit*—"Then how did you know the way here?"

OBSERVATIONS ON THE MORAL CONDITION OF THE AUSTRALIAN ABORIGINES— CHIEFLY THOSE OF WESTERN AUSTRALIA.

Mr. Samuel Gason, a Police-Trooper, who was stationed from the year 1865 until recently in the vicinity of Lake Hope, some six hundred miles north from Adelaide, states that the tribes in the vicinity of Cooper's Creek number about 1,030 persons. He represents them as being very treacherous and lying, but adds that they possess in an eminent degree the three great virtues of hospitality, reverence for old age, and love for their children and parents.*

The same traits of character are more or less conspicuous in the natives of Western Australia, though they are certainly not remarkable for their treachery, and I have very seldom known any of them accused of it.

The following reminiscences and notes may convey some idea of their general moral character, which is doubtless at a very low ebb indeed, though it should not for a moment be supposed that they are less capable of moral training than any other people. Nothing has been added to the moral code since the commencement of the Christian era, and I presume the moral sensibilities of man under similar circumstances are the same everywhere as ever they were, making allowance, of course, for individual idiocrasies.

The following account of *Wengal*—the lad who lived with me for six years, and who was a type of his people—will give some idea of the development of his mind, both intellectually and morally, under culture. He belonged to the Middle Swan tribe, and to a family famous for their courage and activity. He was endowed with originality, confidence, good natural abilities, and an excellent memory. When his mother consigned him to us, at six years of age, he was a very handsome child, quick and intelligent, and soon learned to speak English fluently. At ten years old he could read and spell well, and had a fair knowledge of geography—better, I think, than most boys who had similar opportunities for learning. He could learn to repeat from memory a chapter in the Bible, or a page or two from any English book, in a remarkably short time; but found much difficulty in working out arithmetical problems, though he could eventually master sums in long division as well as most boys of his age. He readily apprehended any simple proposition, but could not easily grasp abstract ideas or follow abstruse reasoning. It would have been interesting to have watched his improvement had his education been continued for some years longer. While living with us, he evinced many good qualities; he was frank, brave, and generally attentive to the duties imposed upon him, and was much attached to his mistress. However, he occasionally became troublesome, and when once he began to be so, it was difficult to bring him back to his generally steady course of life. Though habitually truthful, he did on one such occasion, when about eleven years old, invent a most extraordinary falsehood, and bore it out with a very ingenious and plausible tale. He had large black eyes, with long curled eye-lashes, and a well-shaped head and features. We could often see the color mount to his face, his skin was so transparent, though of a dark chocolate-brown. After I left Western Australia, *Wengal* obtained a good situation at a squatting station, and in the course of time married. He led a regular life, and never at any time evinced any desire to return to his own people; indeed he did not like them. His grandfather, *Beedite*, a fine old man, was greatly respected by his tribe. He had nine children, of whom

---

* Manuscript book. Gason was recently wounded in the attack on the telegraph station on the overland line.

I can mention *Molimegget*, *Molidobbin*, *Narran*, and *Weeban* as brave men and notable warriors, though always friendly with the white people.

Weeban was the father of *Wengal*, and in the year 1840 it devolved on him to avenge the death of a relative, which he did by killing a little black girl belonging to the tribe of the aggressors, who was in the service of Capt. Shaw, of the Upper Swan. For this deed *Weeban* was tried, convicted, and sentenced to banishment for life to the island of Rottnest. Having proved himself one of the best behaved of the prisoners in that penal establishment, at the end of five years, Governor Hutt was pleased, at my solicitation, to grant him a reprieve. We were residing at Fremantle at the time he was liberated, and I saw him just after he landed. The color of his skin was a sort of iron-grey—unlike any native I had before seen. This was because he had not been allowed any grease to anoint himself with, in accordance with the custom of both men and women.

As soon as he had been set free by the Resident Magistrate he hastened to see his son, who, however, was not aware of his father's return. I was anxious to witness the meeting after a five years' separation. Some Fremantle natives had congregated to receive *Weeban* on his landing, and as soon as possible led him to our house, and pointed out *Wengal*, who had just dressed for dinner, and was walking into the house, when his father rushed at him, hugged him in his arms, and kissed him nearly all over. *Wengal*, not knowing who the half-naked, grey-skinned old man was, shrieked with terror, and did not appear less agitated when told that he was held by his own father. He afterwards informed me that his father had once speared him in the leg when he was being carried on his mother's back, and he had been afraid of him ever since.

An offender is sometimes outlawed by his own or a neighbouring tribe, and he then takes to an unfrequented part of the country, often with a stolen wife, but is seldom able to bear the banishment for more than a few months, when he returns, and braves the punishment that awaits him.

I remember seeing a large, stout young man named *Yungher* thus surrender himself. He stood in front of a large tree, without clothes or weapons, other than a single spear and *miro*, or throwing-board. Before him, at a distance of about fifteen or twenty yards, sat some thirty or forty men and women in a semicircle facing him, many of them talking loud and rapidly; while in the open space nearer to him a little man with a spear seemed to be making frantic efforts to work himself up into a passion; but *Yungher* cared not for him; all his attention was directed to two men behind the lookers-on, who, with their spears quivering, were pacing rapidly to-and-fro, every now and then making a feint to throw the spear, but seldom uttering a word. They seemed to be incited by an old hag, who, perfectly naked, but grasping a *wanna** in both hands, was running backwards and forwards before her hut, violently gesticulating and pouring forth a volley of invective, or rather keeping up a monotonous harangue; the rapidity of her speech and her physical exertion were

---

* Yam-stick.

quite surprising. *Yungher* all this time was standing up against the tree, slapping his head first on one shoulder and then on the other. I noticed that he did this more rapidly as he expected an attack.

In about half an hour the little man's passion seemed to have spent itself, and the two fighting-men threw their spears simultaneously, and continued to do so from time to time, *Yungher* dodging them with great coolness and dexterity for nearly an hour, until at length a spear pierced him in the leg, and the affair was over. He was then received as a friend among them, and they had a dance in the evening.

The foregoing is an illustration of a common occurrence among them. The little old man may have been a *Bulya-gadak;* and, if so, he was endeavouring by his imprecations to exert an occult influence with the unseen world to devote *Yungher* to inevitable destruction, in the same way that Goliah cursed David by his gods; and in similar cases we read of the Romans devoting a person to the infernal deities. In the present day, the Indian nations have always their magicians with them in their wars, to use incantations against the adverse party.

I once saw two or three hundred natives, in the York district,[*] fighting in open ground, the adverse parties facing each other. I saw great numbers of *kylies* or boomerangs flying through the air, but had no opportunity of making any observations worthy of record.

Yagan, whom I have mentioned before, was a daring patriot. During the period that a mortal feud existed between some of the settlers and the Aborigines, a party of the former rode out from the Upper Swan on a shooting excursion in pursuit of a tribe whom they expected to find down the river. The late Mr. James Drummond, senior, the Western Australian botanist, who was one of the party, related the anecdote to me. After a great deal of riding about the bush and mistaking the grass-trees[†] for black men, they halted, and while some were preparing the lunch, Mr. Drummond, as was his habit, walked about with his hands and gun behind his back, in search of new plants. Having wandered rather far from the rest of the party, he was suddenly surprised by a naked native man jumping from behind a tree a little in advance of him, and crying "*Tchoot! tchoot!*"[‡] and at the same time leaping into the air as he would have done to avoid a spear. This man Mr. Drummond at once recognised as *Yagan*, who was evidently daring him to shoot at him, in order to show how he could avoid a bullet as he would a spear; but Mr. Drummond was too humane to take advantage of the ignorance of fire-arms of this brave man.

The natives seem to have no proper conception of truth, and would doubtless lie when it suited them to do so; yet, as a rule, the men are candid, frank, cheerful, confiding, and independent. The late Mr. G. F. Moore, when Advocate-General of the colony, wrote—" Fortunately for the ends of justice,

---

[*] In Western Australia.
[†] The grass-trees after this were called "*black boys*."
[‡] "*Shoot! shoot!*" They do not pronounce the letter *s*.

when a native is accused of any crime, he often acknowledges his share in the transaction with perfect candour, generally inculpating others by way of exculpating himself. Were it not for this habit, there would be a total failure of justice in the great majority of cases of aggression committed by them against the white people."

I have said that they are frank, cheerful, and confiding; but I should explain that these terms are scarcely applicable to any but those who are in the full possession of their natural vigor and independence, and who are uncontaminated by the vices of the Europeans. It is not an uncommon occurrence for such an Aboriginal man in his own district, on meeting a gentleman whom he had previously known, to approach him with a firm elastic step, a cheerful independent air, and, in imitation of the English custom, hold out his hand in a confiding, if not a patronizing manner.

Here is an instance of confidence, as related to me by Mr. Bland, and which would rarely if ever be met with in a European:—A tribal murder was committed at King George's Sound by three natives who were appointed to the task. They caught a boy, took him to the end of the jetty and wrung his neck. They then buried his body in the sand, but it was rooted up by some pigs. Two of them escaped in an American whaler, but the third, named *Lindol*, went into the bush, and would not be taken. Mr. Bland, in his capacity of Protector of Aborigines, having arrived at the Sound, sent a message to *Lindol* to come to him. He was afraid to go into Albany, but met him on the York road on his return journey. Mr. Bland said—"You know you ought to be in gaol." He replied—"I will go along with you;" and accordingly walked with him 240 miles to York. Thence Mr. Bland sent him by himself with a warrant of commitment 60 miles down to Perth. He walked straight down to gaol, and faithfully delivered himself up to the authorities. He was tried and transported to the island of Rottnest—the gaol for natives.

These primitive people have no ideas of the rights of property such as we have. In fact they have no separate property in any living animal, except their dogs—of which they are very fond—or in any produce of the soil. The habit of the men from youth to old age is to spear every living animal they come across, and of the women to dig up every edible root they find. The only property claimed by a native is his wife, his weapons, his cloak, girdle, ornaments, and his name; for this last he sometimes sells. It was not therefore surprising that they occasionally speared the sheep and robbed the potato gardens of the early settlers before they understood their views with regard to property; but, as I have before remarked, only entrust a native with property, and he will invariably be faithful to the trust. Lend him your gun to shoot game, and he will bring you the result of his day's sport; send him a long journey with provisions for your shepherd, and he will certainly deliver them safely. Entrust him with a flock of sheep through a rugged country to a distant run, and he and his wife will take them generally more safely than a white man would.

I believe the members of a tribe never pilfer from each other. Yet, like the Bedouin Arabs and other Asiatics, they would not consider the act of pillaging base when practised on another people, or carried on beyond the limits of their own tribe.

Generosity is not a virtue often found among savages, yet I have always known these people share their food with each other. The following instance of forbearance is worthy of note :—Soon after the settlement of Swan River, an outlawed native, remarkable for his intelligence, courage, and patriotism, had been implicated in some homicide, and the Government offered thirty pounds for his head. He quite understood this, and that, if taken, he would be brought up and shot in the public square in Perth. Yet, on hearing that his old father had been lodged in prison as a supposed accomplice in the robbery of some flour at Fremantle, he deliberately walked about Perth one afternoon,* in the hope of seeing his father; but failing in this, he returned, and the next day, when on his way to the Upper Swan, he asked a man whom he saw baling out a boat to ferry him across the river. The man acceded to his request, but when they were half across he heard the sound of a volley of musketry come reverberating up the river, and immediately jumped up in the boat, exclaiming—" They have shot my father!" and holding up three fingers before the face of the boatman, added, " I will kill three white people." He rightly surmised; his father was then shot by a picket of soldiers. However, on reaching the other side, he strode up the bank grasping his eight spears, and never looked back on the terrified boatman who had done him a kindness, but who fully expected to be the first victim. He proceeded at once to the Upper Swan barracks, where six soldiers were stationed, not one of whom happened to be at home. Seeing a soldier's wife inside at a wash-tub, he threw a spear at her and killed her. He spared the man who had shown him a kindness, and walked about fourteen miles in order to confront the fighting-men in their own barracks.

Many of the natives are doubtless treacherous, and the homicides committed by them are probably generally attended with treachery. The following is an instance :—

Molimeygget, one of *Wengal's* uncles, arrived one day from the Swan district at the Half-way House in the Darling Range, where he found a few natives from the interior encamped. After going through the usual form of sitting at a distance, silent, for some time, he approached, and being, as he supposed, on friendly terms with these people, sat down at their fire. One of them asked him to go for a piece of bread to the house. He rose, leaving his spears on the ground, but had not proceeded many steps before he turned to pick them up, when he saw the hand of another man on them, and he was then instantly speared to death. This murder may have been committed as a satisfaction for the death of one of the tribe, with which occurrence *Molimeygget* may have been wholly ignorant.

Homicide with them was not only a savage vindication of the law of life for life taken by the hand of man, but of their superstitious belief that a death from disease is caused in some occult manner by a neighbouring tribe.

---

* I published this anecdote in the *Church News* some years ago, signing myself " An Old Australian."—P. C.

Numerous instances of personal fidelity might be adduced. I have already referred (page 225) to that noble youth *Jacky*, who accompanied Mr. Kennedy in his expedition towards Cape York in 1848, and was with him when he was murdered. *Wylie* also, who accompanied Mr. Eyre, in 1841, in his perilous journey from Port Lincoln to King George's Sound, deserves a record in a historical work for his faithful attendance on his patron, when the rest of the party forsook him, and when the other two natives murdered Mr. Colin Campbell, the overseer, and tried to persuade *Wylie* to accompany them when they ran away. I knew *Wylie* well, and took his likeness.—(See Fig. 252, No. 7.)

I give the following account of a very barbarous murder, and of the punishment which followed, as an illustration both of the savage manner in which revenge is sometimes taken, and also of the practical influence that the superstitious belief of the tribe concerned in the resurrection and after-life of persons buried has on their conduct.

The tragedy was enacted between York and Beverly, in Western Australia, about the year 1839. I remember being shown the place where it occurred, but am indebted for the following particulars to Mr. Bland:—

The wife and child of a shepherd, named Cook, residing in the Avon district, were killed in revenge for the murder of a native by a white man near Green Mount. When Mr. Bland reached the spot, he found the roasting bodies in the smouldering hut, which had been set on fire after the murders had been committed. The poor woman had been wounded and rendered insensible, and then further maltreated by the blacks, who afterwards speared her to death, and, seizing the child by the ankles, dashed its brains out against the wall; they then set fire to the hut, and burned the remains.

Barrabong and *Yughite*, two of the principal murderers, were shortly afterwards apprehended, tried, convicted, and sentenced to be hung in chains on the spot where the deed was committed. This was carried out, and had an effect the result of which was not anticipated at the time. No other murder was ever afterwards committed in that district.

It was subsequently discovered that the natives believed that unless they were buried there was no future existence for them—that they would never "jump up" again. This indicates that savages, even of the low type in which some eminent English writers class these people, have an idea of a future life. They consider that if the body is devoured by crows and native dogs it cannot live again. They distinctly said this. So that the prisoners begged to be shot and buried rather than to be hung in chains; and they tried to provoke the soldiers who accompanied them in the cart to the place of execution to shoot them.

The Australian natives, like the desert Arabians, display a wonderful patience when in pursuit of game or of an enemy. Their avidity, acuteness, and perseverance are equally surprising. They never relinquish the object on account of delay in its attainment, nor until they feel assured that ultimate success is hopeless. While in pursuit, they are continually turning their regards to every quarter, endeavouring to obtain some indication of the object sought for. For this purpose, the slightest and most distant indication of smoke or dust, and the faintest track on the ground, is instantly perceived, and conveys to them the information they desire. They display extraordinary patience, as well as skill, in creeping upon and spearing emus, kangaroos, native "turkeys,"* and wild-ducks—the most vigilant of birds.

Mr. Wake says† "There seems to be an almost total absence from the mind of the Australian native of any idea of abstract morality, or even true instinct of moral propriety." There is no doubt that their normal condition is a most degraded state of barbarism; but I believe the obstacles to the civilization of the young people are attributable to the gross sensuality of their habits, and not to a want of capacity for becoming moral. It is because their associations with the white people have so often tended to encourage sensuality that so little success has attended the efforts to reclaim them. The result of the occupation of their country by our race is that they have been compelled to abandon their old barbarous habits, and, instead of them, they have adopted our vices.

I think the natives of Western Australia have no abstract ideas of truthfulness and honesty as virtues, though they are habitually honest among themselves, if not truthful. I mean they very seldom steal or lie with a sense of guilt. Moral turpitude was in no way connected with the pillaging which was sometimes carried on in the early days of the settlement, as may be seen by the address of *Yagan* to Mr. Moore.‡ And during my many years' acquaintance with them I do not remember ever hearing a native utter a falsehood with a definite idea of gaining anything by it. If questioned on any subject, he would form his reply rather with the view of pleasing the enquirer than of its being true; but this was attributable to his politeness, like that of the Asiatics, and not to any desire to deceive.

Finding among the guests at a recent evening party at a friend's house an educated and gentlemanly Chinese doctor, I had a long conversation with him on some of the customs of his people, and found that he assented in the most good-humoured way to all I said when asking him if so-and-so was what he meant, when I did not quite comprehend him—for he spoke English but indifferently; and yet, immediately afterwards, he would tell me exactly the opposite of what I had said. He would say what was not true rather than contradict me, and would tell the truth afterwards without any sense of shame at contradicting himself. And so with a native. Ask him if he is going to the north, and he would say, "Yes, yes," though presently after he would tell you he is going to the south.

The following anecdote will further illustrate their character in this respect:—

In the year 1844, I returned from King George's Sound to the Swan, in the colonial schooner *Champion*. We had on board some native prisoners, to be tried in Perth, three of whom were *Dennin*, *Webbinburt*, and *Koron*, whose likenesses are engraved in Fig. 252.

---

* The Australian bustard.
† *Journal Anthropological Institute*, vol. 1., No. 1, p. 80.   ‡ Page 228

These men were severally charged with robbery or cattle-stealing; they were from outlying districts, and had had but little communication with the Europeans. I took their likenesses, and was present at their trial, and give the following particulars from notes made at the time. *Dennin*, about forty years old, was a wily savage, charged with several offences. First, with stealing rice from Mr. Belcher. When put into the prisoner's dock, he at once stated that he and another man scratched a hole in the ground and got through into the store-room where the rice was kept, some of which he carried off and ate. He also confessed to stealing flour from Candyup, Mr. Taylor's station. He said he was asleep during the robbery of sugar from Mr. Warburton's station, but another man put some of it into his mouth! *Webbinburt*, a fine-looking young man, confessed to having speared and partly eaten a calf. *Koron*, without hesitation, owned to having killed a sheep belonging to Mr. Gillam. He said he ate the inside, and next day returned and ate part of the leg. Addressing the Clerk of the Court, whom he took to be the principal personage present, immediately he was put in the dock, he stretched out his arm and called out, "Me eat him."

With regard to marriage, a common mode of obtaining a wife was to abduct or carry one off from another tribe. In such a case the woman was in danger of losing her life; for, if she already had a husband, he would, if possible, kill her for adultery; or, if she refused to accompany her new suitor, he would seek her life. Otherwise, a man's wives consist either of the females who have been betrothed to him from their birth, or those whom he has inherited from a deceased brother. A man may never marry a woman of the same name or family division as himself.

The following are instances of revenge which I remember:—

A fine young Irishman, the son of one of the first Swan River settlers, took to the bush and lived for about two years with the natives. On one occasion, he took the young wife of *Marabunda*, a Swan native, and eloped with her over the Darling Range into the Far East. *Marabunda* followed their tracks day after day, until at length he came up with them in one of the great *quangans*, or sand-plains. In accordance with the native practice in such cases, *Marabunda* crept towards them one morning, just as the day was dawning, when people are supposed to sleep the soundest, and was in the act of quivering his spear for the deadly aim, when "Betty," hearing his approach, silently twirled a little piece of stick in her paramour's hair. He had just time to seize the gun at his side, and, raising himself in a sitting posture, pulled the trigger at the same moment that *Marabunda* let fly his spear. It was a remarkable coincidence that the bullet and spear met in mid-air, when the latter was shivered by the concussion, and *Marabunda* went off declaring that his enemy was the devil—*Genga*.

The young Irishman, notwithstanding the vagabond life he thus led for a time, was generous and brave, and never joined with the other colonists in any vindictive or cruel practices against the natives. For twelve months after the occurrence of this incident, whenever he and *Marabunda* met, it was on equal terms—the one cocked his gun and the other raised his spear as they passed, until at length a reconciliation took place. This colonist was afterwards appointed by the Governor chief of the native police at York, and while I was in that district information was brought to him by some native couriers that his younger brother had been killed by a blackfellow, under similar circumstances to those in *Marabunda's* case. He immediately mounted his horse, and rode a hundred and fifty miles, to the Victoria Plains, until he reached the tribe in which he found the slayer of his brother. The native, on seeing a white man approach on horseback, ran towards a grass-tree thicket; the other pursued at full speed, and shot him dead just as he was turning round to throw his spear. For this act the Governor suspended the Police Inspector, but some months afterwards reinstated him, on evidence being adduced that he had shot the native in self-defence.

A third similar example of the summary mode adopted by the natives in punishing an aggressor, and which will likewise be remembered by the old Swan River settlers, is as follows:—The son of a landed proprietor on the Upper Swan took off a native woman to the valley of the Toodyay, whither he was pursued by the husband, who found him asleep lying on his back on the ground. The native stealthily approached him, and chopped his face in two with an axe, severing the nose and cheek-bones. He, however, so far recovered that he lived for many years afterwards.

Some tribes are very careful and jealous of their women, while others are often willing to barter them. The women sometimes quarrel among themselves, and fight desperately with their *wannas*, while the men look on with apparent indifference.

I have not observed that the natives usually bear malice towards an aggressor after the wrong has ceased to exist. Their acts of retaliation, if not committed to punish a present offence, are perpetrated for the sake of conformity to their traditionary customs rather than for the purpose of gratifying a vindictive spirit for some past aggression against the individual offender. The cases of Mr. Kennedy, Mrs. Cook, and perhaps nearly all the murders that have been committed by the natives, are instances of this. The real offender seems never to have been sought for; but acting under the influence of a natural feeling of revenge for some great wrong committed against them, they have attacked the first white person they could get at. Their idea was that all the white people were cognizant of and approved of the acts of each other.

Though the men make drudges of the women, and often treat them in a harsh and sometimes a brutal manner, yet they are capable of strong affection. I have always observed at a native camp that the women appear as hilarious and independent as the men. Husband and wife are often much attached to each other, and continue to be so when they grow old.

I remember an old man named *Dugebub*, at the Middle Swan, who used generally to be encamped with his wife and children near the Rev. Mr. Mitchell's parsonage. They made this their head-quarters for many years. At length the old woman died, and *Dugebub* so took her death to heart that he pined away and died a few weeks after her. His affection and care for her were well known to the neighbouring settlers.

The natives are kind and attentive to their sick, and are very fond of their children, especially the boys.

I have observed that some of the young people are vain of their personal appearance, and fond of adorning themselves; the men as much, or more so, than the women. When fresh *wilghied*, and decorated in their own fashion, they are often really handsome—with a dignified air, a fine figure, and a pleasing countenance, which is always expressive. Some of the faces are quite of the Asiatic type. Some of the young people of both sexes are fond of imitating the dress of the white people. So great was the vanity of a certain lad on the Swan, that failing to obtain a hat or cap, he wore a cast-away iron saucepan, which had lost its handle, for several weeks, although he was put to great inconvenience in continually pushing it up, to prevent it from slipping over his eyes. They do not, however, like incongruity in dress. When a white shirt is given to a Swan native, he smears it over with *wilghee* before putting it on.

They are strongly impressed with the idea of their superiority to other dark people, especially to the Chinese. The following amusing illustration of this conceit took place a few years ago in Heathcote, Victoria:—A Chinaman was making a purchase in a grocer's shop, when an Aboriginal man came in, and passed on higher up the counter. The shopman turned to him and said, "What you want, John?"* The native instantly replied—"Me not John; that fellow John;" and seizing the Chinaman, he flung him into the street.

They have no idea of cleanliness. Except the tribes who live by large rivers, or near the sea, they never wash themselves from their infancy to the day of their death.

The new-born infant is rubbed over with sand, and the adults plaster their hair and anoint their persons with *wilghee*, made of red ochre and grease. This seems to keep them in health, and protect them from the assaults of flies and mosquitos, which otherwise would be intolerable.

---

* The colonists have fallen into the absurd practice of calling the heathen Chinese by the name of the beloved disciple of our Saviour, and which is also the national name of an Englishman.

APPENDIX B.

TRADITIONS OF THE AUSTRALIAN ABORIGINES ON THE NAMOI, BARWAN, AND OTHER TRIBUTARIES OF THE DARLING.

(COMMUNICATED BY THE REV. WILLIAM RIDLEY, M.A., ETC.)

I.—BAIAME.

"BAIAME" (pronounced like the three words "By-a-me," and in the Wellington district south of the Namoi "By-a-my") is the name by which tribes scattered over a great portion of the north-west and west of New South Wales designate the Supreme Being. The blacks there who are acquainted with English, if asked what *"Baiame"* is, reply, *"Carbon-massa,"* *i.e.*, the Great Master; and to further enquiry as to what they and their fathers know of *Baiame*, they reply that He made earth, and water, and sky, animals and men; that He makes the rain come down, and the grass grow; that He has delivered their fathers from evil demons; that He welcomes good people to the great *"Warrambool"* (watercourse and grove) in the sky—the Milky Way—a paradise of peace and plenty; and that He destroys the bad.

The Rev. James Günther, of Mudgee, long a Missionary in the Wellington district, has recorded in his grammar of the *"Wiradhurri"* language that the thoughtful blackfellows ascribe to *"Baiamai"* these three attributes—immortality, power, and goodness. They say that *Baiame* is present at their *Cora*—the periodical assembly at which young men are initiated into the privileges of manhood. Among the ceremonies of the *Cora* is the exhibition of a sacred wand, which they say was given to their people by *Baiame*, the sight of which is essential to impart manhood.

"Baiame" is derived (as the Rev. C. C. Greenway has shown) from *"baia,"* to make, cut out, or build. Like many other words, it is variously pronounced—sometimes aspirated, sometimes sharpened. The "b" which is generally heard at the beginning of words sometimes becomes "bh," or almost "v," sometimes "p."

For ages unknown this race has handed down the word signifying "Maker" as the name of the Supreme.

II.—IDEAS OF THE STARS.

King "Rory," an old chief of the *Wailwun* (*Wile-one*) tribe, on the Barwan, near the junction of the Namoi, gave me the following account of stars:—

The Northern Crown is "*Mullion wollai*," the eagle's-nest ("*wollai*" means "camp"). The several stars in the Crown are the young eagles. When this constellation is on the meridian, Vega rises, and shortly before it Altair. These are the two old eagles springing up to watch their nest. It was a startling word of the old chief when Altair (in Aquila) appeared, to hear the name "*Mullion*."

Arcturus they call "*Guembila*" (red); Canopus is "*Wumba*" (deaf); Benemasch, and the next star in the tail of the Great Bear—the only bright stars of that constellation visible in this latitude, which rise about N.N.E., and set N.N.W., never rising high, but moving, as it were, under the branches of the high trees—they call "*Nyŭng-yū*" (white owls).

The Milky Way they call *Warrambool*, that is a strip of land abounding in fine trees and shrubs, with a stream of water running through it—the home or promenade of the blessed dead. The Pleiades are *Worrul* (bees'-nest); Bungula and Agenor, *Murrai* (cockatoos); the Southern Cross, *Ngŭŭ* (tea-tree); the dark space under the Cross, *Gao-ergi* (emu); Magellan Clouds, *Buralga* (native companions); Antares, *Guddar* (lizard); two stars across the Milky Way, near Scorpio, *Gijeri-ga* (small green parrots); a dark space near them, *Wurrawilbŭrū* (demon, or ghost); the "S"-shaped line of stars in Serpentarius between the Northern Crown and Scorpio, *Mundēwur* (notches cut on a tree to climb up); Spica Virginis, *Gŭriē* (small crested parrot); Fomalhaut, *Gāni* (small iguana); Corvus (4), *Bundar* (kangaroo); star in Peacock's Head, *Murgu* (night cuckoo); Venus, *Ngindigindōer* (you are laughing); Mars, *Gumba* (fat); Saturn, *Wungal* (a small bird).

III.—LAWS OF DESCENT AND MARRIAGE.

A social classification, carried out by means of family names, and embracing every human being of the race, is known to exist all over the tributaries of the Darling, including the Balonne and the Maranoa, and over the Wide Bay district of Queensland. This classification is the basis of strict laws of marriage and descent. The same class-names are in use among tribes speaking different dialects, and the system is known to be established even beyond the extent over which the same names are used. Among the *Kamilaroi*, *Wolaroi*, *Wiradhurri*, *Wailwun*, and *Pickumbul* tribes, the class-names are, for men, *Ippai*, *Murri*, *Kubbi*, and *Kumbo*; for women, their sisters, *Ippăthā*, *Mātha*, *Kubbothā*, and *Būta* (or *Būdha*). Besides these, they have other class-names, derived from animals, which also come by inheritance. The mother's name determines that of the child, and generally, not always, the child's class-name may be known from the father's. This will be seen by the subjoined rules. Besides the names that come to them by birth, the Aborigines have other distinctive names, commonly taken from some personal characteristic, as long-arm, short-leg, sharp-eye. *Murri (Murry)* is the name of the race—meaning Australian Aboriginal. *Murri (Murree)* is the most important of the four classes.

Rules of Descent.

1. The mother's second name descends to all her children. Thus all the children of *Budha nurai* are "*nurai*" (black snake); her sons are *Ippai nurai;* her daughters, *Ippatha nurai*.
2. The sons of *Matha* are *Kubbi;* her daughters, *Kubbotha*. (*Matha murrūra's* sons are *Kubbi murriira* (paddy melon); her daughters, *Kubbotha murriira*.
3. The sons of *Budha* are *Ippai;* the daughters, *Ippatha*.
4. The sons of *Ippatha* are *Kumbo;* her daughters, *Budha*.
5. The sons of *Kubbotha* are *Murri;* her daughters, *Matha*.

    N.B.—*Murri* and *Matha* are the highest grade: but *Matha's* children are *Kubbi* and *Kubbotha*, the lowest. Again, *Kubbotha's* son is *Murri*, of the highest grade. So every family passes, in two or three or four generations, through the highest and lowest grades—a curious combination of the ideas of aristocracy and levelling; but the difference of rank is slight.

Rules of Marriage.

1. *Murri duli* (iguana) may marry a *Matha murriira*, or any *Budha*.
2. *Murri murriira* may marry a *Matha duli*, or any *Budha*.
3. *Kumbo dinoun* (emu) may marry a *Budha nurai*, or any *Matha*.
4. *Kumbo nurai* may marry *Budha dinoun*, or any *Matha*.
5. *Ippai dinoun* may marry *Ippatha nurai*, or *Kubbotha duli*, or *Kubbotha murriira*.
6. *Ippai nurai* may marry *Ippatha dinoun*, or *Kubbotha mute* (opossum).
7. *Ippai bilba* (bandicoot) may marry *Ippatha nurai*, or *Kubbotha murriira*.
8. *Kubbi mute* may marry *Kubbotha duli*, or *Ippatha dinoun*.
9. *Kubbi murriira* may marry *Kubbotha duli*, or *Ippatha nurai*.
10. *Kubbi duli* may marry *Kubbotha murriira*, or *Ippatha bilba*.

A man may have many wives of the names that are legally open to him, if he has the art or force to get them. But if he attempts to take one whose name is not allowed to one bearing his name in these rules, the tribe will kill him, or at least attack him with deadly purpose. The law is sacred; curses and spears fall upon him who dares to violate it.

From the above rules, it follows that generally the children of *Kumbo* are *Kubbi* and *Kubbotha;* those of *Murri* are *Ippai* and *Ippatha;* those of *Kubbi* are *Kumbo* and *Budha;* those of *Ippai* are *Murri* and *Matha*. But if *Kumbo*, instead of marrying a *Matha*, takes a *Budha* (with a different *totem*), his children are *Ippai* and *Ippatha;* and if *Murri*, instead of marrying a *Budha*, takes a *Matha* (with a different *totem*), his children are *Kubbi* and *Kubbotha*. So, in all cases, the mother's name determines that of the children.

Among the *Kogai* tribes, west of the Balonne, and also at Wide Bay, Queensland, the feminine names are derived from those of the brothers, by affixing -*un* or -*gun*. Thus, among the *Kogai*, the names (answering to *Ippai*, &c.) are these:—*Obūr, Wungō, Urgilla, Unburri;* and their sisters, *Oburugun, Wungogun, Urgillagun, Unburrigun*. And at Wide Bay the names are *Derwun, Bārāng, Bundar, Tandor, Balkoin;* and their sisters, *Derwungun, Barangun, Bundarun, Tandorun, Balkoingun*—the only case I have heard of where there are five names to each sex.

Brothers and Sisters.

Daiādi is elder brother; *Gullami*, younger brother. *Boadi* is elder sister; *Buri*, younger sister.

Among eight brothers, the first-born has no *daiadi*, seven *gullami;* the youngest has seven *daiadi* and no *gullami;* the fourth has three *daiadi* and four *gullami*.

So the eldest sister among eight has no *boadi* and seven *buri;* the third has two *boadi*, five *buri*.

Father is *Bŭbā*, sometimes "*Papa*."

Mother is *Ngumba*. But its appellative, used by children in calling on their mothers, is *Guni* (pronounced just as γυνη is pronounced at Oxford).

IV.—NAMES OF LANGUAGES.

Most of the languages are named from their *negative*. Thus in *Kamilaroi*, "*kamil*" means "no" or "not;" in *Wolaroi*, "*wol*" is "no;" in *Wailwun*, "*wail*" is "no;" in *Wiradhurri*, "*wira*" is "no." But in *Pikumbul* "*pika*" means "yes."

APPENDIX C.

NOTES ON THE NATIVES OF AUSTRALIA.

(By Albert A. C. Le Souëf.)

The natives are much more numerous in some parts of Australia than they are in others, but nowhere is the country thickly peopled; some dire disease occasionally breaks out among the natives, and carries off large numbers. This was the case among the Goulburn, Devil's River, and Upper and Lower Murray tribes some few years before the country was peopled by the whites;— the small-pox, or some very similar disease, made its appearance, and played havoc among the tribes. But there are two other causes which, in my opinion, principally account for their paucity of numbers. The first is that infanticide is universally practised; the second, that a belief exists that no one can die a natural death. Thus, if an individual of a certain tribe dies, his relatives consider that his death has been caused by sorcery on the part of another tribe. The deceased's sons, or nearest relatives, therefore start off on a "buccccning" or murdering expedition. If the deceased is buried, a fly or beetle is put into the grave, and the direction in which the insect wings its way when released is the one the avengers take. If the body is burnt, the whereabouts of the offending parties is indicated by the direction of the smoke. The first unfortunates fallen in with are generally watched until they encamp for the night; when they are buried in sleep, the murderers steal quietly up until they are within a yard or two of their victims, rush suddenly upon and butcher them. On these occasions they always abstract the kidney-fat, and also take off a piece of the skin of the thigh. These are carried home as trophies, as the American Indians take the scalp. The murderers anoint their bodies with the fat of their victims, thinking that by that process the strength of the deceased enters into them. Sometimes it happens that the "buccccning" party come suddenly upon a man of a strange tribe in a tree hunting opossums; he is immediately speared, and left weltering in his blood at the foot of the tree. The relatives of the murdered man at once proceed to retaliate; and thus a constant and never-ending series of murders is always going on. Not now in Victoria (for the tribes are nearly extinct), but in the more distant part of the country, I have no doubt the same thing is still going on.

I do not mean to assert that for every man that dies or is killed another is murdered; for it often happens that the deceased has no sons or relatives who care about avenging his death. At other times a "buccccning" party will return without having met with any one; then, again, they are sometimes repelled by those they attack. I remember an instance of this kind many years ago on the Goulburn. There were a large number of natives encamped close to the station at the time. One night about ten or eleven o'clock, just as I was going to bed, I heard a woman's shriek, followed by the excited cries of the men. In an instant the whole camp was in an uproar, and every man, snatching up a fire-brand and spear, rushed to the river, and they spread themselves over the fallen timber which choked the stream. It was a wild, weird scene—the dusky forms of the blacks holding their spears aloft, ready to strike the foe; their numerous torches, as they moved quickly over the fallen timber, reflected in the black water beneath, and lighting up the spreading trees above. As I stood wondering what it all meant, I heard some natives on the opposite bank of the river shouting defiance as they retreated. I then guessed the cause. Next morning I was told that the woman whose shriek I had heard had been sent to the river by her husband—too lazy or frightened to go himself—for water. On her way she was attacked by a "buccceening" party in ambush. Her shrieks at once brought the men to her rescue, who, being numerous, were bold. The "buccceeners" at once plunged into the river and swam across, and it was in the hope of intercepting them that the men spread themselves over the fallen trees. The unfortunate woman got off with a severe blow on her head from a waddy, but, no doubt used to such treatment, she seemed to care little about it, and was greatly rejoiced at having escaped with her life. I recollect a case on the Loddon where a camp was attacked; the men fled, and a number of unfortunate women were murdered. I could tell of cases where weak tribes have been almost annihilated by their stronger and treacherous neighbours.

The constant treachery practised prevents the different tribes from often leaving their own territory; if they do, they are never sure of their lives; for the same reason they do not like going about after dark, or leaving their camps, unless several are together;—there may be a lurking foe behind every tree or bush.

I have mentioned infanticide as being prevalent. This is not practised so much from want of affection for their offspring—on the contrary, those they rear they are very fond of—but simply as a matter of convenience. If a woman has a child before a former one can take care of itself, it stands but a poor chance of its life, especially if a girl. I once asked a young woman who shortly before had dashed her infant's brains out against a tree why she had done so. "Oh!" she coolly replied, "too much cry that fellow." On my telling her that was no reason for killing her infant, she said, pointing to a child of two years of age, "Oh, too much young fellow Jimmy; no good two fellow pickaninny."

The River or fish-eating tribes are the most numerous and the most robust. I have seen many six-foot men among them, well built and stout in proportion. The tribes who inhabit country with no rivers, and but little water, are miserable creatures, repulsive in appearance, stunted in growth, without vigor, having more primitive encampments, fewer appliances, and ruder weapons, and altogether inferior to the fish tribes. The dialects are indeed widely different; the words signifying the same object having no similarity whatever in tribes not far removed; but it is a singular fact, showing the common origin of the language, that although an individual of a tribe may not be able to understand the dialect of the natives a hundred miles from his birthplace, yet, take him considerably further, and he will probably meet with those speaking a very similar language to his own, and with whom he can converse.

The girls are betrothed when very young, sometimes as infants; and at the age of thirteen or fourteen are taken possession of in a very summary manner by their future lords. If they will not go quietly to his mia-mia, they get a tap over the head with a waddy to enforce obedience. They are often promised to men of a neighbouring tribe. In that case, they are taken at some general meeting. In all my long experience of native life I have only met with one instance of anything like love being shown. This was in the case of a pretty young girl, who was given to a man old enough to be her father, and who already had one wife, showing a most decided preference for a young man of her tribe. Charley—for that was the favored one's name—took possession of his lady-love when her intended husband was absent on a hunting expedition. On the return of the latter to the camp, he vowed vengeance, and at once endeavoured to recover the girl by force of arms. He armed himself, and approached Charley's mia-mia, waddy and malka in hand. Charley arose, and, taking up his weapons, coolly awaited his opponent—the poor girl cowering and trembling behind him, for well she knew what her fate would be if her lover was defeated. A desperate fight now took place between the two men. Charley was much the smaller of the two, but younger and very active, and I am glad to say victory declared for him, as he gave his opponent a terrible thrashing. However, as he had committed a breach of tribal usage, all were against him, and he had to take himself off with his fair one until the affair had blown over. The Goulburn and Murray blacks had a curious custom or superstition with regard to betrothment. The mother of the betrothed girl would never look at or meet her intended son-in-law if at all possible to avoid him; but if compelled to pass close to him, she would cover up her head and face with her opossum cloak and shuffle past in a most ridiculous fashion. I never could get at the meaning of this apparently absurd custom, called by the Goulburn tribe *Ulandibe* or *Ulandibo*.

Polygamy is universal; but it is generally the old men of the tribe who have the greatest number of wives. The reason of this is that they exchange their young daughters for young wives for themselves. Many of the young men are consequently without any, and the result is perpetual fights and quarrels about the women. They, unfortunate creatures, lead a wretched life of drudgery. They have to collect yams for their husbands—which alone is no joke, as they eat an immense quantity—fetch wood and water, and when on the move carry everything—the man walking along majestically with his tomahawk and a few spears, his poor lubra trudging behind loaded. Their life depends much upon the temper of their generally morose and sullen masters, who beat them brutally with the first thing they can lay their hands on, tomahawk or waddy, for the veriest trifles. When eating, the man sits in front, devouring all the choice parts, occasionally throwing a half-picked bone or some entrails to his lubra behind.

In the many fights which take place, I am sorry to say that the women, especially the old ones, always make matters worse by taunting the men. They work themselves into a perfect fury, lashing the ground with their yam-sticks and opossum cloaks, throwing dust into the air, yelling and screaming, and looking like very fiends.

Although each tribe is confined to its own territory, they have assemblies at different times, at which several tribes assist. On these occasions there are great feastings and corrobboree—the national Aboriginal dance of Australia—and the meeting generally ends in a fight. When any recent cause of quarrel exists, a fight ensues almost as soon as the tribes meet. I have frequently been present at these native gatherings. I remember once strolling up to the camp of the *Pangarangs*, who had arrived about an hour before on a visit to the *Oorilim*. I had been told that a fight was likely to take place, as a *Pangarang*, rejoicing in the name of *Neptune*, had recently lost a son, and he suspected his death had been caused by one of the *Oorilim*. I went to *Neptune's* mia-mia, where he was sitting cross-legged roasting an opossum, his two lubras squatted behind him. In a few minutes the mother of the dead boy commenced a low, mournful dirge; directly she did so, her husband, who up to that moment had been laughing and talking to me, became grave and silent. The woman gradually worked herself into a rage, until I knew, from my knowledge of the language, that she was cursing the *Oorilim* for causing the death of her child, and taunting her own people, and her husband in particular, for not avenging his death. Gradually the noise of the camp became hushed, and several other women joined in the mournful chant. *Neptune*, who had sat motionless as a statue until now, suddenly sprang to his legs, as if he had received an electric shock, and with a wild cry seized his spears, and dashing his cloak to the ground, rushed into the open space between the two camps, and threw a reed-spear high into the air. As it fell quivering in front of the *Oorilim* camp, every man arose and ran to his weapons. In a minute the two tribes, about thirty men in each, stood opposite to each other. The conflict now commenced in earnest; spears and boomerangs whizzed through the air, the men shouted and yelled defiance, while the women hung on the outskirts of the combatants, lashing the ground with their yam-sticks and dancing like very maniacs—as they were for the time—taunting and spitting at the opponents, and urging on their respective tribes to the combat; every now and then the vixens would rush at each other, and smash each other's fingers with their long sticks. After a time the spears were thrown aside, and the men rushed on each other with their waddies and leangles, and a general hand-to-hand fight took place, and lasted for some time, until a third tribe, who were camped close by, but not mixed up in the quarrel, separated the belligerents, and succeeded in making peace after much loud talking.

When the fight commenced, I got behind a tree and watched the combat. I thought that some would have been killed; but, when quiet was restored, I found that no great damage had been done; one man was severely cut in the thigh by a boomerang, another had a spear through his leg, and a few broken heads made up the sum total of the casualties. At night, a grand corrobboree was held, and the tribes seemed to have forgotten their quarrel, and to be on the best possible terms again. On another occasion I witnessed a desperate fight among those same *Pangaranys*, which took place after dark, from some dispute which had arisen in camp. They fought with tomahawks and waddies, holding torches in their left hands. The shouts and curses of the combatants, the screams and yells of the women and children, the howling of the dogs, the whole camp enshrouded in darkness, excepting where the apparently deadly fray was going on, which was lighted by the glare of fire-brands—made up the most unearthly scene I ever witnessed; and the thought struck me, as I gazed on the savage sight, that if any one unaccustomed to bush life had been suddenly transported to where I stood, he would have thought himself in the infernal regions. It was not safe to go near them, and so they fought the matter out by themselves. After a time they became exhausted, and quiet was gradually restored. In the morning some showed ghastly wounds; but, as they were all on the head, it did not much signify, as a blackfellow's skull seems to be impenetrable.

They are fond of wrestling, and, when two tribes meet, often amuse themselves in this manner. They all collect and sit or stand in a circle about a clear space, and the best wrestlers on either side try their skill. When a fall is given, a shout of approval greets the winner; but these games sometimes lead to serious results, as it seems to be thought a disgrace to be thrown three times in succession. On one occasion when I was a looker-on at a trial of skill of this kind, a native, named Davy, was thrown three times heavily by a man of another tribe named Long Bill. Davy took it all in good part until the third time; then, as he rose from the ground, he left his opponent, and walked towards his mia-mia, and an ominous silence at once settled on all present. I was standing in the circle, and Long Bill, seeing me, ran over to where I stood, and said—" You pull away, plenty boomerang fly about directly." I took his friendly advice very quickly. On reaching shelter, I turned to watch. Davy had reached his mia-mia, and was again advancing with his weapons in his hand. The two tribes now rose and separated. As soon as Davy got near enough, he threw a boomerang right among Long Bill's tribe. They opened out in a crescent, and the missile passed through without striking any one. All now rushed for their weapons, and, in a few minutes, those who had just before been apparently such good friends were engaged in a fierce fight. After a while another tribe, who were neutral, interfered, as neutral tribes generally do, and the fight was stopped; but the disagreement led to a general break-up of the encampment—each tribe retiring to their own territory.

I could describe numbers of fights I have witnessed, but they are all very much alike. I can only say I never saw a man killed in one of them; thanks to their great quickness of vision and agility, they escape many a spear that would transfix a white man in the same position. The corrobboree is common to all Australian tribes, although there is a great difference in the way in which it is danced. The following is the manner in which it is usually performed by the Victorian tribes.

It is generally danced when two tribes meet, one dancing one night, the other the next. The lookers-on congregate about the large fires made to light up the scene, and admire or criticise the performers. The women seat themselves in a body, with their opossum cloaks tightly rolled up before them, on which they beat with their right hands, keeping perfect time, at the same time chanting one of their corrobboree songs. One of the oldest men, generally a man of note, acts as leader. Suddenly, through the gloom, the dancers one by one glide upon the scene, each man painted with white streaks of pipeclay on his face, legs, and body, and a large bunch of green leaves tied tightly round his ankles, which make a peculiar rustling noise as he dances. They commence by beating time simultaneously with their corrobboree-sticks (short pieces of green wood which give out a loud ringing sound when struck), and shaking or quivering their extended legs in the manner peculiar to the corrobboree. As the performers become excited, the vigor of the dance increases, and, with loud shouts, they advance in a body towards their leader, who, chanting at the top of his voice, with his face turned to the dancers, slowly retires before the advancing mass—vigorously beating time meanwhile—until the large fire is reached. The dancing now ceases, and the men, rushing into a compact body, stamp with their right feet until a cloud of dust arises, when, with a wild shout, each one at the same moment throws up his arms above his head, and they then retreat to commence again. The perfect time that is kept is wonderful. If fifty men are dancing, they strike the corrobboree-sticks as if they were but one pair, and they exhibit an extraordinary degree of elasticity and grace in their movements—indeed some seem to have no joints in their legs, so supple and pliant are they. Sometimes they perform with spears in their hands, but not often; and sometimes around the rude figure of a man cut out of bark. This latter dance is connected with some of their superstitions.

As I have stated, the corrobboree is differently danced in other parts of the country, and some tribes have a greater variety of dances than others. In Western Australia they represent the hunting of the kangaroo.—(*See* Mr. Eyre's work.)

They lead a rude, simple kind of life. The day is spent in hunting and fishing, and the women go out and gather yams, or fish in the lagoons with small nets they make for the purpose. As evening advances, the hunters return, and the produce of the day is cooked and eaten. After nightfall, the elders of the tribe often address the rest on some subject interesting to them. They speak in a loud tone of voice, so that the whole camp can hear them, for the mia-mias are built close to each other for protection. Whenever the speaker makes a point, a loud shout of approval is raised. After an hour or two, they cease, and sleep gradually overcomes them, and all is hushed for the night, unless indeed, which often happens, some unfortunate woman offends her brutal husband, and is beaten or speared by him, in which case her piercing *ya-ki! ya-ki!* is heard a long distance; or that most melancholy and depressing of all native chants, the wail for the dead, rising and falling on the still night air, breaks the silence of the otherwise sleeping camp. Summer is their busiest time. It is then the tribes meet together and hold their corrobborees and settle their disputes. Spring is also a time of rejoicing, for their yams and roots are plentiful and good, and the ground being soft, the kangaroo and emu are more easily captured; but in winter they do nothing more than they can possibly help. In July, emus' eggs are eagerly sought after; and from that month until the end of the egg season is the time when they obtain the greatest quantity and variety of food.

A good deal has been written and said about chieftainship, but nothing of the kind exists; there are certainly a few men—generally the boldest and strongest and very often the most mischievous—who acquire some ascendancy in their tribe, but they have no recognised authority as the American Indian chiefs have. Each tribe is bound together by a common cause and a common danger; unity is their only safety from their neighbours. They have some curious superstitions and customs. Any theft or breach of tribal usage is generally enquired into by the leading men of the tribe, and punished. The culprit, if found guilty, has either to stand at a certain distance and receive three spears aimed at him in rapid succession, or to receive a blow on the head from a waddy. The spears are generally avoided, but the other punishment is more serious in its results. I have more than once seen both punishments inflicted. In the latter, the culprit has to hold his head down, and he stuffs his beard into his mouth, to take off the jar of the blow; the executioner then deliberately strikes full on the head. Sometimes, among the South Australian tribes, when they use for the purpose a heavy two-handed sword, the skull is smashed, and the man dies. In other cases, the offender is an idiot for the rest of his days; but among the Goulburn and Murray tribes, where most of my experience of native life has been gathered, it is seldom such results ensue. I remember one case especially, where a man had stolen a small quantity of sugar from one of his fellows. The tribe took it up, and condemned the thief to receive a blow on the head from the man he had wronged. The culprit stood as I have described, and the other walked quickly up to him, stopped for a few moments, and then dealt him a blow which would have smashed a white man's skull. The man who received it, however, never stirred, but simply looked up, the blood streaming down his face. The man who struck him now burst into a violent fit of crying, and, lifting his waddy, struck the pointed handle again and again into his own head until it was covered with blood; then, turning round, he threw his waddy from him as far as he could, and, still crying violently, threw his arms round the neck of the man he had struck. It was a most touching sight, and one I shall not easily forget.

I never could discover anything among them approaching to religion; they certainly have a vague idea that when they die they will, as they express it, "jump up whitefellow," but the superstition must of course be of recent origin. They also believe in evil spirits, which roam about at night; and in others which cause sickness, and which the doctors of the tribe try to exorcise by placing their mouths on the part affected, and speaking or chanting in a singular and rapid manner. But all their superstitions bearing on this subject are so utterly vague—they being unable to explain anything themselves—that it is impossible to make head or tail of it. My opinion is that they have no religious notions or ideas whatever.

The natives of Australia are cannibals in a modified sense; they do not often eat their fellow-creatures, but there is no doubt that occasionally they do. I have myself seen the hands of a man in the *moogger-moogger* or bag of a native; the same man had also a large piece of human fat, with which he anointed himself all over, warming it by the fire and rubbing it well in. I have read of some revolting and well-authenticated cases of cannibalism; but as the theme is not a pleasing one, I will say no more about it.

In every tribe there is a doctor, always an elderly man, and sometimes there are several; and there is no complaint they will not attempt to cure. For cuts or wounds, they apply bandages and often earth poultices, which, by-the-by, often have a marvellous effect. They are also skilled in the art of bleeding; they open a vein with a piece of sharp flint or shell; they often rub and knead with their knuckles the affected part. For rheumatism, they plunge the patient into cold water. But if all their usual remedies fail, they proceed to incantations, in the hope of driving the evil spirit out.

They are very superstitious. Comets are their peculiar aversion. The first night the great comet of 1842 [1843] appeared, there was dreadful commotion and consternation among the Australian tribes. A large number were encamped close to the station where I resided, and I remember the intense alarm it created—different spokesmen gesticulated and speechified far into the night; but as the comet still remained, and all their endeavours to explain the unusual appearance were fruitless, they broke up their camp in the middle of the night—the only time I ever remember its being done—and crossed the river, where they remained huddled up together until morning. Their opinion was that the comet had been caused and sent by the Ovens blacks to do them some direful harm. They left the station, and did not return until the comet disappeared.

Many tribes follow a singular custom of knocking out the two front teeth of the upper jaw. This is done to the young men only. They also tattoo, which is a most painful operation. In some tribes the whole back and part of the chest are covered, and the women are also tattooed, but not to the same extent. Among others, the men only have a single row, high up on the back. The operation is always performed by a man, and consists in making a number of broad and deep gashes in the flesh: those on the men are generally about an inch and a half in length. It is astonishing how stoically this horrible operation is borne. I once saw a young man undergoing the operation, and he bore it with the greatest fortitude, although his back was literally cut to pieces. By some process, with which I am not acquainted, the cut, when healed, protrudes half an inch from the skin, forming large lumps, which are considered a great adornment. Circumcision is not known among the Victorian or New South Wales tribes, but is common among those on the north coast. Among the tribes to the north-west of Adelaide a very singular custom prevails—an incision is made at the base of the scrotum. It is common among the Gawler Range blacks. At the age of seventeen or eighteen, the boys are inducted into manhood by a singular custom, called by the Goulburn natives "*Jibbogoop*." The noviciate is painted in a fantastic manner, and for some weeks is the butt and fool of the tribe. After the absurd ceremony is completed, he becomes a man, and can take part in the counsels of the elders, and take a wife, if he can get one. In some tribes the boy is started off with a tomahawk naked into the bush, and cannot return until he has clothed himself in a cloak of opossum skins, made by his own hands. But, although now a man, he cannot touch the flesh of the emu; that is only for the elders of the tribe; it is fat and oily, and considered a great luxury, which accounts for the old fellows keeping it to themselves.

They have different modes of disposing of their dead. Some tribes burn the body, carefully collecting the ashes into the centre of a small cleared space; others bury, first tying the body into a ball; others place the body on a scaffold some distance from the ground; and others put them into hollow trees. Sir Thomas Mitchell mentions in one of his works that he once saw a regular grave-yard prettily laid out, the paths kept perfectly clean; it was situated in a beautiful grove of acacia, and had evidently been the burial-place of the tribe to whom it belonged for a long time. I recently observed that one of the parties now engaged in erecting the telegraph line across the continent met with a similar grave-yard on the Finke.

When a death occurs, the relatives cover their heads with clay, and daub their faces with the same material, and the most intense grief is exhibited. If a man dies, the women (his wives) cut and burn themselves in a most shocking manner, and the camp at night resounds with their mournful lamentations. The wail of the women on these occasions is intensely melancholy and depressing, especially when heard on a calm, still night. They will never, if possible, unless for the purpose of revenge, mention the departed by name, and I have often made them very angry by doing so.

Before the advent of the whites, I do not think human life was shorter among the natives than it is among Europeans. I have seen many old men with hair as white as snow; at least it would have been so had it been clean. I am sure they were upwards of eighty years of age. I know several instances where men were grey in 1841, when I, as a child, first made their acquaintance, and they really looked but little older when I last saw them in 1861.

Before they became so degenerated by contact with the whites, they were excellent huntsmen. The kangaroo and emu were speared—the hunter stealing on his game against the wind, under cover of a bush held in his left hand, the womerah and spear being grasped in the right. When the black had crept up within spearing distance, the bush was suddenly thrown aside, and before the astonished animal or bird could escape, it was transfixed by a spear. Some of the River tribes—those on the Darling—catch numbers of wild-fowl by stretching a net across the river, from tree to tree, close to the water. A native then ascends a tree, and when a flight of ducks approach, he imitates the cry of the hawk; the ducks immediately drop close to the water, where they strike the net and become entangled.

They are also expert in spearing fish at night from their canoes. The canoe —which is simply a sheet of bark cut off a tree with a bend in it—is allowed to drop silently down the stream; a small fire is lighted in the bow, on a raised piece of clay, of a peculiar resinous wood, which burns with a clear, bright flame; the fish, attracted by the light, swim up to it, and are immediately speared. The canoes, being so frail, require great steadiness in their management, though on the Lower Murray I have seen them large enough to carry a dozen men at once. These large canoes are cut off the giant swamp-gums. They also snare the wild turkey or bustard. They approach as they do when stealing on an emu; but instead of a spear, they carry a long light stick, at the extreme end of which is tied a fluttering moth, as well as a strong running noose hanging just below. The bustard is so intent on looking at the moth that he does not notice the noose, which the cunning black at last succeeds in slipping over his head.

They cook their large game in ovens made in the following manner:—A hole is made in the earth, and lined with stones; in it they make a fierce fire, until the stones become almost red hot; the kangaroo, or what they intend to cook, is then placed in the oven, on the top of which some more hot stones are placed, and the whole covered with earth; the heat of the stones and the confined steam together cook the meat.

The natives, as a rule, are splendid swimmers, though there are tribes living in dry country who will not go near the water, and cannot swim a stroke; but among River tribes water is second nature—children hardly able to walk swim like ducks. It is strange to watch a blackfellow catching ducks by diving. He drops down the stream with merely a small portion of his head above water. When he is close to the flock, he quietly dives, and draws one or two birds under the surface; these he at once kills and tucks them under his belt; he then rises to the surface, but only shows his nose; in a moment he is down again, and another duck or two disappear. I have seen a black take seven ducks in this manner without creating any suspicion in the flock. They are also expert in noosing wild-fowl.

Their weapons consist of different kinds of spears, some being jagged on both sides, others on one; others again are jagged with flint, especially among the northern tribes. These are all most dangerous weapons, for, once in the flesh, they cannot be extracted or drawn back. Some spears are thrown by the hand only, being held in the centre; but all the light spears, especially those used for hunting, are those thrown by the womerah; at the throwing end there is about a foot or eighteen inches of grass-tree, which causes the spear to fly straight.

The Murray and Lower Goulburn natives used principally reed-spears, the reeds being found in large quantities in certain parts of the rivers mentioned. In former years, there was a regular system of barter going on—the tribes owning the country about what is known as Lancefield used to exchange large quantities of greenstone, for making tomahawks, for reed-spears. There is a large native quarry still to be seen on Mount William, near Lancefield, where this stone was quarried. It is extremely hard and tough, and well adapted for stone tomahawks. The same kind of stone was universally used, and I have no doubt the Mount William stone found its way from tribe to tribe for hundreds of miles. They also use the waddy, the leangle—a peculiar weapon not unlike the miner's pick—spear and waddy shields, and a variety of that most singular weapon the boomerang. All their weapons, with the exception of the spear, are more or less carved, and covered with white and red ochre. The natives generally have a considerable taste for carving and drawing. I have repeatedly seen the inside of their mia-mias covered with rude etchings of the kangaroo or emu, or anything else that might occur to them. The sheets of bark are first blackened in the fire, and the drawings are made with a piece of pointed stone or a nail, and some are really very well done.

APPENDIX D.

NOTES ON THE ABORIGINES OF COOPER'S CREEK.

(BY ALFRED W. HOWITT, F.G.S., P.M. AND WARDEN OF THE GOLDFIELDS AT BAIRNSDALE.)

A GREAT central chain of Salt Lakes extends from the Flinders Range northward. Into these lakes flows the surplus water of Cooper's Creek. The Aborigines living on these waters and extending to the eastward on the various watercourses may be said to be numerous, when the nature of the country is considered. I estimated them at about 1,200. They are divided into tribes; and again subdivided, and I am inclined to think that every lake and permanent water may be regarded as having its sub-tribe. I am acquainted with four tribes. The *Deeries*, who live at Lake Hope (*Bando Pinna;* or the Big Lake); the *Yantruwunter*, who live at Cooper's Creek proper; and two other tribes who live towards Lake Lipson (*Bando Patchaditti*); and Sturt's Desert (*Murda Pinna*, or the Big Stones).

The natives living at Strezelecki's Creek are called the "*Tingatingana*" blacks, from the native name of the creek; they are, I believe, a subdivision of the *Deeries*, and have a very bad name. Perhaps it is worse than they deserve, for all the misdeeds done by blacks on the border are laid to the charge of the *Tingatingana* blacks.

The language is the same from Sturt's Desert down to Flood's Creek, in the Barrier Ranges; and from the chain of Salt Lakes eastward, I know not how far up the rivers.

A small family of the *Yantruwunter* go from the end of Strezelecki's Creek down to Flood's Creek, and there meet natives of the Darling back country. I think that the native mentioned by Sturt as coming to his camp (I think at Fort Grey) was probably one of this family. Capt. Sturt mentions that he made signs of great waters to the west or north-west, and also represented the paddling of canoes; I think this really represented the hauling in of a net or "*Yamma*." I have seen such a pantomime, but I never saw a canoe or any place where bark for a canoe had been stripped in Central Australia. This small tribe meets the Darling natives as I have said, and some of them have spoken to me of them derisively as being so ignorant as to call a snake "fire." The *Yantruwunter* call fire "*Touro*." The Darling blacks use the same word for "snake"—for instance, on Burke's track there is a swamp called "*Tourowato*," meaning "To catch hold of a snake;" or, in the broken English of the tame blacks, to "Man-em-snake." "*Wattoley*" is to take hold of anything.

The Salt Lakes form a line, on one side of which water is called "*Appa*" and on the other side "*Owie*" or "*Cowie*;" the blacks are themselves called "Salt-water" blacks and "Hill" blacks; the former living about the lakes, and the latter among the hills forming the extreme northern end of the Flinders Range and the plain between the hills and the lakes. The word "*Owie*" or "*Cowie*" extends through South Australia to the great Australian Bight, and possibly still further towards West Australia. For instance, "*Owie-andinna*" (jump-up water, or spring) at Mount Serle, and "*Yereumban-cowie* (a water) at the head of the Great Bight. This seems to me to point out the migrations of blacks spreading over the country and meeting at the Salt Lakes.

The language also changes on crossing the watershed between the creeks flowing into Cooper's Creek and those falling towards Bulloo Creek and the Darling River.

The different families seem to have distinctive names. Many seem to have no present meaning to the blacks; at any rate I could not find out from them that they had any meaning. Some of the names are *Tchukurow*, a kangaroo; *Mungallee*, a lizard; *Purdee*, an ant; *Pitchery*, a native narcotic herb, &c. The individuals are distinguished from each other, as in the case of the *Pitchery* brothers—one being *Pitchery pinnarou*, the old man *Pitchery*, or the elder *Pitchery*; and the other being *Pitchery coono mielkee*, or *Pitchery* with the one eye.

I estimated the number of Aborigines living on the waters derived from Cooper's Creek (the Barcoo, &c.) as about 1,200 souls. There were numbers of children at some of the camps, and their parents seemed very fond of them. There were numbers of old men, and I saw one of great age; he was very feeble and almost childish. He was covered from head to foot with a fell of grizzly hair. The utmost respect was shown him, and he was brought to see me by a deputation of old men. They spoke of him as a "*Pinna pinnarou*," that is an "Old, old man." Many of the old men were quite bald, but the sun's heat did not at all seem to affect them.

As I remember now, the sexes were disproportioned. The males predominated, and the young men seemed to me out of all proportion to the young women. I was struck with the fact that it was quite rare to see young girls—middle-aged and old women there were, and also quite little girls—infants; but of girls and young women between these ages there were not many. At any rate I did not see them. Does this not point to the killing and perhaps eating of the young girls?

One custom is universal—namely, that strangers visiting the tribe have women given them as a piece of hospitality. I used to find it most troublesome, and I often had great difficulty to make the blackfellows at new camps where we made friends understand that we did not want their women.

The Aborigines do not differ much in appearance from the Coast blacks, but their hair is straighter, and I think they are slighter in build. The curly hair so often seen on the Darling, the Murray, and elsewhere, is not common. The hair is sometimes worn rather long, and done up in a head-net; perhaps with a bunch of crow's feathers, stripped from the quills, tied on the top. I have seen the hair on one individual long, and very shortly afterwards cut quite short. I have imagined this done to provide hair for the hair-cord which is used for several purposes. I have seen it used for twining round the waist, and also for working into nets and bags with the common cord made from rush-fibre. I have always seen it used in the kidney-shaped bags used for bringing down "*Pitchery*."

The usual scars on the back and breast and elsewhere are seen on most

FIG. 256.

blacks. I do not remember that they knock out any teeth; but I think not. A hole is bored through the cartilage of the nose, and in it is worn a long pointed bone, which has two uses—to extract thorns from the feet and to scratch the head. I sometimes have seen, instead of the bone, two feathers stuck through; and this gives them a strange appearance (Fig. 256), particularly when the beard is tied with string round and round to a point, and a bunch of feathers is tied on the top of the head.

Charcoal, red-ochre, pipeclay, and grease are used to smear themselves with on various occasions. On great occasions I have seen them ornamented thus:— Some blood is obtained from a bird or small animal perhaps, or else by cutting themselves; this is dotted over the body, on a groundwork of red-ochre, with the point of the finger, and then, while still moist, is dusted with bird-down. It has a most singular appearance. This is done for "corrobborees," called there "*Wimma*." "*Wimmalcy*" means "to dance."

The dress of the men consists of a head-net, and a very long cord wound round and round the waist like a belt; a large tassel hangs in front. The women wear nothing at all but dirt. They have no 'possum or any other kind of rugs; and I only once saw a covering used. It was a single pelican skin belonging to an old woman near Konatie, who was suffering from elephantiasis.

Their huts are of two kinds—summer and winter huts. The former are mere break-winds of branches or the stalks of marsh-mallows. The latter are made like bee-hives of sticks, then covered with tufts of grass or weeds, and finally with earth or sand thrown on the top and beaten down. The inside is generally scraped out a little hollow. They are wind and rain proof, and are often large enough to hold several people. Large numbers of these huts are sometimes met with near the permanent waters.

Their food may be described as consisting of every thing having life. It is principally of fish and seeds, which are pounded and then mixed with water, and either eaten raw or baked in the ashes. Nardoo is now well known. It may be called their "stand-by" when other food is scarce. In many places, miles of the clay flats are thickly sprinkled with the dry seeds. Seeds generally are called "*Bowar*," of which the *Portulac*—the "*Manyoura bowar*"—is the most prized. It is collected in large quantities by the natives after rains. It is even sometimes collected in such quantities as to be preserved for future use. Near Lake Lipson, one of my party found about two bushels contained in a grass case daubed with mud. It looked like a small clay coffin, and was concealed. The "*Bowar*" is ground on a slab of sandstone by another stone held in the hand,

and water is sprinkled with the other hand from a wooden bowl or "*Peechee*." The ground seed runs out like thick batter. The "*Manyoura bonar*" tastes like linseed-meal, and is by no means unpleasant when baked in the ashes and eaten hot. Seeds of the "*Pappar*" grass are also beaten out in large quantities.

The green *Portulac*—the native spinach (strongly resembling the New Zealand spinach of our gardens)—various plants, native melons, and some fruits—of which the native orange is the best—are eaten raw. The roots of the *Portulac*, roots like radishes, small bulbs called "*Yowar*," are baked in the ashes. Other food includes fish of three or four kinds, which are caught in nets, or in grass weirs placed across runs of water when the floods subside ; birds of all kinds, eggs, lizards, snakes—which they will eat although not killed by themselves—a kind of black ant about as large as the sugar ant, baked in the ashes ; rats ; even lice caught on their own persons and the persons of their friends. They are omniverous, and eat everything having life. I once saw them, however, refuse to eat a deaf-adder. At Lake Hope I saw them eat with great gusto a pelican which had been shot the day before, and had drifted across the lake. It was very "high." All the pieces of rich fat were collected and placed in a membrane bag they got from some part of the bird. This was baked in the ashes, and when quite melted, a hole was made in the membrane, and each of the blacks had a suck—every drop was treasured, and what ran over was rubbed on their faces. The rankest train oil was sweet compared to this rotten pelican oil.

They catch frogs, even in dry places, by searching under the bushes on the margins of dried-up clay-pans. The frogs' feet tracks are visible, and near them is found a small kind of tank, a few inches below the surface—it is smooth inside, and oval, and full of water ; and in this is the frog. I have seen them dug out. The blackfellow dug with a pointed stick, and pulling out the frog, turned him inside out, preparatory to cooking him on the coals. I was told that blacks had even crossed bad country in droughts by digging out frogs and getting the water.

I remember seeing a blackfellow with his girdle full of unfledged *Budgerygars* (shell parrakeets), which he had stuffed under by the heads. The trees on the edge of Sturt's Desert were small box-trees, full of holes, and were full of birds and their nests.

The Aborigines cook their food in the ashes, and have no idea of boiling. I have more than once seen blacks astounded at the quart pots boiling. I remember one being much astonished when he tried to take one up by his toes.

When our food has been given to wild blacks, they have, in many cases, gone through the pantomime of putting it in their mouths, chewing, swallowing, and rubbing their stomachs while saying "*Monalley*," and all the time holding the food in their hands, or having, with complete legerdemain, got rid of it some way or another. They fear being poisoned ; but, on being detected, have laughed ; and being told not to fear but to eat, have actually done so, but with every sign of distaste and dislike. It often took days to accustom some of them to our food. They called it "*Malingkee*," or nasty.

Pitchery is a vegetable substance which I believe to be a narcotic. It appears to be the dried and broken-up twigs of some narrow-leaved shrub. It is chewed by many of the blacks, principally by the older men; I do not remember to have seen the women use it. The mode of using it is, to prepare the twigs of a dwarf kind of acacia, which grows on the sandhills, by drying them in hot ashes; then, to break them up small, and mix a little *Pitchery* with them. This is then chewed. I have tasted it, and found it slightly pungent, and resembling some kind of mild tobacco. I was informed that it was procured eight or ten days' journey to the north-west, and I conclude from this that somewhere near or beyond Eyre's Creek is where it is found. The blacks told me that they went now and then to procure it.

Their only manufactures are weapons, girdles, bags, cords, nets, &c.

The weapons are, generally, the shield and boomerang; one in the hand, and one or two in the girdle; sometimes waddies and spears are also carried. The spears are of hard wood; some are simply pointed; some are jagged. Nowhere did I see the formidable reed-spears. A singular weapon is the great boomerang, about five feet long. It is made of heavy box-wood, and is used, I believe, as a club or broadsword in close quarters. It does not seem to be carried about. I have only seen it in the camps, or hidden near them. The shields are of the usual shape, and of a soft white wood, which does not, I think, grow in the country. On one end is often found a small hemispherical cavity, in which fire is made by rapidly turning a hard stick with the hands until the dust ignites; sometimes a little sand and charcoal-dust are added.

Stones are also used as weapons, and are thrown with great force and dexterity with either hand. I have seen them thrown with great accuracy; and it is a common amusement for the children to roll a round piece of bark down a sandhill and throw stones at it.

Oblong wooden bowls are made by cutting off the knees from a box-tree, and then thinning out with a kind of adze or gouge. Water is carried in them; seed cleaned; or sand dug round the huts.

Adzes or gouges are made by fixing a piece of the stone, which breaks with a flat conchoidal fracture, into the end of a piece of wood, and fastening it as mentioned before. It is used by the workman sitting down upon the ground, holding the piece of wood between his feet, and then adzing it, with the tool held towards him. Flakes of this stone are used for scrapers and knives. —(Fig. 257.)

FIG. 257.

Axes and tomahawks (*Bomako*) are made principally from a very hard cream-colored siliceous limestone;* they are sometimes also made of greenstone. They are carefully ground, and were much valued until iron tools became known. I have seen them produced for us from hiding-places in the sand.

The large axes are used in the hand without a handle. The tomahawks are either fixed in the split end of a piece of wood, or are fastened by twisting

---

* According to Mr. Selwyn, who examined one.

a piece of wood round them as a withe is twisted round some blacksmith's tools. In both cases it is fastened by cord, and then covered with a black hard gum, called "*Pinta*," obtained from a medium-sized tree with oval dark-green leaves and a rough bark.

Cord is made from the bark of a shrub, and is used for girdles; and for nets from the fibre of a rush which grows universally on the edges of the lakes and in flooded ground; the rushes are soaked and then scraped; the fibre is very tough and strong. The nets are large, and are of two kinds; one, which is set on stakes out in the shallow lakes, and in which the fish become entangled, and another which is a drag-net, and expands in the centre into a bag. Immense quantities of fish are caught in this way. I have seen, after the blacks had taken away the large fish, the banks of a water-hole covered with small fish in thousands which had been thrown away.

The red-ochre, or *Pocarto*, I was informed, is brought from somewhere in the western plains in South Australia, from whence also (on the edge of the hill country) they bring the sandstone slabs for grinding grass and other seeds. I was told that a number of young men went down to bring these slabs under some kind of permit from the intervening tribes, and that they returned each one carrying a stone slab on his head.

Some kind of traffic between the tribes seems certain, because I was also told that the shields were given to them by tribes to the east, in return for girdles which they themselves made. Near Kycjeron, I saw the section of a conch-shell, evidently brought from the north or north-east coast. It was perforated and hung to a cord. It was highly valued. I believe it to be the shell ornament called by the Queensland blacks "*Tuleen*."

Connected with this is the fact that there are certain old men who were described to me as "walk-about old men," who travelled among the neighbouring tribes carrying news, and were not meddled with. In fact, a sort of herald. I saw two at Konatie, who had come up-country. The tribe were holding a grand festival. The men were all collected round a fire—the council fire, it may be—where speeches were made. I remember a long oration by one of the visitors; he spoke fluently and at length. The women all the time were busy pounding the grass and nardoo seed. The sight was very strange, and the speeches of the blacks, accompanied by the monotonous tap! tap! of the pounding-stones, lasted till past two in the morning.

The natives are in many things just like children. I have seen a young man, on leaving his camp with us for a trip of about a week, burst into tears, saying to himself all the time—"My country—my people—I shall not see them"—(*Mitta archanic—kurnai archanic—watta arto milkele!*). In five minutes he was laughing and as gay as a bird.

Another time, at Lake Hope, a little boy had been brought by his father to the camp, and had during the day been my "Man Friday"—fetching water, wood, and doing various little errands I set him. The following morning, when we were going to start—indeed, were in the act of starting—the old father came up, weeping and in sad trouble. "Where is my boy?—he is in your bags;" and nothing would satisfy him but to feel all over our packs and see that the little boy was not rolled up in one of them. It was almost ridiculous to see his distress; he was a tall bony old fellow, with grizzly hair, crowned with a circlet of red feathers. One moment he was crying "Where is my little boy?" —the next, he seemed to have forgotten him, and was begging for a "*Bomako.*"

More than once the natives near whom we have camped, and with whom we have become friendly, have asked us to shoot some other tribe, saying that they would take the gins and bury the men. I remember—particularly at Lake Hope, when we were returning—a deputation of old men came to me, and proposed that we should go with them and shoot the blackfellows at Coonaboora; that they were bad blackfellows; and that, if we would shoot the men, they would bury them, and take the women. The deputation was so importunate that I could only get rid of them by saying we would go round the lake in the morning, and I would see about it. The following morning all the blacks accompanied us, full of the proposed expedition, to our camp, a distance of six or seven miles, and from whence I proposed to myself the next morning to start, a distance of forty miles across the sandhills, to Lake Torrens. When we were encamped there, I suddenly heard the blackfellows cry out—"*Coonaboora kurnai; Coonaboora kurnai!*—(Kill them; here they come!)." They seemed so excited that I fully expected we were in for a skirmish with the redoubtable Coonabooros; but to my surprise, as they drew near, I saw some of the Lake Hope men meet them with great cordiality, and, on coming nearer, I recognised them as men whom I had seen before with these very Lake Hope blacks. Coonaboora was, in fact, only a few miles distant.

The graves are just such as are spoken of by Capt. Sturt—large mounds of sand, covered with logs and brush. I believe them to be graves of great men (*Pinnarou*), or of people slain in war. They are not, as I think, numerous enough for the burial-places of the commonalty. Several were shown to me near Merrimoko, near Lake Lipson of Sturt, and I was told that in them were buried the blacks killed in a great battle fought between three tribes at that spot.

In many places where the ground was bare—as on extensive clay flats—I have seen circles and circular figures formed with stones of various sizes, generally about as large as a two-pound loaf. They are laid on the ground, and were explained by the blacks to me as being play. I think they require more explanation.

I must give the natives credit for keeping their agreements with us. On forming the depôt, I got a number of the blacks together, and marked out a piece of ground round our camp. I made them understand that inside the boundary was ours, and outside theirs. They strictly observed this; and when we left, several came and asked whether we were coming back, and if the blackfellows might "sit down" there again. They never used to fish (with the net) in our water at Callioumarou without sending a deputation first to ask permission. I also required that they should, when coming to us, lay their weapons down at a distance, and that at nightfall all blacks should go to their camps, and remain there till morning. This last stipulation was made because blacks had twice tried to get into our camp at night.

The natives of Cooper's Creek do not seem to fear walking about at night. The general impression among them is that we can kill at any distance, and that revolvers never require "feeding" like guns—called by them universally "*Mucketty*"—clearly a corruption of "musket." I have heard them change "bucket" into "*bucketty*." They have not the letter "s," and all their words end with a vowel.

There are native doctors among them. I saw one who conjured with a rock-crystal like a small pigeon's egg. He seemed to swallow it, and bring it out of several parts of his body. This kind of conjuring-stone is called "*Bulk*," amongst the blacks in Gippsland. I believe they use it for "bewitching" other blacks.

I found the belief among the *Yantruwunter* natives that white men were once blacks. I was once asked by some old men how long it was since I was a blackfellow. I believe this must arise from this—that they cannot imagine how we can travel from place to place in straight lines, or how we can speak any of their languages, without having at one time been blacks in their country. I was told that I had once been a *Yantruwunter*—one of the *Mungalle* family. It was often remarked by the natives that we travelled in straight lines across the sandhills, while the natives took the easiest line through them; and, according to my experience, scarcely any blacks go straight from one place to another. I only found one native guide who could make a straight course. Generally, they went twenty or thirty degrees on either side of it. I found this the case everywhere.

On nearing any camp, when accompanied by a guide, we have had to halt while he went forward. He got on some high ground in sight of the camp, and began to bawl out something, holding a branch in his hand. The other blacks from the camp would bawl out in reply for some minutes; the women and children would be seen to scurry off in haste. Then several blacks would come forward and hold a conference with our guide; after which we were called forward, and a camping-ground shown to us.

In one instance, after a most friendly meeting and the best understanding the natives took fright in the night and decamped silently. I heard afterwards that they were alarmed at our watch parading round the camp all night. The next day we were obliged to beat up their quarters, and finding them hidden in a scrubby creek, two miles off, caught two for guides.

Another time a guide ran away; but, finding his track in the sandhills, I ran him to earth in a native camp, and got him given up to me. He was dragged out of some bushes, and delivered up by some of the elders of the camp. This was among my own blacks, at Cooper's Creek. After this I had no more trouble about guides; I could get them anywhere. I had only to go down to the camp, wherever it was, and say I wanted to go in such-and-such a direction. Some black who knew the country, who had probably been there lately, and who had friends among the natives living there, would agree to go for such-and-such a time, and on his return he always received good pay—a suit of clothes and a tomahawk, for instance.

I once had one of these, and also a South Australian black—a Hill blackfellow from Blanchewater—with me. The South Australian bolted north of Sturt's Desert, and made his way in after very great hardships. He told me afterwards he travelled by night until he got among his friends near Lake Hope. The wild blackfellow stayed with me, and was the first to give the alarm when "Black Charley" bolted. He ran off suddenly from the camp with nothing but his blanket; he was chased on horseback for some hundred yards, but escaped in the gigantic marsh-mallows. I would rather have wild blacks any day to deal with than half-tamed ones.

Signs are used among the natives.

One is a sort of note of interrogation. For instance, if I were to meet a native and made the sign Fig. 258—by turning the hand palm upwards as

FIG. 258.

I met him—it would mean, "Where are you going?" In other words, I should say, "*Minna?*"—(What name?).

The next sign means "*Pannie*" (none or nothing). For instance, a native says, "*Bomako ingina*"—(Give a tomahawk). I reply by shaking the hand held in the position shown in Fig. 259.

FIG. 259.   FIG. 260.

Another (Fig. 260) is "*Minnie-minnie*"—(Wait a little). It is shaken downwards rapidly two or three times. Done more slowly, towards the ground, it means "Sit down."

Sign used to express the "hospitable custom" spoken of in page 301.—(Fig. 261.)

FIG. 261.

There are numbers of other signs that I do not now remember.

Quære? Were not the "Masonic signs" spoken of by Stuart possibly such as these?

The only times I found any trace of any tradition or superstition, besides the "jumping-up of blackfellows as white men," which may be ranked with them, was at a camp where I was talking with a blackfellow, in the evening, when a bright falling-star was visible. He said—" An old blackfellow has fallen down there." It may have meant that the spirit of a blackfellow had fallen down, or that some black had died. I could not ascertain which.

All the stars and constellations have names.

I have heard the whites often called "*Pirri wirri coochee.*" When we suddenly came upon a camp, I have heard a yell of "*Pirri wirri, Pirri wirri.*" It was explained to me by the South Australian black I had with me as meaning "*Debbil, Debbil,* what come long way."

The word "*Coochee*" is also applied to an animal living in the deep water at Callioumarou, which drags down blackfellows—evidently the Bun-yip.

Among the back-country blacks, at the Barrier Ranges, there is a custom of making "rock-paintings." That is, the figure of an out-stretched hand—sometimes colored, sometimes plain on a colored ground. When the former,

FIG. 262.

the hand is daubed with red-ochre or pipeclay and printed off. The latter mode is to place the extended hand on the rock, and to squirt color over it out of the mouth; on the hand being removed, the print is left on a colored ground.—(Fig. 262.)

APPENDIX E.

NOTES RELATING TO THE ABORIGINES OF AUSTRALIA.

(By John Moore Davis.)

It is the fashion among many persons to speak of the Australian Aborigines in terms of the greatest contempt, as being far below us in every qualification, both mental and physical; and no doubt the degraded creatures met loafing about the bush public-houses deserve all that may be said of them; but experience teaches that it is no more fair to judge the whole of the Aborigines by the specimens alluded to than it would be to judge the Celt or Anglo-Saxon races by the police reports, or the scum met with in the haunts of vice and infamy; and those persons who have seen much of the blacks in the early days of these colonies can recall many instances of chivalrous daring, benevolence, and patient endurance of hardship and suffering, which perhaps may yet, in the hands of some Australian Cooper, "serve to point a moral or adorn a tale."

That the whole of the blacks scattered over the Australian continent believe in a future state is indisputable; for go where you will—east or west, north or south—you will still find them strong in the belief that though they will die, they will rise again in the flesh, stronger, aye, and wiser than ever.

Their mode of disposing of the bodies of deceased persons differs in various localities. At Encounter Bay in South Australia, and along the coast in that vicinity, the bodies are put on platforms in trees, and so allowed to remain till they fall to pieces. And in cases where a person belonging to another tribe had died among them, the body is gradually smoke-dried in a sort of loft made in their wirley, or temporary abode of the family he lived with; and the body is carried about from place to place, till it is ultimately claimed by the tribe of the deceased. Burying the dead is, however, the most common, particularly in New South Wales, the body being tightly swathed in bark, and placed in the grave in a sitting position, with the face to the east. The grave is then filled up with alternate layers of timber and earth, so as to prevent the body being injured by wild dogs, or exhumed by hostile tribes. Great taste is often shown in the choice of a burying-place, and the writer has often in his travels come upon a grave, or cluster of graves, in some romantic spot—the hieroglyphics carved on the surrounding trees pourtraying, no doubt as truly as our tombstones generally do, all the virtues of those who slept below.

I recollect once, on the banks of the Murrumbidgee, coming suddenly upon a grave in a most picturesque situation; and that the tenant was once who had been great in his day was evident by the care taken on the subject, the ground having been marked out and raised for about three inches in the shape of a canoe, and in the centre stood a little house made of bark in and out, between the upright sheets of which were placed the nets of the deceased, and inside were the weapons used by him. There was also a bed made of nice soft grass inside, and, as I afterwards ascertained, the nearest male relation of the deceased had there to sleep, and keep watch and ward over the body of his kinsman till such time as it had become too far decomposed to admit of being removed by any enemy.

That cannibalism is sometimes practised by the blacks I have been often told; but I believe that in those cases the bodies of deceased persons only have been eaten, and not any one killed on purpose; and I knew one instance where the body of an old woman was eaten, and her own son partook of part of it. I have also on various occasions seen blacks during a corrobboree gnawing a human thigh-bone—doubtless of an enemy—and thereby exciting themselves to a pitch of madness. I have also known a lubra, as a punishment for her misconduct and negligence, made to carry about for months the body of her dead child, wrapped up in an opossum rug; and on one occasion I happened to sit down on a bundle near a wirley, and finding an unpleasant smell, I enquired what was in the bundle, and soon learned to my great disgust that it contained the body of a child which had died some months previous. The blacks, as a rule, avoid camping near any grave, and never mention the name of any deceased member of the tribe, and regard any enquiry after them by the whites as an insult. In parts of New South Wales, such as Bathurst, Goulburn, the Lachlan, or Macquarie, it was customary long ago for the first-born of every lubra to be eaten by the tribe, as part of a religious ceremony; and I recollect a blackfellow who had, in compliance with the custom, been thrown when an infant on the fire, but was rescued and brought up by some stock-keepers who happened accidentally to be passing at the time. The marks of the burns were distinctly visible on the man when I saw him, and his story was well known in the locality. In early years, when intercourse took place between the blacks and whites, and children were the result, the boys were invariably destroyed, but the girls kept; and it was not till the whites became numerous, and the blacks began to dwindle away, that the practice fell into disuse, and the boys were allowed to live.

As a general rule, both fathers and mothers are very kind to their children, and very rarely indeed strike them; and I have been often amused at seeing a rebellious urchin of perhaps eight or nine years of age take up his mimic spears, run a few yards away, and then hurl them with all his force at his mother, who, good woman, would make a buckler of her opossum rug, and thus ward them all off, laughing all the time at the harmless rage of the would-be warrior. That they are very fond of their children and will at any time venture their lives for them is also beyond a doubt; and I knew an instance where, in a skirmish which took place many years ago at New England, the blacks, after being worsted in the fight, swam across a river, leaving in their confusion a child behind them. A Maori who was living at the station, and had been engaged in the struggle, seeing the child, took him up, and held him out to the blacks at the other side of the river. The father, on observing the child, seemed almost frantic, and held out his arms eagerly towards the child, making at the same time signs for it to be given to him. The Maori pretended to be willing to restore the child, and entered the river with it, at the same time carefully concealing his tomahawk, making signs to the black to meet him. The man eagerly waded into the river and swam across, and when he got within reach of the Maori, the treacherous monster immediately brained him with the tomahawk, and the body, with that of the child, which was also killed, was left to whirl down the seething waters, a sad return for parental love and devotion.

When a male child was born, a name was given him referring in general to the locality where his advent took place. On attaining puberty, a second name was conferred; and on arriving at manhood, the third and final one, by which he would be after designated. Many tedious and in some cases painful ceremonies had, however, to be passed through before the young man was duly qualified to take or steal a wife, set up on his own account, and earn for himself a reputation for good or evil as a brave and determined warrior or a mean and despicable coward.

All the Aborigines along the coast from York's Peninsula in South Australia to Western Australia are not only circumcised but are mutilated also in the manner mentioned by Mr. Eyre.* The rite of circumcision has, no doubt, been perpetuated by the Malays, who, in days past, visited the Australian coast in search of the trepang or sea-slug, an article prized as much by them as the edible swallows'-nests by the Chinese; and the other practice was perhaps introduced by some Aboriginal Solomon to prevent the too rapid propagation and thereby starvation of the race; and it certainly is surprising how, under the circumstances, there are any children at all. The rite is supposed to be practised when the boy is about seven years old; but I have known some who had managed to evade it till about fifteen, but were then pounced upon; and as the operation was performed with either a sharp stone or shell, it must have been both a painful and critical affair for the patient. During the last year previous to arriving at manhood, the unfortunate novice had to live a solitary life away from the tribe, procure his own living, and not come near any place where the women were; no doubt to teach him habits of self-dependence, and leave him some green spot for memory to dwell upon when, in after years, he would be harassed by the cares consequent on being a family man.

About Adelaide, Encounter Bay, and the neighbouring localities, the young man was distinguished during the last year of his novitiate by being plentifully besmeared, from head to foot, with red-ochre and grease mixed, which gave him the advantage of not only being impervious to the attacks of mosquitos, gnats, &c., but of being duly advertised as a marrying man. Both men and women were marked on the back, shoulders, chest, and belly with raised ridges

---

* " Finditur usque ad urethram à parte inferâ penis."

formed by making incisions and then filling the cut with charcoal, which answered as a styptic, and also kept the lips of the wound apart and formed the desired ridges. The arrangement of these marks differed amongst different tribes, each tribe having its own peculiar and distinct coat-of-arms; so that those versed in such lore could at once, in looking over a body, decide to what tribe it belonged, and send the information, if required.

Along the Murray, Murrumbidgee, and Lachlan, and in New South Wales, all the males, on arriving at manhood, have either one or two teeth knocked out of the left side of the upper-jaw, as a distinguishing mark; and at certain seasons of the year certain ceremonies are gone through at a distance from the main body of the tribe. These ceremonies occupy several days, are performed in covered-in wirleys, where only the initiated are admitted, and from which the females are most carefully kept a long way off. Certain signs are also used amongst the initiated, and it may therefore be fairly presumed that a species of rude Freemasonry exists amongst the Aborigines, the bequest perhaps of some amongst the many strange visitors who visited these coasts in the far-off days of yore. It is a well-known fact amongst the old settlers, that Aborigines, both old and young, who were in their employ and apparently perfectly comfortable and satisfied, would yet, on the receipt of the summons, insist upon going away immediately; and no temptation, however great, could ever induce them to stop, nor, on their return, could any information be obtained from them as to what had been done at the meeting.

It has always been the practice amongst the Aborigines for the warriors of one tribe to make incursions into the territories of another, either to steal lubras, or to surprise and attack males, who, after being struck down, had an incision made in their sides, through which the caul-fat was drawn, and which fat was carefully kept and used by the assassin to lubricate himself—the belief being that all the qualifications, both physical and mental, of the previous owner of the fat were thus communicated to him who used it. On the Upper Murray, a cord, about the thickness of ordinary whipcord, was formed out of the sinews obtained from the tail of the kangaroo; this cord had a running noose at one end, also two small bones, each sharpened to a very fine point, so fixed that when the noose was drawn tight the points would enter the jugular vein at each side of the neck. Armed with one of these, a black would steal at night up to the camp of another tribe, and, having selected some sleeping man, slip the noose round his neck, strangle his victim, and depart with the coveted caul-fat, without creating any noise or alarm. That these nooses were not used by the Aborigines on the men of other tribes alone, but also on Europeans, is beyond a doubt, as I recollect an instance of a shepherd who, having, at the expiration of his term of service, left the out-station at which he was employed to go to the head-station, and several days having expired without his arrival, an alarm was caused, and a search made, when the body was found, with his faithful dogs lying beside it, with the mark of the fatal noose round the neck. It was afterwards ascertained that the man had engaged a blackfellow and his lubra to carry his swag, and most probably the sight of the blankets had been too much of a temptation to the black; the noose had been used at some favorable juncture with deadly certainty, and the coveted booty taken possession of. The whites of the locality found out who was the murderer, and he shortly disappeared; and for many years afterwards the lonely spot on the plains where the body was found and buried was an object of interest to the European traveller who passed that way.

The patience shown by the blacks in snaring game is very great, and I have known a man spend hours in catching a turkey. The usual plan is for the man to put boughs round him till he looks like a mass of leaves. He then makes a running noose out of a piece of cord, fastens it on to the end of his spear, and sallies forth in quest of game. The turkey is only found in open country, and is a most wary bird; but the black is equal to the occasion, and particularly patient when on his success depends his dinner. When the bird puts down his head to feed, his enemy moves towards him, and as the bird raises his head, the black stops quite still; the bird sees what is apparently a bush, is satisfied, and again lowers his head to feed, when the black again moves closer; and so on till the noose is thrown round the neck of the unsuspecting bird, and he is secured. Quail are also caught in the same manner. Ducks were sometimes caught in narrow creeks, by fixing nets from side to side in the branches that grew along the banks. The blacks then imitated the cry of the hawk, causing the birds to fly upwards in alarm, and thus get entangled in the net above them. A favorite way to take ducks on a lake or large sheet of water was to put some small bushes carefully round the head, and then tread water noiselessly till the black arrived amongst the ducks; when he would pull one at a time under water, twist its neck, and secure it in his girdle till he got a sufficient number, when he would glide quietly away and go on shore.

The tribes along the Murray made splendid nets, which they used most successfully. The Billybongs which run inland for miles, and served as reservoirs to hold the waters which were brought down by the floods, had weirs placed carefully across their mouths in summer, when the water was very low; and these weirs, which were formed of stakes interlaced between with little twigs, served most effectually to retain the fish which had passed over them during the floods, and which, when the water got low, were secured with ease. In order to secure the old men who were unable to get their own food from the danger of starving, it had been wisely decreed that animals of a certain sex, such as the she opossum, &c., and particular descriptions of fish and other game, could not be eaten by the able men of the tribe; but, when taken by them, should be given to the old men, under pain of incurring the penalties duly provided, and in a manner losing caste.

The largest article in the shape of a covering of any sort which I have known them to manufacture—with the exception of the opossum rug—is a circular mat, about three feet six inches in diameter, made out of rushes by the lubras, on the banks of Lake Alexandrina, into which the Murray empties, and used by them and not by the men. These lubras also make rafts out of the reeds which grow on the banks, and on them go out sometimes miles on the lake to fish with nets. Both men and women are very expert at diving and catching the large fish, which lurk amongst the stones and timber at the bottom of the rivers. On the coast it was quite a picturesque scene of a night, when the waters of some little bay were lit up with scores of lights, which were continually moving and forming a variety of fantastic groups. These lights were pieces of blazing bark, carried by men, women, and children, who, each armed with a spear formed of a straight pointed young sapling, waded about the shallow waters in pursuit of the fish brought in by the rising tide.

The blacks appear to enjoy a certain immunity from the sharks; for although I have known numbers of men and women to swim in and cut off a large quantity of fish from the schools of schnapper, extending sometimes more than a mile each way, which visit these coasts about December, and which schools are invariably followed by a host of sharks, ever on the watch to pick up the weakly fish, yet I never knew of an instance where a black was injured. That may, however, most probably be owing to the sharks being in a manner gorged at the time, as I have also known the blacks to swim off to the stranded carcass of a whale to get the coarse meat—or *Kreng*, as it is called—when the sharks have been almost as thick round it as flies on meat during summer. The blacks are very expert in getting the schnapper alluded to. For days previous, scouts are posted on the various look-out places to give notice of the approach of the fish; and as soon as the alarm is given, the greatest excitement prevails—men, women, and children rush recklessly into the water, swim towards the school, cut off a lot of the fish, and then, forming a semicircle, swim behind the fish and drive them into shallow water, where they are dexterously and quickly speared. To give you an idea of the quickness of the blacks, I can mention an instance in which three blacks, another white, and myself, speared upwards of thirty large schnappers in about twenty minutes.

Another common way of catching mullet and whiting, and such sized fish, is, at the time the tide is coming in, for a black to take a bough in one hand, a spear in the other, and a piece of lithe sarsaparilla root—which abounds on the coast—round his neck; he then gets behind a school of fish, moves the bough with his hand, causing a shadow to fall on the water, before which the fish rush away in terror, till he gradually gets them into water from two to three feet deep, where he can deal with them to a certainty, for every time he darts his spear he is sure to strike a fish. The black gives each a bite at the back of the neck, and strings it through the gills round his neck till he gets enough, when he walks ashore, broils his fish, takes his meal, and under the shade of a tree rests from his labors.

The blacks along the coast from Yorke's Peninsula to King George's Sound will not eat pork, owing, no doubt, to the prejudices acquired by their intercourse with the Malays, who are Mahomedans. They are also more jealous of their women, and more cautious and treacherous, owing, most likely, to the same cause. Numbers of white men belonging to whaling vessels which have been wrecked at different times have perished owing to their getting embroiled with the natives about their women. I know of one instance, where we noticed on the beach the tracks of some white men, who had evidently landed from a boat, and gone into the bush with a lot of natives; but there were no traces of their ever having returned, so that in all probability they were murdered; and, in support of such belief, we found some time after a boat on one of the islands, about ten miles from the main, a hut, and the remains of a man in it. On searching the place, we found a diary, by which it appeared that the dead man had been one of a boat's crew which had been left at another part of the coast, in charge of the property saved from the whaler which they had belonged to, and which had been wrecked, the rest of the crew having sailed away in the boats to Hobart Town for another vessel in which to carry away the oil, &c. The six men in charge, being tired of where they were, had gone for a trip in their boat, and landed at the place mentioned, where four out of the number had been induced by the natives to go on shore and into the bush after lubras. The others, who remained in the boat some distance off the shore, were surprised shortly after at seeing a party of natives, who came down to the beach, after vainly inducing them to land, suddenly throw a lot of spears at them. Both men were wounded, but they, however, managed to slip their anchor, and hoist the sail, which soon took them beyond the reach of the natives. Finding that they were both badly hurt, they sailed to the island alluded to, where one man died shortly after landing; but the other lived for some time, and evidently did not die of starvation, there being a small cask of salted mutton-birds in the hut, and also a dog at large, who looked quite fat. The poor animal seemed quite tired of his solitary life, for he barked and pranced about in great glee when he saw us, and was evidently determined not to be left behind, as he jumped into the boat when we were getting ready to leave.

When a female child is born, she is affianced to some man of the tribe, generally a warrior of repute; and when of sufficient age, she is taken by him, provided she has not been previously stolen by some enterprising youth of either his own or some neighbouring tribe. Should the girl have been taken by a warrior of his own tribe, the question has to be fought out between the rivals, and the girl falls to the lot of the victor; but if the abduction has been committed by a member of another tribe, then the friends on each side take part in the quarrel, and, in some instances, several tribes thus become involved.

The modes of stealing lubras differ in various localities. In New South Wales and about Riverina, when a young man is entitled to have a lubra, he organizes a party of his friends, and they make a journey into the territories of some other tribe, and there lie in wait, generally in the evening, by a water-hole where the lubras come for water. Such of the lubras as may be required are then pounced upon, and, if they attempt to make any resistance, are struck down insensible and dragged off. There is also this peculiarity, that in any instance where the abduction has taken place for the benefit of some one individual, each of the members of the party claims, as a right, a privilege which the intended husband has no power to refuse. But in cases where one tribe has attacked another and carried off a lot of the lubras, those unfortunates are common property till they are gradually annexed by the best warriors of the tribe. The horrors endured by the various white women who have been stolen from stations in the early days, or, having been wrecked upon the coasts of the colony, have thus fallen into the possession of the natives, may therefore be conceived.

I have known several instances of the abduction of both women and girls. In one, the daughter of a wealthy settler was taken away by a tribe at Gippsland, and although every exertion was made by the whites, and a party composed of volunteers and the native police, under the command of Capt. Dana, sent to her rescue, the tribe who had her managed to elude every attempt, and she was at length—which must have been a happy release—speared by one of the blacks who had previously possessed her, and from whom she had been taken by another warrior. I also knew another instance of the daughter of a settler being taken away and never recovered. Her course was traced by a party of volunteers for a long distance by the letters she had managed to cut on the trees. These traces, however, ceased after a time, owing most probably to having been observed by the blacks, who prevented her from making any more. Nothing more was, however, ever heard of her, and her subsequent fate is still a mystery. On one occasion, about twenty-nine years ago, when out on the Murrumbidgee, with two other lads, looking after cattle, we came suddenly on a camp of blacks, and amongst those present we noticed one who, though much sunburned, squalid, and dirty, was yet evidently a white woman. Whether from shame at being found in such a situation, dread of the consequences of holding any communication with us, or through being contented with her lot, she would not answer any of the many questions addressed to her by us; and as we were totally unarmed, and the blacks numerous, it was out of our power to then take her away, even provided that she was willing to go. Many enquiries were subsequently made by us on the subject, and different attempts made to see her, but all in vain, the blacks being evidently on their guard and determined to baffle us. On another occasion, a young and pretty women, the wife of a man named Cummings, was stolen from a station at New England, New South Wales, and it was only by the most energetic exertions on the part of the whites resident in the locality, and after a desperate encounter, in which the blacks were defeated with great slaughter, that the woman was recovered.

One day, during the time that Moreton Bay—now known as Queensland—was a penal settlement, information was brought in by the blacks of a vessel having been wrecked at Wide Bay, and that amongst the few survivors was a white woman. There happened at the time to be at the settlement, as it was then called, a prisoner of the Crown, who, years before, had absconded and lived with the Wide Bay tribe, but subsequently, having become tired of life among the Aborigines, had come into the settlement and given himself up to the authorities. This man was sent for by the Superintendent, and the matter having been explained to him, he volunteered to go alone and rescue the unfortunate woman; because, as he stated, to send a party out after her would be almost certain to end in disappointment and her death, as the blacks would kill her at once if they found themselves hard pressed by the whites and likely to lose her.

The proposition, after mature deliberation, being agreed to by the Superintendent, the man, having divested himself of his clothing, painted and armed himself with spear, waddy, &c., in the Aboriginal style, departed on his mission, and, after a long and weary journey, reached the hunting-grounds of his quondam associates and brethren-in-arms; and, on falling in with the tribe, was received with great joy, under the impression that he was come again to live with them. Upon making enquiries, he learned that several men and one woman were saved from the wreck, but that the former had, politely speaking, been used up; but the latter had, after the usual preliminaries, been annexed by a distinguished warrior to soothe his cares and grace his wirley. Watching his opportunity, one day he arranged a rendezvous with the woman for that evening, and meeting her there at the appointed time, he started away with her. The journey back was most difficult; for not only had he to take the woman, who was the widow of the captain of the ill-fated vessel, on his back, and swim across several wide, deep, and rapid rivers, but he had also to elude the pursuit of the blacks, who were after him hot-foot to recapture the woman. His knowledge, however, of bush life enabled him to baffle all pursuit, and to bring the unfortunate lady to within a short distance of the settlement, where he left her concealed while he went in and acquainted the Superintendent with the successful accomplishment of his mission. The Superintendent's lady, accompanied by several women, and provided with a supply of clothing, were guided to the spot, where they found the unfortunate in a state of nudity, and almost dead from hunger and exhaustion. She was conveyed to the settlement, where she remained at the Superintendent's house for a considerable period, till her shattered health was restored, when she left her hospitable entertainers to return to her friends in England. The memory of the time she spent among the blacks of Wide Bay, and the terror of that journey, when she was momentarily expecting to be again captured and led back to the horrors from which she had escaped, were never obliterated from her memory; and many a night after, while sleeping at the house of some of her friends, she has awakened all there by her screams, fancying in her dreams that she could hear the wild and unearthly yell of the blacks in pursuit.

Promiscuous intercourse between the sexes is not practised by the Aborigines, and their laws on the subject, particularly those of New South Wales, are very strict. When at camp, all the young unmarried men are stationed by themselves at the extreme ends, while the married men, each with his family, occupy the centre. No conversation is allowed between the single men and the girls or the married women; and about Riverina I have seen the young men make a considerable detour to avoid going near a station where the lubras were present. Infractions of these and other laws were visited either by punishment by any aggrieved member of the tribe, or by the delinquent having to purge himself of his crime by standing up protected simply by his shield, or a waddy, while five or six warriors threw, from a comparatively short distance, several spears at him. The man was often severely wounded, and sometimes killed; but occasionally, however, a very agile warrior escaped untouched; and the activity and nerve displayed by the man in evading and parrying at the same time the different spears thrown at him were really wonderful, and I have often watched with breathless interest the issue of these expiatory trials.

[Mr. Moore Davis adds some facts which are interesting only to the ethnologist. At great corrobborees the practices of the natives are remarkable:— Uxoribus plerumque licet eorum bellatorum quibus sunt duæ pluresque uxores —nec in ulla tribu desunt multi ejusmodi bellatores—cum juvenibus cœlibibus coire. Unaquæque femina incendio parvo locum indicante circiter pedes trecentos abest ab choreâ atque aliquoties juvenis a commissatione excedet feminam adibit cum ea coibit et ad saltationem redibit. Nec aliter quum amicum accipiunt Aborigines (ut fecerunt temporibus antiquis clariorum Romanorum nonnulli) unam ei ex suis uxoribus præbent.

On the same authority, the following facts and customs may be accepted as reliable, detailing features in the mode of life of the natives which are not without value:—

Utrisque sexibus fit coitus initâ ætate; puellæ quidem novem fere aut decem annos natæ.

Ad Glenelg et prope Portland anus in secreta virginum si minora quam ut penem acciperent anguillæ caput inserebant. Multisque in temporibus albi viri quum eo habitatum venissent rogabantur ut causâ gratiæ virginem ararent.

Volunt plerumque Aborigines uxores suas albis hominibus pretio commodare sed quominus uxores omnino relinquant causâ alborum hominum suos viros fere recusabunt. Trucidati sunt plurimi nigrique et albi cupiditate horum quum illorum uxores ut pellices retinere conati sunt.

Haud quaquam autem semper feminæ cum albis hominibus coire volunt: in regione Tattiara albus quidam quum feminam etiam invitam coercebat ab eâ interfectus est. Prope ad Portum Veneris et in orâ maritimâ Regisque Georgii Sinum versus Aborigines moribus minus commodis quam in aliis regionibus plerumque nolunt uxores albis præbere et quum quidem id viri concedunt uxores id ipsum forsitan voluntes se esse invitissimas simulant nec sine vi cum albis abiguntur. Hoc eâ causâ faciunt quo viri suas uxores abire nolle existiment.

Ad fluvium Darling omnes nonnunquam etiam ad duodecimi nigri si albus cum feminâ nigrâ coeat eandem in feminam successive inibunt. Nec mirum si gonorrhœa in eis locis tantopere valet; hic morbus autem haud acutus aut pestifer est hominesque et feminæ spectatu infirmissimo post solitudinem per dies viginti unum plerumque convalescunt. Per cum spatium herbâ longe latéque in virgultis quâ florem album effert uti dicuntur eam herbam in camino partim coctam mandunt.]

Where a white man joined a tribe, and was adopted into it—as was very common during the old times, when penal servitude existed—it was the custom to give him a lubra to set up with, leaving him, if he wished, to afterwards secure as many more as he could get; and that the women are susceptible of strong attachments is evident by the many instances shown. I knew of one where a lubra used to visit the different stations within a radius of twenty miles to obtain food for the white man—a bushranger—she was living with, and who, having been severely wounded in an encounter with the mounted police, was lying quite helpless in a covert in the mountains. No promises of reward could induce her to reveal where the man was concealed, and she evaded every attempt to follow her; and when at length he died, her grief knew no bounds, and she was inconsolable.

George Clarke, *alias* "The Barber," was a noted man amongst the blacks at Liverpool Plains, New South Wales. He was an escaped convict, who lived with them for many years, and taught the blacks to make large stockyards in a triangular form, so that the cattle, when driven into the apex of the triangle, could be readily speared by the blacks; and, in consequence of these and other similar practices, became most obnoxious to the squatters in the locality. Large rewards were offered for his apprehension, and many attempts made to capture him. He, however, succeeded for years in baffling his pursuers, and so well could he imitate the blacks, that on several occasions, when actually seen by the police, he was allowed by them to get away, they being under the impression that he was a blackfellow. He was at length captured by the celebrated and daring Sergeant Sandy, of the mounted police, who with a party of men were in search of him. On it becoming known among the tribe that their great friend and benefactor had fallen into the power of his enemies, the blacks mustered in great force to rescue him, and threatened to destroy all the police if Clarke was not given up. Sergeant Sandy, however, was equal to the occasion, and putting a pistol to his prisoner's head, he told him that the first spear which was thrown should be the signal for his death; and although the blacks might in the end destroy the whole party, yet his escape was impossible. Clarke, finding that Sandy was a determined man, gave up all hopes of escape, and, standing up, harangued the blacks, advising them to disperse and leave him to his fate, and not to lose their lives in vain. They, however, remained obdurate for a considerable time, but at length, in deference to Clarke's wishes, they dispersed with great lamentations. Four lubras belonging to Clarke would not, however, leave him, but followed him all the way to Bathurst; and during all the time he was kept in prison there they remained outside, patiently waiting for a chance to see him; and on his removal to Sydney they made their way there. Clarke told the Government that he knew of a very large inland lake, and offered to accompany Sir Thomas Mitchell on an expedition, and show him the lake. The Government seem, however, to have been afraid of giving Clarke a chance of escaping, for they declined his proposals, and he was transported to Tasmania, where he again took to the bush; and the laws there, in Governor Arthur's time, being very severe in reference to such weaknesses, Clarke, though he had never committed any murders, was hung; and thus the locality of the great lake, if it did exist in reality, remains to this day unknown.

I knew another instance where a lubra called Charlotte, who had been taken away off the coast when a girl by a party of sealers, and was living with a man named Manson on an island called St. Peter's, about fifty miles from Coffin's Bay, was on one occasion proceeding in a boat on a sealing expedition to another island, with her man, her two children, and another white man named

Jackson, when the boat was upset by a sudden squall, and sank. Charlotte and Jackson rose to the surface, but neither Manson nor the children could be seen. Charlotte swam about for a considerable time in search of Manson and the children, whom she was to rescue, if possible, at any sacrifice; but finding no signs of them, she turned to Jackson and said—"I will take you on my back and swim ashore." Jackson, however, was equally generous; and, although they were then out of sight of land, refused her offer, saying that he would do the best he could for himself. Charlotte then got one of the oars, which was floating close by, and stripping herself of the woollen and cotton shirts which she had on, she rolled them round the oar for Jackson to lay his breast on. They thus floated on for some time, till the distance between them gradually increased. Charlotte eventually lost sight of Jackson, and never saw him again. On nearing the coast, near Avoid Bay, where the surf breaks with awful violence and a noise like thunder for miles off the land, she met with great difficulties, practised and wonderful swimmer as she was, and had to dive time after time repeatedly, to prevent being dashed to pieces against the rocks. She succeeded at length, after almost superhuman efforts, in reaching the land about dusk, after being in the water from the early part of a summer's day till then. She assured me, and I did not wonder at it, that when she made the land, and attempted to walk up the beach, she fell down quite exhausted. To increase her troubles, she shortly afterwards saw at a distance some of the blacks belonging to that part of the coast, and being afraid of being captured by them, concealed herself in the scrub, and remained there all night. Next morning she started, and travelled cautiously on, till, finding some cattle tracks, she followed the tracks till she came to the herd, which were in charge of a white man, who kindly took her to the hut, and clothed and fed her; and, when sufficiently recruited, she went into Port Lincoln, where I saw her, and listened to her recital of the loss of her husband and children, and her own narrow escape.

In the earlier days of these colonies, parties of men used to band together, get whale-boats and other requisites, and visit the islands and other places along the coast in search of the fur-seal, which then abounded in those localities, and which was a valuable article of commerce, the price per skin ranging from £1 to £1 5s. These men used to fix upon some island favorably situated for the purpose as their head-quarters, and from thence visit the different seal-rookeries and occasionally the mainland also, from whence they often carried off young lubras, whom they kept as companions during their roving life. The woman Charlotte, alluded to in my last, had been one of those thus abducted; and having lived for years with a white man named Bryant, who had formerly been a sealer, she had become most useful, and was equally at home whether washing a shirt or killing a seal, cooking a dinner, or managing a boat in a heavy sea. Charlotte and another elder lubra lived with this man Bryant on St. Peter's, an island about fifty miles off Coffin's Bay. They had quite a snug little farm there, and Bryant, who was a cooper by trade, and also an ingenious man, constructed a windmill to grind their corn, and a number of other mechanical contrivances to save manual labor. He had likewise a fine garden, and the different American whalers who frequented those seas often called upon Bryant for a supply of vegetables, giving him tobacco, liquor, and money in exchange; and of the latter Bryant seems to have accumulated a goodly sum, as Charlotte has often told me of the quantity of what she afterwards knew to be money which the old man had in a box, and which he kept concealed from the knowledge of the two lubras. In course of time Bryant, who was well stricken in years, died, and was gathered, not to his fathers, but, like many another ancient mariner, laid to sleep by the kindly hands of his lubras with the cry of the penguin and the roar of the ocean round his sea-girt home for his lullaby. The lubras—Charlotte and Sally—with two of their little boys, went on cultivating their small farm, and lived very happily for some years, when the island was visited by a gang of desperadoes, under the command of one John Williams (an escaped convict from Tasmania), a most notorious scoundrel, who had for years infested the islands in the Great Australian Bight.

These worthies had been shipwrecked on Thistle Island, and from thence made their way in a whale-boat round the coast to St. Peter's, where they knew there was material enough left from previous wrecks to build a small schooner, with which they intended sailing back to their old haunts near King George's Sound. Williams and his men, after building the schooner, sailed away from St. Peter's, taking the two lubras and the children and a good stock of provisions with them, but failing to find the box of coin which had been hidden by Bryant. The two lubras lived amongst the crew for a long time, but at length made their way back to within a short distance of their old island home, St. Peter's. The parties alluded to were composed, in general, of escaped convicts, and many a sad scene was enacted by them during their reckless career as sealers, and often wreckers.

The navigation of these seas was then comparatively but little known, and many a goodly craft was lost amid the coral reefs and islands. These wrecks afforded good plunder, and in cases where a few unfortunates had escaped the disaster, their lives were ruthlessly sacrificed by the wreckers.

Sally told me of an instance where a mulatto, named Antonio, who used to babble in his cups rather strangely of some tragic occurrences, was disposed of. Being a powerful and determined fellow, they were afraid to quarrel with him, and therefore determined to get rid of him the first opportunity. On one of their cruises, they came upon a seal-rookery, which could only be approached by descending the rocks from above—a great height, and a considerable part of which the man employed would have to be lowered down by a rope, and then drawn up again. Antonio volunteered to perform the perilous task; descended in safety, killed a number of fur-seals, skinned them, and sent up their skins, and then, at a given signal, began to ascend by the rope. His treacherous companions, after pulling him up some distance, stopped, and then Williams began to revile him for what he had said during his maudlin moments, and after taunting him for some time—while thus hovering on the brink of eternity—with the doom they had assigned him—in order, as they said, to keep his tongue quiet—they cut the rope, and the wretched man fell some hundreds of feet into the boiling abyss beneath.

APPENDIX F.

NOTES ON THE SYSTEM OF CONSANGUINITY AND KINSHIP OF THE BRABROLONG TRIBE, NORTH GIPPSLAND.

(By A. W. Howitt.)

In undertaking to communicate a paper on the system of consanguinity and kinship of the Australian Aborigines, it had been hoped by the Rev. Mr. Fison and myself that we should be able to collect and discuss a large amount of systematized information from all parts of the Australian Continent. Experience has, however, proved to us that the time required to gather together such a mass of materials will be much longer than we had anticipated. We had hoped to have received aid from others in our enquiries; but the result has proved our expectation to be almost unfounded. In addition to these unforeseen difficulties, my valued colleague in the investigation has been compelled by ill-health to leave Victoria, at least for a time. Our work has, therefore, made but little progress, and the publication of our results must, of necessity, be postponed to some future undetermined time.

In order, however, that the promise made by us may not altogether fall to the ground, I have proposed to myself, as an example of the subject, to consider one system, namely, that of the Brabrolong tribe of North Gippsland. It has been carefully compiled, and thrown into shape in a series of diagrams, some of which will be embodied in these notes.

The knowledge which I may have acquired of the branch of ethnological research must be credited to the pioneer labors of Mr. Fison; but the conclusions at which I have arrived in this instance are my own, together with any imperfections or inaccuracies in the mode of treatment; and would not, I believe, as regards the latter, have arisen had I been so fortunate as to have had his co-operation.

Before entering into the subject of these notes, it may be well to lay down some classification to which the Brabrolong system may be referred.

I propose to avail myself of the classification used by Mr. Morgan, the well-known American ethnologist, whose opinion in these researches is of the very greatest weight and authority. I have not his works now at hand for reference, but I extract the following from communications which he has made to Mr. Fison and to me:—

1. *Consanguine Family*—founded upon the intermarriage of brothers and sisters in a group. The Malayan system of consanguinity was created by this family, and proves its antecedent existence.

2. *Punaluan Family*—founded upon the intermarriage of several brothers to each other's wives in the group, and upon the intermarriage of several sisters to each other's husbands in the group; the brotherhood of the husbands in the one case, and the sisterhood of the wives in the other, forming the base of the relation. The Punaluan family created the Turanian system of consanguinity.*

3. *The Turanian Family.*—This is a form of the Punaluan family, in which a man is married to a group of sisters, or a woman to a group of brothers. This system is found to exist now in Thibet.

4. *The Pairing Family*—founded upon marriage between single pairs, but without an exclusive cohabitation. The marriage was during the pleasure of the parties. It had no monogamic character. The husband claimed fidelity, under penalties; but did not admit reciprocal obligation. This system is in existence among the Aborigines of Australia.

5. *The Patriarchal Family*—founded upon strict polygamy. This existed among the Semitic pastoral peoples.

6. *The Monogamian Family*—founded upon marriage between single pairs, with an exclusive cohabitation; the latter being an essential element. The existing system of European nations.

If we consider the present state of any organization, such as the social condition of any people, we may perceive that the existing conditions are the direct result of accumulated minute changes from somewhat different previous conditions; for instance, the present social condition of the English people may be traced from that of the Ancient Britons. In the same way we may look at the system of consanguinity and kinship of any people—that is, the terms denoting the intersexual relations. For instance, such as that of the Jewish people, who are now eminently a "Monogamian" people, but who in the time of Abraham were in the Patriarchal family. Moreover, from passages in the Sacred History of that people, we may infer that they were once in the Turanian system. For instance, from the custom under which a brother took to wife the widow of his deceased brother—which is a modification of the principle embodied in the Turanian family system.†

Were we able to review and discuss the records of a people which is now in the Patriarchal system, we might expect to find evidence pointing to the former existence among them of the Pairing family, the Punaluan, or even the Consanguine systems. In the same way, we might expect that the records of a people in the Pairing family system—did such records exist—would show us evidence of the former existence among those people of the earlier systems of consanguinity. But the only records belonging to savage races are those embodied in their customs and beliefs, and therefore in their language, in which the terms designating the inter-relations of the sexes, together with the customs and beliefs connected with those relations, may be found.

---

* The term "Punaluan" is adopted, I believe, by Mr. Morgan from Hawaii, where a woman not a wife, but in the position of a wife, was called "*Punalua*," meaning "Particular friend."

† A similar custom exists among the Brabrolongs.

In the following notes I shall only touch upon the systems of kinship. I shall only allude to the division of the tribe into classes, without entering upon the interesting subject of the class-names, or the laws regulating marriage in accordance with them under the Punaluan system. Nor can I now mention any of the customs and beliefs which are intimately connected with the systems of consanguinity, and many of which appear to me to have been contemporaneous with, and to have perhaps arisen out of, the changes of system which may be observed, if not the very cause of these changes. The materials for such a full discussion are not yet completed; and I have, therefore, restricted myself, as I have before said, to the system of consanguinity and kinship of the Brabrolongs, and to such conclusions as it seems to me may be justly drawn as to the position which may be assigned to it in the classification already given.

The Brabrolong tribe of Gippsland Aborigines inhabit—or, rather, did inhabit, for they are now nearly extinct—that tract of country bounded upon the south by the Gippsland Lakes, on the west by the Mitchell River, on the north by a line passing somewhere near Tabberabbera, Mount Baldhead, the mountains at the sources of the Tambarra River and Fanwick (on the Buchan or Native Dog River), and thence on the east by a line from Fanwick through Bruthen to the Tambo Bluff.* The tribe was divided into three classes:—The Brabrolongs of Wy Yung, those of Bruthen, and those of Bullum Ware.† The members of each class were only permitted to marry members of the other two classes and not of their own.

The Aborigines of Australia having, during long ages, inhabited a continental area, shut off from external influences, have had, as regards their social condition, a homogeneous development. A parallel to this general statement is found in the Aborigines inhabiting Gippsland. Their country was bordered by the sea to the south; on the east and west they were hemmed in by vast and almost impenetrable jungles; to the north their boundary was the Great Dividing Range, across which two or three "*trails*" led to the northern slopes. In an isolated area such as this we might expect to find, either that the social conditions of the tribes maintained an archaic type elsewhere obscured, or that, in accordance with conditions peculiar to the area, the type had assumed some aberrant form. Among the Gippsland Aborigines, I believe the former to have been the case. The existing family system of the Brabrolongs was, that single pairs cohabited. The man required exclusive fidelity from the woman, under the severest penalties, even death; but he recognised no reciprocal obligation towards the woman.

Here we have the essential part of the Pairing family. Among the Brabrolongs, however, the system was not quite complete, for a man was not restricted to one wife, but might have two or more at the same time, and the

---

* No such actual *line* existed; but I indicate merely the direction stated to me by the names of places given by my Aboriginal informants.

† Wy Yung, now the name of an agricultural area; Bruthen, now the name of a small township on the Tambo; and Bullum Ware, the post town of Boggy Creek. Bullum Ware means "two spears"—Mount Taylor and Mount Look-out.

wives might be, and even were occasionally, sisters, thus retaining a Turanian element.

DIAGRAM I.—*Paternal Grand Ancestors.*

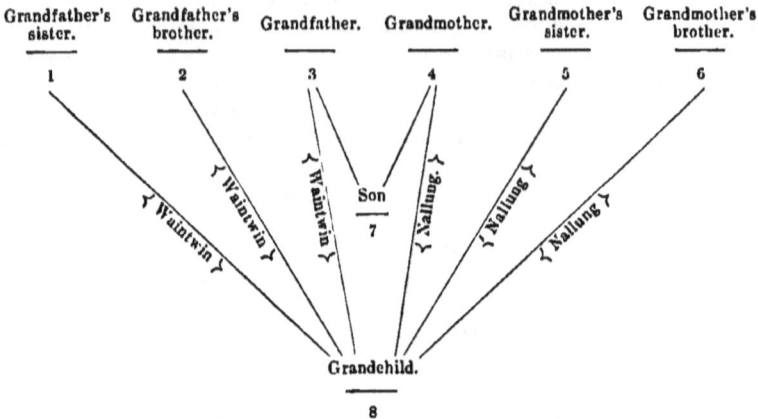

DIAGRAM II.—*Maternal Grand Ancestors.*

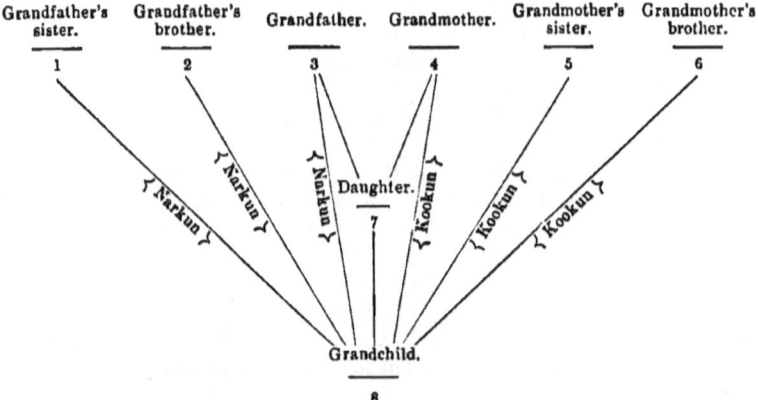

In the diagrams the mark ⟩ indicates the direction in which the term of relationship to which it is affixed is used.

The term "*child*," or "*grandchild*," includes both sexes, no distinction being drawn before the age of puberty.

In Diagram I. it is to be noted that the terms used between Nos. 4, 5, 6, and 8 denote the Malayan system, for it is only under it that brothers and sisters in a group can bear the same relation to a child or grandchild.

CONSANGUINITY AND KINSHIP. 327

The term used between Nos. 2 and 3 and 8 differs from that used by Nos. 1 and 8, and this may be regarded as Punaluan or Turanian; and it is to be noted that the change takes place here on the side of the male in advance of the side of the female.

In Diagram II. the basis is evidently Malayan; and here we may observe the same feature of less tendency to change in the maternal descent than the paternal.

DIAGRAM III.—*Parents and Children.*

Father's sister.	Father's brother.	Father.	Mother.	Mother's sister.	Mother's brother.
1	2	3	4	5	6
Mummuog Balugun	Mungan Leet	Mungan Leet	Leet Yukkan	Leet Yukkan	Leet Barbuk

Child.

7

Here, Nos. 2, 3, 4, 5, and 7 form a Punaluan group—for we have the brothers married to the sisters, the children being common to all; and, according to this system, we should expect to find the term denoting the *father's sister* and the *mother's brother* to differ from that applied to the *father's brother* and the *mother's sister*.

Nos. 2, 3, 4, and 5 form the Punaluan group, while No. 1 and No. 6 are units of two other and separate groups.

No. 7 is the child of No. 3 and No. 4; No. 7 is, however, also the child of No. 4 and No. 6. Therefore we may conclude that No. 4 and No. 6 have at some period cohabited. But No. 4 and No. 6 are sister and brother, and this is according to the Consanguine system. But while No. 7 is the child of No. 6, the latter is the "uncle"[*] of the former. In this, therefore, the relation of No. 6 towards No. 7 is an advance on the relation of No. 7 towards No. 6, and is Punaluan or Turanian.

We may notice here that the change on the side of the male parent is complete, while on the side of the female parent it is incomplete.

---

[*] If we take *Barbuk* = mother's brother, the term "uncle" is justified as a matter of convenient expression.

328   APPENDIX:

DIAGRAM IV.—*Brothers and Sisters—Brothers-in-Law and Sisters-in-Law—Cousins.*

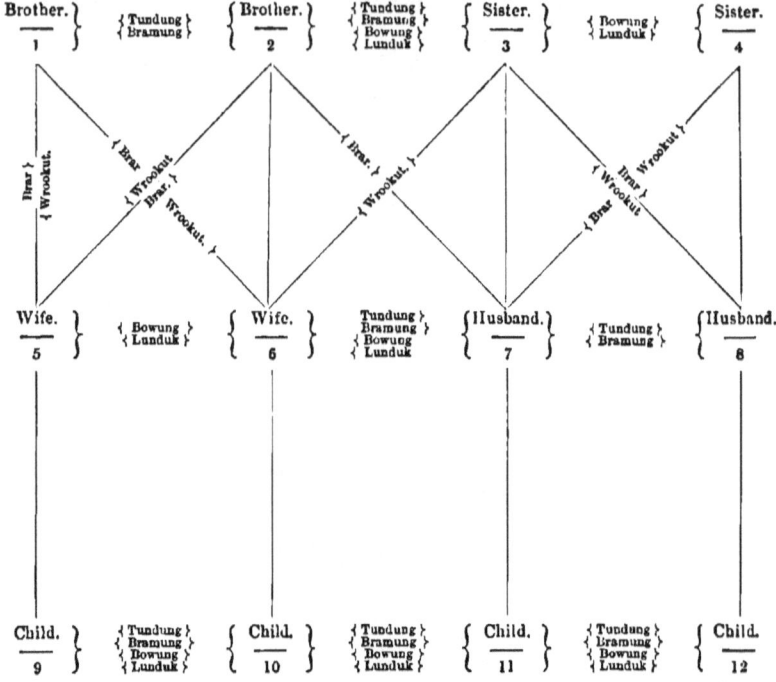

Each vertical column forms the group—father, mother, child. The upper horizontal line consists of brothers and sisters; the middle line of their respective wives and husbands; and the lowest line of their respective issue.

It will be seen that distinctive terms are used for elder brother, younger brother, elder sister, younger sister; namely, *Tundung, Bramung, Bowung, Lunduk*. The terms denoting the marital relations are given in respect to No. 1 and No. 5. It will be seen that the term "*Brar*"—*i.e.*, husband—is also applied by No. 2 to No. 7, or by the woman's husband and brother reciprocally; while the term "*Wrookut*"—*i.e*, wife—is applied by No. 3 to No. 6, or by the man's wife and sister reciprocally. The terms "*Brar*" and "*Wrookut*" may, however, be regarded as probably meaning "male" and "female," or "man" and "woman;" used, for example, as the German terms "Mann" and "Frau." "*Brar*" is found in a number of Brabroloug words. For instance, "*Brewit*," a young man; "*Brewin*," a supposed evil being who is said to afflict them with disease; "*Brajerak*," an Aboriginal of any other tribe than those of Gippsland. Here the explanation of the term may be well traced in "*Brar*" = a man; and "*Jerak*," or "*Yerik*" = angry, quarrelsome, wild.

If we look at the horizontal lines of Diagram IV., we shall perceive a complete Consanguine group, in which the parents are all brothers and sisters;

and consequently all the children of the group bear the same relation to each other. If we look at the vertical columns of the diagram in connection with Diagram III., it will be evident that it falls into two Punaluan groups, consisting of two brothers and sisters, with their respective wives and husbands and children. The distinction is seen here between this and the preceding family in the relations of the brothers and sisters and their respective children; for the brothers and sisters are no longer the parents of each other's children. Even here, however, we can trace a last link connecting the two systems; for the child of the sister is also the child of the brother—for which *see* Nos. 4, 6, and 7 of Diagram III.

I think the following conclusions may be arrived at from the preceding statements :—

1. The existing system is a not quite complete form of the Pairing family.
2. Some of the terms used denote a previous condition in the Punaluan family.
3. Other of the terms used denote a previous condition in the Consanguine family.
4. The actual intersexual relations are in advance of the relations denoted by the terms used.
5. We have here, therefore, indicated an apparent advance from the Consanguine family system at some early period to the Pairing family system of the present time.

I have pointed out, by an instance taken from the Jewish people, that we may trace the progress of a civilized people who are now in the Monogamian family system from an earlier system—the Patriarchal family, with indication of still earlier systems of consanguinity, which are now only to be met with as existing among savage races.

From the Brabrolong tribe, I have endeavoured to point out that we may, with some reason, conjecture that at a former period they were in the Punaluan system, and at a still earlier in the Consanguine system. It is, I think, difficult to conceive of any earlier social system than that adopted by Mr. Morgan as the starting point of his classification—namely, the "Consanguine." But, if we are justified in concluding that the preceding statements point to the Brabrolongs having at one time been in the Consanguine family system, it would, I think, follow that we must regard them as having risen through the successive stages to the actual system in existence. The question would then present itself, whether we should conclude that the Consanguine family was the starting point of the race; or whether their earlier progenitors were under other intersexual conditions? If they were under other conditions, then I think it would be admitted that those other conditions must probably have been either of a lower or of a higher type. The gradual progression from the Consanguine family upwards might imply a probable progression from some still lower family system upwards to the Consanguine.

Very different replies might be given to such questions by those who hold to the principles of evolution as being applicable to man and to man's social conditions; and by those who regard the principles of evolution as not being thus applicable, or who do not admit the truth of the evolution hypothesis at all.

It seems to me that the Brabrolong system, when regarded from the evolution stand-point, becomes a coherent whole, and highly suggestive of the past history of this race of savages; while under any other view the terms used would be senseless and without meaning. When it is further seen, as it has been seen by me in working out the systems of other tribes from distant parts of Australia, that similar conclusions to the above may be drawn from their systems, while no two are precisely similar in detail, the evidence as to the truth of the conclusions drawn becomes much strengthened.

Still there may be many who will demur to these conclusions. As regards this, I think it may well be left to those who are of opinion that the principles of evolution are not applicable to man or to man's social organizations to show what other and adverse conclusions may be legitimately drawn from an independent consideration of the systems of consanguinity and kinship, not merely of the Brabrolongs, but of any or of the whole of the Australian Aboriginal tribes.

The following table of relationships is taken from the Rev. George Taplin's work,* and should be studied in connection with Mr. Howitt's paper :—

Description of Relationship.	Native Term.	Translation.
My father - My father's brother -	Nanghai	Father.
My mother My mother's sister - My father's second wife - My stepmother -	Nainkowa	My mother.
My father's sister - My mother's brother's wife -	Barno	My aunt.
My mother's brother - My father's sister's husband -	Wanowe	My uncle.
My son or daughter - My brother's children -	Porlean	My child (I being a male).
My grandson - My granddaughter - My brother's grandson - My brother's granddaughter - My father's brother's son's son - My father's brother's son's daughter -	Maiyarari	My grandchild (I being a male).

* *The Narrinyeri*, p. 38.

CONSANGUINITY AND KINSHIP. 331

Description of Relationship.	Native Term.	Translation.
My elder sister - My father's brother's daughter (if older than myself) My mother's sister's daughter (if older than myself)	*Maranoxi*	My sister.
The relations last mentioned (if younger than myself); also my younger sister	*Tarte*	My younger sister.
My elder brother - My father's brother's son - My mother's sister's son -	*Gelanowe*	My elder brother.
My younger brother, and the relations last mentioned (if younger than myself)	*Tarte*	My younger brother.
My younger brother's son - My brother's daughter -	*Ngoppari*	A title to distinguish them from my own children.
My elder brother's son -	*Waiyatte*	(The same).
My son's wife - My brother's son's wife -	*Maiyareli*	My daughter-in-law. They call me the same.
My daughter's husband - My brother's daughter's husband - My wife's father -	*Yallundi*	A reciprocal term by which a father-in-law and a son-in-law address each other.
My sister's son (I being a male) - My mother's sister's grandchildren - My sister's daughter - - My father's brother's daughter's daughter	*Nanghari*, addressed as *Ung*	A term for a nephew or niece of this kindred.
My daughter's husband -	*Kutyi*	My son-in-law.
My sister's son (I being a female) - My sister's daughter (I being female) -	*Ngarra*	A term to distinguish them from my own children.
My brother's son - My brother's daughter - My mother's sister's son's sons and daughters (I being a male)	*Mbari*	A nephew or niece of this kindred.
My mother's brother's child - My father's sister's son - My father's sister's daughter -	*Nguyanowe*	Cousin.

APPENDIX.

Description of Relationship.	Native Term.	Translation.
My sister's son's wife		
My sister's grandson		
My sister's granddaughter (I being a female)		
My sister's grandson (I being a female)		
My sister's granddaughter		Grand relation. This is nearest term we have in English.
My father's sister's son's wife (I being either male or female)	*Mutthari*	
My mother's brother's son's wife		
My mother's brother's son's son		
My mother's brother's son's daughter		
My mother's brother's daughter's son		
My mother's brother's daughter's daughter		
My father's brother's daughter's husband		
My father's sister's daughter's husband	*Ronggi*	Brother-in-law.
My mother's sister's daughter's husband		
My wife's brother		
My mother's brother's daughter's husband	*Wurungelrop*	No equivalent.
My mother's sister's son's wife	*Ngulbowalle*	Sister-in-law.
My father's brother's son's wife		
My sister's son's wife (I being a male)	*Rinanowe*	Sister-in-law.
A woman's brother's wife		
My wife's sister's husband	*Ngauwiruli*	Relation-in-law.
My wife's sister		
My father's father		
My father's father's brother	*Maiyanowe*	Grand relation.
My father's father's sister		
My father's mother		
Her brother	*Mutthanowe*	Grand relation.
Her sister		
My mother's father		
His brother	*Ngaityanowe*	Grand relation.
His sister		
My mother's mother (I being a female)	*Bakkano kurukunu*	Grandmother.
My daughter's child (I being a female)	*Bakkari*	My grandchild.
My son-in-law		A reciprocal term. No equivalent in English.
My daughter-in-law; also (I being a male) my wife's mother	*Karinye*	
Twins	*Lalumpe*	

APPENDIX G.

NOTES ON THE LANGUAGE AND CUSTOMS OF THE TRIBE INHABITING THE COUNTRY KNOWN AS KOTOOPNA.

(BY WILLIAM LOCKE.)

Campbellfield House, 5th December 1876.

DEAR SIR,—The following is a corrected copy of a letter of mine which appeared in the *Argus* some years ago on the above subject. If it is of any use to you in the compilation of your book, I shall be pleased.

I am, dear Sir,
Yours faithfully,
WILLIAM LOCKE.

R. Brough Smyth, Esq.

WHEN a very young man, I held a large tract of country, called in the native language *Kotoopna* (now wrongly spelled *Kotupna*), extending nearly across the angle formed by the Goulburn and Murray. This portion of country belonged to a small tribe of blacks called *Pangorang*, or *Waning-otbun*. The men were very fine specimens of the Aboriginal, many of them being considerably upwards of six feet in stature, and exceedingly active and warlike in appearance. At that time they subsisted principally upon fish and wild-fowl, which they procured in great abundance on the Lower Moira. The ducks were caught wholesale in the following manner:—A large net was stretched across a narrow neck of a lagoon, when a blackfellow would go some distance up or down the creek, and drive or frighten the ducks towards the net, when numbers in their flight would be caught in the meshes. I have also seen them catch ducks by diving underneath them, and suddenly laying hold of them by the legs.

In consequence of my being located, as it were, in the midst of these darkies, I, of necessity, became intimately acquainted with their manners and customs, and became a great favorite. I always treated them with great kindness, and they were only too glad to prove their gratitude at every opportunity. The fact of my being able to converse with them in their own tongue gave me considerable influence. They used to say—"No stupid, Mr. Locke; always yabba the same as blackfellow." On one occasion a gentleman made his appearance on the back portion of the run, intending to "sit down" there with a flock of sheep; but my sable friends would not have it at any price. They said to him—"What for you comballee along-a this one country? This one country all about belong-a to Mr. Locke." Eventually he had to depart, the blacks, at my request, cutting bark canoes, to enable him to cross his sheep. Although at that time these blacks were perfectly wild, I never had the slightest apprehension of suffering any personal injury from them. I have often gone out with them in the bush, perfectly unarmed; although as to this I once got a piece of advice from one of the tribe. He said—"When you walk in bush along-a blackfellow, you make him blackfellow walk first time" (in front). I said—"What for?" He replied—"I den know; I believe debil debil jump up, want him blackfellow spear whitefellow." It is hardly necessary to add that upon this hint I acted in future.

Several strange superstitions existed amongst them. I once went to the Moira, accompanied by a blackfellow, and on our return I expressed to him my opinion that it would be dark before we reached home, whereupon he alighted from his horse, and, without saying a word, proceeded to cut a small sod of grass, which he placed in a fork of a tree, exactly facing the setting sun, remarking—"Plenty quambee (stop) sun now. No pull away." As it happened, we got home before it was dark, when Sambo exultingly exclaimed—"No gammon ground" (meaning the sod of earth). If a young baby died, the mother had to carry the body on her back till her husband procured the kidney-fat of a strange blackfellow. This is a very horrible custom. I have seen a lubra so carry about her dead child. The kidney-fat is wrapped up in several bits of rag, and worn round the neck as a charm. They told me that a blackfellow would linger from six to eight days before death ensued after the removal of the kidney-fat. The victim is first stunned by a "waddy," a small incision made in his side, and a portion of the kidney-fat carefully removed, when he is left to his fate.

The language of this tribe is very euphonious, and, strange to say, at a distance of only about fifty miles from Kotoopna, the idiom, indeed the language itself, is quite different. Most of the names of places end in "pna," as "Kotoopna," "Tarigoroopna," "Jillinupna," "Ulupna," &c. Kangaroo—*Koyeemar.* Emu—*Bigorumja.* Young emu—*Woola.* Opossum—*Bunna.* Kangaroo-rat—*Arenewtha.* Dog—*Bocka.* Horse—*Corkitarnook* (this name for horse is the same in Gippsland and other parts of Victoria). Sheep—*Jumbaya.* Supposed bun-yip—*Tanutbun.* Little—*Ingarnaka.* Least—*Inga.* Great—*Turneja* (as great heat, *Turneja daideja*). Extensive—*Boymee* (as extensive plain, *Boymee natcha*). Nice—*Kulnia.* Beautiful—*Kalimna* (this word I think has a very sweet sound; I have named several of my friends' estates after it). No, or none—*Uta* (same nearly all over Victoria). Lightning—*Kernyara.* Thunder—*Manena.* Come here—*Cockiaroo.* Go away—*Berriaroo.* Very hot, me too much lazy—*Turneja daideja, marrilatchimut neynee.* What is it?—*Min-the-lay?* Where—*Woonul.* Knapsack—*Belshula.* Fishing-net—*Jegoga.* Gum-tree—*Bela.* Box-tree—*Tharmia.* Bark—*Yalmin.* Tomahawk—*Aanu.* Reed-spear—*Gaumur.* Jagged spear—*Jikola.* Spear with glass—*Coico.* Woomera—*Ulewar.* Boomerang—*Wadeenia.* Creek—*Bormea.* Plain—*Natcha.* Mountain—*Uleela.* Sandhill—*Maloga.*

Goulburn River—*Koyeela*. Murray River—*Fingola*. Campaspe—*Yalook*. Hut—*Mano*. Father—*Baapoo*. Mother—*Cana*. Sister—*Thajuba*. My dear brother—*Thoma nien boynupa*. My dear sister—*Thoma nien thajuba*. Little brother—*Kidjika*. Acquaintance—*Jucada*. White woman—*Malawa uniar*. Blackfellow—*Ainbootha*. Teeth—*Derrara*. Very hungry, stomach empty—*Turneja malunwick, cetumut boolie*. Give me some bread—*Mitther eeyanook*. Be off to your camp, all of you—*Berumja beriarroo, mano noothiga*. Go and cut some bark for me—*Beriarroo wabuja yalmin neence*.

The three following were favorite corrobborees :—

1.

Berri berri ma jildomba,
Berri berri ma jildomba,
Berri berri ma jildomba-naga.
Athen jindema, no goi-cela ;
Jindema, jindema, O-en-dethen-o.
Warrim bang-e, berri berri ma jildomba-a,
Berri berri ma jildomba, berri berri ma jildomba.

2.

Aree muthe-e, aree mutho-o,
Aree mutha, comaug-a thalitanga magoouba ;
Malaug-oree, malang-oree.
Mullin mullin jing-a magoonbang-a jilitang-a,
Jing-a jing-a, gothanga, magoontanga thalato.

3.

Thunda irra tha, thunda ra-oo,
Gra imalaug-a imee-e ;
Thunda irra tha, thunda re-e,
Gra imalaug-a, imme-e-e.

Some years ago I revisited the scenes of my youth. The once powerful tribe of *Pangorangs* had dwindled down to eight or ten men and four women. They did not recollect me at first; but when I mentioned my name, the old men were delighted. As a proof of the march of civilization, the women were engaged at the camp playing with cards—the intellectual game of "All Fours." *O tempora, O mores!*

APPENDIX H.

HUNTING THE BLACKS.

(BY THE HONORABLE A. F. A. GREEVES.)

"It was when I was Chief Constable of the Port Macquarie district," said Mr. D—— "The blacks had been very troublesome; among other murders they had committed was one of Mr. ———'s stockmen, whom they seized and sawed up into junks while he was alive. We found the cross-cut saw; but more of that by-and-by. I was only turned nineteen then, and was delighted to be appointed to head the party to track and punish the miscreants. The party consisted of two half-civilized blacks for guides—you know one tribe will always betray and attack another; one better sort of young fellow named Meade, a sort of second or lieutenant; and four Government men, with two soldiers. Well, we beat about a long time before we could get on their track."

"And pray how did you find out their trail?"

"Oh why, after several days' reconnoitring, at last we found a little bit of bark on fire, and one fire smouldering away. It was cold weather, so that all were carrying bark torches to keep themselves warm; but they were cunning enough either not to light fires or to cover over the ashes with bark, so that we should not find them. However, in this way, we went on day after day until we came into the wildest country you can imagine. All rocks and stones; no horses could have gone there."

"What; were you on foot?"

"On foot! Every man of us. Horses won't do to track the blacks; they take too much looking after; they occasion too much noise in trampling on dry leaves and rotten sticks; besides, when the natives are pursued, they resort to precipices and ravines where horses could not go twenty yards. I think it was the second day after we found their track that one afternoon, on turning the corner of a rock, we found ourselves in a long valley, bounded by rugged precipices on each side. The bush was open; there were only a few large trees here and there. There were copses of brushwood scattered about of stunted Banksias and mimosas, like thickets of hazel at home. Well, just as we entered the valley, we saw the whole party of blacks defiling a great height above us, in a zig-zag direction, among the precipices. They did not appear to see us, and we hurried on after them. At last we began to hear their voices. Sunset was near, and we presently heard them breaking off branches to construct their mia-mias—or gunyahs, as those tribes call them—for the night. We went very cautiously a little further, until we could, by glimpses through the wood, just ascertain they were about to encamp a few hundred yards ahead on the opposite side of a narrow scrub of young trees. We halted in silence until it was quite dark, and then I gave the signal to move on. We crept stealthily along, one of our guides hovering about a little ahead to reconnoitre their exact place. I was very near him; in fact, in the scrub itself; and we were cautiously prowling forward, when he trod upon a rotten twig—unavoidable in the dark. Snap went the twig, sounding in the silent dark solitudes like a pistol shot: instantly, within a few yards of me, jumped up about a dozen or score blacks. I was taken very much aback, for in the dark we had not thought them so near. They had all spears, and I had never been in war before. I must confess I felt rather qualmish at the sight of those stout fellows so near me; however, I had resolution enough to cry out—'Now, boys, fire away.' The men fired—the natives uttered a fearful yell, shouting 'white fellow,' threw down their spears, and ran off like kangaroos. I now found my courage much restored, and ordered to reload; but, in my anxiety to lose no time, I put the wrong end of my cartridge into my piece, so it was of no use just then. We then set a watch, and waited until morning. I don't think many of us slept for fear of a surprise. Nothing, however, occurred, and in the morning we found we had killed three big fellows. They had left several of their spears and liangles and other things; amongst the rest was the cross-cut saw with which they had murdered the poor stockman, all covered with blood. We concluded we had now driven them off our side of the country, and taking off the tip of the ears of the dead blacks, according to orders, set off back, and without further adventure got to the settlement.

"When I reported progress to old Major ———, the head Government officer there, he swore we had only half served them out; they were too daring to be easily driven away; and ordered me to recruit my party, and, with fresh supplies, to be after them again, and make an example of them. I had had quite enough for one spell. However, go I must."

"But how," interrupted I, "did you get food?"

"Why, this time we had two extra men—*Weenick* named them our pack-bullocks—to carry an extra supply. The first expedition each man carried his own."

"And water?"

"Oh, we never found any difficulty. The blacks know every spot of the country, and always take care to travel where there is water. Besides, we had a favorable season for it: it was winter. Well, we set off and reached the limit of our former journey, and got again upon the trail of the blacks. The long and slender kangaroo-grass, trodden down as here and there it occurred in their line of march, had not yet sprung up again. It is not so difficult to follow a track in the bush after all; but it's keen work, too, and wants a quick and practised eye. Anything eatable quickly disappears with the wild dogs and wild cats, as well as by the natives themselves and their dogs. But a little twig lying on the ground CUT off, or merely with the branches and leaves stripped off, which show that man had done it, and the condition of freshness or dryness, would tell how long since he was there. The notched trees—nicks they make in the trees in order to ascend them—are very conspicuous guide-posts. Occasionally you come upon a foot-mark in a miry place, or a dry and sandy one; and it is amazing how the blacks will infer the size, age, and sex of the persons who imprinted it. In short, they recognise the features of a foot-mark just as we do those of the countenance; and as they are clearly defined, or obliterated, as the minute blades of grass are crushed down, or erecting themselves again, can they tell how long since the person passed. For seven days did we travel in this manner following the fugitives. Little did we think of their manœuvre, as will presently appear. Every evening, at sunset—the time they camp—did I ascend some eminence, to see if we could observe the minute little cloud of curling smoke which indicates their fires. We could see nothing, and yet we knew they were not very far off. That night some of the party fancied they heard a chopping of branches, as when the blacks construct their gunyahs at eventide. However, next morning, before the party started, I went to the top of an eminence with Meade, to reconnoitre the day's journey and direction. It was a fine cloudless morning in July. The air was chilly, as it always is in winter at morning. The sun was just clear above the fogs of the horizon, and the dew glittered on the leaves. The parrots were wakening up with noisy welcomes to day, and sucking the honey from the early-flowering trees. The squirrel and opossum had gone to sleep in their holes—for the Australian animals *live* only at night; and the shy kangaroo might be seen slowly hopping away to his lair, having filled his pouch since dawn, to ruminate his hastily-got food. I sat down on the brink of the precipice which looked towards the country we expected to traverse. There was a fog in the valley below rapidly clearing off; but beyond that was the wide wild forest, over which I could not detect a symbol of life. Suddenly my companion exclaimed—' My heavens, what a lot of blacks!' I looked down the precipice—the mist had cleared off—and sure enough there was the sable company in vehement agitation. They saw the two white men against the sky, on the rocks above them, and they were for off. I hastened down to our camp, summoned the party, and off we set.

"We set off direct for the mountains, and after two days we came to some ashes, which were quite warm. Towards evening we heard the sound of the chopping of branches (preparing their gunyahs) and children playing. It came on snowing, and we halted until morning. At dawn a dog came and smelt and snuffed around, and then retired a little distance to a big log and began to howl. Up jumped the blacks, and rushed towards us; we let fly; several blacks fell; and a *mêlée* ensued. We had to use the butt-end of our muskets. One young lad was shot through the chest and both arms, after which he ran some three hundred yards before he dropped. Not a woman of them was hurt, except one who got her head grazed. The children made holes, and buried their heads, looking like black burnt stumps. One fine tall fellow appeared on the top of the hill, shouting—' Bail me coolah long with white fella.' Two of my men went towards him. I shouted—' Take him, he'll be of use;' but in a moment one knocked him down and the other shot him through the head.

All the women and children then fled. We cut off his left ear, wrapped it in salt, and I carried it in my waistcoat pocket to take to our superior officers as a trophy of our success.

"We now determined to return, our provisions all being done but a piece of damper.

"We set a watch every night. We began to feel the pangs of hunger, but were afraid to shoot any game for fear of directing the blacks; so, having caught a native bear, we killed him for food. Next night we halted; it was a beautiful night, and there was a beautiful fall of water on the spot. It was Meade's watch, though we all watched alike. I went to wash my shirt in the creek; I was busy there when I fancied I heard a crackle—perhaps it was a kangaroo; again I fancied I saw a star or two, or a spark; then another. 'Here's the blacks,' called out all hands; and, crossing the creek above the falls, we saw the lights coming nearer, and then a shower of spears fell into our mia-mias, already deserted by us.

"'Let fly,' was the word; there was a great cry; and next day sixty spears were found, all where we had been lying. This was the ambush into which the party of blacks had wished to draw us from the first. If I had not taken charge of the watch, I believe we should all have been killed.

"We now pursued our return march, and for many days suffered intensely from hunger; but arriving at an out-station, we killed a bullock, upon which we fared sumptuously on broiled beef; we left, however, the tips of the ears unconsumed; and, resuming our march, arrived safely at head-quarters. The blacks were never troublesome in that neighbourhood any more. Since then they have been subject to ordinary law; but previously all they understood was '*force*,' and that retaliation is a virtue."

This was written down by me from the lips of the above head of the party, Mr. J—— D——, then reporter to the *Port Phillip Gazette*, and now one of the Members of Assembly for Hobarton, in 1844-5.—AUGUSTUS F. A. GREEVES.

APPENDIX I.

THE CRANIA OF THE NATIVES.

(By GEORGE B. HALFORD, M.D., PROFESSOR OF ANATOMY AND PHYSIOLOGY IN THE UNIVERSITY OF MELBOURNE.)

HAVING been requested by Mr. Brough Smyth to superintend the drawing of some Australian skulls, and to append to them a few notes, I have done so in as simple a manner as possible, and have afterwards added some measurements suitable to the strictly scientific enquirer.

The reader may depend upon the accuracy of Major Shepherd's drawings; and of the manner in which they were done he shall speak for himself.

G. B. H.

NOTE.

The series of drawings from the skulls committed to my care comprises four drawings of each, viz.:—

1. A front view.
2. A side view or profile.
3. A view of the base of the skull.
4. A view of the skull from above.

There is also a drawing of the skull of (M), and of the Australian Aboriginal (A) seen from behind.

The method adopted to secure a perfectly similar position and point of view for each specimen in the different aspects chosen was as follows:—

A board was adjusted with its upper surface quite level. On the front edge of this board, and rising perpendicularly from it, a frame was placed, with crossed threads (perpendicular and horizontal) an inch apart, the lowest thread coinciding with the surface of the board.

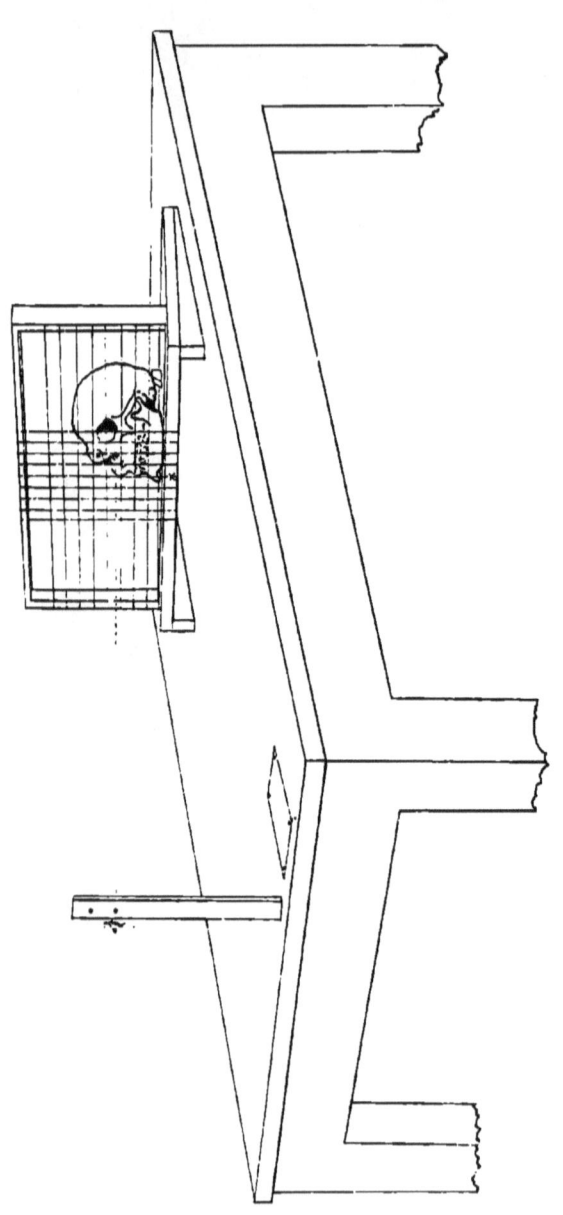

At a distance of 33 inches in front of and exactly opposite to the centre of the front edge of the level board an upright lath of wood was fixed, with an aperture for the eye at the same height as the middle of the object to be drawn. In this series of drawings two apertures were used, one for the *front* and *side* views, and the other for the views from *above* and *below*.

It may be mentioned that, having to use a sloping drawing table, allowance had of course to be made for its inclination in fixing the level board and the point of view.

1. In adjusting the skull for a front view, the lower edge of the *body* of the under-jaw rests on the level plane of the board with its symphisis touching the middle thread of the frame, the hinder portion of the skull being supported in position by a wedge. The longitudinal axis of the skull coincides with a line drawn from the point of sight through the middle upright thread of the frame.

The drawings were all made upon paper ruled in half-inch squares, consequently the portions of the object that touched the plane of the threads are half the size of the originals, the retiring portions being perspectively diminished in proportion to their distances from that plane.

2. In the side view the skull was turned round until the longitudinal axis was at right-angles to the line of sight, the ridge of the temporal bone touching the middle thread of the plane.

3. In drawing the basilar aspect, the skull rested on the cerebellum, the middle thread touching the spine of the occipital bone and the points of the incisors of the upper-jaw.

4. The view of the skull from above was drawn with the line of sight in the same plane, but at right-angles to the front view, the crown of the skull touching the middle thread of the frame.

In the posterior views the skull as adjusted for a front view was turned completely round, its longitudinal axis coinciding with the line of sight, and the hinder part of the skull touching the middle thread.

The whole arrangement will best be understood from the accompanying diagram.

RICHD. SHEPHERD.

10th October 1876.

(A.)

SKULL OF AUSTRALIAN.

Fig. 263.—*Front.*

The observer will notice—

1. The large superciliary ridges, overshadowing the orbits, which are very extensive, with somewhat angular circumference. These superciliary ridges, when cut into, were found to be solid bone.
2. Above these ridges, the small cramped retreating forehead.
3. Short concave nasal bones, forming the upper boundary of the broad front opening of the nostrils.
4. Downward and outward sloping of the malar (cheek) bone.

Fig. 264.—*Side View.*

1. Very prognathous jaws.
2. The abrupt indentation between the superciliary ridges and the nasal bones.
3. Small mastoid process.
4. The length of this skull from the brow to the occiput is diminished internally by quite $1\frac{1}{4}$ inch, owing to the thickness of the bones.

Some other features in this view will be referred to when (M) 2 is described.

(A.)

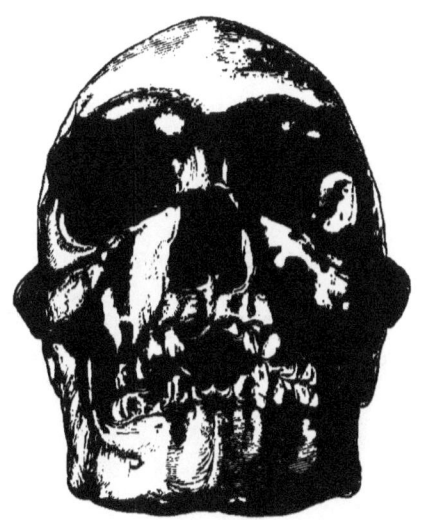

FIG. 263.

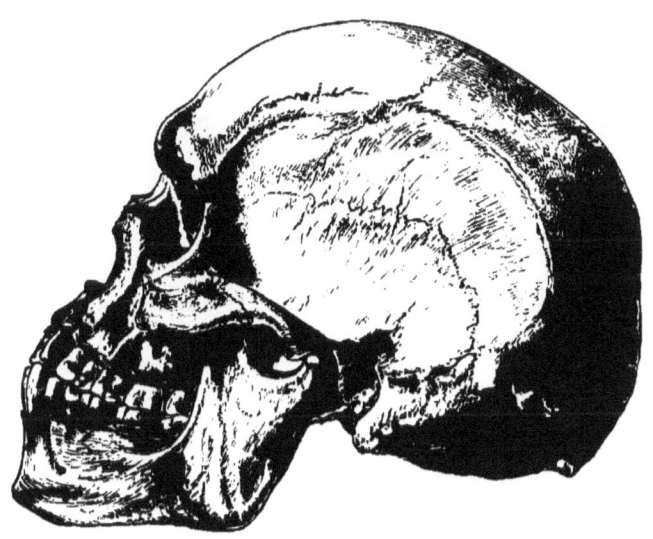

FIG. 264.

(A.)

SKULL OF AUSTRALIAN.

Fig. 265.—*Posterior View*.

1. Narrowing of the anterior parietal and frontal regions of the skull. This feature is not so well represented as it exists in the original skull.

Fig. 266.—*From above*.

1. Shows the narrow frontal, temporal, and anterior parietal regions, with the coarse bowed zygomata.
2. Pits for the front teeth in upper-jaws not hidden by the nasal bones.

(A.)

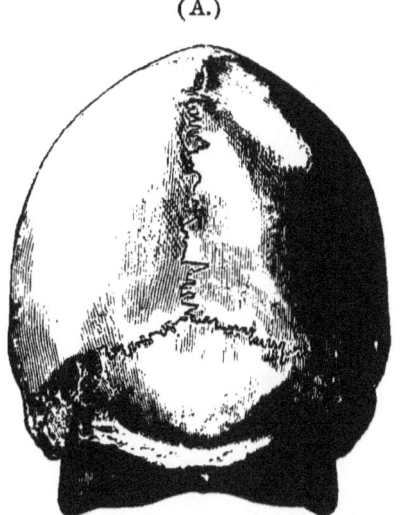

FIG. 265.

FIG. 266.

(A.)

SKULL OF AUSTRALIAN.

Fig. 267.—*Inferior View.*

1. Somewhat circular outline of the occipital hole (foramen magnum).
2. Very oblique occipital condyles.
3. Bowed coarse zygomata.
4. Narrow alisphenoid region.
5. Deep zygomatic fossa.
6. Elongated palate.
7. Cusps of the teeth nearly obliterated.

(A.)

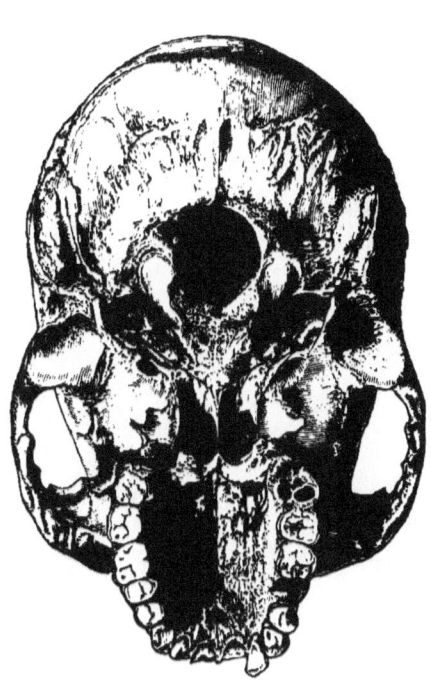

FIG. 267.

(M.)

SKULL OF MORGAN, THE BUSHRANGER.—(EUROPEAN.)
To be compared with Australian Skull (A).

Fig. 268.—*Front.*

1. Greater development of the frontal and temporal regions.
2. Less prominent zygomata.
3. Larger mastoid processes.
4. More circular circumference of orbits.
5. Narrower anterior nasal aperture.
6. More vertical alveolar processes for holding the teeth.
7. Arch formed by the teeth less prominent.

Fig. 269.—*Side View.*

1. Superciliary ridge prominent, containing a large frontal sinus.
2. Far greater height of skull.
3. Posterior development about equal with (A).
4. Floor of temporal fossa more convex.
5. Facial bones less brutal in shape.
6. Long nasal bones.
7. Prominent chin.

(M.)

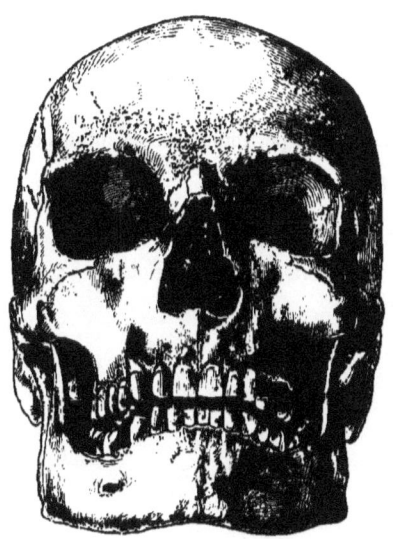

FIG. 268.

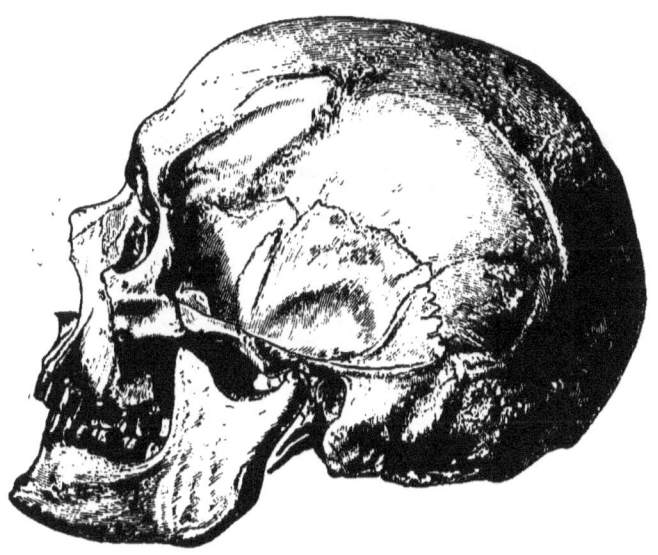

FIG. 269.

(M.)

Fig. 270.—*Posterior View.*

1. Greater extent of the vertical portion of the occipital bone.
2. Greater size of mastoid processes.
3. All the diameters of this region of the skull greater.
4. Greater fullness of the superior parietal regions.

Fig. 271.—*From above.*

1. Every possible diameter of this skull of greater extent.
2. Space between the brain-case and the zygomata greatly reduced.
3. Alveolar processes of the central incisor teeth quite hidden by the nasal bones.

THE CRANIA OF THE NATIVES. 351

(M.)

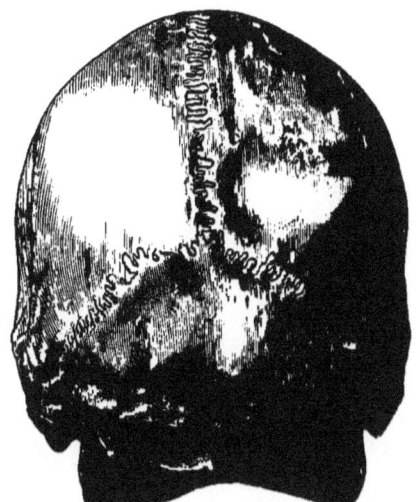

FIG. 273.

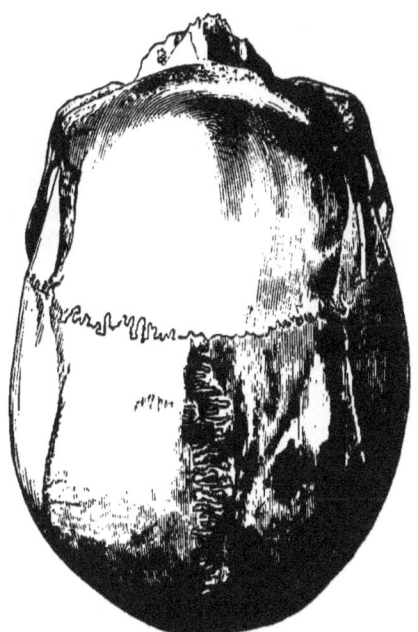

FIG. 271.

(M.)

Fig. 272.—*Inferior Aspect.*

1. Occipital region far more extensive, both transversely and longitudinally.
2. Mastoid processes larger.
3. Foramen magnum more oval.
4. Occipital condyles less oblique.
5. Greater width of the sphenoidal region.
6. Less bowed zygomata.
7. Palate less extensive from before backwards.
8. Crowns of the molars smaller, the cusps not being worn away, as is usual in Australians' teeth, owing to the amount of sand mixed with their food.

(M) AND (A).

REMARKS.

When these skulls were bisected longitudinally, it was found that the superciliary ridges in (M) bounded large frontal sinuses. In (A) they were the anterior boundaries of very close diploë between the external and internal tables of the skull. The phrenologist's perceptive faculties would therefore have been in (M) air and mucus; in (A) solid bone six-eighths of an inch thick.

Measuring from the internal occipital protuberance to the foramen cœcum, both skulls were found to be of the same length, viz., $5\frac{5}{8}$ inches; and the longest diameter above this of the brain-case was found exactly alike in both, viz., $6\frac{3}{8}$ inches. But the width and height of the cavity above the floor of the skull was much greater in (M) than in (A); so that however equal the contained brains might have been as regards those parts forming their bases and their cerebella, still in all that constitutes cerebral development (M) must have been superior to (A).

The reader will do well to look now at the following drawing of the skull and face of a Chinaman.

Although the cranial dimensions are less extensive than in (M), they are greatly superior to (A), and the whole aspect is much less brutal.

(M.)

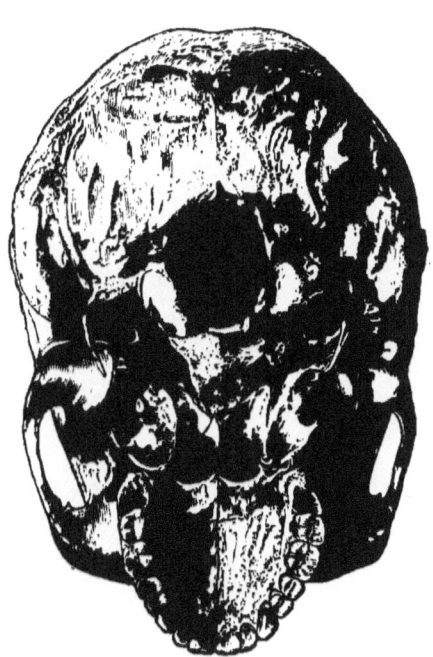

FIG. 272.

Fig. 273.

SKULL OF A CHINESE.

For comparison with Australian skull (A).

SKULL OF A CHINESE.

FIG. 273.

(B.)

SKULL OF AUSTRALIAN (PROBABLY FEMALE).

Fig. 274.—*Front View.*

1. Low frontal region, sloping away from above outwards and downwards.
2. Posterior lateral bulging of the parietals visible.
3. Circumference of the orbits less angular than usual in Australian skulls
4. Anterior nasal opening wide.
5. Teeth very even; crowns worn smooth.

Fig. 275.—*Side View.*

1. Very small superciliary ridges, the bone in this region being solid.
2. Want of height in the middle fronto-parietal region.
3. Good development of the posterior cerebral region, verified by examination of the cavity afterwards.
4. Parietal eminences prominent.
5. Zygomata very delicate.
6. All the bones of the skull and face very smooth.

(B.)

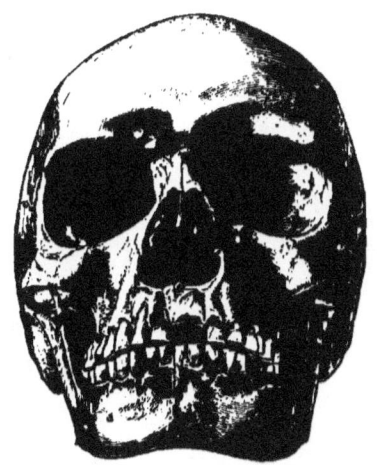

FIG. 274.

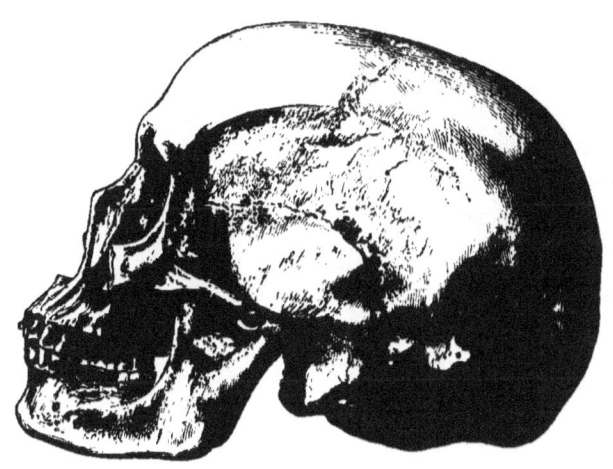

FIG. 275.

(B.)

Fig. 276.—*From above.*

1. Narrow frontal region.
2. Comparatively broad posterior cerebral region.
3. Alveolar processes of central front teeth not hidden by the nasal bones.
4. Indent on the right side, probably from a blow during life.

Fig. 277.—*Inferior Aspect.*

1. Very narrow occipital region.
2. Prominent parietal eminences.
3. Somewhat circular outline of foramen magnum.
4. Very oblique occipital condyles.
5. Very narrow anterior temporal and alisphenoid regions.
6. Crowns of the teeth worn even by attrition.
7. Palate more elongated than in European.

THE CRANIA OF THE NATIVES. 359

(B.)

FIG. 276.

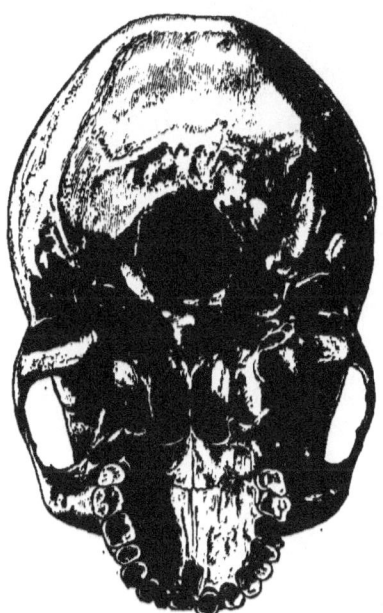

FIG. 277.

(C.)

SKULL OF AUSTRALIAN.

Fig. 278.—*Front View.*

1. Forehead tolerably broad.
2. Good breadth and height in the frontal and lateral regions.
3. General features less brutal than in (A).

Fig. 279.—*Side View.*

1. Great posterior development of the skull.
2. Sloping frontals.
3. Small mastoid processes.
4. Abrupt concavity below superciliary ridge.

(C.)

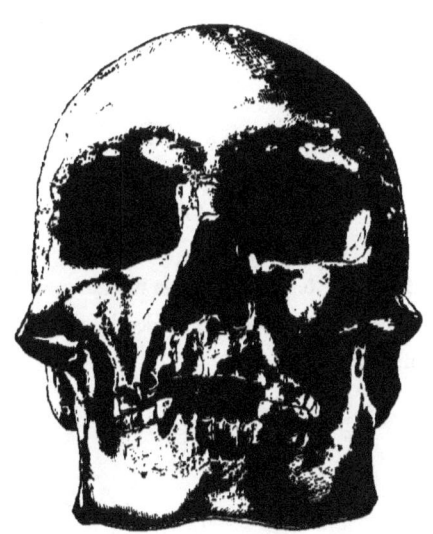

FIG. 278.

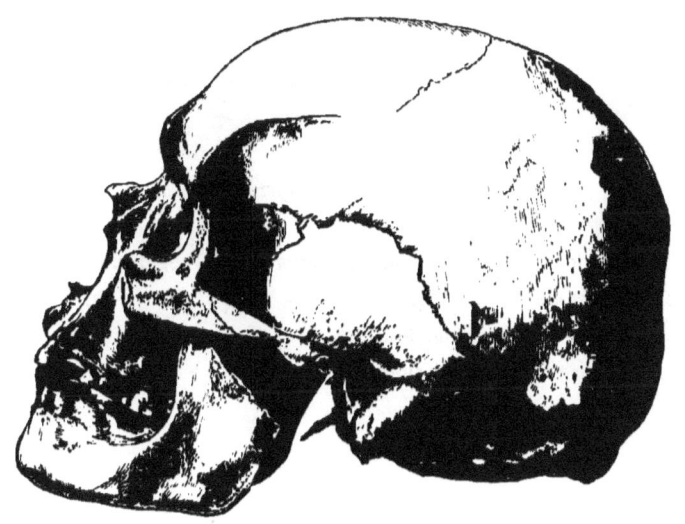

FIG. 279.

(C.)

Fig. 280.

1. Frontal and anterior temporal regions tolerably well developed.
2. Alveolar processes of incisors not hidden by the nasal bones.
3. Zygomata not much bowed.

Fig. 281.—*Inferior Aspect.*

1. Well-developed occipital and posterior parietal regions.
2. Narrow alisphenoid region.
3. Oblique occipital condyles.
4. Crowns of teeth worn smooth.

(C.)

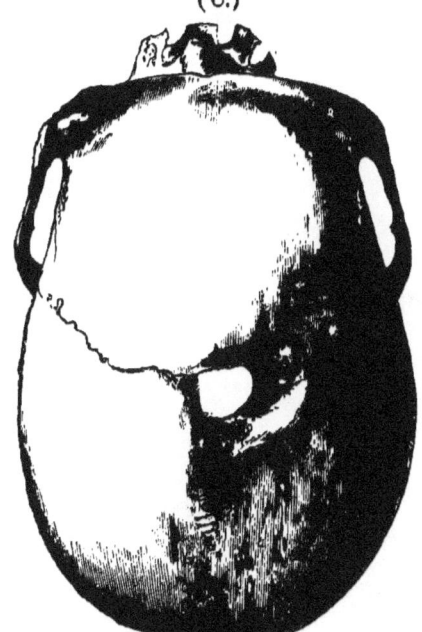

FIG. 280.

FIG. 281.

(D.)

SKULL OF AUSTRALIAN.

FIG. 282.—*Front.*

1. Narrow and retreating forehead.

FIG. 283.—*Side View.*

1. Superciliary ridges large, and containing well-developed frontal sinuses.[*]
2. Narrow sloping frontal and anterior parietal regions.
3. Great height in the centre.
4. Large development of posterior cerebral region.
5. Large temporal region.
6. Thin and delicate zygomata.

[*] In examining six other Australian skulls than those referred to in this work, I found three with good frontal sinuses, and three without any trace of them.

(D.)

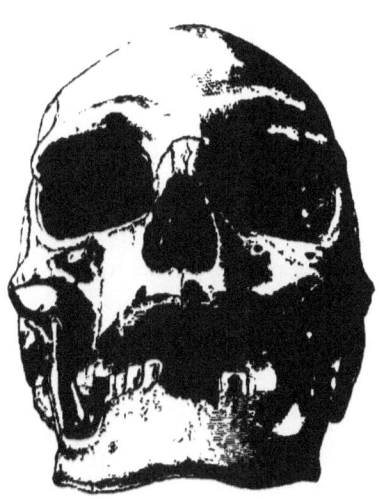

FIG. 282.

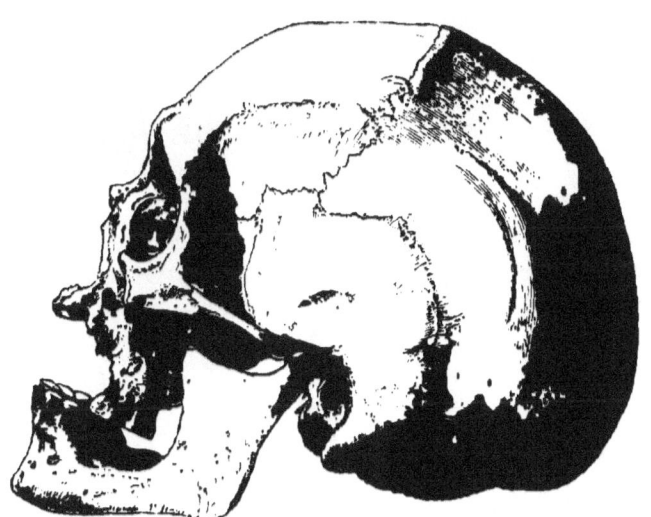

FIG. 283.

(D.)

Fig. 284.—*From above.*

1. Narrow frontal and anterior parietal regions.
2. Bowed zygomata.
3. Alveolar processes for teeth seen beyond the nasal bones.

Fig. 285.—*Inferior Aspect.*

1. Nearly circular outline of the foramen magnum.
2. Small occipital condyles.
3. Bowed zygomata.
4. Pointed elongated palate.

THE CRANIA OF THE NATIVES. 367

(D.)

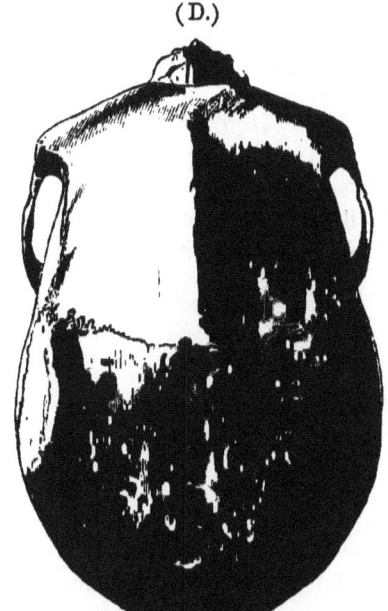

FIG. 284.

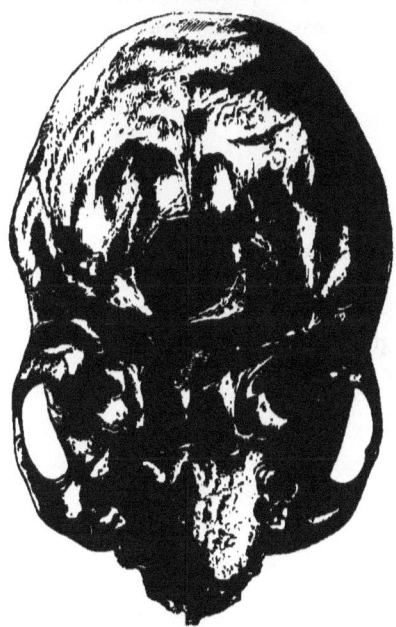

FIG. 285.

(E.)

SKULL OF KING JIMMY, OF THE MORDIALLOC TRIBE.

This Australian chief died lately, and, through the kindness of Dr. Cooke and of one of my students (Mr. Brownless), his skull was given to me. There being some very peculiar points about it, I think it fit to include a description of it in this work.

Fig. 286.

Represents the anterior aspect of the skull, which in the original was even more brutal than here represented. The sort of mid-rib running along the top of the skull, like the crest of the gorilla, and bounded on each side by a temporal ridge, gives the skull a most ape-like appearance. The immense orbits and nasal fossæ with prognathous upper-jaw complete the picture.

Fig. 287.—*Side View of the same Skull.*

The brutal aspect has disappeared; we have apparently a skull of large capacity. We notice the height to which the temporal fossa reaches and its backward direction.

(E.)

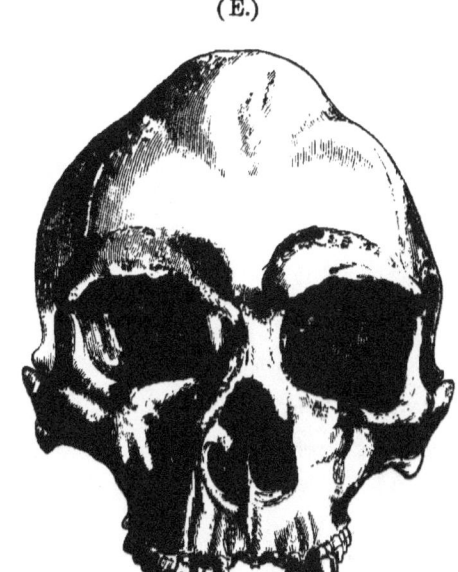

FIG. 286.

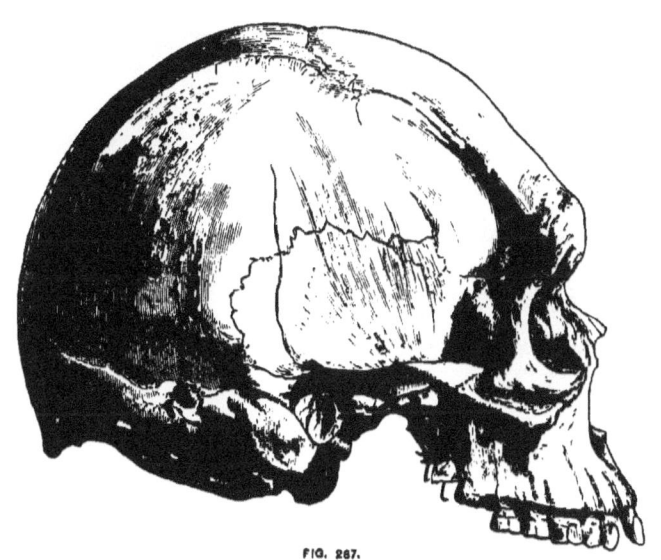

FIG. 287.

(E.)

Fig. 288.—*Upper View, showing—*

1. The extent to which the temporal ridges rise.
2. The middle and posterior breadth of the skull.
3. The prognathous upper-jaw unhidden by the nasal bones.

Fig. 289.—*Posterior Aspect.*

1. The posterior and middle breadths.
2. The longitudinal central elevation of the skull.

THE CRANIA OF THE NATIVES.

(E.)

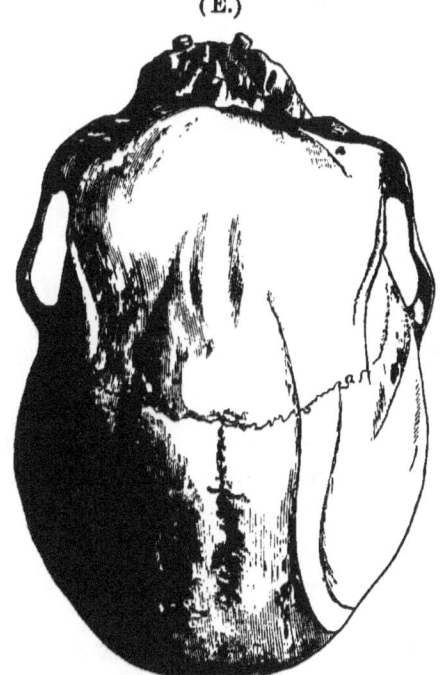

FIG. 288.

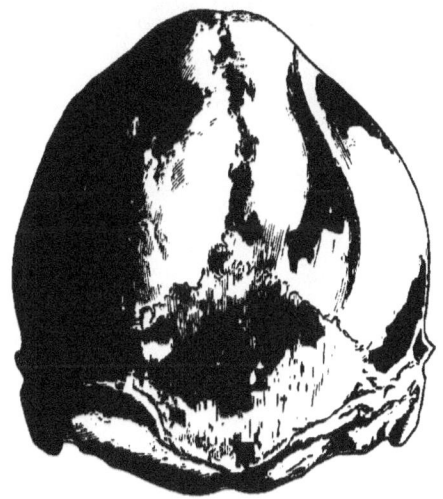

FIG. 289.

(E.)

Fig. 290.—*The same Skull bisected longitudinally, showing—*

1. Large frontal and sphenoidal cells.
2. Respectable capacity, and internal contour, whereby it asserts its claims to humanity.

After the foregoing drawings had been completed, I bisected five of the skulls, and, with Major Shepherd, measured with the greatest care the angles, base lines, arches, &c., on the plan recommended by Professor Cleland in the *Journal of Anatomy and Physiology*, July 1877. I have done this in the hope that it may, in however trifling a way, assist the craniologist in "obtaining national distinctions of a most exact description."

SECTION OF THE SKULL OF KING JIMMY (E),

Showing the base lines, radii, chords, angles, &c., referred to in the lists of measurements recorded in the following pages.

(Fig. 291.)

- a–f. Foramen magnum.
- d. Fronto nasal suture.
- a–d. Base line.
- g. Points corresponding to the centre of the external auditory meatus.
- g–1. Mid occipital radius.
- g–2. Mid parietal radius.
- g–3. Mid frontal radius.
- a–b. Occipital arch.
- b–c. Parietal arch.
- c–d. Frontal arch.
- a–b. Occipital chord (line not drawn).
- b–c. Parietal chord.
- c–d. Frontal chord.
- d–h. Frontal base.
- h–f. Middle base.

THE CRANIA OF THE NATIVES.

(E.)

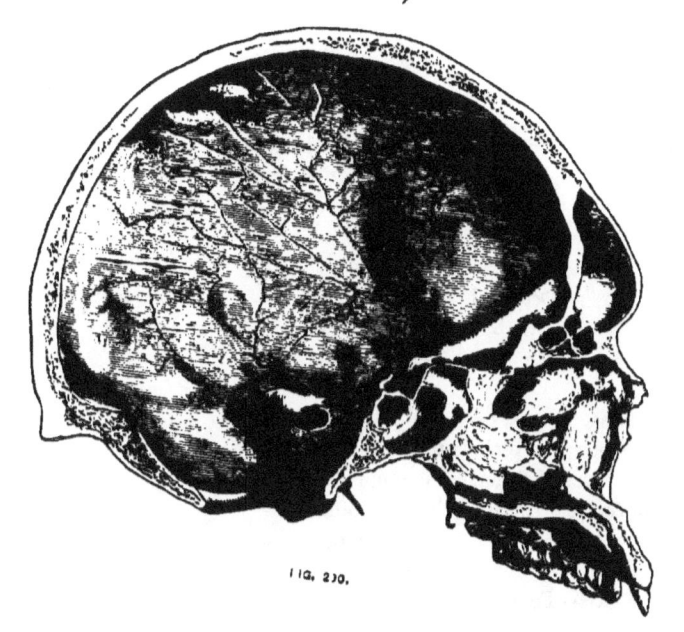

FIG. 230.

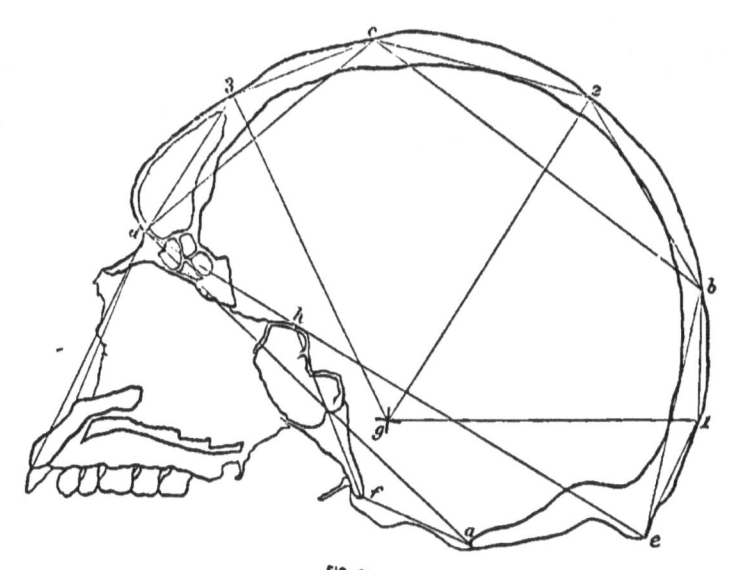

FIG. 231.

SKULL (A).

Breadths—Greatest breadth, close to but a little below the squamous suture in the part of its course where it turns down behind - - - - - 5·1 inches
        Coronal breadth - - - - - - 4·1 ,,
        Zygomatic - - - - - - - 5·4 ,,
        Arch—Occipital - - - - - 4·4
               Parietal - - - - - 4·8
               Frontal - - - - - 5·1
                                                                  —— 14·3 ,,
        Base line - - - - - - - 5·4 ,,
Length from occipital probole to fronto nasal suture - - - 7·05 ,,
Height from front of foramen magnum - - - - - 5· ,,
Radii from centre of meatus—Mid occipital - - - - 3·7 ,,
                           Mid parietal - - - - 4·35 ,,
                           Mid frontal - - - - 4·45 ,,
Portions of base—Foramen magnum - - - - - 1·25 ,,
              Middle base - - - - - 2·05 ,,
              Frontal base - - - - - 2·35 ,,
Chords—Occipital - - - - - - - 3·45 ,,
        Parietal - - - - - - - 4·4 ,,
        Frontal - - - - - - - 4·45 ,,
Angles—Between foramen magnum and mid base - 142° 0'
        Between mid base and frontal base - - 145° 0'
        Orbito frontal - - - - - 78° 0'
        Orbito nasal - - - - - 88° 0'
        Mid parietal - - - - - 138° 0'
Proportion of arch to base line - - - - - 2·65
Proportion of height to length - - - - - 0·71 nearly
Proportion of breadth to length - - - - - 0·72

SKULL (M).

Breadths—Close to squamous suture to the part of its course where it turns downwards behind	5·45	inches
Coronal breadth	4·75	,,
Zygomatic	5·2	,,
Arch—Occipital — 4·0		
Parietal — 4·55		
Frontal — 4·75		
	13·39	,,
Base line	5·8	,,
Length from fronto nasal suture to occipital probole	7·1	,,
Height from front of foramen magnum	5·5	,,
Radii from centre of meatus—Mid occipital	4·	,,
Mid parietal	4·9	,,
Mid frontal	4·8	,,
Portions of base—Foramen magnum	1·55	,,
Middle base	2·2	,,
Frontal base	2·45	,,
Chords—Occipital	4·2	,,
Parietal	4·3	,,
Frontal	4·35	,,
Angles—Between foramen magnum and mid base — 133° 30′		
Between mid base and frontal base — 137° 30′		
Orbito frontal — 79° 30′		
Orbito nasal — 81° 0′		
Mid parietal — 140° 30′		
Proportion of arch to base line	2·3	
Proportion of height to length	0·77	
Proportion of breadth to length	0·77	

SKULL (B).

Breadths—Just above and behind the squamous suture in the part of its course where it turns down behind -	5·05 inches
Coronal breadth - - - - - - -	4·2 ,,
Zygomatic - - - - - - -	4·7 ,,
Arch—Occipital - - - - - 4·2	
Parietal - - - - - 4·7	
Frontal - - - - - 4·8	
	13·7 ,,
Base line - - - - - - -	5·1 ,,
Length from occipital probole to fronto nasal suture - -	6·75 ,,
Height from front of foramen magnum - - -	4·85 ,,
Radii from centre of meatus—Mid occipital - - -	3·7 ,,
Mid parietal - - -	4·3 ,,
Mid frontal - - -	4·3 ,,
Portions of base—Foramen magnum - - - -	1·4 ,,
Middle base - - - - - -	1·8 ,,
Frontal base - - - - -	2·1 ,,
Chords—Occipital - - - - - - -	3·5 ,,
Parietal - - - - - - - -	4·35 ,,
Frontal - - - - - - - -	4·2 ,,
Angles—Between foramen magnum and mid base - 142° 0'	
Between mid base and frontal base - - 143° 0'	
Orbito frontal - - - - - 82° 30'	
Orbito nasal - - - - - 93° 30'	
Mid parietal - - - - - 136° 30'	
Proportion of arch to base line - - - - -	2·6
Proportion of height to length - - - - -	0·72 nearly
Proportion of breadth to length - - - - -	0·75 ,,

SKULL (D).

Breadths—3-10 inch below the squamous suture in the part of its course where it turns down behind - - -		5·05 inches
Coronal breadth - - - - - - -		4·2 ,,
Zygomatic - - - - - - -		5· ,,
Arch—Occipital - - - - -	4·55	
Parietal - - - - -	5·2	
Frontal - - - - -	5·	
		14·57 ,,
Base line - - - - - - -		5·3 ,,
Length from occipital probole to fronto nasal suture - - -		6·75 ,,
Height from front of foramen magnum to the most distant part of the vertex - - - - - - - - -		5·3 ,,
Radii from centre of meatus—Mid occipital - - -		3·7 ,,
Mid parietal - - -		4·5 ,,
Mid frontal - - -		4·5 ,,
Portions of base—Foramen magnum - - - -		1·25 ,,
Middle base - - - - -		2·05 ,,
Frontal base - - - - -		2·3 ,,
Chords—Occipital - - - - - - -		3·8 ,,
Parietal - - - - - - -		4·85 ,,
Frontal - - - - - - -		4·45 ,,
Angles—Between foramen magnum and mid base - 143° 0'		
Between mid base and frontal base - - 137° 30'		
Orbito frontal - - - - - 79° 30'		
Orbito nasal - - - - - 85° 30'		
Mid parietal - - - - - 140° 30'		
Proportion of arch to base line - - - - -		2·75 nearly
Percentage proportion of height to length - - -		0·78
Proportion of breadth to length - - - -		0·75 nearly

KING JIMMY (E).

Base line - - - - - - - - - - -	5·65 inches
Length from fronto nasal suture to external occipital probole -	7·5 ,,
Breadth, 0·25 inch below the squamous suture, in the part of its course where it turns down behind, and 1·35 inch above the posterior root of the zygoma, in a line drawn downwards to the centre of external auditory meatus - - - -	5·5 ,,
Proportion of arch to base line - - - - - -	2·7 ,,
Height from front of foramen magnum - - - -	5·75 ,,
Percentage proportion of height to length - - -	76·5
Greatest breadth in the course of coronal suture - - -	4·7 ,,
Greatest breadth between zygomata - - - - -	5·85 ,,
Proportion of breadth to length - - - - -	0·73
Middle base - - - - - - - - -	2·3 ,,
Frontal base - - - - - - - - -	2·25 ,,
Arch—Occipital - - - - - - - 4·8	
Parietal - - - - - - - 5·3	
Frontal - - - - - - - 5·3	
	15·4 ,,
Angles—Between mid and frontal base - - 143° 0'	
Between foramen magnum and mid base - 137° 5'	
Orbito frontal - - - - - 81° 30'	
Orbito nasal - - - - - 87° 0'	
Mid parietal - - - - - 130° 30'	
Radii from centre of meatus—Mid occipital - - -	3·8 ,,
Mid parietal - - -	4·75 ,,
Mid frontal - - -	4·8 ,,
Portions of base—Foramen magnum - - - -	1·4 ,,
Middle base - - - - -	2·25 ,,
Frontal base - - - - -	2·25 ,,
Chords—Occipital - - - - - - - -	3·85 ,,
Parietal - - - - - - - -	5· ,,
Frontal - - - - - - - -	4·75 ,,

The Aborigines of Tasmania.

PHYSICAL CHARACTER.

THE natives of Tasmania differed in appearance from the people of the continent; but, as has been remarked of the people of the continent, they were not all alike, and there is reason to believe that the members of some tribes were scarcely distinguishable from the Australians.

Cook saw the Tasmanians in 1777. "They were quite naked," he tells us, "and wore no ornaments, unless we consider as such, and as a proof of their love of finery, some large punctures or ridges raised on different parts of their bodies, some in straight and others in curved lines. They were of the common stature, but rather slender. Their skin was black, and also their hair, which was as woolly as that of any native of Guinea; but they were not distinguished by remarkably thick lips nor flat noses. On the contrary, their features were far from being disagreeable. They had pretty good eyes, and their teeth were tolerably even, but very dirty. Most of them had their hair and beards smeared with a red ointment, and some had their faces also painted with the same composition."*

"The Aborigines of Van Diemen's Land," according to Mr. R. H. Davies, "are a full average height, very sinewy and wiry. Stout, muscular men occur but rarely; this is in accordance with their habits, in which activity rather than strength is called into action. Their color is bluish-black—less black than that of African negroes, but slightly more so than Lascars. Their hair is black and woolly, but apparently not so much so as that of negroes. The hair of the female appears more woolly than that of the male; this is probably owing to the female keeping her hair cut extremely close, leaving a narrow circle all round, as if a basin had been put over the head and the hair inside of it cut away. The men allow their hair to grow very long, matting each lock separately with grease and ochre. The eyes are dark, wild, and strongly expressive of the passions; forehead high, narrow, running to a peak; nose flat and nostrils wide; the jaw-bones are large, strong, and prominent, and show a great width in front; the mouth is very wide, and the teeth large, strong, and even; the lips are not *full*, like those of negroes—at least not generally so. The men grease their bodies, and streak them with red-ochre and a variety of plumbago; this is partly done for ornament; but they say that it in a great measure protects them

---

* *Third Voyage*, B. 1., ch. vi.

from the inclemency of the weather. Unconnected with this besmearing, a very peculiar odour proceeds from their bodies. Their skulls must be very thick, judging from the blows which they receive on them with impunity."*

Lieut. Breton thus describes them :—" They have woolly hair, features flat and disagreeable, and a perfectly black complexion, and it struck me that their eyes were more deeply seated than I ever observed in any other people. They are more strongly formed than the New Hollanders, being neither so slight nor so long in the limbs; their aspect, I consider, if anything, inferior."†

Péron has given the following account of the natives he met with :—

"Sur la terre de Diémen sur l' île de Maria qui l'avoisine, il existe une race d'hommes tout-à-fait différente de celle qui peuple le continent de la Nouvelle-Hollande. Pour la taille les individus se rapprochent assez des Européens; mais ils en diffèrent par leur conformation singulière. Avec une tête volumineuse, remarquable sur-tout par la longueur de celui de ses diamètres qui, du menton, se dirige vers le sinciput, avec des épaules larges et bien développées, des reins bien dessinés, des fesses généralement volumineuses, presque tous les individus présentent en même temps des extrémités faibles, alongées, peu musculeuses, avec un ventre gros, saillant et comme ballonné."‡

And comparing the race with the natives of Australia, he says :—

" En effet, si l'on en excepte la maigreur des membres, qui s'observe également chez les deux peuples, ils n'ont presque plus rien de commun, ni dans leurs mœurs, leurs usages, leurs arts grossiers, ni dans leurs instrumens de chasse ou de pêche, leurs habitations, leurs pirogues, leurs armes, ni dans leur langue, ni dans l'ensemble de leur constitution physique, la forme du crâne, les proportions de la face, &c. Cette dissemblance absolue se reproduit dans la couleur; les indigènes de la terre de Diémen sont beaucoup plus bruns que ceux de la Nouvelle-Hollande : elle se reproduit même dans un caractère que tout le monde s'accorde à regarder comme le plus important de ceux qui servent à distinguer les diverses races de l'espèce humaine ; je veux parler de la nature des cheveux ; les habitans de la terre de Diémen les ont courts, laineux et crépus ; ceux de la Nouvelle-Hollande les ont droits, longs et roides."§

The following account of the natives of Tasmania, written at the time of the first colonization of the island by the whites, contains a description of a wild black. His deportment affords grounds for the belief that, if this people had been differently treated, their relations with the English would have been peaceful :—

"In their way up, a human voice saluted them from the hills on which they landed, carrying with them one of several swans which they had just shot. Having nearly reached the summit, two females, with a short covering hanging loose from their shoulders, suddenly appeared at some little distance before them ; but, snatching up each a small basket, these scampered off. A man

---

* *Tasmanian Journal of Natural Science*, &c., January 1846, pp. 409-10.
† *Excursions in New South Wales, Tasmania*, &c., by Lieut. Breton, R.N., p. 398.
‡ *Voyage de Découvertes aux Terres Australes*, 1800-4, par M. F. Péron, vol. I., p. 448.
§ *Ibid*, vol. II., pp. 163-4.

then presented himself, and suffered them to approach him without any signs of fear or distrust. He received the swan joyfully, appearing to esteem it a treasure. His language was unintelligible to them, as was theirs to him, although they addressed him in several of the dialects of New South Wales, and some few of the most common words of the South Sea Islands. With some difficulty they made him comprehend their wish to see his place of residence. He pointed over the hill, and proceeded onwards; but his pace was slow and wandering, and he often stopped under the pretence of having lost the track, which led them to suspect that his only aim was to amuse and tire them out. Judging, then, that in persisting to follow him they must lose the remaining part of the flood tide, which was much more valuable to them than the sight of his hut could be, they parted from him in great friendship. The most probable reason of his unwillingness to be their guide seemed to be his fearing that if he took them to his women their charms might induce them to run off with them, a jealousy very common with the natives of the continent.

He was a short slight man, of a middle age, with a countenance more expressive of benignity and intelligence than of that ferocity which generally characterized the other natives; and his features were less flattened, or negro-like, than theirs. His face was blackened, and the top of his head was plastered with red earth. His hair was either naturally short and close, or had been rendered so by burning, and, although short and stiffly curled, they did not think it woolly. He was armed with two spears, very ill made, of solid wood. No part of their dress attracted his attention, except the red silk handkerchiefs round their necks. Their fire-arms were to him objects neither of curiosity nor fear.

This was the first man they had spoken with in Van Diemen's Land, and his frank and open deportment led them not only to form a favorable opinion of the disposition of its inhabitants, but to conjecture that, if the country was peopled in the usual numbers, he would not have been the only one they should have met. A circumstance which corroborated this supposition was, that in the excursions made by Mr. Bass into the country, having seldom any other society than his two dogs, he would have been no great object of dread to a people ignorant of the effects of fire-arms, and would certainly have been hailed by any one who might have seen him.

They fell in with many huts along the different shores of the river, of the same bad construction as those of Port Dalrymple, but with fewer heaps of mussel-shells lying near them.

The natives of this place probably drew the principal part of their food from the woods; the bones of small animals, such as opossums, squirrels, kangaroo-rats, and bandicoots, were numerous round their deserted fire-places; and the two spears which they saw in the hands of the man were similar to those used for hunting in other parts. Many trees, also, were observed to be notched. No canoes were ever seen, nor any trees so barked as to answer that purpose." *

---

* *An Account of the English Colony in New South Wales*, by Lieut.-Col. Collins, p. 480.

A careful comparison of the photographic portraits of the natives of the island with those of the natives of the continent shows that the difference in appearance is due chiefly to the character of the hair. In the one it is woolly, or inclined to grow in small spirals, and in the other waved or curled. The forehead, eyes, nose, and mouth remind one, in all the portraits of the Tasmanian females, of the natives of the southern parts of Australia. Yet there is a difference. The Tasmanian has unquestionably—altogether apart from the appearance given to the face by the hair—a certain resemblance to the negro, while the Australian not seldom has a European cast of features.

A photographic portrait of *Wuntinyeri*, a woman of the Mundoo tribe, which appears in the Rev. Mr. Taplin's work, might readily be mistaken for that of a Tasmanian woman; but none of the others in the same work have any likeness to them.

The Tasmanians, like some of the Australians, are said to have had a great deal of hair on the body.

No very accurate measurements have been made of the height of the adult Tasmanians; but, in 1849, Mr. Hugh M. Hull had all the Aboriginal children then in the orphan schools at New Town weighed and measured; and the result showed that they were shorter than the white race of the same age, but much heavier. One young female eleven years of age weighed 102 pounds; another of eight, 86 pounds. The average weight of European children of these ages is stated to be 78 pounds and 60 pounds respectively—60 as compared to 86; 78 as compared to 102.*

Mental Characteristics.

The natives that were met with by the early voyagers appear to have manifested little of that ferocity which subsequently distinguished their intercourse with the whites. They appear to have shown no hostility when a ship's company visited their coasts. They were indifferent, they exhibited little curiosity, and were rather timid than distrustful.

Cook observed that they received every present made to them without the least appearance of satisfaction. When some bread was given, and as soon as they understood it was to be eaten, they either returned it or threw it away without even tasting it. They refused some elephant-fish, both raw and dressed, but they accepted the birds that were offered, and made it understood that they liked them. "We had not been long landed," says Cook, "before about twenty of them, men and boys, joined us, without expressing the least sign of fear or distrust. There was one of this company conspicuously deformed, and who was not more distinguishable by the hump upon his back than by the drollery of his gestures and the seeming humour of his speeches, which he was very fond of exhibiting, as we supposed, for our entertainment." †

The Rev. T. Dove formed a very low estimate of their character. "Every idea," he states, "bearing on our origin and destination as rational beings

---

* *Lecture on the Aborigines of Tasmania,* by Hugh M. Hull, Esq., 1870.
† *Third Voyage,* B. i., chap. vi.

seems to have been erased from their breasts." He adds, however, that, looking to "the methods which they devised of procuring shelter and subsistence in their native wilds, to the skill and precision with which they tracked the mazes of the bush, and to the force of invention and of memory which is displayed in the copious vocabulary of their several languages, they claim no inconsiderable share of mental power and activity." *

The same writer observes that "their social history was rather characterised by the absence of what is venerable and lovely than by the prevalence of what is dark and revolting. Harmony and good humour seem generally to have reigned among the members of the same tribe. The force of the parental instinct was usually strong enough to render the maintenance of their offspring a care and a delight. Instances, however, have occurred in which the child has been wantonly sacrificed to the dread of famine. When it is borne in mind that polygamy prevailed among them, the abject condition of the female sex may be easily conceived." †

From all that can be gathered respecting this now extinct race, it appears that the people were originally—when they first came into contact with the whites—mild, diffident, willing to be friendly, and rather afraid of the invaders of their territory. But when the convicts were let loose; when those who had tickets of leave and those who had escaped from confinement began to steal the wives and daughters of the natives, and to slaughter the warriors; when the settlers began to occupy their lands—they evinced stronger feelings, and, if not greater courage, certainly a greater ferocity than the inhabitants of the continent. They attacked the settlers whenever an opportunity occurred; and their energy and persistence, if they had succeeded in ridding themselves of their enemies, would have placed them high in the ranks of patriots. But they were beaten, and consequently they are despised.

A few warriors—ten or twelve—overawed, terrified a colony that could send out several hundreds of white fighting men; and if cunning, and something very like treachery, had not been employed, a large number of the natives would be living in their native forests at the present time. They were slaughtered in order that room might be made for the sheep and cattle of the settlers; and when these were in undisturbed occupation of the soil, the few men and women remaining were sent to an island in the Straits, where, scantily supplied with—what were to them—the necessaries of life, and cut off from all the pleasures that it was possible they could enjoy, they lingered awhile and died. ‡

---

* *Tasmanian Journal of Natural Science*, &c., 1842, vol. i., p. 250.

† *Ibid*, p. 252.

‡ The following extracts from a lecture on the Aborigines of Tasmania, by Hugh M. Hull, Esq., the Clerk of the House of Assembly in Hobart Town, tell sufficient of the melancholy story of the extermination of the natives. Mr. Hull says:—" A friend once described to me a fearful scene at which he was present. A number of blacks, with the women and children, were congregated in a gully near town, under the shade of some flowering tea-trees, and the men had formed themselves into a ring round a large fire, whilst the women were cooking the evening meal of opossums and bandicoots; they were surprised by a party of soldiers, who, without giving warning, fired upon them as they sat, and, rushing up to the scene of the slaughter, found there

If they had not been men and women, if they had not been human creatures —if they had been quadrumanous, every detail connected with them would undoubtedly have been investigated and recorded. But they were indeed human; and they were the enemies of the white man because they wished to live in places where cattle and sheep would thrive, and it was deemed necessary to exterminate them; and they have been exterminated. It is said that there is not one now living. Some half-castes are living; and it is nearly certain that the blood will mix with that of the whites, and never be lost. But the race, the traditions of the race, and the language, are lost for ever.

NUMBERS.

Tasmania, like Australia, was sparsely peopled. Many parts of the island are unfitted for the abode of savages. The western districts are in most places thickly timbered; there are dense scrubs; and the country is damp, cold, and inhospitable. The larger animals are scarce, and such tracts never could have supported any large number of Aborigines. The central and eastern areas were those in which the blacks found food, and where they were comparatively numerous.

The area of the island is approximately 24,000 square miles; and if it be assumed that the number of square miles required to support one native was the same as in the more fertile parts of the continent, the population would amount to no more than 1,400. Dr. Milligan thinks that the Aboriginal population, at the time the colony was first occupied by Europeans, did not exceed 2,000; and this estimate he gives apparently with some hesitation, as being perhaps excessive. Altogether erroneous ideas were formed of the numbers inhabiting Tasmania by the voyagers who visited the island in early times, and by the first settlers. Dr. Milligan informs us that "the open grassy plains and thinly-timbered forest ground along the eastern and central portions of the island were the most eligible for the purposes of the early settlers, and were therefore the portions of the territory first occupied; but these fine tracts of

---

wounded men and women, and a little black child crawling near its dying mother. The soldier drove his bayonet through the body of the child, and pitchforked it into the flames. It was *only a child*, he said!"

"It is stated also," Mr. Hull adds, "that it was a favorite amusement to hunt the Aborigines; that a day would be selected, and the neighbouring settlers would be invited, with their families, to a pic-nic. Husbands and wives, sons and daughters, would come in to the social gathering, and after dinner all would be gaiety and merriment, whilst the gentlemen of the party would take their guns and dogs, and, accompanied by two or three convict servants, wander through the bush in search of blackfellows. Sometimes they would return without sport; at others they would succeed in killing a woman, or, if lucky, mayhap a man or two. . . . . As the white settler spread his possessions over the island—over the natives' favorite camping-grounds, driving away their kangaroos, and replacing them with bullocks and sheep—the natives objected in their own way to the inroad. In many cases, no doubt, the blacks were sacrificed to momentary caprice or anger, and suffered much wrong. Indeed one of the Governor's proclamations states that cruelties had been perpetrated repugnant to humanity and disgraceful to the British people."

It is not strange that the outraged natives sought every opportunity to murder the white settlers and to emulate them in cruelty.

country were precisely those which naturally yielded the means of subsistence in the greatest profusion to the Aborigines, and they were accordingly the districts chiefly frequented by the natives at that time." In these tracts the settlers saw occasionally large numbers of natives, and the smoke of numerous fires were observed along the coast, and they almost unavoidably formed erroneous estimates as to the Aboriginal population of the whole island.

Mr. Hugh M. Hull, the Clerk of the House of Assembly, says that he has "records of many of the tribes and their habitats.

The Eastern Coast tribes spoke a different language from the western.

The Ben Lomond tribe was a large and savage body of blacks on the north-east.

The Oyster Bay tribe on the south-east.

The Stony Creek tribe, a murderous lot, in the centre of the island, roving about Campbelltown, Ross, and Saltpan Plains.

The Western tribe about the Westbury and Deloraine districts; also a murderous lot.

The Circular Head tribe on the north.

The Eastern Marshes tribe near Oatlands.

The Bruni Island tribe.

The Adventure Bay tribe.

In 1824 we had 180 men and 160 women on the roll—all known by name; in 1844 they were reduced to 60 in all; and in 1847, when removed to Oyster Cove, they were 45 all told, and 10 of these were children."

In a very short time these perished.

Birth, etc.

The Tasmanians seem to have had but little affection for their wives. They were treated as slaves, and, whether young or old, had to work hard for their masters. Little care was bestowed on the wife at the most interesting periods of her existence. "When a woman was taken in labor, the tribe did not wait for her, but she was left behind with another woman, and afterwards followed as best she could."*

As soon as the mother was able to move, which would be probably a few hours after the birth of the child, she placed the infant in the kangaroo skin which hung at her back, and resumed her journey. When the child required nourishment, the breast was thrust over the shoulder, and the mammæ of the married women were "consequently preposterously long." †

They suckled the infants for a long period; sometimes, Mr. Davies believes, for upwards of two years.

In their treatment of infants, the blacks of Tasmania did not differ much from the natives of the continent. If a child was permitted to live, it was tended with some care; but children were not seldom destroyed. Mr. Davies says—and he writes cautiously—"I have no reason to suppose that infanticide

---

* R. H. Davies, in the *Tasmanian Journal of Natural Science*, &c. † *Ibid.*

existed amongst the Aborigines in their former wild state. There is little doubt, however, that it was common of later years—driven to it, as they in all probability were, by the continued harassing of the whites."

It is not reasonable to suppose that the natives of Tasmania, with but a scanty supply of food—and much of that procured by the labors of the females—did not rid themselves of their burdens in the same manner as the inhabitants of the continent. There is no doubt that the same pressure of want was felt everywhere amongst the savages of this part of the world, and that the women had recourse to the same means to alleviate their distresses. They killed their infants because it was impossible for them to tend them and nourish them.

The male children that were spared were taught to throw the spear, to use the waddy, to climb trees, and to throw stones. They were educated by their elders, and made fit to take part in fights and dances.

Some ceremonies attended the initiation of the young males into the rights and privileges of manhood; but if the information afforded by the first settlers is correct, these differed altogether from those practised on the continent. The young men, it is said, were given over to the old women, who cut them on the thighs, shoulders, and muscles of the breast with stone-cutting implements, and thus raised cicatrices. Mr. Davies states that when he witnessed the operation a female was the performer, and he had reason to believe that females in all such cases were chosen for the office. "The subject," he says, "was a young man named *Penderoine*, brother to the celebrated Western chief *Weymerricke*. The instrument was a piece of broken bottle; and although the fat of his shoulder literally rose and turned back like a crimped fish, he was during the whole operation in the highest glee—laughing, and continually interrupting his operatrix by picking up chips to fling at our party in play. These scarifications are intended as ornaments."

The women had raised cicatrices on their bodies; but it is not known whether they were purposely made and intended as ornaments, or were the result of the cuttings and bleedings to which they were subjected when sick.

It is said that circumcision was unknown to the natives.

Marriage.

There were restrictions on marriage amongst the natives. A man was not permitted to marry a woman of his own tribe. Little or nothing beyond this is known of the customs which the men followed in selecting wives. A man had usually but one wife; but there are reasons to believe that polygamy was not unknown. Polyandry, or something very like it, existed; and widows, it is affirmed, were, unless given in marriage, the common property of the males of the tribes into which they had married.

Mr. Hugh M. Hull speaks doubtfully on the subject of marriage. He says "they usually selected wives from other tribes than their own," and that a black never had more than one wife at a time.

It may be said that they had passed out of the communal system nearly, out of the endogamous system nearly, and no more can be said. From what is known of them, so much is certain. They had not reached the higher and more complex system under which women are given in marriage in Australia, but the germ of that system was apparently existing.

The women were seldom accompanied by many children; but there is no reason to suppose that they were less prolific than people of other races.

The condition of a wife in Tasmania was abject. She was required to labor unceasingly. She had to provide food for her master, to keep his fire ready for cooking, and to cook his food; and, when marching, to carry whatever was deemed necessary for his proper entertainment and pleasure at the new encampment. With one or two children, and a heavy load, consisting of weapons and utensils, her progress was painful.

Death and Burial.

The practices of the natives of Tasmania when a death occurred, and their ordinary mode of disposing of the bodies of the dead, greatly resembled those observed in many parts of Australia.

"During the whole of the first night after the death of one of their tribe," says Davies, "they will sit round the body, using rapidly a low continuous recitation, to prevent the evil spirit from taking it away. They are extremely jealous of this ceremony being witnessed by strangers; but I had upon one occasion an opportunity of being an ear-witness of it the whole night." The same writer says "they place the body upright in a hollow tree, and (having no fixed habitation) pursue their avocations. When some time has passed, say a year or upwards, they return to the place and burn the body, with the exception of the skull; this they carry with them, until they chance (for I do not think that they lose time in seeking it) to fall in with a cemetery, in which a number of skulls are heaped together, when they add the one with them to the number, and cover them up with bark, leaves, &c. They do not bury them in the ground. I have never been able to ascertain that they put either weapons or food in the tree with the dead."[*]

In some parts of Northern Australia a similar practice prevails. Skulls are heaped together until at last a mound is formed; and these mounds are seen mostly in rather conspicuous places.

The bodies of the dead were not always placed in the hollows of trees. They were not seldom buried in natural holes or burnt. It is probable that the ceremonies were not the same in all parts of the island, and that greater care was taken in disposing of the remains of deceased warriors than in the case of women or young natives, whose bodies probably were quickly put out of sight. This is the more likely, as Péron found rather elaborate tombs, which he thus describes:—

"Tandis qu'avec intérêt je me livrois aux sensations pleines de charmes qu'un lieu semblable devoit inspirer, et que je portois, avec une douce inquiétude,

---

[*] *Tasmanian Journal of Natural Science*, &c.

mes regards autour de moi, j'aperçus, à peu de distance, un monument dont la construction me surprit et m'intéressa : je m'avançai précipitamment ; et voici ce que j'observai.

Sur une large pelouse de verdure, à l'ombre de quelques Casuarina antiques s'élevoit un cône grossièrement formé d'écorces d'arbres plantées en terre par leur partie inférieure, et réunies à leur sommet par une large bande de la même substance. Quatre longues perches fixées en terre par une de leurs extrémités, servoient de soutien et d'appui à toutes les écorces au-dessous desquelles elles se trouvoient placées ; ces quatre perches paroissoient encore avoir été destinées à l'ornement de l'édifice ; car, au lieu de ne se réunir qu'à leur extrémité supérieure comme les écorces, et de ne former alors qu'un simple cône, elles s'entre-croisoient à peu de distance de la moitié de leur longueur, c'est-à-dire, précisément à l'endroit de leur sortie de la toiture du monument. De cette disposition, il résultoit une espèce de pyramide tétraèdre, dont le sommet se trouvoit justement opposé à celui du cône. Ce contraste de formes et d'opposition dans les deux parties de l'édifice, produisoit un effet assez gracieux, et qui le devenoit davantage encore par la disposition suivante. A chacun des quatre côtés de la pyramide correspondoit une large lanière d'écorce, dont les deux extrémités se trouvoient inférieurement embrassées par cette grande bande que j'ai dit réunir toutes les autres à leur sommet : il en resultoit que chacune de ces quatre lanières formoit une espèce d'ovale plus aigu vers son extrémité inférieure, plus large et plus arrondie dans sa portion supérieure : et comme chacun de ces ovales correspondoit à chacun des côtés de la pyramide, il est aisé de concevoir tout ce qu'une semblable disposition pouvoit offrir d'élégant et de pittoresque.

Après avoir donné quelques instans à l'observation de ce monument, dont je cherchois vainement à concevoir l'usage, je me déterminai à pousser plus avant l'examen que je voulois en faire ; j'enlevai plusieurs grosses écorces, et je pénétrai facilement jusque dans l'intérieur de la toiture. Toute la portion supérieure en étoit libre : dans le bas se trouvoit un large cône aplati, formé d'une herbe fine et légère, disposée avec beaucoup de soin par couches concentriques et très profondes. . . . . Mon intérêt s'accroissoit avec mon incertitude. Huit petites baguettes de bois croisées entre elles au sommet du cône de verdure, servoient à le contenir ; chacune de ces baguettes avoit ses deux extrémités fichées en terre, et consolidées elles-mêmes par l'application d'une grosse pierre de granit aplatie.

Tant de précautions me donnoient l'espoir de quelque découverte importante ; je ne me trompois pas. . . . . A peine j'eus soulevé quelques-unes des couches supérieures de gazon, que j'aperçus un gros tas de cendres blanches, et qui paroissoient avoir été réunies avec soin ; je plongeai ma main au milieu des ces cendres ; je sentis quelque chose qui résistait plus fortement ; je voulus le retirer ; c'étoit une mâchoire d'homme, à laquelle des lambeaux de chair tenoient encore. . . . . Un sentiment d'horreur me pénétra. . . . .

Cependant, en réfléchissant un peu sur tout ce que je venois d'observer dans la composition du monument, je ne tardai pas à éprouver des sensations bien différentes de celles que j'avois eues d'abord ; cette verdure, ces fleurs, ces arbres protecteurs, cette couche profonde de jeunes herbes qui recouvroient les cendres ; tout se rénnissoit pour me convaincre que je venois de découvrir un tombeau. . . . .

A mesure que j'enlevois les cendres j'apercevois un charbon très noir boursouflé, friable et léger ; je reconnus un charbon animal ; dans le même instant je retirois une portion de fémur avec quelques lambeaux de chair; on y distinguoit encore des tronçons de gros vaisseaux remplis d'un sang calciné réduit à l'état où ce fluide rapproche d'une substance résineuse. A ces premiers ossemens en succédèrent d'autres non moins reconnoissables ; des vertèbres, des fragmens d'humerus, de tibia, des os du tarse, du carpe, &c. ; tous étoient profondément altérés par le feu, et se reduisoient facilement en poudre : j'en possède toutefois quelques debris, avec des portions de la chair grillée qui leur étoit adhérente. Ces ossemens ne se trouvoient pas, ainsi que je l'avois cru d'abord, appliqués simplement à la surface de la terre ; ils étoient tous réunis au fond d'un trou circulaire de 40 à 48 centimètres de diamètre (15 à 18 pouces) sur 21 à 27 centimètres de profondeur (8 à 10 pouces)." *

ENCAMPMENTS, ETC.

Dove says that the encampments of the natives were always formed on the margin of a stream or lagoon, so that they might have at all times a plentiful supply of water. They did not dig wells, it is said; and their vessels for containing water, whether large shells or bags of bark, did not contain sufficient to admit of their staying in any spot remote from rivers or lakes. They erected break-winds in the more open parts of the country. These consisted of large branches of trees, fastened together and supported by stakes, and arranged in the form of a crescent, the convex side of which was so placed as to oppose itself to the wind. A fire was kept burning in the open space to leeward. Near the sea-shore and in the mountainous parts of the country they sought shelter in caves and natural hollows. †

It is stated by Davies that near " Pieman's River, on the west coast, one tribe was discovered living in a village, if it may be so termed, of bark huts or break-winds, of a better description than usual, and having somewhat the appearance of a fixed residence. It is probable, however, that being good hunting-ground, they merely intended making a lengthened stay there." ‡

The natives had no domestic animals. It is believed that it was only after the colonization of the island by the whites that they adopted the practice of keeping as pets the young of the kangaroo. They did not have dogs until they were introduced by the colonists. After they became possessed of them, they kept numbers around their encampments, and the women very often suckled the puppies.

There was no chief of any tribe, though the name was often applied by the whites to some man whose skill and valor raised him somewhat above his

---
* *Voyage de Découvertes aux Terres Australes*, 1800-4, vol. 1., pp. 265-6.
† *Tasmanian Journal of Natural Science.* ‡ *Ibid*, p. 418.

fellows, and who exercised authority. The men were lazy and selfish. The women had to carry such goods as they possessed from camp to camp, while the men would pace slowly in front; and, if the nature of the ground admitted of it, they would cunningly trail their spears after them, the point being held between the toes. They could almost instantaneously transfer the spear to the hand. Davies, in mentioning these facts, remarks that the spears were trailed by the toes in order that their hands might be free to throw the waddy at any small object that might appear.

The same writer observed that the blacks could not stand continued fatigue, and that in respect to endurance they were inferior to a hearty European— " nor," says he " what will appear singular, can they, like him, bear constant exposure to bad weather ; when such sets in, they will cower round their fires, under the lee of their break-winds, in a sheltered situation, until a change takes place."

The natives were superstitious, and did not like to move about after dark. They believed that their deceased relatives would appear again on earth. Lieut. Jeffery says that when the women were left by their husbands—who, as sealers, had often, in pursuit of their occupation, to be absent for several days —these affectionate creatures would sing or chant a hymn or song, addressing themselves to a deity who, they said, presides over the day. An evil spirit or demon rules the night. " The hymn or song," this writer says, "they address to him during the absence of their husbands or protectors is intended to secure his divine care over them, and especially to bring them back with speed and safety. The song is accompanied with gracefulness of action, and is poured forth in strains by no means inharmonious ; on the contrary, the voice of the singer, and in many parts the sweetness of the notes, which are delivered in pretty just cadence and excellent time, afford a species of harmony to which the most refined ear might listen with pleasure."

This statement is in accordance with the experience of Mr. Geo. Hull, who, on the 24th March 1871, wrote a letter to his son, Mr. Hugh M. Hull, of Hobart Town, containing some information relating to the natives, which he had arranged expressly for this work. Mr. Hull's letter is as clearly written and as well composed as if he had been a young man; but at that time (1871) he was eighty-four years old, having taken charge of the Commissariat in Tasmania as Deputy Assistant Commissary-General in 1819. Respecting their singing he says—" It was, I think, in the year 1824 or 1825 that some ten or twelve natives appeared on the west bank of the Tamar, opposite Launceston. They coo-ed and made signs to be taken across, which was instantly complied with. There was not a man or a boy among them. It was a most singular occurrence. They were from sixteen to thirty years of age—all disgustingly dirty. I ordered my storekeeper to give them food. We made signs for them to sing and dance. The former they did in a manner which led me to think that they were at least one remove from the monkey tribe. They sang, all joining in concert, and with the sweetest harmony ; the notes not more than thirds. They began say in D and E, but swelling sweetly from note to note, and so gradually that it was a mere continuation of harmony—very melancholy, it is true. It was like what it would be if you began one chord on the organ before you took your fingers from the keys of the other. Their dances are a mere wriggling motion of the hips and loins, obscene in the extreme."

The dances of the men are thus described by Davies:—"Their principal amusement consists in their corrobborees or dances. These are sometimes held in the day-time, but far more generally at night. They light a large fire, round which, quite naked, they dance, run, and jump, keeping time to their own singing, which is far from unmusical. These songs are various, each having its own peculiar dance, intended to illustrate some action or effect from causes. One is called the kangaroo-dance, and is, along with some others, most violent. In this the party (I have seen as many as ninety joined in one corrobboree) commence walking round the fire slowly, singing in a low monotonous tone. After this has continued for some time, they begin to get excited, singing in a higher key, walking faster, striking their hands upon the ground, and springing high in the air. By degrees their walk becomes a run; their solitary leaps, a series; their singing, perfect shrieking: they close upon the fire, the women piling fresh branches upon it. Still leaping in a circle, and striking the ground with their hands at every bound, they will spring a clear five feet high, so near to the fire, so completely in the flames, that you fancy they must be burnt. Excited to frenzy, they sing, shriek, and jump until their frames can stand it no longer, and they give up in the uttermost state of exhaustion. Some of their dances are evidently lascivious; some are medicine, &c.; though, had I not been told by themselves that they intended to represent making bread—taking such was the case—I never should have perceived any analogy."

The following is a song, Davies says, of the Ben Lomond tribe. It is not fit for translation, the subject not being very select:—

   Ne popila raina pogana
   Ne popila raina pogana
   Ne popila raina pogana

   Thu me gunnea
   Thu me gunnea
   Thu me gunnea

   Thoga me gunnea
   Thoga me gunnea
   Thoga me gunnea

   Naina thaipa raina pogana
   Naina thaipa raina pogana
   Naina thaipa raina pogana

   Naara paara powella paara
   Naara paara powella paara
   Naara paara powella paara

       Ballahoo, Ballahoo, Hoo, hoo!
       (Their war-whoop, very guttural.)

Dr. Milligan has given an account of the manner in which the natives of Tasmania believed that fire was brought to them (see *Vocabulary*), and has added two or three songs. There were, no doubt, many stories, legends, and myths that afforded amusement to the natives when told by the old men over the camp-fires at night, and it is much to be regretted that so little has been preserved. That in Dr. Milligan's paper reminds one of some of the stories told by the natives of the continent.

Food.

The food of the natives of Tasmania, like that of savages in other parts of the world, was yielded spontaneously by the land and the sea.

There was scarcely an animal of any kind that was not deemed fit to be eaten; and in the central and eastern parts of Tasmania the blacks could find kangaroos, bandicoots, wombats, and opossums, as well as snakes, lizards, grubs, and worms. Birds, too, were numerous; and they had feasts, like the natives of the continent, at the season when the pupæ of ants were to be obtained.

The opossum, however, afforded them food at all times. This animal was usually caught by the women. Provided with a rope made of kangaroo sinews or of grass, twisted, and with wooden handles fastened to the ends, they rapidly ascended even tall trees. "They first, as high as they could conveniently reach, cut a notch with a sharp stone in the side of the tree; then, throwing the bight of the rope up, and leaning back, it held against the tree by their weight, until with its assistance the climber got her right toe into the notch that had been cut; then, grasping the tree with her left arm, the rope by a sudden jerk is thrown higher up the tree, a fresh notch is cut for the left toe; and so the climber proceeds. If branches interfere, they are a hindrance to the climber; but she then throws the end of the rope over it, and, holding both ends, raises herself up."*

They climbed trees in the same way to procure honey, the women carrying with them grass baskets in which they placed the spoil.

In the western parts of the colony, where animals were scarce, the natives lived chiefly on shell-fish; and in obtaining food of this kind, though the pursuit was laborious, and not always free from danger, the women were almost exclusively employed. A woman with a grass basket slung round her neck would dive in the sea, and grope about until, after successive efforts, she had procured more than sufficient for her husband; what was left would be thrown to her and to the children. Davies states that by this method they took most commonly the haliotis and cray-fish; but they gathered likewise mussels, oysters, limpets, &c.

They speared sea fish in shallow water, and caught them also in nets and with hooks made of bone or shell. Whether the nets and fish-hooks were invented by the natives or copied from those used by the Aborigines of the continent after the colonization of the island is uncertain.

---

* Davies. *Tasmanian Journal of Natural Science,* &c.

Mutton-birds, the eggs of birds of all kinds, seals, and occasionally a stranded whale, supplied the tribes of the coast with the materials for rich banquets.

"Their only mode of cooking," says Davies, "is by roasting on the fire, whole; they do not take out the entrails until after it is done, which is supposed to be when heated through."

They were gross feeders. They ate enormous quantities of food when they had the opportunity. The same writer states that "a native woman at the settlement at Flinders Island was one day watched by one of the officers, and seen to eat between fifty and sixty eggs of the sooty petrel (*Procellaria sp.*), besides a double allowance of bread; these eggs exceed those of a duck in size."

Certain kinds of food were prohibited, but under what regulations is not known. Some tribes, or certain people of some tribes, would not eat the female wallaby; others would not eat the male. One set would not eat scaled fish; and Davies believed that the western natives did not eat the smooth-shelled haliotis, though those of the eastern coast had no objection to that shell-fish. "The smooth-shelled haliotis," Davies says, "is more numerous on the east coast than the other species, and the reverse on the western coast; but that seems scarcely a sufficient reason to induce the western natives to reject it."

Certain kinds of food were rejected, and certain kinds prohibited, no doubt in obedience to superstitions like those which have such a strong hold on the minds of the natives of the continent. Nothing, however, is known of the laws relating to food as they existed amongst the Tasmanians.

Backhouse says he is not aware of any custom of the Aborigines of Van Diemen's Land common with the Jews, except it be that of their not eating fat. "This they so much abhor as even to reject bread that has been cut with a buttery knife. On my companion offering some soup to a poor emaciated woman on board the cutter, who had a baby who looked half-starved, she tried to take it, seeing it was offered in good will; but having a little fat upon it, she recoiled from it with nausea. J. R. Bateman, master of the brig *Tamar*, once had some soup made for a party of these people whom he was taking to Flinders Island; they looked upon it complacently, skimmed off the floating fat with their hands, and smeared their heads with it; but they refused to drink the soup. They thought it was only made for greasing their heads."

The vegetable food that the natives could have procured was various rather than abundant. I had compiled from Hooker's *Flora Cibaria* a list of the more common fruits, seeds, and roots that might have afforded them sustenance during certain seasons: but knowing that the Government Botanist of Victoria had given much attention to this subject, I applied to him for information, and he at once furnished the following list.*

---

* In the *Tasmanian Journal of Natural Science* (1842; pp. 35-52) there is an excellent paper entitled *Remarks on the Indigenous Vegetable Productions of Tasmania available as Food for Man*, by Ronald C. Gunn, Esq., F.R.S. The plants are arranged according to their natural orders, as they follow in the system of De Candolle.

PLANTS THAT COULD HAVE BEEN USED FOR FOOD BY THE ORIGINAL
TASMANIAN NATIVES.

1. For succulent fruits :—

Billardiera scandens.
Mesembrianthemum æquilaterale.
Muehlenbeckia appressa.
Rubus parvifolius.
" Gunnianus.
Sambucus Gaudichaudiana.
Gaultiera hispida.
" antipoda (and perhaps of the allied Pernettya).
Styphelia sapida.
" adscendens.
" humifusa.
" oxycedrus.
" lanceolata.
" Richei.

Styphelia Australis.
" abietina.
" Billardieri.
" straminea.
" Hookeri.
Trochocarpa Gunnii.
" thymifolia.
" disticha.
" Cunninghami.
Myoporum insulare.
Solanum vescum.
Leptomeria Billardieri.
Exocarpus cupressiformis.
" humifusa.
" stricta.
Astelia alpina.

2. For roots :—

Geranium dissectum.
Rumex bidens.
Microseris Forsteri.
Dipodium punctatum.
Gastrodia sesamoides.
All species of Thelymitra.
Spiranthes Australis.
Calochilus campestris.
All species of Diuris.
Cryptostylis longifolia.
All species of Prasophyllum.
Microtis porrifolia.
Corysanthes pruinosa.
All species of Pterostylis.
Caleana major.
" minor.
All species of Acianthus.
Eriochilus autumnalis.

Lyperanthus nigricans.
" Burnetti
Cyrtostylis reniformis.
All species of Caladenia.
Chiloglottis diphylla.
" Gunnii.
Glossodia major.
Arthropodium strictum.
" paniculatum.
Bulbine bulbosa.
Triglochin procera.
Typha Muelleri.
" Brownii.
Heleocharis sphacelata.
Scirpus maritimus.
(Probably also the roots of Hypoxis, Cæsia, Anguillaria, and Burchardia.)

Medullar substance of stem of Dicksonia antarctica and Cyathea medullaris (possibly also of Alsophila Australis).
Flowers of all species of Xerotes (for their sweet taste).
Base of leaves and young flower-stem of Xanthorrhœa Australis and X. minor.

Herb of *Nasturtium terrestre*, *Barbarea vulgaris*; all *Cardamines* and *Lepidiums* for cress.
Herb of *Apium prostratum* (native celery), of *Eryngium vesiculosum*, of *Mesembrianthemum Australe* and *M. æquilatorale*; *Sonchus oleaceus*; probably also of various salt-bushes (*Atriplex*, *Rhagodia*, *Salicornia*, &c.), as these are used by the Australian race.
Herb of *Oxalis corniculata* and *O. Magellanica*, as sorrel.
Seeds (mealy) of all species of *Polygonum* and *Rumex*.
Seeds of some *Acaciæ*.
Seeds of *Linum marginale*, *Ehrharta distichophylla* and *E. tenacissima*, *Festuca fluitans*.
Fungi :—
Mylitta Australis.
Cyttaria Gunnii.
Agaricus campestris, *A. procerus*, *A. mutabilis*; *Polyporus frondosus*, *Hydnum lævigatum*, *H. repandum*; *Clavaria Botrytis* (and probably many other mushrooms, occurring in Tasmania, but the edible kinds of which seemingly not tested or recorded by Europeans).
Gum of *Acacia decurrens* (and perhaps other species also).
Manna of *Eucalyptus viminalis*.
Saccharine sap of *Eucalyptus Gunnii* (turning soon into a kind of cider).
Sweet sap of the flowers of *Banksia marginata* and *B. serrata*.

Bunce states that the natives obtained from the cider-tree of the Lakes (*Eucalyptus resinifera*) a slightly saccharine liquor resembling treacle. They ground holes in the tree at the proper season, and from these the sweet juice flowed plentifully. It was collected in a hole at the root of the tree. These holes were kept covered over with a flat stone, apparently for the purpose of preventing birds and animals from coming to drink it. When allowed to remain for a length of time, it fermented, and settled into a coarse sort of wine or cider, rather intoxicating if drank to excess.*

The native of Tasmania used, according to Davies, a hunger-belt, made of kangaroo sinews, which he tightened when deprived of his usual supplies of food.

The following valuable paper *On the Heaps of Recent Shells which exist along the Shores of Tasmania*, by Ronald C. Gunn, Esq., F.R.S., appeared in the *Tasmanian Journal of Natural Science* in 1845 :—

"The Aborigines of Tasmania have left behind them such faint traces of their existence—so few indications by which their having so long inhabited this island could be known—that it may not be deemed altogether uninteresting or unimportant to draw attention to the only permanent memorials they have left us; namely, the large heaps of shells formed by them along the shores of our coasts, bays, and estuaries, wherever *testaceæ* abound; being the accumulated remains of their feasts.

---

* *Austral-Asiatic Reminiscences*, by Daniel Bunce, p. 47.

Some years ago, when I first observed the immense quantity of comminuted shells mixed in the soil of certain portions of the Government garden at Hobart Town, I could not be informed by those of whom I enquired how they had arrived there; and I was led to infer that they had been artificially and recently applied as a manure. It was not until long after, when I had an opportunity of observing some lately-formed heaps of shells on the west coast of the island, that I ascertained the truth. As some persons, otherwise well informed, still believe that changes in the relative levels of land and sea may have led to the appearance of the shells in their present places, I have thought it best to record my observations on the subject.

The Aborigines of Tasmania appear at all times to have derived a considerable portion of their food from the sea; and as they seem to have had no effectual means of catching fish in any quantity, the testaceæ and crustaceæ constituted the principal and almost only supply they drew from that element.

From the reports of the early navigators, it would seem that the Aborigines existed in considerable numbers along the coast of Tasmania; and we may thence infer that the consumption of shell-fish must have been very great, as they ate no vegetables or substitute for bread. In cooking, the shells appear in all instances to have been merely roasted in the simplest manner, as I never could trace any indications of ovens, or stones arranged to be heated. This burning of the shells has hastened their decay, and, in the course of a few years the identity of the species of which the various heaps and mounds are composed will with difficulty be traced.

In obtaining the shell-fish, &c., the women were, I believe, almost exclusively employed, wherever diving was requisite, as for the species of haliotis or oyster; these being brought to the surface in baskets formed from various sedge-leaved plants. In the majority of cases, they consumed their food as near as possible to the fishing stations, occasionally going a little inland, to avail themselves of a spring or stream of fresh water. I have, however, observed in a great number of instances that there were unusually large accumulations of shells on projecting points, headlands, and places commanding extensive views —even where apparently not the most eligible for cooking; whence I have supposed that they adopted these sites for their repasts to protect themselves from the sudden attacks of hostile tribes. The want of good water in the vicinity seems to have been sometimes immaterial, as La Billardière, in his *Voyage in Search of La Perouse*, observes, with reference to a repast of the Aborigines of Recherche Bay: 'Their meal (consisting of haliotis and cray-fish) had continued a long time, and we were much surprised that not one of them had yet drank; but this they deferred until they were fully satisfied with eating. The women and girls then went to fetch water with the vessels of sea-weed, getting it at the first place they came to, and setting it down by the men, who drank it without ceremony, though it was very muddy and stagnant.'

Heaps and mounds of shells, of sizes varying from what might be supposed to be the *débris* of a family dinner, to accumulations several feet in thickness, and many yards across, abound on all our shores, and up every indentation of the coast; the species of which these heaps are composed varying according to locality; the constituent species being wholly influenced by the greater or less abundance of the different kinds upon which the natives subsisted existing near the particular spots.

On the estuary of the Derwent these remains are found for several miles above Hobart Town, towards New Norfolk, until they disappear altogether at about three miles above the latter town. On the Tamar they are found at still less distances from the sea; and it does not appear that the Aborigines at any time were in the habit of carrying their shell-fish many miles inland, the farthest I have observed being two or three miles.

The principal kinds of testacea used by the Aborigines as food, exclusive of the smaller kinds, were—

Two species of *Haliotis* (*H. tuberculata* (?) and *lævigata*), which both attain to a large size, and are common on the rocks on the north-west coast, in Bass's Strait, and at Recherche Bay, &c. They were removed from the rocks (to which they closely adhere) by means of a wooden spatula-shaped instrument. The haliotis is called mutton-fish by the colonists.

The *Mussel* (*Mytilus sp.*), of which only one species of large size is abundant and easily procured. It is very common on the Derwent, on the Tamar, the north-west coast, &c., and is excellent eating. The heaps on the Derwent and Tamar consist principally of this shell.

Oysters (*Ostrea sp.*).—These are now rather scarce in many situations where their remains are abundant, which would indicate, as has indeed been found to be the case, that some causes, either diseases or otherwise, lead to the destruction of certain species of mollusks in some localities. All the oysters in the Derwent and Pittwater were thus destroyed some years ago, but I have recently learned that they are again appearing. The large mussels in the Tamar have, in the same way, disappeared of late years.

The *Warrenah* (*Turbo sp.*), which is very common in many situations, seems to have been a favorite article of food. At Cape Grim there is a heap several feet in thickness of this shell, formed on the top of the Cape.

Limpets (*Patellæ sp.*).—On the south and west coast these attain to a very large size. I do not recollect to have observed any shells of the *Parmophorus Australis* in the heaps, although, from the size of the fish, I would have expected to have found them much prized.

Fasciolaria trapezium (?)—This shell I saw principally in the small heaps, on the north coast; it is there abundant in the crevices of the rocks.

A species of *Purpura* occurs occasionally in the heaps near Circular Head.

A species of *Cardium*, and some of the smaller bivalves, were used on the Derwent, where these shells are common; but, as already observed, the beds of shells usually consist of those still existing close by.

Some of these heaps—as at Spring Bay, on the east coast—have recently been opened out and burnt for lime; but they are, in general, too much mixed with earthy matter, charcoal, &c., to make the lime of good quality; and the period of time which has elapsed since the shells were removed from the sea (in most cases the latest must be upwards of thirty years), joined to their partial calcination by the Aborigines in roasting, has caused their decomposition to be considerable. . . . ."

DISEASES.

The diseases most common amongst the natives were due to cold, neglect, and to the filthy condition of their persons. They suffered likewise from complaints arising out of their habits of gluttony. When food was plentiful, they would indulge their appetites to excess, and then perhaps for a long period they would suffer from want. Scarcely any of the natives were entirely free from skin diseases, and some suffered severely, their bodies being covered with sores. "In the children," says Davies, "these are dreadful and disgusting in the extreme; with them, all parts of the body are affected; with the adults, the sores are more confined to the head; these are doubtless caused by their coarse living aided by their dirty habits." *

The most fatal disease was inflammation of the lungs; but it is conjectured that prior to the colonization of the island by the whites a large number of persons had been carried off by the small-pox, conveyed, perhaps, by some exploring vessel.

The adults were afflicted with swellings of the face, and some were crippled by rheumatism.

All the sufferings that have to be endured by those who neglect their persons, and are without the means of preserving their bodies in a state of cleanliness, were felt as severely by the Tasmanians as by their neighbours on the continent.

Their methods of cure were not very different from those practised by the Australians. They usually resorted to bleeding, the flesh being cut with flakes of stone prepared for the purpose.

They seem to have had a belief in the efficacy of charms. Davies, Dove, and Hull make mention of superstitions like those elsewhere referred to in this work. "There are two customs of a superstitious kind still retained among them, neither, however, bearing the slightest reference even to low and misguided views of religious homage. The one is an anxiety to possess themselves of a bone from the skull or the arms of their deceased relatives, which, sewed up in a piece of skin, they wear round their necks, confessedly as a charm against sickness or premature death. The other is a fear of pronouncing the name by which a deceased friend was known, as if his shade might thus be offended. Nothing is more offensive to them than a departure from the rule which they have prescribed to themselves on this point by the white people with whom they may be drawn into converse. To introduce for any purpose whatever the name of any one of their deceased relatives calls up at once a frown of horror and indignation." †

Davies states that the bones he has seen carried by them were most commonly the jaw-bone, or the bone of the thigh; as also the skulls of children,

---

* *Tasmanian Journal of Natural Science*, &c. † *Tasmanian Journal*, 1842.

the latter wrapped up in a skin. "These bones," he adds, "are worn by people in perfect health, most probably as mementos of deceased relations; but, if so, they lend them to others of their own tribe when ill, who wear them as charms round the neck."*

It is said that they carried sacred stones, with which they could cause diseases amongst their enemies, and cure those that afflicted their friends; and that they had the same belief in the evils that could be worked by any one who might possess himself of a portion of their hair.

Dress and Ornaments.

The males amongst the Tasmanians wore no clothing of any kind when in good health. When sick, they covered themselves with a rug made of the skins of the opossum or of the kangaroo. The opossum skins were laced together with sinews of the tail of the kangaroo, and the woolly side was worn next the body. The women generally wore a covering of skins, and carried, like the men, the belt made of sinews, but for use only, not as a part of their clothing or as an ornament.

They used red-ochre, a kind of plumbago, and powdered charcoal for ornamenting their bodies.

The necklace shown in Fig. 292 was formerly in the possession of the late Mr. A. F. A. Greeves, to whom it was given many years ago by Chief Protector

FIG. 292.

Robinson. It now forms part of my collection. It was worn by a principal woman of a Tasmanian tribe. The shells—565 in number, and all of the same species (*Elenchus Bellulus*)—are strung on thin well-made twine, formed apparently of the fibre of some root.

Only a part of the necklace is shown in the figure.

The shells were cleaned by hanging them over a wood fire, and subsequent rubbing and polishing with the hands. The shells are of a greenish color, the nacre showing prismatic hues.

The necklace is beautiful, and must have been much prized by the owner. Its length is eighty-nine inches.

---

* *Tasmanian Journal.*

Mr. Dove says that the cluster of these glittering shells was termed *Merrina*. Some, according to information furnished by another correspondent, were named *Terri*.

He adds that "a similar love of ornament was displayed in the flowers and feathers with which the heads of both sexes were generally found to be attired."*

Weapons, Implements, Canoes.

The weapons of the natives were few, and of rude construction. The heavy spear was about fifteen feet in length and an inch in diameter; it was merely a sapling of tea-tree, dog-wood, or curryjong; one end brought to a point and hardened in the fire. The lighter spears were about ten feet in length and three-quarters of an inch in diameter. The native names of the spears were *Pena, Perenna, Prenna, Rugga* (southern tribes); and *Racah* (northern tribes).

The waddy was made of hard heavy wood (perhaps blackwood); it was nearly two feet in length, and about one inch and a quarter in diameter. Some of the waddies were pointed at both ends, and the part to be grasped was roughly notched, so as to afford a secure hold for the hand.

Mr. Ronald Gunn, F.R.S., informs me that the natives never had any other weapons except their spears and sticks. Their spears, he adds, were merely straight pieces of wood, made from young plants of a species of *melaleuca*, without barbs or carving of any kind; and the waddies were equally plain. They had no throwing-sticks or boomerangs, nor had they any shields. Reed-spears, similar to those in use on the continent, were unknown to the islanders.

Davies states that "in personal quarrels each party fights with a waddy, standing each other's blow on the head without defending it. If an offence be committed against the tribe, the delinquent has to stand whilst a certain number of spears are, at the same time, thrown at him. These, from the unerring aim with which they are thrown, he can seldom altogether avoid, although, from the quickness of his sight, he will frequently escape unhurt. He moves not from his place, avoiding the spears merely by the contortions of his body. Another mode of punishment is to place the offender upon a low branch of a tree, point at, and jeer him."

The same writer states that each tribe claimed a certain tract of country, but trespasses were common, and wars were frequent.

Cook, being desirous of knowing the use of the stick which one of the natives carried in his hand, caused a piece of wood to be set up as a mark, and induced the black to aim at it, at the distance of about twenty yards. He threw the stick several times, but without success, "for after repeated trials, he was still very wide from the object." Lieut. Breton, on the other hand, states that the stick was a dangerous weapon, that it could be thrown with ease and precision a distance of forty yards, and that it was observed to go horizontally, describing the same kind of circular motion as the boomerang, and with the like whirring noise.

---

* *Tasmanian Journal.*

The character of the weapons made by the natives of Tasmania, the absence of ornament, their using their clubs as missiles, and throwing stones at their enemies when all their clubs were hurled, or when they desired to keep their clubs for protection, indicate a condition so much lower than that of the Australians, that one is not unwilling, with Dr. Latham, to seek in other lands than those from which Australia was peopled for their origin.

Their implements were a vessel of bark, very neatly made, for holding water, and baskets of different forms, like those used by the natives of Australia. The native names of the baskets were *Treena*, *Tillé*, and *Trughauna*.

Large shells were kept for holding water and for conveying it to the sick.

The natives necessarily had occasionally to cross rivers and arms of the sea. Dove says that "the contiguous islands of the Straits were frequently visited by the tribes located on the northern coasts of Tasmania. A species of bark or decayed wood, whose specific gravity appears to be similar to that of cork, provided them with the means of constructing canoes. The beams or logs were fastened together by the help of rushes or thongs of skin. These canoes resembled, both in shape and in the mode by which they were impelled and steered, the more elegant models in use among the Indians of America. Their peculiar buoyancy secured them effectually against the usual hazards of the sea."

From another source I learn that when, during their excursions in the autumn, which were supposed to be from west to east, and in the spring from east to west, and they came to an arm of the sea, or a large river, or a lake, they made a kind of raft, somewhat like the catamarans of the people of Torres Straits. This raft was formed of the trunks of two trees, about thirty feet in length, and laid parallel to one another, and at a distance of five or six feet. The logs were kept together by four or five smaller pieces of wood, laid across at the ends, and fastened by slips of tough bark. In the middle was a cross timber of considerable thickness, and the whole was interwoven with a kind of wicker-work. This raft was propelled by paddles with amazing rapidity. Such a vessel—if vessel it can be called—would carry six or ten persons. When it had served its purpose, it was usually abandoned; and when Tasmania was first colonized, the whites not unfrequently discovered these rafts or their remains on the sea-shore, or on the banks of the rivers and lakes.

The names of the canoes were *Malanna*, *Munyana*, and *Munghana*.

Mr. Hull says that there were formerly many accounts of the drowning of natives who embarked in these catamarans for the purpose of visiting the neighbouring islands. Their bodies were found on the beaches.

Stone Implements used by the Natives of Tasmania.

When engaged in investigating the character of the stone implements of the Australian natives, it was but natural to look to the neighbouring isle —Tasmania—and to enquire whether the people who once inhabited it had used the stone-tomahawk, the stone-chisel, and other tools of stone similar in form to those found in Victoria and over the whole extent of the island-continent of

Australia. It might appear to the reader that no difficulties would present themselves in the attempt to obtain accurate information on a point of this kind. The natives of Tasmania were numerous within the memory of a great many persons now living, and it is but—one may say—a few days since the last of them was buried; yet, as those who knew them best were not the best of observers, it happens that facts connected with their customs and their arts are not easily gathered. But for the assistance given by the Rev. H. P. Kane, Dr. Agnew, the Honorary Secretary of the Royal Society of Tasmania, Mr. Ronald Gunn, F.R.S., and others, I could not have had the opportunity of comparing the stone implements of Tasmania with those of Australia. To these gentlemen I am deeply indebted. As soon as the Honorary Secretary of the Royal Society was informed of the nature of my investigations, he sent me specimens of the stone implements which had long been treasured in the Museum of the Society. These, as soon as they were received, were figured and described, and, in order that I might have their forms at all times before me for comparison, I caused *fac-similes* to be made of them.

Five of these specimens are figured. Before returning these stone-axes to the Royal Society, I made a careful examination of them, with the object of determining the character of the rocks of which they are fragments. In doing this, I had help from Mr. Cosmo Newbery, B.Sc. They are nearly all chert, or cherty varieties of metamorphosed sedimentary rocks, obtained in all probability from the neighbourhood of granite or porphyry. Mr. Cosmo Newbery agrees with me in the opinion, that while some of them have been split by hand from larger blocks, others are fragments of rock occurring naturally, and selected because they were of suitable form. These fragments, whether detached by blows or got from the beds of streams, have been treated in one way only: having selected that which appeared to be the best for a cutting edge, the native has improved it by simply striking off small flakes all along the edge and from one side of the edge only. This has been done, however, in all cases with so much skill as to keep the line straight. It is not a serrated edge. It would appear that the fragment was held in the palm of one hand, with the edge outwards, and that with a piece of stone in the other hand blows were given towards the palm and away from the edge, until flakes were detached in such a manner as to leave it even and sharp. Some specimens, however, have been detached by one blow from a larger rock. These exhibit a semi-conchoidal fracture, and having a good edge, have not been subsequently altered by chipping.

The implements sent to me by the Honorary Secretary of the Royal Society sufficiently show the character of these tools; but I have had also the opportunity of examining nineteen samples from the collection of Mr. Ronald Gunn, and seventeen collected for me by the Rev. Mr. Kane.

Amongst Mr. Ronald Gunn's specimens there are two scalpriform implements, very skilfully made. One—the best—of a triangular shape, and with a remarkably sharp cutting edge, has been improved by striking off flakes—in size from a sixteenth of an inch to a quarter of an inch—from the base of the triangle; and the other, a smaller stone, about three inches in length and two inches in breadth, formed in the same way, is scarcely inferior. These were evidently struck off by hand from some larger blocks, and afterwards improved in the manner described. The first was found near Westbury and the other near Ross. In the collection presented to me by the Rev. Mr. Kane there were two or three beautiful specimens, one not inferior to any I have ever seen.

The largest stones do not weigh more than six or seven ounces, and the smallest are not much heavier than the chips of black basalt used by the natives of Victoria for cutting and cleaning skins.

Those used for skinning animals are said to have been called *Mungana* and *Trowutta* by the natives.

These stone implements are all of one character; none of them were provided with a handle; and it is not probable, judging from the shape of them, that the native had even the protection of the opossum skin for his hand.*

One or two, Mr. G. H. F. Ulrich thinks, may be flakes of black basalt, but this could scarcely be determined without fracturing the implements. The greater number—nearly all of them—may be classed as fragments of metamorphosed rocks, cherts, and porcelainites. Owing to having been buried for a lengthened period, many are coated with a thin yellowish-brown or grey skin.

I can state with certainty that not one has been ground, and that no attempt has been made in any case to give an edge by grinding.

I have received the following letter and memorandum from Mr. Ronald Gunn respecting these implements:—

Newstead, 30th May 1873.

MY DEAR SIR,—I forward per steamer the stone implements of the Aborigines of Tasmania. You will find them of the very rudest description. Those resembling tomahawks were held in the hand, and under no circumstances, as far as I know or can learn, were they ever fixed in any handle. The smaller stones were used for scraping and forming their spears and waddies. I send a copy of a memorandum received from Mr. J. Scott, Surveyor, who kindly procured me the implements. The locality from whence

---

* Mr. James Rollings, in a letter addressed to Dr. Agnew, and dated the 5th May 1873, says that in his youth he was constantly in the habit of seeing the Aborigines of Tasmania, and mixing with them occasionally, and that he had many opportunities of seeing how they used their stone knives and tomahawks. The knives, similar to those in the Museum [*see* figures in this work], when used for skinning kangaroos, &c., were held by the forefinger and thumb, and the arm, being extended, was drawn rapidly towards the body. The carcass was afterwards cut up, and the knife was held in the same way. In cutting their hair, one stone was held under the hair, another stone being used above, and by this means the hair was cut, or rather, by repeated nickings, came off. A larger stone, well selected, about four or five pounds in weight, was used for a tomahawk, a handle being fastened to it in the same way as a blacksmith fastens a rod to chisels, &c., for cutting or punching iron, being afterwards well secured by the sinews of some animal. The handles were strong saplings of wattle or curryjong. These were the only stone implements he saw used among the natives, and very expert they were in using them.

Mr. Rollings, no doubt, may have seen the natives using tomahawks similar to those of the Australians; but it is certain that they were introduced after the island was peopled by the whites. They were probably obtained from the Port Phillip natives. If anything like the stone tomahawk of the Australians had been used in Tasmania prior to the colonization of the island, numerous specimens would have been found. As far as can be ascertained, not one has been discovered anywhere.

they were obtained by the Aborigines, he states to be a spot on the west side of the Great Lake, and there is no rock (which he terms "flint") of a similar description, so far as he knows, for many miles round where he picked them up.

The natives of Tasmania had no weapons except spears, and sticks about two and a half feet long, used as waddies. Their spears were merely straight pieces of wood, made from young plants of a species of *melaleuca*, without barbs or carving of any kind. The waddies were equally plain. They had no throwing-sticks, shields, or boomerangs, nor had they any spears partly formed of reeds, as in Victoria. If there is any other information you require, I shall be glad to furnish it. I may add that I have been in this colony upwards of forty-three years, and saw a good number of the Aborigines in 1830 and few subsequent years.

Yours very sincerely,
R. Brough Smyth, Esq., &c., &c., &c.   Rd. Gunn.

Memorandum on the Stone Implements used by the Aborigines of Tasmania, found at Mount Morriston, eight miles south from Ross, on the east bank of the Macquarie River, on lot 78, Parish of Peel, County of Somerset:—

The space over which they were found is about three by five chains, or one and a half acres, in a sheltered bend of the river, at the head of a deep lagoon, above one mile long, the Saltpan Plains lying to the west, and the hills rising suddenly to the east. The original place where these were first obtained by the Aborigines is between the "Split Rock" and the west shore of the "Great Lake," about forty miles distant, where Mr. Pitt has seen the ground covered with stones partly broken and shaped—"like a workshop," by his statement to me. It would be worth while to have the spot re-discovered and fixed properly. In using the flints, the thumb was placed on the flat surface, and held by the other fingers resting in the palm of the hand, and the sharp edges used to cut the notches in the trees for climbing, cutting spears, and making the handles of the waddies rough, so as not to slip from the hand. They devoted much time to chipping the edges of the flints, and the small pieces broken off show very distinctly in good ones; the pieces not so marked, and smaller, are probably the pieces left in making them into ship-shape at first. Whilst the flints were used to cut notches in the trees for the great toe to rest in, for climbing, the body was supported against the tree by a strong grass rope, passed round the tree and the body, held by one hand, whilst with the other they used the flint. In making this grass rope, some eight or ten men would all begin to pull long wiry grass (a native species of *fescue*), and when they had a quantity, two and two would twist a fine rope with a crooked stick, and, when all finished, come and join the whole eight or ten ropes into one strong one, sufficient to support a native against the tree. I have frequently found single flint stones lying over the country adjoining the Saltpan Plains, but never in quantity, except at the spot referred to here, which from its shelter and convenience to water, and the open plains, yet close to the trees, has been a favorite place of resting, &c.

The number of stones of the same material (but different shades in color) which I found at that spot was upwards of 218, viz. :—150 now in my possession; 24 left at Mount Morriston; the remainder given away, some to the Museum in Hobart Town, and others as curiosities.

I believe if the ground were turned over at the spot, that more might yet be found. Adjoining the spot where the flints were found there were also some common water-worn stones broken in the edges, as if used for chipping, but of no interest otherwise.

JAMES SCOTT, Surveyor.

Launceston, 12th May 1873.

In the report of the proceedings of the Royal Society of Tasmania, at a meeting held on the 8th July 1873, attention was called to the enquiries which had been made respecting the character of the stone implements used by the natives, and a letter was read from Mr. James Scott, M.H.A., of Launceston, in which, on the authority of the late Mr. Thomas Scott, his brother, who for some time held the office of Assistant Surveyor-General, and from his own observations, he makes statements strictly consistent with those contained in the memorandum just quoted.

It is highly creditable to the Royal Society that they should have devoted so much attention to this subject, a subject of the highest importance to those who make the history of mankind their study.

The facts contained in this brief account of the stone implements of the Tasmanians, and the descriptions of the stone tomahawks, knives, and chisels of the Australians, will probably cause scientific men who have collected data relating to the savage races that once peopled Europe to re-investigate these data, and perhaps to modify the inferences drawn from them.

It is apparent that savages living but a few hundred miles apart, and having many customs in common, exhibited in their implements of stone all the forms from the rudest chip of chert to the highly-polished tomahawk of greenstone.

The following figures and descriptions relate to the implements sent to me by the Honorary Secretary of the Royal Society of Tasmania.

The cutting implement Fig. 293 is a fragment of cherty rock — a fragment detached, apparently, without the aid of man's hand, from some larger mass. It was selected, probably, because it was fitted for the purposes to which it would be put by the Aborigines. The cutting edge shown on the left-hand side of the figure was formed by

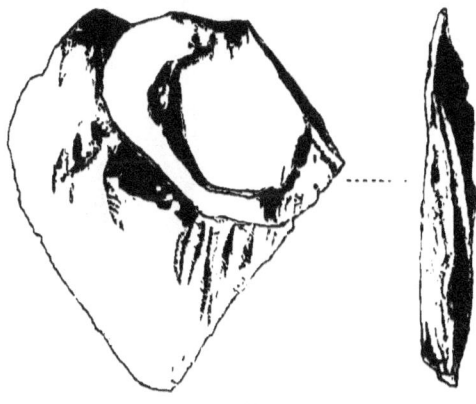

FIG. 293.—(Scale ¼.)

striking off thin flakes about a quarter of an inch in width. In this figure the numerous indentations made by striking off the flakes are not depicted. The irregularities occur on the side not shown in the engraving, but, instead, the even cutting edge is presented. The marvellous skill of the workman in striking off flakes so as to preserve an even edge, as shown in the figure, is worthy of notice and admiration. This implement bears a label, from which it appears that it was presented to the Royal Society of Tasmania by Dr. Milligan, and was used, according to his statement, for skinning the kangaroo, &c., and was usually carried in their baskets by the natives.

The weight of this implement is six ounces.

The specimen Fig. 294 is said by Dr. Milligan to have been used for cutting spears and sticks. The cutting edge is not good. It is a very rude implement. It is a fragment of a dense, very heavy siliceous cherty rock pre-

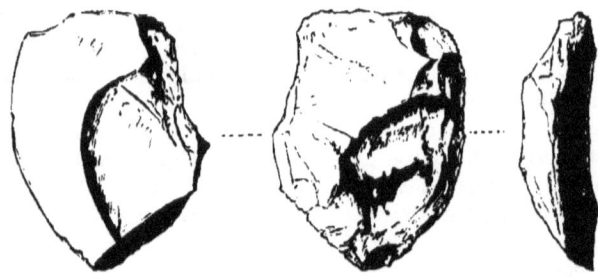

FIG. 294.—(Scale ½.)

senting a semi-conchoidal fracture. Its color on the surface is light bluish-grey, but where splintered approaching to black. It has been improved by striking off small flakes, so as to form a cutting edge, but the work has been done rudely, yet not without skill. Its weight is three and a half ounces.

This (Fig. 295) is a fragment of rock struck off from some larger block,

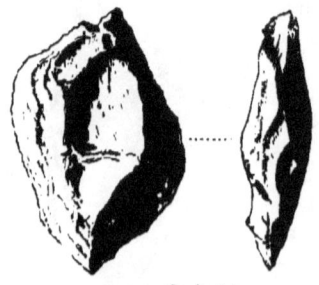

FIG. 295.—(Scale ½.)

which has had given to it a cutting edge by knocking off flakes from and not towards the edge. It seems as if the native had selected the best side for cutting, and then, by striking that side with another stone, split from it small chips, working towards the stone and not from it. In this way only—as I imagine, looking at the fragment—could the work have been performed. This is a serviceable implement. Its weight is two and three-quarter ounces.

The implement here shown (Fig. 296) is one of the best in the collection. It was used probably for cutting holes in the bark of trees when climbing. It

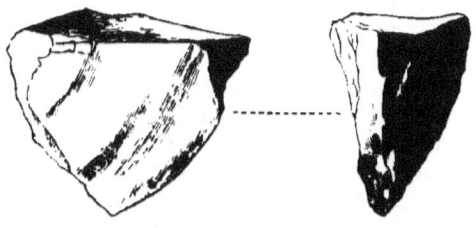

FIG. 296.—(Scale ½.)

has a good cutting edge. Whether found in the form it presents, or struck off by the native from some larger block, is difficult to determine. It certainly has not been altered as the other implements have been by striking off flakes.

It is very heavy, and, like the others, a dense siliceous cherty rock. The color of the skin is light brownish-grey, and the interior a very dark-bluish grey, nearly black. The weight is five and one-quarter ounces.

This stone (Fig. 297) has been brought into shape by striking off fragments. It has a good but rather rough cutting edge, and has been used perhaps for

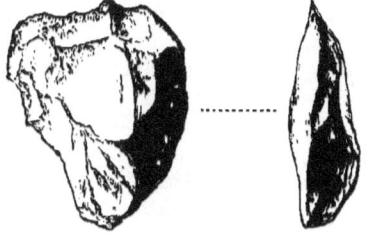

FIG. 297.

forming clubs, fighting-sticks, or spears. It is a good, sharp, useful stone, and evidently, from the appearance of the surface, more recent than the other implements.

The other specimens received from the Royal Society of Tasmania are of the same character as those figured and described. One—a heavy thick stone, with a rough edge—was probably used for cutting wood. It is a fragment of a dark bluish-grey siliceous rock. Small flakes have been struck off to form a cutting edge.

Another—a thinner and broader fragment and triangular in shape—is formed of the same kind of rock, and the cutting edge is in like manner made by striking off thin small flakes.

The weight of each is a little less than seven ounces.

FIRE.

It is not anywhere clearly stated how the natives produced FIRE. Dove states that they were always careful to carry in their hands the materials of kindling a fire. "Their memory," he says, "supplies them with no instances of a period in which they were obliged to draw upon their own inventive powers for the means of resuscitating an element so essential to their health and comfort as flame."

Davies, however, apparently much more careful in making statements and in drawing inferences, states that, "When they move from place to place, they carry fire with them: when they had it not, I have been informed that they obtained it by rubbing round rapidly in their hands a piece of hard pointed stick, the pointed end inserted into a notch in another piece of dry wood." It would be contrary to all experience of savage races to suppose that the means of kindling a fire by the use of two pieces of wood was unknown to this people. At the same time it is certain that the natives would rarely have occasion to resort to friction for such a purpose.

LANGUAGE.

The language of the natives of Tasmania was, like that of the Australians, vocalic, but in their words, unlike the Australians, there are few re-duplicates. Latham thinks that the affinities of language between the Tasmanian and the New Caledonian are stronger than those between the Australian and Tasmanian. This brings us to the consideration of the question of the peopling of Tasmania, which is discussed elsewhere.

I give here a vocabulary of the dialects of some of the Aboriginal tribes of Tasmania, compiled by Joseph Milligan, Esq., F.L.S., together with his notes. This vocabulary appeared originally in the journals of the Royal Society of Tasmania, and was subsequently reprinted with an introductory note by Sir Robert Officer, who states that the compiler was for many years Medical Superintendent of the Aborigines Establishment, first at Flinders Island, and afterwards at Oyster Cove, to which the remnant of the race was removed in the year 1848. Sir Robert adds that ample opportunities were afforded to Dr. Milligan of acquiring a knowledge of the language of the race, and that, as known to all, his character and attainments are a guarantee of the fidelity and accuracy of his work.

To Dr. Milligan's paper is appended a list of words in use amongst the Oyster Bay tribe, compiled in 1826, by Thomas Scott, Esq., late Assistant Surveyor-General of Tasmania.

Mr. R. H. Davies, in his paper on the Aborigines of Van Diemen's Land (published in 1844–5), makes some judicious observations which I shall here transcribe. He says—"Their language is, in all probability, extremely limited, or at least was so before their intercourse with whites; but so many words have since crept in, and been naturalized as above, that it would now be impossible to find out to what their original language was confined. I much doubt their ever having separate names for all the different kinds of birds with which they were conversant; *Iula* (a bird) appeared to answer for most. The *lingua franca* before alluded to as spoken at Flinders Island is a mixture of English, words from the different tribes, and a number of words from the New Holland tribes, and even from other countries; these last have been introduced by the women, Aborigines of Van Diemen's Land, who have lived for many years with sealers, and been with them to the continent; even negro words have been introduced. From these circumstances, it may be perceived how difficult it would be to separate their absolutely primitive language from that now in use."

Though, as stated by Dove, the Aborigines of Tasmania have been usually regarded as exhibiting the human character in its lowest state of degradation, yet he admits that, when we take note of the force of invention and of memory which is displayed in the copious vocabulary of their several languages, they can claim no inconsiderable share of mental power and activity.

What they knew and what they did not know cannot now be ascertained. Low as they were, they were human in all that they did and did not do, and nearer to ourselves—and not to the worst amongst us—than the so-called civilized peoples of the cities would be willing to admit.*

---

* A paper *On the Aboriginal Languages of Tasmania* appears in the *Tasmanian Journal of Natural Science*, where a number of words are given from the MSS. of Jorgen Jorgenson and the Rev. Thomas Dove.

ON THE DIALECTS AND LANGUAGE OF THE ABORIGINAL TRIBES OF TASMANIA, AND ON THEIR MANNERS AND CUSTOMS.

(By Joseph Milligan, F.L.S.)

The day is not far distant when, according to the ordinary course of nature, the last of the surviving remnant of the Aboriginal inhabitants of Tasmania, now maintained at a Government establishment, and little more than a dozen in number, must be removed by death, and a distinct people cease to exist. The entire extinction of a population, an isolated stirp of the human family, is neither a matter of every day occurrence nor of trivial import.

When Van Diemen's Land was first occupied by Europeans, half a century ago, its Aboriginal population spread in tribes, sub-tribes, and families over the length and breadth of the island, from Cape Portland to Port Davey, and from Oyster Bay to Macquarie Harbour; and their aggregate number at that time has been variously estimated at from 1,500 to 5,000.

The early navigators make frequent mention of rencontres with numerous groups of "the natives," and of fires, and of "smokes" seen in the bush, which were considered to indicate their presence in considerable force in the neighbourhood. But experience has taught us that such evidence is, at the best, fallacious and untrustworthy; we all know that bush-fires may smoulder and rage in turns for months together at certain seasons, and over a great extent of country, without the actual presence of any human being in the vicinity; we also know very well that a mere handful of Aborigines appearing, shifting their ground, and re-appearing on the edge of a thick scrub, or in the recesses of forest ground, variously grouped and under different aspects, may easily be, and have often been, mistaken for a formidable number. We therefore receive with some allowances the higher estimates formed of the Aboriginal population of this island at or about the time of its discovery.

Assuming that the number of tribes and sub-tribes throughout the territory was then about (20) twenty, and that they each mustered, of men, women, and children, 50 to 250 individuals, and allowing to them numbers proportioned to the means of subsistence within the limits of their respective hunting-grounds, it does not appear probable that the aggregate Aboriginal population did materially, if at all, exceed 2,000. For it is to be borne in mind that all along the western side of the island the face of the country is thickly covered with dank and inhospitable forests, and that other physical conditions most unfavorable to a natural abundance of animal life prevail there, while our traditionary knowledge of the tribes known to have existed along the east and centre is sufficiently accurate to enable us to form a close approximation to their actual strength. The estimates which fixed the native population at 5,000 or upwards when the colony was first settled are therefore obviously in error.

LANGUAGE.

The open grassy plains and thinly-timbered forest ground along the eastern and central portions of the island were the most eligible for the purposes of the early settlers, and were therefore the portions of the territory first occupied; but these fine tracts of country were precisely those which naturally yielded the means of subsistence in the greatest profusion to the Aborigines, and they were accordingly the districts chiefly frequented by the natives at that time. The first colonists were therefore unavoidably brought into contact, and frequently into immediate and familiar intercourse, with the tribes belonging to the districts in which they had located themselves; they thus enjoyed peculiar facilities for becoming acquainted with their disposition and habits, and acquiring from the more intelligent of them some knowledge of their history and traditions. Few comparatively of these original settlers—the pioneers of colonization in Van Diemen's Land—remain to communicate the information which they may thus have obtained. A fortunate few returned home, enriched with the legitimate fruits of industry and good management; others, less successful here in the first instance, migrated early to a neighbouring province, and reaped largely of the golden harvest with which it has been blessed; while many have "passed that bourne whence no traveller returns," and left no record of the simple race whose position, rights, and very existence they had come to usurp and to supersede.

As, under such circumstances, every scrap of authentic information respecting the Aborigines of Van Diemen's Land may be regarded as of some value, I avail myself of the opportunity afforded by the publication of the vocabulary of certain Aboriginal dialects of Tasmania, and of some remarks necessary thereupon, briefly to make record of such particulars illustrative of their habits, manners, and customs as have fallen under my notice, or been gathered directly from their statements to myself.

In order that ethnologists and others interested in the vocabulary of Aboriginal dialects referred to may be inclined to place perfect confidence in their accuracy, I have to explain that every word before being written down was singly submitted to a committee (as it were) of several Aborigines, and made thoroughly intelligible to them, when the corresponding word in their language, having been agreed upon by them, was entered. This, of course, was a most tedious method to pursue, but it was the only plan which gave a fair chance of precision and truthfulness. On being completed, the manuscript was laid aside for two or three years, when it was again submitted, *verbatim* and *seriatim*, to a circle of Aborigines for their remarks: a revision which led to the discovery and correction of numerous blunders originating in misapprehension, on the part of the Aborigines in the first place, of the true meaning of words which they had been required to translate.

But I found the fault had oftentimes been my own, in having failed to seize the exact and essential vocal expression, which, on being repeated to the Aborigines at any time afterwards, would infallibly reproduce the precise idea which it had been stated to imply in the first instance.

This circumstance has strongly impressed upon me the conviction that much of the discordance apparent in the vocabularies of the same language or dialect, published by different travellers, is attributable to similar causes. For instance, a zealous naturalist, knowing nothing whatever of the language the words of which he desired hurriedly to secure, would point to a tree and repeat the word "tree," the reply to which, in all probability, would be not the equivalent for tree, but the specific name by which that particular sort of tree was known there; and so with other things. Abstract ideas are unfamiliar to and not easily comprehended by untutored Aboriginal minds, and hence numberless mistakes which, from want of verification and correction, become fixed and permanent errors.

The language of a people, whether it be possessed of a copious or spare vocabulary—whether it consist of a plain collocation of a few simple and arbitrary sounds, or be characterized by elaborate inflexions and a complex arrangement of words of analogical import—ought to be accepted, one would say, as the index of the degree of mental culture and social and intellectual progress attained by those who make use of it, and find it sufficient for the expression of their various thoughts, feelings, and desires. A glance at the vocabulary of Aboriginal dialects of Tasmania, and at the condition of the Aborigines themselves, will perhaps be thought to lend confirmation to the opinion.

The words or vocal sounds of the unwritten language of rude predatory tribes are liable to more frequent and to more violent and arbitrary changes than are incident to a tongue embodied in the symbolic forms of letters, the various inflexions, combinations, and analogies of which have been recognised by the eye as well as the ear, and stereotyped, as it were, by the printing press.

The circumstance of the Aboriginal inhabitants of Van Diemen's Land being divided into many tribes and sub-tribes, in a state of perpetual antagonism and open hostility to each other, materially added to the number and augmented the energy of the elements and agents of mutation ordinarily operating on the language of an unlettered people: to this was superadded the effect of certain superstitious customs everywhere prevalent, which led from time to time to the absolute rejection and disuse of words previously employed to express objects familiar and indispensable to all; thus imperiously modifying nomenclature and the substantive parts of speech, and tending arbitrarily to diversify the dialects of the several tribes.

The habit of gesticulation and the use of signs to eke out the meaning of monosyllabic expressions, and to give force, precision, and character to vocal sounds, exerted a further modifying effect, producing, as it did, carelessness and laxity of articulation, and in the application and pronunciation of words. The last-named irregularity, namely, the distinctly different pronunciation of a word by the same person on different occasions to convey the same idea, is very perplexing, until the radical or essential part of the word, apart from prefixes and suffixes, is caught hold of. The affixes, which signify nothing, are *la, lah, le, leh, leah, na, ne, nah, ba, be, beah, bo, ma, me, meah, pa, poo, ra, re, ta, te, ak, ek, ik,* &c. Some early voyagers appear to have mistaken the terminals *la, le,* &c., as distinctive of sex, when applied to men, women, and the lower animals. The language, when spoken by the natives, was rendered embarrassing by the frequent alliteration of vowels and other startling abbreviations, as well as by the apposition of the incidental increment indifferently before or after the radical or essential constituent of words. To defects in orthoepy the Aborigines added shortcomings in syntax, for they observed no settled order or arrangement of words in the construction of their sentences, but conveyed in a supplementary fashion by tone, manner, and gesture those modifications of meaning which we express by mood, tense, number, &c. Nor was this a matter difficult of accomplishment amongst a people living in a state so primitive that animal wants and gratifications, and the exigencies of the chase and of war, comprised the sum total of events which characterized their existence either as individuals or as members of the communities to which they belonged. Barbarous tribes, living in isolated positions, antagonistic to and repellant of each other, would each, within its own sphere, yield to various influences, calculated to modify language, and to confirm as well as create dissimilarity. New words introduced into the language of civilized and lettered communities betray their origin and relationship to pre-existing words in the same or in cognate and kindred tongues: but rude savage people often adopt the most arbitrary and unmeaning sounds, through caprice or accident, to represent ideas in place of words previously in use; a source of mutation, as respects the various dialects spoken amongst the Aborigines of Van Diemen's Land, fertile in proportion to the number of tribes into which they were divided, and the ceaseless feuds which separated them from one another. Hence it was that the numerous tribes of Tasmanian Aborigines were found possessed of distinct dialects, each differing in many particulars from every other.

It has already been implied that the Aborigines had acquired very limited powers of abstraction or generalization. They possessed no words representing abstract ideas; for each variety of gum-tree and wattle-tree, &c., &c., they had a name, but they had no equivalent for the expression "a tree;" neither could they express abstract qualities, such as hard, soft, warm, cold, long, short, round, &c.: for "hard," they would say "like a stone;" for "tall," they would say "long legs," &c.; and for "round," they said "like a ball," "like the moon," and so on, usually suiting the action to the word, and confirming by some sign the meaning to be understood.

The elision and absolute rejection and disuse of words from time to time has been noticed as a source of change in the Aboriginal dialects. It happened thus:—The names of men and women were taken from natural objects and occurrences around, as, for instance, a kangaroo, a gum-tree, snow, hail, thunder, the wind, the sea, the Waratah, or Blandfordia or Boronia, when in blossom, &c.; but it was a settled custom in every tribe, upon the death of any individual, most scrupulously to abstain ever after from mentioning the name of the deceased—a rule the infraction of which would, they considered, be followed by some dire calamities: they therefore used great circumlocution in referring to a dead person, so as to avoid pronunciation of the name; if, for instance, William and Mary, man and wife, were both deceased, and Lucy, the deceased sister of William, had been married to Isaac, also dead, whose son Jemmy still survived, and they wished to speak of Mary, they would say "the wife of the brother of Jemmy's father's wife," and so on. Such a practice must, it is clear, have contributed materially to reduce the number of their substantive appellations, and to create a necessity for new phonetic symbols to represent old ideas, which new vocables would, in all probability, differ on each occasion, and in every separate tribe; the only chance of fusion of words between tribes arising out of the capture of females for wives from hostile and alien people—a custom generally prevalent, and doubtless as beneficial to the race in its effects as it was savage in its mode of execution.

The Tasmanian Aborigines made use of some vocal sounds not met with in the English language; one, for instance, corresponds to the sound of *u*, as pronounced by the French; others are equivalent to *ch* and *gh* in the Scotch and Irish *loch* and *lough;* and there are some curious combinations of nasal and guttural sounds.

The orthography of the Aboriginal vocabulary agrees as nearly as possible with the ordinary phonetic expression of the English alphabet, with the following qualifications:—The vowel *a*, when it stands alone, is to be pronounced as in *cat, rap,* &c., but *aa* is sounded nearly as *aw* in the word *lawn; e* is pronounced as in the English word *the,* and *ee* as in *thee, me, see,* &c., but *é* is to be sounded like *a* in *potato* and in *day; i* is to be pronounced as in *sigh, fie,* &c.; *o* is to be sounded as in *so, go, flow,* and *oo* as in *soon, moon,* &c.; *u* is never to be sounded as in the English word *flute,* its usual sound being that in the French words *une, usage, usurier, fumer,* &c., but when followed by a double consonant, or by two consonants, it is to be sounded as in the English words *musk, lump, bump,* &c.; *y* is to be sounded as in the English words *holy, glibly, yonder, yellow,* &c.; *i* before another vowel has a full sound as in the English words *shine, riot; ei* coming together are to be pronounced as in *Leipsic, ou* as in *noun, oi* as in *toil,* &c. Consonants have their usual sounds when single; *ch* and *gh* are pronounced as in the German word *hochachten* and in the Irish *lough.* When a double consonant, or two consonants stand together, the first carries the accent, as in the English words *cunningly, peppery, cobbler, pipkin.*

VOCABULARY OF DIALECTS OF ABORIGINAL TRIBES OF TASMANIA.

(By Joseph Milligan, F.L.S., etc.)

English.	Tribes from Oyster Bay to Pittwater.	Tribes about Mount Royal, Brune Island, Recherche Bay, and the South of Tasmania.	North-West and Western.
Abscess	Licemena	Limeté	Wallamalé
Absent	Malnmbo	Taggara	Wakannara
Abstain	Miengpa	Parrawé	Wannabea tongh
Abstract (to deduct)	Nunamara		
Accompany	Tawé		Tawélea mepoilea
Acid (taste)	No-wicack	Noilce	'Gdnlla
Aerid (taste)	Peooniack	Mené wuttá or Mené ruggara	
Add to or put	Prolonè	Poggona nee wughta	Poilabea
Across (to put or place)	Prolon-unyeré	Wuggara tungalé	Tienenable poingh
Adult man	Puggana minyenna	Pallawah	Pahlea
Adult woman	Lowalla minyenna	Nienaté and Lowanna	Noallea
Afraid	Tianna coithyack	Tiennawillé	Camballeté
Afternoon	Kaawntto	Nunto-né	Kaoonyleah
Aged (literally rottenboned)	Tinna-triouratick	Naggattaboyé	'Gnee-mucklé
Agile	Menekarowa	Narra warraggara	
Ah !	Ah !	Mile-né !	
Air	Oimnunla	Rialannah	
Altogether	Nnntyemtick	Mabbylé	
Aloft	Muyanato	Crougana wughata	
Amatory (rakish)	Riunyowalinya	Lingana loaa renowa	
Anger	Miengeonnenechana	Poiné moonalané	
Angle (crooked like the elbow)	Wien-powenya	Wiena and Wienenna	
Ankle	Munnaghana	Munnawana	
Anoint	Yennemee	Ruggara	
Another	Tabboucack	Neggana	
Answer (to)	Ouneeprapé	Oghnemipé and Oghnecprapé	
Ant, blue	Pugganeiptictta		
Ant, small black, strong smelling	Ouiteitana	Moyberry	
Ant, largest black, venomous	Tietta	Tité	
Ant, red body with black head and tail	Nowateita	Lalla and Loattera	
Ant-eater (*Echidna setosa*)	Mungyenna	Munnyé	
Apparition	Wurrawena krottomicentoneack	Ria-wurrawa	
Aquiline (Roman nosed)	Muunna puggawinya	Maitingulé	
Arm	Wu'hnna	Wu'hnna	
Ashamed	Leienntonnyack	Lienuté	
Aha ! you are sulky all of a sudden	Annyah ! Teborah !	Keetrelbea-noomena, Peniggomaree !	
Ashes	Tontaiyenna	Toiberry	Ronghtaly né
Ask	Ongheewammeno	Oghnamileé	Onabeamahbelé
Asleep	Tugganick	Longhana	Nenarongabea
Awake (to open the eyes)	Cranny-mongtheé		
Awake, ditto	Wennymongtheé	Nunneoine-roidukaté	
Awake him, rouse him	Identiapé		Illetiapé
Ay (yes)	Narramuna	Narrawa	Narro baro
Azure (sky)	Noorblack	Warra-né	Lourannelcah
Awake (rouse ye, get up)	Llentable, tagga muna !	Nawaté, pegrate, wergho !	Takkawugh né !
Babe	Cottrnluttyé	Puggata riela	Rikenté
Bachelor	Pugganara mittyó	Lowatimy	Paponnewatté
Back (the)	Me-inghana	Talinah	Teerannelee-leah
Backward	Lenere	Talire	Kelabateeorah
Bad (no good)	Noweiack	Noile	Eo-ayngh-la-leah
Bandy-legged	Lackaniampaoick	Kentroueté	
Bandicoot	Tiennah	Tenghanah or Tenna-ne	Lugoileah mungoinah leah

VOCABULARY OF DIALECTS OF ABORIGINAL TRIBES OF TASMANIA.

English.	Tribes from Oyster Bay to Pittwater.	Tribes about Mount Royal, Bruno Island, Recherche Bay, and the South of Tasmania.	North-West and Western.
Bark (of a tree)	Poora, Poorah-nah	Warra	Poora leah
Barren (woman)	Kaceto kekrahouah	Lowa puggatimy	Lopiteneeba
Barren ditto	Nangemoona	Luakennamalú	
Baskets	Tughbranah	Trenah	Tillé
Bat	Peounyenna	Lérynah	
Battle	Miemyenganah	Mialungana	Mungymeni leah
Beard	Comena purennah	Cowinné	Comené waggelé
Beardless	Comena-ranyah	Co-win-timy	Cominerah leah
Beat (to strike)	Legganegulumpté	Lugguna	Menghboibee raté
Beau (coxcomb)	Pugganaterectyé	Pallowah-tutté	Papponné tughte leah
Beauty (fine-looking woman)	Lowanna-claphatyé	Nire-lowa	Noa noughanoatté
Beauty, ditto	Lowanna-eleebana-leah	Loa-minery	
Bark of tree flapping	Poorakunnah	Lowarinnakunnah	
Bed (sleeping-place in the bush)	Oortrackeomee	Orragurru wurina	
Bed, ditto	Noonameena	Orragurra nemony	
Before	Mealtetriangule-beah	Prungee	
Behind	Mealtitta lerrentitta	Talina	
Belch (to)	Luonua-kunna	Loona kanna	
Belly	Tree-érina	Lomate	
Big (large)	Teeunna	Papla	
Bill (bird's)	Meunna	Peegra	
Bird	Puggunyenna	Punna	
Bite	Rulkwomma	Rebkarranah	
Bitter	Laiceriack	Poina noily	
Blandfordia nobilis	*None in the district*	Iteminé	
Black	Maback *or* Mabauna	Loaparte	
Blood (my)	Warrgata meena	Coeeah	
Blossom	Malectyé	Nannee purillabenannee	
Blow-fly	Mongana	Monganah	
Blow (with the mouth forcibly)	Loyuné	Loinganah	
Boil (*Furunculus*)	Lieemena	Licematah	
Bosom (woman's)	Parugganna	Parugganah	
Bosom (man's)	Puggamenyera	Parrungyenah *or* Liatimy	
Boy (small child)	Malangyenna	Puggatah paw-awé	
Boy (large child)	Cotty-mellityé	Poilahmaneenah	
Bread	Pannaboo	Pannaboo na	
Bread (give me some)	Tieuna miapé pannaboona	Tieugana má pannaboo	Tunghmbibé tungaringalea
Breast (chest)	Meryanna	Toorinah	
Brook	Manenge-keetanna	Wayatinah	
Broom (a besom)	Perruttyé	Beroieah	
Brother (little)	Nietta mena *or* Nietarrana	Piembucki	
Brother (big)	Puggana tuantittyah	Peegennah	
Brow (forehead)	Rogoona	Roic-runnah	
Brushwood	Weena-keetyenna	Looranah	
Burn (hurt by fire)	Punna meena	Wuggatah	
Bury (to)	Parrawé peanglunta-poo	Pomannencluko	
Buttock	Liengana	Nunnah	
By-and-by	Piyeré	Gunnyem waubberaboo	
Buzz (like a fly; also name of fly)	Mongana	Monganah	
Come along, I want you	Talpyawadyno tuyenacunnamee	Tattawattah onganeena	
Call	Ronnie	Ronnypalpee	
Canoe (catamaran)	Mallanna	Nunganah	Nunghuna
Carcass	Miackbouraek	Micpoiyenah	
Cat (large native)	Luyenna	Luyenna	Lunna *or* Laboibé
Cat (small native)	Pringreenyeh	Lapuggana	Labaggyna *or* Naboineenélé
Catarrh	Teachrymena	Manah	Teachreena

VOCABULARY OF DIALECTS OF ABORIGINAL TRIBES OF TASMANIA.

English.	Tribes from Oyster Bay to Pittwater.	Tribes about Mount Royal, Bruné Island, Recherche Bay, and the South of Tasmania.	North-West and Western.
Catarrh	Teaknonyak	Tekalieny	Tecakunny
Catarrh with dyspnœa	Takkaruttye	Mannah larree	Poorannacallc
Caterpillar (small)	Rianna	Peenga	
Cavern	Liclle wolingana	Poatina	
Caul	Roongreena	Meena or Loarinah	Mena lowallina or Kuttamoileh
Cease (to)	Myeemarah	Parrawé	
Charcoal	Maweena	Loarra	
Chase (to)	Rhinyetto	Lerypoontabee	
Chirrup (to)	Tetyenna	Telita	
Chin	Comnienna	Wahba	
Chine (back-bone)	Myingana-tenena	Turarunna	
Cider from eucalyptus	Way-a-linah	Way-a-linah	
Circle	Lowamachana	Riawnnna	
Claw (talon)	Kurluggana	Kuluggana	
Clay	Pannogana malittyé	Pappalye mallee	
Crazy (cranky)	Tagantyeuna or Muggana puggoonyack	Tannatea	Wayenoeele, or Poietanaté, or Konga tuné, or Kongatuccle
Clean	Pannycaleebna	Mallea	
Climb (to)	Kronyé	Kroanna	
Clutch (to)	Tiackboorack	Tigyola	
Cold	Tunack	Mallané	
Come (to)	Talpeyawadeno	Tutta watta	
Come (to)	Tallya-lea		
Conflux (crowd)	Tirranganna menya	Palabamabbylé	
Conflagration	Kawaloochta	Loiny or Una paroina	
Conversation (a great talking)	Rhincowa mungonagunea pogganakarné	Poyara kunna nuemena	
Conversation, ditto	Karnyalimenya	Karnamoonalané	
Conversation, ditto	Karnalirya	Karnalaré	
Cord (a small rope)	Metakeetana	Mité	
Corpse (a dead carcass)	Myack boorrnck	Moyé or Mungyé	
Correct	Onnyneealeebyé	Nirabe	
Cough	Tachareetya	Mannaladdy	
Coxcomb (a fine-looking fellow)	Puggana tareetya	Pallawah tutty	
Coxcomb, ditto	Puggatimy pena	Pallawahpamary	
Cockatoo, white	Weeanoobryna	'Nghara	
Cockatoo, black	Menuggana	'Nghay rumna	
Crevice or fissure in rocks	Liellowullingana	Riengeena	
Creek	Manenya keetanna	Liapota	
Cross	Ocilupoonia urapoonie	Poiré tungaba	
Crow	Lietenua	Taw wereiny	
Cry (weep)	Naoutagh bourack	Moi-luggata	
Cry (weep)	Tagara toomiack	Tarra toone	
Cut (to)	Lowgoone	Toagarah	
Cape Portland (language)	Tebryeunna		
Creak (from friction of limbs of trees)	Temata kunna	Retakunna	
Dance	Klanna riacunha	Rialangana	
Dark	Taggremapack	Nune meene larraboo	
Daughter	Neantyména	Loggatalé meena	
Daylight	Taggre maranny é	Luggaranialé	
Dead	Mientung bourrack and Merack bourrack	Moyé	
Deaf	Guallengatick guanghata	Wayeebedé	
Deep (water)	Loa maggalangta	Kellatic	
Demon	Mienginya	Ria warrawah noilé	Pawtening-eelylé
Demur (grumble)	Kokoleeny konqua		
Den (of wild animals)	Lienwollingena	Riengena poatina	

VOL. II.   3 G

VOCABULARY OF DIALECTS OF ABORIGINAL TRIBES OF TASMANIA.

English.	Tribes from Oyster Bay to Pittwater.	Tribes about Mount Royal, Brune Island, Recherche Bay, and the South of Tasmania.	North-West and Western.
Depict (draw a design in charcoal)	Macooloona	Pallapoirena	
Deplore (to lament, as at an Irish wake)	Tagrunah kamulug-gana	Moaluggata kannaproie	
Desire (to)	Oonaeragninek	Poykokarra	
Desist (to)	Parrawureigunepa	Parawnree	
Dine (to)	Pooloogoorack	Tuggara nowe	
Dirt (mud of a whitish color)	Panogana maleetya	Mannana mallyé	
Dirt (mud dried)	Pengana rutta	Mannana rullé	
Dirt	Pengana	Mannana	
Dirty	Mawpack	Mawpa	
Displease (to make angry)	Licneghi miawero, or Kukunna poipugge-apa	Poinawallé	
Dispute (to)	Rinnea guanettya	Kanna moonalané	
Distant	Manlumbéra	Kantogganna wébbery	
Dive (to)	Toné lunto	Togana lea-lutah	
Diversion (sport, play)	Leenyallé	Luggara riawé	
Dizzy	Mongtantiack	Nubretanyté	
Dog	Kaceta	Panoiné	
Dove (wild pigeon)	Mongalonerya	Moatah	
Draw (to pull)	Ko-uiopu	Menghana	
Dream	Neacha puggaroamee	Neaggara	
Drink	Lougholee	Nugara	
Drop (water)	Liemkaneack	Mikany	
Drown	Tong bourrak	Tong poyeré	
Drowsy	Tugganémónuinck	Nuccnédy	
Dry	Rongoiulong bourrack	Karnaroide	
Dry	Roungeack		
Duck (gender not distinguished)	Wickennya	Woaroiré	
Dug	Paroogualla	Paruggana	
Dull (stupid dolt)	Koullangtaratta	Poyetannyté	
Dumb	Manemmenéna	Menawély	
Dung (excrement)	Tiamena	Tiena	
Dusk	Knoota	Panubratony	
Dust	Pughrenna		
Dwarf	Wughwerra pacetya	Nuggatapawé	
Dysentery or diarrhœa	Tiaquénnyé	Tiamahbylé	
East Bay Neck	Luecualang'ta	Lucenalaughta	
Eaglehawk Neck	Teeralinnick	Teralinna	
Eagle	Gooalanghta	Weelaty	
Eagle's nest	Licemunetta	Licewughta	
Ear	Mungenna	Wayee	
Early (in the morning at twilight)	Tuggamarannye	Nunawenapoyla	
Earth (mould)	Pengana	Mannena	
Earthquake	Wughyranniack	Munna potrunne	
Earth-worm	Lollah	Lollara	
Eat heartily	Telbetelceben		
Eat (to)	Tughlee	Tughrah	
Eat (to)	Tuggana	Tuggranah	
Echo	Kukanna wurrawina	Kannamyété	
Eel	Lengomenya	Lingowenah	
Effluvia	Mebrene	Polné noilé	
Egg	Liena punna	Pateenah	
Elbow	Wieninnah	Wayeninnah	
Elf or fairy (fond of children and dances in the hills, after the fashion of Scotch fairies)	Naug-inya	Nungheenah or Noilo-wanah	
Eloquent (talkative)	Munkannára walah	Kannamoonalané	
Ember (red hot)	Toneetea	Weealuttah	

VOCABULARY OF DIALECTS OF ABORIGINAL TRIBES OF TASMANIA.

English.	Tribes from Oyster Bay to Pittwater.	Tribes about Mount Royal, Bruné Island, Recherche Bay, and the South of Tasmania.	North-West and Western.
Embowel (to dis-)	Parrawé tiakrangana	Parratibe	
Embrace (Platonic)	Talwattawa, or Rugana wurranaree, or Ramuna relugance	Tallawatta	Moilatené
Emmet (small ant)	Ouyeteita	Lallah	
Emu	Punnamoonta	'Ngunannah	
Encampment	Lena wughta rotaleebana	Line rotali	
Enfeeble (to)	Meingotick	Mungawelé	
Enfeeble (to)	Mienkomyack		
Enough (sufficient)	Miemerémelé	Narramoiewa	
Entrails	Regana tianna or Tiakrangana	Poiné	
Evening	Kaoota	Kawootah	
Exchange	Tientewatera nenté or Tiangtetewemyna	Tayenebé or Tayene nye-lntera	
Excrement	Tianiena	Tiannah	
Expectorate	Teagarea kraganeack	Manna méredé	
Extinguish	Parlieré	Patingnnabé	
Exudation	Wialina, or Wallenah, or Wallamenula	Wialiné	
Exuvia (skin of a snake)	Lierkanapoona or Lierkapoona	Liergrapoinena	
Eye	Mongténa	Nubré or Nubrenah	
Eyebrow	Lyeninua poorinna	Leeininné	
Eyelash	Mongtaliuna	Nubré tongany	
Eyelid	Moygta genua	Nubre wurrine	
Fyry	Malauna meena	Linenah	
Falmouth and George's River	Kunawra kunna		
Face	Niengheta	Noienenah	
Face (fine)	Niengheta elapthatea	Noiena niré	
Facetious	Poigneagana	Pené or Penamabbelé	
Faint	Mongtauiack	Nubretanueté	
Fairy	Murrumbuekannya or Nanginya	Murrumbukannya	
Falsehood	Maneentayana	Laninga noilé	
Fang (canine tooth)	Wugherinna rugotoleebana	Payee rotylé or Coorina	
Far	Tongoomela	Lomawpa	
Far	Lewatenoo or Nangumnera	Tomalah	
Fat	Niennameena	Pangana wayedeé	
Fat man	Poonamena moonta	Pallawah proina	
Fat woman	Nienna langhta	Lowa proina	
Father	Noonalmeena	Nanghabee or Nanghamee	
Feast	Tuggely pettaleebea	Tuggety proibee	
Feather	Puggerinua	Lowinné	
Feces	Tianana	Tianah	
Feeble	Tuggemboonah	'Ngattai	
Feel (to pinch)	Wughanee	Winghanee	
Fern	Lawitta-brutea	Tughanah	
Fern-tree	Nowarracomminea	Lapoinya	
Fetch (to bring)	Kunnywattera	Kanua watta	
Fetch (a spirit)	Preolenna		
Fever	Miempecouiack	Mic luggrata	
Few	Luowa	Potalughyé	
Fiend	Winnya wainettea or Mienginnya	Winneluaghabaru	
Fight	Miamengana	Moymengana	
Filth	Lenymebryé	Line poine noilé	
Fin (of a fish)	Wunlia	Purgha lamarina	
Finger	Ri-ena	Rye-na	Reeleah
Fire	Tonna	'Ngune'	Winnaleah
Fire-tail (bird)	Lyenapontendiah	Lyekah	

Vocabulary of Dialects of Aboriginal Tribes of Tasmania.

English.	Tribes from Oyster Bay to Pittwater.	Tribes about Mount Royal, Brune Island, Recherche Bay, and the South of Tasmania.	North-West and Western.
Fire in the bush grass	Kawurrinna	Lienah	
Firm (not rotten)	Weerutta	Weerullé	
Firmament (sky)	Warratinna	Warrangalé lorunna	
Fish (a)	Mungunna	Peeggana	
Fish (cray)	Nunnya	Nubé	Nubyna
Fist	Ree-trierrena	Ree-mutha	
Five	Pugganna	Marah	
Flambeau	Poorena maneggana	Leewurré	
Flank	Poolomina	Poolumta *and* Tiawalé	
Flay	Relbooce trawmea	Lergara leawarina	
Flea	Lowangerimena	Noné	
Fleet (swift)	Warrangata poonalareetyé	Loongana	
Flesh (meat)	Wiangata	Palamuena	
Fling	Peawé	Pákara	
Flint	Trowutta	Mungara	
Flint (black)		Mora trona	
Float (to)	Lia ruoluttea	Puggata *or* Rannyana	
Flog	Luggana poograué	Lunghana	
Flounder (flat fish)	Lerunna	'Ngupota-metee	
Flow (as water)	Lia tariglitea	Lia teruttena	
Fleece (or fur of animals)	Poocerinna	Longwinny	
Fly (like a bird)	Koomela	Coaggara	
Fly (insect)	Mongana	Monga	
Foam (froth)	Kukamena-mena	Lia láratame	
Fog	Mainentayana	Warratie	Pulangalé
Foolish (or fool)	Mungana paonyack	Noilee	Lonneeaté
Foot	Luggana	Lugganah	Lugh
Foot, right	Luggana eleebana	Lugga worina	Malleearé
Foot, left	Luggana acota	Lugga oangta	Oolatyneealé
Footmark of black man	Puggalugganna	Pallowa lugganah	Pah lug
Footmark of white man	Ria luggana	Reea lugganah	Matyena lugh
Ford of a river	Teeatta kannawa	Penghana	
Forehead	Raoonah *or* Rogounim lienya	Roee rocerunna	Rioona
Forest ground	Teeatta kanna marranah	Wayraparattee	Pallanyneené
Forget	Poeenabah	Wannabayoocrack	Lyluneragoo
Four	Paguntu	Wuliyawa	
Fragrant (smell)	Noya leebana	Poiné niré	Polimganoanaté
Freestone	Boatta *or* Potha malleetyé	Potta mallya	Poningalee
Fresh water	Liena eleebana	Liéniré	Lié nonghaté
Friend	Kaeetagooanamenah	Lapoile lu nagreenah moolanah	Mateté loguattame
Frigid (cold)	Tunnack	Mallané	Ptunarra
Fright	Tian-cottiack	Tianawilly	Micumoolaka
Frog	Rallah	Tattounepuyna	Lora
Frost	Parattah	Oorattai	Oolrah
Frost, hoar	Parattiana	Oorattai	
Fuel	Wielurena	Oocena *or* Winna	Ooee
Full (after a meal)	Riawaeeack	Ma teelaty	Mapilriagunara
Full (a vessel filled)	Rueeleetipla	Kanna	Yeackanara
Fun (sport)	Riawena	Luggara	Riawé
Fundament	Leieena	Loié loiningé	
Fur of animals	Pooarenna	Longwinny	Waggelé
Fury	Leenangunnyé *or* Koananietya	Liapooneranh	Neenubrulatai
Gale	Ralanghta	Rallana proiena	Loweeny rulloi leah *or* Loweeny loileah
Gape	Grannacunna	Granna canaibee	'Ngana kankapea oolralaheah capueeleah
Ghost	Wurrawana	Riawarawapah	Teeananga winné
Girl	Lowana keetanna *or* Kottomalletye	Longatylé	Noamoloibee

VOCABULARY.

Vocabulary of Dialects of Aboriginal Tribes of Tasmania.

English.	Tribes from Oyster Bay to Pittwater.	Tribes about Mount Royal, Bruné Island, Recherche Bay, and the South of Tasmania.	North-West and Western.
Glutton	Lemyonterittya	Pamoonalantutte	Tuggattapecatto
Good person	Kckanna clangoonya	Nirree	Kanna noaugaté
Go	Tawé	Tawkwábee	Tawé
Goods (things)	Noona meena	Ooraimabilé	Noonamoy
Goose (wild)	Weicnterootya	None	None
Gosling	Kaceta boena		
Grandmother	Lowan kareimena	Ooaimena or Wyemena	Neenambee
Grass	Rouninna	Nemoné	Probluah
Great-bellied (with child)	Lowallaomnena	Puggata lowatta lutta	Lomalleé
Green	Norabeetya	Nobeetya mallya	Mallabeabu
Greeting (a)	Yah! tahwattywa!	Yah! nun'oyné!	Yah!
Grin (to make faces)	Monapaooniack paorectye	Moyetuugali	Boabenneetea
Grinder (back tooth)	Wuggarinna ryana	Payelughana	Yennaloigh
Gristle	Comyenna	Wéyalé	Péngai
Groin	Mungalarrinna	Tramina	Tarrané
Ground	Pyengana	Manuina	Nattie
Grow (as a tree, child)	Myallanga bourack	Mangapoieré	Mallacka
Growl	Nannéaquanhe	Nunnaquannapeiere	Dyekka nameenera
Grub	Menia or Mungwenya	Larraminnia	Langwé
Gull	Lueeteianna	Lieppetah	Payugh
Gulp (to)	Tongwanma	Tongané	Tonnabea
Gum (wattle-tree)	Munganna	Reeatta	Reeattawee
Gum-tree (eucalyptus)	Lottah	Moonah	Loyké
Gums (of the mouth)	'Ngenna	Carena	Kattamoy
Gun (musket)	Leryna or Le langta	Pawleena	Rullé
Gunpowder	Lerytiana	Pawleenatiana	Lughtoy
Glow-worm or phosphorescence	Pugganga lewa or Munghtamena	Payaleena	
Hen (native)	Mienteroonyé	Riacooné	Recakallingalle
Hold your tongue, be patient, by-and-by	My-elbeerkanima or Mealkammah	Kanna moona lané mentakuntiby or Konnyab	Wannabee or Kannebo
Hail	Pratteratta	Turéhai	
Hair	Poinglyenna	Poieté longwinne	
Hair (matted with ochre)	Poinghana	Poina	
Halo (round the moon)	Weetaboona	Panoggata	
Halt (limp on leg)	Ungunniack	'Nganee	
Ham or hough	Pryenna	Tabba	
Hamstring (the)	Metta	Tapmita	
Hand	Riena	Reemutta	
Harlot	Pugganatingana or Menoternityc	Patingana	
Hastily (quickly)	Lemya or Tnggana	Cothé	
Hawk	Nierrina	Peugana	
Head	Oolumpta	Poieté	
Headache	Oongena liack	Poieté merede and Poingata	
Heal	Raick hourrack	Niré	
Heap (to make)	Prolmy nunty mente	Tecaté	
Hear (to)	Toieuook boorack	Wáyee	
Heart	Teeaekana warrana	Teggana	
Heat	Peooniac	Lughrah	
Heave (to pant)	Tengoonyack	Teggalughrata	
Heavy	Miemooatiek	Moorah	
Heel	Tokana or Toggana	Tokana	
Help	Nelunie	Lagrah	
Hide (to conceal kangaroo)	Lyeemena kamei	Muggrah	
Hide one's self	Mur kamiah	Muggrah	
Hill (little one)	Poimena	Layeté paawé	
Hill (mountain)	Poimena tyenkanganarrah Tienare warrah	Layeté proigh	
Hit	Menny	Merrhé	
Hither and thither	Pughawee nyawee	Tackra, tungalé, tungalé	

VOCABULARY OF DIALECTS OF ABORIGINAL TRIBES OF TASMANIA.

English.	Tribes from Oyster Bay to Pittwater.	Tribes about Mount Royal, Brune Island, Recherche Bay, and the South of Tasmania.	North-West and Western.
Hoar-frost	Tyeebertia crackana	Warattai	
Hoarse	Lonypeack	Lonnabeeadé	
Hole (like wombat burrow)	Lowa lengana	'Ngeanali	
Hot	Peooniack	Lughrata	
House	Lenna	Line	
Howl (in distress, like a dog)	Tuggermacarna or Myluggana	Cockata	
Humid (wet, damp)	Mallecack	Layekah	
Hunger	Mecoongyneack	Teccotte	
Husband	Puggan neena	Pah-neena	
Hurt (with spear)	Mayance rayerec	Roaddah	
Hurt (with waddy)	Payalee	Loipuné	
Ice	Paratta	Rullai ungaratine	Ralloileah
Ill (sick)	Crackannaceack	Mérédé and Merydyneh	Managauurrah
Imp	Winya waumetya	Ria warappé noilé	
Impatient	Telwangatea leah	Kannamoonalanné	
Inactive (indolent)	Meallee tonerragetta	Rannah moorinah	
Indolent (lazy)	Mimooneka nentaca nepoony	Rannah moorinah	
Infant	Malangenna	Puggetta	
Infant (female)		Lowa luggeta	
Infant (newly born)	Cotruoluttye	Poggata riale	Lapoitale or Lapoittendaylé
Inform (to tell)	Oana	Oanganah	
Inform (tell me)	Oana mia	Ongana meena	
Instant (quick)	Krottee	Koatté	
Instep	Lugga poola mena	Lugga umené	
Intimidate	Tieneootyé	Tienwealé	
Intersect	Unginnapuee	Poany pueré	
Intestines	Tiaerakena	Lomatina	
Invigorate	Neingtera teroontee		
Jaw-bone	Yangena	Wahba and Wabranna	Ninenna leah
Jealous	Pachabrea-longhe	Mahrewealai and Poinéwealai	
Jerk	Co-ule	Cokura	
Juice of a plant, red	Miangatentyé	Miengaleena	
Juice of a plant, white	Tuggara maleetyé	Taramena	
Jump	Wughallee	Warrakara	
Juvenile	Croatta meleetyé		
Keep	Tialapué	Tiagarra	
Kill (deprive of life)	Mienémiento	Lungana	
Kiss (to)	Miewallé	Moce miré	
Knee	Mienna	Ranga	Rawinna leah
Kneel	Meallé mianaberré	Leetarangah	Wannabya raminnaerybee
Knuckle	Reekateninna	Ria puggana	Releenula leah
Kangaroo, brush	Lyenna	Lena	Kn leah
Kangaroo, joie	Tumnanna	Rartyna	Piaclummé
Kangaroo	Nawittyé	Tarra na	Tarra leah
Lad	Puggannaereebana	Pa-ga-talina	
Lake (lagoon)	Miena, mena	Lia mena	
Lame	Playwarruugana	Luggamutte or Raggamuttah	
Lance (wooden spear)	Perenna	Pena	
Large (big)	Pawpela	Proina nughabah	
Last (to walk last in file)	Loente wannela	Mituggara murawamena	
Laugh	Poeenyeggana	Pœnghana	Peninna
Lax (diarrhœa)	Tiacroinnamena	Tia noileh	
Lazy (see Indolent)	Mienoyack	Ruété	Rudanah
Leaf	Poruttyé	Proié	Parocheboina
Leafless	Poruttye-mayeck and Paruye-noye-maeck	Paroytimena	Purochyateemua
Lean	Tughenapoonyac	'Ngattai	'Ngatta

VOCABULARY. 423

VOCABULARY OF DIALECTS OF ABORIGINAL TRIBES OF TASMANIA.

English.	Tribes from Oyster Bay to Pittwater.	Tribes about Mount Royal, Brune Island, Recherche Bay, and the South of Tasmania.	North-West and Western.
Leap (see Jump)	Waighalleh	Wurragara	
Leech	Pyenna	Pangah	Liawena
Left hand	Riena-aoota	'Ngotta	Oottamutta
Leg, left	Leoonyaua	Luggunagoota	Luggrangootta
Leg, right	Leoonya eleebana	Warrina niré	Luggra-niré
Lick (with the tongue)	Neungulee	Nugra mainre	
Light of a fire	Tonna kayinna	—	Unamayna
Lightning	Poimettyé	Poimataleena	Rayeepoineé
Limp (see lame) right foot	Wughuna eleebana		
Limp, ditto, left foot	Playwughreua	Raggamuttah	
Load	Mangeluhwa	Munghe mabbely	
Lobster (fresh-water)	Tayatea	Tay-a-teh	
Log (wood)	Wyee langhta	Weea proingha	
Long	Rogoteleebaua	Rotuli	
Look (to gaze)	Reliquamma	Lutubrenemé	
Loud (to speak)	Kuggana langhta	Kanné proine waggaba	
Low	Lunta	Pranako	
Lie (falsehood)	Manengtyangha - Tyangamonceny rapparé	Linughé noilé	
Locust (V.D.L.)	Ganammenyé	Ganemmanga	Rowé leah
Long way	Murramanattya onamarumpto	Noina muttaina	
Maria Island	Tiarra marra monah	Tiarerrymeealonah	
Magpie	Poierrynienna	Reninna	Curraillylé
Maim	Mennanwee		
Man (black)	Pugganna	Pallawah	Pah-leah
Marrow	Moomelinah	Lebrana	
Me	Mina	Meenah	
Menstruate	Teebra wanghatamena		
Midday (or noon)	Tooggy malangta	Toina wunna	
Milk (of Aboriginal woman)	Proogwallah	Prooga ueannah	
Milt (of fish)	Lowalinnamelah	Perina	
Mirth	Leenealé	Penamoonalane	
Mischief	Puoynoback	Tannate	
Moon	Wiggetena	Weetah	Weenah leah
Moonlight	Wiggetapoona	Weetapoona	Weenapooleah
Moss	Lagowuunah		
Mother	Neingmenna	Neeminah	Neena moygh
Moth	Commeneana		
Mouse	Terangaté munuggana	Pugganarottah	Ptoarah leah
Mouth	Kakaunina	Kaneinah	Kapoughy leah
Mud (sediment)	Kokerea kokeleetyé	Manannywayleh	
Murmur	Mannyaquanee	Kanaroiluggata	
Mushroom	Neatyranna	Neúrana	
Mole-cricket	Nawywemena		
Mutton-bird (sooty petrel)	Yolla	Yolla	
Mutton-fish (smooth)	Magrannyah		
Mutton-fish (rough)	Yowarrenah		
Mount Royal (country intervening between there and Port Cygnet)	—	Tuluné	
Nail (finger)	Tonye	Ryeetonyé	Waute leah
Nail (toe)	Peyerrena	Lugga-tonnyé	Perrarunne
Navel	Mienanuggana	Tunoh	
Near	Malumnyella	Réné	
Nautilus shell (argonaut)	Wietatenana	Weettah	Weena runnah
Nettle	Miatowunnameena	Miny	
Nest (bird's)	Malunna	Liné	
Nest (little bird's)	—	Puné liné	
Never	Noye myack or Noceaek	Timeh or Timy	
New (not old)	Croatte	Bollé	
Night	Tagrummena	Nuné	Dayna leah
Nip (to pinch)	Reloyé tonyeré	Redeekatah	

VOCABULARY OF DIALECTS OF ABORIGINAL TRIBES OF TASMANIA.

English.	Tribes from Oyster Bay to Pittwater.	Tribes about Mount Royal, Brune Island, Recherche Bay, and the South of Tasmania.	North-West and Western.
Nipple	Prugga poycenta	Pruggapogenna	
No	Parra garah	Timch or Timy or Pothyack	Mallya leah
Noise	Kukanna wallamonyack	Kanna	
Nose	Mununa	Muye or Muggenah	Muanoigh
Now (at this time)	Croattee		
Ochre, red	Ballawiné	Ballawiné	
One	Marrawah	Marrawah	
Orphan	Kollyenna	Wah-wittch	
Outside	Tulenteena	Pratty-toh	
Owl (large)	Tryeenna	Kokatah	Tayaleah
Owl (little one)	Laoona	Wawtronyte	Kokannaleah
High land behind Oyster Bay	Pottry munatta		
Opossum (black)	Nualangtamabbena	Tonytah	Temytah temyta malughlee
Opossum (ring-tail)	Tarripnyenna	Pawtella	Pawtellunna nuckelah
Opossum (mouse)	Lowowyenna	Leena	Paponolearah
Ore of Iron, Iron Glance (used by the Aborigines as a black paint)	Latta	Lattawinné	
Pain	Crackanyeack	Mayrude	
Palm of the hand	Rielowolingana	Reea-rarra	
Parrot	Cruggana	Cruddah	
Paroquet	Welleetya	Wellya	
Paw	Luggantereeua	Togga-né	
Peak (St. Valentine's)			Natone
Peak (a hill)	Poymalangta	Letteené	
Pelican	Treooutalangta	Toyné	
Penguin	Tomenyenna	Tong-wynne	
Perspire	Regleetya	Laywurroy	
Pet (pettish)	Lowabereelonga	Poyneh	
Pigeon	Mooaloonya	Mootah	
Place (a)	Lenna	Linch	
This place		Liné poynena	
Plant	Mellangbourack		
Play	Lyanclé	Luggarrah	
Point of spear	Poycenta	Poyeenna	
Pool or lagoon	Mienameena	Kannah	
Porcupine	Mungyenna	Mungyé	Mungynna kanagale
Porpoise	Minga-oinyah	Poyrennah	
Pregnant	Lowalloomanyenea	Lomatilutta	
Prickly	Mona-meenee	Moynéna	
Punk	Wullugbetye	Rarra	
Pebble rolled quartz	Kughaweenya	Tramutta	
Piper's River district	Oramakunna	Oramakanna	
Port Davey		Poinduc	
Penis	Lubra, Mattahprenna	Leena	
Pubes (mons veneris)	Maga	Magana	
Quaff (drink)	Lowelly	Nugarah	
Quail	Terranguatta	Téna terrangutta	Tena teewarrah
Run together (race)	Réné uunempté	Loongana	
Rage	Neoongyack	Leecoté	
Rain	Pokana or Pogana	Porrah	
Rain (heavy)	Progga-langhta	Porra	
Rainbow	Weeytena	Wayatih	
Rascal	Nowettye-cleebana	Pawee	
Rat	Lyingauena	Tooarrana	
Ray (stingaree)	Leranna	Piremé	
Red	Tendyagh or Tentya	Koka	
Repair	Trulee	Peruggarch	
Respire	Tynckanoyack	Taykalyngana	
Retch (to vomit)	Nutyack	Nukatah	

VOCABULARY OF DIALECTS OF ABORIGINAL TRIBES OF TASMANIA.

English.	Tribes from Oyster Bay to Pittwater.	Tribes about Mount Royal, Bruné Island, Recherche Bay, and the South of Tasmania.	North-West and Western.
Rib	Tolameena	Tené	
Rise	Takumuna	Peggaruggarua	
Ripe	Crang-boorack	Pegarah	
Root (tree)	Remeenyé	Monalghana or Pughweady	
River (little)	Menace keetannah	Lia-pootah	
Rock (large)	Lonah or Loelaughta	Loynce broyee	
Rod (small)	Weenah keetannah	Weea pawee	
Roll (to)	-	Wangana weepootah	
Roe (of fish)	Leena bunna		
Rotten wood	Tréoratick	Tawnah	
Rough	Payralyack	Rullé	
Round like a ball	Micawinck	Mattah	
Row (a long one)	Raoudeleeboa	Reekara	
Rub (rub in fat)	Mungaunemoce	Ruggarra	
Ruddy cheeks	Miypooetanyack	Koka	
Ruddy cheeks	Mientendyack		
Run	René	Legara	
Rush	-	Roba	
Ringlets (corkscrews, with red-ochre)	Pow-ing-arootelee-bana	Poeena	Poenghana
Sexual intercourse	Loanga metea or Poanga metea		
Sea-horse (*Hippocampus*)	Lay-ao-unea	Poolta	
Salt on the rocks by the sea-side	Lienowittye		
Salt on the rocks by the sea-side	Liopackanapoona		
Sand	Mungara mena	'Nguna	
Sap	Miangatentya		
Sap	Miangmallcetya		
Sap (milk-white)	Poor-wallena		
Scab	Loryomena or Loiamena	Lowidé	
Scales (of fish)	Poerinna	Lowinna	Nangennamoi
Scar	Trugatepoona	Mungerapoona	Toolengennaleah
Scarify	Lowooné	Towatté	
Scent	Mebryack	Poanoilé	
Scratch	Larré	Larré	
Sea (ocean)	Lienna wuttya and Lyaleetea	Pananuna	Leah lé
Seal (*Phoca*), black on sandy beach	Naweetya	Wayanna, *white belly*	
Seal, black on rocks, white-bellied	Pienrenya		
Seal, sandy beach	Prematagomoneetya		
See (to behold)	Mongtone	Nubratoné	
Serious (sad gaze)	Lelgaoy-guonga	Manatta rulla	
Serpent	Loiena or Lounabe	Loina	Rau-anah
Shallow	Waylearack	Roheté	
Shadow	Wurrawina tietta	Maydena	Belanyleah
Sharp (like a knife)	Lyetta	Nenah	
She-oak tree	Luggana-brenna	Luh-be	
Skin	Lurentanena	Lurarunna	
Ship	Lotomalangta loomena	Luné poina makkaba	Loallybé
Shore	Malompto	Loccota	
Shore (sandy beach)	Koynaratingana		
Go ashore	-	Tawé loccoto	
Shoulder	Puggarenna	Parangana	
Shout (yell)	Kukanna wurrarenna	Palla-kanna	
Shower (of rain)	Pokanna kuanna	Tungatinah	
Shrub	Tarra coonce	Tarrara manné	
Sick	Micrackanyach	Miméredé	
Sick	Miycracknatareetya		
Side (the)	Lieteliuna	Taynna	

VOL. II.   3 H

VOCABULARY OF DIALECTS OF ABORIGINAL TRIBES OF TASMANIA.

English.	Tribes from Oyster Bay to Pittwater.	Tribes about Mount Royal, Bruné Island, Recherche Bay, and the South of Tasmania.	North-West and Western.
Sinew (kangaroo)	Metah (met-ah)	Mitah	
Sing	Lyenny	Lyenné	
Shag (cormorant)	Moora	Moora	
Sing a song	Lyenny riacunna		
Sink	Tomla, Tome, Boorcka		
Sit down	Mealpugha		
Sister	Nowantareena		
Skin	Tarra meenya		
Skull	Pruggamoogena		
Sleep	Lony		
Smile	Pughoncoree		
Smoke	Progoona or Prooana		
Sneeze	Lonughutta		
Smooth	Panninya		
Snore	Teakanarra loneah	Roggara	
Snake	Loiena	Loinah	Rounna rawannah pallawa royanah roallabcah
Snow	Parattianah	Turrana	
Snow	Paratta		
Sole (of foot)	Lug-yenna	Lugga-lunnah	
Song	Riacunnah	Lunariabe	Riacannah
Soon	Leenya	Kothé	
Son	Malangena	Puggatah	
Sour	No-wiyack	Noile	
Spark	Tonypeprinna	Powitté	Pughweenyna weimyale
Spawn	Manunghana	Manungana	
Spear (wood)	Perenna	Pe-na	Pana, Pilhah
Spew	Nuka	Nukara	Nugryna
Speak	Pucellakanny	Poeerakunnabeh	Pooracannaby
Spider	Tangana	Waytauga	
Spine	Myingeena terrena	Tuherarunnah	
Spit	Tynckaree-meena	Kamena meena	Kaimonamoce
Sport (play)	Riawena	Riawé	Riawé wayboree
Spring (wattle blossom season)	Pewenya poeena	Luggarato pawé	Lughra-pawee
Squall	Ralangta	Rallana proce	Raali poyngnah
Stamp (with the foot)	Taoonteckapé	Taoonteckapé	
Stand (stand up)	Tackamuna	Cracka-wughata	Pegretty wergho
Starlight	Teahbertyacrackna	Oarattih	
Shooting star	Puggarectya	Paeharcah	
Star	Teahbrana	Romtenah	Rhomdunna or Miabeemenah
Steal	Maneena langatick	Maneena layawé	
Step	Luggana marah	Luggacanna	
Stomach	Teenah	Teena	Teenah
Stone	Loantennina	Loinah, Lonna	Loiné
Stoop	Puggana narratyack	Puggana narrangabé	
Stop	Poyeeré	Kuneeamé	
Straight	Ungoyeleebana	Tunghabé	
Strike	Luggana golumpté	Lunghana	
Strong	Oyngteratta	Rulla rullanah	Ramanarralé
Stump (of a tree)	Pomya kunnah	Ortawenah	Weealynghana
Stupid	Koallangatick	Oyelarraboo	Wayeelarraboo or Puggytemoorah
Sun	Pugganoobra nah pukkanehrenah	Pallanubra nah	Panubrynah, Tonah leah
Suck	Molé	Mokrá prugh	
Sullen	Lowattobeolo kakannecté monna perinua lowaperee longha	Poininna	
Summer	Wingytellangta	Lughoratoh	
Sunrise	Puggalena parrack boorack	Panuboine rocelapoerack	

VOCABULARY. 427

Vocabulary of Dialects of Aboriginal Tribes of Tasmania.

English.	Tribes from Oyster Bay to Pittwater.	Tribes about Mount Royal, Bruné Island, Recherche Bay, and the South of Tasmania.	North-West and Western.
Sunset	Wictytongmena	Panubra tongoiccrali	
Suspiration (sigh)	Teangonyack	Takoné	
Survivor	Lugga pocrannca		
Swallow (a bird)	Waylelinna	Papalawe	
Swallow (act of deglutition)	Tony quamma	Touganah	
Swan	Kélangunya	Pugherittah	
Sweat	Mallecack reglcetya reglec poona	Leghrouina	
Swell	Licnyack	Linch	
Swim	Poggely	Pughrah	
Switch	Tarra koona	Tarraweenah	
Tail	Manna poonce	Pugghnah	
Take	Nunné	Nunnabch	
Talk	Pueelcanny	Poieta kaunabch	
Tall	Takkaro delecabano righ elcebana	Rotulih	
Talon	Kuluggana	Kuhluggana	
Tame	Riaputheggana	Tiagropoiuccna	
Tarantula (large spider)	Ne-ungalangta	Temmatah	
Taste	Wnghné	Weené	
Teal	Ryennatiabrootca	Weahwanghrutah	
Tear	Tagarrena	Tarragatté	
Teat		Pruggana	
Teeth	Wugherrinna		
Thirsty	Rukannaroouyack	Kukannaroiteé	
Throw	Myengy	Menghana	
Thumb	Rianaoonta	Ryanaootta	
Thumb-nail	Tonyé	Toiena	
Thunder	Poincttya	Papatonguné	
Tick	Loangaritea	Prammanah	
Tie (a knot)	Kukannabocc	Pilangootah	
Tide	Luggatick	Lughruttah	
Tiger (V.D.L.) (Thylacinas cynocephalus)	Laguuta	Ka-nunnah	
Timber (large)	Wyelangta	Wee a proinah	
Timber (small)	Wyena	We'rapawé	
Tired	Pryennemkoottiack	Kakara wayalee	
Three	Lea winnawah	Talleh	
Toothless	Wugherinna normyak	Payeatimy	
Tooth	Wughrinna	Pay-ee-a	
Talk (much speaking)	Mealpeal kamma or Kukannah liéreah	Kukanna moonalane, or Kunrare, or Kunmoonera	
Tongue	Kayeuu	Menné, or Mayna, or Maynerinah	
Top	Tulendeeno	Waghata	
Topaz (crystal)	Tendeagh	Mughra mallee	
Tor (a peaked hill)	Poymalyetta	Layatinnah	
Torch	Poorena moneggana	Lee wurrá	
Touch	Neungpa	Winganah	
Touch-wood (rotten wood)	Weitree ouriatta	Weeawanghratta	
Tough	Lughteeac	Rnlli	
Track (foot-mark)	Puggataghana and Tughanaloumeno	Luggaboiné	
Trample (to)	Tyentinh	Tecantibe	
Transfix (to)	Myenny-pingater-reluteo	Menaoitete	
Travel	Tackamoona	Tackramoonina	
Tree	Loatta		
Tree (fall of a)	Poenghoorack	Moona punganæ	
Tremble	Mienintyae	Tienéwelch	
Trickle	Kukkamena meena	Truggara	
True	Gonyncealeehya	'Nghana kanna niré	
Try (to)	Wughneé	Weené	

VOCABULARY OF DIALECTS OF ABORIGINAL TRIBES OF TASMANIA.

English.	Tribes from Oyster Bay to Pittwater.	Tribes about Mount Royal, Brune Island, Recherche Bay, and the South of Tasmania.	North-West and Western.
Tug (to, at a rope or string)	Koyule	Kottubé	
Tumble	Mientongka	Mieparragana	
Turn (to)	Wughannamee	Miewangana	
Tusk (canine tooth)	Wuggerinna rotaleebana	Payee, á rotylé	
Twig	Loatta keetana	Weea wunna	
Twins	Muiynabkeek	Meinna-na	
Twilight	Teggrymony keetana narra longboorack	Nuuto neenah	
Twirl (twist)	Wughannemoe	Oaghra	
Twitch (pluck)	Kolé	Ko-kra	
Two	Pia wah	Pooalih	
Ugly	Nowatty nieleebana	Noailee nnggabah	
Urine	Mungana	Munghate mungbabeh	
Uxorions	Lowa puggelannye		
Vale or valley	Ma-ra cominya	Mara-way-lee	
Vanish	Poyena potattyack	Tiembugh	
Vassal (serf)	Puectoggana mena	Potaigroee narana	
Venomous	Ree puaneré nunghapa	Nunghboorack nnngabah	
Venom	Mana mena	Kamona moina	
Vent	Loa lingana	'Ngeenah	
Vertex	Togance	Togari	
Warratah (plant, *Telopea truncata*)	Kinntah		
Wallabee	Lukangana	Taranna	Noguoyleah
Warm even to perspiration	Reggooleetya	Lewurra moina	
Water (fresh)	Liena	Liawence	Lia winne *and* Lileah
Water (cold)	Lietinna	Liawence	
Water (warm)	Liena peoonya *or* Liena peeonyack	Lialughrana	
Wood (firewood)	Wiena *and* Winna	Muggrawebé *and* Mattawebé	
Woman	Lowanna	Ne-eanta *and* Lowanna	Nowaleah
Woman (handsome)	Loanna eleebana *and* Loa niry	Loa-niré lyadywaiack	
Woman (young)	Krotto meleetyé	Loalla puggana	
Woman (adult)	Puggya malleetya	Longatallinah	
Woman (aged, old)	Payanna	Nena ta poiena	
Wombat	Raoompta rowoomata	Rowitta	
Wake	Lientiack	Weeny	
Wale	Woimenniac	Mowerrenah	
Wail (to lament)	Tegryma kannnnya	Mocluggrana	
Waist	Pooalminna	Pooaryumena	
Wait	Myelpoyeré	Krattabé	
Walk	Tahlyooneré	Lawtaboorana	
War	Kennamoimenya	Moi mengan mabeli	
War (skirmish, one or two killed)	Marana	Mocemutté	
War (battle, all killed but one or two)	Moeelughawa	Mocemabbylé	
Warm	Peoonyack	Lughreto	
Wart	Créman poona	Ta winné	
Wash (to)	Nonelmoi	Mannugra	
Wattle-tree	'Nghearetta	Manna	
Wave	Legleetya mengyna	Leaturi	
Weak	Koomyenna	Mia wayleh	
Weed	Pannabon bruttyé	Tallaratai	
Weep	Tagarramena	Tarra wayleh	
Well (spring)	Loy-ulena	'Ngyena	
Wet (rainy)	May-niack	Lay-ka	
What?	Telingha? Tebya?	Pallawaleh?	Tarraginna?
What's that?	Telingha?		
When and where?	Namelah nayeleh?	Wabbara?	

VOCABULARY.

Vocabulary of Dialects of Aboriginal Tribes of Tasmania.

English.	Tribes from Oyster Bay to Pittwater.	Tribes about Mount Royal, Bruné Island, Recherche Bay, and the South of Tasmania.	North-West and Western.
Whisper	Kukana punyepara	Poeta kanna pawaybah	
Whistle	Purra kunna	Munnakanna	Plubeah
White	Malleetyé	Mallee	Mungyanghgarrah
Whiz (like a ball, &c.)	'Ngona kunna	Payngunnana or Poyngunna kunna	Nangoinuleah
Whore, fornicatrix		Pannbré mabbylé	
Widow	Wurrawa noattyé, Wurrawa lowanna	Nena tura tena	
Wife (newly married)	Kroatla langunya	Poya lanuné	Waggapoonynurrah
Wind	Rawlinna	Rallinganunné	Lewan
Wind (high)	Raalanghta	Rallinga proiena	Lewanhock
Windpipe	Lonna	Lonna and Loarinna	
Wing	Poilinna	Maykana poungbra	
Wink	Mentroiack	Nubra rotté	
Winter	Tunna	Turra	
Wrinkle	Niangté nepoony	Pelanypoonch	
Wrong	Miengana	Nuyeko	
Wrist	Rapoolmena	Riapoolumpta	
Woe's me! ah me!	Paygra wayleabeh kum leah!	Taqueaté!	
Yawn	Granna kunna	Leakanny	
Yes	Murramoona, Narrawallee	Narra warrah, Narraway narra luawah	Narro barro
Yesterday	Nentegga menyena	Neca numnawa	
You	Neena	Neena or Nee	
Young (little) boy	Kacetenna mallang yenna	Puggata paweena	
Young (little) girl	Lowauna kacetenna		

Short Sentences in the Native Language.

Give me a stone	Lona or Loina tyennabeah mito.
Give him a stone	Lonna tyennamibeah.
I give you some water	Lina tyennamibeah.
I will not give you any water	Noia meahteang meena neeto linah.
You give me food	Tyennabeah tuggené.
You do not give me food	Noia meah teang meena neeto tuggené.
Give me some bread	Tyeuna miapé pannaboona, or Teenganana ma pannaboo, or Tunghmbibé tungaringaleah.
We will give you a stick	Tyennamibeah weena.
We will not give you a stick	Noia tyennamibeah weena.
Give me some bread to eat, I am hungry	Teeanymiape tuggané, Meeongyneeomé, or Teeanymeiape teeneottym'na, or Teeanupiapé matugluala mapilreeottai.
This is my hand	Reena narrawa.
Sing a song	Lyenné riakunna or Rialinghana.
Where is your father?	Ungamlea nangéena?
My father is here	Nangamea numbé.
He is my father	Nangamea numbé.
He is not my father	Miangunana.
Tell your father of this	Onnabea nangato.
We go to see the river	Nialoiniah nanaiah.
I like to drink the water	Monna langarrapé.
I make the boat go fast	Parapetaleeben malanna talea warrangaté.

English	Tasmanian
The ship goes upon the sea	Tiretya tecakalummala.
The waves make the sea rough	Leea leetyah poinummeah.
You see the sea over the hill	Roogoomalé linoiyack.
Go down from the hill	Rongtané tyungerawa.
Run over the ground	Ringápyanganaweberé.
Do not run along the road	Parrawé ringapé.
The man feeds the dog	Tyénnabeah kaeetabeah.
The woman makes a basket	Lowanna ollé tubbrana.
The woman is very fair	Lowa maleetya.
The child eats his food	Teeana malangeebeah.
The child is small	Malangeebeah.
The horse runs on the ground	Pangooneah réne pateleeben.
The horse kicks the child	Pangooneah paraingumenah.
One	Marrawah.
Two	Piawah.
Three	Luwah.
Four	Paguntawulliawah.
Five	Pugganna marah.
I shall go to my house	Tugganna lunameatah.
I strike the horse	Pella pangooneah.
Touch his hand	Rientonnabeah.
Do not touch his hand	Tallé-tallé parrawé.
Cut down the tree	Ungana puyé loté.
Tell him to go to the house	Tallé lenutoo.
Speak to the man	Oonah beah.
He is in the house	Lunaretah.
They jump over the river	Wuggala menayé.
They walk through the river	Yangé menayé.
Run along the side of the river	Tawé ranté weberé.
They swim in the river	Puawé menayé.
They sink in the river	Tongé menayé.
We drink water	Loa liyé.
He cuts his hair with flint	Tuggana pugheranymee trautta.
My brother has a long arm	Nietta mena oon root' cleebana.
My sister is very tall	Nienta mena tuggara root' cleebana.
He has two children	Malang-piawah.
Take a stick and beat the dog	Tial wee pella kaeeta.
The dog is beaten with a stick	Pella kaeetah naootamena.
The sun is rising	Puggulcéna paréebara.
The sun is set already	Puggulcéna toomla pawa.
The moon is risen	Ooeeta poona.
The moon is not seen	Ooeeta mayangti byeack.
The moon is behind the cloud	Ooeeta toggana warratena lunta.
You stand behind the tree	Maugana lutena.
They climb up the tree	Crongé lotta.
The swan swims in the water	Kalungunya tagumena liyetitta.
The water is very warm	Lia pyoonyack lé !
The water is not warm	Lia tunnack.
Salt water	Lia noattye.
Fresh water	Lian cleebana, or Liana cleebana.
He is a good man	Puggana tareetyé.
He is a bad man	Tagantyaryack.
Come and drink the water	T'allé le loolaka lia.
This water is salt	Lia noattyé.
That water is fresh	Liana cleebana.
Milk comes from the cow	Prughwullah packalla.
Send him to get milk	Rangé prughwullah.
I saw the tree yesterday	Lotta monté meena cotté.

VOCABULARY. 431

I have cut my finger	Rié poyé pueningyack.
He limps with one leg	Raggamuttah.
He sees with one eye	Tagguonah.
My face is very black	Raoonah mawpack.
Make the horse run fast	Pangoonya rené wurrangaté.
When the warm weather is come	Nente pyoonta.
It is now cold weather	Tunna.
They are white men (the men are white)	Riana. Rianowittyé.
This woman is very white	Lowana elecbana.
Bring him and put him down here	Nunnalea pooranamby, or Kannawattah ponnawé, or Kannawuttah ponnapoo.
Come along, I want to speak to you	Talpyarwadeno tuyena kunnamee, or Tutta wuttah onganeenah, or Tunneka makunna talmatieraleh.
Aha! you are sulky all of a sudden	Anyah! teborah! keetrelbya noomena peniggomaree.
Hold your tongue, or be patient, by-and-by	Mealkamma, or Metakantibe, or Kannyah mielbeerkammah, or Kanna moonalané wannabee kannybo.
Come here	Tia neberé or Tialleh.
Walk naked	Tia reea lugungana.
Go ashore	Tawé loccato.
Make a light, I want to see you	Mené le monghtiapee monghtoneelé, matangunabee nubratonee.
Run together (a race)	Rene nunempté or Leongana.
Stay or keep a long way off	Onamarrumnebere, or Crackné lo maba, or Kelaba rowé.
Awake, rouse ye, get up!	Tientable taggamunna, or Nawatty! pegraty! wergho! or Takka wughra!
Don't wake him, let him sleep	Tialengbpa lontun-narra, or Kunnyam tilanga bah, or Kunnyam narraloyea.
Whisper, speak low, let nobody hear	Kukanna lenagangpa nunty pateinuyero, or Onabeah dayaleah.

Some Aboriginal Names of Places in Tasmania.

Cape Portland district	Tebrakunna.
Country extending back from Ringarooma township	Warrentinna.
Douglas River	Leeaberryack or Leeaberra.
Nicholas's Cap	Mita winnya, Kuruuna poima-langta.
Doctor's Creek (East Coast)	Wuggatena menennya.
Long Point	Wuggatena pocenta.
Saltwater lagoon near the Coal mines	Muogarattya.
Governor's Island	Tittanarlack.
George's River district	Kunarra-kunnah.
Maria Island	Tiarra-marra-monah.
Mount Royal and Port Cygnet, country lying between	Taluné.
Oyster Bay	Poyanannupyack.
High lands behind ditto	Pothy munatta.
"St. Valentine's Peak, ou Surrey hills, peak like a volcano," of Flinders	Natoné.
Piper's River district	Orramakunna.
Port Davey	Poynduc.
East Bay Neck	Lueena langhta muracomyiack.

Eaglehawk Neck	Teeralinnack *or* Tera-liuna.
Hampshire Hills district, in the north-west	Pateena.
Barren Joey Island	Roobala mangana.
Glamorgan district	Tebranuykuuna.
Port Arthur	Prémaydena
Macquarie Harbour	Parralaongatek.
Recherche Bay	Leillateah.
Port Esperance	Raminea.
Southport	Lamabbéle.
Bruni Island	Lunawanna-clonuah.
South Arm	Reemeré.
Huon Island	Prahree.
Betsy Island	Temeteletta.
Three-hut Point	Taoonawonna.
Tinder-box Bay	Renna kannapughoola.
Brown's River	Promenalinah.
Arch Island	Poora tingalé.
Tamar River	Ponrabbel.
Piper's River	Wattra karoola.
Swan Island	Terelbessé.
Arthur River	Tunganrick.
Schouten Island	Tiggana marraboona.
Cape Grim	Kennaook.
Mount Cameron (West Coast)	Preminghana.
Mount Hemskirk	Rocinrim *or* Traoota munatta.
Mount Zeehan	Weiawenena.
Circular Head	Mouattek *or* Romanraik.
Frenchman's Cap	Mebbelek.
Albatross Island	Tangatema.
Hunter's Island	Reeneka.
Pieman's River	Corinna.
District north of Macquarie Harbour	Timgarick.
Lake St. Clair	Leeawulena.
Huon River	Tahuné-linah.
Satellite Island	Wayaree.
Derwent River	Teemtoomelé menennye.
Mount Wellington	Unghaniahletta *or* l'ooranetteré.
Clarence Plains	Nannyelcebata.
Crooked Billet and on to the Dromedary	Unghanyenna.
Range of hills between Bagdad and Dromedary	Rallolinghana.
Jordan River	Kuta linah.
Lovely Banks	Tughera wughata.
Ben Lomond	Toorbunna.
South Esk River	Mangana lienta.
Lagoon on summit of Ben Lomond	Meenamata.
St. Patrick's Head	Lumera genena wuggelena.

VOCABULARY.

SOME NAMES OF ABORIGINES OF TASMANIA.

MEN.

Tonack	A native of Macquarie Harbour.
Paoblattena (literally, wombat)	A native of North-West district.
Kakannawayreetya (literally, joey of the forester kangaroo)	A native of Oyster Bay.
Bonep	A native of Macquarie Harbour.
Kellawurumnea	A native of Pittwater.
Lanney	A native of the North-West.
Kunnarawialeetyé	A native of Oyster Bay.
Meenapeekameena	A native of Lovely Banks.
Maywedick or Maywerick	A native of Port Davey.
Redaryioick	A native of Circular Head district.

WOMEN.

Taenghanootera (literally, weeping bitterly)	A native of George's River.
Worromonoloo (literally, boughs)	A native of Piper's River Road district.
Rammanaloo (literally, little gull)	A native of Cape Portland.
Wuttawantyenna (literally, nausea)	A native of east bank of Tamar River.
Plooranaloona (literally, sunshine)	A native of George's River.
Tenghanoop	A native of Port Davey.
Trooganeenic	A native of Mount Royal.
Metakartea	A native of North-East quarter.
Tiabeah	A native of Bruni Island.
Koonya	A native of Sorell.
Pueelongmeena	A native of Oyster Bay.
Unghlottymeena	A native of North-East.
Rayna	A native of Pieman's River district.
Penghanawaddick	A native of Pieman's River district.

ABORIGINAL VERSES IN HONOR OF A GREAT CHIEF.

(Sung as an accompaniment to a Native Dance or Riawé.)

Pappela Rayna 'ngonyna, Pappela Rayna 'ngonyna,
 Pappela Rayna 'ngonyna!
Toka mengha leah, Toka mengha leah,
 Toka mengha leah!
Lugha mengha leah, Lugha mengha leah,
 Lugha mengha leah!

Nena taypa Rayna poonyna, Nena taypa Rayna poonyna,
 Nena taypa Rayna poonyna!
Nena nawra pewyllah, Pallah nawra pewyllah,
 Pellawah, Pellawah!
Nena nawra pewyllah, pallah nawra pewyllah,
 Pellawah, Pellawah!

Fragment of another song.

Wannape Wappere tepara,
Nenname pewyllah keilape,
 Mayngatea.
Maynapah Kola maypelea,
Wappera Ronah Leppakah,
 &c., &c., &c.

THE ABORIGINES OF TASMANIA.

Fragment of another song.

Kolah tunuame neanyme,
Pewyllah puganarra ;
Roonah Leppaka malamatta,
. . . Leonalle.
Renape tawna newurra pewurra,
Nomeka pawna poolapa Lelapah,
Nongane mayeah melarootera,
Koabah remawurrah,
&c., &c., &c.

LIST OF WORDS IN USE BY THE OYSTER BAY TRIBE OF ABORIGINES.

(*Copied from a Manuscript of* 1826 *by* THOMAS SCOTT, *late Assistant Surveyor-General of Tasmania, by* J. R. SCOTT.)

English	Native	English	Native
Toom's Lake, Upper Macquarie River	Moyentelcea.	Forehead	Druan a malla.
A knife or flint	Teroona.	Hair	Nukakala.
A knife or flint	Trawootta.	Neck	Loobeyera.
Water	Mookaria.	Arm	Nanimpena.
Fire	Nooena.	Head	Neenapena.
The sun	Pagannbrana.	A scar or mark on the arm	Troobenick.
The moon	Wee-etta.	Bread	Taoorela.
A white man	Ragina.	A bird	Darwalla.
A white man	Ragi.	Boomer kangaroo	Rena.
A white man	Rytia.	Brush kangaroo	Lena.
Marrow of a bone	Moomelena.	Emu	Padanawoonta.
Blood	Balooyuna.	Kangaroo skin	Bleagana.
Hand	Dregena.	Stone	Peoora.
Hand	Reegebena.	Shell	Kaa-ana.
Thumb	Manamera tagina.	Dog	Booloobenara.
Ear	Roogara.	Dog	Kuayetta.
Eyes	Nepoogamena.	Spear	Preana.
Nose	Megrooera.	Trees	Moogootena.
Mouth	Moonapena.	Dead wood	Weegena.
Chin	Coomegana.	Grass	Rawinnina.
		Feather	Kna-oo-legehra.

The legend of the Origin of Fire and of the Apotheosis of Two Heroes, by the Aborigines of Tasmania, as related by a native of the Oyster Bay tribe, appears under the head of "MYTHS," vol. I., page 461.

INDEX.

A.

	VOL.	PAGE
Abduction of white women	II.	317
Aborigines of Australia, notes relating to (Appendix E)	II.	310
Abuse, terms of	II.	23
Activity, ingenuity, perseverance, customs, weapons, &c.	II.	248
Adjectives, Lake Hindmarsh	II.	58
——— numeral	II.	16
Adverbs, Lake Hindmarsh	II.	58
Affection, instances of	I.	138
——— instances of	II.	283
Affray with natives	II.	227
Africa	I.	49, 54, 58
Agility and skill	II.	244
Albinism	I.	7
Amusements	I.	176
Animals, habits of	I.	xxxviii, 247
——— native names of, Lake Hindmarsh	II.	54
——— native names of, Lake Tyers	II.	38
Ants, pupæ of	I.	207
Araucaria Bidwilli	I.	xxxiii, 218, 220
Areas common to various tribes	I.	219
——— occupied by tribes in Victoria	I.	36
Astronomy of the natives	I.	432
Athletic exercises	II.	244
Australia, how peopled	I.	lxiv
——— natives of	I.	20
——— North-Western	I.	16
——— notes on the natives of (Appendix C)	II.	289
Australians, form, color, and general character of	I.	xviii
——— intermixture of Chinese with	I.	xvii
——— intermixture of Malays with	I.	xvii
——— intermixture of Papuans with	I.	i
——— numbers of	I.	xix, 31, 45
Avenging a death	I.	102
Aversion to strangers	II.	231
Axe, stone, Pitcairn's Island	I.	377

B.

Bags and baskets	I.	343
——— carried by natives	I.	276
Baiame	II.	285
Ball, game of	I.	176

	VOL.	PAGE
Bam-er-ook	I.	332
Bandicoot	I.	191
Banksia	I.	210
Bark, cutting	I.	123
——— delineations on	I.	286
——— for canoes	I.	411
Barn-geet	I.	313
Barter	I.	180
Barter	II.	298, 305
Bats	I.	191
Beal	I.	210
Bear, native	I.	lxi, 191, 446
Beard	I.	7
Bedouins	I.	55
Bees	I.	206
Belief in a future state	II.	285, 310
Bellingen, natives of	I.	18
Ber-buk	I.	272
Berries	I.	215
Betrothal of children	I.	78
——— of children	II.	291, 316
Birds, catching	I.	xxxii, 196
——— catching	II.	314
Birth and education of children	I.	46
Black-fish	I.	203
Blindness	II.	253
Bolgan, history of	I.	479
Bool-la-min-in	I.	273
Boomerang	I.	xlvii, 310
——— Egyptian	I.	324
——— essay on the	I.	325
——— flight of the	I.	319
——— invention of the	I.	316
——— or Kylie	II.	251
——— peculiarities of the	I.	317
——— theories respecting the	I.	321
——— uses of, in hunting	I.	195
Boomerangs, ornamented	I.	329
Bone awls	I.	241
——— magic	I.	102, 103
Bones of deceased relatives, carrying	I.	98
Boor-a-meel	I.	450
Borneo	I.	49
Bottle-tree	I.	222
Bowkan, Brewin, and Bullundoot	I.	471
Brabrolong tribe, classes of	II.	325
——— family system of the	II.	325
——— language of the	II.	46
——— North Gippsland	II.	323
——— terms used to denote relationship in the	II.	326
Bream	I.	203
Brothers and sisters	II.	288
Bubburum	I.	258
Bucceening	II.	289
Buk-ker-til-lible	I.	456
Bulk or sacred stones	I.	386
——— or sacred stones	II.	307

INDEX 437

	VOL.	PAGE
Bungan tribe	I.	18
Bungeleen, Thomas	I.	22
Bungil, a term of respect	I.	xxii, 57
—— or " Mister"	I.	57
Bunya-bunya	I.	xxxiii, 218, 220
Bunyip, the	I.	435
Burial	II.	273
—— various modes of	I.	xxvi, 108
—— various modes of, amongst savages	I.	121
Burning dead bodies	I.	99, 109
By-yu	I.	xxxiii, 215

C.

	VOL.	PAGE
Cannibalism	I.	xxxvii, 49, 130, 244
Cannibalism	II.	296, 311
Canoe-dance	I.	174
Canoes	I.	lviii, 407
—— cutting bark for	I.	409
—— form of	I.	408
—— letters respecting	I.	415
—— of the Andaman Islanders	I.	415
—— size of	I.	412
—— suitable bark for	I.	411
Canoes	II.	298
Cape York, natives of	I.	19
Cat, native	I.	191
Catching wild-fowl	I.	193
Cateia	I.	326
Cat-fish, Murray	I.	203
Caves, painted	II.	222
Cemeteries	I.	99
Ceremonies attendant on the burial of a corpse	I.	xxvi, 101
Character, mental	I.	22
Characteristics, mental	II.	256
—— physical	II.	236
Chark, invention of the	I.	403
Chieftainship	II.	295
Children, color of, &c.	I.	6
—— education of	I.	50
—— mode of carrying	I.	48
—— mode of carrying, &c.	II.	243
—— naming	I.	xxi, 55
—— naming	II.	312
—— not beaten	I.	129
—— number of, in a family	I.	78
—— treatment of	II.	311
Children's toys	I.	49
Chimera	I.	203
Chinese	I.	15
Chips for cutting, opening, and dressing animals	I.	382
—— for cutting scars, &c.	I.	381
—— for skinning opossums, &c.	I.	381
—— for spears	I.	380
—— for various purposes	II.	250

	VOL.	PAGE
Cicatrices	I.	xli, 295
Circumcision	I.	xxiii, 66, 74
——— South Australia	I.	75
Circumcision	II.	272, 296, 312
Classes	I.	86
Climbing trees	I.	150
Club or Waddy	I.	xlv, 299
Cockatoos, killing	I.	195
Cod, Murray	I.	203
Cod-perch, Murray	I.	32
Color, hair, &c.	I.	5
——— of the skin	II.	243
Colors, names of	I.	293
——— used in painting the body	I.	xli, 281
——— used in painting the body	II.	302
Color-types, Broca's	I.	5
Comets, fear of	II.	296
Coming of age of young men and young women	I.	xxii, 58
Companion, native	I.	193
Compungya	I.	214
Condah, Lake, language of the natives of	II.	63
Condition, barbarous, of the natives	II.	223
Confidence reposed in a white man	II.	278
Conger eel	I.	203
Consanguine family	II.	323
Consanguinity and kinship of the Brabrolong tribe, North Gippsland (Appendix F)	II.	323
Cooking	I.	xxxvii, 125, 187, 188, 190, 191, 192, 194, 204, 208
Cooking	II.	250, 298, 303
Cooper's Creek, natives of	I.	25, 75
——— notes on the Aborigines of (Appendix D)	II.	300
Coranderrk	I.	64
Corrobboree	I.	167
——— dress for the	I.	275
——— song	I.	170, 173
Corrobborees	II.	293, 335
Crab	I.	205
Crania of the natives (Appendix I)	II.	340
——— of the native, method of drawing figures of the	II.	340
Cray-fish	I.	205
Crows, catching	I.	197
Cucumber, sea	I.	205
Cups, drinking	I.	348
Cure of wounds	I.	155
Customs and superstitions	II.	267
——— of the Aborigines of Cooper's Creek	II.	301
——— remarkable, of the natives of the Western district	II.	319
——— remarkable, of widows	I.	106

D.

	VOL.	PAGE
Dams for taking fish	I.	201
Dances	I.	166
——— of girls	I.	178
Darling, natives of	I.	18

INDEX.

	VOL.	PAGE
Deafness and dumbness	I.	30
Death	I.	428
——— and burial of the dead	I.	xxvi, 98
——— avenging a	I.	102
——— of a man	I.	99
——— superstitious beliefs connected with	I.	110
Death	II.	289
——— and burial of the dead	II.	297, 310
Declension of noun, use of possessive pronoun, &c.	II.	96
Decorations for the corrobboree	I.	167
Defensive weapons	I.	330
Defiance and contempt, modes of expressing	I.	28
Deformity	I.	30
Deluge, legend of a	I.	477
Descent and marriage	II.	286
——— rules of	II.	287
Dew, collecting	I.	222
Dhabba	I.	340
Dialect of the Ja-jow-er-ong race	II.	154
——— of the natives of Wagga Wagga	I.	lxviii
Dialects	II.	290
——— of Gippsland	II.	14
——— of the Murray	II.	8
——— of the Western district	II.	12
——— of the Wimmera district	II.	10
——— of the Yarra and Western Port	II.	13
——— of tribes arranged geographically	II.	8
Dialogues, Yarra and Western Port	II.	128
Dieyerie tribe, ornaments worn by the	I.	281
Diseases	I.	xxxviii, 253
——— cure of	I.	259
——— curing	II.	296
——— reports of guardians on	I.	263
Diving and swimming	II.	249, 298
Djee-ball-djee-ball	I.	258
Dog, the native	I.	479
Dog-fish	I.	203
Dogs	I.	147, 191
Dow-ak or Dun-ah	I.	340
Dress	II.	314
——— and personal ornaments	I.	xxxix, 270
——— and personal ornaments	II.	302
Drinking cups	I.	348
Drum	I.	174
Drummung	I.	330
Dual, examples of the	II.	24, 43
Ducks and other wild-fowl	I.	193
Dugong	I.	204

E.

	VOL.	PAGE
Eagle, mopoke, and crow	I.	451
Earth, eating	I.	xxxiv
Earth-worms	I.	208
Eastern Australia	I.	31
Echeneis remora	I.	198

	VOL.	PAGE
Education of children	I.	xxi, 50
——— of children	II.	259
Eel	I.	203, 249, 251, 252
——— conger	I.	203
Eels, spearing, &c.	I.	388
Eggs	I.	208
Emu	I.	191
——— fat of the	I.	238, 450
——— stalking	II.	248
——— the, and the crow	I.	450
Encampment and daily life of the natives	I.	xxv, 123
Endurance, powers of, &c.	II.	244
——— under suffering	II.	253
Essington, Port, names of	I.	19
Exchanging wives	I.	77
Exercises, athletic	II.	244
Exogamy	I.	86
Eyes, color of	I.	5

F.

	VOL.	PAGE
Fasting	I.	xxxiv
Fat	I.	xxxv, 237
Fat	II.	315, 393
Feet, using the	I.	8
Female children, betrothal of	I.	78
——— children, betrothal of	II.	291, 316
Fidelity	II.	230
——— of natives	I.	26
Fights	I.	154
Fights	II.	292
Figures and paintings in caves	I.	289
——— carved on trees	I.	292
Fiji	I.	49
——— ornamentation in	I.	297
Fire, as used at funerals	I.	106
——— carrying	I.	396
——— due to meteoric agencies	I.	406
——— how first procured	I.	405, 462
——— how lost and regained	I.	478
——— method of producing—by the Aztecs	I.	401
——— by the Chinooks	I.	401
——— by the Dacotah	I.	401
——— by the Dyaks	I.	399
——— by the Esquimaux	I.	402
——— by the Greeks and Romans	I.	404
——— by Kaffirs	I.	397
——— by the Lepcha	I.	400
——— by the Maori	I.	399
——— by the natives of Tierra del Fuego	I.	402
——— by the Red Indians	I.	401
——— by the Tahitians	I.	399
——— by the Tongusy	I.	401
——— in Japan	I.	400
——— in Java	I.	400

INDEX.

	VOL.	PAGE
Fire, method of producing in New South Wales	I.	400
——— methods of producing	I.	lvii, 393
——— myths relating to	I.	458
——— producing	II.	250
——— stolen	I.	lx
Fires, signal	I.	153
Fire-sticks	I.	393
Fish	I.	xxxii, 199, 248, 251
——— catching	I.	388
——— catching by hand	I.	199
——— catching by nets	I.	199
——— cooking	I.	204
——— names of	I.	204
——— shell	I.	205
——— spearing	I.	200
——— various methods of catching	II.	248, 298, 314
Fish-hook, New Zealand	I.	392
Fish-hooks	I.	lvii, 391
Fishing, Lake Tyers	I.	413
Fishing-spears	I.	306
Five-corners	I.	217
Fiz-gig	I.	201
Flat-head	I.	203
Flounder	I.	203
Flying squirrels	I.	191
Food	I.	xxxi, xxxiii, 183
——— animal and vegetable, Cooper's Creek	I.	223
——— animal and vegetable, Cooper's Creek	II.	302
——— forbidden	I.	xxxv, 234
——— forbidden	II.	297
——— how procured by children	I.	48
——— joint ownership in	I.	xxxv
——— vegetable	I.	208
——— vegetable, of natives of Northern Queensland	I.	227
Fragments of tomahawks	I.	381
Frog, the Port Albert	I.	478
Frogs	I.	199
Funeral rites	I.	xxvi, 100
——— rites	II.	273
Future state, belief in a	II.	285, 310

G.

	VOL.	PAGE
Gal-gal-la	I.	255
Games and amusements	I.	176
Gar-fish	I.	203
Gee-am	I.	332
Geebung	I.	217
Geelong, natives of	I.	41
Generation, theory of	I.	93
Generosity	II.	279
Gesture-language	I.	lxiii
Gesture-language	II.	4, 308
Gippsland, areas occupied by tribes in	II.	36
——— naming children in	I.	56

VOL. II.   3 K

	VOL.	PAGE
Gippsland, native population of	I.	36
Girls, initiation of	I.	65
Glenelg tribe, words in the dialect of the Upper	II.	62
Glenisla, words in the dialect of the natives of	I.	63
Government of a camp	I.	126
Graves	I.	100
——— of the natives of the Goulburn	I.	109
Graves	II.	310
——— Cooper's Creek	II.	306
Grief, modes of expressing	I.	105
Grubs	I.	207
Gudgeon or trout	I.	203
Gum	I.	214

II.

	VOL.	PAGE
Hair	II.	242
——— character of	I.	6
——— on the body	I.	7
——— superstitions connected with	I.	83, 112
Half-caste Tasmanian	I.	94
Half-castes	I.	3, 20
Hand-net	I.	389
Hands	I.	8
——— figures of, in caves	I.	291
——— figures of, on rocks	II.	309
——— of Australians	I.	xviii
——— signs made by the	II.	338
Head-dress, Cooper's Creek	II.	301, 302
——— Port Lincoln, Cooper's Creek, Macleay River, and River Bogan	I.	xl, 280, 289
Head-man, duties of a	I.	129
Height, weight, &c., of natives	I.	1
Herring	I.	203
Hindmarsh, Lake, language of the natives of	II.	50, 55
Hindoo paintings	I.	289
Homicide	II.	279
Hooks used in fishing	I.	lvii, 202, 391
Hunger-belt	I.	272
Hunting	II.	297
——— the blacks (Appendix II)	II.	336
Huts and Miams	I.	125
——— and Miams	II.	252, 302
Hymn	II.	133

I.

	VOL.	PAGE
Idiots	I.	30
Iguana	I.	248
Implements and manufactures	I.	lii, 343
Infanticide	I.	xxi, 51
Infanticide	II.	272, 290, 311
Infants	I.	xx
Influence of the old women	II.	270
Ingenuity	I.	222
Ingenuity	II.	248

INDEX.   443

	VOL.	PAGE
Initiation	I.	58
——— Macleay and Nambucca Rivers	I.	72
——— New South Wales	I.	69
Initiation	II.	312
——— Goulburn natives	II.	297
——— near Adelaide	II.	271
Injuries, rapid recovery from	I.	155, 257
Inquest	I.	102
Insanity	II.	254
Instruments for taking fish	I.	391
Intelligence of natives	I.	28
Interjections, cries, &c.	II.	20
Interring a corpse	I.	xxvi, 104, 108, 121
——— a corpse	II.	273
Invention, readiness of	II.	265
Islands in the Straits inhabited by sealers and native women	II.	320

J.

	VOL.	PAGE
Jerryale, &c.	I.	62
Jimbirn	I.	274, 295
Judicial combat in England	I.	82
Justice, native idea of	II.	228

K.

	VOL.	PAGE
Kadjo or hammer	I.	li, 339
——— or hammer	II.	249
Kaffirs	I.	54, 55
Kangaroo	I.	xxxii, 248, 250, 252, 449
——— bag	I.	273
——— names of	I.	187
——— rat	I.	353
Kangaroos, hunting	I.	184
——— increase of	I.	184
Kan-nan	I.	350
Kerreem	I.	332
Khonds of India	I.	54
Kidney-fat	I.	102, 107, 246, 469
Kidney-fat	II.	289, 313
Kiley or Boomerang	I.	195
Kindness of natives	I.	25
——— of natives	II.	229
King George's Sound, natives of	I.	17
Kinship	I.	xxv, 89
——— Brabrolong tribe	II.	323
Knives and adzes	I.	379
Kon-nung	I.	302
Koonkie	I.	262
Koorn-goon	I.	356
Kootchee	I.	262, 457
Kotoopna, notes on the language and customs of the tribe inhabiting the country known as (Appendix G)	II.	323

	VOL.	PAGE
Kourn-burt	I.	271
Kour-ur-run	I.	271
Koy-yun	I.	307
Kud jer-oong	I.	299
Kuldukke	I.	261
Kul-luk	I.	xlv, 301
Kur-bo-roo	I.	446
Kur-ruk	I.	xlvii, 309
Kwon-nat	I.	219
Kylie or Boomerang	I.	li, 335
—— or Boomerang	II.	251

L.

	VOL.	PAGE
Labors devolving on wives	I.	85
Land, property in	I.	144
Language	I.	lxi
Language	II.	{1, 266, 300, 334}
—— Avoca	II.	80
—— Balmoral	II.	83
—— Barnawartha	II.	68
—— Boort	II.	82
—— Camperdown	II.	88
—— Colac	II.	89
—— Corio and Colac	II.	165
—— Carngham	II.	87
—— Daylesford	II.	81
—— Echuca	II.	68
—— Flooding Creek, &c.	II.	91
—— Glenorchy	II.	79
—— Goulburn	II.	115
—— Goulburn, Murray, and Campaspe	II.	166
—— Gunbower	II.	69
—— Hamilton	II.	84
—— Horsham	II.	77
—— Ja-jow-er-ong race	II.	154
—— Jhongworong, Pine-gorine, and Gnurellean natives	II.	166
—— Kulkyne	II.	70
—— Lake Condah	II.	116
—— Lake Hindmarsh	II.	76
—— Lake Tyers	II.	93
—— Lake Wellington	II.	92
—— Mildura	II.	74
—— Morcovia Creek	II.	72
—— Portland	II.	85
—— Sandford	II.	84
—— Swan Reach	II.	95
—— Tangambalanga	II.	67
—— Tyntyndyer	II.	73
—— Upper Richardson	II.	80
—— Warrnambool	II.	86
—— Western Port	II.	90
—— Wickliffe	II.	87
—— Witouro, Jajowrong, Knenkoren, Burapper, and Ta-oungurong tribes	II.	167
—— Woddowrong, Koligon, and Dautgart natives	II.	165

	VOL.	PAGE
Language, Yarra	II.	90, 99
——— Yarra and Western Port	II.	120
——— Yotta	II.	74
——— English-Native	II.	67
——— gesture	II.	4
——— Native-English	II.	133
——— native, Gippsland and Murray	II.	33
——— of the Brabrolong tribe, &c.	II.	49
——— of the natives, Lake Tyers	II.	24
——— of the natives near Wickliffe	II.	58
——— of the natives of the Crawford, Stokes, and lower parts of Wannon and Glenelg	II.	64
——— of the natives of Lake Condah	II.	63
——— of the natives of Lake Hindmarsh	II.	50
——— of the natives of the Western district	II.	60
——— of the Pine Plain tribe, &c.	II.	39
——— succinct sketch of	II.	118
Languages, distinguished by their negations	II.	8
——— names of	II.	288
Larap, larp, or lerp	I.	211
Laws affecting marriages	I.	xxv, 77, 86
——— affecting marriages	II.	287
Leange-walert	I.	349
Leek-leek	I.	271, 272
Length of legs and arms	I.	5
Leon-ile or Langeel	I.	302
Leopard, sea	I.	203
Letters, sounds of	I.	lxii
——— sounds of	II.	2
Lies, punishment for telling	I.	129
Life during the four seasons	I.	xxxi, 139
— — duration of	II.	297
——— of a native	I.	130
——— of natives, ordinary	II.	294
Li-lil	I.	xlv, 314
Lincoln, Port	I.	66
Liquors	I.	210
List of vegetables eaten by natives of Victoria	I.	212
——— of words, English-Native	II.	67
Lizard	I.	251, 252
Lizards	I.	198
Loo-errn	I.	453
Loss of life in war	I.	32, 153

M.

	VOL.	PAGE
Magpie	I.	452
Mallee (Weir-Mallee)	I.	220
Man with a tail	I.	429
Mankind, the dispersion of	I.	427
Manna	I.	211
Maori	I.	6, 12
Marks on trees	II.	232
Marm-bu-la	I.	469
Marn-grook	I.	176
Marriage	I.	76

	VOL.	PAGE
Marriage, Fraser's Island, Queensland	I.	84
—— laws of	I.	xxv, 86
—— at Mackay, Queensland	I.	91
—— at Port Essington	I.	89
—— in North-East Australia	I.	88
—— in Port Lincoln district	I.	87
—— in West Australia	I.	87
Marriage	II.	266, 282, 316
—— rules of	II.	287
Marriages	I.	xxiii
—— between black men and white women	I.	97
Mar-rung-nul	I.	276
Marsupials, small	I.	191
Mauke, natives of	I.	14
—— language of natives of	I.	14
Measurements of skulls	II.	374
—— of the bodies of Europeans	I.	5
—— of the bodies of natives	I.	4
Mecro	I.	li, 302
—— or Womerah	I.	338
Men, modes of representing	I.	285
—— the first	I.	424
Mental character	I.	22
—— characteristics	II.	256
Message-stick	I.	133
—— sticks	I.	liii, 354
Messengers	I.	133
Messengers	II.	305
Methods of producing fire	I.	393
Miams, arrangement of	I.	124
Mice	I.	191
Middens	I.	xxxvi, 241
Min-der-min	I.	271, 350
Mintapas	I.	260
Mirnyongs or native ovens	II.	232
Mirra	I.	258
Mirram and Warreen	I.	449
Mirrn-yongs, shell-mounds, and stone-shelters	I.	xxxvi, 238
—— shell-mounds, and stone-shelters	II.	232, 233
Mission, Roman Catholic	II.	262
Moneys expended for the benefit of the Aborigines	I.	xx
Mongile	I.	xlvi, 304
Monogamian family	II.	324
Moo-gro-moo-gro	I.	273
Moon, the	I.	431, 433
Moora-moora	I.	253
Moral condition	II.	240, 275
Mornmoot-Bullarto Mornmoot	I.	452
Mother-in-law, superstitious avoidance of a	I.	xxv, 95
Moths	I.	207
Mounds, shell	I.	238
—— shell	II.	234
Mourning	II.	297
—— colors used for	I.	294
Mulga	I.	330
Murders	II.	279
Murgon and Marr-aga	I.	332

INDEX. 447

	VOL.	PAGE
Murray cat-fish	I.	203
—— River, natives of	I.	16
—— the River	I.	456
Murri-guile	I.	271
Murr-uong or Mirrn-y'ong	I.	209
Mur-rnm Tur-uk-ur-uk	I.	58, 61
Music and singing	II.	266
Mussel-shell or U-horn	I.	349
Mutilations	I.	xxiii
– – – Cooper's Creek	I.	75
Mylitta Australis	I.	209
Myndie	I.	444
Myths	I.	lx, 423

N.

	VOL.	PAGE
Names of hills, rivers, lakes, and other natural features in Victoria	II.	192
—— of hills, rivers, &c., Western district	II.	216
—— of localities near the Crawford, Wannon, &c.	II.	66
—— of places—in Victoria	II.	174, 217
—— Belfast	II.	187
—— Carngham	II.	178
—— Gippsland	II.	188
—— Glenelg	II.	176
—— Glenorchy	II.	177
—— Hampden and Heytesbury	II.	180
—— Lake Hindmarsh	II.	176
—— Lake Tyers (Gippsland)	II.	191
—— Lake Wellington (Gippsland)	II.	190
—— Lower Murray	II.	175
—— River Yarra Yarra	II.	188
—— Talbot	II.	180
—— Wannon	II.	177
—— Warrnambool	II.	186
—— of places, &c., Kerang, Lower Loddon	II.	218
—— of rivers and lakes in Gippsland	I.	37
—— of the dog	I.	149
—— of trees, shrubs, plants, &c.—Condah	II.	174
—— Coranderrk	II.	170
—— Lake Hindmarsh	II.	172
—— of tribes in Victoria	I.	36–42
—— of vegetables	I.	210
—— of wild-fowl	I.	195
—— (various), Hampden and Heytesbury	II.	185
Naming children	I.	xxi, 55
Nandum	I.	305
Nardoo	I.	209, 214, 215
Narra-mang	I.	62
Narrinyeri	I.	65
Native bear	I.	191, 446
—— companion	I.	193
—— dog not recent	I.	149
—— family	I.	131
—— story	I.	lx, 423
—— story	II.	32, 44, 49, 53
—— wells	II.	245

448 INDEX.

	VOL.	PAGE
Native women and half-castes married to white men	II.	320
Natives, behaviour of, at Cooper's Creek	II.	306
——— King George's Sound	II.	237, 247
——— not always improvident	I.	143
Necklaces	I.	278
Necklaces	II.	251
Need-fire	I.	404
Neolithic age	I.	lv
Nerum	I.	351
Nets and fish-hooks	I.	lvii, 389
——— fishing	I.	200, 389
——— fishing	II.	249, 305, 314
New Guinea, ornamentation in	I.	296
New South Wales, natives of	I.	18
New Zealand	I.	54
——— ornamentation in	I.	297
New Zealanders	I.	12
Ngargee or Corrobboree	I.	167
Ngobera	I.	xxvii
Nicknames	I.	xxii
——— of early settlers	II.	66
Ni-yeerd	I.	277
Nonda	I.	217
Noom-bine	I.	341
Noose and bones	II.	313
Nose ornaments	I.	277
Notes and anecdotes of the Aborigines of Australia (Appendix A)	II.	221
Nouns and verbs, Gippsland	II.	32
Noute-kower	I.	271
Nruug-a-Narguna	I.	456
Nruwi	I.	257
Nulla-nulla	I.	301
Number of children in a family	I.	78
Numbers and distribution of the Aborigines—Cooper's Creek	II.	301
——— in Victoria	I.	xix, 31, 45
Nurp	I.	219

O.

	VOL.	PAGE
Oaths	I.	153
Ochre	I.	294
Odour	I.	7
Offences, how dealt with	I.	129
Offensive weapons	I.	299
Old man, respect paid to an	I.	136
——— women, influence of	II.	270
Omeo, Lake	I.	37
Onomatopœia	II.	3
Oogee or head-dress	I.	xl, 280, 289
Ophthalmia	I.	253
Opossum	I.	188
——— names of	I.	189
——— rugs, ornamenting	I.	288
Opossums, catching	II.	248
Ordeal	I.	79
Ordeal	II.	276

	VOL.	PAGE
Ornamentation	I.	xlii, 283
——— common forms of	I.	284
——— in Fiji	I.	296
——— in New Caledonia	I.	298
——— in New Guinea	I.	296
——— in New Zealand	I.	296
——— of Boomerangs	I.	329
——— of shields	I.	331
Ornamentation	II.	299
Ornaments	II.	251
——— worn by females	I.	273, 275
——— worn by the Dieyerie tribe	I.	281
——— worn by the natives of Cooper's Creek	II.	302
——— worn by the natives of the Lower Murray	I.	276
——— worn in the nose	I.	277
Ounep	I.	xlvii
Outrages	II.	224
Ovens, native	I.	xxxvi, 240
——— native	II.	232
——— native, at Lake Connewarren	II.	233
Oyster	I.	205, 237
Ozier-nettings for taking fish	I.	201

P.

	VOL.	PAGE
Painted caves	II.	222
Painting the body	I.	167, 174
Paintings, rock	II.	309
Pairing family	II.	324
Palæolithic age	I.	lv
Papuans	I.	19
Paroo	I.	74
Parrots, names of	I.	196
Parturition	II.	243
Patriarchal family	II.	324
Per-bo-re-gan	I.	176
Per-re-ber-it	I.	178
Perseverance	II.	248
Physical character	I.	1
——— character of the country, influence of	I.	179
——— of the natives of Cooper's Creek	II.	301
——— characteristics	II.	236
——— powers	I.	8
Pictures	I.	liv, 286
——— in caves	I.	285
——— on bark	I.	292
——— on rocks	I.	293
Pictures	II.	257
Pigments	I.	294
Pinjarrah, battle of	II.	225
Pinya	I.	103
Pitcheric	I.	xxxiv, 222
Pitcherie	II.	304
Platypus	I.	248, 249, 251, 252
Poison, fear of	II.	303

VOL. II.   3 L

	VOL.	PAGE
Polygamy	I.	78
Polygamy	II.	291
Polynesia	I.	54
Polynesians	I.	6
Population, estimate of	I.	35
—— native	I.	31
Porcupine	I.	191
Pork and pork fat	I.	xxxv, 237
—— and pork fat	II.	315
Porpoise	I.	203
Port Essington, natives of	I.	19
—— Lincoln	I.	66
Pottery	I.	296
Priests and sorcerers	I.	178, 462
—— and sorcerers	II.	270
Prohibitions against marriages in certain classes	I.	86
—— against marriages in certain classes	II.	266
Pronouns and substautives	II.	43
—— Lake Hindmarsh	II.	15, 56
—— Lake Tyers	II.	15
—— personal, sameness of	II.	19
Property carried by a native	I.	130
—— in land	I.	144
Proportions of figure	II.	243
Prostitution	I.	86
Punaluan family	II.	324
Pund-jel	I.	423
Punishment of wives	I.	85
Purslane	I.	213
Purslane	II.	303
Puzzle, native	I.	178

Q.

	VOL.	PAGE
Quirriang-an-wun	I.	xlvii, 315

R.

	VOL.	PAGE
Races	I.	9
Raspberry	I.	xxxiii, 219
Rat, water	I.	191
Reed-spears	I.	305
Relationship, terms used to denote, amongst the Narrinyeri	II.	330
—— terms used to denote, in the Brabrolong tribe, North Gippsland	II.	326
Relics	II.	232
Religion	II.	295
Remarkable customs of widows	I.	106
Reptiles	I.	198
Retribution	II.	229
Revenge	I.	103
Revenge	II.	282
River or fish-eating tribes	II.	290
Rock paintings	II.	309
Roebuck Bay, natives of	I.	17
Rugs, ornamenting	I.	294
Rules of descent and marriage	II.	287

S.

	VOL.	PAGE
Savage Island	I.	54
Scars	I.	295
Scars	II.	296, 302, 312
Schnapper	I.	203
Schools, native	II.	259
Sea, origin of	I.	429
Seal	I.	203
Seeds, gathering and grinding	I.	214
Senses	I.	7
Shark	I.	203
Sharpening-stones	I.	383
Shell-fish	I.	205
——— names of	I.	205
Shell-mounds	I.	xxxvi, 238
Shell-mounds	II.	234
Shield, Western Australia	I.	li, 330
Shields	I.	xlix, 330
——— Queensland	I.	l, 334
Shields	II.	251
Sight	I.	7
Signals	I.	152
Signs	II.	313
——— used at Cooper's Creek	II.	308
Singing and music	II.	266
Skate	I.	203
Skins, preparing	II.	249
Skull of Australian (A)—		
front view ; side view	II.	342
posterior view ; from above	II.	344
inferior view	II.	346
measurements of	II.	374
——— of Morgan, the bushranger, European (M)—		
front view ; side view	II.	348
posterior view ; from above	II.	350
inferior aspect	II.	352
measurements of	II.	375
——— of a Chinese	II.	354
——— of Australian, probably female (B)—		
front view ; side view	II.	356
from above ; inferior aspect	II.	356
measurements of	II.	376
——— of Australian (C)—		
front view ; side view	II.	360
from above ; inferior aspect	II.	362
——— of Australian (D)—		
front view ; side view	II.	364
from above ; inferior aspect	II.	366
measurements of	II.	377
——— of King Jimmy, of the Mordialloc tribe (E)—		
front view ; side view	II.	368
from above ; posterior aspect	II.	370
bisected longitudinally	II.	372
section of the, in outline	II.	372
measurements of	II.	378
Skulls (M) and (A), remarks on	II.	352
——— of natives and others	II.	239

	VOL.	PAGE
Skulls used as drinking cups	I.	348
Sleep, sound	I.	179
Sleeping in a hole in sand	I	48
Small-pox	I.	xix, 253
Small-pox	II.	254
Smell	I.	7
Smoking	I.	223
Snake	I.	249, 251, 252
Snakes	I.	199
——— with two heads	I.	199
Snow	I.	428
Son-in-law, superstitious avoidance of a	I.	xxv, 95
Song, corrobboree	I.	170
——— Yarra tribe	II.	111
Sorcerers	II.	307
——— and priests	I.	178
Sorcery	I.	102, 465
Sorcery	II.	289
Sow-thistle	I.	214
Spear, mode of throwing the	I.	310
——— throwing the	I.	180
Spears	I.	xlvi, 304
——— Central and North Australia	I.	308
——— West Australia	I.	336, 339
Spears	II.	251
Squirrels, flying	I.	191
Stars, ideas of the	II.	286
Stature	I.	1
Stature	II.	238
Stefano, loss of the bark	II.	230
Sting-ray	I.	203
Stone axe, Pitcairn's Island	I.	377
——— boilers	I.	xxxvii
——— circles, Cooper's Creek	II.	306
——— circles, Western district	II.	235
——— getting, for tomahawks	I.	378
——— implements	I.	lv, 357
——— implements	II.	249, 304
——— implements, forms of	I.	358
——— implements, rocks used for	I.	358
——— mia-mys or shelters	II.	234
——— shelters	I.	238, 242
Stone-headed spears	I.	xlvi, 308
Stones for pounding and grinding seeds, &c.	I.	382
——— for ruddle	I.	386
——— sharpening	I.	383
——— used in fishing	I.	385
——— used in making baskets	I.	385
Storms	I.	452
Story, native	I.	lx, 423
——— native	II.	32, 44, 49, 53
Strange tribes, reception of	I.	133
Sucking-fish	I.	198
Suffering, patient endurance of	II.	254
Sun, the	I.	430
——— the, the moon, and the stars	I.	431
Superstitions	II.	224, 267, 296, 308, 335

	VOL.	PAGE
Superstitious avoidance of a son-in-law	I.	xxv, 95
Supreme Being	II.	285
Swimming	I.	49
—— and diving	II.	247, 298
Swine, fat of	I.	xxxv, 237
—— fat of	II.	315
Sword, wooden	I.	303

T.

	VOL.	PAGE
Tarnuk	I.	347
Tartengk	I.	261
Tasmanian half-caste	I.	94
Tasmanians	I.	lxix, 12
—— Aboriginal names of places	II.	431
—— birth, &c.	II.	385
—— death and burial	II.	387
—— dialects and language, manners and customs, &c.	II.	410
—— diseases	II.	398
—— dress and ornaments	II.	399
—— encampments, &c.	II.	389
—— fire	II.	408
—— food	II.	392
—— language	II.	408
—— marriage	II.	386
—— mental characteristics	II.	382
—— names of Aborigines	II.	433
—— numbers	II.	384
—— physical character	II.	379
Tasmanians, shell-mounds	II.	395
—— short sentences in the native language	II.	429
—— songs	II.	433
—— stone implements	II.	401
—— vocabulary	II.	415
—— weapons, implements, canoes	II.	400
—— words in use by Oyster Bay tribe	II.	434
Taste	I.	7
Tattooing	I.	295
Teeth, knocking out the	I.	61, 62, 64, 65, 69, 71, 74
—— knocking out the	II.	296, 313
Throw-sticks	I.	310
Tibbut	I.	58, 60
Til-bur-nin	I.	272
Toes, using the	I.	8
—— using the	II.	243
Tomahawks	I.	359
—— uses of	I.	379
Tomb, design for a	I.	298
Touch	I.	7
Toys, children's	I.	49
Trackers and tracking	I.	7
—— and tracking	II.	264, 337
Traditions of the Australian Aborigines on the Namoi, Barwan, and other tributaries of the Darling (Appendix B)	II.	285
Traffic amongst the tribes	I.	180

	VOL.	PAGE
Traffic amongst the tribes	II.	305
Translations, Yarra and Western Port	II.	130
Travelling	I.	123
Treatment of women	I.	xxiv
—— of women	II.	293, 315
Trees, figures carved on	I.	292
—— water-yielding	I.	221
Tribes, gathering of, at Merri Creek	I.	136
—— names of, in Victoria	I.	36–42
Truffle, native	I.	209
Truth, no proper conception of	II.	277, 281
Tuin-tuin	I.	271
Turanian family	II.	324
Turkey	I.	192
Turtle, &c.	I.	xxxii, 197
Twins	I.	78
Twins	II.	272
Two, the words for	II.	19
Tyers, Lake	I.	65

U.

	VOL.	PAGE
U-born (mussel-shell)	I.	349
Unio	I.	205, 237

V.

	VOL.	PAGE
Vegetable food	I.	208
—— of natives of Northern Queensland	I.	227
Vegetables, list of, eaten by natives of Victoria	I.	212
—— names of	I.	210
Victoria Lake	I.	39
—— natives of	I.	15
Vocabularies of Australia	II.	16
Vocabulary—Crawford, Stokes, and lower parts of Wannon and Glenelg	II.	64
—— Gippsland and Murray	II.	36
—— Goulburn tribe	II.	115
—— Ja-jow-er-ong race	II.	157
—— Lake Condah	II.	116
—— Lake Hindmarsh	II.	55
—— Wagga Wagga, New South Wales	II.	218
—— Western district	II.	44, 60
—— Yarra and Coast tribes	II.	133
—— Yarra tribe	II.	99

W.

	VOL.	PAGE
Waal-bee	I.	341
Wagga Wagga, dialect of the natives of	I.	lxviii
Wallaby	I.	xxxii
—— snaring the	I.	186
Waller-wal-lert	I.	271
War, loss of life in	I.	32, 153
Waropa or drum	I.	174
Warra-warra	I.	301

	VOL.	PAGE
Water, how first obtained	I.	429
——— means of obtaining	II.	246, 253
——— procuring	I.	221
——— vessels	I.	346
Water-rat	I.	191
Water-yielding trees	I.	220
Wawoorong or Yarra tribe	I.	32
Weapons	I.	xliv
——— defensive	I.	330
——— offensive	I.	299
Weapons	II.	298, 304
Weet-weet	I.	352
Weir, great, Upper Darling	I.	202
Weir-Mallee	I.	220
Weirs for taking fish	I.	xxxii, 201
Wells, native	II.	245
Wer-raap	I.	462
West Australians, weapons and implements of the	I.	1, 335
Whale	I.	203
Whale	II.	315
Whiting	I.	203
Widow at the grave of her deceased husband	I.	105
Widows	I.	97
——— remarkable customs of	I.	106
Wild-fowl, catching	I.	193
——— names of	I.	195
Wilghee	II.	238
Will-fire	I.	404
Wirotheree	I.	206
Wirrullume	I.	258
Witarna	I.	69, 260
Wittcha	I.	258
Wives, exchanging	I.	77
——— labors devolving on	I.	85
——— punishment of	I.	85
Wiwirri	I.	261
Wi-won-der-rer	I.	455
Wombat	I.	189, 449
Women as ambassadors	I.	165
——— as doctors	I.	xxxix
——— influence of the old	II.	270
——— native	I.	29
——— the first	I.	427
——— treatment of	I.	xxiv
——— treatment of	II.	283, 315
——— white, stolen by natives	II.	317
Wonguim	I.	xlvii, 310
Words and sentences—Jajowrong and other tribes	II.	165
——— Wagga Wagga, New South Wales	II.	218
——— Yarra and Western Port	II.	127
——— Yarra tribe	II.	109, 112
——— new	II.	4
——— resembling English	II.	6
——— those of the Aryan race	II.	5
Wounds, easily cured	I.	155, 257
Wrestling	I.	177
Wrestling	II.	293

Y.

	VOL.	PAGE
Yel-un-ket-ur-uk	I.	271
Yepene Amydeet	I.	167
York, Cape, natives of	I.	19

Z.

Zamia	I.	xxxiii
Zeuzera	I.	207

www.ingramcontent.com/pod-product-compliance
Lightning Source LLC
Chambersburg PA
CBHW051858300426